The Power of Your Life

The Power of Your Life

The Sanlam Century of Insurance Empowerment, 1918–2018

Grietjie Verhoef

OXFORD
UNIVERSITY PRESS

OXFORD
UNIVERSITY PRESS

Great Clarendon Street, Oxford, OX2 6DP,
United Kingdom

Oxford University Press is a department of the University of Oxford.
It furthers the University's objective of excellence in research, scholarship,
and education by publishing worldwide. Oxford is a registered trade mark of
Oxford University Press in the UK and in certain other countries

First Edition published in 2018

Impression: 1

Published in the United States of America by Oxford University Press
198 Madison Avenue, New York, NY 10016, United States of America

British Library Cataloguing in Publication Data
Data available

Library of Congress Control Number: 2018942484

ISBN 978–0–19–881775–8

Printed and bound in Great Britain by
Clays Ltd, Elcograf S.p.A.

Dedicated to Verity Roussouw

PREFACE AND ACKNOWLEDGEMENTS

To do business in global markets emerging from humble parochial beginnings in the scope of a hundred years testifies to a determination to succeed. The rise of global companies has had a profound impact on domestic politics, the economy, and society, but multinational enterprise has also shaped the global environment. In the globalized world of business and society, new entrants can only succeed by strategic market selection and operational competitive advantage. Studying internationalization offers a range of possibilities to new entrants, but context changes so dynamically, that it has become almost impossible to predict the exact course of business expansion. When the opportunity arose to study the century of development of an anchor Afrikaner financial services enterprise, Sanlam, it was apparent that it would be a study in business sustainability, the adaptability of ethnic culture to the globalized world of business, and the changes those trends implanted in peripheral polities, economies, and societies. When taking on the history of a century of Sanlam, the aim was to explore business adaptability in the context of globalization. The history of Afrikaners in South Africa is complex. The history of Sanlam allows insight into the complexities of political, economic, and social empowerment of not only Afrikaners, but also those South Africans who exercised a distinct choice to put South Africa first. The centenary history of Sanlam is a history of South African home-grown entrepreneurship, business vision, and the inextricable socio-political development of the country from anti-imperialism, through competing nationalisms through to a society responding to the forces of globalization and international business. Sanlam responded in the domestic South African market to global trends in market deregulation and subsequently emerged as a global enterprise. This is an important achievement. Sanlam made this transition from humble but confident beginnings in the Cape into global markets capitalizing on its firm-specific advantages.

Empowering the marginalized and creating a century of sustainable wealth in Africa—this is the African success story of Sanlam, the only emerging market multinational company to adapt an inward-looking nationalistic business model to become a global player. Sanlam relied on its institutional learning of a century ago to conduct global business from Africa. A history of embeddedness in an economic and political environment of racial segregation and white power, was transformed into the firm-specific competitive advantage of understanding the business of mobilizing marginalized people in emerging markets to take ownership of their own destiny.

This history is good news from Africa. It explains how a financial enterprise rooted in a developing market, within an ethnically and culturally circumscribed community, utilized social capital and mobilized its community for empowerment. It offers insights into successful transformation strategies for companies in African and other emerging markets. The historical institutional perspective is important, since other global financial service enterprises such as Barclays failed to capitalize on its DCO (Dominion, Colonial and Overseas) legacy in devising a new African strategy. The perspective from humble African beginnings presents an important dimension to future financial service provision in Africa and other emerging markets.

This is the history of the South African National Life Assurance Company (*Suid-Afrikaanse Nasionale Lewens Assuransie Maatskappy*—Sanlam), established in 1918 amidst the international turbulence of World War I, the growing marginalization of poor Afrikaners in South Africa, and emerging nationalisms in the British Commonwealth. Afrikaner entrepreneurs consciously chose insurance to mobilize the people's savings towards their own economic empowerment. First the South African National Trust and Insurance Company (*Suid-Afrikaanse Nasionale Trust en Assuransie Maatskappy*—Santam) was established in March 1918. Soon the short-term trust and insurance business separated from the long-term life business. Sanlam was established in June 1918 and made inroads into an industry controlled by English- and foreign-owned life offices. Sanlam leaders supported the call for the supremacy of South Africa's interests above loyalty to the British Crown. Sanlam leaders aligned themselves to the politics of white supremacy since the formation of the National Party in 1914. This history provides a unique perspective in Business History. It illustrates the business of using nationalism to mitigate risk in deeply divided societies progressing through socio-economic transformation. Sanlam used strategies to enter the life market in South Africa through actively canvassing the non-insured segment of the white population and ultimately grow an inclusive business able to outgrow the ethnic enclave. This is an exceptionally complex, but inspiring business history, unprecedented in the history of insurance and financial services development in developing markets.

The unique Business History case is this transformation from an enclave to a global business focus. The complex political and economic environment of the first decade of the twentieth century presented limited strategic alternatives to an insurer aspiring to enter the market. These environmental complexities only intensified in the course of the century. The importance of excellence in top management for the performance of the company, as well as for the national economy, was consistently emphasized by Alfred Chandler in his study of industrial corporations in the United States. This is equally true for the role of management in the insurance company, Sanlam, since 1918. Marginalized Afrikaners were mobilized to trust Sanlam in growing their personal destiny as inevitably interlocked with the future of a sovereign South Africa in the British Commonwealth. Economic empowerment was the ultimate aim. Management was the agent providing the intellect and impetus for organizational innovation and performance improvement at the enterprise level. Sanlam mobilized savings, created an Afrikaner-controlled corporate business network alongside the existing English- and Jewish-controlled South African corporate world. Afrikaner business employed social capital to construct a significant position in the South African economy by the 1970s. Distinct Afrikaner-controlled business groups (Sanlam, Federale Volksbeleggings, and Federale Mynbou Beperk, later Gencor as one group, and Rembrandt as another group) emerged and established a distinct presence among the big English business groups centred around the mining industry. Sanlam outperformed competing long-term insurers to take up the position as the second largest life office in South Africa within forty years—through the development of competitive products, superior agent training, innovative computer technologies, and building broad trust amongst all South Africans. Fundamental environmental transformation in Africa and South Africa again altered the strategic options to Sanlam. Sanlam reconsidered its nationalistic 'culture' since the late 1970s as intra-Afrikaner voices rose against the hegemony of white rule. The study also debunks the myth of 'Afrikaner' unity or homogeneity, since intra-Afrikaner business competition displayed opposing ambitions, personality clashes, and a lack of some mythical united nationalist force. The fundamental transformation of the South African political economy at the beginning of the 1990s led to radical changes. The next level of contextual complexities manifested: transformation of the initial business model, focusing on white policy holders, was directly adapted to the political transition of black majority rule in 1994. Management devised the strategy of responding to global and domestic trends by determining long-term goals and objectives for the enterprise. Sanlam aligned to the trends in the global long-term insurance industry. Domestic regulation and global industry trends dictated a fundamental revision of the Sanlam business model. Domestic underperformance followed global industry experiences. The significant Business History case study is how management effected this strategic transition to sustain the company in the wake of potentially threatening contextual turbulence.

Global financial deregulation, the declining demand for traditional life assurance products, and the rising demand for innovative wealth products, signalled structural change to the mutual life industry. In 1998 Sanlam followed the global trend: it demutualized and entered the market as a diversified financial services company. This constituted a radical business model overhaul. It took almost five years to implement a new business strategy. Sanlam relied on its roots in the empowerment of marginalized people by realigning itself as an emerging market conglomerate with its firm-specific advantages from the home base as competitive advantage. Several South African conglomerates exited the local market through foreign primary listings—Sanlam chose deliberately not to pursue that strategy. The history of Sanlam leading from 1918 into the twenty-first century is the only case study of a successful emerging market financial services conglomerate from Africa illustrating the benefits of strong domestic market embeddedness, dynamic managerial capabilities, and socio-cultural adaptability in business sustainability and expansion.

The study covers a century of Sanlam's history from establishment, through crises, building capacity, and diversification, to threatening disaster caused by over-exposure to unfocussed conglomerate activities, the insulation caused by international isolation, sanctions and anti-apartheid pressures, to functional business restructuring, which resulted in responding to global trends in insurance—demutualization and business refocussing. The outcome is the creation of a diversified financial service enterprise able to operate in developed and developing markets. In entering other emerging markets, Sanlam relied on its understanding of emerging market dynamics, the empowerment of the marginalized by addressing human risk as a tool towards empowerment—socially and economically.

The study concludes with an explanation of the broad business mix in Sanlam, delivering sophisticated financial services to the broad spectrum of shareholders and policy holders—from the wealthy to those aspiring to be wealthy. This study shows how a business moved with the *mentalité* of Western European civilization—from European domination under colonialism, rising European nationalism, decolonization and independence—to respond to the pressures of globalization. These trends unfolded with a certain lag in South Africa under Afrikaner leadership and international isolation, but unmistakably in similar sequence, resulting in the twenty-first century universal democracy. The history of Sanlam is intertwined with this history. The adaptive capabilities of the Afrikaner leadership, the transition from Afrikaner mutuality to inclusive South African and international stakeholders, the capacity to deliver on promises and the strength to turn back from legacy decisions undermining progress, created the space to innovate and compete effectively. Sanlam went from highly centralized bureaucratic management to strategic division of authority on operational level in the diversified M-form of the Group. The golden thread through this history is leadership, management capabilities, and vision.

The opportunity to research and write this history is a privilege. The accolade in moving the life office to commissioning a comprehensive research project on the history of a hundred years old Sanlam, goes to the former Group Archivist, Verity Rossouw. She liaised with the executive management, especially the Group Secretary, J. P. Bester, in 2007 to commission a research project comprising two Masters' dissertations and four doctoral theses. I supervised these studies with the capable co-supervision of colleagues from the University of Stellenbosch and the University of Johannesburg. The research team received the assistance of several former Sanlam employees, who conducted research reports on aspects of the development of Sanlam. The following academic studies comprise the basis of in-depth research on aspects of the history of Sanlam. Randall Adams completed a MA degree in History at the University of Stellenbosch in 2010 with a dissertation, *Die ver-Suid-Afrikanisering van die Suid-Afrikaanse ekonomie, 1918–1985*. (The South Africanization of the South African economy, 1918–1985). Victoria Laburn completed a minor dissertation in Economics at the University of

Stellenbosch in 2011, titled *The Economics of Corporate Social Investment: Sanlam and Corporate Social Responsibility expenditure, 1970 to 2008*. In 2013 Simone Halleen completed a PhD in History at the University of Stellenbosch on, *From Life Insurance to Financial Services: A Historical Analysis of Sanlam's Client Base, 1918–2004*. In 2017 two theses were completed. Yolande Hagedorn-Hansen completed a PhD in Financial Management at the University of Johannesburg in 2017 on *The Transformation of the South African Short Term Insurance Industry as Represented by the Development of SANTAM, 1918–2012*. Wynand Beukes completed a PhD in History in 2017 at the University of Stellenbosch, titled, *Van Afrikanerkultuur tot Korporatief: die geskiedenis van Sanlam se Hoofkantoor-personeelkorps,1918–2008*. (From Afrikaner Culture to Corporate: the History of the Sanlam Head Office Corps, 1918–2008). Shaun de Wet has completed a PhD in Financial Management at the University of Johannesburg on *The Role of Asset Management in the Transformation of a Life Insurance Company to a Financial Services Group: the Case of Sanlam*. Supporting research was undertaken by Abie du Plessis on *Die Veldpersoneel van Sanlam. 1919–2013* (The Agents/Field Staff of Sanlam 1918–2013); Adri Drotskie and Grietjie Verhoef on *Management and Sustainability: the Development of Management in Sanlam, 1918–2015;* Leon Venter on *The History of Sanlam Broker Distribution*, and on *Regional Head Offices of Sanlam*, as well as a compilation of the human resource development programmes under the supervision of Frederick Stroebel; The Sanlam Computer Group Research report (compiled by Barry Leo, Andre Prins, Andre Hoffman, Nico Ras, Marinda de Waal, Jaco du Plessis, Herman du Plessis) compiled an extensive report on *The IT Journey: A History of IT Development in Sanlam 1990–2014*. Nick du Preez completed a research report on Sanlam's medical schemes, *Sanlam Gesondheidsorg* (Sanlam Health Care). The final integration of the vast historical material collected by means of the academic studies and research reports, as well as my own research on aspects of the history of Sanlam, was my privilege. The pioneering work by Sanlam in commissioning such research on an arms-length basis underlines the corporate responsibility of the Group as well as its sense of civil citizenship. Sanlam has taken the lead in corporate South Africa by making its well-organized archive accessible to bona fide researchers. The current Group Secretary, Sana-Ullah Bray, was instrumental in formalizing the legal structure of the research project, final publication avenues, as well as invaluable support in arranging access to Salam management for the purpose of interviews, questions, and clarification of processes in Sanlam.

Many aspects of the development of the insurance industry, of which Sanlam is a case study, were presented to numerous international scientific conferences and research projects. At successive congresses of the International Economic History Association, at Utrecht in 2009 (WEHC 2009), at Stellenbosch (WEHC 2012), at Kyoto (WEHC 2015), and at meetings of the Business History Congress in the USA, the European Business History Association in different locations across Europe, and at meetings of the Economic History Society of South Africa, scholars from across the globe participated in comparative insurance research presentations. After the 2009 meeting in Utrecht, Robin Pearson (ed.) published *The Development of International Insurance* (London: Pickering & Chatto). As part of the Dai Ichi Life Insurance project on Corporate Forms of Organization co-ordinated by Robin Pearson and Takau Yoneyama, comparative work on the organization of international insurance business were deliberated at workshops between 2011 and 2014. The outcome of this enterprise was the publication of R. Pearson and T. Yoneyama (eds) *Corporate Forms and Organisational Choice in International Insurance* (Oxford: Oxford University Press). Ongoing international engagement with the dynamically changing context of the insurance industry on matters of regulation, different cultures of risk, and insurance globalization is in process and will result in future international conferences and research projects.

The history of Sanlam offers a case from the emerging market context. This book invites the global readership into the unique history of an African emerging market financial services conglomerate. This enterprise seeks to bring scholarly interest to the world of business, finance and economic transformation in Africa. I hope to be the intermediary between this highly complex environment, that is simultaneously a world of opportunity. It was a journey of endless learning. I am indebted to all my students who completed their academic studies to assist the mining of the vast archival material on Sanlam and the insurance industry in South Africa. I also thank the loyal and dedicated Sanlam staff who assisted in submitting research reports on topics they had lived through as employees in Sanlam. I am forever indebted to Verity Roussouw for her vision and confidence in the company, the project, and the humble hands writing it all up. The executive management in Sanlam since the inception of the project, has given unfaltering support. The other Sanlam archive staff Jalynn Fortuin and Catherine Snel (current archivist) were the friendly assistants on call to find sources. I am also indebted to my international colleagues for the penetrating academic discourse on comparative insurance research. I wish to express a special gratitude to Monica Keneley, who has been an intellectual partner and friend over an extended period of insurance and business history research. Research assistants in the Department of Financial Management, Milan de Wet (doctoral candidate) and Waldo Oberholzer, assisted with econometric research methodology in analysing the Sanlam share price performance. The University of Johannesburg allowed me the academic freedom to engage in this project. The usual disclaimer remains: the responsibility for the contents is mine.

The history of Sanlam's first hundred years is testimony to the quality of the human capital of the people of South Africa and the success embedded in vison, strategy, and work. This book is dedicated to the vision of entrepreneurs from Africa.

Grietjie Verhoef

Johannesburg
May 2018

CONTENTS

LIST OF FIGURES

LIST OF TABLES

LIST OF ABBREVIATIONS

AAC	Anglo American Corporation
ABSA	Amalgamated Banks of South Africa
ACVV	Afrikaanse Christelike Vrouevereniging (Afrikaans Christian Women's Association)
AECI	African Explosives and Chemical Industries
AHI	Afrikaanse Handelsinstituut (Afrikaans Chamber of Commerce)
AHT	African Homes Trust
A&M	Automation and Mechanization
AMP	Australian Mutual and Provident
ANC	African National Congress
ARC	African Rainbow Capital
BAAM	Business Adopt a Municipality
BDM	Business Development Manager
BEE	Black Economic Empowerment
B-BBEE	Broad-based Black Economic Empowerment
BoP	Bottom of the Pyramid
BSB	Boere Saamwerk Beperk (Farmers' Collaborative Organization)
CAI	Corporate Africa Investments
CAMAF	Chartered Accountants' Medical Aid Fund
CANSA	Cancer Association of South Africa
CAR	Capital Adequacy Ratio
CMT	Cash Management Trust
COSATU	Congress of South African Trade Unions
CPIX	Consumer Price Index Excluding Mortgages
CRAF	Central Retirement Annuity Fund
CRM	Client Relationship Management
CSA	Country Specific Advantage
CSI	Corporate Social Investment
CSR	Corporate Social Responsibility
DCO	Dominion, Colonial and Overseas

DCoG	Department of Cooperative Government
DRC	Dutch Reformed Church
DT	Demutualization Trust
EDP	Electronic Data Processing
EE	Employment Equity
EFT	Electronic Funds Transfer
EGL	Empowerment Group Leader
ELM	Entry Level Market
EO	Equal Opportunity
EV	Embedded Value
EVK	Ekonomiese Volkskongres (Economic Congress of the People)
FAIS	Financial Advisory and Intermediary Services
FET	Further Education and Training
FFA	Fellow of the Faculty of Actuaries
FM	Federale Mynboumaatskappy (Federal Mining Company)
FPI	Financial Planning Institute
FSB	Financial Services Board
FSC	Financial Sector Charter
FSV	Financial Soundness Valuation
FVB	Federale Volksbeleggings (Federal People's Investments)
GAAP	General Accepted Accounting Principles
GDFI	Gross Domestic Fixed Investment
GDP	Gross Domestic Product
GEMS	Government Employees Medical Scheme
GFC	Global Financial Crisis (2008)
GFSA	Gold Fields of South Africa
GNI	Guardian National Insurance
GRI	Global Reporting Initiative
HSBC	Hong Kong Shanghai Banking Corporation
IDC	Industrial Development Corporation of South Africa
IFRS	International Financial Reporting System
ILPA	Institute of Life and Pension Advisers
INSETA	Insurance Sector Training Authority
IRR	Internal Rate of Return

JCI	Johannesburg Consolidated Investments
JSE	Johannesburg Securities Exchange
KMB	Korporatiewe Maatskaplike Betrokkenheid (Corporate Social Responsibility)
KWV	Koöperatiewe Wynbouers Vereniging (Wine Farmers' Co-operative)
KZN	Kwa-Zulu Natal
LAMA	Life Assurance Management Association
LID	Lid Identifikasiestelsel (Member Identification System)
LISP	Linked Investor Service Provider
LOA	Life Offices Association
LTRR	Long-Term Rate of Return
MIA	Merchant Investors' Assurance
MOU	Memorandum of Understanding
MSV	Modified Statutory Valuation
NAIL	New Africa Investments Limited
NEC	National Empowerment Commission
NIPR	National Institute of Personnel Research
NMASA	National Medical Aid Society of South Africa
NP	National Party
NPO	Non-Profit Organization
OB	Ossewa Brandwag (Ox Wagon Guard)
OFS	Orange Free State
OLS	Ordinary Least Squares
PAC	Pan Africanist Congress
PFA	Pension Fund Administrator
PIC	Public Investment Commissioner
P4RR	Partnership for Risk and Resilience
PPS	Professional Provident Society
PSG	Private Securities Group
PwC	PricewaterhouseCoopers
RDB	Reddingsdaadbond (Self Redemption League)
RDP	Reconstruction and Development Plan
RDR	Retail Delivery Review
REAL	Real Africa Holdings Limited
RFA	Retirement Fund Administrator
RFR	Risk Free Return

RHO	Regional Head Office
RoA	Return on Assets
RoC	Return on Capital
RoCE	Return on Capital Employed
ROCO	Register of Co-operation between commercial banks
RoE	Return on Equity
RoEV	Return on Embedded Value
RoOGEV	Return on Group Equity Value
SABC	South African Broadcasting Corporation
SABES	South African Business Ethics Survey
SACEE	South African Council for English Education
SAD	South African Druggists
SADTU	South African Democratic Teachers' Union
SAICA	South African Institute of Chartered Accountants
SALGA	South African Local Government Association
SAM	Sanlam Asset Management
SAM	Solvency Assessment Management (regulatory regime of the FSB)
SAMA	South African Medical Association
SAMAS	South Africa Association of Medical Aid Schemes
SANSOM	Suid-Afrikanse Nasionale Siekte- en Ongevallemaatskappy (South African Sick and Casualty Company)
SAP	South African Party
SAQA	South African Qualifications Authority
SARB	South African Reserve Bank
SASOL	South African Oil and Gas Corporation
SATMAR	South African Torbanite Mining and Research
SBIC	Standard Bank Investment Corporation
SC	Sanlam Corporate
SCM	Sanlam Capital Markets
SDM	Sanlam Developing Markets
SEM	Sanlam Emerging Markets
SEMIL	Sanlam Emerging Markets Ireland, Limited
SF	Sanlam Foundation
SFAS	Statement of Financial Accounting Standards
SFP	Sanlam Financial Planners

SFS	Sanlam Financial Services
SGI	Shriram General Insurance
SHRM	Sanlam Health Risk Management
SHAM	Sanlam Health Administration Management
SHQM	Sanlam Health Quality Management
SIIP	Sanlam International Investment Partners
SIM	Sanlam Investment Management
SMMI	Sanlam Multi Manager International
SNH	Sanlam Netherlands BV
SOA	Service Oriented Architecture
SOE	State Owned Enterprise
SPC	Strategic Planning Company
SPF	Sanlam Personal Finance
SPW	Sanlam Private Wealth
SSS	Sanlam Sky Solutions
STFC	Shriram Transport Finance Company
SUT	Sanlam Unit Trusts
TCF	Treat Customers Fairly
TCFS	Thebe Community Financial Services
TCOA	Transvaal Coal Owners' Association
TIC	Thebe Investment Corporation
TRC	Truth and Reconciliation Commission
UB	Ubuntu–Botho
UBCDT	Ubuntu Botho Community Development Trust
UDF	United Democratic Front
UP	United Party
UBFS	Ubuntu Botho Financial Services

1 Growing opportunity on African soil

A world of opportunity: the new century

Western nations were looking towards the twentieth century with hope, expecting prosperity and progress as scientific and technological advancement had already brought them higher living standards. The Western nations moulded their progress on the model of 'liberal capitalism'. This model secured material advantages, but was grounded in a very specific political framework that promoted the freedom of speech, freedom of commercial exchange, democratic self-government based on an ever-extending franchise, freedom of scientific enquiry, and the mobility of the factors of production. Progress and accumulation of wealth gradually led to the adoption of innovative technology in industry, commerce, and communications and the expansion of financial services.[1] The world population of the new millennium became more urbanized, more secular, and more materialistic. Business responded, either by driving or following this global expansion, but the accompanying social democratization and political liberalization were far from universal.

As Western influence spread across the globe, Africa was the subject of deliberations at the Berlin Conference of 1884/1885 where the colonial powers agreed on the terms of occupation, settlement, and control over territories. As the century drew to a close, British imperial ambitions marched towards the resource-rich independent Boer Republics. By 1902, Britain had just emerged victorious from an unprecedented challenge to its power. In the Southern African territories under British control, liberal capitalism unfolded selectively only as far as the imperial goal was served. Britain steered the four colonies, the Cape Colony, the Natal Colony, the Orange River Colony (formerly the *Republiek van de Oranje Vrijstaat*), and the Transvaal Colony (formerly *De Zuid-Afrikaansche Republiek)* under its authority towards the Union of South Africa in 1910. However, it was primarily those of European descent who participated extensively in the capitalist economy and the political liberties incrementally granted under stages of political emancipation. British reconstruction in the former Boer Republics between 1902 and 1909 engineered the emergence of a white-controlled state in South Africa.

[1] Skidelsky, R. 1998. 'The growth of a world economy', in *The Oxford History of the Twentieth Century*, eds M. Howard and W.M. Louis. Oxford: Oxford University Press: 50–61.

Afrikaners and the English-speaking settlers in the colonies shared a similar outlook on racial co-existence. The Natal Colony implemented racial segregation resembling the policies of the Union since the 1880s and during the National Convention (the successive meetings deliberating on the structure of the planned Union—an all-European affair) the delegates from Natal opposed the extension of the franchise model of the Cape Colony universally in the new Union. In the Transvaal Colony the British High Commissioner, Alfred Milner, was advised by Godfrey Lagden in 1903 (heading up a Commission to advise Milner on the proposed restructuring of the former Boer Republic)[2] that land should be divided on racial lines—a framework closely resembling the core of the Natives Land Act. No 27 of 1913.[3]

Economic and business development occurred in the context of British imperial preference. The Afrikaner community constituted reluctant subjects in the British Empire. With Britain at the height of its imperial power, Afrikaners in South Africa sought to regain lost sovereignty, but were caught between Empire and national pride. While most of the British colonies in Africa were not even contemplating independence from the Empire, or even any degree of autonomy compared to what was granted to the Union of South Africa, British commercial interests in the newly established local mining industry mandated the protection of their economic interests. British imperial pragmatism allowed the unfolding of a dichotomy between liberal capitalism and the paramount interests of the Empire. South Africa was permitted to build the Union on European political supremacy.[4] Black people harboured expectations of British recognition after the South African War, but their concerns were considered a different matter altogether, a matter to be dealt with at a later stage. None of the African, Coloured or Indian leaders were invited to unification negotiations. When the British Parliament considered the South Africa Bill in 1909, their voices were disregarded. A delegation of black leaders went to London, consulted widely with members of Parliament, journalists and the Aborigines Protection Society, but to no avail.

The British Parliament passed the South Africa Act in both houses with a substantial majority on 20 September 1909.[5] Business development mirrored this political dualism. The victorious political party at the first Union elections in 1910, the South African Party, delivered a moderate reconciliatory message of collaboration between the 'two

[2] W. Beinart (2001): *Twentieth Century South Africa,* Oxford University Press: 7–12; J. Grobler (2014): 'Black political awakening': 316.

[3] H. Giliomee (2014): 'Afrikaner nationalism 1875–1899' in F. Pretorius (ed.) *A History of South Africa: From distant past to the present day.* Pretoria: Protea Book House: 263–4.

[4] The British-sanctioned constitution of the Union of South Africa did not grant equal franchise to all inhabitants of the new Union. People of non-European descent were only granted representation by a qualified vote through European representatives in the Cape Province. This right was not extended to any of the other provinces in the new Union.

[5] J. Grobler (2014): 'Black political awakening, 1875–1949' in F. Pretorius (ed.) *A History of South Africa: From distant past to the present day.* Pretoria: Protea Book House: 316–17.

white races' of South Africa—the English- and the Afrikaans-speaking people of South Africa. The first Union Government included most of the former Boer Generals. General Louis Botha was the first Prime Minister and two other former generals, General J.C. Smuts and General J.B.M. Hertzog, formed part of the first cabinet. Afrikaners were in a relatively powerful position politically, but not in the emerging economy.

By 1911 the South African population consisted of 5.972 million people, 1.4 million of whom were Europeans (21.4 per cent), 525 466 (8.6 per cent) were Coloured, 152 094 (2.4 per cent) were Indian, and just over 4 million (67.5 per cent) were African. Afrikaners made up 51.8 per cent of the whites (661 700). Almost half of the African population lived in the Eastern Cape, in the Transkeian and Ciskeian territories, which were rural areas, and almost a million each in the Natal and Transvaal, which were also primarily in rural areas. A total of 51.6 per cent of the white people but only 12.6 per cent of African people were urbanized by 1911. By the end of World War II around 74.5 per cent of the white population and 23.7 per cent of the African population were urbanized. At the end of the war around 60.4 per cent of Afrikaners were urbanized. Literacy rates of the African population were very low in 1911—only 6.8 per cent of African people of all ages could read and write. However, by the end of World War II, the literacy rate had risen to 21.3 per cent.[6] It is against this demographic background that the socio-economic order of South African politics emerged at the beginning of the Union. It was the only territory in Africa where, at the beginning of the twentieth century, the British faced a settler population consisting of loyalists and anti-British nationalists. It was also the only territory in Africa at that time with mineral resources so rich and strategically significant for the Empire.

In South African business non-Afrikaner interests controlled the core of commerce and industry. Afrikaners needed to reposition themselves economically after the war, but only a minority were capable of taking on the challenge. At the beginning of the twentieth century business in South Africa was dominated by English speakers, often British loyalists, and other foreigners such as Jewish, German, or Dutch entrepreneurs. Afrikaners made up a negligible portion of the business community despite constituting more than half of the European population.

Those Afrikaner businessmen who were successful, were primarily from the Cape. At the turn of the century around 52 per cent of Afrikaners lived in the Cape Colony, 19.5 per cent in the Free State and 26 per cent in the Transvaal, with only 2 per cent in Natal. The economies of the *Zuid-Afrikaansche Republiek* and the *Oranje Vrijstaat* were primarily agricultural, with the post-1870 mining sector introducing small industrial developments—the latter firmly in the hands of foreign capital. Influential and wealthy Afrikaner families such as the Graaffs, Kriges, De Waals, Kohlers, Weges, and the De

[6] Union Statistics for Fifty Years (1961): A3–A5; A10; A18; A22.

Villiers family, slowly came to have an important presence in Cape Town. Many joined the Afrikanerbond established in 1883 by J.H. Hofmeyr (*Onze Jan*) to promote the interests of Afrikaners as a community in the Cape. The growing presence of Afrikaners in Cape public life and the commercial environment led to comments such as the following by John X. Merriman, describing David Graaff as 'one of the new breed of pushy Afrikaners'.[7] The South African War exacerbated the polarization between English-speaking colonists and Afrikaners in the Cape Colony. The negotiations leading up to the formation of the Union brought some reconciliation between the two white population groups. A sense of South African loyalty was nurtured by *Onze Jan* who, through the Afrikanerbond, fostered the notion that people to whom he referred as 'Afrikaners' were everybody who owned up for themselves the cultural heritage of the Dutch and English peoples. After the formation of the Union, Hofmeyr declared in 1913 that politically Afrikaners included '*een ieder die, zich in dit land neergezet hebbende, hier wensde te blijven, onze gemeenschappelike belange te verzekeren*...'[8] *Onze Jan* made it clear that the Afrikanerbond recognized no nationalism but that of Afrikaners, and that Afrikaners included everybody who had the well-being of South Africa at heart.[9] The sense of a separate social entity in South Africa, a society with a distinctive destiny, ambitions, and loyalties, had developed among inhabitants of the former British colonies. This notion of a people grounded in the culture and legacy of the European communities from whom they descended, was shared also by Afrikaner leaders of the South African Republic. General Piet Joubert considered the '*uitlanders*' as potential Afrikaners and fellow-citizens of the Boer Republic. The distinction between them and other inhabitants lay in final loyalty—was it with the British Crown or was it with the new settler society? These national sentiments were gradually taking shape and impacted on the emerging society. The Afrikaners occupied a more prominent position in public life after 1910, but public life entailed more than political power. Afrikaners began to assert themselves in other public spheres, such as the press, commerce, and education.

The opportunity of defeat

Opportunity is recognized by inspirational visionaries and transformed into reality—that is the nature of creative entrepreneurship. From the devastation caused by warfare rose the opportunity to rebuild the British colonies and ultimately to give birth to the

[7] *The Cape Times*, 1 August 1882.

[8] J.H. Hofmeyr (1913): *Het leven van Jan Hendrik Hofmeyr (Onze Jan)*. Cape Town: Van de Sandt Villiers: 574. [Afrikaners include everyone who have settled in this country, who wish to reside here and who wish to secure the common interest of all.]

[9] Ibid., p. 712.

new unitary state. Reconstructing the Afrikaner society psychologically and materially at the turn of the century called for visionary leadership to rise and inspire. Rebuilding was bound to be a demanding and protracted endeavour. A sizeable portion of Afrikaners who emerged from the war were poor and marginalized. Nevertheless, there was a will to take on the challenge. It was characteristic of Afrikaners to stand up to existential challenges. White poverty was a reality: more than 77 per cent of all livestock in the Transvaal and 58.5 per cent in the Orange River Colony were wiped out by the war. Anywhere else on earth such circumstances would have reduced those dependent on livestock for agricultural purposes to dependency. Fellow-Afrikaners from the Cape offered monetary and material assistance such as livestock, seed, and money. This sense of mutuality among Afrikaners developed as a recurrent theme in the history of Afrikaners in South Africa. Among the Cape Afrikaner elite, entrepreneurs in agriculture, commerce, professional services, and cultural engagement created a base from which to restore pride and power. Entrepreneurial enthusiasm for business was a distinguishing characteristic of the influential and wealthy Afrikaner families from the Cape. Their entrepreneurial spirit wove a fibre of optimism as a foundation for the rapidly growing economic prosperity of the area. The first entrepreneurs at the Cape were the Free Burghers who since 1657 had battled to ensure free markets and liberal economic policies to facilitate thrift, enterprise, and profitable business. This spirit was the force behind their cultural and religious organizations. Building a future in the country they called their motherland became a collective effort, a '*volkstaak*'.

The South African economy recovered slowly after the South African War. It was only by 1906 that the long post-war depression eased. By 1910 political unification assisted the upward movement in the business cycle, stimulated by mining production and gold exports. World War I offered unexpected opportunities, which lasted until around 1920, when post-war depression struck again. Fortunes were recovering again after two years, only to be shattered by the worldwide depression of 1929. The impact of this global catastrophe hit South Africa as a country dependent on the export of primary products, exceptionally badly. To the Afrikaner community these cyclical business swings presented both opportunities and potentially devastating risks. An entrepreneurial opportunity presented itself, as Afrikaner social marginalization could be addressed by establishing Afrikaner enterprises across the different sectors of the economy.

The ongoing attempts by Alfred Milner to prevent the publication of Afrikaans newspapers in the British colonies after 1902, motivated Afrikaners to establish numerous Afrikaans language papers. *De Volkstem, Het Westen* (later *Het Volksblad*), and *Ons Moedertaal* emerged to voice the Afrikaans views in the language of the people. When World War I broke out, even the Afrikaans newspaper in the Cape, *Ons Land*, enthusiastically supported the decision of the South African Party (SAP) Botha-led government to declare South Africa's allegiance to Britain. The timing was terribly wrong as many nationalist Afrikaners harboured a deep-seated feeling of resentment towards

Britain. There was no national newspaper to express this message. This sense of rejection fuelled the emergence of self-empowerment strategies. After 1902 Afrikaner women formed their own welfare organizations. Afrikaans teachers established their own teachers' unions, and when Afrikaners moved their savings from the imperial banks to smaller Afrikaner-controlled financial institutions (the Stellenbosch District Bank, and numerous trust companies and local boards of executors in the Cape), the way was paved for Afrikaner self-empowerment strategies.

The time had come for Afrikaners to address the growing sense of nationalism that was gaining a new dimension under the leadership of Hertzog. Even before the formation of the Union, Hertzog had insisted on equality of both English and Afrikaans as the medium of instruction in schools. After 1910 Hertzog championed the principle of South Africa's autonomy in international relations, when he stated unequivocally at a meeting at De Wildt in late 1912 that a British decision to declare war would not automatically commit South Africa to that war. Hertzog insisted on the principle of 'South Africa first', meaning that the Dominions would only follow Britain if such a decision to go to war served the best interests of the individual Dominion. Young people were inspired by Hertzog's leadership. In a telegram to Hertzog in December 1912, Jannie de Waal, Willie Hofmeyr, and Fred Dormehl wrote: '*Jong Zuid-Afrika waardeer uw mannelijk gedrag en sal uw poginge tot opbouw van een suiwer Afrikaans nationalisme verder eendragtig ondersteun. Ons wens u alle sukses.*'[10] Tension regarding Hertzog's position resulted in Botha leaving Hertzog out of the cabinet when reshuffling it in an not unexpected move in 1913. In 1914 Hertzog formed a new political party, the National Party, clearly making national South African interests paramount in opposition to allegiance to the British Empire.

Tension was mounting between South Africans who supported the British war declaration (generally but not exclusively the English-speaking population), and those resisting being drawn into a war on the side of the former enemy, Britain. World War I created a crisis of loyalty: the British declaration of war against Germany unleashed Afrikaner opposition among those nationalists rejecting British supremacy. This socio-political division presented a potential threat to stability in the newly formed Union, but also an opportunity to mobilize South African nationalism in the interest of national economic goals.

Afrikaner rebels organized themselves under former Boer Generals to resist the official mobilization of South African troops. The rebels invaded South West Africa (then a German colony, now Namibia) to prevent the occupation by South African armed forces loyal to the British crown. Afrikaner rebels' military mobilization and armed confrontation

[10] C.F.J. Müller (1990): *Sonop in die Suide. Geboorte en groei van die Nasionale Pers, 1915–1948*, p. 75. [Young South Africa admires your brave conduct and will unanimously support your efforts to building a truly Afrikaans nationalism. We wish you all the best.]

with the South African Defence Force caused the loss of life and destruction of property. Rebels were captured and tried and some were sentenced to death. Others were jailed or received heavy fines. Afrikaner sympathizers joined forces to effect the release of rebels and pay fines in order to secure their freedom. An unprecedented voluntary fund-raising effort known as the *Helpmekaarbeweging* (Mutual Aid Movement) was organized to address the legal and financial costs incurred by the rebels. The *Helpmekaarbeweging* collected more than £330 000 from Afrikaners from all walks of life, paid all rebel fines and legal costs and contributed to an overwhelming sense of achievement and pride. A surplus in excess of £92 000 was finally put into a fund, later to be used for education bursaries.

Around the same time as the looming war in Europe, Afrikaners in the Cape grew increasingly dissatisfied with their lack of a public voice. There was no newspaper expressing their views. Cape Afrikaner leaders again mobilized nationalist sentiments to secure a Dutch public medium of expression, debate, and opinion on matters newsworthy in their own community. They needed a mouthpiece to spread the nationalistic ideas of Hertzog since none of the existing Dutch newspapers in the region were sympathetic to his patriotic ideas. It was apparent that the growing countrywide support for Hertzog mandated a newspaper. On 12 May 1915 the Afrikaner-controlled newspaper company *De Nationale Pers* was established. The first newspaper, *De Burger,* was published on 26 July 1915. This development caused sharp division among Afrikaners in the Cape. Many Afrikaners were directly involved in the publication of *Ons Land,* the Dutch newspaper which was openly critical of the nationalist policies of Hertzog.[11] *De Burger* constituted the second leg of the Afrikaans language movement in the Cape and received support from Afrikaners across the country—even letters of support from rebels still in jail. As a new business venture, the establishment of a newspaper in the wake of strong opposition by the government and the upcoming war was risky.

Financially, *De Burger* ran very tight operations during its first three years. Hostile English newspapers organized a boycott of advertisements in *De Burger,* which almost brought the paper to its knees. Founding members invested personally in the newspaper and were on the verge of losing all within the first two months of going to press. Prudent management secured the survival of the paper and eventual success simply led to greater achievements. Its success set a benchmark for the development of new entrepreneurial ventures. The case of *De Burger* served as an excellent example when the establishment of a permanent trust and insurance company was considered. The launch of a newspaper strengthened Afrikaner nationalism and in the editorial column Dr D.F. Malan, the newspaper's first editor, advocated strategies for economic empowerment. He wrote, 'a people able to maintain themselves materially, ought to be able also to do so politically

[11] C.F.J. Muller (1990): *Sonop in die Suide*, pp. 116–64.

and socially'.[12] Confidence in the ability to succeed in business, specifically a financial enterprise, was growing.

Important forces converged between 1914 and 1918. Hertzog expressed a growing dissident voice against a prevailing British sentiment of superiority. Afrikaner nationalism gained confidence in self-mobilized actions, such as the formation of a new political party, resistance against the declaration of war, self-redemption of convicted fellow-Afrikaners during the 1914 Rebellion, and the formation of a new Afrikaans language newspaper. Afrikaners displayed a clear South African patriotism, as they called for equality for both English and Afrikaans in the church, legal, and public spheres. The key was self-empowerment. On the occasion of the establishment of a branch of the *Afrikaanse Taal- en Kultuurvereniging* (ATKV—Afrikaans Language and Cultural Association) in Stellenbosch in 1907, N.J. Hofmeyr, professor at the Theological Seminary in Stellenbosch, advised his nephew, W.A. Hofmeyr, that Afrikaans as a language would only gain full equal standing once it acquired commercial value.[13] Afrikaans undoubtedly did not enjoy that status by 1918. Willie Hofmeyr resigned his established position as a partner in a law firm to take up a full-time organizing position for the newly formed National Party in 1915, and subsequently the Chairmanship of *De Nationale Pers.*

Enter insurance

A group of enterprising Afrikaners met in Cape Town on 5 December 1917 to establish an insurance and trust company. This initiative followed informal conversations among Afrikaner business, cultural, church, and community leaders about the ever-growing problem of persistent poverty, especially among white people. This social phenomenon had been gaining momentum since the devastating droughts of the late nineteenth century, the scorched earth tactics of the British forces during the South African War, and a growing deterioration of the social fabric among those in abject poverty. The Smuts[14] government's policy was a neo-liberal market approach, following the Cambridge economist Alfred Marshall's advocacy of the corrective measure of the market. The poor-white problem added yet another dimension to the emerging nationalism—Afrikaner leaders were thinking about measures to provide employment for impoverished fellow-Afrikaners. All of the founding members attending the meeting had been involved in some business initiative and had participated in the wider Afrikaner cultural

[12] N.J. le Roux (1953): *W.A. Hofmeyr*, p. 123. [13] Ibid., p. 119.

[14] J.C. Smuts succeeded Louis Botha as Prime Minister of South Africa after Botha passed away on 27 August 1919.

and community initiatives. These initiatives, developed from a South African perspective, were driven by ambitions to strengthen the country's independence.

The meeting was attended by C.G. Fichardt (Charlie), W.A. Hofmeyr (Willie), C.R. Louw (Charlie), P.A. Malan (Piet), F.H. Dormehl (Fred), A.J.F. Benning (Antoon), and A. MacDowall (Alfred). Apart from MacDowall, all the founding members were keenly involved in the Afrikaans language movements, the launching of a new newspaper, and the rising nationalist political tendencies. These men had developed social capital on three levels: the reformed protestant religion, which instilled a sense of social responsibility towards fellow-Afrikaners, nationalism and cultural pride in response to British political domination, and visionary entrepreneurial ambition to strengthen Afrikaner participation in the South African economy. As members of the Afrikaner elite, they were engaged in the Dutch Reformed Church initiatives seeking solutions to the problem of white poverty. The success of the *Helpmekaarbeweging* boosted the confidence that it might be possible to mobilize Afrikaner savings to support other ventures motivated by the emerging nationalist South African sentiments. The close solidarity of poor Afrikaners was aptly illustrated by the scope of the *Helpmekaarbeweging*. By venturing into an insurance company Afrikaner leaders devised a new strategy to address the overall position of Afrikaners in South Africa.[15] A stronger role in the political and socio-cultural context was beginning to take shape, but Afrikaner participation in the economy still left much to be desired. The strengthening of the South African economy was premised on the Afrikaners assuming a dignified role in the economy, and making a contribution to building a future for the fatherland. Unless all the components of the white society could participate and contribute equally to the economy, the full potential of the country would remain compromised and subject to foreign domination.

Choosing the insurance industry as a vehicle for economic empowerment and domestic economic development was a strategic decision. These men knew very well that foreign insurance companies dominated the local market. In a letter to *The* Star on 22 May 1960, R.I.C. Scott-Hayward, an Irish-born former Accident Manager at Santam, commented on the employment opportunities open to Afrikaners in Johannesburg during the first two decades of the twentieth century: 'At this time there was no senior place for any "Colonial", irrespective of language group, in any Bank or Insurance Company, for these avenues of employment were the close preserves of "overseas-born men". This offended my sense of justice and I did everything possible to teach the South African-born young men all I could.' Scott-Hayward referred to the exclusion of Afrikaners, irrespective of their abilities, from all positions higher than chief clerk in

[15] Verhoef, G. (2008) 'Nationalism, social capital and economic empowerment: SANLAM and the economic upliftment of the Afrikaner people, 1918–1960', i, Special Issue: Putting Social Capital to Work, 50 (6): 694–713.

any financial institution. Only foreigners were appointed to positions of management and control.[16] An entrepreneurial opportunity seemed to present itself for Afrikaner entrepreneurs: they had superior market knowledge and could navigate the local context at a time when this knowledge intersected with a business opportunity and social mobilization. The success of the *Helpmekaarbeweging* pointed towards an entrepreneurial opportunity: Afrikaners' underestimated savings capacity. An awakened nationalistic patriotism appealed to many Afrikaners aspiring to rise from the defeat at the hand of the British. The business opportunity lay in building a strong insurance company while simultaneously addressing social and economic marginalization under the slogan of 'South Africa first'.

The seed of entrepreneurial action germinated during the dark period of the so-called 'bitter legacy of the war of freedom'. The eight founding members shared a sense of patriotism and sympathy with the loss of political sovereignty by the former Boer Republics. They were appalled by Afrikaner impoverishment and social marginalization. Charlie Fichardt had fought in the South African War, was captured and sent in 'exile' to the Cape (Mowbray) until the end of the war. Willie Hofmeyr, who had joined the Boer commandos during the war, was also captured and 'exiled' from Johannesburg (where he had practised as a lawyer) to Cape Town until the end of the war. Charlie Louw had also joined the Boer commandos at the beginning of the South African War, but was captured in 1901 and sent back to his home town of Paarl. Hofmeyr and Fichardt developed useful business connections during their stay in Cape Town.

Fichardt, the son of a German immigrant from Crentz, north-eastern Germany, had an English governess, was educated in Germany and Britain (at Blair College Scotland), and started his career with an English firm, W. Dunn, in London. Fichardt returned to Bloemfontein in the Orange Free State to work with his father in G.A. Fichardt General Dealer, but soon took up the management of Fichardt Estate, Private Bank, and Financial Agents. He then entered public life in Bloemfontein, where he was city councillor and mayor, as well as a close friend of the former Orange Free State President, M.T. Steyn. While in exile in the Cape, he maintained frequent contact with prominent politicians and business people. He met John Daniels, a member of the Cape Town municipality, with whom he entered into a business association upon his return to the British-controlled Orange River Colony in 1902. Fichardt re-established his business interests with the aim of restoring Afrikaner political power. This he achieved by serving as director on the Board of Directors of the newspaper *The Friend*, the mouthpiece of Free State citizens appealing for self-government for the colony—granted in 1908 under the political leadership of the *Orangia Unie*. Fichardt was elected member of the Union Parliament for the constituency of Ladybrand. On his annual attendance of Parliament

[16] SA: 6/5/2: *Die Sanlam-Fakkel*, 7 May 1936, p. 3, 1 November 1948, p. 3.

in Cape Town he engaged with fellow-Afrikaner leaders and businessmen, including Willie Hofmeyr.

William Angus (Willie) Hofmeyr was born in Montagu in the Cape, the son of Dr Servaas Hofmeyr, a *dominee* or minister in the Dutch Reformed Church (DRC). He studied law at Victoria College (later University of Stellenbosch) with J.B.M. Hertzog (former Boer General in the South African War, and later Prime Minister of South Africa) and finally established a legal practice with his brother in Johannesburg. During the South African War, Hofmeyr was captured and exiled to Cape Town. After the war he established his practice as attorney in Cape Town. As an Afrikaner patriot and member of the '*oude Kaapsche familiën*' (old Cape families), he became involved in the Second Afrikaans Language Movement, calling for full recognition of Afrikaans. His mother was Anna Georgina Morgan, daughter of a Scottish minister, but the six Hofmeyr children were brought up as Afrikaners, although they spoke English fluently, both at the dinner table and in their education. As an Afrikaner 'aristocrat' Hofmeyr was destined to play a leading role in Cape public life. As the son of a minister of the DRC, he was acutely aware of the poverty among fellow-Afrikaners, but his vision was to foster Afrikaner agency to create employment opportunities through business enterprise. One such initiative was the formation of the Afrikaans publishing house, *De Nationale Pers*, with its newspaper *De Burger* in 1915. Hofmeyr was Chairman of the Board of Directors of *De Nationale Pers,* and from 1918 Managing Director. Willie Hofmeyr had travelled across the country as organizer of the National Party. During these visits to remote rural areas, he was appalled by the destitution of many poor Afrikaners. His impressions were strengthened by the so-called 'Poor White' Congress of the DRC in November 1917. At these church meetings the severity of the poverty problem was highlighted and a serious plea made to fellow-Afrikaners to address the problem as the responsibility of the '*volk*' (people) themselves. Hofmeyr had the vision of Afrikaner economic empowerment. The means were not yet clear, but powerful events were signalling the opportune time to do so. The success of the *Helpmekaarbeweging* was an important turning point. The establishment of Sanlam was the calling of the people, a '*volkstaak*', to give effect to much-needed economic initiatives of Afrikaner economic salvation.[17]

The Cape Afrikaner elite shared a genuine sense of solidarity with their fellow-Afrikaners in the Transvaal and the Free State. Since Victoria College was the only tertiary institution of Dutch instruction, it emerged as a place of convergence for many future leaders in the Afrikaans cultural and political movement—Willie Hofmeyr, J.B.M. Hertzog, C.W. Malan, P.A. Malan. Stellenbosch became a place of intense discourse about equal language rights for Afrikaans, stimulated by the rise of nationalism among theologians at the Theological Seminary. The public belittling of Afrikaners and

[17] H.R. Malan (1977): William Angus Hofmeyr, *South African Biographical Dictionary*, 3. Tafelberg: Pretoria: 416–18.

their language aroused these nationalistic sentiments. Sir Alfred Milner expressed his intention in 1902, 'to absorb and ultimately getting rid of them [the burghers] as a separate, exclusive caste'.[18] In the editorial of the *Cape Times* of 4 May 1901 it was asked 'why forego it [English] its glorious privilege for the sake of kitchen Dutch, an ungrammatical *taal* which is only fit for peasants and up-country kraals?'[19] Through these and other jingoist inferences and a general anti-Afrikaner mentality, the market value of Dutch/Afrikaans was destroyed, and with it also its economic value. Sadie noted that there was little or no empathy in the private sector with the Afrikaner and no feeling of responsibility or compunction towards him. Jobs were allegedly deliberately withheld from Afrikaners, as revealed in a petition which stated 'Jingo's do not want to give jobs to Boers'.[20] The result was an induced feeling of isolation: 'their language, culture and sense of belonging fractured, they began to suffer an inferiority complex'.[21] This observation was indeed valid for those Afrikaners still suffering from the post-war destruction and impoverishment, but the *Helpmekaarbeweging* sparked an opportunity.

That opportunity needed ignition. The Cape Afrikaner elite's social capital was embedded in capitalism: the Cape was 'one part of South Africa in which Afrikaners had a clear and long-established stake in capitalism. Indeed, the wine and wheat farmers of the Western Cape formed the oldest stratum of the ruling class: Powerful and affluent elite... [which] came into existence around 1700 and were the major beneficiaries of Willem Adriaan van der Stel's fall from grace as governor in 1707 as the result of his attempts to monopolize Cape economic life. Two centuries later, these farmers were still determined to preserve the social relations that ensured their wealth.'[22] Striving to extend wealth went hand in hand with Afrikaner leaders' insistence on the recognition of their rightful place as equals in society. The time of isolation of fellow-Afrikaners was behind them. In a unified South Africa, Afrikaner leaders occupied positions of political prominence. The time was ripe to push aspirations forward into the economic sphere.

Piet Malan practised as a lawyer in Bloemfontein and used Willie Hofmeyr as correspondent in Cape Town. Malan had already discussed the possibility of the establishment of an insurance company in the Free State with former President M.T. Steyn and Fichardt in 1916. Piet Malan was aggrieved that the absence of a local Afrikaans insurance company left him no choice but to conduct his insurance business

[18] G. Joubert, 1997: Afrikaans: is dit ons erns? *Die Burger*, 28 April 1997, p. 10; N.C. Weideman: *Politieke naweë van die Anglo-Boereoorlog 1899–1902*. Unpublished DPhil Thesis, University of Pretoria, p. 166.

[19] *Cape Times*, 4 May 1901: 4.

[20] J.L. Sadie, 2002: *The Fall and Rise of the Afrikaner in the South African economy*. University of Stellenbosch Annals, 2001/2002, p. 12; A.N. Pelser, 1941: Die Arm-blanke in die Suid-Afrikaanse Republiek tussen die jare 1852–1899, *Historiese Studies*, 2(4):184.

[21] G. Leach, 1989: *The Afrikaners: Their last Great Trek*. Macmillan: London: 28.

[22] A. Nash (1997): Wine-farmers, heresy trials and the 'whole personality': The Emergence of the Stellenbosch philosophical tradition, 1916–1940, *South African Journal of Philosophy*, 16(2): 56.

through the foreign companies. This situation, he noted '*het modderspore in my siel getrap*' [it treaded muddy footprints in my soul].[23] In the Cape, Hofmeyr had already tested the waters with other Afrikaner business leaders as well as well-disposed English-speaking persons with experience in the insurance business.

One such Afrikaner businessman, who was not part of the established Cape Afrikaner elite families but had developed extensive independent business interests, was Frederic Hansen Dormehl. Dormehl was actively involved with Hofmeyr in the Second Afrikaans Language Movement, specifically to terminate English sermons in the DRC Wynberg congregation, where they both attended church services. Dormehl married the daughter of a DRC 'dominee'. He had worked as a clerk at the London and Lancashire Insurance Company in Cape Town since the age of sixteen. Later he joined Alliance, but after qualifying as an accountant he was appointed in that capacity at the *Algemene Eksekuteurskamer* (General Trust Company). At the time of his departure from Alliance, he had already expressed the desire to establish an Afrikaans insurance company, since all the companies offering fire and accident insurance were owned by foreigners. In 1915 he joined *De Nationale Pers* as general manager and secretary and was inspired to promote Afrikaner involvement in the broader South African economy.

Willie Hofmeyr proved to be the link between inspired Afrikaners in the Cape. He knew A.F.J. Benning (Anthony Frederik Jacobus—known as Antoon), who as the son of a Dutch immigrant established extensive business interests in the construction industry. Benning also served in the Cape Town municipal council and joined Dormehl and Hofmeyr in advocating the interests of Afrikaners in Cape Town. He attended the meeting in the Royal Hotel to discuss the formation of Santam.

A third Cape lawyer was Charles Robert (Charlie) Louw. He was the son of a DRC 'dominee', and his mother was a sister of Reverend Andrew Murray, the Scottish reverend who came to the Cape in the 1820s. He studied law at Victoria College, but completed his articles of clerkship in Pretoria. After the war he returned to Ermelo in the south-eastern Transvaal to practise law, but was disturbed by the destruction and impoverishment caused by the South African War. He responded by organizing the first agricultural co-operative to assist farmers in rebuilding their farms and resuming subsistence agriculture to maintain destitute families. In 1916 he returned to Cape Town with the explicit intention of using his business skills to establish Afrikaner business enterprises to grow their participation in and contribution to the South African economy, which at that stage, i.e. the first decade of the twentieth century, stood at a mere 13 per cent of the total economy.[24]

[23] *Die Fakkel*, September 1953, p. 8.

[24] J. Venter (1987): Charles Robert Louw, *South African Biographical Dictionary*, 5. Human Sciences Research Council: Pretoria: 495–7; *Die Fakkel*, December 1966: 5–7.

These members of the Afrikaner elite were ambitious, and had good intentions, but they knew very little about the insurance industry. They were primarily legal practitioners and would rely on Dormehl's experience in the industry to provide grounding to their aspirations. Hofmeyr also met Alfred MacDowall, a Scot who had immigrated to the Cape as an employee of Standard Bank. MacDowall was a Fellow of the Scottish Institute of Bankers. He married Elizabeth de Vaal, an Afrikaans woman from Fraserburg. MacDowall worked in the Transvaal for a short period, before returning to the Cape to take up employment with the General Accident Company where he was employed as a senior accountant from 1912. In that position he recognized the untapped potential in the Afrikaners' sense of a 'calling' in South Africa, so aptly displayed in the savings mobilization of the *Helpmekaarbeweging*. He commented to Hofmeyr: 'You must capitalize on the wave of nationalism.' MacDowall discussed the idea of establishing an insurance company with Afrikaner capital with G.F.S. (Gys) de Villiers, an Afrikaans lawyer at the firm PAM Cloete, but nothing came of that. MacDowall subsequently discussed his ideas with National Party members of the House of Assembly, Charlie Fichardt, Tielman Roos, and Piet Grobler. It soon became clear that such an initiative would need the support of the Cape Afrikaner elite. MacDowall met with Willie Hofmeyr, Piet Malan, and Fred Dormehl to discuss the possibility. Although MacDowall claimed to have been the originator of the idea of an Afrikaner-capitalized insurance company, it was later challenged by Piet Malan. Nevertheless, MacDowall supported the initiative of Hofmeyr and fellow-Afrikaners. He attended the meeting to establish such a company as an interested Cape businessman.[25]

The meeting in the Royal Hotel in Cape Town on 5 December 1917 prepared for the establishment of the *Suid-Afrikaanse Nasionale Trust en Versekeringsmaatskappy* (Santam—South African Trust and Insurance Company) on 28 March 1918. The attendees were Charlie Fichardt, Willie Hofmeyr, Antoon Benning, Charlie Louw, Piet Malan, and Fred Dormehl, as well as MacDowall. They agreed to serve as the 'Provisional Board of Directors' of Santam in preparation of the official launch in March 1918. The group discussed a plan to embark on an insurance venture, engaging in life and short-term insurance, such as fire and accident insurance and trust business. Thorough planning was done for the meeting: a draft prospectus was discussed, including the appointment of directors and staff. It was also envisaged that the insurance company would buy the trust, estate, and insurance business of Fichardt and Daniels in Bloemfontein. Daniels was Fichardt's business partner and the meeting proposed to offer Daniels a position as manager of Santam in the Free State. The meeting appointed MacDowall as General Manager and Secretary. Systematic planning followed to give effect to the new insurance initiative. The provisional board met six times during December 1917 to finalize

[25] SA 6/6/1: Biography A. MacDowall; SA 6/1/5 Interview P.A. Malan, March 1965.

preparation for the publication of the prospectus on 28 January 1918. On 11 December 1917 Jan S. de Villiers was appointed to prepare the Memorandum of the Articles of Association. Attempts to register the company in both English and Afrikaans failed because the Registrar of Companies did not allow dual registration. On 21 January 1918 the name of the new company was decided—*Suid-Afrikaanse Nasionale Trust en Assuransie Maatskappy*. By the end of December 1917 four more people were invited to join the Provisional Board of Directors. They were C.W. (Charlie) Malan, T. J. (Tinie) Louw, T.J. (Tielman) de V. Roos and P.G.W. (Piet) Grobler. The significance of the new additions was the greater geographical representation of the board—Roos was an advocate in Pretoria and Grobler was a Member of Parliament for a rural constituency in the Transvaal. Their inclusion enhanced the geographical inclusivity of Afrikaner leadership. Broad representation of leaders across South Africa was crucial for a new insurance competitor in South Africa. Preparing the minutes of the planning meeting in English displayed goodwill towards MacDowall, the only English-speaking member 'in attendance' at the first meeting. It was also in full agreement with the intended vision of the founding fathers, namely that the company should be a truly South African company.

It was significant that Antoon Benning was not a member of the established Cape Afrikaner elite families, but a well-respected businessman. He was the son of a Dutch immigrant, but his father passed away at an early age, leaving him to support the family. Antoon qualified as a carpenter, spent some time on the mines in the Transvaal and finally entered the construction industry as a qualified tradesman. He was responsible for the construction of large buildings in Cape Town, inter alia, the Cape Supreme Court and part of the building occupied by *De Nationale Pers*. Benning had invested in the company that printed the newspaper *Ons Land*, which had given him valuable experience he could pass on to Willie Hofmeyr during the planning and establishment of *De Nationale Pers*. Benning shared the Afrikaner nationalist sentiments, but was of particular value as an independent and respected Afrikaner businessman in Cape Town.[26]

The prospectus of the new company was published on 28 January 1918. Provision was made for total nominal capital of £300 000, of which shares of £1 each to the value of £200 000 were offered to the public. On 29 January 1918 *De Burger* welcomed the publication of the prospectus, especially noting the clear and meticulous outline of the proposed business plan, conveying an impression of a truly South African national spirit. Unfortunately the negotiations for the takeover of the Fichardt and Daniels business in Bloemfontein took an unexpected turn. Daniels declined the offer of a managerial position at Santam, and Fichardt felt torn between two loyalties—on the one hand to his business partner and on the other hand to the new insurance company he had helped to conceptualize. In private correspondence Fichardt noted that the failure to

[26] *Die Fakkel*, July 1963, pp. 15–17.

incorporate this business in Santam, left him no choice but to withdraw from the planned new insurance company. He was not prepared to sit on the board of a company that would compete directly with his own existing business in Bloemfontein.[27] Fichardt resigned as Chairman of the provisional board of Santam on 26 March. A corrective note was immediately printed as addendum to the prospectus, announcing the replacement of Fichardt by Willie Hofmeyr as Chairman of the provisional board. The Administrator of the Orange Free State, C.T. (Carl) Wilcocks, replaced Fichardt on the board. The company was finally registered on 28 March 1918. The certificate was issued in terms of Section 57 of the Companies Act and was the first to be issued to a company in Afrikaans.[28] Santam was registered as an insurance company undertaking all forms of trust work, life assurance, fire and accident insurance, health, marine, animal stock, and related insurance business.

The strategic positioning of Santam points to the careful planning and intelligent assessment of the insurance environment in South Africa. The Articles of Association prepared by Jan de Villiers, the lawyer responsible for Santam's legal compliance, provided an avenue to separate short-term insurance business from long-term life insurance. De Villiers cautioned the planning committee that it could be very difficult to keep long-term life funds separate from short-term liabilities. The risk of impairment of the long-term life funds by general claims against Santam creditors presented a real risk. Section 16 of the Articles of Association provided for the conduct of life insurance on the basis of the mutual principle, and Section 18 also made provision for life business. No mention was made of a separate life insurance company, but Section 22 provided for the establishment by Santam of any company it saw fit to promote its business, and to fund such a company or to apply the capital of Santam to stand surety for such a company. Formal legal provision was therefore made for the formation of a separate life insurance company, but the first step was to register the company and then to explore strategic expansion. The planners noted the Government report on the insurance business in the Cape Province in 1915: insurance premiums had risen from £24 263 572 in 1911 to £30 727 747 in 1915—an increase of £6 464 175. Of this new insurance business, the six local companies wrote 60.7 per cent of the increase in premiums and the twenty-nine foreign companies 39.2 per cent. Although these figures only explained the developments in one province, it was taken as a clear indication of the vast potential in the South African insurance market for new local competitors. By 1918 foreign insurance companies undoubtedly still dominated the short-term market. They collected 73.2 per cent of premium income in all short-term classes. The high profitability in the industry, broadly calculated by considering claims only, was around 69 per cent in

27 SA: Letter Fichardt—Santam Provisional Board, 12 April 1918.
28 Santam Bank. *50th Annual Report* 1967, p. 4.

1918.[29] What motivated the Santam men was the growth in the domestic market. In long-term life assurance the reverse was the case—local companies dominated the market by far. It would therefore make good business sense to enter both categories of insurance business from the outset. One matter that seemed non-negotiable was that the life business had to be undertaken on a mutual basis. The dominant South African life offices were mutual in organization. The strategic direction of Santam was therefore to develop life insurance through a mutual form in a separate life insurance company.

When the Fichardt connection failed to materialize, was the prospective new insurance venture at risk? Three major risks presented themselves: market risk, capital risk, and human capital risk. The market risk was the number of insurance companies operating in the small South African market. By 1910 the minority of insurance companies operating in the Union were incorporated in South Africa and the majority had head offices in Britain. By 1918, when Santam was about to enter the market, a total of seventy-four insurance companies operated in the South African market—forty-four with head offices in Britain, fifteen in South Africa, eight in other British dominions, three in the USA, and four in other parts of the world.[30] The only consolation was the institutional memory of former insurance companies established by Dutch colonists in South Africa—the *Zuid-Afrikaansche Brand en Versekeringsmaatskappij* (established in 1831 and sold in 1894); the *Commercial Marine and Fire Assurance Company*, established in 1849 and of which ten of the thirteen directors were Dutch colonists; and *De Protecteur Brand en Levens Assurantie Maatschappij* (established in 1838 and sold in 1896). Keen market competition was to be expected. New entrants needed to offer a clearly distinguishable product.[31] The only mitigation to the steep challenge was the fact that there were only four South African companies in life insurance and three in fire insurance by 1918—of the latter, two were confined to localized rural areas. The opportunity presenting itself was in choosing an entrepreneurial competitive advantageous position—target a well-defined uninsured market segment and operate on a nationwide geographical basis. Official statistics proved the growth in the insurance market, and Santam had reason to believe that with careful strategic planning it could ride the wave.

The capital risk was to mobilize sufficient capital to enter and sustain operations in the highly competitive market. Local insurers were generally well capitalized. The timing of Santam's entry was good since World War I had boosted local food and general agricultural and resource prices, which raised inflation, and created surplus funds

[29] *Official Year Book of South Africa*, 1925, p. 841.

[30] *Official Year Book of the Union of South Africa*, 1910–1924—various tables consolidated.

[31] R. Vivian, 1995: *The story of Mutual & Federal, Johannesburg*, pp. 17, 28, 69; G. Verhoef, 2015: 'The world insures South Africa: Early insurance activities of Insurance companies in South Africa, 1820–1910' in R. Pearson and T. Yoneyama (eds) *Corporate Forms and organizational choice in international insurance*. Oxford: Oxford University Press, p. 164.

seeking good investment returns. The confidence that sufficient capital would be raised was based on a meticulous planning process to prevent a human capital risk. Before the end of 1917 the planning committee had employed experts from the insurance industry to head up key divisions of the new company's operations. Dormehl was engaged as Managing Director. MacDowall was appointed General Manager and Secretary, supported in operations by J.H. Harris as Agency Manager, Simon J.P. West as Fire Manager, Reginald I.C. Scott-Hayward as Accidents Manager and Geo Patterson as Actuary. Dormehl and MacDowall were qualified insurance men. Dormehl had worked with West, an experienced fire manager, at the London and Lancashire, and Allianz. Scott-Hayward was an Irish nationalist and experienced insurance manager who had inquired from Fichardt, Oswald Pirow, and Tielman Roos about the possibility of establishing a truly South African insurance concern. Harris was a former colleague of MacDowall at the General and Accident Insurance Company and offered to assist the new concern in raising its capital.[32] With an experienced complement of insurance men, the public could be approached to invest with confidence in a truly South African concern.

The proposed Board of Directors of Santam, as published in the prospectus, added human capital of a different nature. This group included lawyers, an advocate, businessmen, farmers prominent in social life, and politicians—seven from the Cape, two from the Transvaal, and one from the Orange Free State. These were prominent leaders in the Afrikaner community, educated men involved in the rising tide of nationalism and patriotism. The Afrikaner leadership accepted responsibility for ordinary Afrikaners' sense of collection as a people with a specific mindset and set of convictions. The leaders took it upon themselves to keep the welfare of their people in trust. One strategy to do so was to devise ways of promoting such well-being. The development of the insurance industry constituted a logical part of the leadership strategy. Despite serious attempts by persons such as Piet Malan to invite prominent Afrikaners who supported the South African Party of Louis Botha to the first meeting in Cape Town in December 1917, only Afrikaners known to be sympathetic to the views of the newly established National Party of Hertzog attended. The conciliatory approach suffered a blow with the public refusal of Louis Botha, then Prime Minister of the Union, to collaborate in the new venture. Piet Malan had invested a lot of energy in promoting the planned new venture among Afrikaners of all political sympathies—including SAP supporters. Piet Malan argued that the idea of a new South African insurance company, without support from both SAP and NP (National Party) Afrikaners, would be an idea stillborn. Willie Hofmeyr himself approached the Prime Minister, Louis Botha, asking for his support for the establishment of an insurance company with Afrikaner capital. Botha refused to render his

[32] SA 6/6/1/5: Interview with P.A. Malan, March 1965. Malan expressed his scepticism about the 'Jew' offering to sell shares in the new company, but Harris did not disappoint.

support or become involved.[33] The strategy to bring Afrikaners out in united support of the formation of Santam was not successful. When branches were later opened, the new Santam management went all out to bring SAP Afrikaners into the organization.[34] Although limited success was achieved in engaging Afrikaners from different political affiliations in the launch of Santam, in the long run a broad base of Afrikaners was eventually integrated into the successful operations of the new company. Raising share capital went satisfactorily.

The first year in business: 1918–1919

Santam was registered as an insurance company on 28 March 1918. It commenced official business on 1 May 1918. On 2 April 1918 the provisional board met in the offices of *De Burger* to constitute the new Board of Directors of the newly registered insurance company, Santam. W.A. Hofmeyr was elected Chairman and C.T.M. Wilcock Deputy Chairman. The other members of the first board were C.R. Louw, F.H. Dormehl, A.F. Benning, C.W. Malan, T. de V. Roos, P.G.W. Grobler, P.A. Malan, and T.J. Louw. The last three directors (Grobler, Malan, and Louw) were absent from this meeting. On 18 April Dr C.F (Colin) Steyn also joined the board. Initially the Board of Directors met at 30 Keerom Street, the offices of Willie Hofmeyr, then Managing Director of *De Burger*. The registered offices of Santam were situated at No. 10 Burg Street, Cape Town and occupied the entire first floor at a rent of £20 per month. In 1920 Santam moved offices to Adderley Street. In 1918, the core business of Santam was its trust business. The trust business was explained by MacDowall in his 11 November 1918 report as the administration of all classes of estates, the consolidation of applications for loans, and the investment of the funds of the trust and life companies. Loans were granted on fixed property (mortgages). The insurance business was in the fire and accident departments, and included the issuing of guarantees.

The composition of the initial staff complement harboured an element of irony. The majority of the officials of the new company were not Afrikaans speakers. Paterson, MacDowall, Harris, Scott-Hayward, and West were all English speakers. The company was not yet fully capitalized, but shares were offered incrementally to new stakeholders as branches were established across the country. Even before the registration of the company Harris and his collaborators had sold 40 000 shares. By 13 April 1918 a total of 52 000 shares had been sold by the Harris connection as well as numerous Afrikaners in legal practice, trust companies, and related business enterprises.[35] The distribution of

[33] N.J. le Roux (1953): *WA Hofmeyr—Sy werk en waarde*: 127.
[34] SA: 6/5/2/1: PA Malan Biographical documents: Interview 1960.
[35] *Santampos*, Maart 1959: 6.

shares was the collective effort of many Afrikaners and non-Afrikaner sympathizers with the vision. Many ordinary Afrikaners as well as influential Afrikaner community leaders and businessmen were mobilized by the successful Afrikaner nationalist initiatives of the recent past. Here the successful collection of contributions to the *Helpmekaar* fund served as inspiration to show a similar enthusiasm and dedication to a cause affecting their own people. The Santam shares were marketed as an investment, not meant for speculation like, for example, mining shares. Shareholders were given two voting rights for twenty-five shares, which increased to ten voting rights for 5 100 shares.[36] By June 1919, the board decided not to issue any further shares; however, an additional 20 000 shares were reserved for three months, at nominal value, for distribution in the Transvaal and the Orange Free State (OFS).[37] Additional shares were provided in respect of branches not yet formed, also at par. By July 1919 the share capital of Santam consisted of 200 000 shares: 166 945 were allocated, 14 300 were available for distribution in the Free State and the Transvaal, 7 275 were available to branches, and 11 480 were available at a premium (see Table 1.1).[38]

The general public bought shares in different allotments. At the Santam board meeting on 26 July 1918 shares were allocated in sets of 25, 50, 100, 250, 300, 500, 800, and even larger lots. Some applications were rejected, but no reasons were provided in the board minutes. Authorization was also given for the transfer of shares from a previous owner to another—twenty-five shares were transferred from A.C. van den Heever to P. J. Malherbe, and sixteen shares from C.H. de B. Joubert to N.C. Krone, who then owned a total of 150 shares. This micro-management by the directors shows how important they regarded careful selection of potential shareholders, since the establishment of Santam was a big venture, harbouring a definite potential risk if shares were acquired by persons not supportive of the larger ideal of the founders. Strict

Table 1.1. Santam statement of shares and expenses 1918 to 1919

	Share capital	Number of shares sold	Shares paid up	Expenses
At 12-6-1918	£42,027:10:0	86,055	£35,325:0:0	£29,865:2:2
At 25-9-1919	Number of shares available 200,000; 173,050 allocated, at value of £104 809:0:0	182,525	£179,695:0:0	

Source: Statement of Share Capital dated 13 June 1918 WCA-A2213-500000.

[36] *Articles of Association, 1918*, pp. 20, 27. [37] Board of Directors meeting 19190605.

[38] Santam Report to Board of Directors, 28 September 1919; also see Y Hagedorn-Hansen (2017) The transformation of the South African short term insurance industry as represented by the development of SANTAM, 1918–2012. Unpublished PhD Thesis, University of Johannesburg.

selection was therefore applied in the allocation of shares. A guarantee by I.J. Marais for £1 000 in lieu of acquiring Santam shares was not accepted.[39] Credit screening could not be watertight, but management exercised care in assessing the quality of applicants. The most important aspect was geographical distribution. The directors wanted to secure countrywide buy-in. It was not advisable to launch the new company as a Cape-based concern, but rather as a national endeavour. The manner in which the board controlled the distribution of shares points to the tight control by these directors of the operations of the company from the start.

In 1918, the Executive Committee was known as the *Dagelijks Bestuur* or *Daelikse Bestuur* and later *Dag Bestuur,* in Afrikaans. At the time the committee comprised three board members, namely Charlie Louw, Antoon Benning, and Fred Dormehl. The General Manager, Alfred MacDowall, was always present. Hofmeyr, the chairman of the board, was also the chairman of the *Dagelijks Bestuur* and by February 1919 four board members made up the daily executive body. Meetings were held weekly and minutes were kept in Afrikaans (except the first set of minutes, which was in English). Hofmeyr was prominent in the governance and day-to-day management. He had attended most meetings since the beginning. The agenda rarely varied. It regularly dealt with the following matters: Loans, branches, premium income (fire and accident), bank reconciliation, cheques drawn, guarantees, bank accounts, new agents, commission on loans, and staff.[40] The prospectus made it clear that preference would be given to the appointment of Afrikaans-speaking applicants, but the dearth of suitably qualified clerical and professional staff mandated a pragmatic approach to appointments. As will be shown below, many capable English-speaking staff joined Sanlam during the formative years—and with positive results for the company. The first two office staff appointments were a clerk, Ferris le Sueur, and a typist (*masjinenschrifster*), Miss Ellen van der Merwe, who addressed the administrative needs of the company and its subsequent subsidiary, Sanlam.

The management structure of Santam closely resembled that of the British insurance industry in as far as the composition and operation of the board and Executive Committee were concerned. As long ago as August 1710, the Sun Insurance office management spent considerable time deciding how the business should be organized, how clients should be recruited, running administration expenses, and sourcing monies for claims. 'They treated themselves as a working body.'[41] They formed two structures, namely a General Court or meeting of all the managers, and a weekly Committee of Management elected from the General Court with a maximum of seven members, two of

[39] SA: Santam Board Minutes, 26/07/1918.

[40] *Leninge; takkantore; premie inkomste opgawes (brand en ongevalle); toekenning Aandele; Oordrag aandele; Tjeks getrek; Waarborgaktes; Bank rekeninge; Nuwe agente; Kommissie op lenings; Staf.*

[41] P.G.M. Dickson: *The Sun Insurance Office 1710–1960*, 1961: 35.

whom were elected Secretary and Treasurer respectively. The Committee of Management met weekly and later fortnightly and was seen as the real controlling and innovating body in the Sun's affairs.[42] The founders of Sanlam surveyed a wide range of insurance companies' organizational form in preparation of their own endeavour. Management was subsequently organized along similar lines at Santam. It was almost impossible to distinguish between the board and the daily management. Hofmeyr was intimately involved in daily managerial responsibilities. The board conducted its responsibilities diligently. Members were not allowed to be absent from meetings without permission and prior notification. Board members who failed to attend three meetings in succession were assumed to have vacated their position and could be replaced.[43] This principle was enforced without regard for the person concerned, because the collective knowledge and experience of a carefully selected group of directors constituted the social and human capital necessary to steer such a new venture through unknown waters. The functional overlap between the board and daily management also signified the caution with which the founding fathers approached their enterprise. This lack of functional distinction later caused friction with management and led to resignations.

The establishment of Santam pulled together the energy, enthusiasm, and ambition of Afrikaner leaders. It was a commercial decision to venture into the insurance industry, seizing a business opportunity with the intention to succeed in an industry dominated by foreign competitors. The insurance business offered the possibility of mobilizing savings to be invested in growth opportunities, which would strengthen Afrikaner involvement in the domestic economy. The strategic advantage these entrepreneurs enjoyed, was the coincidence in history of a growing Afrikaner nationalism and an emerging South African identity. This nationalism was spurred on by social marginalization, widespread poverty among fellow-Afrikaners, and proven success in mobilizing savings among a people generally perceived to be poor, relatively backward, and not fit for the world of business and finance. The short period between the decision in March 1918 to establish Sanlam, a separate life office, and the actual registration on 8 June was testimony to the latent managerial capabilities of the Afrikaner elite. The new life insurance company was officially registered as *Die Suid-Afrikaanse Lewens Assuransie Maatskappij, Beperk (Sanlam).*[44] The management of Santam again attempted to secure simultaneous registration of the new company in Afrikaans and English by petitioning the High Court on

[42] The Sun: 49.

[43] SA: Minutes of Board meeting, 27/09/1918; 24/12/1918.

[44] The acronym 'Sanlam' for the life office was first used on 20 June 1919. This was exactly one year after the first meeting of the Board of Directors and the Daily Management was held. At this meeting the minutes referred to the life office as 'S.A.N.L.A.M.' (Minutes of Sanlam Daily Management, 20/6/1919). The first use of the acronym without the full stops was in the minutes of the Sanlam Daily Management meeting of 3/12/1920. The first use of the acronym 'Sanlam' by the Chairman in his annual address was on 21 December 1921. See SA: 5/2/1: Sanlam Annual Reports, 1919–1924.

10 May 1918. The Judge Hon. A.J. de Villiers rejected the petition, stating that he found no reasonable grounds for such an 'unusual' request. It is therefore apparent that language equality was neither informally accepted nor officially sanctioned. This in itself provided the new company with a valuable strategic tool in the development of a market. Santam and Sanlam marketed their business in Afrikaans and English, a service not offered by any other insurance company in South Africa.

The Santam board established Sanlam with capital of £25 000, consisting of shares to the value of £1 each, 24 985 of which were held by Santam. The remaining fifteen shares were kept by the Santam board for allocation of one each to the new members of the new Sanlam Board of Directors. This Board of Directors was comprised of the same people as the Santam board. Management was also a mirror of Santam—MacDowell and Dormehl were appointed in positions at Sanlam similar to those occupied in Santam. Sanlam's business was life insurance, both industrial as well as individual. Sanlam's Articles of Association distinguished explicitly between an 'industrial fund' and the 'ordinary branch'. The industrial fund referred to life policies for an amount less than £100, whereas the ordinary branch issued policies exceeding £100. The actuary appointed to both companies was G.W. Paterson, with M.S. Louw (a teacher from Paarl) as his (apprentice) assistant. D.P de Klerk (an attorney from Marquard in the Orange Free State) was appointed Agency Manager. Sanlam was run as a mutual life insurance company, a choice that followed from the earlier decision by the Santam board to conduct the life insurance business on a mutual basis. Investment returns on policyholders' funds were distributed among policyholders and profits from the short-term fire and accident insurance were paid to shareholders - in the case of Santam, these were the holders of Santam shares.

After the registration of Sanlam in June 1918, the Sanlam board met for the first time on 20 June 1918. The management, which consisted of the exact same persons as those of the Santam management, was acknowledged as being people of standing. Since a life office needed medical expertise, Dr H.D Max Ackermann was appointed Chief Medical Officer of Sanlam. The General Manager of Standard Bank, with which Santam and Sanlam soon dealt, commented as follows: 'The directorate of the Company consisting of... is highly influential.'[45] The social capital unleashed with the formation of Sanlam provided an inspirational drive to many. De Klerk wrote about his motivation to take the position of manager at Sanlam: 'I was primarily motivated by the idea of building a purely Afrikaans company, with capital of approximately £30 000. In those days you hardly ever heard about companies with such vast capital.'[46]

[45] Standard Bank Archives (SBA): GMO 3/1/62: Report to Standard Bank of South Africa, Ltd. London: 13/12/18: 802.

[46] SA 5/2/4/2: Geskiedkundige Memos en Briewe: 'D. P. de Klerk: Eerste Trustbestuurder van Santam.'

For the first twenty years of business Santam and Sanlam operated very much in tandem, sharing a common vision, strategy, management, administrative staff, directors, and markets. The wartime economic fortunes (primary product price inflation, pent-up demand, surplus funds) afforded the new companies a smooth start. The first Sanlam life policies were issued at the initial meeting of the Sanlam board on 20 June 1918. The first Sanlam life policy was issued to Servaas Daniel de Wet. He worked as an administrative manager at *De Nationale Pers* and was well acquainted with the founders of Sanlam. He took out a whole-life policy for £500 with a premium of £11.8s.4d.[47] During the first six months of business in 1918 an estimated 93 per cent of Sanlam's client base was Afrikaans.[48] The second life policy was issued to Alfred MacDowall and the third to Mr and Mrs H. Marcus. The first seven policies issued had a total value of £5 250. Sanlam placed an advertisement in the daily press announcing 'a triumph for South Africa'—Sanlam was a triumph for South Africa. The company was ready to offer all classes of life insurance and called on Afrikaners to support 'a national institution'.

From a business perspective this advertisement was significant. At first the business announced itself as a South African institution. Secondly, the business announced confidently that it was a fully-fledged insurance enterprise and not a second-class company or agent for a foreign insurance concern. Thirdly, the company called on fellow-Afrikaners to trust the institution as a national institution and to support it on those specific grounds. The company was appealing to the first tier of nationalism, namely South African nationalism based on a pride in the achievement of South Africans, and secondly on the narrower Afrikaner nationalism, confined to South Africa. Some Afrikaans-speaking people had been clients of the established life offices in South Africa. None of those offices appealed directly to Afrikaners on the grounds of their South African nationalism, nor on them being Afrikaners. A great deal of goodwill existed towards Santam and Sanlam, but the challenge to the new insurance companies was to earn the public trust in their ability to deliver on the promise of superior service.

Sanlam was fully committed to bilingualism as a matter of principle. It would be an important strategic advantage. As Sanlam positioned itself as a 'South African national' company, it targeted the entire white population. Right from the first policy issued, Sanlam made policy documents available in the language of the policyholder. The company firmly supported the position of 'South Africa first'. In a letter by Alfred MacDowall to Reverend P.W.A. de Klerk in October 1919 he claimed: '*Een van ons sterkste punte is dat die Maatskappij suiwer Suid-Afrikaans is. Ons leuse is "Suid-Afrika eerste". Ons streef na gesonde besigheidsmetodes, eerlike rondborstige behandeling teenoor ons kliënte. Onse beste dienste en advies word altijd aan iedereen wat daarvan gebruik*

[47] Sanlam: Policy Register, 1; SA 6/5 6/5/1, Biographical notes on Servaas Daniel de Wet; *Die Fakkel*, June 1968, p. 1.

[48] Sanlam: Policy register, 1.

wil maak, toegestaan.'[49] Additional costs were incurred as a result of the policy on bilingualism. M.S. Louw recalled that he spent long hours translating policy documents into Afrikaans soon after he joined the company as actuarial clerk. Charlie Louw and Fred Dormehl reported to the board that the policy on bilingualism caused additional work for staff since quite a number of staff members were not proficient in Afrikaans. Letters and policies were drafted in English and then translated into Afrikaans.[50] When M.S. Louw reflected on those early years, he reiterated that Sanlam's position on bilingualism was vital, because Sanlam was there to serve not one, but all sections of the population, each in his own language.[51] Sanlam even advertised in German, acknowledging the presence of a sizeable German community in South Africa. Inclusivity was aimed at making the English-speaking section of the population feel part of the overarching goal of Sanlam to contribute directly to the development of South Africa.[52] The important mission of the company to develop a culture of saving that would ultimately contribute to the development of the country, was directed at both language groups. In 1943 it was stated in *Die Fakkel* that the education of both sections of the population on the general benefit of insurance, should be of advantage to the oldest and to the newest company, and was of incalculable benefit to the country in general terms, since it instilled habits of thrift and systematic saving.[53]

Sanlam was undoubtedly attempting to change the well-established trend of insurance business in South Africa being conducted only in English. Its Memorandum and Articles of Association that were registered in Afrikaans, were the first such technical documents in the insurance industry available in Afrikaans. The predominantly Afrikaans policyholder base was because Afrikaans people could identify with Sanlam, the first company communicating with them in Afrikaans and delivering technical documents to them in Afrikaans. Management argued that the company sought to reverse the trend in South Africa, namely that if one wanted insurance it would be available only in English. Sanlam pioneered offering policy documents in Afrikaans and English. One way of attracting English-speaking clients was to offer them policies in their mother tongue—thus Sanlam insisted on bilingualism as company policy from the outset.[54]

Insurance for South Africa was Sanlam's business. Just as much as the leadership of Santam and Sanlam were active in Afrikaner nationalist causes in society, the church, and politics, they were also fully aware of the financial liability that contractual savings through insurance, placed on households. In the first Chairman's report Hofmeyr underlined the fact that Sanlam conducted good and prudent business and intended to

[49] SA 6/5/1: Letter MacDowall—De Klerk, 23/10/1919. [One of our strengths is that we are a truly South African company. Our motto is 'South Africa first'. We strive to maintain sound business principles, and treat our clients with honesty. Our best service and advice are available to all desirous of making use thereof.]

[50] SA 6/5/1 Letter C.R. Louw—W.A. Hofmeyr, 3/10/1918.

[51] *Die Fakkel*, 1 June 1942: 2.

[52] *Die Fakkel*, 6 January 1941: 5.

[53] *Die Fakkel*, 1 July 1943: 5–6.

[54] *Die Fakkel*, 7 February 1936: 5.

sustain that. That was how the company planned to contribute to the growth of 'our country' and the South African economy. The company acknowledged its task of educating those outside the insurance net, such as fellow-Afrikaners, to take up their responsibility towards their families, those dependent upon them, and in the broader sense to their country. He stated, 'it is our aim, not only to build rapidly, but to build a solid foundation capable of supporting a large building... it is our aim to assist in the development of our country using the money entrusted to us. What a pleasant thought to policyholders that they contribute to the development of the country.'[55] The sound first-year financial results of Sanlam, he explained, resulted from co-operation among Afrikaners in 'the broadest sense of the word', because Sanlam was the big South African life insurance co-operative association.[56] The publication of Sanlam's annual report in Afrikaans and English since 1922 enhanced the notion of a business serving the interests of the whole nation. The Chairman repeatedly referred to Sanlam serving the development of the country, *'diensbaar vir die ontwikkeling van ons land'* [in the service of the development of our country],[57] since economic independence was dependent on the building of own South African institutions.[58] The concept of mutuality was used to motivate and educate people. Sanlam was a South African life office, to distinguish it from the majority of foreign insurance businesses operating in the country. Sanlam belonged to its policyholders, who shared in the profits. Afrikaners were encouraged to take out policies as their 'sacred duty' to provide for their dependants.[59] While Sanlam was serving the nation by offering young people training and employment, it mobilized capital and distributed the proceeds of prudent management in the form of bonuses among policyholders and invested in local opportunities.

Into the market

The world was in the fourth year of the Great War in 1918. Surplus capital in the country as a result of the war-induced inflation, made the timing of the entry of Sanlam into the insurance industry, most opportune. The success of any new insurance company lay in reaching the uninsured. There was only one way to do that—establish a presence across the entire country. The natural market seemed to be the Cape, but success in Cape Town and the immediate surroundings where foreign companies were well established, was not a foregone conclusion. Supporting nationalistic causes and cultural campaigns was not synonymous with confiding hard-earned savings to the new player in an industry

55 Sanlam Chairman's Report, 22/12/20: 3.
56 SA: Sanlam Chairman's Report, 21/12/21: 3; 30/09/25: 3.
57 SA: Sanlam Chairman's Report, 21/12/21: 3; 30/09/34: 3; 30/09/25: 3.
58 SA: Sanlam Chairman's Report, 21/12/21: 3.
59 SA: Sanlam Chairman's Report, 23/12/19: 2.

in which Afrikaners failed to present a track record of success. As Afrikaners were increasingly divided politically following Hertzog's formation of the National Party in 1914, posters with the following slogan in red writing against a black background were displayed in a rural Transvaal town: 'Sanlam for the nationalists! To hell with Sanlam. Damn the Nationalists!'[60] Equally adverse sentiments were expressed by English-speaking interests. MacDowall conveyed the negative comments published in *The Cape* (a Cape weekly newspaper) to Fichardt, 'If you have seen this week's *Cape*, you will have observed that the campaign has begun.'[61] A report in *The Cape* of 4 January 1918 stated: 'We should like to receive some assurance that the new South African insurance company, to whose advent we have referred more than once in recent issues (it is to be called by the way, the "South African Mutual Trust and Assurance Company") is not an outcome of the recent failure of a Hertzogite group to capture seats on the "Old Mutual", and eventually, no doubt, to control the full board of that institution.' The report insinuates that the new company was a co-operative undertaking, similar to the *Afrikaanse Handelshuis* (a failed hardware business in which Hofmeyr had an interest), but if that was not true, the paper called on MacDowall to issue a statement to that effect. The report concluded, 'We offer the remarks not out of mere curiosity, but in the public interest; for, as we have often said, we cannot think of anything more likely to perpetuate racialism and ill-feeling in South Africa than making party politics a commercial business. It is the next worst thing to make a commercial business of party politics.'[62] Market suspicion was rife.

Then an unforeseen catastrophe struck: Spanish influenza swept across South Africa between September and November 1918. South Africa was the fifth most affected country in the world, with around 500 000 people dying as a result of the epidemic. The global epidemic started in March 1918 and killed more than 50 million people worldwide. The highest mortality rate was in the Cape, where 62 per cent of the deaths occurred. In the course of six weeks between September and mid-October 1918, 140 000 people died. In Cape Town and surrounding magisterial districts 122 720 cases and 6 342 deaths were reported. In Kimberley another 1 348 people died and in Bloemfontein 1 291 casualties were reported.[63] The impact on Sanlam was both devastating and opportune.

Frederic Hansen Dormehl passed away on 20 October 1918 in Cape Town. The Afrikaans community and Santam as well as Sanlam lost a stalwart, its Managing Director.[64] Willie Hofmeyr took over the responsibilities as Managing Director between

[60] *Die Transvaler*, Supplement, 8 June 1968. [61] N.J. le Roux: *W.A. Hofmeyr*: 131.

[62] *The Cape*, 4 January 1918: 4. The different 'races' to which reference is made, are the English-speaking and the Afrikaans-speaking people.

[63] H. Phillips (1990): *'Black October': The impact of the Spanish influenza epidemic of 1918 on South Africa*, Government Printer: Pretoria:28, 53, 68, 167.

[64] SA; Minutes of Sanlam Board, 2/12/1918: The Santam Board decided to pay six months' of Dormehl's salary to his widow, and Sanlam offered to take responsibility for half of the amount. This gesture signified the overwhelming sense of loss experienced by the company and the vacuum left by his death.

the time of Dormehl's death and 1920, when Charlie Louw succeeded him as acting Managing Director. The disruption caused by the influenza epidemic had an important stimulating impact on the insurance industry as a whole. Statistics on the demand for insurance products rose unprecedentedly in the months directly following the Spanish flu. The demand was both for new life policies as well as for increased benefits on existing policies. It was estimated that in 1919 new life business had amounted to around £20 million.[65] The opportunity did not necessarily secure a captive market for Sanlam products. There was still the issue of placing sufficient trust in the new entrant in the high-risk market.

Sanlam moved fast after Dormehl's death: stability in the management structure was vital. Hofmeyr stepped into a managerial position despite the fact that he was Chairman of both Santam and Sanlam. The absence of the division of executive and governance positions was not uncommon in the early twentieth century, but in Sanlam it would soon lead to friction in management at Head Office. The first goal was to get out into the market. For that Sanlam needed agents and branches beyond the immediate magisterial district of Cape Town. The resignation of Harris as the first Agency Manager on 13 June 1918 could potentially have been very disruptive, because his successor H.H (Heinrich) de Villiers was only appointed as the new Agency Manager on 2 August 1918. MacDowall and Dormehl therefore assumed shared responsibility for the organization of agents in the meantime. Agents were only appointed after persons had been nominated for consideration, and their candidacy considered by the *Dageliks Bestuur* and ratified by the board. No official policy was in place, but the conduct of management displayed the direct bureaucratic management style of the formative years. The first appointments were made from nominees by individuals familiar to members of Head Office staff, or by specific members of the managerial team. Agents were not employed by Sanlam, but earned commission on the sale of policies. Sanlam realized people did not 'buy' life insurance, but that a policy had to be 'offered and sold' to a prospective buyer. Policies were primarily marketed by lawyers and notaries in Santam branches as a result of the Santam trust business, and by boards of executors. Personal contact was the only distribution channel and Sanlam worked through the network of legal practitioners' trusts and boards of executors where Afrikaner social capital was established. These networks were primarily extended in the *platteland* or rural areas where Afrikaners, the initial primary target market, lived in farming communities, small towns, and perhaps larger towns or 'cities' such as Bloemfontein, Kimberley, and Pretoria. Urbanization was in its infancy. Distances were far and the target market dispersed.

The primary constraint was the lack of transport and communication infrastructure. By 1918 the best long-distance means of transport into the interior was trains. A journey

[65] Ibid., 213.

to Johannesburg from Cape Town took two days by train and three days by ship between Cape Town and Durban. By 1918 the most frequent form of transport was horse-drawn carts. The privileged few who owned motor vehicles had difficulty travelling on the limited and inferior-quality roads. Automobiles were also not very reliable. One of the first Sanlam agents, Alexander Duncan Struthers, an agent in Pretoria, noted: 'Our mode of travel (I speak of the few Transvaal agents) was either by pushbike or by two good, sound legs (Dapper en Stapper); or, if you had to get to some other dorp, by train—second class, because there was no third class!'[66]

Communication was seriously limited by a lack of telephone lines. Telephone communication was more frequent in cities, but on the *platteland* the telephone lines were either non-existent or unreliable. Meeting with a prospective client by appointment was far more successful than simply 'blind canvassing'. The unreliable nature of telephone communication is illustrated by the exchange of telegrams between Hofmeyr and Charlie Louw in 1921 to finalize matters concerning management.

The first candidates for agents were considered by the *Dageliks Bestuur* in June 1918. The first agents appointed were P. J. de Villiers and G. Koenig from Cape Town, followed by T.D.T. von Moltke and C.W. Mallinick. The first *platteland* agent appointed was P.G. Groenewald from Paarl, appointed on 8 July 1918. Two very productive agents entered the market by the end of July 1918. They were J. van Voorn from Humansdorp and P.H. Malherbe from the *Bo-Karoo* in the Hanover district. Van Voorn wrote the first two policies in the office of the member of the board of Santam/Sanlam, C.W. Malan, a lawyer in Humansdorp. Van Voorn most probably had earlier experience in the insurance industry because he was successful as an agent right from the beginning. P.J. Malherbe was an entrepreneur in Tulbagh where, after leaving school, he worked as a shop assistant until he could establish his own business at the age of twenty-one. Malherbe suffered from ill health and had to sell his business, but then offered to sell subscriptions in *De Nationale Pers*, which meant he travelled the country. He had travelled the northern parts of the province, especially De Aar and other parts of the *Groot Karoo*. After the establishment of Santam he was very successful in selling Sanlam shares in the Northern Cape regions. He had no experience in the insurance industry and was taken aback when asked to sell Santam fire policies—something he regarded as inferior to selling life products. He turned out to be a very productive Sanlam agent.[67]

Attracting suitable agents to the insurance industry was problematic. Despite being enthusiastic about the new venture, few Afrikaans people had a suitable background in the industry and few were fully bilingual. In June/July 1918 Sanlam attracted the services of fifteen agents, fourteen of whom were active and sold thirty-five policies to a total value of £13 044. The largest number of policies were sold in Cape Town and

[66] *Die Fakkel*, September 1948: 6.

[67] Santam Board Minutes, 4/04/1918.

Stellenbosch, but the agents also succeeded in Rhodesia (Zimbabwe, where they sold policies to people working at the Shamva Mine), Paarl, Humansdorp, and Moorreesburg. The influenza epidemic affected these statistics to the extent that production shifted more deeply into the *platteland* and the Transvaal. Production improved between August and October 1918, with up to twenty-seven agents selling 264 policies to a value of £90 487 by the end of the year. The shift in distribution to the Transvaal was encouraging, but the largest number of policies were still sold in the Cape Province, albeit a growing number outside Cape Town. The first female agent was Miss Sarah Goldblatt, who started as one of the first three administrative appointees at Head Office, but three months later also assumed the role of agent. Her performance was less than satisfactory and she was politely returned to her teaching position at the Tokai Public School. The productivity of agents was low: only eight of the twenty-seven sold more than ten policies that year. Before his untimely death Dormehl expressed the view that if Sanlam wanted to grow rapidly, the opening of branches in each of the four provinces was imperative.

Success in the competitive insurance industry could not simply be managed from the central location of the Agency Manager at Head Office. In the Orange Free State Gordon Fraser, a lawyer, was appointed the Santam Branch Manager on 18 April 1918. It took him two months to register the company and he then had difficulty with the services of an inexperienced assistant until finally Jan Feenstra, the Chief Clerk at Head Office visited Bloemfontein towards the end of the year. The influenza epidemic disrupted progress in the province, but Feenstra's involvement set some agents to work. By the end of 1918 J.J. Rittenburg delivered good productivity in the southern districts of the province. In Bloemfontein A.W. Stead, and in Bethlehem, Douw van der Merwe got the Sanlam presence established. The board kept a close eye on the progress in the Orange Free State and in January 1919 advised the *Dageliks Bestuur* to appoint a local board for the Orange Free State without delay.[68] Feenstra had raised serious concerns about the mounting stream of complaints by clients as well as agents and warned management that the company was placing the trust of the public in serious jeopardy. He called for the much-improved organization of agents and the administration of applications.[69]

The first branch in the Transvaal was established by Harry van Dam, who had been employed by the Australian insurance firm Colonial Mutual. Sanlam appointed Van Dam on 29 July 1918 to take up his duties on 1 September 1918 as the first Branch Manager in the Transvaal located in Johannesburg. The benefit to Sanlam was that Van Dam brought a number of his experienced colleagues from Colonial Mutual along to Sanlam, thereby adding the much-needed experience to the new company. According to

[68] Santam Board Minutes, 24/01/1919. [69] SA 6/5/1: Feenstra correspondence 9 June 1920.

agency reports J.C. Haines, A.D. Struthers in Pretoria, H.A. Alberts and A. Pienaar in the Witbank district, A.R. Smit in Potchefstroom and L.F. Haak in Volksrust were part of this group.[70] Agents were not always assigned to specific geographic locations. However, Sanlam did appoint Miss J. van Niekerk with specific assignment 'for ladies and children'.[71] It was apparent within the first year of operations that the travelling agents contributed substantially more to production, e.g. 89 per cent in March 1919 in the Cape Province—a trend that was sustained for a very long time.[72]

The operations of the company outside the district of Cape Town were strengthened by the appointment of a local board in geographical areas far removed from Cape Town. This was a common practice followed by insurance companies in South Africa. Sanlam appointed a local board in Johannesburg for the Transvaal in December 1918, but the disruptions caused by the influenza epidemic delayed the first meeting until 28 January 1919. The board performed duties similar to those of the company board—ratifying agent appointments, lease agreements for the acquisition of motor vehicles, subject to the authority of the company board. When agent E. Keyzer applied for permission to purchase a cart and two horses, it was turned down and he was advised rather to invest in an automobile. The Transvaal board drew on the experience and networks of local leaders to advise the Sanlam board on strategic direction in the Transvaal, since the depth of the Sanlam board lay in the Cape. Regular reports from the Transvaal local board were tabled and discussed at length in the characteristically bureaucratic management style of the board at that time.

By the end of 1918 Sanlam policies sold in the Cape Province totalled eighty-two, the Transvaal fifty-six, and the Orange Free State fifty-six. This meant that Sanlam had made better inroads in the Cape. The most successful regions were not Cape Town, but the more remote *platteland* areas of the Southern Cape, Swartland, the North-eastern Cape, the *Groot Karoo*, and the North-western parts of Upington and Kakamas. The total amount insured of £30 850 was indeed higher than the £21 700 in the Orange Free State and £17 950 in the Transvaal. Pretoria and the central Highveld region delivered the highest production, while in the Orange Free State the *platteland* districts delivered the bulk of new policies, not Bloemfontein.

The Sanlam management realized the pivotal role of good-quality travelling agents. This constituted the axis of success of the new life office and would take time to establish. The strategy to achieve a stable, competent, and a successful agent network was systematically constructed by attracting suitable agents from all walks of life, from all language groups, and from all races. No doubt, most of Sanlam's agents were white Afrikaners, but the company gladly appointed capable persons irrespective of culture or race.

[70] Santam Board Minutes, 29/07/1918.

[71] WCA: A2213: Private Collection C.R. Louw, Band 3: File Santam 1918, 1919.

[72] SA: Compiled from Policy Registers.

It was remarkable that in the first year of Sanlam's business English-speaking agents made up a notable component of the travelling agents—Mallinick in Cape Town, Struthers in Pretoria, Stead, Hogan, and Rittenburg in the Orange Free State, Miller, Dix, Black, and Reiffin in Johannesburg, as well as Weeks in Potchefstroom. Women were welcome as agents—Sarah Goldblatt was perhaps less successful, but Cato le R. van Niekerk was a well-performing agent at the age of thirty-two. Agents were drawn from all backgrounds, such as teachers, farmers, millers, persons who assisted with the selling of shares in *De Nationale Pers* and Santam, influential community leaders such a General A.P.J. Bezuidenhout[73] and Senator Nicolaas Serfontein,[74] and railway workers.

The organization of agents was not yet firmly established after the first year of business. Following the resignation of Harris, Feenstra performed a dual function as Manager of the Western Province region as well as Chief Clerk at Head Office until Heinrich de Villiers' appointment in 1921. There was no set criterion for the selection of agents, but performance was closely monitored. Agent production was intermittent. The *Dageliks Bestuur* incentivized agents by means of a competition announced in May 1919, where a monetary prize was awarded to the agents with the highest production in the following five months.[75] The competition had the desired effect—the winner brought in £46 300 in new business, but systemic problems were recurring. Fraudulent activities occurred within the first year, leading to the dismissal of agents. The system of premium collection was such that agents collected relatively large amounts of cash (since they often received applications from numerous applicants before returning to the branch to deposit the premiums collected) and sometimes failed or delayed to deposit the money. The board discussed each contravention of ethical conduct and decided on appropriate action—in one case the agent was allowed to repay the funds stolen after submitting a written admission of guilt, as well as agreeing to the terms of repayment.[76] The Board insisted on strict ethical conduct on all levels of operation. Decisive action on matters of commission claimed by staff for submitting policies to Sanlam was enforced from early on. A case was discussed in February 1919 where a local member of the Transvaal board claimed commission on policies introduced by him. The board refused such commission, but asked the Agency Manager to develop company policy to be implemented at the discretion of his office.[77]

[73] J.C.G.Kemp (1942): *Die pad van die veroweraar*, pp. 149, 204, 285. General Bezuidenhout participated in the South African War, was appointed to the Union Armed Forces in 1910, but resigned to serve under General Kemp during the Rebellion of 1914/15 and was later proposed by Piet Grobler to be chief agent in Western Transvaal.

[74] *South African Biographical Dictionary*, 4, pp. 589–90. Serfontein also fought in the South African War, was appointed to the Union Armed Forces in 1910, but was elected to the Provincial Council in the Orange Free State in 1911. He joined Hertzog's National Party in 1914 and was elected to Parliament for the constituency Frankfort in 1914, but during the Rebellion of 1914/15 he was captured, jailed, and later freed. He lost his seat in Parliament, but was appointed to the Senate in 1921.

[75] SA: Sanlam *Dageliks Bestuur*, 2/05/1919.

[76] Santam Board Minutes, 30/09/1918.

[77] SA: Minutes of Sanlam Board, 12/02/1919.

Swift and decisive action in such cases was critical, because it was clear that public trust had to be earned. Competitors spread suspicion that because of its limited capital, Sanlam might not be able to pay out when policies matured. Other insurance companies were reluctant to provide reinsurance to Sanlam. In confidential circulars to policyholders, other companies warned their clients to be wary of Sanlam policies, because the company would be unable to honour its commitments in case of war or epidemics. The stability of Sanlam was placed under suspicion by cautioning clients that Sanlam might not be able to sustain bonuses of any significance.[78]

The distribution via an agent network was still precarious after one year in business. Another opportunity to expand the distribution channel had been part of the Santam business plan since its inception. In the Santam prospectus, the company stated that it would engage in industrial life insurance, which was explained as life policies to a value of less than £100. This undertaking was included in the Articles of Association of Santam (sections 34 and 35). These sections stipulated that Santam's business would be conducted via two separate branches—the 'Ordinary' branch and the 'Industrial' branch. Industrial policies were issued on the life of any person, providing for any condition, and were payable on a weekly or monthly basis. The industrial branch was therefore an integral part of Santam's vision to extend life policies to all strata of society. Santam established an industrial department on 3 June 1918 by appointing Christian M. Dantu from Johannesburg as Manager. He was to assume duty on 1 July 1918 in Cape Town. The operations of the industrial branch served the life cover needs of working-class people, especially (but not exclusively) the Coloured and black communities. As Sanlam was established to conduct the planned life business of Santam in June 1918, the industrial department was transferred to Sanlam. Agents and officials for this dedicated business were appointed from those communities. Dantu thus took office as an employee of Sanlam in July 1918. In the ordinary life department of Sanlam, T. la Fleur was the first Coloured agent. The first policy La Fleur sold was to Andrew Niekerk, a plasterer from Kensington Estate, Maitland, and his wife Florence, to whom the policies were issued on 1 February 1919.

Prior to the official establishment of Santam in March 1918, it became known that African Homes Trust (AHT), established in 1899, was in the market. AHT was initially a company providing life insurance, which could be used to obtain a mortgage on a house when the cash value of the policy had increased sufficiently. Loans were extended to buy the house against security of a mortgage and a life policy. AHT soon also ventured into industrial policies and by 1918 that business had overtaken home financing. The Johannesburg financier I.W. Schlesinger had developed the only other competitor in the industrial insurance field in his company African Life. Schlesinger was eager to

[78] H.S. Marais (1962): *Die Sanlam Gedenkboek*: 16.

acquire AHT since that would secure him an undisputed monopoly in industrial insurance in South Africa. On the other hand, the owners of AHT were not too well disposed towards the idea of being absorbed into African Life, but preferred a transaction which would allow AHT to maintain a separate entity. To the leaders contemplating the establishment of Santam, the opportunity of acquiring AHT promised a perfect fit. Santam could acquire an established industrial insurance business, where the inexperienced newcomers to the market of insurance could benefit from an established concern. The Santam actuary, George Paterson, assessed the possibility to acquire AHT and on 29 May 1918 declared: 'I believe we have an opportunity of a lifetime.' The Santam auditor, Harry Gibson, reported to the board on 19 June 1918 that the acquisition of AHT would strengthen the competitive advantage of Santam in that particular branch of insurance, that AHT was a well-organized business and would save Santam the costs of establishing a new industrial business. Santam was not interested in absorbing AHT, but intended to maintain AHT as a separate concern as a Santam subsidiary. A bold step was needed: Santam offered to purchase AHT for £129 285.10s.0d (£10 000 higher than the rejected Schlesinger offer made in January 1918). Santam entrepreneurs secured a loan from the imperial bank Standard Bank against the security of the AHT shares. On 1 August 1918 Santam acquired AHT. The former AHT directors resigned and Willie Hofmeyr was appointed Chairman of the AHT board. The other directors were Alfred Benning, Fred Dormehl, C.R. Louw and Victor Dormer. Alfred MacDowall was appointed General Manager, thereby bringing AHT into the Santam fold.[79] AHT secured Santam an additional distribution channel with the added benefit of an established network of clients and experienced staff. The Santam board considered the possibility of liquidating AHT and organizing the industrial department of Sanlam into two sections—one for white business and one for Coloured business. The decision of managing AHT as a subsidiary was motivated in particular by the publicity advertising AHT as a reputable company, one that had paid out very large death benefits during the influenza epidemic. In the market, a record of honouring contractual responsibilities was of enormous value to Santam. In 1918 this acquisition was a notable achievement by the Afrikaner entrepreneurs. It indicated the confidence of the market as well as other established financial institutions in the abilities of the new management.

The business plan of Sanlam was simple. The company offered basic life insurance products. In the life market competitive advantage was found in cost management and efficiency of delivery and service.[80] The life insurance market was especially conservative. The responsibility to deliver on promised investment outcomes, to provide the greatest level of security to the policyholder, and to reduce the debilitating effect of uncertainty, made conservative policies and adherence to the principles of prudence imperative.

[79] SA 6/1/7: M.S. Louw Personal Document File: Memorandum of African Homes Trust, 13/04/1959.

[80] L. Dennett: *A Sense of Security*, pp. 36–7; C. Trebilcock: *Phoenix Assurance, Vol. 1.*

The profile of the company leadership was the keystone in building the trust in the policies offered. Social connections and network developments underpinned the construction of trust.[81] The life insurance industry was changed fundamentally by the introduction of endowment policies—a product that enhanced security as a precautionary investment product.[82] Generally, product innovation in the life industry was also constrained by the tense relationship between 'prudence and speculation'.[83] Sanlam began cautiously.

Sanlam's life policies were issued in both Afrikaans and English because Sanlam targeted all South Africans. The first policies were the following: Ordinary whole-life policies for persons from the age of twenty-one to the age of sixty. Premiums were payable either annually, half-yearly, quarterly, or monthly; whole-life policies with premiums terminating at a certain chosen age; child inheritance policies, taken out on the life of a parent and devolving to children; child inheritance policies without the termination of premiums after the death of the parent; and endowment policies payable at maturity after fifteen, twenty, twenty-five, or thirty years.[84]

The policies offered were the standard ones, but Sanlam immediately introduced two innovations in the life industry in South Africa. The company paid annual reversionary bonuses, based on annual valuations as from September 1919. The Stone & Cox Life Insurance Tables of 1920 noted that Sanlam was the only insurance company established in South Africa to conduct such annual valuations.[85] Another innovation was disability benefits. These benefits provided for the cessation of premiums and the payment of the sum insured in a lump sum in the case of total and permanent disablement—the latter being interpreted 'liberally', according to Stone & Cox, as the loss of two limbs, blindness, etc.[86] While disability benefits were nothing new in the industry, Sanlam was the first South African life insurer to pay lump-sum disability benefits as opposed to the industry norm of instalment payments. Sanlam ran a higher risk of unexpected high payouts, but it was argued that a disabled person needed immediate relief due to sudden unexpected expenses.[87]

These policies endorsed the vision of the Chairman, Willie Hofmeyr, that the company sought to assist policyholders in providing for their families in case of the breadwinner not being able to do so, for the education of their children, and the broad

[81] O. Westall: *The Provincial Insurance Company*, pp. 3.12–13; M. Keller: *The Life Insurance Enterprise*; 16–24.

[82] O. Westall: *The History of Insurance*: 98.

[83] G. Clark: *Betting on lives: The culture of life insurance in England, 1695–1775* (Manchester: Manchester University Press, 1999).

[84] SA 1/2/1/3 Rate Book 1931–1936).

[85] SA 1/2/1/1/2 Stone & Cox Life Insurance Tables, 1920: xi.

[86] SA 1/2/1/1/2 Stone & Cox, 1927: xiii.

[87] SA 1/2/1/3: Stone & Cox Tariefboek, 1921: xi; *Sanlammer* 61(40) 5/03/93.

development of the economy of the country. The concept of 'mutuality' was central in the marketing of insurance and found a sympathetic audience among the growing South African nationalist and patriotic society. Sanlam supported the notions of 'duty' and 'pride' that would grow in policyholders as they contributed to the well-being and development of their families, their communities, and the country at large.[88]

The first year of business had mixed results. A record number of policies were sold compared to the performance of other insurance companies' first year of operations. Sanlam issued 3 228 policies, delivering a total premium income of £39 466.6s.11d. The company had only eight claims as a result of the Spanish flu and paid death claims of £2 205 only.[89] A healthy £4 627.15s.6d was paid into a life insurance fund (reserves), which showed that the company could be trusted to deliver on its contractual liabilities. Sanlam invested funds only in government stock and kept small amounts of cash at the four banks where accounts had been opened shortly after commencing business. These banks were The Standard Bank of South Africa Ltd, The National Bank of South Africa Ltd, the African Banking Corporation, and the Netherlands Bank for South Africa Ltd.[90] Market penetration did not occur without frustrations and criticism. The board often dealt with complaints about the delay in the delivery of policy documents, delays in the processing of policy applications, funds paid on first instalments but not reaching Head Office, and higher insurance tariffs than competitors. The board referred to the actuary's statement that his calculations of policy fees were based on the payment of an annual bonus on those policies. Sanlam's whole-life policies were cheaper than SA Mutual's, but the matter was referred to the *Dageliks Bestuur*.[91] A case of the delay in submitting a policy application by the agent resulted in a death benefit being forfeited. This case could seriously affect the reputation of Sanlam and the board decided to pay an ad hoc amount to settle the claim and reprimanded the agent.[92] These matters were all discussed at board level because of the potential adverse implications such incidents could have for the company. It was symptomatic of the foundation phase where the agency manager had not yet implemented strict rules and procedures in the organization.

Despite minor organizational problems, the overall performance justified the declaration of an annual bonus as soon as the actuarial report was received. The annual actuarial report, due four months after the end of the financial year, was not available upon the release of the financial statements and Chairman's report, because the actuary, George Paterson was ill. Hofmeyr described the results as '*sukses sonder weerga*' [success beyond compare], but the industrial department underperformed. Establishment costs of the industrial department were £12 157.15s.6d, while the costs for the establishment of the ordinary department only amounted to £2 390.14s.11d. Income only marginally

[88] SA JV 5/2/1 Sanlam Annual Report, 23/12/19: 2; 22/12/20:3; 21/12/21:3.

[89] SA JV 5/2/1: Sanlam Annual Report, 1919.

[90] SA: Minutes of Sanlam Board, 20/06/1918.

[91] SA: Minutes Sanlam Board, 24/01/1919.

[92] SA: Minutes of Sanlam Board, 2/12/1918.

exceeded expenditure in the industrial department. A total of 24 114 policies were issued, but sixty death claims were paid. Administrative costs constituted 277 per cent of income. (In practice this meant that the industrial business was not profitable but business was nevertheless sustained because of the expectation that that form of insurance would in the long run provide access to an extended market.) Total income at the end of the 1919 financial year was £7 261, while agency and executive expenditure amounted to £17 860. A shortfall of £12 157.15s.6d was transferred to establishment costs.[93] Decisive action on the business of the industrial department was required soon.

At the end of the first year in business Sanlam was on a relatively stable footing—except for the industrial department. The largest number of policyholders were resident in the Cape Province, but the Orange Free State was most disappointing. The Transvaal business was promising. Sanlam positioned itself at the centre of the emerging South African nationalism and Afrikaner enthusiasm about a business vehicle promising economic empowerment. Management was capable, but exercised strong centralized control because they were inexperienced in the world of insurance. Much older and larger competitors in the market indirectly spread suspicion about the new entrant's ability to deliver on its contracts or even survive in the competitive insurance market.

A relatively stable workforce representing Afrikaans and English speakers generally converged into an enthusiastic team. Many of the office staff and senior officials in Sanlam were first-language English speakers early on, because there were simply too few Afrikaans-speaking people with experience in the insurance industry. *The Star* newspaper noted that Afrikaans-speaking persons were not yet proficient in conducting clerical work in Afrikaans, since the language was still in the developmental phase of formulating official vocabulary suited to the world of business. Companies realized they could not advertise for an Afrikaans-speaking clerk or typist, because 'Afrikaners throughout the Union were learning to write their language as they spoke it, . . . So Sanlam started its career as an Afrikaans company with staff predominantly English speaking.'[94] During the first decades of Sanlam's operations its accountants and actuaries were predominantly English speaking. They included Harry Gibson (1918–19), George W. Paterson (consulting actuary 1918–19), D. Spence Fraser (consulting actuary 1920–2), C.L. Anderson (accountant 1919–23) and the consulting auditing firm H. Gibson & Son (1919–22).[95] Working relations among the small band of office staff were excellent and bilingualism remained characteristic of the Head Office *esprit de corps*. The management and Board of Directors realized that first-class staff were a prerequisite for success and there were no compromises on the appointment of well-qualified able people to secure the company's entrance into the industry.

[93] Ibid. [94] *The Star*, 11/05/1960.
[95] *Die Fakkel*, 1/11/48, p. 6; 2/12/46, p. 4; 7/08/37, p. 13; 7/20/36, p. 19; 7/07/36, pp. 4–5.

The death of Dormehl was a heavy blow to the company, not only because of his exceptional leadership and managerial capabilities, but also his presence as a community leader active on various fronts of Afrikaner repositioning. The departure of Harris was less disruptive, but placed additional responsibilities on Head Office officials, which impacted negatively on some individuals. A strong team of young inspired Afrikaner men soon converged on Head Office to give support to the *Dageliks Bestuur*. These men were: M.S Louw, who joined Sanlam shortly after its formation, but then departed to pursue actuarial studies in Scotland in November 1919. He returned to Sanlam after qualifying as Fellow of the Faculty of Actuaries (FFA) in Edinburgh. The next young man was Jan Feenstra, who joined Sanlam in October 1919 as Chief Clerk at Head Office. He emerged as a key role player in organizing agents in the Western Province, while simultaneously taking charge of the administrative management of the field staff (the agents). Towards the end of 1919 a third person, G.F.S. de Villiers, also joined Sanlam as Branch Manager in De Aar. M.S. Louw, Jan Feenstra and Gys de Villiers performed important roles in developing a South African insurance company capable of contributing to a mature local industry. The most pressing matters Sanlam had to address were the image of the company as an undisputed South African life office of standing, the professionalization of its field staff, sophisticated and efficient organizational processes, and growing market share.

Conclusion

A business was born in a highly competitive industry in 1918.[96] Sanlam ventured out with an ambitious vision. The founding fathers took a bold step to enter into an industry with more than thirty companies, some performing short-term insurance business, some long-term life business, and some both, relying on impressive histories of experience and success in foreign markets. By 1930 Sanlam was not yet listed among the top three life offices, but almost a century after venturing into the market, in 2015, the company was the second-largest South African diversified financial services group. To build a company able to sustain its business and diversify operations for a century in a settler economy as part of the British Commonwealth and expand operations from a peripheral market into international markets, is premised on firm foundations. The success is captured in the adaptability to dynamically changing conditions in the home market. Sanlam started out to serve a marginalized segment of the South African society. A century later the

[96] The first statutory regulation of the insurance industry on a Union-wide basis only came with the passing of the Insurance Act of 1923. Incomplete statistics on the industry prior to the mid-1920s are available. It is only possible to make general claims regarding the number of companies operating in the industry.

company has the ability to address financial needs of both the top end of the wealth market as well as aspiring low-income clients in emerging markets. It has done so based on a century of rich learning, its foremost asset. During the establishment year, Sanlam management acted pragmatically in choosing strategies to arrive at a vision that mobilized human capital potentially outside the core of South African economic development. Management was bureaucratic, centralized, and integrated with the business of Santam and AHT. The initial target market, the Afrikaners, were divided, generally undereducated, and lacked business acumen. The complex and exclusive political economy of South Africa offered a temporary laboratory to conduct an experiment in empowerment, which, if managed strategically, harboured its own transformation. Insurance and financial services are universal, but also contextually embedded. As global markets were transformed by deregulation and globalization, Sanlam management prepared the company to follow that market. By commencing business with a strong focus on building the domestic economy and empowering marginalized Afrikaners, Sanlam was perfectly positioned to call on markets outside its traditional geographical sphere of operation. From a South Africa where Afrikaners and the English-speaking population were seen as 'two races', to a South Africa in the rising African market, Sanlam has emerged as the only successful emerging-market financial services conglomerate to address risk by selling trust and empowerment through financial services.

2 Setting down the footprint: from war to war, 1919–1945

After the Great War, European reconstruction set the backdrop for international economic recovery and in South Africa war demand was supplemented by demand for reconstruction. The recovery was slightly delayed by the post-war depression, which impacted adversely on business towards the ends of 1921 and 1922. The cycle bottomed out by August 1922. Local drought exacerbated tight market conditions for Sanlam, which experienced a decline in new business volumes. Sanlam's success of its first year was enhanced by the post-war economic prosperity, but the delinking of the British currency from the USA dollar in March 1919 led to inflationary pressures in the UK as well as in South Africa.[1] In 1921, new business at Sanlam fell by £31 381 to £1 116 589.[2] A new low of only 1 993 new policies to a value of £702 792 were issued in 1922, followed by a slow recovery. The slowdown in the sales of new policies during 1921/22 was accompanied by low claims payments in 1922. This allowed the company to strengthen its insurance fund to £90 026 by the end of that year. This performance made it possible for Sanlam to reintroduce the annual bonus, which was then paid uninterruptedly at a rate of '£1.6%' until 1929, when it was increased to '£2%'.[3] These bonus declarations were an invaluable marketing mechanism for the company.[4]

The entire insurance industry was on the verge of regulatory innovation, as the volatility in the market and a growing South African nationalism mobilized by Hertzog's call for 'South Africa first' raised voices canvassing for the regulation of the insurance industry. Insurance augments economic growth by mobilizing society's total savings. These savings reduced the cost of borrowing. The Union Government addressed the lack of statutory regulation of the domestic insurance industry by the promulgation of The Insurance Act, No. 37 of 1923. This Act followed the British Assurance Companies' Act of 1909 in consolidating earlier colonial insurance statutes in force in the Cape Colony

[1] E.H.D. Arndt (1928): *Banking and Currency Development, 1652–1927*. Juta: Cape Town: 412; De Kock: *Selected Subjects in Economic History*, pp. 131–2.

[2] SA, Minutes, General Management, 12 December 1921.

[3] The notation '£1.6%' was used in the annual reports. The meaning of this notation was the payment of £1.6 bonus per every £100 assured. By writing '£1.6%' the company indicated that £1.6/100 was paid as the bonus on policies. See Sanlam Annual Report, 1921: 3. This style of reporting on the bonus paid was used until the 1950s.

[4] SA, Minutes, General Management, 18 November 1922.

since 1891 (Life Assurance Act, No. 13 of 1891 Cape Colony). The 1923 Act made registration of all companies operating in the insurance industry, whether long-term or short-term insurance, compulsory. Registered companies paid a licence fee, deposited a maximum amount of £25 000 with the Treasury and submitted annual actuarial reports on the condition of their business. The statutes acknowledged the principle of 'freedom with publicity', granting operational freedom on the grounds of full disclosure of the nature of business.[5]

The domestic market was lucrative for insurance companies. After the first submissions to the Treasury in 1925, thirty-four registered life offices operated in the market—nine local firms and twenty-five foreign-based enterprises. In 1934 the life offices established the Life Offices Association of South Africa (LOA) to advance the professionalism of the industry. Despite the dire economic conditions the long-term insurance industry was booming and local companies dominated the market. Four companies were dominant: The African Life Assurance Society Pty Ltd, the South African Mutual Life Assurance Society of the Cape of Good Hope (Old Mutual), the Southern Life Association, and Sanlam. The total assets of insurance companies in 1925 were £822 435 000. The South African companies' assets were £26 698 000 (3.42 per cent of the total assets of long-term insurance companies operating in South Africa) and those of foreign companies £795 737 000 (96.7 per cent of total assets). This distribution should be understood by taking into account that the foreign incorporated companies held vast assets outside South Africa and were much older than the local companies. The local insurance companies nevertheless collected 65.3 per cent of total premium income accruing to the long-term business in South Africa. A total of 74 per cent of all new policies issued were with South African companies. This showed local trust in and support for the local insurance companies.

This market grew by 6.4 per cent per annum between 1929 and 1945 under adverse economic conditions, including a post-war depression, drought, the 1929 world depression, slumping primary product prices, and the drawn-out decision of South Africa to abandon the gold standard in 1932. Economic recovery took off with the increased demand for local products during World War II.[6] Politically, the years between the two world wars were only marginally stable. The rise of the National Party (NP) and an embattled economy resulted in a change in government in 1924. Hertzog's NP and the Labour Party entered into an election agreement, won the general election and established the Pact Government in 1924.[7] The world depression and the gold standard crisis had long-lasting adverse effects on the primary production-based economy as the prices

[5] G. Verhoef (2010): *Life offices to the rescue*: 149. [6] Ibid., 150.

[7] The Pact Government is the government formed as a result of the election pact between the National Party and the Labour Party prior to the 1924 general election to defeat the South African arty of J.C. Smuts—C.F.J. Müller (1987) *Vyfhonderd jaar Suid-Afrikaanse Geskiedenis*, Pretoria: Academica: 419–22.

of minerals and agricultural commodities plummeted. When Britain abandoned the gold standard in September 1930, the Hertzog government insisted on demonstrating the independence of the Union by adhering to the standard. Hertzog used the gold standard to illustrate to Britain the independence of the Union and to demonstrate that a British decision on the gold standard did not automatically imply that South Africa would follow suit. Hertzog wanted to confirm the confidence of the South African government in gold (having the largest gold-mining industry in the world). As sterling depreciated, so did the other currencies in the Commonwealth, resulting in a dramatic collapse in South Africa's primary product exports. Tielman Roos, a former member of the Sanlam board and leader of the National Party in Transvaal, announced in December 1932 that he would return to active politics to challenge the Pact government's stand on gold. Hertzog responded on 28 December 1932 by following the international community in abandoning the gold standard. The sudden and sharp rise in the gold price immediately reversed the flow of capital into South Africa and restored the competitiveness of local exports. Under weakened economic conditions, political realism triumphed over intra-Afrikaner political divisions. In 1933 the NP merged with the South African Party under General J.C. Smuts to establish the United Party (UP). Disenchanted members of the NP refused to follow Hertzog into the UP. Dr D.F. Malan, leader of the NP in the Cape Province, broke away to form the Purified National Party. As the Second World War drew to a close, white politics would soon reconfigure again. Afrikaners made up around 56 per cent of the white population by the late 1930s, which explains the direct impact of intra-Afrikaner dynamics on the domestic political system.

These divisions reverberated in the Sanlam boardroom, but management firmly refrained from permitting such divisions into its business. At the time, Sanlam had just opened a branch in Southern Rhodesia (now Zimbabwe) where a predominantly English-speaking policyholder base was being nurtured. The second half of the 1930s was also the time when Feenstra worked tirelessly to weather the storm of agent-hopping, slower production following the depression of the late 1920s, and stabilization of the network of branch offices and agents. The Sanlam management displayed strategic insight in assessing potential synergies with a broad base of local business interests. The official policy was that political intrigues were not to be allowed to derail sound business. Emerging synergies could not be risked by engagement with the day-to-day party political development. Strong voices by local businessmen called for tariff protection of domestic infant industries from 1919. These businessmen were English industrialists, but their calls dovetailed neatly with growing Afrikaner economic nationalism. The Board of Trade and Industry was established in 1920 and soon afterwards protective tariffs were introduced to nurture domestic industries.

South African industrial development took off during the interwar years in the context of policies of racial segregation. Labour legislation gave priority to white labour. African labour was accommodated in controlled segregated urban locations. The Land Act of

1913 and 1936 restricted African access to land ownership to traditionally owned communal land. The 1936 Native Representation Act gave African people political representation by means of a council with advisory powers. Only African and Coloured people who had qualified to vote before the formation of the Union retained the vote, but were represented by white representatives in the Union Parliament. Racial segregation was the norm in society, but people of all races interacted on different levels of society, albeit not with equal power or authority. The insurance industry developed in this racially divided society, although no person was excluded from sharing in the benefits of the industry. None of the insurance companies openly challenged the status quo. However, in the management structure there were people with long standing personal connections to the ruling party. Sanlam overtly sanctioned the status quo and advanced Afrikaner empowerment encapsulated within.

Vision and strategy: management

Sanlam progressed through the first year of business with relative stability. During the interwar years the company encountered turbulent times despite the overall favourable developments in the local and international industry. Sanlam had the benefit of relatively stable management built around the relationship of trust and a shared vision for the company. The leadership of Willie Hofmeyr as Chairman since 1918 up to 1953 was instrumental in focusing the company on growth through the delivery of industry-leading service and products. Hofmeyr was highly respected in broader Afrikaans business, political, and cultural circles. His stature contributed to a sense of security and direction for the company as well as the growing community of policyholders.

Willie Hofmeyr was the image, voice, and conscience of Santam and Sanlam from 1918. His deep understanding of the condition of his people, the Afrikaner, in South Africa and his drive to contribute constructively towards the progress of South Africa as a newly independent Union, equipped him with both insight and visionary strategy. To overcome persistent poverty and social marginalization Hofmeyr understood that personal agency held the key, but people also had to be motivated and believe in the potential of transforming the vision into reality. Life insurance offered people the opportunity to take control of their predicament. The alignment of the newly found personal power with rewards feeding into visible progress, was the transformation of despondency into hope. This idea constituted a golden thread through the entire century of Sanlam's history as company leaders in succession understood the context and the mechanisms of redemption. From the first Chairman's report, Hofmeyr underlined the usefulness of life insurance to provide for the future of families, the entire '*volk*' and the country as a whole. He explained the strategy—national economic development and progress through personal upliftment and empowerment as a collective effort of people's buy-in and a responsibly managed enterprise. He referred to 'the development of our fatherland' and the 'personal contribution' of each policyholder through savings.[8] Personal gain was connected to national gain, since life insurance was laying the foundation of the largest building policyholders can construct—a prosperous South Africa.[9] The 'Afrikaners' he addressed, included within the widest sense of the meaning of the word 'all those South Africans who put South Africa first'. He capitalized on the statement by the President of the Cape Town Chamber of Commerce in October 1923, pointing out the negative invisible exports/remittances from South Africa, fueled largely by the expatriation by foreign insurance companies and other businesses, of profits earned in the domestic market. Sanlam sought to reverse that trend by investing local savings in local development and local ownership.[10] In the wake of the division fostered by war and social inequality, he emphasized mutuality, employment creation, and education to those outside the market, and the most up-to-date policies and benefits to achieve the vision. Sanlam observed international trends in modern-day life insurance, namely the tendency towards mutualism, and the recognition in business of the principle of service to the community.[11] Service to the community was directly linked to local economic advancement. Building the national economy amid uncertainty, he argued, could only be achieved through 'Life Assurance... the only way of providing compensation for the uncertainty of human life.'[12]

There was no doubt that the vision of the company was embedded in nationalist Afrikaner aspirations. In 1934 Hofmeyr underlined the aspirations of management for the company—to grow to the benefit of the country, to serve as inspiration to the *Afrikanervolk,* and to inspire wider entrepreneurial opportunism. He expressed himself in the vocabulary of the Afrikaner countryman—'*die veld lê braak*' [the fields were lying fallow], talent was there, but courage and unity were required to take up the challenge.[13] When Sanlam celebrated the first decade in business, Hofmeyr invited the people of South Africa 'to grow with Sanlam' because the company was firmly rooted deep in the South African soil.[14] Throughout the depressing economic environment of the late 1920s, Hofmeyr refused to be drawn into negative doomsday speech, but drew policyholders' attention to the stability of the company's sustained growth and the fact that the life insurance fund had exceeded the £1 million mark during those trying times.[15] As if to

[8] SA: 5/1/2/: Chairman's Report, Annual Report 1921: 2.
[9] SA: 5/2/1: Chairman's Report, Annual Report 1920: 4.
[10] SA: 5/2/1: Chairman's Report, Annual Report 1923: 4.
[11] SA 5/2/1: Chairman's Report, Annual Report 1922: 5; Chairman's Report, Annual Report 1925: 5.
[12] SA: 5/2/1: Chairman's Report Annual Report 1924: 6; Chairman's Report Annual Report 1927: 5.
[13] SA: 5/2/1: Chairman's Report, Annual Report 1934: 12.
[14] SA: 5/2/1: Chairman's Report, Annual Report 1928: 4.
[15] SA: 5/2/1: Chairman's Report Annual Report 1931: 6.

vindicate these claims, the South African Treasury released statistics showing the growing demand for life insurance in South Africa. For Sanlam the good news was that while the average premium growth of life offices in the country between 1930 and 1935 was 17.7 per cent, Sanlam's premium growth was 69.6 per cent. The performance of the company was proudly described in quasi-biblical terminology, '*Aan sy vrugte sal jy hom ken*' [you will recognize it by the fruit it bears].[16] In 1929 Hofmeyr expressed his appreciation for the team-like spirit and dedication of the staff in building a truly South African company, a company born from the people to serve the people.[17] It was significant that the 1937 official annual report of Sanlam carried the motto '*Uit die volk gebore om die volk te dien*' [From the people, to serve the people] as the official motto for the first time.[18]

The year 1938 was a commemorative year for the Afrikaner people, since it was the centenary celebrations of the *Groot Trek* (Great Trek—or mass emigration of Afrikaners from the British-controlled Cape Colony into the interior, which ultimately resulted in the establishment of the two consolidated Boer Republics—*Republiek van de Oranje Vrijstaat* and the *Zuid-Afrikaansche Republiek*. These republics were officially recognized by Britain in 1852 and 1854 respectively). Afrikaner nationalism was publicly mobilized and gave a fresh impetus to the economic empowerment idealism of the early Afrikaans companies, *De Nationale Pers, Santam,* and *Sanlam.* Hofmeyr noted the awakening of a renewed national consciousness coinciding with Afrikaner urbanization. Despite the difficult decades of the 1920s and 1930s, Sanlam doubled its size between 1933 and 1938. In 1938, the company's twentieth anniversary, it boasted that it was the first year in its history that more than £5 million in new business had been written. The nationalism of 1938, the impressive performance of the company, and the confidence in the managerial capabilities of the Sanlam leadership converged in new business ventures shortly after the beginning of World War ll.

As the world economy contracted during the war years (1939–45), adverse conditions such as rising inflation and declining interest rates dampened industry growth prospects. Far from being isolated from global developments, Hofmeyr delivered a compassionate argument for life insurance as social security provision. The appointment of the commission chaired by Sir William Beveridge in Britain in 1941 to investigate social security provision in the United Kingdom, sparked a Commonwealth-wide discussion. In South Africa, the government appointed the National Health Service Commission in 1944 to investigate public health provision in South Africa. The Beveridge Report was finally released in December 1945,[19] but in 1943 already Hofmeyr had sensed the opportunity

[16] *Die Fakkel*, January 1935: 1. [17] SA: 5/2/1: Chairman's Report, Annual Report 1929: 4.
[18] SA: 5/2/1: Chairman's Report, Annual Report: 6.
[19] G. Verhoef (2006): The History of Medical Aid provision in South Africa's public sector, *Social Science History*, 30(4): 601–27.

to address policyholders on social security provision as an individual responsibility. Acknowledging the basic human need for social security, Hofmeyr questioned the capacity of the state to provide universal social security and reiterated the Sanlam approach to social security needs—that is empowerment of the individual towards self-provision. He aligned the human need for security with the desire for human dignity, self-respect, and independence. Life insurance, especially within the mutual model, offered the ultimate mechanism of social security provision and the retention of self-respect and pride. Sanlam policies were said to be tailored to provide for the uncertainties of death, disability, retirement (pensions), education, and medical expenses. Sanlam even offered interest-free loans for medical procedures. The overall capital formation through collected premium income invested in all the sectors of the economy, represented the contribution of life insurance to the entire spectrum of economic activities in the national economy: '*Uit sulke gelde voorsien dorps- en stadsrade hulle inwoners van water, elektrisiteit, strate en ander geriewe. Ook die staat trek hoofsaaklik uit hierdie fondse die kapitaal vir sy spoorweë en hawens, sy nasionale paaie, sy openbare geboue en sy besproeiingskemas... So word die spaargelde van die volk... gemobiliseer en gebruik vir die ontwikkeling van die land.*' [Municipalities use such funds to supply water, electricity, streets and other amenities. The state also draws from these funds the capital for the construction of railways and harbours, national roads, public buildings and irrigation schemes... this is how the savings of the people are mobilized and applied towards the development of the country]. To be able to provide universal social security ultimately implied a redistribution of national income, which made it imperative to grow national income—which was exactly what Sanlam had set out to achieve. The tool was empowerment initiatives, including stimulating entrepreneurial activity by offering venture capital to those inspired by the vision.[20] It was this deep social engagement of the Sanlam management, articulated in the Chairman's Report, which constituted the unique combination of entrepreneurial responsibility in business, civic duty, and a deep-seated alignment with the *volk* in a late-comer life office in South Africa. It would be easy to describe these sentiments simply as nationalist jargon. However, the realities of the Afrikaner people as a South African constituency in the British Commonwealth during two world wars and intense international economic distress, explain the entrepreneurial insight to capitalize from it.

The disruption in management caused by the passing away of Dormehl and the resignation of MacDowall unsettled the new company, especially since both men were experienced insurance men. A high level of stability was nevertheless maintained through the management structure, the managerial style, and the social cohesion among the management team. Day-to-day management was inextricably linked to the

[20] SA: Chairman's Report, Annual Report 1943: 3.

Chairman and the Board of Directors. Willie Hofmeyr's presence in multiple positions up to 1953 (as Chairman, acting Managing Director, Chairman of Santam as well as Chairman of *De Burger*) was instrumental in establishing the company and guiding it through the vital first years. The members of the Board of Directors and the local advisory boards were all influential community leaders and often held public political office. Most of the directors served on the board for periods of almost thirty years. On the initial Board of Directors, Charlie Malan was the National Party Member of Parliament (MP) for Worcester and Minister of Railways and Harbours between 1924 and 1935 when he passed away, Dr Tielman J. de V. Roos was the National Party MP for Lichtenburg in 1915, while Dr Colin Steyn (only son of former President M.T. Steyn) was at first the National Party MP for Vredefort and Bloemfontein, and after the formation of the UP, the United Party MP between 1938 and 1948. He also served as Deputy Minister of Justice under Tielman Roos and during the war as Minister of Justice in the Smuts Cabinet. Mr Piet Grobler was a founding member of Sanlam, who participated in the Rebellion of 1914, was caught, sentenced and had to pay a fine of £500. Grobler supported Hertzog and was elected MP in 1922 and served as Minister of Lands in the Pact Government and Minister of Native Affairs from 1933 and subsequently followed Hertzog to the merged United Party in 1934. He was a member of the Sanlam Board until 1940.

Where the social capital of participation in the South African War and nationalist Afrikaner language initiatives moulded cohesion among the founding fathers, the social capital network was expanded and reinforced by those who joined the Board after the Great War. Afrikaner nationalism, mobilized in support of Hertzog's 'South Africa First' slogan, resonated in the Sanlam boardroom. C.T.M. Wilcocks was Administrator of the Free State and Vice-Chairman of Sanlam until his death in 1935. Wilcocks was succeeded by Dr J.F.J. van Rensburg as Administrator of the Free State as well as a member of the Sanlam board. Van Rensburg was a qualified land surveyor and lawyer, with a doctorate in Law from the University of Stellenbosch. He resigned his position as Administrator of the Free State soon after the beginning of World War II to become the Commandant General of the *Ossewa Brandwag*, an organization of Afrikaners opposing the South African government's decision to join the Allied Forces in the war. The organization disbanded after the war and Van Rensburg retired to his farm, but he remained a member of the Sanlam board until his death in 1966.[21] Mr J.H. Conradie, who served on the Sanlam board from 1922, was elected National Party MP in 1920 and appointed Administrator of the Cape Province in 1929. Mr S.F. Malan, also a National Party MP, joined the board in 1936, and in 1939 Advocate Eric Louw, an MP and later Minister of Foreign Affairs in the National Party Cabinet, was elected to the board.

[21] Die *Fakkel*, October 1966: 3.

Prominent NP members of Parliament who served on the Sanlam board before 1945 were Dr J.F.J. van Rensburg and Dr P.D. Rousseau, the son of a *dominee* of the DRC. Rousseau qualified as a teacher, participated in the South African War, was captured and sentenced to death, but exiled to St Helena for the duration of the war. Upon his return he completed advanced studies in Education and was later appointed Inspector of Education in the Cape Province. He was the father of Dr Pierre Etienne Rousseau, who later became Managing Director of Sasol (South African Oil and Gas Corporation) and also a member of the Sanlam board.[22] Other members included Dr I.P. Schabort (gynaecologist, founder of the South African Medical Council and a member of the Transvaal Local Board[23]), and Mr S.F. Malan (brother of the later Prime Minister Dr D.F. Malan, and member of the Cape Provincial Council and later member of the Executive Committee, while also a member of the agricultural union and the *Koöperatiewe Wynbouers Vereniging (KWV)* in the Western Cape). Before 1945, Dr Colin Steyn was the only non-NP member of the Sanlam board, but shared the inspiration of the company from the beginning. The pragmatism of the leadership was not often rewarded. P.A. Malan noted many years later that the founding fathers experienced great difficulty convincing Afrikaners who did not support Hertzog to join the Board, because the initial leadership did not want the political divisions to derail the ambitions of the company.[24] That proved very difficult. P.A. Malan nevertheless remembered the request by Eric Louw, his long and loyal friend who later entered politics, to keep an eye on a possible directorship should a vacancy arise. This happened when Mr Pieter Neethling passed away in 1939. Eric Louw was then appointed to the Sanlam board.[25]

On the local advisory boards Sanlam's pragmatism was better rewarded. In Natal, the company succeeded in availing itself of the services of influential community leaders outside the Afrikaner circle. These included Advocate George Hulett, a respected English-speaking jurist and businessman, who had served as a member of the Natal Provincial Council since 1910 and was a member of the Union Senate from 1919. R. Ellis Brown, born in Natal in 1880, fought against the Boer forces in the South African War as a member of the Natal Volunteer Corps (held in the siege of Ladysmith during 1899), later became mayor of Durban, and served on the Sanlam local board from 1941. On the Transvaal local board, General J.C. Kemp, NP member for Wolmaransstad (1920–46), and General C. Muller, NP member for Pretoria district from 1920–5, served with P.G.W. Grobler. On the Free State provincial board was Senator W.J. Brebner who had served in the South African War and was a member of the National Party, as was Senator M.J. Vermeulen.

[22] SA: 6/2/1 Biographical files PD Rousseau; *Die Fakkel* May 1940: 8–9.
[23] *Die Fakkel*, December 1942: 6; December 1966: 23; April 1971: 1.
[24] SA: 6/1/19: P.A. Malan biographical papers.
[25] SA: 6/1/19: P.A. Malan biographical papers: Letter E. Louw—P.A. Malan, 9/9/1939.

Willie Hofmeyr, Charlie Louw, Piet Malan, and Piet Grobler were the stalwarts who constituted the core of the board through the interwar years. Ambiguity on politics in the company was glaring. While the board comprised almost exclusively sympathizers and members of the National Party, the official policy since the early 1930s with respect to Head Office staff and agents was a complete ban on active participation in party politics in public. On 27 July 1929 Sanlam sent out an instruction to all staff members to refrain from any public participation in party politics 'without prior permission from the Board of Directors'. In 1935 A.J. Coertse (inspector in Kimberley) requested permission from the *Dagelijks Bestuur* to make himself available for election to the Kimberly City Council. It was refused.[26] In 1937 Mr Lambrechts, a member of Head Office staff, who had joined Sanlam in 1927 as a member of the Labour Party, chaired a public meeting of the Labour Party in Stellenbosch. *De Burger* reported on the meeting and when Feenstra got wind thereof, Lambrechts was reprimanded and asked to resign his position in the party.[27] Similarly agent B.L. Mitchell's request to stand for election in a municipal ward was rejected.[28] The application of this policy continued and in 1943 the board authorized the termination of a contract with agent P.W.A. Nel following public political participation.[29] This drastic action led to a revision by the board of the company's policy on participation in politics and in the Staff Policy on officials' and agents' participation in party politics. The following rules were laid down: Full-time officials and agents had the civil right to be members of political parties or organizations with political aims and could attend meetings, but could not engage in propagating such causes, actively participate in public actions, or serve on the representative bodies such as municipal councils, regional councils, school boards, or any related bodies (section 2 Staff Rules).[30] The broad South Africanism frequently articulated in Hofmeyr's Chairman's addresses confirmed this policy in section 2. It stated that Santam and Sanlam were general Afrikaans people's institutions with economic goals, seeking to serve all sections of society. These goals could only be achieved if all Sanlam officials refrained from any public party political conduct. Officials were explicitly forbidden from any degrading or public-enticing conduct, either at work or after hours. At the June 1943 meeting of the board the rules were amended to exclude unanimous election of staff to school boards or committees, following written permission from the board.[31]

The firm policy position by the board was significant for two reasons. Firstly, the direct influence of the board comprising well-known National Party supporters and representatives could be interpreted as a double standard. It was actually clear pragmatism, since

[26] SA: Sanlam Minutes of Dagelijks Bestuur, 19/1/1935.
[27] SA: Minutes of Dagelijks Bestuur, 13/5/1937.
[28] SA: Minutes of Dagelijks Bestuur, 9/9/1937.
[29] SA: Minutes of Dagelijks Bestuur, 27/1/1943.
[30] SA: Minutes of Dagelijks Bestuur, 17/3/1943.
[31] SA: Minutes of Dagelijks Bestuur, 16/6/43.

the company was only just stabilizing the agent network and stemming the tide of agents attracted to competitors. It had also just come to light that new business growth had gained steady momentum. Secondly, intra-Afrikaner political division was growing and could destabilize business prospects. The reconfiguration of Afrikaner politics from Hertzog's National Party to Smuts' United Party (UP), then Malan's Purified National Party, was potentially destabilizing. Afrikaner division was driven further when Smuts won a Parliamentary vote to align South Africa with the Allied Powers in World War II, defeating Hertzog's opposition to South Africa's participation in the war. This decision led to the formation of the *Ossewa Brandwag.* All of these factions were represented on the board. In Sanlam the policy of non-public party political participation was timely and made business sense.

The potential disruptive impact of intra-Afrikaner strife was ameliorated by the 1938 Great Trek Centenary celebrations and the mobilization of Afrikaner economic initiatives to the next level of Afrikaner empowerment in 1939. Despite the policy on public political participation, Sanlam overtly supported and collaborated in the Great Trek celebrations, since it was argued that it was a national cultural event bringing all Afrikaners together. The Great Trek celebration mobilized Afrikaner nationalism across the country as nine ox wagons followed the exact routes of the 1838 treks to Pretoria, where the foundation stone of the massive Voortrekker Monument was laid on 16 December 1938 during the Day of the Covenant commemorations. Sanlam capitalized on the emotive nationalism of the time. *Die Fakkel* of 7 November 1938 was a special '*Voortrekkeruitgawe*' (Voortrekker Edition). Hofmeyr made direct reference to the centenary celebrations in the Chairman's address. The event, he claimed, mobilized Afrikaners as never before in history, bringing a sense of unity and a desire to be worthy of their cause. In 1938, the twentieth anniversary of Sanlam, new business exceeded £5 million for the first time—an achievement, he claimed, resulting from its dedication to job creation, training, and education of young people, and pioneering the second trek of Afrikaners, that is the trek to the cities. In *Die Fakkel,* Hofmeyr reiterated that Afrikaners had to disentangle themselves from their social and economic inferiority by building a future for their descendants. That goal would not be realized through negative forces, but only through the inherent power that was in the *volk.*[32] At Head Office, *Die Fakkel* opened with the words '*Sanlam op die pad van Suid-Afrika*' [Sanlam on the road of South Africa]. The first article on the first page of the magazine acknowledged the unique event in the history of the Afrikaner people, and also the endless fire of people's enthusiasm, 'ignited by a few ox wagons on the Road of South Africa, but also the trek of 1918 when the Sanlam wagon departed towards the economic liberation of our people'. Staff were allowed to participate in all events, from the departure of the ox wagon from

[32] SA: Sanlam Annual Report, Chairman's Address: 2–6.

Cape Town on 8 August 1938, to the actual celebrations on 16 December in Pretoria. They were even allowed to take their annual leave in December in order to attend the festivities. The Sanlam staff participated in several centenary initiatives, such as the men growing beards and the women refraining from wearing make-up. Non-compliance led to a fine. The fines were collected and contributed to the fund for the construction of the Voortrekker Monument.[33] There was no mistaking this event as a valuable marketing opportunity for Sanlam.

The company experienced mixed results in the market. Sanlam did not enjoy unqualified support from Afrikaners. In 1937 Feenstra wrote to Charlie Louw, alluding to the lack of support for Sanlam in the agricultural society *Boere Saamwerk Beperk* (BSB), and asking for the intervention of board members to put Sanlam's case to BSB. Of the nine members on the BSB board only three were sympathetic towards Sanlam.[34] This experience showed management that loyalty to Afrikaner causes did not automatically translate into support for Sanlam. Sound management and quality competitive products would drive market growth.

Doing good business came down to management

Sanlam management remained remarkably stable throughout the interwar years. However, the naming of designated managers was very confusing and remained so until the late 1940s. The early minutes of Santam and Sanlam reflected the ambiguity in assigning authority. At first the company appointed two managers—a Managing Director (Fred Dormehl) and a General Manager (Alfred MacDowall). Dormehl passed away in October 1918 and MacDowall resigned his position in 1920 and was succeeded as General Manager on 17 March 1922. Willie Hofmeyr acted as Managing Director after the death of Dormehl between 1918 and 1920, when he was succeeded by Charlie Louw, who served as acting Managing Director between 1920 and 1922. Hofmeyr was also Chairman of the Board of Directors of Sanlam from 1918 until 1953. He was both Managing Director and Chairman of the board between 1918 and 1920. The title of General Manager was again bestowed on G.F. de Villiers (Gys), a position he held until 1927. Between 1927 and 1935 M.S. Louw (Tinie), the actuary of the company, was appointed Manager of Sanlam and then between 1935 and 1946 De Villiers and Louw were joint General Managers. The title '*Hoofbestuurder*' was used for the first time in 1935, but then in 1948 when De Villiers retired, his successor was again referred to as

[33] *Die Fakkel*, 7/11/38 :1, 4; 7/9/38: 19; 7/10/38: 14: SA: Minutes of Dagelijks Bestuur, 4/8/1938; 22/9/1938; 25/9/1941.

[34] WCA: C.R. Louw Collection: Feenstra–Louw, 1/7/1937.

Managing Director of Sanlam. The seeming indecisiveness in the use of titles was an indication of the concern about control and hierarchy in the new insurance operation. So much was at stake. Management appealed to policyholders' trust as it sought to engineer a strategy of personal and community empowerment. A firm hold on the execution of each step of that vision depended on trust among the managerial team and the Board of Directors, and their ability to control the roll out of the growing enterprise.

The relatively inexperienced Sanlam insurance management team suffered a heavy blow when Alfred MacDowall, one of the three experienced insurance managers appointed in 1918, resigned his position on 18 May 1920. MacDowall criticized the *Dagelijks Bestuur* for not appointing enough staff. He criticized the executives for not understanding the actual insurance environment. Explaining his reasons, on 25 May 1920 MacDowall wrote that his management was unfairly criticized due to policies laid down by the Executive Committee (to which he had objected from the outset), such as a lack of staff and the executives not getting out of the office enough. MacDowall believed the Agency Manager blamed him for the accounts of agents being overdue and the Accidents Manager blamed him for the state of the bookkeeping in Johannesburg. Members of the Executive relied on these reports when responding to MacDowall's conduct. When asked if the Executive was satisfied with his management, no comments were made. He referred to the majority report of 3 October 1918 as well as his minority report, disagreeing with the findings on his managerial capabilities. The majority report was accepted without incorporating his objections. MacDowall recognized the difficulty in attracting experienced staff and therefore proposed the appointment of local boards where the expertise of attorneys could be acquired to facilitate the bridging of the problem. Finally, he stated that he was suffering from a work overload. He was physically incapable of performing all the duties imposed upon him. He blamed the Trust Manager for being incapable of acting in his absence, therefore making it impossible for MacDowall to leave him in charge.

MacDowall suggested that the company suffered from 'overmanagement'.[35] To him the *Dagelijkse Bestuur* was formed to oversee the flotation of the company and be a permanent loan committee; however, it had developed into a management committee, instead of management performing their duties. This led to directors losing their policy breadth, vision, and foresight. He reiterated that for eighteen months he had advocated the formation of a bank:

> it is the only weapon with which we can fight Schlesinger with the facilities at this command . . . None of the members of the *Dagelijks Bestuur* has time to investigate the banking scheme owing to immersion in detail. The same with the opening of a Trust Office in Pretoria which I strongly advocated in my Report of 12th July 1918.[36]

[35] A. MacDowall to Chairman, Santam, dated 25 May 1920.
[36] A. MacDowall to Chairman, Santam, dated 25 May 1920.

MacDowall was striking directly at the core of managerial inexperience and subsequent centralization of responsibilities leading to his frustration at not being permitted the work he was qualified to do. Management initially requested MacDowall to vacate his office by 30 June 1920 but on 3 June 1920 Hofmeyr announced that MacDowall's services had been terminated at 6.00 pm as his behaviour since his resignation had not been in the interest of the company. The following day C.R. Louw was appointed Managing Director and Gys de Villiers succeeded MacDowall as acting Secretary.[37] Nothing in the MacDowall statements was untrue or unreasonable, but during the formative years of the new insurance enterprise such conduct was viewed as a breach of confidence that resulted in undesirable tension.

Management wanted to grow the company. A shared vision within the hierarchy of leadership addressed the difficulties of the successful mix of management systems, products, agents, and society. The pioneering managers in Sanlam between 1920 and 1945 were Tinie Louw, Gys de Villiers and Jan Feenstra. De Villiers was born in Beaufort West on 12 August 1888 and attended the same school as the later Minister of Foreign Affairs, Eric Louw. De Villiers then studied law at the Victoria College at the same time as M.S. (Tinie) Louw studied mathematics. Gys de Villiers was admitted as a lawyer in Cape Town where he practised as an attorney, notary, conveyancer, and accredited translator. He performed legal work for the General Accident, Fire and Life Corporation Ltd in Cape Town—an important recognition of his abilities, since few Afrikaans lawyers were ever entrusted with legal work for English companies. Between 1916 and 1917 De Villiers regularly encountered Alfred MacDowall, who was employed at General Accident. After the establishment of Santam, De Villiers accepted an appointment as Branch Manager of Santam at De Aar, then in Prins Albert. He finally moved to Head Office in January 1920 as Trust Manager. When MacDowall resigned, De Villiers acted as Secretary of the company and from December 1921 he was officially appointed Secretary of Santam. His career in the central management team is significant since he fitted the profile of a professionally qualified person sharing the vision of Afrikaner upward mobility amid a skeptical English-speaking dominated business community.

Tinie Louw was also born in 1888—on 15 August in Ladismith in the Cape, where his father was a minister in the DRC. His career in Sanlam started as Assistant Actuary and after qualifying as Fellow of the Faculty of Actuaries (FFA) in Scotland, he stepped into the shoes of George Paterson as the Sanlam Actuary on 1 January 1922. He emerged as an exceptional inspirational business leader across the broad spectrum of emerging Afrikaner business ventures.

Johannes Pieter Feenstra was born in Cape Town on 17 October 1885, where his father was a Dutch immigrant owner of a general trading enterprise. Feenstra had to

[37] Death letter de Villiers, 19/11/1957.

leave school at the age of sixteen to take up employment. He entered the service of the Australian insurance company, the Colonial Mutual Insurance Company, in Cape Town. The Colonial's business language was English, resulting in Feenstra developing a comfortable acquaintance with the language. For many years during his career in Sanlam his correspondence with colleagues was in English, since he mastered the technical vocabulary of the industry in English, and signed his letters as 'John Feenstra'. His energetic abilities as an experienced insurance man were a saving grace to Sanlam. The overall performance of the company as published in the annual report, was relatively favourable, but Feenstra was on the receiving end of the actual developments. In correspondence to the Managing Director in June 1920, Feenstra noted that the life department of the company was in a state of great disarray when he was appointed. He dealt with complaints from agents and policyholders alike and had to fend off the threats of the Southern Life Assurance Company to withdraw all reinsurance of Sanlam's policies unless Sanlam got its house in order. Matters were aggravated by the inability of the Actuary, Paterson, to carry out his responsibilities. Feenstra afforded extensive attention to reducing the lapsed policy rate from 12 per cent in 1919 to 8 per cent by September 1920. Feenstra devoted many hours to rectify matters, and did so very successfully, enabling him to comment that 'the results were so satisfactory, that I was inspired to do more and be more enthusiastic'.[38] By mid-1920 Feenstra was satisfied that all the internal Sanlam records were in order and that the company had acquired the nature of a 'modern office' managed on the best business principles of quick service and professional abilities. With industrial policies managed by the oldest industrial insurance company in the country, management addressed the question of distribution channels.

Agent network

Sanlam's penetration into the market the company was developing depended on strong management and a successful agent network. When the business was launched, the *'reizende agenten'* were organized centrally. The Spanish flu interrupted both the canvassing and appointment of agents, but also the marketing of policies. For almost two months in 1918 the marketing of policies came to an almost complete standstill. The flip side of the coin was that a renewed interest in life insurance was awakened. This trend was described as follows by Howard Phillips:

> statistics show that in the months after the Spanish 'flu epidemic there was a consequent and unprecedented rise, both in the number of new life insurance policies taken out and old

[38] SA 6/5: Feenstra biographical papers: Letter Feenstra–MacDowall, 9/6/1920.

ones extended. In 1919 new life business alone was estimated as worth £20 million, easily a South African record.[39]

Sanlam benefited from this heightened demand for insurance, but a special effort was required to improve the geographical spread of its market. During the first four months of operations thirty-five policies were sold, only three of which were outside the immediate Cape Town district. Sales during August and October 1918 included new policyholders from the Transvaal, Orange Free State, and the northern parts of the Cape Province, but there was no interest in Natal. The actual problem was inexperience in organizing the agents or field staff. De Villiers, who was appointed the Agency Manager, confined his attention only to the management of business in the Western Cape. He left Sanlam in 1921 to pursue further studies in law. His successor, S.M. Goodson, was appointed Manager of Agents one year later and then he also resigned in 1923 to take up employment with another insurance company. Finally, it was Jan Feenstra who was appointed Chief Clerk in the New Business Department of Sanlam on 1 October 1918 who established that function at Head Office. Feenstra could see that the organization of field staff was in dire straits. He was sent to the Orange Free State (Bloemfontein) to establish why the manager in that region, the lawyer Gordon Fraser, failed to make progress. Feenstra succeeded in breathing some life into the Orange Free State, but again not because he was the responsible manager at Head Office. The building of a successful agent corps during the establishment years was finally linked directly to Feenstra's insistence on the permanent appointment of agents only once a proven record was established. Sanlam had no dedicated training programme for agents, since the company was hitting the ground running, but Feenstra used the publication of Sanlam's first tariff schedule in 1919 to add basic guidelines on agent conduct. The *General Instructions to Agents and Tariff Book*, published in 1919, was the first introduction of inexperienced agents to the world of insurance. It contained general guidelines on the completion of applications, medical examinations, professional loading, and 'friendly reports' (a polite way of presenting personal information). Considering the inexperience of many agents, the book explained professional conduct, unacceptable conduct, and the underlying Sanlam ethical values.

In correspondence with MacDowall in March 1920 Feenstra insisted that an agency manager be appointed for the Transvaal. The *Dagelijks Bestuur* finally appointed a temporary organizer for agents in the Orange Free State in March 1920 and a manager for the Transvaal at the same time. It is clear that the Sanlam management was undecided on how to structure the countrywide organization of agents. In June 1920 a directive to all agents requested them to submit 'regular statements' to the manager of

[39] Howard Phillips: *'Black October': the Impact of the Spanish Influenza Epidemic of 1918 on South Africa*, p. 213.

the branch under the auspices of which they were working.[40] Feenstra's experience, infused with inspiration for Afrikaner empowerment, brought a business-like approach to the organization and operation of agents. He told MacDowall that the time had come for Sanlam to stop the experimentation with agents. The company had attracted some first-class people with valuable experience from other insurance companies, as well as professionally qualified persons such as teachers, ministers of religion, missionaries, farmers, railway workers, mining engineers, and jurists. He insisted on experienced bilingual persons, but experience was lacking among the enthusiastic new recruits.

Smooth progress in the Free State remained complex. Sanlam had to deal with weather conditions, agents, and its parent company. The close relationship with Santam (the parent company with which it shared management and board members) added to the complexities in that market. Santam as the parent company carried the flag in expansion into the interior. Santam offices accommodated agents distributing both short-term insurance, as well as agents engaged in marketing Sanlam life products. Penetration into the Free State market was slow and cumbersome despite the expectation of it being a valuable market given the early involvement of Fichardt in launching the company. The strong Afrikaner population in agriculture and the Free State towns made it a logical market to cultivate, but similar aspirations were harboured by competing concerns. Santam's difficulties expanding into the Free State market resulted in closer alignment with trust companies and boards of executors across the province. This strategy alerted the Schlesinger Organization of Mr I.W. Schlesinger to the potential threat lurking in Santam's expansion ambitions. Schlesinger sought to expand his insurance empire by acquiring the trust and agency business of attorneys in the Free State with the aim of establishing an all-powerful Free State Trust Company. If that strategy succeeded, it could have stalled all Santam's ambitions in the Free State. Concerned persons wrote anxious letters and sent deputations to meet with the Santam management, requesting action to attempt to put a halt to the Schlesinger ambitions. For Santam to challenge the Schlesinger Organization from its own branch network in the Free State would be an extremely uneven battle. The alternative was to align itself with existing Free State trust companies to present a stronger presence. Santam management argued that collaboration with existing trust businesses would be cost efficient and allow access to a well-developed Free State network of trust business. For that purpose Santam acquired an interest in the Free State Board of Executors, hoping to strengthen the resistance to the Schlesinger expansion ambitions. Santam's management was satisfied with the due diligence conducted on the Free State Board of Executors, since annual dividends had been paid for at least five years and the Board of Executors enjoyed the support of an extended network of Free State attorneys. Santam invested in the Free State Board of

[40] Minutes of Dagelijks Bestuur, 24/6/20.

Executors on condition of exclusive distribution of Santam products and Sanlam life products. Santam invested £32 000 in the Free State Board of Executors in 1920, but soon afterwards economic growth ground almost to a halt as a result of a severe drought, putting pressure on the trust business. To complicate matters the Law Society of the Free State approached the Supreme Court to prohibit attorneys from managing trust and executor businesses. When the court ruled in favour of the Law Society, many capable attorneys resigned from their managerial positions in the trust and executor businesses. Under these adverse economic conditions, the cost saving brought about by the resignation of attorneys was actually a positive development. The persistent nature of the economic downturn depleted the capital base of the trust companies, including the Free State Board of Executors in which Santam had a substantial stake. Santam made a further advance of £30 000, but could not salvage this investment. In May 1923 the Free State Board of Executors was in provisional liquidation.[41] Santam dealt with the loss (as well as a loss of around £10 000 in the Sanlam industrial department) by writing down its capital of £135 705 to issued capital of £42 282 (consisting of 211 410 shares of 14/- at 4/- paid up) and a new reserve fund of £15 000. Although the loss was a heavy blow to Santam, the company was not even close to terminating operations. Sanlam and African Homes Trust were delivering a stable flow of funds (premiums).[42]

The first seven years proved challenging, especially in the Transvaal and OFS. The three main problems were a relatively high policy lapse rate, variable agent productivity, and the bad debts of agents themselves. The Area Manager in the Free State, D.J. Marais, proved incompetent and unable to manage his own finances. He was demoted to the position of ordinary agent in 1923 and replaced by J.M. de Ville in the Transvaal and J. Blanckenberg from Colonial Mutual as OFS Manager.[43] Advertisements for a manager for Natal met with the interest of 'shady characters', with whom Sanlam had no desire to enter into any relationship. Harry van Dam, then Area Manager in Cape Town, was subsequently despatched to Natal in 1926,[44] after which the Natal business stabilized. Sanlam made significant inroads in the rural areas, such as the Overberg area north-east of Cape Town, the Karoo and Namaqualand areas of the Northern Cape Province, the Transvaal *platteland* and the western Free State region. It was interesting that Cape Town and its direct surrounding areas did not offer the new company similar success. In the Free State, strong growth was experienced in Bloemfontein, the capital, as well as the agricultural districts of the northern and western regions, and in the Transvaal it was also

[41] SA 6/1/1/5; W.J. Bezuidenhout Biographical documents: Minutes of Special Annual General Meeting of shareholders, 1 May 1923; *Africa Insurance Record*, July 1924: 36.

[42] SA 6/1/1/5: W.J. Bezuidenhout Biographical documents: Minutes of Special Santam AGM, 1 May 1923; Y. Hagedorn-Hansen (2017) 'The transformation of the South African short term insurance industry', 109–12.

[43] SAQ: Minutes Dagelijks Bestuur, 27/6/23; 25/7/23.

[44] SA: 5/2/4/2/1: Letter Secretary—General Manager, 30/11/25.

the *platteland* of the Western Transvaal, the eastern escarpment and Southern Transvaal summer crop areas, where policyholder numbers grew steadily. Between 1919 and 1945 the value of Sanlam's new policies rose steadily by 9.94 per cent annual compound growth. This was significant, since the formerly uninsured segment of society (also the most vulnerable to volatile climatic conditions) formed the backbone of the new business. The flip side of rural success was rural volatility.

The adverse economic conditions of the early 1920s slowed down the issuing of new policies, but by 1928 slow but steady growth was restored. The board considered various mechanisms to stabilize the agent network, such as improved remuneration to counter competitors' higher commission offerings. In the Transvaal alone Sanlam lost almost half its agents in 1925. Cases were reported of the Colonial Mutual offering successful Sanlam agents 95 per cent commission on first-year business, while Sanlam paid only 60 per cent.[45] In 1927 alone, seven Free State agents, four from Natal, five from the Transvaal and eight from the Cape Province with active commission accounts, left Sanlam for competitors. This trend became specifically challenging during the troublesome years of the mid-1930s. Sanlam's agents were worth luring away—a phenomenon Feenstra described as the 'butterfly phenomenon'.[46] While it was apparent that Sanlam agents were in high demand with competitors, this caused operational instability by the mid-1930s. The Colonial Mutual was especially active in attracting Sanlam agents.

The sustained growth trajectory in new business depended on improved stability in the agent network and on incentives. Management offered monetary rewards to the top-performing agents during the crucial establishment years 1919 and 1920,[47] and in subsequent years similar incentive schemes towards the end of the financial year (September) served as an important source of encouragement. The competition was for a shield, the Silver Shield, supplemented by cash bonuses.[48] Incentives were supplemented by the introduction in 1932 of inspectors. These officials were added to the organizational structure between branch managers and Head Office management. Feenstra submitted a very detailed report to the board explaining the shared experience of competitors such as The South African Mutual, Colonial Mutual, and National Mutual reporting that their business in the Free State 'has gone to pot'.[49] Tinie Louw delivered a well-considered response: agents lost could not be replaced, some agents were 'fair weather' agents lacking the fighting spirit to take on changing conditions, and attempts to outbid Colonial Mutual's excessive offers to Sanlam agents amounted to reckless business. He therefore devised a plan to strengthen the agents, to empower and equip

[45] SA: 5/4/2/1/2 Correspondence Johannesburg Branch manager—Secretary, 11/7/27.

[46] The 'butterfly phenomenon' referred to the Sanlam agents' being perceived as attractive and successful operators in the insurance market, worthy of being lured away by competitors.

[47] SA: 5/2/6: Annual Agent statements, 1929.

[48] SA: 5/2/6: When Jan Feenstra retired in 1946, the shield was renamed the Jan Feenstra Shield.

[49] SA: 5/3/1: Monthly Report 1930–1935: Memorandum Feenstra on Orange Free State.

them with the capacity to take on the challenges of adverse economic conditions and competition. This plan was the introduction of inspectors, sanctioned by a decision of the board in 1932. The basic organizational structure of the agent network was as follows:

Head Office General Manager → Assistant Manager: Agents → Branch Manager → Inspector/Organizer → Agent.[50] The inspectors were instrumental in stabilizing the Sanlam agency network. They were seen to be the link between the company and the agent and were responsible for ensuring that an entire area assigned to an agent was cultivated thoroughly. They were given the responsibility to advise the board on the appointment of new agents, train new agents, and support them with advice and guidance both on the distribution mechanism and on managing their own personal finances. The inspectors were the public image of Sanlam's sense of responsibility to build and sustain trust and pride in the ability of the new player to succeed in the industry.[51] In each of the branches a number of inspectors were appointed in 1932. In the Western Province branch six inspectorates were mapped and placed under the supervision of one inspector; in the Eastern Province branch four inspectorates were mapped and allocated to four inspectors; three inspectors were assigned to the Free State branch, including the northern Cape region of Griqualand East; the Transvaal was organized into five inspectorates and Natal into three areas; and one inspector was assigned to South West Africa (now Namibia). This organizational innovation laid the foundation for the subsequent growth. For the first time the agent network covered the entire geographical area of South Africa in an orderly and firmly structured manner, directly reporting to branch managers who reported to Head Office. The overlapping of agents' operations was thereby systematically terminated and operational boundaries formalized.

As experienced insurance men Feenstra, Free State branch manager John de Ville, and Western Cape manager Harry van Dam realized that the market was volatile, competitive, and challenging, thus requiring innovative imagination to pre-empt potential agent despondency. It was decided to introduce the *Saamwerk-week* (Collaboration Week) during the week coinciding with the birthday of Tinie Louw (15 August) annually—a 'production gift' to him. During the *Saamwerk-week* agents competed to submit the most successful policy applications. The gold medal to the first winner in 1930 went to S.J. van der Merwe of the Johannesburg branch, with policies to the value of £10 000. The following year Van der Merwe shared the medal with J.A. Delport from Port Elizabeth, both with policies to the value of £20 000. In 1932 the *Saamwerk-week* delivered a total of

[50] SA: Sanlam Board Minutes, 15/3/23. This elementary structure of agents' organization remained operational until the 1990s. The titles 'inspector' and 'organizer' were used interchangeably during the first decade of operation.

[51] *Die Fakkel*, June 1937, pp.1–2.

new policies to the value of £275 000—which translated to £14 million per annum.[52] The *Saamwerk-week* developed into a powerful tool, reinforcing ambition, teamwork and the sense of 'doing it for our company'.

The initiative was supplemented by the introduction of the annual conference of agents in 1932. Sanlam proudly moved into its new Head Office on the corner of Waal and Burg Streets, Cape Town, in December 1932. To the Sanlam management the building symbolized the confidence and ideals of the founders, and the success in establishing a people's financial institution able to reach into all corners of the country. It also symbolized the achievement of the firm and its position in the business environment of Cape Town. The building represented financial stability and commitment to the well-being of its policyholders, who were no longer only from the *platteland*, but had migrated and had become citizens of the city.[53] This move coincided with the first annual conference of agents, inspectors, and managers. The tone was inspirational and pedagogic. Willie Hofmeyr called for the trustworthiness of agents with the public and their company, Tinie Louw outlined the growing professionalism of the industry, the sophistication of sales techniques and 'service to the public through the best advice', and Harry van Dam (the Australian-born Dutchman) spoke about 'enthusiasm and emulation'.[54] More social mobilization tools were devised, especially by Tinie Louw. He sought to encourage agents to communicate with him in confidence, directly, about any issues concerning their work. To this end he established 'Club 21', a confidential correspondence club comprising 'Head 21' and all agents interested in engaging with him. Agents were invited to write to 'Head 21' concerning troublesome matters. Correspondence was treated confidentially and a unique number was allocated to each agent to protect the identity of the correspondent. Louw addressed matters raised confidentially and encouraged agents to buy into the slogan 'Smile, darn you, smile' as the motto of public conduct. Each participant received a unique number. It was later disclosed that Feenstra's number was 121 and Harry van Dam's 221—number one of Club 21, and number two of Club 21. With personalized member certificates, Club 21 was a unique tool of communication

[52] *Die Fakkel*, December 1932, p. 5: 'die uitslag van die saamwerkweek 1932 [het] ons stoutste verwagtings oortref. Die totale besigheid gedurende die week afgehandel het £275000 bedra. Dit is teen'n koers van £14 miljoen per jaar. Die les wat ons daaruit leer is dat, as ons personeel gedurende een week teen die koers van £14 miljoen per jaar kan produseer, dan is die skatting van £2500000 seker maklik in ons bereik vir die lopende finansiële jaar.' [The outcome of the Saamwerk Week exceeded our expectations. Total business of the week was £275 000. That is at a rate of £14 million per annum. The lesson we learnt from that was that if we can inspire our agents to produce at a rate of £14 million per annum in one week, then an estimated £2 500 000 per annum is surely within our reach].

[53] SA: 5/2/2: Geboue, 1–20: 1919–1938; See F. Freschi (2010), 'The business of belonging: Volkskapitalisme, modernity and the imaginary of national belonging in the decorative programme of selected commercial buildings in Cape Town, South Africa', *South African Historical Journal*, 61(3).

[54] *Die Fakkel*, February 1933, pp. 7–10.

between Louw and agents, individually and collectively, to motivate, challenge, guide, and to attend privately to individuals' concerns.

Tinie Louw often published anonymous challenges and directives under the pseudonym 'Head 21' in the in-house periodical *Die Fakkel*, calling on agents to aim high and work tirelessly. In personal correspondence to each member of Club 21 he set annual production targets in bronze, silver, and gold categories. Quarterly and annual prizes were linked to performance and sometimes Head 21 reported that none of the agents had achieved the targets. When targets were reached or improved, this news was prominently displayed in *Die Fakkel*. In response to the inspiration from Head 21 an inspector reported in *Die Fakkel* that agents' organizations under his auspices were growing 'inspired and enthusiastic', and that he would keep the flame of the 'Sanlam-fakkel' burning perpetually higher.[55] The tight managerial control of the early years of Sanlam was significantly mitigated through such personal engagement with agents. It paid off. Growth in total premium income had declined from 12 per cent between 1930 and 1931, to 5 per cent and 6 per cent per annum up to 1933, after which a 24 per cent growth was achieved between 1933 and 1934. Thereafter double-digit annual growth was sustained up to World War II.

A momentous event was the 1937 *Saamwerk-week*. This was the only meeting in the history of Sanlam where all agents and inspectors got together. The meeting was held in Johannesburg during the first week of December 1937 to coincide with the inauguration of the new Sanlam building in the city. Groups of vehicles, all carrying the Sanlam emblem on little green flags on the front engine cap of the vehicles, drove from Cape Town, Port Elizabeth, Bloemfontein, and Durban, joining the 'trek' to Johannesburg. The meeting was addressed by Professor H.F. Verwoerd, then professor of Sociology at the University of Stellenbosch, on the importance of savings to build the domestic economy, and Professor J.C. van Rooy from the Potchefstroom University College for Christian Higher Education, on service as the duty of all men. Of special significance was the address by Mr Vernon Fairbrass, the world-renowned agent from Sun Life of Canada, on the strategy and techniques of successful life product marketing. It was apparent that the conscious process of training, discipline, structure, and teamwork overcame the earlier lack of selection and training of agents. There was a drastic decline in agents leaving the service. Sanlam management was alert to international developments and went to great lengths to expose agents to the state of the art in the industry.[56] At the 1937 meeting, reference was made for the first time to the '*Sanlam-spangees*' (Sanlam team spirit). Similar conferences planned for 1938 were called off in the wake of the threatening world war.

[55] *Die Fakkel*, October 1936, p. 20.

[56] *Die Fakkel*, November 1937: 7; February 1938: 4–5.

Table 2.1. Sanlam financial performance, 1918–1945

Year	Premium income £	% growth	New policies	Life assurance reserve fund £	Assets £	Return on assets %	Death and disability claims paid £	Branches	Bonus	Administrative cost £
1918	-							1	1.00	
1919	35 966		3 228	4 627	53 077		2 205	1	1.00	5 188
1920	55 286	54	3 193	19 292	86 977		7 492	1	1.00	11 913
1921	71 363	29	3 160	45 104	60 562		10 817	1	1.13	13 285
1922	83 343	17	1 993	90 025	98 908		3 949	1	1.25	14 254
1923	96 086	15	2 278	141 531	149 824		7 450	1	1.38	16 591
1924	101 305	5	2 580	195 271	203 635	3.17	9 222	2	1.50	18 496
1925	121 130	20	2 668	265 473	273 908	4.2	13 023	2	1.63	21 476
1926	154 730	28	3 613	357 845	368 324	4.12	13 407	3	1.75	22 538
1927	178 142	15	4 076	461 663	474 658	4.29	19 148	3	1.88	26 950
1928	212 267	19	3 951	598 146	619 103	4.45	20 584	3	2.00	27 549
1929	240 999	13	4 314	753 735	775 468	4.42	26 616	3	2.00	44 706
1930	270 123	12	4 925	910 748	947 026	4.47	30 105	3	2.00	41 031
1931	283 659	5	4 821	1 068 246	1 113 792	4.63	38 761	3	2.00	45 046
1932	297 208	5	4 792	1 231 706	1 267 241	4.63	41 496	5	2.00	47 756
1933	321 357	8	6 984	1 379 406	1 401 027	4.44	47 880	5	2.00	49 858
1934	391 219	22	7 109	1 516 195	1 608 365	4.01	53 765	6	2.00	62 471
1935	458 031	17	8 076	1 803 449	1 854 094	3.92	56 069	6	2.00	74 504
1936	531 326	16	9 191	2 053 931	2 171 517	3.92	60 914	6	2.00	81 436
1937	619 445	17	9 889	2 533 481	2 597 809	3.86	68 802	6	2.00	89 388
1938	707 598	14	10 763	2 919 368	3 079 268	3.80	101 307	7	2.00	102 289
1939	796 908	13	11 840	3 394 165	3 582 329	3.72	77 518	7	1.50	93 069
1940	871 870	9	10 703	3 980 099	4 196 783	3.75	104 805	7	1.50	113 809
1941	994 259	14	12 595	4 598 779	4 844 838	3.83	132 651	7	1.50	122 651
1942	1 152 388	26	14 791	5 337 049	6 683 573	3.80	188 099	8	1.50	188 099
1943	1 355 424	27	17 793	6 375 783	6 689 829	3.59	158 989	9	1.50	158 865
1944	1 611 699	28	10 311	7 565 172	7 926 065	3.42	184 344	4	2.00	187 022
1945	1 888 766	29	19 959	8 770 978	9 394 751	3.35	215 186	9	2,00	209 961

Source: Sanlam Annual Financial statements, 1918–1945.

The structure of agent organization did not change during World War II, except that fewer new agents were appointed and wartime rationing of petrol and tyres curbed travelling and therefore production. A dramatic increase in the value of new policies was achieved through the mobilizing effect the *Saamwerk-week* had on agents' productivity. The value of new policies rose from £1 893 904 in 1932 to £2.4 million in 1933, £3 million in 1934, £3.5 million in 1935 and £4.1 million in 1936. New policies to the value of £11.8 million were written in 1939, exceeding those written in 1938 by more than £1 million, and reaching £13.7 million by the end of the war in 1945. A different measure of the growing enhanced performance was net premium income: total net premium income rose from £297 208 in 1932 and reached £796 908 by 1939 and £1 888 766 in 1945—a growth of 137 per cent during the war (see Table 2.1). At the end of 1939 Club 21 was dissolved, having achieved its aim. The organizational structure, the quality of people and the collectively mobilized team spirit moulded successfully to the benefit of the new company, much to the personal acclaim of Feenstra and Louw. The latter harboured a deep personal sense of responsibility to assist the relatively inexperienced well-meaning team of agents as market conditions deteriorated, to build confidence and grow strong businesses together with Sanlam.

Products to grow the market

When Sanlam entered the long-term insurance market, more than thirty other companies sold life cover.[57] Successful market penetration depended on the identification of a niche market. That was undoubtedly the marginalized uninsured people of South Africa, of which Afrikaners constituted a considerable part. The bottom line remained to do good business. The Sanlam policies were marketed to the broad public in different languages right from the start.[58] The first Sanlam policies targeted two market segments—the ordinary life market and the industrial policy market. After 1921, the industrial business shifted to AHT.[59] The Sanlam industrial business was unimpressive and non-inspirational, especially at a time when the company was forced to reconsider the declaration of an annual bonus.

By the end of 1920 the prerequisite size of the insurance reserve to justify a bonus declaration fell short of the target. Management was bound by its adherence to prudent managerial principles and actuarial advice, and decided to withhold the declaration

[57] The most important competition for Sanlam was the South African Mutual Life Assurance Society (Old Mutual, as it was later known). This was a South African mutual life office established in 1845.

[58] S. Halleen: From Life Insurance to Financial Services: A Historical Analysis of Sanlam's Client Base, 1918–2004, PhD thesis, Stellenbosch, 2013, pp. 87–93.

[59] Sanlam Archives (hereafter SA), A, 5/2/1, Sanlam Annual Report, 1919.

of a bonus in 1921—a very depressing decision to both management and agents, but a wise one. Other cost-saving measures were considered. One was to rationalize operations by consolidating expertise. The Sanlam industrial department was on thin ice and Santam owned the oldest industrial insurance business in South Africa, AHT, with all the capacity to conduct such business successfully. On 20 December 1920 the Sanlam management therefore decided to transfer the industrial department's assets and liabilities to AHT as from 1 January 1921. This move was conducive to the development of improved business focus in Sanlam. The focus on whole-life policies endorsed the vision of the Chairman, Willie Hofmeyr,[60] that the company sought to assist policyholders in providing for families bereft of a breadwinner, for the education of children and the broad development of the economy of the country. Hofmeyr emphasized the concept of 'mutuality', 'duty', and 'pride' that would be engendered in policyholders as they contributed to the well-being and development of their families, their communities, and the country at large.[61]

Business and nationalist inspiration induced creative policy innovation, embodied largely in the person of Tinie Louw.[62] He was entirely absorbed by the potential of actuarial science to create the policy options required to achieve the multiple goals of South African economic advancement and the empowerment of his people. He devoted his professional career to enhance life products to deliver a better and more appropriate service to policyholders. As a young actuary at Sanlam, and an inspired Afrikaner nationalist, he used every opportunity to enhance the competitiveness of the company. In 1922 Sanlam announced a first for the South African life insurance industry and Louw was the mastermind behind it.[63] This new policy was called the Ideal Policy. It introduced the concept of income protection through insurance, a brand-new concept M.S. Louw had been introduced to during a conversation with an employee of the National Insurance Bank of Rotterdam in the Netherlands in the summer of 1920.[64] The idea was that families were not fully secured by the receipt of a lump sum at the death of a breadwinner, but could be better provided for by receiving regular payments

[60] See H.R. Malan: William Angus Hofmeyr, *South African Dictionary of Biography, Vol. 3* (HSRC, Pretoria, 1977), pp. 416–18; N.J. le Roux: *W.A. Hofmeyr: Sy Werk en Waarde* (Cape Town, 1953), pp. 108–10 and 163–4; *Die Sanlam Fakkel*, December 1947, p. 2; *Die Sanlam Fakkel,* November 1953, pp. 24–31.

[61] SA, JV 5/2/1, Sanlam Annual Reports, 23 December 1919, p. 2; 22 December 1920, p. 3; and 21 December 1921, p. 3.

[62] See *Dictionary of South African Biography*, Volume 1, p. 471.

[63] SA, Minutes of Board of Directors, 21 December 1921.

[64] Louw visited the Netherlands after completing his actuarial training in Scotland. The Sanlam management maintained close contact with the international insurance industry. References were made in the minutes of the Board of Directors to participation in congresses and maintaining other links with insurance companies overseas. See SA, 6/5/1, Minutes of Board Meetings, 29 April 1921 and 4 April 1922. Sanlam was also a member of LIAM (an international non-profit organization of life insurers) and attended regular training and research meetings of LIAM (see SA, *Die Sanlam Fakkel*, December 1962, pp. 8–9).

to replace the weekly or monthly income of the deceased. This policy, launched on 1 May 1922, provided death benefits as family income benefits, while ordinary endowment policies could also be issued to a family. The 'Ideal Policy' was advertised as 'the latest triumph for actuarial science'. This policy introduced income protection, a much-needed support during the economic downturn of the early 1920s. Sanlam moulded access to the benefits of these policies to encapsulate as many uncertainties that could possibly affect full benefits. An example of such an additional benefit was the automatic maintenance of a policy in the event of an interruption of premium payments. In 1922, the Sanlam Board also authorized the first 'non-medical' policies—policies capped at £250 or less without the mandatory medical examination. The value was soon increased, but opened the door to enhance the development of a relationship of trust with Sanlam.

When Sanlam opened its office in the Transvaal in June 1918, it was in Johannesburg, home of a large contingent of poor, newly urbanized Afrikaners working in the mines, industries, or on the railways. This uninsured and marginalized market was the explicit target of the company. Why not in Pretoria, Feenstra was asked. His response was that the concentration of marginalized Afrikaners on the Witwatersrand determined the direction of the company's 'calling'.[65] When typical mining diseases such as miner's phthisis manifested from the early 1930s, Sanlam developed the Phthisis Policy. It was an endowment policy with additional phthisis benefits. It paid out a cash amount equal to 50 per cent of the sum insured if the policyholder contracted silicosis or tuberculosis during the policy term.[66] The restrictions to manage the risks of mining diseases led to a limited demand for those policies, but Sanlam maintained that the business must be conducted in accordance with sound business principles. Too high risks would undermine the ability of the company to honour liabilities across the full spectrum of its policy liabilities.

In 1927 Sanlam introduced a pension scheme for its Head Office staff (thirty-six people) and in 1928 extended it to the agents and staff operating in the branches across the country. In 1927 pension provision by a company for its employees was the exception rather than the rule. When the Sanlam Pension Fund was finally established on 1 October 1927, Sanlam progressed another step towards social security provision for its young employees, often first-time entrants to the labour market. Sanlam then used the experience gained from its own pension fund to advertise this service to public organizations, such as municipalities or provincial authorities. Since no statutory provision required public institutions to acquire external pension fund provision, legislation to that effect was passed only in 1929. Sanlam subsequently actively cultivated the market for pension provision. In the despair of the 1929 depression, Sanlam added more safety-net products for families. In 1929 and 1931 Sanlam added the income benefits to whole-life

65 SA: Minutes of Board Meeting, 8/7/1919; *Die Fakkel*, November 1938: 26–8.
66 SA: Minutes of Board meeting, 21/3/1932; Brochure: Gold Miner's Policy, 1935.

policies, and the family income protection insurance with limited instalments and family income benefits at death.[67]

In 1929 Sanlam took the lead again by introducing the first-ever group pension scheme for institutions, such as municipalities, provincial councils, or other organizations unable to set up their own pension schemes. In the absence of statutory provision for such schemes, Sanlam staff assisted the Cape Provincial Administration in preparing ordinances providing for municipalities and regional councils to contract with insurance companies to set up and administer group pension schemes on behalf of such authorities. Sanlam was the first South African assurer in the managed pension scheme market. Despite a slow take-off, new business volumes rose from 1930. Sanlam also pioneered the long-term life industry in South Africa by becoming the first company to pay annual bonuses based on compound interest calculations. In practice this meant that all policyholders received a 'bonus on a bonus'.

Sanlam's strategy was developed to address market shortcomings. The local insurance industry was unfamiliar with the concept of group employee benefits or social security. The South African state had not engaged in comprehensive social security programmes and other British Commonwealth countries also only rolled out the implications of the Beveridge Report systematically after World War II. Sanlam identified the collective entity of teachers as a potential market to offer products addressing self-sufficiency and responsibility of the breadwinner for his/her dependants. The Departments of Education of the different provinces were reluctant to establish a provident fund for widows and orphans of teachers. This was the opportunity Sanlam snapped up by extending the new-generation Ideal Policy to the organized teaching profession. The Family Income Policy, the Income Protection Policy, and the Family Protection Policy were endorsed as the official policies to these associations. These policies were marketed on a group basis to the organized teaching profession—in September 1933 to the Transvaal Teachers Association, in May 1934 to the Free State Teachers Association, and in December 1934 to the South African Teachers Association. This product innovation was a strategic marketing move and enabled access to a specific distribution channel of stakeholders. By 1934 Feenstra announced that Sanlam had officially become the insurer of choice of the Transvaal teachers' community as well as employees of the South African Railways.[68] In the aftermath of the depression and social dislocation resulting in unprecedented Afrikaner urbanization, the individual policies and the group benefit schemes secured Sanlam a distinct competitive advantage. A carefully planned set of policies, targeted at the identified market eventually built the policyholder base to sustain the new enterprise. As Sanlam approached the end of the interwar period, the company experienced a sense of achievement.

[67] SA, 1/2/1/3, Rate Books of 1922 and 1929.

[68] *Die Fakkel*, 15/11/34: 9–10.

The Sanlam family of policyholders

Undisputedly Afrikaans in foundation and driven by the plight of impoverished and marginalized members of its people, Sanlam was primarily a South African company. The composition of its policyholder base was a reflection of the socio-political stratification of South Africa and the direction of success in marketing the enterprise. Before 1945 the Afrikaans segment of society constituted around 85 per cent of the Sanlam policyholder base. Between 1918 and 1939 the client base was 93 per cent Afrikaans,[69] primarily because the Sanlam policies were the only policies available in Afrikaans in the South African market. The corps of employees at Head Office or as agents in the field was overwhelmingly, but not exclusively, Afrikaans. Sanlam advertised widely in Afrikaans newspapers and periodical publications, such as *Die Burger, Die Volkstem, Die Volksblad, Dagbreek, Brandwag, Die Huisgenoot, Landbouweekblad, Die Vaderland, Die Kerkbode, Ons Land, Die Taalgenoot, Die Volksgenoot, Volkshandel, Die Unie, Die Kerklike Skoolblad, Die Hervormer* and several regular publications. The company often advertised in school year books, e.g. in the annual publication of the *Hoërskool Jan van Riebeeck*, the first Afrikaans-language high school in Cape Town—an institution established inter alia through the endeavours of Willie Hofmeyr and Charlie Louw.[70] As Afrikaner urbanization escalated, the notion of providing for the future, for possible insecurity and unforeseen calamities found a captive audience, especially when delivered in the mother tongue. English-speaking South Africans did their business either with the local life offices, or with foreign companies operating in the country. It was only by the 1960s that Sanlam could report a significant English client base.[71]

The primary access to the African or Coloured market was in the industrial department of Santam, later Sanlam and subsequently in AHT after 1934. In the stronghold of Coloured people in the Cape, many spoke and read Afrikaans. This market was addressed in the Afrikaans policy documents, but the African people were not proficient in Afrikaans. This market was addressed using the English documents. The first life policy issued to an African policyholder was to Mr C. Ncinitwa, purchased by his mother as an industrial policy and underwritten by Sanlam in September 1919. Sanlam used African agents, such as Mr Godlo from East London, to market its industrial policies. The Coloured population had a lifestyle resembling much of the Afrikaans way of living (the food they consumed, inherited health conditions), which made them a similar risk

[69] S. Halleen, From Life Insurance to Financial Services: A Historical Analysis of Sanlam's Client Base, 1918–2004, PhD thesis, Stellenbosch (2013), p. 96; W.P.G. Koen (1986) *Sanlam tussen twee Wêreldoorloë*, p. 317.

[70] SA: RN 3/6/2: Selected advertisements, 1918–1945.

[71] S. Halleen, From Life Insurance to Financial Services: A Historical Analysis of Sanlam's Client Base, 1918–2004, PhD thesis, Stellenbosch (2013), p. 113.

cohort of clients.[72] Few applications were received from other people, such as from Indian people. In June 1919 an application for a life policy to the value of £500 on the lives of two Indian people was turned down[73]—no reasons were minuted. Management was concerned about the risk profile of certain race groups and the matter was referred to the actuary on 3 September 1920, requesting guidance and advice.[74] A death claim was paid out on an African life in October 1921,[75] but Sanlam's proportion of African business remained around 5 per cent throughout the interwar years.

The African market was generally associated with a higher risk premium. The African people maintained a much lower standard of living than whites and had a higher mortality rate, resulting in more strict approval criteria for such applications.[76] Screening of African lives was general practice in the South African insurance industry: 'Most companies required Non-Europeans to furnish particulars of their living conditions upon application for life cover. In cases where overcrowding, lack of adequate sanitary facilities, insufficient means, or exposure to infection are apparent, an extra premium is likely to be imposed.'[77] This additional 'loading' of premiums was referred to as 'a race load' and was practiced across the industry in South Africa because the African population had a higher mortality rate than that included in the British mortality tables used locally for the calculation of premium rates.[78] Insurance companies also had some difficulty to establish the exact age of applicants, since applicants often misstated their age. The Registrar of Insurance noted this phenomenon in correspondence to the LOA, requesting the advice of the insurance companies on the feasibility of legislation to address the matter.[79] There was considerable variation in the mortality rates of the different races and the domestic industry followed similar loading guidelines. Applications by Africans were mentioned fairly regularly in the Sanlam management minutes. The report of the Medical Officer of Health for the Cape Colony in the late 1890s had, for example, found that 'the mortality at each year throughout the whole term (i.e. between the ages of 15 and 45) is higher than the English standard by 33% in the case of Europeans and by nearly 200% in that of the coloured deaths'.[80] Insurance companies also loaded premiums of owners residing outside the Union or travelling outside the Union regularly—this applied to all policyholders, white and non-white, since such conduct was considered to raise the risk profile of policyholders. In 1932 the Sanlam

[72] A.C. Macintyre: *The South African Insurance Red Book*: 23.

[73] SA: Minutes of Dagelijks Bestuur, 20/6/1919.

[74] SA: Minutes of Dagelijks Bestuur, 3/9/1919.

[75] SA: Minutes of Dagelijks Bestuur, 20/10/1921.

[76] R.J. Miller: *Life Assurance in South Africa:* 52–4; SA: Minutes of Dagelijks Bestuur, 30/8/1950; Memorandum to Sanlam Board, 22/8/1959; Minutes Dagelijks Bestuur, 26/8/59.

[77] R.J. Miller: *Life Assurance in South Africa*, 54.

[78] A.C. Macintyre: *The South African Insurance Red Book*: 23.

[79] SA: 7/5/2: LOA; Minutes of Management meeting 4/5/1948.

[80] A.C. Macintyre: *The South African Insurance Red Book*: 23.

board decided to accept only male Indian applicants born in South Africa and those belonging to 'the higher social class'.[81] Coloured persons' applications for endowment policies were accepted on condition that the applicant was male, of a higher social class and the policy did not include disability benefits.[82] Insurance companies made no distinction purely on the basis of race, but on the basis of risk profile. Sanlam was no different. Applications by Africans, Coloured people, or Indian people rarely qualified for disability benefits or non-medical business because of their frequent exposure to hazards in the course of employment and ordinary life.

Sanlam was more willing to accept Africans with a high standard of living, such as African teachers, rather than whites of the lowest stratum.[83] Conditions for the approval and insurance of these lives were more lenient. In 1933 Sanlam decided to accept non-medical business for Indian and African teachers up to £200.[84] In the same year the confidential report that had to accompany African applications was removed for teachers because they were regarded as having a standard of living similar to that of most whites and therefore displayed a similar risk profile. Such applicants no longer had to provide additional proof of insurability.[85] Sanlam was prepared to accept African and Coloured female teachers on certain conditions.[86] A similar trend can be identified in the United States with the North Carolina Mutual Life Assurance Company—a black life insurance company insuring teachers: 'Durham folklore argues that the Mutual endured the Depression because it held so many ordinary policies on black schoolteachers, whose incomes remained relatively stable during the panic.'[87]

In the 1930s, Sanlam introduced group life schemes specifically for African teachers and other Africans of a high social standing, such as missionaries, ministers, and government officials.[88] These schemes were introduced at the same time that Sanlam became the official insurer of the Transvaal, Orange Free State, and Union Teacher's Associations. The introduction of these schemes allowed Sanlam to include Africans in its group insurance for teachers while addressing the specific needs and risks associated with this section of the market. Insuring Africans as a group eliminated some of the risks associated with this market. The black population preferred to be insured as a group

[81] SA: Minutes of Board meeting, 21/4/32. See also R.J. Miller, *Life Assurance in South Africa*: 50–6.

[82] SA: Minutes of Sanlam Board, 19/5/1932.

[83] Sanlam: Board meeting, 18/2/1932: 99; Sanlam: Board meeting, 21/4/1932: 101; Sanlam: Board meeting, 19/5/1932: 102.

[84] Sanlam: Dagelijks Bestuur, 19/10/1933: 423; Sanlam: Board meeting, 27/10/1933: 119.

[85] Sanlam: Daily Management meeting, 23/2/1933: 391; *Die Fakkel*, 1/4/1933: 13; *Die Fakkel*, 1/12/1938: 33.

[86] Sanlam: Board meeting, 17/5/1934: 126; Sanlam: Daily management meeting, 5/5/1936: 281.

[87] W.B. Weare: *Black business in the New South: A social history of the North Carolina Mutual Life Insurance Company*: 157–8.

[88] Sanlam: Dagelijks Bestuur, 23/9/1934: 213; SA RM 3/6/2, Selected advertisements, 1934–1938; SA B1/2 1/2/13/2, Selected brochures, 1935–1938.

because of its sense of collective identity.[89] Sanlam made use of black agents and white agents who were proficient in African languages to canvass clients in this market. These agents operated in areas with large black populations, such as the Transkei and Queenstown.[90] A special organization was established in the Transkei to canvass black teachers. In 1933 Jan Feenstra and Mr Kusche, the chief inspector of schools, visited a black school in Rouxville in the Free State to canvass teachers for pension schemes. The school's principal, Mr Mciteka, recalled how the visitors informed his staff about the importance of life insurance. He also recalled that provision for retirement was a major concern among black teachers at the time. The school signed a group pension scheme with Sanlam.[91] Sanlam's African client base peaked at 5 per cent of its policyholders by the end of the 1940s. The peak period coincided with the marketing of policies to African teachers, but as the National Party rose to power towards the end of the 1940s, the relative ration of new African policies declined and Sanlam shifted its attention to the emerging Afrikaans civil servant community.

The policyholder profile of Sanlam by the end of the interwar period was around 45 per cent in the early breadwinner age group of twenty-four to thirty-three years and around 23 per cent in the next age group of thirty-four to forty-four years. These were primarily the so-called 'breadwinner' market segment. Men signed policies on the lives of their wives or children, but by the early 1930s almost 20 per cent of policies were joint policies, that is endowment policies on the lives of both spouses, paying out at the death of the first spouse.[92] Women were therefore beneficiaries of life insurance, but as independent policyholders they constituted a different category. Women qualified for life cover at Sanlam, but they did not qualify for the same benefits as men as a result of their different risk profile. A special 'Pregnancy Clause' was introduced in 1919, similar to the provisions of other life offices such as Southern Life and Old Mutual. This clause made the issue of life cover for an applicant who was pregnant or fell pregnant within three months of the application, subject to the woman surviving childbirth, or it was stipulated explicitly that the company was not liable in case of death at childbirth. If a female applicant was less than six months pregnant, the company was also discharged from any liabilities in case of death at childbirth, or the premium was loaded, but only on the recommendation of the chief medical officer. Women with a history of miscarriages, or who were older than thirty years, were subject to the same loading as pregnant women.[93]

89 *Die Fakkel,* February 1959: 12.

90 Sanlam: Dagelijks Bestuur, 25/1/1934; Sanlam: Dagelijks Bestuur, 16/6/1930; *Die Fakkel*, 1/5/1933: 12–13; Sanlam: Dagelijks Bestuur, 22/6/1933; 23/9/1934; *Die Fakkel*, 7/12/1938: 13; Sanlam: Dagelijks Bestuur, 13/11/1945; 29/7/1947.

91 *Die Fakkel,* October 1959: 2.

92 S. Halleen (2013) From Life insurance to Financial services: 154.

93 SA; Minutes of Dagelijks Bestuur, 20/6/1919; 14/8/1929; Minutes of Sanlam Board, 23/5/191; *Die Fakkel*, 15/4/1934: 16.

Female policyholders also did not qualify for interest-free loans for medical procedures if the operations resulted from pregnancy or childbirth. Only unmarried women, divorcees, or widows qualified for disability benefits or income protection benefits.[94] Between 1918 and 1940 the proportion of female policyholders remained around 14 per cent of the Sanlam policyholder base.[95] The Life Insurance Act (1923) determined that 'A married woman is allowed to take out a policy on her own life or on her spouse and the policy is her property not her husband's. She may complete an application form and it will be accepted with her signature.'[96] Two of Sanlam's earliest policyholders were women—policy 7 and policy 11 were issued to women. Women were active in public life, but in a patriarchal society where women were only granted the right to vote in May 1930, they were not targeted as a designated category for Sanlam policies. This changed only much later during the 1960s when the international women's movements rose to prominence. Sanlam was no champion for gender equality, but conducted its business with women within the parameters of the social consensus of the day.

The collective: Head Office and company

For an Afrikaner enterprise to erect a skyscraper in the central business district of Cape Town on the back of the worst depression in world history, was interpreted as success. When Sanlam occupied its new offices on 3 September 1932, *De Burger* described its significance 'not in the stone and mortar, but in the rise and growth of a true Afrikaans enterprise . . . a monument of massive creativity in the economic sphere and an architectural symbol of the beauty in the soul of the people' [translated from Afrikaans]. This was the first Sanlam-owned newly erected home of the company.

A distinctive feature of Sanlam as a long-term insurer in South Africa was the constant belabouring of the shared vision and inspiration. The field staff were perceived to be a 'family' and so were the Head Office employees—although distinct levels of authority were strictly observed. Once the production targets had been achieved via Club 21, Harry van Dam suggested the introduction of an in-house magazine for all staff and not only agents. On 15 December 1932 the first issue of *Die Fakkel* [The Torch] was published. *Die Fakkel* was the internal communication vehicle. Staff submitted letters, management posted messages, performance in different spheres of the company was applauded, and training was disseminated on all aspects of Head Office administration, agent ethics, and new marketing tools. It was used as a powerful tool for training, building collaboration, and inspiring competition 'to motivate individual performance

[94] SA: Sanlam Rate Books 1922, 1941.

[95] Ibid: 182, 188.

[96] *Die Fakkel*, 7/6/1936.

by praising the successful, whereby the quality of our work is improved'—the message in the first editorial in December 1932. *Die Fakkel* published product information, praised the success of agents, served to bring the nationwide agent network closer every month, and introduced management to the staff. This monthly publication served as the pride and inspiration for many years, reflecting the character of Sanlam. Jan Feenstra himself published guidelines for agents on approaching prospective clients, while a Memorandum for Agents was circulated in early 1933 to supplement training material. The tone was paternalistic, but inspirational and a source of encouragement to all. *Die Fakkel* was an important organizational tool that replaced Club 21 in cementing the agent network, but also constructing and nurturing a company culture.

The culture of the Head Office was unmistakably Afrikaans, despite the fact that first-language English speakers were appointed from 1918 on condition that they become fully bilingual—therefore learn to use Afrikaans in the workplace. Some applications were submitted in English, others in Dutch, but all had to indicate their ability to read, write, and speak both Afrikaans and English.[97] The notion of facilitating the transition of rural Afrikaners into the urban business environment was indirectly engineered by management by emphasizing that it was Sanlam that brought the young Afrikaners from the *platteland* to the city, and there it performed the role of surrogate parent. The Afrikaner sense of a people with a shared nationalism, language, religion, and therefore a total shared destiny, was epitomized in the organization and management of Head Office. In 1933 Hofmeyr made it clear that Sanlam was a unique company, which would have failed if it had not displayed the characteristics of an Afrikaans enterprise. While Feenstra worked tirelessly to get the agent network organized and operating in an orderly way, he taught the agents industry Afrikaans vocabulary to conduct their business professionally in correct Afrikaans. In 1935 Hofmeyr claimed categorically that Afrikaans and the Afrikaner had been established in the insurance industry purely as a result of the employment opportunities Santam and Sanlam offered young Afrikaners from the *platteland*.[98] The paternalistic nature of Afrikaans society was woven into staff conduct at Head Office as management exercised close control over such conduct. Staff members were advised not to 'bother' their superiors, since their time was valuable. Submission to the authority of the superior was non-negotiable. Unless a male employee earned a minimum of £25 per month, he should not even contemplate getting married. The remuneration level was increased to £30 after the war. Single men needed written consent from management to get married. Single women had to resign when entering

[97] SA: 6/5/1: Letter of application Fanie Cloete, 6/11/1920; 5/2/4/2 C: Application J. Bezuidenhout, 15/3/1920. The establishment of Santam and Sanlam coincided with the Afrikaans language movement, of which Willie Hofmeyr was a prominent member, calling for the recognition of Afrikaans as the official language alongside English. In 1918 English and Dutch were the official languages of South Africa, but in 1925 Afrikaans replaced Dutch as the second official language.

[98] *Die Fakkel*, 15/1/34, p. 12; 12/5/35, pp. 12–14.

into a marriage. Written consent from management was even needed to buy a car.[99] In January 1934, Mr J.C.W. Louw wrote to Tinie Louw, explaining that he had been dating a Miss le Roux for five years, that she had a good occupation earning a steady income, but that her mother had passed away and therefore they considered the time opportune to get married. The employee acknowledged that management had the interests of Sanlam's employees at heart and, as his salary was only £16, Miss le Roux intended to keep her job until he had earned enough for them to start a family. Tinie Louw's permission for them to marry was requested.[100] Similar correspondence crossed the desk of Sanlam management frequently, sometimes without success. This control was rationalized as securing the company a stable, reliable, and well-disciplined workforce.

Die Fakkel subtly published information on healthy living, hygiene, and a neat appearance. In 1934 *Die Fakkel* advised men to take a bath daily, and if that was not possible, at least twice a week, but their clothing had to be clean at all times.[101] For good healthy social activities Head Office staff were treated to staff excursions, the first on 18 December 1922, to the 'mountain', to wine farms, river resorts, and the beach—always using organized bus transport. A social club for Sanlam employees organized social activities. These activities reinforced the authority of management and served to develop subservient Head Office staff. The patriarchal approach to Head Office as an operating unit in the business distinguished Sanlam from other companies in the industry. The low turnover at Head Office—124 appointments up to 1932 and only twenty-six resignations (20 per cent)—shows the general acceptance of the culture. The predominantly rural origin and Afrikaner cultural background of many employees, allowed the company to organize relations in the head office to resemble that context of submission to authority, respect, and discipline. It was possible to define the company culture from the top down. With many employees at Sanlam being new in the industry, often in any form of wage employment, provided the company with 'a clean sheet', an inexperienced employee, susceptible to the organizational culture of Sanlam. Management moulded this culture to the advantage of the new business, though never forcefully imposed it in the workplace. There was a special relationship of shared destiny. Afrikaners' submission to the authority of the head of the household assisted management in establishing the new venture relying on a relatively loyal workforce.

As Sanlam entered the insurance market, the company used its official seal as logo. When Sanlam and Santam moved into their first building in 1932, it was considered an appropriate time to introduce a dedicated Sanlam logo. It was designed by the cartoonist T.O. Honiball, advised by Professor Blommaert from the University of Stellenbosch. The logo consisted of three sections: a large white bird with wings opened wide to protect four chickens, a middle section with three spears in flight, and a bottom section with a

[99] SA: 4/10: Staff administration papers; Minutes of Dagelijks Bestuur, 27/5/43.
[100] SA: 4/10: Letter J.C.W. Louw–M.S. Louw, 2/01/1934. [101] *Die Fakkel*, 15/8/1934, p. 12.

springbok on a black background. The bird symbolized the company protecting the people of South Africa residing in four provinces; the three spears symbolized speed and progress; and the springbok symbolized the country of South Africa. The new logo sought to convey a nationalistic and patriotic message of a strong connection to South Africa. A slogan '*Uit die volk gebore om die volk te dien*' [born from the people to serve the people] was proposed by Tinie Louw. He explained his choice as signifying the sentiment of a company with a close connection to the Afrikaner people, from whom it emerged with the clear vision to serve the people. The colours of the Sanlam logo were dark green, gold, and black.[102] Explaining the meaning of the Sanlam logo, the first *Die Fakkel* encouraged Sanlam agents and Head Office employees to embody the '*esprit de corps*' of soldiers, since 'our personal welfare is so closely bound up in that of Sanlam that on close inspection we find that the man who promotes the latter, at the same time achieves the former'.[103] The logo was symbolic of that '*esprit de corps*' and was presented as such to the staff, for whom *Die Fakkel* was exclusively intended. The management team used a number of different slogans. Alfred MacDowall used 'South Africa first' in correspondence in 1919, Jan Feenstra used the slogan 'Each year a bonus year' in his correspondence in 1926, and in 1926 a brochure advertising the Sanlam policies used the slogan 'Born from the people to serve the people'.[104] These subjective verbalization of the moods of employees can simply be understood as the expression of dedicated stakeholders.

To celebrate Sanlam's 21st anniversary in 1939 the existing logo was adjusted [See Appendix 1]. The springbok head was enhanced and the company name was added in ornamental lettering, with the words 21 years below it. In general speech, reference was made to the logo as 'the vase'. This 'vase' remained the official logo until 1953. In 1940, the '21 years' was removed from the logo, as was the '*Uit die volk gebore*' slogan, and replaced by a decorative ribbon at the bottom. The use of symbolism and the accompanying nationalistic slogan was a powerful tool in the marketing of Sanlam products. The decision to drop the slogan in 1940 was a business decision to move away from the emotive nationalistic Afrikaner appeal and allow the patriotic South African symbols to portray the intentions of the company as a South African organization. A slogan 'Sanlam our company' was sometimes used after 1939 and in 1947 the logo was sometimes accompanied by the slogan 'For growth . . . for service . . . for safety'.[105]

Notwithstanding the family-like, conservative, chauvinistic, and authoritarian culture instilled at Head Office, the company adopted advanced technology early on to enhance

[102] SA: 5/3/4; Sanlam Logo History: *Die Fakkel*, December 1932: 2; 17/9/1973: 4.

[103] *Die Fakkel*, December 1932: 7.

[104] SA: 5/3/4: Sanlam Brochure 1926; SA 6/5/1: MacDowall correspondence 23/10/1919; SA 5/3/4: Huisgenoot 3/12/1926.

[105] SA 5/3/4: Sanlam brochures, 1939–1947.

administrative productivity. Management was not deterred by the potential risks of the three factors regulating the adoption of new technology, namely the trade-off between price and technical performance, the uncertainty of the performance of the new technology or the actions of competitors, and the market structure of the industry.[106] Cost was always a consideration, but management considered it carefully and justified price by the proven performance record of the new technology. The oligopolistic structure of the long-term insurance industry mandated calculated risk taking to outperform the market, therefore Sanlam considered the adoption of the most advanced office technology as a key strategy of competitiveness. From 1929 new typewriters were added to the office equipment, while addressographs, Multigraph printing machines and Marchand calculators were regularly added to the modern office environment. In November 1932 the *Africa Insurance Record* noted that 'everything in fact of the latest and most efficient' was in operation at Sanlam Head Office.[107] In 1934, a Powers-Samas calculator was introduced at Head Office—the first of its kind in South Africa.[108] The modern office equipment filled the staff with a sense of pride and contributed to improved efficiency in processing new applications and despatching policy documents. In the business environment of the post-war era, Sanlam management proved progressive and pragmatic and the company has remained at the forefront of industry technology throughout its history.

Capture the moment: empowerment and earnings growth

The sources of income of the long-term insurance company were primarily interest on investments in government and municipal bonds, loans to public entities, personal loans, and mortgages on farms/real estate. Business diversification could only be considered once relative stability in the long-term business was achieved. The 1923 capital loss by Santam led management to decide against the integration of AHT operations into Santam. The decision was rather to retain AHT as a separate entity. It was soon apparent that it would make strategic sense to sell AHT to Sanlam, whereby all life business would be consolidated in Sanlam. In 1934, Sanlam acquired AHT from Santam for £153 541, the value of AHT in the Santam books. The name was changed to African Homes Trust and Insurance Company, with M.S. Louw as General Manager and actuary. Functional

[106] R. Barras (1986): Towards a theory of innovation in services, *Research Policy*, 15: 161–73.
[107] SA: Minutes of Dagelijks Bestuur, 18/4/1928; 15/1/1930; 30/9/1931; 7/10/1932; AIR, 1/11/32:4–5.
[108] SA: Minutes of Dagelijks Bestuur, 12/1933; *Die Fakkel*, 15/5/1934: 8; 15/10/1934: 21.

reorganization was taken further by the introduction of funeral policies, a variety of industrial insurance, through AHT.[109] AHT had experienced the able competition by the funeral industry to its industrial business and after 1934 it was decided to take on the market offering enhanced funeral cover with the Sanlam backing. For this purpose, AHT acquired established funeral enterprises in Cape Town (Goodall & Williams) and in Johannesburg (Wasserfall & Hardick). This strategy resembled the decision to acquire AHT—to buy the leading enterprise in the industry and to develop from that position of strength. The two funeral businesses made good progress, with the latter acquiring further interests and finally changing its name to Morton & Wasserfall. AHT delivered a funeral service under its life policies through its subsidiaries in Cape Town and the Johannesburg and Pretoria regions, while independent service providers were contracted elsewhere. AHT also established Funeral Proprietary Ltd, an enterprise manufacturing coffins, thus making the company fully independent in many respects. Where funeral service providers could not supply coffins, they were sourced from other suppliers. The ordinary life department of AHT was also developed to a level where the ordinary life business in AHT almost equalled the industrial and funeral business by the end of the 1950s.

By the end of World War II in 1945, AHT had contributed significantly to the Sanlam revenue. Total premium income rose from £198 231 in 1936 (industrial branch, ordinary life branch, and funeral branch) to £395 019 in 1945. The insurance fund increased from £557 747 in 1936 to £1 262 057 in 1945. The actuarial surplus rose from £16 370 to £40 271 at the end of the war.[110] Income from this subsidiary supplemented the other sources of income, namely interest earnings from loans and investments. Those asset classes were preferred for their security and low risk. Since the 1923 Insurance Act did not prescribe compulsory investments, insurance companies could invest where returns were most attractive. Before acquiring AHT, Sanlam's sources of funds were premium income and interest on loans and investments. Sanlam invested primarily in government stocks and personal loans, mortgages, and fixed property, and managed a fairly balanced portfolio. When the company decided to acquire AHT, management was unanimous except for one member, Charlie Louw. To his mind the acquisition of AHT would be a divergence from the company's investment policies. The acquisition constituted a too substantial investment in a single business entity. He was in favour of a balanced investment portfolio, which would be jeopardized by the acquisition of AHT. Hofmeyr thought the time was opportune for insurance companies to liberalize former conservative investment policies.[111] The AHT transaction signalled the gradual emergence of a

[109] SA: Sanlam Annual Report, Chairman's address: 4; SA: 6/1/7: M.S. Louw biographical papers, Memorandum, 13/4/59.

[110] SA; 6/1/7; M.S. Louw biographical papers: Memorandum G.D. Wilson: AHT, 8/2/56.

[111] SA: Minutes Dagelijks Bestuur, 12/12/1934.

growing appetite for risk, especially in the private entrepreneurial segment of the market. Sanlam gave the first step towards organic growth.

The AHT transaction was a turning point in the history of Sanlam's growth. Up to 1935 management followed a cautious line and invested in a disciplined and conservative fashion only in fixed-interest-bearing instruments, such as mortgages, property (from which rental income could be earned), and government and other public bodies' bonds or debentures. With the AHT transaction management showed signs of disagreement about when the time would be opportune to supplement the conservative investment strategy by growing organically. The acquisition of AHT widened the scope of Sanlam's life business, while a gradual movement towards higher risk equity investments started to emerge. Charlie Louw preferred a gradual transition into the higher-risk world of ordinary shares. In 1935 Sanlam invested in ordinary shares as part of its investment portfolio for the first time.[112]

A significant shift into substantial volumes of government stocks and securities of other public institutions followed the promulgation of the Insurance Act, No. 27 of 1943. Based on the rationale of improved protection to policyholders, the office of a Registrar of Insurance was introduced to control the industry. The new Registrar required annual actuarially compiled financial statements. Those enabled the Registrar to assess the solvency and stability of each insurance company operating in South Africa. The compulsory deposits with the Registrar varied according to the level of solvency of the company to its assets. Insurance companies were compelled to keep assets equal to the liabilities of their domestic business. Younger businesses were required to keep larger ratios of assets to liabilities to protect the solvency of those enterprises. A fixed proportion of the domestic assets had to be invested in government and other public utilities' paper. This ratio was 53.5 per cent in 1943, but was changed as domestic demand fluctuated. The dual purpose was to secure access to the funds of insurance companies for domestic development and to ensure solvency of insurance companies, many being incorporated outside South Africa. In Figure 2.1 the surge in government securities since the early 1940s is the most remarkable aspect of the change in Sanlam's allocation of its funds before 1945. Strong domestic demand for capital contributed to rising returns on official stocks, which made them an attractive investment. Mortgages were the most important asset class until 1938, when returns on stocks and the statutory compulsory investments since 1943 made government and other public stocks the leading investment instrument. Sanlam's substantial exposure to mortgages—37.8 per cent of its assets was in mortgages by 1931—was much higher than the 32.2 per cent of the industry, but by 1945 Sanlam's 25.6 per cent was in line with the industry average.[113] Investment in

[112] SA: Minutes of Executive Management, 20/4/1939.

[113] E.H.D. Arndt, 1938, *An analysis of the investment policies of life insurance companies in the Union of South Africa*: 15–18; SA: Sanlam Annual Financial Statements, 1919–1945.

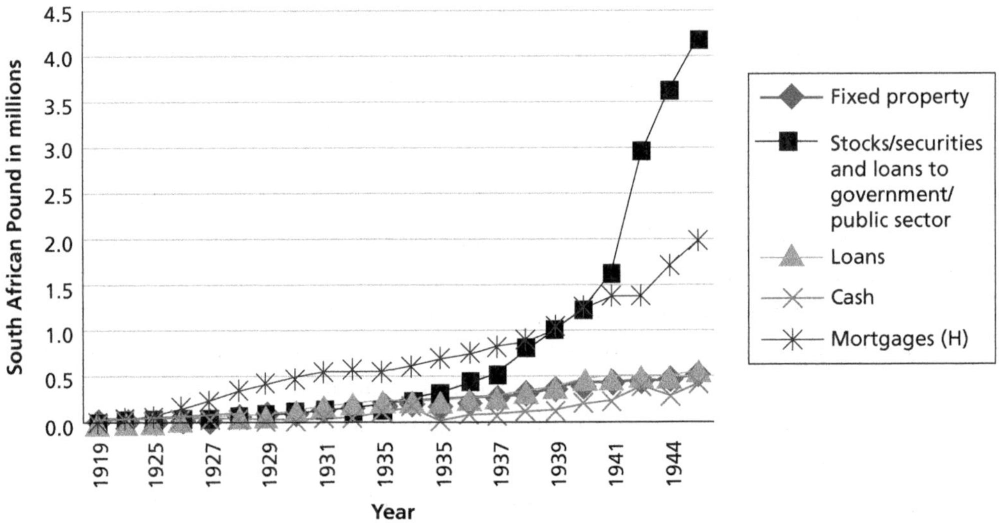

Figure 2.1. Application of funds, Sanlam 1919–1945 (£)

Source: Sanlam annual financial statements, 1919–1945

listed equities or shares had risen steadily since 1935 to become the third most significant asset class in the Sanlam portfolio. As is reflected in Figure 2.1, investment in property was paramount, until the 1943 Insurance Act mandated higher investment in government securities. Sanlam did not maintain high volumes of cash, but rather extended loans to policyholders. The investment in property rendered higher and more stable return.

Sanlam supported in principle the investment in government securities as necessary to grow certain sectors of the economy and supported the development of the public sector. The company was the champion of domestic economic growth by directing investments inward rather than outward.[114] Hofmeyr and succeeding chairmen of the company were critical of the level of mandatory investments. These investments often delivered lower returns than investments in listed equities. Suboptimal returns were to the detriment of policyholders, while discretionary investments in private equity supported the private entrepreneur and thereby provided domestic investment capital.[115]

Tinie Louw was the great protagonist of increased investment into ordinary and preference shares. In public addresses he motivated the channeling of savings into listed equities rather than into deposits with financial institutions or into mortgages, as the driver of economic growth. He criticized the volumes of capital lying idle in credit markets, rather than being in productive investments, such as trade finance and

[114] SA; Annual Report and Chairman's address, 1944: 3.
[115] SA; Annual Report and Chairman's Address, 1945: 4.

industrial production.[116] The opportunity to change Sanlam's investment policy arose in the later 1930s when an uptake of Afrikaner nationalism together with a stabilized and motivated agent network delivered excellent production. At the time various Afrikaner cultural and church leaders mooted ideas on how to address persistent white poverty. Domestic economic growth offered the only solution to white poverty, which had been addressed by the Carnegie Commission Report, released in 1932. The Dutch Reformed Church had concerned itself at successive church meetings with the growing and non-abating problem of white poverty since the end of the nineteenth century. After the South African War the barren war-torn land was described as being 'as wasted as the edge of the Sahara'.[117] Several church gatherings addressed the welfare need of the impoverished and the challenges of adjusting to urban life after flocking to cities in the hope of finding employment. White poverty was not a post-war phenomenon, but was exacerbated to the point where the Carnegie Foundation of the USA provided £4 000 funding for a systematic in-depth investigation into the nature and extent of white poverty in South Africa. The report, released in 1932, claimed the existence of 300 000 white people in South Africa in abject poverty—the majority being Afrikaners.[118] The historian C.W. de Kiewiet described the condition as follows: 'At the base of white society had gathered, like a sediment, a race of men so abject in their poverty.'[119] The Carnegie Report ascribed the state of poverty to the inability of the people to adjust to the modern economic environment. The solution was to be sought in education and training to facilitate entry into the emerging domestic industrial sector. Since 1914 the Government had introduced protectionist measures to support the development of domestic industries.[120] White labour was also afforded statutory protection in designated employment categories deemed fit only for 'whites'.[121] Reserving employment was meant to assist whites in succeeding in the market, but the prerequisite was still ability. Many whites simply did not have the required skills or training to take advantage of the statutory protection. An extensive network of Afrikaner cultural organizations

[116] SA: 6/1/7: M.S. Louw biographical documents; Speeches.

[117] R. Macdonald (1903): *What I saw in South Africa*: 3.

[118] Carnegie Commission, 1932: vii; J.F.W. Grosskopf, 1932: 1:20–1:22.

[119] C.W. de Kiewiet: *A history of South Africa: Social and Economic* (Oxford: Clarendon Press, 1942), pp. 162–9, 181–2; M.H. de Kock: *Selected Subjects in the Economic History of South Africa* (Cape Town: Juta, 1924), pp. 455–6; C. Feinstein: *An Economic History of South Africa* (Cambridge: Cambridge University Press, 2005), pp. 82–5.

[120] F.S. Jones & A.L. Müller, 1992: *The South African economy, 1910–1990*: 422–6. The Customs and Excise Act, No. 26 of 1914 as amended by Act 36 of 1925 afforded extensive tariff protection to designated domestic industries.

[121] The Mines and Works Act, No. 12 of 1911, reserved certain employment categories for skilled labour, thereby indirectly reserving certain jobs for whites. Similar protection was afforded by means of The Industrial Conciliation Act, No. 12 of 1924, the Amendment Act on Mines and Works, No. 25 of 1926, and the Labour Act, No. 27 of 1925. See Jones & Müller, 1992: 422–6.

subsequently joined forces to devise an appropriate strategy. Many of the leaders and management in Santam and Sanlam were members of such organizations.

The *Federasie van Afrikaanse Kultuurverenigìnge* (FAK) (Federation of Afrikaans Cultural Associations), established in December 1929 to preserve and develop Afrikaans as a language and Afrikaans cultural activities, sowed the seeds of organizing a meeting of Afrikaners from all walks of life to brainstorm the problem and deliver solutions. An *Ekonomiese Volkskongres* (EVK) (Economic congress of the people) met in Bloemfontein in October 1939, almost a year after the successful Great Trek centenary celebrations, to develop the strategy of Afrikaner empowerment through the mobilization of all possible means to succeed in eradicating poverty and empowering Afrikaners to a rightful position in the economy of their fatherland. At the meeting, the message in the opening address by Reverend J.D. Kestell, known as *Vader Kestell* (Father Kestell), was that a people should redeem themselves from poverty (*'n Volk red homself*). The only solution to poverty and marginalization was work, education, and collaboration. Kestell said that it was not the responsibility of the government to secure the upliftment of those who have fallen. Emotive language was used in almost all the addresses delivered to the delegates.

Several speakers addressed proposals for a workable solution to effective empowerment. Professor Schumann from the University of Stellenbosch pointed to the fact that the South African GDP (Gross Domestic Product) in 1937 was around £280 million, to which Afrikaners had contributed an estimated £100 million. This he interpreted as a significant amount of capital under Afrikaner control. A collective effort of all Afrikaners could potentially mobilize even more capital towards the establishment of investment and operational structures to address poverty and economic marginalization.[122] Several ministers of the Dutch Reformed Church reiterated that attempts by the state after similar meetings in 1934 to alleviate poverty by means of statutory protection of white labour, had failed to resolve the problem of white poverty. Dr P. du Toit called for Afrikaner organizations to help themselves, '*Daar moet 'n inheemse eie Afrikaanse ekonomiese stelsel opgebou word*' [an own Afrikaner indigenous economic system must be constructed] and Du Toit was convinced that Afrikaner capital would suffice.[123] Dr Eben Dönges called for a much-intensified savings culture and the mobilization of savings.

These voices culminated in the proposal Tinie Louw offered the congress. He told the delegates stories of Afrikaners who attempted in vain to raise capital for their own enterprises, but failed, for several reasons—lack of security, no references, unfriendly

[122] C.G.W. Schumann (1939): 'Die huidige posisie van die Afrikaner op ekonomiese gebied', Address delivered at the EVK, Bloemfontein, in *Referate, Besluite en Presensielys van die Ekonomiese Volkskongres*: 50.

[123] P. du Toit (1939): 'Van die breë beleid van die Volkskongres (1934) tot die ekonomiese selfstandigmaking as kernvraagstuk', Address delivered at the EVK, Bloemfontein, in *Referate, Besluite en Presensielys van die Ekonomiese Volkskongres*: 25–9.

financial institutions, etc. His solution was the establishment of an Afrikaner-controlled finance house. By the end of the 1930s Sanlam celebrated its twenty-first year in business. It had achieved significant market penetration, acquired its first subsidiary, and was searching for avenues to arrive at its goals of enhanced domestic economic development and a more significant Afrikaner stake in that economy. Co-operative and socialist sentiments were alien to the Afrikaner business elite from the Cape. Tinie Louw wanted entrepreneurial empowerment. He wanted Afrikaner businessmen to take on the market. He had been thinking about this as an ideal for a very long time and wanted to run the idea by the Sanlam board in 1938. In a carefully worked out memorandum he motivated the establishment of a finance house to provide start-up seed capital for entrepreneurs desirous of taking on the opportunities and the risks of the market. The finance house was intended to provide seed capital, not to manage enterprises. The managerial capabilities were to be nurtured though university studies, experience in the workplace, and collaboration among Afrikaner businessmen.[124] Tinie Louw's long-standing concern about the unproductive nature of savings in bank deposits or mortgages was finally given concrete meaning when he proposed to the congress the establishment of a financing house for industrial development. He suggested a finance house similar to the finance houses of the big mining companies, because access to risk capital was a prerequisite for Afrikaner business take-off. Louw wanted an enterprise, capitalized by Afrikaner savings, issuing shares on which dividends could be earned and reinvested to secure Afrikaner participation in the emerging industrial sector of South Africa. Such an enterprise would challenge Afrikaners to take on the risk of equity investments, to be the entrepreneurs themselves, and thereby to learn to conquer the market they thought inaccessible to them.

The standing of Tinie Louw in the Afrikaner society was impressive—as the first Afrikaans-speaking actuary he was a role model and inspiration to many young Afrikaners. In Sanlam he witnessed numerous loans and mortgages granted to policyholders—the minutes of the Sanlam Board read like a loan bank register. While Sanlam assisted policyholders by means of access to loans, Louw wanted Afrikaners to be educated in taking the risk of operating in the industrial market. His proposal was accepted by the congress and in 1940 led to the establishment of *Federale Volksbeleggings, Bpk* (FVB) (Federal People's Investments).

The EVK gave rise to a massive mobilization of Afrikaner energy towards their own economic progress. The congress decided to take several measures. The first was that the FAK would establish an Economic Institute to oversee the implementation of congress decisions and establish the *Reddingsdaadbond* (RDB) (Association for self-redemption).

[124] SA: 6/1/7/; M.S. Louw papers: Memorandum aan die Raad insake finansieringsmaatskappy, 20/10/1938.

The RDB was the vehicle to mobilize Afrikaner savings and other fund raising to support Afrikaans enterprises, to fund the education of members' children and technical training, while encouraging women's organizations and agricultural co-operatives. Furthermore, Afrikaner savings should be mobilized towards significant participation in the domestic industrial sector. The co-operative movement was hailed as a vital strategy for the general economic development of South Africa.[125] It was apparent that two opposing ideological positions were held—co-operative socialist sympathies and hard-core capitalist entrepreneurial ideals. The latter was advocated by Tinie Louw, Dr Eben Dönges, and Professor C.G.W. Schumann.

Sanlam did not establish FVB, but was asked by the EVK to direct the process towards its formation. The intellectual capital in Sanlam gave birth to the idea and provided the organizational infrastructure to set up, register, and get the enterprise operational. In terms of the Companies Act, No. 23 of 1939, FVB was registered as a company in 1940 and received authorization from the Registrar of Companies on 17 October 1940 to commence business.[126] Sanlam acted completely outside the conventional scope of business of a life office, but thereby set its foot on the path of the economic awakening of Afrikaners. Sanlam had know-how, organizational infrastructure, and access to capital. To establish FVB, seven men met in April 1940 to compile the Statutes and Articles of Association. The meeting consisted of Tinie Louw, Joint General Manager of Sanlam; Dr E.G. Jansen, Speaker of the House of Assembly; Dr J.N. Claassens, a medical doctor; Dr T.E. Dönges, advocate of the High Court of South Africa; Mr Charlie Louw, member of the Sanlam Board of Directors; Mr A.P.J. Fourie, director of companies; and Prof C.G.W. Schumann, Professor in Economics at the University of Stellenbosch. Each was assigned ten ordinary shares in FVB, which was subsequently registered as a company with £300 000 capital. The capital was made up of 100 000 preference shares of £1 each and 200 000 ordinary shares of £1 each. Holders of preference share were entitled to an annual dividend of 5.5 per cent on paid-up capital, but would not share in the profits of the company. Preference shares were not offered to the public, but to institutions such as Santam, teachers' unions, *Boeresaamwerk Beperk*, the *Helpmekaarbeweging*, and the *Reddingsdaadfonds*. Ordinary shareholders were entitled to dividends payable after each annual general meeting of the company. The prospectus for FVB was issued and the public invited to buy shares. By the time of the first report of directors in June 1941, 115 560 ordinary shares and 42 500 preference shares had been paid up. The undertaking by Santam to underwrite 50 000 preference shares was in place, but not yet

[125] G. Verhoef (2006a): 'Die stigting van instellings as werktuie in die ekonomiese opbouproses van die Afrikaner sedert die Anglo-Boereoorlog', *Tydskrif vir Geesteswetenskappe*, 46(2): 381–91; G. Verhoef (2005): 'Afrikanernasionalisme in die besigheidswêreld. 'n Verenigde front?', *Joernaal vir Eietydse Geskiedenis*, 30(1): 44–64.

[126] SA: 6/1/7: Personal documents M.S. Louw: FVB Statutes and Articles of Association, 27/11/1940.

paid up. Among the preference shareholders were the *Helpmekaar* branches of the different provinces, teachers' associations from the Free State, The Economic Institute of the FAK, the *Reddingsdaadfonds*, and the *Afrikaner Broederbond*, leaving only 7 000 shares unallocated. The directors of the company were Charlie Louw as Chairman, C.G.W. Schumann, C.M. van der Merwe, D.J.D. Jordaan, A.P.J. Fourie and T.E. Dönges.[127] Charlie Louw was the only Santam/Sanlam representative on the board, with Van der Merwe, Jordaan, and Fourie private businessmen. Sanlam bought the Santam shareholding in FVB as the vehicle of preference to provide mentorship to the new enterprise.[128]

The relationship between FVB and Sanlam developed as mutually beneficial and empowering. Declining interest rates adversely affected returns on investments and therefore impacted directly on insurance companies' revenue. The 1943 Insurance Act included specific guidelines on compulsory investments in government and related securities, but allowed a fair proportion of discretionary investments. The adverse interest rate trend encouraged Sanlam to consider more lucrative investment opportunities, such as investments in ordinary shares. The capabilities of Sanlam's small investment department were very much in its infancy. As FVB was established primarily to finance industrial initiatives, it was anticipated that the skills would be developed in FVB to assess the quality of companies, the growth potential of investment products, such as debentures, preference shares, and equity. Sanlam therefore negotiated an agreement with FVB to provide the company with technical advice on investments. Sanlam required FVB to advise the company on investment opportunities, to acquire such investment instruments, and appoint an official to oversee those investments on behalf of Sanlam, without compromising existing arrangements with Santam.[129] An agreement was finally entered into between Sanlam and FVB in terms of which FVB would render technical advice on equity and other investment opportunities to Sanlam. Sanlam paid £50 per month to FVB from 1 July 1943 as a retention fee for the advice and investigation into investment opportunities, as well as a further 0.5 per cent commission on investments Sanlam made on FVB's advice.[130] Sanlam immediately requested FVB to make investments in Imperial Cold Storage preference shares. A symbiotic relationship developed whereby FVB developed investment expertise, Sanlam gained access to the opinion of trusted investment specialists, and FVB secured its first investment client.

In June 1942 a building society, *Unie Bouvereniging*, was established by Afrikaner initiative, but the name was soon changed to *Saambou (Permanente) Bouvereniging* (Saambou Permanent Building Society). Building societies in general operated in a very competitive market. Interest rates were highly competitive and the public shopped

[127] SA: 6/1/7: FVB Report from Directors, 27/11/1940.
[128] SA: Minutes of Executive management, 20/4/1939.
[129] SA: Minutes of Sanlam Board Meeting, 19/5/1943.
[130] SA; Minutes of Sanlam Board meeting, 16/6/1943.

around for better interest on deposits. Building societies were competing with banks for deposits, and insurance companies had also entered the home-loan market by offering mortgages to policyholders. The Sanlam weekly management and monthly board meetings dealt with applications for mortgages as a standing item. When *Saambou* entered the market in 1942, more than twenty established building societies populated the market. Sanlam was approached to salvage the ailing building society and sought FVB's advice on the prospects of the transaction. The FVB report advised Sanlam to secure representation on the *Saambou* board, to suggest changes in staff appointments, and request that board meetings be held in Cape Town on a rotation basis. *Saambou* was a rescue operation, but once restored to profitability proved a vehicle to address the growing demand for urban housing. On 22 September 1943, Sanlam invested in *Saambou* indefinite subscription shares to the value of £35 000 on condition that a further investment by individuals and enterprises of £25 000 was secured. Sanlam also insisted on an enlarged Board of Directors at *Saambou*, which would allocate two seats to Sanlam.[131] This proved a sound turn-around strategy. Sanlam refrained from involvement in active day-to-day management, but through board representation performed a supporting role to stabilize operations and secure a good return on its investment. Tinie Louw described the vision of the Afrikaans building society as undisputedly Afrikaans in character and service aims, but simultaneously also serving all members of the South African society, irrespective of race or language.[132] By the end of the 1940s, Sanlam had invested more than £387 000 in *Saambou* subscription shares, exercising its commitment to Afrikaner empowerment through the support of Afrikaner entrepreneurship.[133] Tinie Louw and the Sanlam director P.D. Rousseau were appointed to the *Saambou* board and by 1946 *Saambou* had accumulated funds of £350 000 and declared a first dividend to shareholders. In 1946 the Sanlam Chairman, Hofmeyr, announced that Sanlam could confidently advise its policyholders to do business with *Saambou*.[134] By 1947 *Saambou's* accumulated funds (share capital and deposits) had risen to £1 million. *Saambou* was firmly established in the wider Sanlam drive to empower Afrikaners. In 1957 Tinie Louw justified Sanlam's involvement with *Saambou* by the contribution the building society made to society irrespective of language or race, in securing housing and thereby security in the urban setting.[135] Sanlam was willing to invest policyholders' funds in investments that yielded a good return, but refrained from actively managing the company.

[131] SA: Minutes of Sanlam Board, 22 September 1944.

[132] SA: 6/7/1: M.S. Louw documents: Address at Sanlam Managers Conference, October 1957.

[133] SA: 5/2/1: Minutes of Sanlam Board meeting, 22/9/1943.

[134] SA: Sanlam Annual Report, 1946: 7.

[135] SA: 6/1/7: M.S. Louw personal documents: Saambou. The aim and purpose of Saambou, address delivered at Sanlam Managers Conference, October 1957: 304.

With these initiatives, Sanlam engaged directly with Afrikaner enterprise development as a second tier of economic empowerment alongside personal empowerment through life insurance. The establishment of FVB was a momentous achievement for Afrikaners, since it was their debut into industry and served as the stepping stone into other sectors of the economy dominated by English or foreign capital. The timing was also significant. Afrikaner political alignment was again disrupted when the NP and the SAP merged, but Hertzog lost the vote in Parliament to keep South Africa out of World War II. As in 1914, many Afrikaners were opposed to participation in an international conflict against Germany, and sided with Britain. General J.C. Smuts succeeded Hertzog as Prime Minister. An organization to mobilize those opposing the declaration of war, the *Ossewa Brandwag* (OB) was formed. Dr J.F.J. van Rensburg resigned from the Sanlam board to become the leader of the OB. Officially Sanlam took a position of neutrality, despite it being known that several of the directors and managers were staunch supporters of Hertzog. By the end of the 1930s Sanlam's policyholder profile included just under 7 per cent non-Afrikaans policyholders and 1 per cent Africans.[136] It was not possible to separate out those sympathizing with the war effort and those against it, but Sanlam would not risk being drawn into such division. Not much publicity was given to the war in *Die Fakkel*, but staff were duly informed about the war and allowed to join the armed forces. On 5 September 1939 *Die Fakkel* reported '*'n Storm bars los!*' [a storm erupts]. No official list of Sanlam staff engaged in the war was ever published, but it could be established that at least ten staff members from Head Office and the field staff joined the South African forces. By 1940, six staff members were in active service. Only one casualty was reported in *Die Fakkel*—Frans Carstens died in Italy on 10 June 1944.[137] Sanlam's virtual silence on the war, apart from reports on the disruption of operations, was in stark contrast to the heroic publicity given by its competitor, SA Mutual, to its staff fighting in the war. More than 300 SA Mutual staff participated in the war; nineteen died, and a bronze plaque bearing their names was erected at Head Office after the war to commemorate their bravery.[138]

For Sanlam the war meant market adjustments. Shortly before the war on 1 September 1939 all non-profit-sharing and family income policies, disability benefits, and double endowment benefits were withdrawn from the market. The LOA immediately mandated the restoration of non-profit-sharing policies, but with increased premiums. All valid policies in the Union were amended under the 1923 Insurance Act (section 21), mandating written notification by the policyholder to the insurer that the policyholder would be outside the Union, south of the equator, or in combat outside the African continent, 'unless in defense of the Union'. Premiums of such policies were adjusted

[136] S. Halleen (2013) From life insurance to financial services: 96, 124.

[137] *Die Fakkel* 1/8/1944: 11; December 1951: 23.

[138] P. Brooke Simons (1995): *Old Mutual 1845–1945*: 137.

upwards. In case of failure by the policyholder to inform the insurer, the latter's liability was limited to that under the premium paid. Uncertainty about when a policyholder was acting 'in defense of the Union' led to statutory amendments in 1940 to limit the insurer's liability to the level of increased premiums paid while outside the borders of the country. The impact of the uncertainty caused by the war was to reduce new business and lower profits. Although Tinie Louw proposed the non-payment of a bonus, the board decided to pay a stable bonus during the war (£1.50.00 in 1939–1944 and £2.00.00 in 1944 and 1945) and strengthen the insurance fund from £3.3 million in 1939 to £8.7 million in 1945. Total productivity of the Sanlam staff responded well to the stimulus of war despite wartime uncertainties. The total number of Sanlam staff members (Head Office, branches and agents) per £100 000 policy income declined from 26.6 in 1933 to 13.4 by 1945, especially at Head Office. In April 1942 a new branch was opened in the Northern Cape, including business in South West Africa (now Namibia). However, in June 1943 an independent branch was opened in Windhoek, the capital of South West Africa, bringing the total number of branches to nine by the end of the war.

The footprint

Sanlam's performance is reflected in Table 2.1. The new player in the market collected premiums in excess of £1 888 766 by 1945, which represented annual compound growth of 16.45 per cent, compared to growth of 6.4 per cent p.a. for the long-term industry as a whole. Sanlam's assets increased from £53 077 in 1919 to £9.4 million in 1945—a growth of 23.7 per cent p.a. between 1922 and 1945, compared to industry asset growth of 10.33 per cent p.a. for the same period. The composition of the Sanlam portfolio, as reflected in Figure 2.1, shows the impact of the 1943 Insurance Act. Before 1943 Sanlam invested primarily in property as a source of secure revenue, but after the change in regulation with increased statutory prescribed investments, Sanlam's exposure to government stock rose beyond that of its exposure to property.

The return on assets remained low—only just above 4 per cent (4.02 per cent in 1925, then rising well above 4 per cent but not yet 5 per cent, falling back to 4.1 per cent in 1934). The return on assets declined during the depressed interwar years, as reflected in Figure 2.2. Growth in assets continued, but yield did not. This improved only after the war. Sanlam expanded slowly through a limited distribution network of nine branches by 1945. The conservative bonus policy was responsible for the slow rise in bonus declaration from £1.00 in 1918 to levels around £4, only to return to £2.00 at the end of the war. Sanlam had only just set down a business footprint by the end of the war and was positioned for growth in the strong growth environment after 1945.

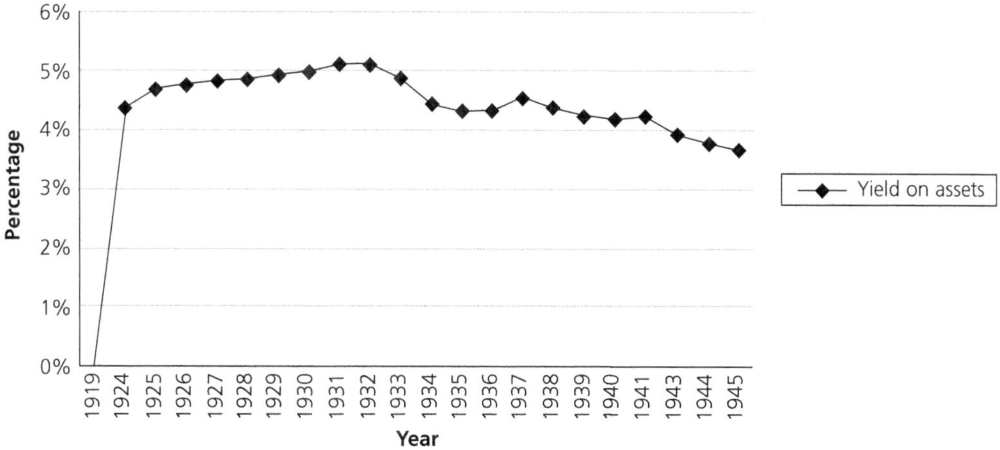

Figure 2.2. Sanlam yield on assets, 1918–1945

The 'two white races' were far apart during the first half of the twentieth century. Smuts hoped to bring them closer, but while there was a marked difference between their socio-economic conditions, separate nationalisms and aspirations were bound to dominate the domestic context. Sanlam enjoyed some appreciation in society, and was especially proud of the recognition afforded to the company by an English-speaking South African, George Wilson, who became the assistant actuary of Sanlam in 1936. Wilson observed, 'I shall never forget the impression which the Sanlam officials and staff made on me when I landed back home in 1936. Their energy and enthusiasm were startling and infectious and I thoroughly enjoyed joining in the thrusting and purposeful attitude of the whole Sanlam organization. Let me put it this way. If the productivity of a normally well-run Life Assurance Office was 60% the productivity in Sanlam must have been 90%. The years 1937, 1938 and 1939 were not easy for Sanlam but the results achieved were really phenomenal.'[139]

Afrikaners by no means presented a united front. Afrikaner leaders in Sanlam positioned the company within Afrikaner destiny as expressed at the beginning of the twentieth century. Some Afrikaners still did insurance business with competitor companies, but management pragmatically developed a business model that was all-inclusive South African, without allowing the strong swells of Afrikaner nationalism to be lost to the company. The Afrikaner empowerment cause was strong and powerful, but the plight of the marginalized was always framed as sound business, inviting anybody interested in their superior products. During the first half of the twentieth century insurance in South Africa was primarily, but indeed never exclusively, conducted with

[139] J.P. Scannell (1968): *Uit die volk gebore. Sanlam se eerste vyftig jaar*. Cape Town: Nasionale Pers: 117.

the white society. Burial societies constituted the general form of insurance engaged in by urbanized Africans and Coloured people. The 1943 Insurance Act compelled burial business to register as industrial insurance, whereby regulatory supervision was extended to the limited form of insurance penetrating the African and Coloured communities. Sanlam had been involved in that market since 1919 and extended that penetration with the acquisition of AHT. The nature of South African society and political dynamics during the first twenty-six years of Sanlam's existence allowed management to position business within that broad consensus. By the time Sanlam celebrated its fiftieth anniversary, Africa had been transformed by decolonization and independent African states. South Africa was soon to become a different country and insurance business was bound to reflect that.

3 Forty years: protection, isolation, and diversification, 1945–1985

Global growth, exclusion, and global entry

The 'golden age of capitalism' commenced with the end of World War II. The boom in the world economy was rooted in the rebuilding of the economies of Europe and Japan. World GDP per capita rose on average by 3 per cent per annum between 1950 and 1973, which outpaced the growth performance of the former decades threefold. Productivity gains, increasing real income levels, and declining commodity prices combined to allow factor mobility, capital, and labour, and financial improvements in social services. The Bretton Woods institutions developed mechanisms to intermediate between the private capital market of the world and capital-short countries. These institutions aimed to achieve macro-economic stability and to negotiate global free trade. Unfortunately, the positive effects of decolonization in large parts of sub-Saharan Africa were offset by state breakdown, recurring civil wars, genocide, and famine.[1] The era of the Cold War brought the stark contrast between developed and developing countries into the international arena. The division of the world after 1945 resulted in what Borscheid calls 'a de-globalization' of the insurance industry. Insurers in foreign markets found themselves faced with a plethora of obstacles to overcome, a type of 'xenophobia' of legal restrictions prohibiting foreign companies from acquiring a majority interest in national firms.[2] The division of the world between capitalist Western nations and the centrally planned nations aligned with the USSR left many African states to negotiate a new position in the non-aligned movement led by Jawarlal Nehru of India. South Africa had a relatively stable white-controlled government, resisting the pressures to relinquish white power to black majority rule. The buoyant economic growth of the 1950s and 1960s seemed unstoppable, until the oil price hike of 1973 brought it to an abrupt halt.

The post-depression Keynesian conviction that government must stabilize aggregate demand in order to avoid high and rising unemployment, prompted states

[1] R. Skidelsky (1998): 'The growth of a world economy' in M. Howard & W.M. Louis (eds) *The Oxford history of the twentieth century*. Oxford: Oxford University Press: 55–9.

[2] P. Borscheid (2012): *World Insurance*. Oxford University Press: Oxford: 20–2.

worldwide to intervene in managing economic activity. In post-colonial Africa, state ownership in almost all the sectors of the economy expanded. The state was seen as the representative of the newly independent people, the owner of the capital means to establish and manage public enterprise. The state was expected to provide a framework of physical and social infrastructure, such as a legal framework and general education, while simultaneously encouraging the entrepreneur, investor, and manager of economic activity. As many of the very high expectations of prosperity after colonization failed to materialize, political systems moved away from Western democracy. Developing countries gradually shifted the blame for poor performance to the organization and regulation of international economic relations. The South African economy was able to sustain strong growth throughout the turbulent times of post-independent Africa between the end of World War II and the early 1970s. Economic growth in Africa declined consistently during this period of political instability. In Tanzania full 'African socialism' was introduced, and democratically elected leaders were ousted by *coups d'états* in many African states. Between 1950 and 1970, twenty-one military takeovers occurred in Africa. In 1971 the democracy of Milton Obote in Uganda was overthrown, and in 1974 Emperor Haile Selassie's feudal regime was toppled by military power. By the mid-1970s more than half of African states were under civil-military rule.

South Africa experienced equally turbulent times on the political front. In 1960, the Prime Minister Dr H.F. Verwoerd led South Africa from the British Commonwealth and in 1961 South Africa became a Republic. This occurred amid rising South African nationalism and support for Verwoerd. Verwoerd gradually strengthened the power base of the National Party government and in 1966 almost swept domestic opposition in Parliament aside, winning 126 seats in the 166-seat House of Assembly. The strengthening of white political power occurred against the backdrop of mounting domestic opposition. Political opposition was banned—in 1950 to the Communist Party of South Africa, and in 1960 the African Nationalist Congress (ANC) and the Pan Africanist Congress (PAC). As these opposition movements went underground, other incidents of civil protests such as the public burning of passes at Sharpeville in March 1960, occurred. Police action resulted in the death of protesters. This incident poised anti-South Africa international sentiment, causing the flight of capital. While the civil war was raging in the former Belgian Congo and Belgian settlers fled the country, the political situation stabilized in South Africa. The political tensions of the 1950s and 1960s in South Africa were controlled by a powerful state, through the policy of separate development. Although the international community criticized South Africa for not implementing majority rule in a unitary democratic state, it was possible to grow the economy on the back of global growth. Between 1948, when the National Party rose to power on the policy of separate development, and 1970, real income per capita had risen by 70 per cent and real GDP rose by an average of 4.2 per cent per annum in the 1950s and

5.5 per cent in the 1960s.[3] Massive speculation on the JSE (Johannesburg Securities Exchange) led to a crash in May 1969, ending a period of sharp increases in equity prices. These fortunes turned as global fortunes were turned upside down.

Relative political stability and sustained economic growth in South Africa could not shield the country, or the continent, from international turbulence. In 1971 the Bretton Woods fixed exchange rate system was terminated when declining USA current account surpluses virtually disappeared, resulting in a mounting USA balance of payments deficit of US$30 billion by 1971. The USA abandoned the fixed exchange rate system, leading the international community into floating exchange rates. Volatility entered global markets. In October 1973 the Yom Kippur War erupted in the Middle East, followed by an Arab embargo on oil sales to the USA and the Netherlands, and a 214.8 per cent increase in the oil price by OPEC (Organization of Petroleum Exporting Countries) in December 1973. This price increase was most probably the largest economic shock the world economy has ever experienced.[4] Rising inflation characterized Western economies, including South Africa, throughout the remaining years of the 1970s. The average annual rate of inflation was around 3 per cent between 1950 and 1970, but then spiked to 13.4 per cent between 1974 and 1975. In 1979 a second oil price increase hit global markets, and Middle Eastern current account surpluses rose beyond US$2 billion by 1978. These were invested in Western markets, allowing lending to escalate to unprecedented levels, especially to developing countries that resorted to borrowing rather than structural adjustment of their economies. Borrowing to balance budgets rather than adjusting expenditure, especially in the countries of Latin America and Africa (notably Mexico and Nigeria), created a time bomb. By 1982 Mexico, an oil-exporting country, announced its inability to service its debt, ushering in the global debt crisis. By the early 1980s Western economies had adjusted to high inflation and slow growth—'stagflation', a term coined in this period. Keynesian economics offered no solution to embattled economies. A return to growth was dependent on liberalizing markets.

A revival of appreciation for the liberal market model of the Austrian school's Friedrich von Hayek was notable in the political groundswell towards the libertarian right. Margaret Thatcher rose to power in Britain in 1979 and Ronald Reagan in the USA in 1980. The liberal market orthodoxy swept across Western economies. Deregulation, contraction of state economic involvement, and a renewed appreciation for entrepreneurial endeavours constituted core elements of the restructuring models of the post-global recession world of the mid-1980s. Africa was especially indebted—with total foreign debt amounting to more than US$162 billion. Debt rescheduling and macro-economic

[3] C. Simkins (1999): The political economy of South Africa in the 1970s, in *South African Journal of Economic History*, 14: 13.

[4] I.M.D. Little, Richard N. Cooper, W. Max Corden & S. Rajapatirana (1993): *Boom, Crisis and Adjustment: The macro-economic experience of developing countries*. New York: Oxford University Press: 17.

adjustment policies challenged African economies to consider the liberal market. South Africa did not escape the turbulence. The international gold price rose sharply in the wake of the global oil-led recession. The gold price rose from US$37.87 in August 1972 to US$675.99 in September 1980. This meant that South Africa was cushioned from the immediate effects of the oil shocks. The South African currency depreciated against the dollar and other foreign currencies. Before the 1970s, South Africa experienced a relatively stable net inflow of foreign capital, but this changed as the political uncertainty following the independence of Mozambique and Angola and domestic unrest in South Africa impacted negatively on investor confidence. It was not only global economic turbulence that made South Africa a very challenging market. The mobilization of black opposition to the National Party Government manifested in so-called student protests, popularly known as the Soweto Uprising of 1976. State repression of sustained domestic unrest led to the declaration of a state of emergency in July 1985.

Domestic growth was under pressure. Inflation was spiralling and no longer in step with that of South Africa's main trading partners. The state fuelled inflation by not implementing restrictive fiscal and monetary policies. Inflation peaked at 18.6 per cent by January 1986. The South African government obtained its first IMF (International Monetary Fund) loan in January 1976. This signified the sustained weakening of the economy. The first annual capital account deficit since the 1960s was recorded in 1977. During the first half of the 1980s there were some large capital inflows into the country again as international markets remained liquid and South Africa remained a credible borrower. The South African government also encouraged foreign borrowing by providing forward cover at attractive rates. A shift occurred from long-term direct investment in the non-monetary private sector to shorter-term borrowing by the public sector and the banks. This borrowing held imminent risks. Borrowing was coupled with large uncovered interest rate differentials and lack of experience by borrowers in dealing with the magnitude of potential losses involved in uncovered forward borrowing.[5] As domestic political instability mounted, a confluence of international and local events occurred. These included the collapse of the gold price after 1980, a sharp decline in exports, unprecedented sharp depreciation of the SA currency, high levels of short-term borrowing on international markets, and contraction in international capital markets. As a result, foreign banks refused to roll over South African short-term debt of US$14 billion in 1985. The expectations in August 1985 that President P.W. Botha would announce radical political reforms towards political power sharing with the black majority were dashed in his speech in Durban on 15 August 1985—the so-called 'Rubicon' address.

[5] B.W. Smit and B.A. Mocke (1991): Capital flight from South Africa: magnitude and causes, *South African Journal of Economics*, 59.(2): 314.

It failed to satisfy the international expectations of fundamental reform in South Africa.[6] In this climate the South African government issued a moratorium on debt repayment in August 1985—the so-called 'debt standstill'. In response, financial sanctions were introduced against South Africa, leading the country to become a capital-exporting country. This was the world in which South African financial services enterprises operated after 1945.

During this period of global turbulence and the accompanying revision of Keynesian macro-economic orthodoxy, the South African government appointed the De Kock Commission of Inquiry into the monetary system of South Africa in 1977. Following global trends[7] the commission recommended the introduction of a market-related monetary policy. Market-related policy instruments such as annual growth targets for the M3 money supply, discount policy, and support for open-market transactions became the main policy instruments of the South African Reserve Bank. Financial institutions took advantage of the less-regulated markets. As foreign insurance companies were required by the 1965 Insurance Amendment Act to be incorporated in South Africa, most foreign insurers complied. This followed the international trend. In a study published in 1971 SwissRe found that the number of foreign insurers operating in non-national markets had steadily declined in absolute as well as relative terms since 1960. Primary insurers had withdrawn behind their countries' borders.[8] In South Africa, insurance companies were afforded similar protection and benefited from financial services deregulation of the mid-1980s. Diversification of operations into other financial services was slow in developing. The full impact of financial services deregulation was only felt after 1990. The excessive liquidity in the South African market during the 1960s and 1970s encouraged functional diversification in the insurance industry. By 1985 this development had direct implications for the focus of Sanlam as a life office.

Managing for growth and diversification

The establishment years had passed. The insurance industry faced the opportunity of post-war growth, while the fruits of the *Volkskongres* of 1939 were gradually taking shape. At the end of the war the total premium income of all insurance companies was £11.8 million, rising to £23.1 million by 1950. In 1945 Sanlam was only the fourth-largest life office in terms of premium income, but moved into second position after 1948.[9]

[6] H. Giliomee (2013): *Die laaste Afrikanerleiers. 'n Opperste toets van mag.* Cape Town: Tafelberg: 202–8.

[7] J. Singleton and G. Verhoef (2010): Regulation, deregulation and internationalization in South African and New Zealand banking, *Business History*, 52.(4): 536–63.

[8] P. Borscheid (2012): *World Insurance*, p. 23.

[9] Registrar of Insurance, Annual Report, 1945, 1948.

The financial services market became more competitive, specialized, and diversified. Management directed Sanlam into a diversified operational environment as the founding generation of managers made way for the second generation of managers. Gys de Villiers and Tinie Louw, joint General Managers, both retired in 1946. Louw stayed on as Managing Director of Sanlam until December 1949, while A.D. Wassenaar succeeded De Villiers as General Manager in October 1948—a position he held until the end of 1965, when the title of the senior manager changed from General Manager to Managing Director. Wassenaar held this position until 1969, when he was succeeded by P.J.F. (Pepler) Scholtz in March 1969 until the end of April 1978. Scholtz was the Managing Director until 1978. When Wassenaar stepped down as Managing Director, he then joined the Board, from which he retired at the age of eighty, bringing to an end a career of sixty years in Sanlam. F.J. (Fred) du Plessis succeeded Scholtz in May 1978 and served as Managing Director of Sanlam until April 1985. Up to 1978 the top managerial positions in Sanlam were occupied by men who had progressed up the company ladder. Wassenaar started his career as an employee of the Department of Census and Statistics in Pretoria. He completed his first degree part-time at the Transvaal University College (TUC). He then joined the South African Air Force as a pilot, but soon accepted employment at the Standard Assurance Company in Edinburgh. While in Scotland he qualified as an actuary. In 1937 he accepted an appointment as Assistant Actuary at Sanlam. In 1947 he was promoted to the position of Assistant General Manager, succeeding Feenstra who had retired. Working with Tinie Louw, Wassenaar emerged as a strong campaigner for the free market, the development of entrepreneurship, and Afrikaner empowerment through market opportunities.

The management team of the 1950s and 1960s were all Sanlam men. It was a stable, ageing and tight-knit team. When Wassenaar succeeded Feenstra, he in turn was succeeded as Actuary by Dr H.G. Hansman. P.J.F. Scholtz was one of the assistant actuaries. When Wassenaar moved into the General Manager's position in October 1948, he handed the responsibility of the agent network to W.J. (Bill) Bezuidenhout. Bezuidenhout (after whom a major arterial road leading from the Sanlam Head Office was named) was a devoted Sanlam employee his entire life. Pepler Scholtz moved into the position of Managing Director after a career of thirty-five years at Sanlam—first as Assistant Actuary, then as Investment Manager, and then as Actuary from 1959. Once these managers retired, their services were often called upon by the board. The Sanlam Private Act, No. 3 of 1954, provided for the incorporation of Sanlam as a mutual life assurance company. The act made no reference to an age limit for directors, but in 1964 the act was amended. Article 41(k) on 'disqualification of directors', was amended to add that a person who reached the age of seventy-five automatically has to vacate his office as director. As soon as the amendment took effect in December 1966, Charlie Louw had to retire as director at the age of ninety-one, Piet Malan at the age of eighty-six, Tinie Louw at the age of seventy-eight, and Eric Louw at the age of seventy-six. In January 1983 the board decided to lower the automatic retirement age of directors to seventy.[10] This tendency perpetuated the longevity of stable management, since the institutional memory of earlier managers was ever-present in the board of directors.

The generation of founding members worked in a close-knit managerial team under the sympathetic leadership of Willie Hofmeyr as Chairman of Sanlam. When Hofmeyr died suddenly in 1953, Charlie Louw succeeded him as Chairman until 1966. He then retired at the age of ninety-one, having served the company, of which he was a founding member, as director for forty-eight years. Hofmeyr was not only a symbol of Afrikaner perseverance and drive, but also succeeded in inspiring able young new managers with a vision to direct future strategies for progress and modernization. The position of Chairman was not an executive one, but Hofmeyr was well on top of operations and strategic direction. He allowed the new generation to grow the company in the challenging post-war era, but provided stability in the core strategic direction. Inward-looking Afrikaner control was illustrated by Wassenaar's ascendancy to the position of Chairman of the Sanlam board in January 1967. He held this position together with his executive position as Managing Director until he retired from the latter in 1969. Wassenaar was Chairman of the board until he turned seventy-five in September 1982. He retired as Chairman, bringing to an end a period of thirty-five years in Sanlam—twenty-two years as General Manager/Managing Director, and thirteen years as Chairman of the board. Fred du Plessis succeeded Wassenaar as Chairman in 1982. In 1982 Du Plessis was made Executive Chairman of Sanlam and assumed the duties of Group Chief Executive in 1985, positions he occupied until his death in 1989.

Sanlam found itself in a boom economy immediately after the war. The aspirations of growing Afrikaner participation across the spectrum of economic activity demanded strategic planning. Hofmeyr and Tinie Louw called on the domestic credit market to invest in local equities, especially risk capital. The calculated and responsible actuary-manager Louw and his successor A.D. Wassenaar operated firmly within the post-war management model of the human resource theory, and later in the 1960s the 'Theory Y' management style, emphasizing the dependence on managerial ingenuity to unlock the full potential of employees.[11] The shared destiny instilled in all employees on all levels of management as displayed in the agents conferences of the 1930s and the Head Office 'family-like' organizational culture, was characterized by the *esprit de corps* in Sanlam also after 1945. Immediately after the succession of Wassenaar, a managers conference was held in December 1948. Attention was drawn to the necessity to grow Sanlam's market among English-speaking South Africans. By 1945, English-speaking policyholders

[10] SA: Minutes of Sanlam Board, 26/1/1983.

[11] G.R. Jones and J.M. George (2011): *Essentials of contemporary management*. 4th edition. McGraw-Hill Irwin: New York: 42.

constituted less than 10 per cent of the total Sanlam policyholder base. The post-war era up to 1978 can justifiably be described as the Wassenaar era, since he exercised executive control in a firmly centralized U form of organization. When he moved on to the position of Chairman of the board with Pepler Scholtz as Managing Director, he remained the captain of the ship. He was an ambitious man. His ascendancy in Sanlam was described as phenomenal, and his leadership was strategic and performance-driven. Married to the daughter of the Lord Mayor of London, Wassenaar found himself fitting comfortably into the Sanlam aspirations of Afrikaner empowerment encompassing a wider strategy of the promotion of local South African business interests. Hertzog's 'South Africa first' slogan embodied his ambitions. He was an Afrikaner nationalist, but he was not an uncritical supporter of the ruling National Party.

The opportunity for expansion under the buoyant economic conditions of the 1950s and the functional diversification of Santam's operations required a fundamental rethinking of the relationship between Santam and Sanlam. By the end of the war Santam and Sanlam were still managed primarily by the same people. At the time shortly before Willie Hofmeyr's death in October 1953, the Santam board consisted of Willie Hofmeyr, Dr J.F.J. van Rensburg, Charlie Louw, Piet Malan, Dr J.P. Schabort, S.F. Malan, D.J.A. Kotze, Eric Louw, P.D. Rousseau, G.F.S. de Villiers, and Tinie Louw as alternate director.[12] The Board of Directors of Sanlam in 1953 comprised the following: Charlie Louw (Chairman) and Piet Malan, S.F. Malan, D.J.A. Kotze, Dr J.F.J. van Rensburg, Eric Louw, P.D. Rousseau, Dr I.P. Schabort, Tinie Louw and G.F.S. de Villiers.[13] The two companies shared the same board members. The business of Santam comprised the trust and executor business, short-term insurance (operating through various companies such as Santam Insurance Company and Brandwag Insurance Company), the bulk of this business being fire, motor vehicle, and employers' liability insurance. By the early 1950s Santam did less than 5 per cent of the total short-term insurance business in South Africa,[14] and Santam did banking business. Sanlam was the subsidiary of Santam, paid no dividends to Santam, but paid Santam commission to manage its mortgage investments at a commission of 1 per cent of the capital allocated and 5 per cent collection commission on mortgage rates. Sanlam had to obtain permission from Santam to start any new commercial initiative, such as the business of short-term insurance.[15] While composite insurance companies (companies conducting both short- and long-term insurance) were prevalent in the industry globally, in the Santam/Sanlam case operational diversification was constrained by the subsidiary relationship, despite the shared oversight structures.

[12] SA: Santam AGM, 1953. [13] SA: Sanlam Annual Report, 1953: 16.

[14] Union of South Africa: Summaries of Returns deposited with the Treasury by Insurance Companies, 1948.

[15] WCA-A2213: Agreement Santam/Sanlam, 19/6/1945.

By the end of the 1940s the assets of Santam represented only 3.7 per cent of the domestic short-term insurers and 1.2 per cent of the total insurance market in the Union. In 1950 Sanlam's assets, in comparison, constituted 10.8 per cent of total industry assets and Sanlam's premium income put the company in the second position of all insurance companies in the Union. The planned mobilization of Afrikaner economic activity that followed the *Volkskongres* of 1939 manifested in an emerging group of Afrikaner-controlled enterprises and business initiatives. The Sanlam/Santam relationship displayed a growing imbalance with respect to the asset base and managerial control. Sanlam's assets rose from £9 394 751 in 1945[16] to £32 901 535 in 1953[17] (an increase of 250.2 per cent within eight years), while Santam's assets amounted to £194 688 in 1948 and increased to £644 157 in 1953.[18] Santam's business was dwarfed by the business expansion of Sanlam. The latter's business was expanding rapidly after the war; the company had just moved into its own head-office building in Bellville in September 1953[19] and was developing a strategic role in the unfolding of the network of Afrikaner-controlled enterprises.

As the new generation ascended to power, management operated in an environment very different from the 1930s and 1940s. They needed to respond to the highly liquid financial market, the change in consumer demand following improved remuneration and living standards, and the opportunities for growth in the rapidly industrializing domestic economy. In December 1952 the Santam board decided to restructure the company as two separate entities—an insurance company and a trust company. Sanlam would receive a stake in the restructured insurance company equal to its premium contribution to the Santam premium income. It was minuted explicitly that Sanlam would refrain from competing with Santam in both short-term insurance and trust business.[20] As Sanlam, the subsidiary, expanded successfully in the long-term insurance market, internal tension in the intimate relationship with the less focused parent company was imminent.

In 1950, SA Mutual initiated proceedings to amend its Private Act (No. 16 of 1915) to extend permission to conduct different forms of insurance business and engage in a wider variety of investment operations. SA Mutual went back to Parliament on different occasions for purposes of wider jurisdiction in operations and geographical locations. As the companies in the Santam Group (Santam, Sanlam, *Federale Volksbeleggings* (FVB), Saambou National Building Society, and Bonuskor) developed the Afrikaner presence in South African business, the legacy relationship between Santam and Sanlam entered the

[16] SA: Sanlam Annual Report, 1945. [17] SA: Sanlam Annual Report, 1953.

[18] Report of the Registrar of Insurance Companies, 1950: 40; Report 1954: 34.

[19] The official opening of the new building was on 16 October 1953. Two days after the grand opening Willie Hofmeyr passed away.

[20] SA: Minutes of Sanlam Board meeting, 29/4 1953.

public domain. Santam sought legal advice on restructuring options. The company was advised that the mutual form of organization would be beneficial to the business of Sanlam in as far as the mutual company would not be liable for income tax. It would take a long time before Sanlam would benefit from a tax-exempt structure. Santam management assumed that a private act would be passed by Parliament with less delay, since fewer stakeholders would feel obliged to comment or object to aspects of the proposed bill. In March 1953 the Santam board therefore decided to restructure the relationship between Santam and Sanlam by means of a private act of Parliament.[21] The Sanlam management acknowledged the state of divergence between Santam's business and its own, which mandated what they called 'constitutional' amendments.[22] Since 1918 Santam and Sanlam had always maintained that the life business had been conducted on a mutual basis whereby all profits accrued to policyholders, but in fact Sanlam had to report to its shareholder (which was Santam) at the end of each financial year.[23]

The two companies entered into an extended agreement. It provided for Sanlam to become an independent legal entity, permitted to conduct only those operations stipulated in the private bill, which excluded all trust and short-term insurance business. Sanlam emerged as a new legal business entity able to conduct the following business: life insurance in all its branches; sinking fund, industrial, and funeral insurance business; issue annuities; engage in reinsurance; trade in securities, movable, or immovable property; lend money; mortgage property; underwrite share issues, stocks, or debentures; create and maintain a pension fund for its officers; and register as an insurer in the Union as well as any other country.[24] In preparation of the Sanlam Private Bill the Sanlam management found that SA Mutual had already commenced more amendments to the SA Mutual Private Act in order to expand the operations of the Old Mutual Life Office, especially to enable the company to engage in trust business.[25] These developments encouraged swift action and the private bill was tabled in the South African Parliament in February 1954. The bill was passed without opposition. To Sanlam the statutory position simply aligned the *de facto* position with the *de jure* position. Sanlam always did its life business on the firm assumption and practice of mutuality. Despite Santam being the only shareholder, no dividends were paid to Santam, but the latter received payments for services rendered to Sanlam. The Sanlam Private Act, No, 3 of 1954, determined that Sanlam had to pay Santam £50 000 as reimbursement for the capital Santam held as sole shareholder in Sanlam (Section 8). Sanlam acquired all

[21] SA: Santam Minutes of Board meeting, 18/3/1953; 25/3/1953; WCA-A2213: Ex parte SANLAM (Bpk): 30/12/1952.

[22] SA S5/1, 5/1/4: Sanlam Management Special Committee Meeting, 17/2/1954.

[23] *Die Fakkel*, February 1953: 2; Sanlam Annual Report, 1954: 1.

[24] Private Act, No. 3 of 1954: Section 5.

[25] WCA-A2213: Memorandum to Sanlam Board, 29/10/1952; WCA-A2213: SANLAM minutes of Board meeting, 28/1/1953.

its assets, liabilities, rights, and responsibilities vested in the company prior to the promulgation of the Act and was permitted to conduct insurance operations as stipulated in Section 5 of the Act.[26]

This Private Act clarified much of the uncertainty about the scope of Sanlam's operations at a time when its development required strategic certainty. In the period up to 1985 Santam's business focus often seemed blurred. Santam restructured itself again in the mid-1960s into a separate insurance company and a bank. Sanlam also diverged operations into substantial shareholdings in non-insurance companies. As a much stronger market player it no longer reported to another parent company. The Sanlam business reported to policyholders, who at that stage were fairly inarticulate, uncritical, and non-activist. The growth in market share and the performance of its subsidiaries were the signals of success or failure, depending on the rapport between management and policyholders. As Afrikaner business penetration gained momentum during the late 1950s and 1960s, the perceived unified Afrikaner front in business began to show a more nuanced character. Most Afrikaner enterprises were operating in the financial services industry and were therefore competing for funds. During the rapid growth era of the late 1950s, the country experienced capital shortage. This situation prompted the state to pass statutes to compel financial enterprises to invest their funds in government stock, which delivered lower returns than other investments. Intra-Afrikaner friction between Sanlam and other companies in the group surfaced in 1954 when FVB (in which Sanlam held a controlling stake) contemplated the formation of a trust company, *Federale Trust,* a pension fund for various other companies and the National Finance Corporation. In a memorandum to the Sanlam board in August 1958, Wassenaar stated unequivocally that if the almost aggressive competition for savings was allowed to continue unchecked, it could impact negatively on Afrikaners' business aspirations ('*Afrikanersaak*' was the word he used).[27] The popular conception of Afrikaners as a monolithic entity was gradually subjected to the forces of the market.

The Sanlam management team emerged during the 1950s as the strategic leadership of Afrikaner economic empowerment. Wassenaar led the team of Sanlam stalwarts: Nico Bonthuys as Secretary, Hansman as Actuary, Karl Ehmke as Accountant (one of the earliest Afrikaans persons to qualify as a Chartered Accountant in South Africa), and Bill Bezuidenhout as Agents Manager. The regulatory context of insurance changed and the complexity of Sanlam's business portfolio escalated beyond the simple long-term insurance business of the pre-war era. The Insurance Act, No. 27 of 1943 (as amended), remained in force until new legislation was passed in 1997. The general monetary policy environment changed fundamentally. In 1972 the Commission of Inquiry into Monetary Policy was appointed under the Chairmanship of Dr D.G. Franszen. The Franszen

[26] WCA-A2213: Union of South Africa, Private Act, No. 3 of 1954.
[27] WCA-A2213: Memorandum to Sanlam Board, 18/8/1958.

Report (RP87/1972) expressed grave concern about the emergence of groups of financial services companies, bank holding companies, and cross-shareholding between banks and insurance companies from the perspective of the protection of depositors' interests. The risk Franszen anticipated was that non-depositors' interests in conglomerate business groups could result in the application of funds to the effect of jeopardizing depositors' interests. This concern was even more alarming if financial services companies were controlled by foreign shareholders. The recommendations of the Franszen Commission were therefore to disallow more than a 10 per cent cross-shareholding between banks and insurance companies and that all bank holding companies had to register as such in terms of the Banks Act of 1965. Furthermore, foreign shareholding in South African banks and insurance companies had to be reduced to less than 50 per cent within a period of five years.[28] In a growing isolated South African market, these developments effectively enhanced an incubator effect of protecting domestic companies from international competition, and strengthened market concentration.

As Santam considered aggressive strategies to grow its business, it was suggested to Sanlam to consolidate the business interests of the two companies in a group structure.[29] The Santam board was enthusiastic about the formulation of joint group goals and policies. The idea was well received in Sanlam. The board immediately agreed to guarantee the independence of the Santam companies (at that stage Santam Bank and Santam Insurance) on condition that contentious matters would have to be ratified by a Sanlam director. The Sanlam decision signified the role of a senior partner to this relationship. However, the recommendations of the Franszen Commission thwarted the plans for such a group structure as that would bring about a holding company owning both banks and insurance interests. Business operations at Sanlam had become much more diversified, which mandated clarity of focus and management.

Functional diversification in a growing economy

The close association of the Santam and Sanlam leadership with the Afrikaner collective action to pull themselves up by their own bootstraps, commencing at the *Volkskongres* in 1939, resulted in various actions to establish industrial, mining, and other financial interests. Tinie Louw's plea for the establishment of a finance house to finance industrial development led to the establishment of FVB. The next step was to apply policyholders' funds for the same purpose. Louw prepared an extensive memorandum to the Sanlam

[28] RP87/1972: Report of the Commission of Inquiry into Monetary Policy in the Republic of South Africa.; G. Verhoef (1987): *Die Geskiedenis van Nedbank, 1945–1973*. Unpublished DLitt et Phil thesis, Rand Afrikaans University: 150–62.

[29] SA: Santam Board meeting, 12/5/1970.

board, motivating the establishment of a vehicle for direct investment in securities, especially in the emerging industrial sector of the economy. He publicly criticized the investment policies of credit institutions in South Africa. He observed that savings in South Africa were primarily flowing to banks that were 'under British influence' and which followed a very conservative credit policy that favoured loans instead of investment in ordinary shares of industrial enterprises. Of the £600 million at commercial banks, savings and small loan banks, trust companies, building societies, and insurance companies, less than 1 per cent was finding its way into ordinary shares. Furthermore, he doubted whether the finance and investment corporations had sufficient funds to finance long-term growth in the mining and manufacturing sector. Louw was not only arguing from the perspective of the Afrikaner's aspirations of meaningful participation in the industrial economy of the country, but also reflected international developments. The establishment of The Finance Corporation for Industry in Britain to assist in the reconstruction of British industry after the war, and The Industrial and Commercial Finance Corporation with guarantees of the Bank of England, specifically to assist small commercial and industrial enterprises, were used as support for his plea for dedicated investment in ordinary shares. Investments in debentures, mortgages, or government securities were not addressing the full commitment to industrial development, since that amounted to loan capital. In contrast, investment in shares made the investor a partner to the enterprise, sharing in the profit of the enterprise and not only fixed-interest-bearing paper. Investment in shares contained an element of risk. The investor was a partner to the business with an interest in its growth. A well-managed enterprise can exceed any return on interest earnings.[30]

Louw was preaching to his own people. Up to the 1940s Sanlam's investment policy was 'safety first'. Sanlam's investments were primarily in interest-bearing securities, debenture, mortgages, and preference shares.[31] This investment behaviour was fully in line with industry best practice, but Louw was a South African patriot: he wanted to support and finance domestic growth from within. It should be noted that the liabilities of Sanlam (and other insurers) were also changing from largely non-profit policies, i.e. all benefits guaranteed, to reversionary bonuses (carrying a 'bonus loading' that could be seen as a risk premium to cover more risky investments) where bonuses were not guaranteed until declared and vested.

The actuary, Tinie Louw, stepped forward as the strategic thinker. In a submission to the executive management in August 1945 he outlined a proposal for a subsidiary to divert cash bonuses from policyholders into direct investment in higher-risk ordinary share investments. During the war Sanlam's premium income rose by 163 per cent

[30] SA: 6/1/7: M.S. Louw address, 12/09/1945, Stellenbosch: Association for Economy and Trade.

[31] SA: 5/2/1: Sanlam Annual Financial statements, 1935–1940; SA: 3/1/2: Memorandum on investment in ordinary shares, 9/02/1951: 1–2.

and total profit by 121 per cent.[32] Access to an enlarged investment pool prompted management to revise the previous cautious investment strategy to provide for the riskier investment in ordinary shares of industrial enterprises. It was also a rising interest rate environment. Sanlam directed more investment funds into industrial enterprises, but Louw motivated a wider investment focus as high liquidity in the post-war period and domestic demand for industrial finance offered lucrative returns. Louw made numerous visits to Pretoria and Johannesburg to consult with the Registrar of Companies on the capital structure of the new venture, and with the President of the Johannesburg Securities Exchange about listing requirements of an investment company. Full agreement was secured from both authorities on the concept of an investment company as a vehicle for the direct investment of policyholders' cash bonuses in industrial equities. Legal opinion was sought on the formation of a dedicated industrial investment company directing voluntary cash bonuses from policyholders into higher-risk, higher-revenue-earning industrial equity. Legal opinion confirmed that the Sanlam Articles of Association permitted the investment of policyholders' cash bonuses provided that policyholders were given a choice of either reinvesting bonuses in the existing policies or withdrawing bonuses as cash for the purposes of investing it in equities.[33] *Bonus Beleggingskorporasie van Suid-Afrika Bpk* (Bonuskor) was incorporated on 20 February 1946 with a capital of £2 million[34] and was later listed on the Johannesburg Stock Exchange. This development signified the progressive strategic leadership in Sanlam.

This action was significant in two respects. It was an innovative strategy whereby policyholders were offered an investment product to supplement ordinary life policies. For the first time an insurance company enabled policyholders to have direct access to investments in equities. Sanlam used this strategy to give effect to its goal of giving South Africans a significant share in the development of their domestic economy. The communication to policyholders described the offer to invest in Bonuskor as a practical means to improve the living standards of all South Africans. Indirectly such investments would contribute to employment creation as the seed capital for new industries. The public, through policyholders, was offered access to the equity market using the knowledge of the Sanlam investment managers to select equity in well-performing listed entities. The unfamiliarity of policyholders with equity investments was backed by the Sanlam knowledge base, which could result in growing the demand for

[32] SA: 5/2/1: Sanlam annual financial statements, 1939, 1945.

[33] SA: 6/1/7: M.S. Louw Documents; Vertroulike Memorandum insake die voorgestelde stigting van 'n beleggingskorporasie die kapitaal waarvan voorsien word deur kontant-bonusse op Sanlam-polisse, [Confidential memorandum on proposed formation of a bonus investment corporation, of which the capital is provided from cash bonuses on Sanlam policies] 26/02/1945: SA: 6/1/7: M.S. Louw Memorandum, 20/5/1945.

[34] SA: Minutes of Sanlam Board, 25/07/1945; 5/10/1945; 21/10/1945; SA: 5/2/1: Sanlam Annual Report 1943: 4; SA: 3/1/2: Beleggingsnavorsing: Hoofbestuurder: Memorandum i.s. SANLAM/Bonuskor verhouding, 5/02/1960.

Sanlam investment products and policies. Insurance companies followed conservative investment policies. Life offices invested on a portfolio basis in safe investment instruments. Never before had an insurer opened up an investment medium to policyholders to exercise a direct option for investment in ordinary shares. The significance of the development was that Sanlam set its foot on the path of direct investment exposure in industrial enterprises—this is apart from ordinary portfolio investments. Bonuskor was established with capital to which Sanlam contributed £400 000 immediately paid-up shares. Policyholders were invited to apply for 'contributory shares'. Each contributory share automatically gave the owner fifty ordinary paid-up shares of 10/- each. Sanlam held the controlling shareholding,[35] appointed the Managing Director (which was M.S. Louw) and the Board of Directors (W.A. Hofmeyr, M.S. Louw, and Prof. W.F.J. Steenkamp). FVB was the issuing company that managed the establishment and share issue. Bonuskor was the first 'managed trust' company in the South African insurance industry. Investments, according to its statutes, were to be made in ordinary and preference shares of mining, industrial, and commercial enterprises. Only holders of profit-sharing policies to a value of £500 or higher were eligible for participation. Policies on the lives of children or issued on the lives of more than one person were excluded. Profits were distributed in dividends to shareholders.[36] Bonuskor declared a dividend of 5 per cent after the first year of business.

The establishment of Bonuskor was significant, as it was yet another innovation in assurance business operations in South Africa. The reason why this development is afforded explicit attention, is because it represented the realization of one of the aims of Sanlam at its inception, namely to contribute to the development of the domestic economy. Bonuskor was another vehicle devised by Sanlam to incentivize its policyholders to invest in the future of the South African economy. It is also significant because it showed the innovative thinking at Sanlam in developing investment products that served a dual purpose—making local savings available for industrial development, and securing policyholders a share in the lucrative market of listed equities. Afrikaner policyholders were not experienced or inclined to invest in the securities exchange. Bonuskor assisted the 'education' towards engagement in the world of shares.

The demand for the investment of bonuses in Bonuskor shares exceeded expectations. Management considered every single application at the weekly meetings of the executive management. This routine was followed until October 1947, when the responsibility to authorize these investments was transferred to the investment manager as it had simply become an extremely cumbersome task. The Bonuskor strategy addressed the 'infertile' capital phenomenon so publicly criticized by Tinie Louw. Bonuskor invested in ordinary shares, preference shares, and debentures of industrial enterprises and participated in the

[35] SA: 6/5/1: Minutes of Sanlam Management, 13/03/1946.
[36] SA: 6/1/7: Sanlam notice to policyholders, March 1946.

capital of new enterprises. Policyholders bought into the opportunity. By September 1947 more than £50 000 had been invested in Bonuskor shares. Bonuskor paid regular dividends. The steady flow of investments of cash bonuses by policyholders in Bonuskor shares reached £750 000 by 1959.[37] Towards the end of 1959 shareholders' interest in Bonuskor had risen to £4.5 million and total assets to £6.5 million.[38] Bonuskor's profits grew from £22 500 in 1947 to £350 150 in 1961, by which time it had equity interests in 148 different companies. The establishment of Bonuskor was a significant contributor to the much-needed venture capital of a growing South Africa, but it also gave Sanlam policyholders the option to supplement their life insurance and retirement provision by investing their cash bonuses. Sanlam kept a close watch on the Bonuskor share price. Trading conditions were sluggish during the early to mid-1950s and that prompted Bonuskor to request the parent company to support the price by buying shares in the market to prevent the price from dipping below the issue price. When Sanlam issued more Bonuskor shares at par to support the issued share value, it in effect led to a dilution of the value of existing shares.[39] This was an unsustainable situation.

As investment conditions improved towards the end of the 1950s Bonuskor was faced with a different dilemma. Investment funds from policyholders were showing no signs of slowing down, but the number of suitable investment opportunities did. Bonuskor invested heavily in companies within the group of Sanlam-linked concerns, such as the mining house *Federale Mynbou Korporasie* (Fedmyn, established in 1953), and the *Sentrale Finansie Korporasie* (Central Finance Corporation). Bonuskor's investments tended to become too concentrated in its own group, which focused the risk instead of spreading it. The management of Bonuskor became increasingly involved in the management of the new enterprises. This was not the original intention, as Sanlam's managers were insurance experts, not managers of industrial companies, mining, or finance houses. Management had two choices: issue more shares at net asset value, or limit the issued share capital of Bonuskor to, say, £5 million and establish another investment vehicle, a 'second Bonuskor'.[40] Management was reluctant to issue more Bonuskor shares at a premium. The issued capital of Bonuskor was fixed at £5 million in expectation of a gradual improvement in the market once the number of shares issued was fixed. A new investment company, *Sanlam Beleggingskorporasie* (Sankor—Sanlam Investment Corporation), was subsequently established in 1959 to succeed Bonuskor as its capital was restricted to £5 million. Sankor was not to invest directly into ordinary shares of industrial and commercial undertakings but rather into ordinary shares of investment companies listed on the stock exchange. Sankor had applied for its stock to be quoted on the Johannesburg Stock Exchange and was quoted under 'Financial Shares:

[37] SA: 6/5/1 Sanlam Annual Financial Statements, 1959.

[38] SA: 3/1/2: Beleggingsnavorsing: Memorandum insake Sanlam/Bonuskor verhouding, 5/2/1960: 1–13.

[39] Ibid., SA: Sanlam Annual Report, 1959: 4. [40] Ibid.

Industrial and General' in April 1962. Sankor then ceased to be a subsidiary of Sanlam; however, Sanlam would remain the largest shareholder in Sankor. Sanlam committed itself by continually investing its funds alongside its policyholders' bonuses in Sankor as it did in Bonuskor, which both resembled diversified portfolios in their own right. The risks of direct involvement in the greenfields enterprise development that resulted from some Bonuskor investments, raised cautionary flags. In the next decade the investment operations in Sanlam placed the company on an empowerment path, but also more extensive investments of functional importance to the company.

Sanlam was the only life office in South Africa conducting its business alongside so-called 'associated' companies. Bonuskor addressed the persistent drive in Sanlam to provide venture capital for domestic industrial development. Sanlam's investment policy was conservative up to 1950. Investments were primarily made in safe, low-risk investments such as mortgages, fixed property, and state/municipal securities (as prescribed by the Insurance Act of 1943). By the end of the 1940s Sanlam had invested only 5.2 per cent of its funds in ordinary shares. Hofmeyr, and later also Wassenaar, criticized state policy prescribing insurance companies to cover liabilities by investing 40 per cent of investment funds in state securities, while the capital demands of the industrial and mining sector exceeded supply. Such prescription was detrimental to the development of the economy. Sanlam engaged in the public outcry against the statutory compulsion preventing insurance companies from more productive investments.[41] Considering the expansion of investments in Bonuskor and the sustained demand by policyholders for investments in ordinary shares rendering inflation-beating returns, in 1951 Sanlam management decided that the time was ripe to embark on a more risk-prone investment strategy. This decision was prompted by two considerations: the economy was in a strong upward trend, but inflation was rising, and the mining and industrial sectors were dependent on foreign capital. A decision to embark on direct investments in ordinary shares was backed by a carefully thought-out framework for the selection of shares. The first principle was that investments were to be distributed among companies and industries. Companies selected for investment had to be well established in the industry, own active products in the market, and have a share price that displayed a consistent upward trend. The company itself had to pursue a conservative investment strategy and control assets in excess of £1 million.[42] A dedicated investment strategy was in the making.

Sanlam invested in a diversified portfolio of shares on the JSE. These shares were spread across a number of prominent local enterprises, such as in Imperial Cold Storage, Tiger Oats, De Beers Industrial, Natal Canvas, O K Bazaars, and in Dorman Long Africa and Hume Pipe in the heavy engineering industry. Local steel industries such as the Union Steel Corporation, the footwear manufacturer Edworks Ltd, the

[41] Sanlam Chairman's Statements, SA: 5/2/1: Sanlam Annual Report, 1951: 5.

[42] SA: 3/1/2: Sanlam Beleggingsnavorsing: Memorandum insake beleggings in gewone aandele, 9/2/1951: 1–5.

packaging company Amalgamated Packaging Industries, and SA Motor Assemblers and Distributors were recipients of Sanlam investments.[43] Locally incorporated industries, despite being owned and controlled by English business, were given the patriotic thumbs-up by Sanlam. By the mid-1950s companies in the industrial and mining sector under Afrikaner control constituted only 6 per cent of the market.[44] By 1960 Sanlam's investments in ordinary shares amounted to £8.4 million compared to £1.2 million in 1950—still only 10.3 per cent of its total assets. The exposure to industry and mining soon gained a life of its own when Sanlam decided to invest more funds in the development of Afrikaner-owned industrial and mining conglomerates.

Functional diversification in the Sanlam strategy was directly linked to the Afrikaner empowerment ideals. The establishment of FVB in 1940 provided the first vehicle to grow a substantial Afrikaner presence, not only as an employee in industry but also as entrepreneur. Under Wassenaar the industrial strategy gradually steered the business of the life office into a diversified group configuration. The upward cycle in the economy favoured growth and investment. These opportunities suited Sanlam's ideals. During the 1950s and 1960s the insurance sector outperformed the commercial bank sector, which was especially significant, since the relative contribution of the entire financial sector to GDP declined consistently between 1950 and 1984.[45] Insurance companies were asset-rich in an economy in which inflation was spiraling. Returns outside the financial sector were offering better long-term prospects, and Sanlam intended to reap those benefits to grow its empowerment ambitions.

Building the economy for the people

Afrikaner idealism, social networks, and human capital came together during the post-war era. A drive to succeed in business allowed the proliferation of Afrikaner-controlled enterprises across the total spectrum of economic activity. FVB was the financing vehicle. Sanlam had a controlling interest in FVB, but did not manage the company. The social capital network of managers and directors of Sanlam formed the matrix of managerial control in the emerging industrial conglomerate. The first employee and later executive chairman of FVB was Christoph Hendrik Brink, a qualified chartered accountant. M.S. Louw employed him at Sanlam and when FVB was established it fell upon him to support entrepreneurs and investors through the acquisition, rationalization of

[43] SA: 3/1/2/: Beleggingsnavorsing: Memoranda insake beleggings, 18/8/1954; 20/10/1954; 14/4/1959.

[44] SA: 6/7/1: M.S. Louw documents: M.S. Louw address to FAK: 'Opkoms van die Afrikaner op ekonomiese gebied', 14/3/1950.

[45] F.S. Jones (1992): 'Introduction: The growth of the financial sector, 1950–1988', in F.S. Jones (ed.) (1992): *Financial Enterprise in South Africa since 1950.* London: Macmillan: 5.

management, and the streamlining of Afrikaner enterprises to full profitability. Brink was a quick thinker, fast in taking decisions and driven by inspiration. As the son of a farmer in the Krugersdorp district in Transvaal, Brink was one of the first young Afrikaners to qualify as a chartered accountant in 1934, and when he entered the employment of FVB he was a first-generation Afrikaner in business. He was supported by a board from the Sanlam/Afrikaner social capital network: C.R. (Charlie) Louw (the first Chairman of FVB), Dr T.E. Dönges (a prominent member of the Sanlam Board and participant in the *olkskongres*), Senator A.P.J. Fourie, D.J.M. Jordaan, C.M. van der Merwe, and Professor C.G.W. Schumann (long-standing supporter of Afrikaner empowerment and participant of the *Volkskongres*). Jan S. Marais was one of the first FVB employees, together with William Bedford Coetzer who was sent to Johannesburg in 1941 to open the FVB office in the Transvaal. Coetzer would later take the leading role in the establishment of a mining subsidiary for FVB. Dr P.E. Rousseau was the industrial adviser to FVB—later in 1950 he was appointed by the Government to start Sasol. When Charlie Louw retired as Chairman in 1966, Hendrik Brink, who had risen to Managing Director of FVB, succeeded him as Chairman. The FVB business plan was simple: financing enterprises, not managing enterprises. Brink and Coetzer had very different temperaments: Brink was more inclined to offer support and rescue plans, while Coetzer was the calculated chartered accountant insisting clinically on maximum returns on investment. FVB formed a subsidiary, Federal Investment Corporation (FIC), as a closed-end investment trust. The bulk of the FIC investment portfolio consisted of the FVB shareholding in other underlying assets. These investments rose in tandem with the rapidly rising FVB investments. Brink took over as Managing Director of FIC and Coetzer of FVB. In 1966, Dr Kerneels Human succeeded Brink as FVB Chairman and was succeeded by I.J. Moolman in 1981.

FVB started by providing loans to emerging industrial enterprises. The first loan was to retailers Kriel & Company of Riviersonderend. This was a point of difference between Brink and Coetzer: the former supported loans to assist the small entrepreneur to get started. The latter favoured investments with prospects for long-term growth. The first FVB investment was in the South African Farm Implement Manufacturers (SAFIM) based in Vereeniging. In 1961 FVB acquired a 28 per cent stake in Massey Ferguson South Africa, while the Canadian parent company retained control of the South African operations. Massey Ferguson soon acquired SAFIM. As a wholly-owned subsidiary of Massey Ferguson, SAFIM manufactured farm equipment and Massey Ferguson managed distribution. During the late 1970s the Canadian parent company ran into difficulties, allowing FVB to acquire outright control.[46] This is how Afrikaner business moved into the agricultural mechanical equipment industry.

[46] G. Verhoef (1995): 'The development of diversified conglomerates: the case of Federale Volksbeleggings—a case study', *Joernaal vir Eietydse Geskiedenis*, 24 (2): 60–1.

FVB also led the Afrikaners into the food industry. It all started with a loan to Jameson Welding Works, a small fishing company from Salt River in the Cape, in 1941. On the Cape's west coast was another small fishing company, *Laaiplek Visserye*, which later changed its name to Marine Products. Marine Products merged with Jameson Welding Works and soon took on the reduction of fishmeal and oil from shoal fish. Marine Products developed into a jewel in the FVB crown, diversifying into other enterprises such as copper mining (Klein Aub Copper Mine), production of insulation wool from slag, and the production of malt and other feedstocks for the beer-brewing industry, as well as vegetable oils and allied products (Nola Industries). By the 1970s Marine Products and its subsidiaries contributed 37.4 per cent of total FVB earnings. The *Financial Mail* commented: 'It is probably FVB's most important money-spinner, and certainly one of its main pillars of prosperity since its inception.'[47] The humble beginnings of farm equipment and fishing provided the foundation for the subsequent development of FVB as a diversified industrial conglomerate, a holding company managing more than thirty companies operating across the entire industrial and mining spectrum of the South African economy by 1970.

In that year the FVB conglomerate included FIC, *Federale Lenings- en Assuransie Maatskappy* (FLAM) (Federal Loan and Insurance Company), *Federale Nywerhede Beperk* (Federal Industries Limited), Fedchem, Transmar, and Champions. The first two subsidiaries were the funding initiatives responsible for finding the capital required to extend the loans to enterprising applicants. This capital was also used to fund the FVB participation in the establishment of new companies. In 1970 FIC's assets stood at R18.4 million. These included FVB's shareholding in Trust Bank, Fedmyn, General Mining, Sentrust, and Klein Aub Copper Mine. By 1970 FLAM had accumulated R15.2 million in assets. FLAM was headed by Dr Jan S. Marais, who later led the new bank in the FVB group, Trust Bank. FLAM issued and traded in debentures to raise working capital for the enterprises on the FVB book. By 1970 it was the only wholly-owned subsidiary of FVB. FVB needed a funding vehicle, since Sanlam refused to manage FVB or act as its source of cash. In March 1946 the Sanlam management refused permission for Tinie Louw to serve on the board of *Federale Nywerhede,*[48] and in September 1946 the board declined an FVB offer to take up £25 000 shares in FVB.[49] Sanlam forced Afrikaner business to develop capacity, secure its own funding, and expand beyond the Sanlam stable.

Federale Nywerhede was a listed holding company in which the fishing and food companies were held, with assets of R8.7 million by 1970. The interests in chemical companies were organized under Fedchem, another holding company. FVB had shares in Klipfontein Organic Products, a small chemical business. In 1967, FVB owned small

[47] *Financial Mail*, 19 June 1970: 17.
[48] SA: Minutes of Management meeting, 13/3/1946.
[49] SA: Minutes of Sanlam Management, 18/9/1946.

interests in BP Chemicals, National Chemical Products (NCP), and the Synthetic Rubber Company of the Industrial Development Corporation. All the chemical interests merged into Sentrachem, the largest chemical conglomerate in South Africa by the end of 1967. Further interests in chemical-related companies included a minority interest in Federal Fertilizer, SA Druggists (SAD), Aerochem, and two pharmaceutical companies, Sana and Petersen. FVB appointed Francis le Riche as Managing Director of Sentrachem. He turned the loss-making companies around and then FVB negotiated the acquisition by SAD of those enterprises in exchange for an increased share in SAD. By the early 1970s the Sentrachem interests were not yet delivering the returns anticipated, but were poised to do so soon. Fedchem, with assets of R19.9 million in 1970, was not an FVB subsidiary, since SA Mutual held a significant stake. This was another example of growing collaboration between the emerging Afrikaner businesses and non-Afrikaner business.[50]

Two smaller holding companies in FVB were Transmar and Champions. Transmar held the FVB interests in trade, tourism, and services companies. The retail stakes in the furniture retailer Morkels, the general clothing retailer Uniewinkels, the petroleum interests in Trek Investments, and Avis, the hotels and vehicle rental company, made up the R6.3 million assets of Transmar. Champions held FVB's property interests and the minority stake in Massey Ferguson, and its total assets were R7.7 million. The complex pyramid holding company structure of the R47.8 million FVB assets was characteristic of the conglomerated business landscape of South Africa. The FVB stable comprised around thirty companies, nineteen of which were listed. FVB's management strategy was to avoid a 51 per cent control, but to exercise effective control in collaboration with partners via the holding company structures. This was a conscious strategy. FVB wanted to build an investment company with a broad exposure to industrial interests, utilizing a minimum cash outlay—it had limited capital to start with. The board thought FVB could build its capital resources better through a reliance on a steady dividend flow, rather than a reliance on operating profit, which had the tendency to fluctuate beyond the control of management. FVB grew by a high rate of income retention in its holding, operating, and intermediate investment companies. It then injected loan and equity capital into its underlying companies. A loss of £1 390 in 1941 was turned around to profits of R2.5 million in 1970 (an 81 per cent annual compound growth), and total dividend payments of slightly more than £90 000 in 1950 rose to R1.2 million in 1970 (an increase of 12 per cent annual compound growth).[51] The rapid expansion of the domestic economy, structural change, and rising equity prices obviously favoured industrial expansion. The relative contribution of agriculture and mining to GNP in 1939 was 33.4 per cent, but this declined to 18.7 per cent in

[50] G. Verhoef (2010): 'The chemical industry' in S. Jones and R. Vivian (eds), *South African economy and policy, 1990–2000*. Manchester: Manchester University Press: 143–58.

[51] SA: FVB Annual Report, 1970.

1970, while the contribution of the industrial sector increased from 17.7 per cent to 24.7 per cent.[52] By 1970 international pressure and exchange control encouraged both massive acquisition exercises and firm control through holding structures. The conglomerates diluted the value of underlying assets, but strategies to restore focus through the break-up of these empires only gained traction much later in the 1990s. What happened in FVB subsequently was not only an FVB managerial strategy, but also indicated the growing integrated strategic vision of Afrikaner business.

Sanlam's investments in industries were not limited to its own portfolio investments and FVB, but extended also to other Afrikaner entrepreneurs seeking a foothold in the economy. The young entrepreneur Anton Edward Rupert shared the Afrikaner nationalist enthusiasm of the *Volkskongres.* Rupert was a son of a Graaff-Reinet lawyer and member of the so-called Cape elite. Rupert studied chemistry and lectured at the University of Pretoria for a while, but he was greatly inspired by the *Volkskongres* initiatives. He joined the *Reddingsdaadbond* (RDB) as head of the small business development unit in 1940. He was moved by the marginalization of poor Afrikaners, but was inspired by initiatives to foster Afrikaner entrepreneurship. With an entrepreneurial mind himself, he opened a dry-cleaning business in Pretoria, but had more ambitious dreams. In 1941 he established the *Voorbrand Tabakkorporasie,* a company that manufactured cigarettes and other tobacco products. He took on an established market with four foreign companies occupying a firm position in the market. Rupert opened his factory in Johannesburg. The early years were difficult. United Tobacco Corporation's representative offered to buy *Voorbrand* several times, but Rupert politely refused. When he needed a market for the snuff tobacco leaves (not used for cigarette manufacturing), he used his social network. Rupert met Yusuf Ahmed Cachalia, an Indian textile trader, and Donath Desai, an Indian general trader, who assisted him in finding an outlet for the snuff leaves. FVB had invested in *Voorbrand,* but by late 1942 developed doubt about the prospects of the tobacco industry. Rupert, of course, did not. He spotted the entrepreneurial opportunity and devised a strategy to buy the FVB shares and establish a vehicle to finance future expansion. He and his partner, Dirk Hertzog, sold the dry-cleaning business they had in Pretoria and bought the FVB shares. In 1944 *Voorbrand* was restructured as a public company with capital of £50 000 and issued shares to the public to the value of £36 980. In the same year he also established a finance company, *Tegniese Beleggings,* to finance further business expansion. By the late 1940s *Voorbrand* owned more than forty registered tobacco trademarks, eleven types of packaged tobacco and eight types of loose tobacco, but was not permitted to manufacture cigarettes. In 1946 the *Rembrandt Tabakkorporasie van Suid-Afrika* was established as the holding company for the tobacco interests of *Voorbrand* and liquor interests, of

[52] H. Jones and A. Müller (1992): *The South African economy, 1910–1990*: 130.

which his partner, Hertzog, had taken control. In 1945 Rupert met Sydney Rothman in London while shopping around for new technology. When it became known that Rothman wanted to sell his cigarette company, Rupert could not resist the opportunity. He entered into an agreement with Rothmans of Pall Mall to manufacture its cigarettes in South Africa in exchange for technical assistance. Rupert established more investment companies and finally organized them in a pyramid structure under *Rembrandt Beherend*, the holding company controlled by him and Hertzog.

It was from this systematically constructed business platform that Rupert acquired Rothmans from London in 1953. Sanlam, through Bonuskor, had taken up preference shares in Rembrandt in 1950. The Sanlam board was especially impressed by the quality of management in Rembrandt, but cautioned against two risks. The first was the highly competitive nature of the cigarette market and the other was the structure of Rembrandt's assets. The Sanlam board expressed confidence in the management of the company and its capital structure, but was less comfortable with its asset structure. It was decided to insist on consultation with preference shareholders prior to any changes to its asset structure. Sanlam took 75 000 preference shares in Rembrandt as well as 100 000 ordinary shares.[53] When Rembrandt clinched the Rothmans deal, the company had a serious cash problem: £750 000 was due to Rothmans in London on Monday, 25 November 1953, but Rembrandt did not have it. Rupert met with A.D. Wassenaar of Sanlam, then General Manager, in Johannesburg asking for Sanlam's assistance. The Sanlam executive management met on 18 November at Sanlamhof, Bellville, to discuss the Rembrandt request for a loan of around £400 000. A special meeting of the executive management was called on Friday, 20 November 1953, for the urgent consideration of the loan.[54] At that meeting Sanlam as preference shareholder in Rembrandt gave permission to Rembrandt to issue £500 000 7 per cent debentures. If the transaction was successful, Sanlam would take up £250 000 7 per cent debentures, secured by Rembrandt's shares in Rothmans, as well as by combined and separate security offered by both the investment companies (*Tegniese en Industriële Beleggings 1* and *2*) in the Rembrandt Group. The Sanlam exposure was spread 50/50 between Sanlam and AHT, Bonuskor and FVB.[55] The remaining funds were supplied by Volkskas taking up debentures. Sanlam's permission to Rembrandt to issue debentures and the decision to take up half of the debentures collectively in the Sanlam group of companies and associated companies, provided Rupert with the means to make its first international acquisition. For the development of Afrikaner business in South Africa this was a major achievement. It was significant in the history of the Rembrandt Group, as well as the collective Afrikaner business effort. The insurance business of Sanlam developed

[53] WCA: A2213: C.R. Louw Collection: Memorandum on Rembrandt, 19/9/1950.
[54] SA: Minutes of Sanlam Executive, 18/11/1953.
[55] SA: Minutes of Sanlam Executive, 20 November 1953.

completely separately from the liquor, cigarette, and luxury goods businesses of the Rembrandt Group, but good relationships existed between the companies and individual leaders. When FVB celebrated its twenty-first anniversary in 1961, Rupert was invited to attend the occasion, leading to correspondence of mutual gratitude and respect.[56]

As part of the growing Afrikaner ambition in business, it was only a matter of time before an appetite for the mining industry would become a driving force. FVB was cautious of entering the mining industry. The high capital intensity of the industry, the dominance of foreign and English capital, the report by The Low Grade Ore Commission in 1932 that the low quality of ore and the deep level of deposits, coupled with rising working costs per ton, had put profitability under pressure, especially since the late 1940s.[57] Afrikaners also had very limited experience in mining. A large number of urbanized poor Afrikaners did work in the mining industry, but Afrikaner entrepreneurs were wary of the industry. Young Afrikaners were gradually qualifying as engineers, for example Pierre Etienne Rousseau from Tulbagh, who qualified as a metallurgical engineer from Massachusetts Institute of Technology (MIT) and chemical engineer from the British Institute of Chemical Engineers. He entered a mining career with Anglovaal in 1938 and was appointed Managing Director of Sasol in 1950. Some entrepreneurial Afrikaners bought shares in small coal mines. Wentzel du Plessis and his brother Jacques established Klipfontein Collieries Pty (Ltd) in 1940, which owned the Klipfontein mine and later acquired the small Acme coal mine. A persistent cash-flow problem forced the Du Plessis brothers to seek financial assistance from FVB. The latter was not interested as mining was considered too risky and fell outside the business plan. FVB was finally persuaded by loyalty to fellow-Afrikaner entrepreneurs and the Du Plessis brothers' close relationship with Professor C.G.W. Schumann, a director of FVB, to assist the company. FVB issued a guarantee to Volkskas in favour of a loan to Klipfontein Collieries, but encouraged Klipfontein to approach the market. In October 1944 Klipfontein Collieries made a public offering of 30 000 shares, underwritten by FVB. Coetzer, the FVB manager in Johannesburg, encouraged the Klipfontein management to locate better-quality coal deposits through exploration. Soon richer deposits were found at Horingkrans and later at Broodsnydersplaats No. 216 (later developed as the Blinkpan mine). In 1945 Klipfontein Collieries acquired options in Horingkrans, in 1947 at the Klippoortjie mine and in 1948 at the Koornfontein mine. Klipfontein Collieries lacked capital to take up all these options. FVB negotiated with the brokerage firm Michel & Bowman to underwrite a Horingkrans share issue—FVB did the sub-underwriting at 5 per cent commission and Bonuskor did the underwriting for 40 000 of the 100 000 issued shares. This was the first joint-venture mining transaction by FVB and Bonuskor. As Klipfontein Collieries

[56] WCA: A2213: Correspondence between C.R. Louw and A.E. Rupert, 20/6/61; 7/7/61; 27/7/61.

[57] Transvaal Chamber of Mines, *61th Annual Report*, 1950: 60.

kept draining capital, and Wennie du Plessis entered politics,[58] FVB moved closer to operations at the Klipfontein Collieries' mines. More detailed investigation into the coal-mining operations convinced FVB that the mines required better management. By 1948 Klipfontein Collieries ran the risk of defaulting on the £40 000 Volkskas loan.[59]

By that time FVB was at a crossroads on mining: either call in the loan to Klipfontein or take full management control of all the coal-mining interests to secure profitability. William Bedford Coetzer was anxious to take on the Anglophone mining establishment in Johannesburg. This ambitious entrepreneurial step was considered even though Professor W.H. Hutt from the University of Cape Town had publicly expressed his opinion about Afrikaners' capacity to succeed in business to a meeting of the Sons of England in August 1946. He claimed Afrikaners had serious deficiencies in engaging successfully in business.[60] Afrikaner entrepreneurs were consequently clearly out to prove their abilities. Coetzer had to convince the FVB directors in the Cape that FVB had the capabilities to succeed in mining. The strategic business issue was to turn the focus of FVB beyond the safe small and medium-sized enterprises in which the bulk of FVB capital had been invested, towards the big business of mining.

The turning point came when Coetzer convinced FVB to grant a further £100 000 loan to Klipfontein Collieries on condition that FVB acquired sole mining rights to coal deposits at Koornfontein and Broodsnydersplaats, while Klipfontein shares held by FVB were retained as security. FVB thereby became directly involved in coal mining with full management control of the mines.[61] In August 1948, FVB for the first time discussed the possibility of a mine holding company. In September 1948, FVB terminated public offerings of coal shares in the Klipfontein Collieries group of mines.[62]

The Koornfontein and Horingkrans coal deposits presented new prospects of successful coal mining operations, but profitability was dependent on access to a larger market. Coetzer then negotiated membership for Klipfontein Collieries with the Transvaal Coal Owners Association (TCOA), which landed Klipfontein Collieries a 2 per cent quota and the Koornfontein mine a 3 per cent quota in the TCOA coal market. TCOA was controlled by the Anglo American Corporation (AAC). The alliance with AAC's Harry Oppenheimer was strategically significant. Coetzer was heavily criticized by his own assistant, Dr A.J. Visser, Wentzel du Plessis (then MP for Standerton, but a member

[58] In 1948 Wentzel du Plessis opposed General J.C. Smuts in the elections of the constituency Standerton and defeated him. Du Plessis then devoted his attention to politics and resigned from the operational responsibilities at Klipfontein.

[59] FVB Minutes of Board Meeting, 8/9/1948.

[60] SA: 6/5/1/8: C.H. Brink papers: *Cape Argus*, 15/8/1946. The Vice Chancellor of the University of Cape Town, Sir Carruthers Beattie, also told a public meeting that the 'poor whites were "intellectually backward" and that there was something inherent in the Afrikaners that resulted in the phenomenon of [poor whiteism] assuming such alarming proportions in their case'. H Giliomee (2003): *The Afrikaners*: 348.

[61] FVB Minutes of Board meeting, 29/9/1948. [62] FVB Minutes of Board meeting, 23/6/1949.

of the board of Klipfontein Collieries), and Mr Jan Steyn (MP for Potchefstroom). Collaboration with AAC was considered in breach of the goals of FVB to secure and promote Afrikaner business. Coetzer argued that doing business with well-intended English businessmen would afford the inexperienced Afrikaners valuable experience. The matter caused an unexpected upheaval at the FVB board meeting, since Visser and Du Plessis had secretly negotiated with the two wealthy Jonker brothers from Bonnievale (Herman and Japie) to buy out the Koornfontein rights from the FVB-controlled Klipfontein Consolidated Collieries. The FVB board then dug in its heels: its flagship mine was not up for sale, but if it was to be acquired, then negotiations were only to be with FVB and all outstanding FVB loans would be called up. The Jonker brothers could not foot the full bill. Visser, Du Plessis, and Steyn then resigned from the Klipfontein board and FVB was left with absolute control of Klipfontein Collieries.[63] Coetzer delivered some sober business advice: he insisted that there was much to be gained from the TCOA's experience and that there was no such thing as English demand for coal or an Afrikaans economy or that an Afrikaans coal-mining concern could be built on exclusive Afrikaner demand for coal.[64] He established links with the leading mining company in the industry and secured the small nascent Afrikaner coal-mining interests access to the powerful TCOA market. He was instrumental in the appointment of the Anglo-Transvaal mining group of the Hersov family as consultants to the new Klipfontein Collieries group of mines.[65] This strategy held the potential for the running of profitable coal mines. Coetzer was ambitious and eager to establish Afrikaners in the mining industry. Successful entry depended on very good management, patience, and much-enhanced technical surveys. He was very business oriented. To him there were no sentimental considerations in business, only profits, which could only be achieved through investment in big industry and mining. He opposed FVB's approach of scattered small investments in mining. Instead, he suggested the formation of a holding company for all the coal-mining interests of Klipfontein Collieries, which by 1953 included Klipfontein, Koornfontein, Klippoortjie, Broodsnydersplaats (Blinkpan), and Horingkrans.

FVB's directors were located in Cape Town, while Coetzer operated in Johannesburg. His business inclination and ambition to secure an Afrikaans mining house finally convinced the FVB board to establish a mine holding company. On 1 July 1953 he resigned from FVB and took up the position of Managing Director of the Klipfontein Consolidated Collieries. (He remained a director of FVB.) Support from Sanlam was forthcoming from Tinie Louw in his capacity as Managing Director of Bonuskor, as well

[63] FVB Minutes of Board meetings, 30/11/1949; 1/12/1949; 11/8/1950.
[64] FVB Minutes of Board meeting, 30/11/1950: Memorandum by W.B. Coetzer.
[65] FVB Minutes of Board meeting, 11/8/1950.

as the secretary, P.R. Rörich.[66] Louw had been the Sanlam manager consistently calling for investment in manufacturing, but he supported Coetzer's ambitions because it was clear that the coal mines under his FVB management had been improving profitability since 1948. Bonuskor did not have the required technical abilities to invest in mining options, but FVB had accumulated a core of expert technical staff to evaluate mining propositions. Hendrik Brink thus proposed an FVB and Bonuskor joint venture by forming a separate mine holding company. Bonuskor provided capital and FVB technically trained staff.[67] The risk of new mining ventures was then situated in a separate mine holding company. A team of qualified technical staff could be brought together to assess propositions and provide expert advice, facilitating decisions to involve the company at the earliest possible stage of mining operations. This strategy would place the mining company in the driving seat of new operations, allowing it to manage operations to profitability. This new company could earn commission by selling its technical, managerial, and secretarial expertise to other mining ventures. Brink estimated that the new company could earn up to £20 000 per annum in commission. Both FVB and Bonuskor transferred all mining shares in their portfolios to the new company. FVB's mining shares amounted to £320 000 and Bonuskor's £130 000. It was agreed that FVB would acquire *de jure* control of the new company, but since Bonuskor would provide the working capital the two companies would be equal partners with equal representation on the board of the new venture.[68] Detailed correspondence was exchanged between Louw, Rörich, and Brink prior to the formal establishment of the mining company. The firm agreement was that should the new company proceed with a capital issue with the aim of involving either the public or any other interested parties, FVB and Bonuskor would have the right to negotiate with, for example, Sanlam on the formation of a holding company for the mining interests to secure control by either FVB, Bonuskor, or Sanlam.[69] The agreement on the formation of the new company was based on strict business principles protecting the interests of each stakeholder. There was a tangible confidence among these Afrikaner businessmen in their ability to venture into the mining industry and succeed.

Federale Mynbou Maatskappy (Fedmyn)[70] was established on 6 June 1953 with authorized capital of £1 million, consisting of two million shares of 10/ each. FVB and Bonuskor were the joint controlling shareholders. William Coetzer was the Chairman,

[66] Rörich was the holder of an MCom degree and had been employed by the Industrial Development Corporation of South Africa and Sanlam. See SA: Sanlam Annual Report, 1946; Chairman's Address: 7.

[67] SA: FVB Memorandum by C.H. Brink. 26/2/1953.

[68] SA: Memorandum P.R. Rörich, Bonuskor, 16/3/1953.

[69] SA: Memorandum P.R. Rörich, Bonuskor, 20/3/1053; Letter M.S. Louw–C.H. Brink, 24/4/1953; Memorandum C.H. Brink, 29/4/1953; Letter C.H. Brink–M.S. Louw, 29/4/1953.

[70] On 1 February 1958 the name was changed to *Federale Mynbou Beperk*.

and Managing Director. Bonuskor was represented on the board by M.S. Louw and P.R. Rörich and FVB by C.H. Brink and G.J. van Zijl. Coetzer insisted on Fedmyn's operational independence from its shareholders' focus on investment management and small business development. He immediately appointed consulting engineers, geologists, and technical engineers to the Fedmyn staff and within a decade the English Sunday newspaper *The Sunday Times* acknowledged that Fedmyn had obtained the services of first-class leaders, managers, and engineering consultants. In 1964 the *South African Mining and Engineering Journal* had to admit that investment in Fedmyn was not an act of sympathy for Afrikaans business, but justified by 'its intrinsic merits as a virile young mining and finance house'.[71] The expansion of Fedmyn's operations soon required further capital. In 1958 intricate negotiations between FVB, Bonuskor, and Sanlam resulted in Sanlam acquiring a third equal shareholding in Fedmyn on 1 June 1958.[72] FVB wanted compensation for its exposure to risks when taking control of the Klipfontein and Koornfontein coal mines. In this period the struggling mines paid no dividends to Fedmyn. Sanlam agreed to the same terms of agreement between FVB and Bonuskor on control of Fedmyn as documented in the correspondence between Tinie Louw and Hendrik Brink prior to the establishment of Fedmyn.

The rapid expansion of Fedmyn's operations and its growing exposure to the gold-mining industry meant a consistent demand for more capital and therefore Sanlam became involved. Once the terms of Sanlam's third equity stake were confirmed, Fedmyn increased its authorized capital to £2 million and listed on the JSE on 29 July 1959. The public issue of Fedmyn shares was 89 per cent oversubscribed before closing.[73]

The participation of Sanlam as third equal shareholder in Fedmyn was significant for three reasons. Firstly, Sanlam was still seen to be the main source of capital for emerging Afrikaner business, despite the establishment of FVB. Secondly, the involvement of Sanlam in the mining industry by direct shareholding in Fedmyn was the beginning of extensive investments in companies later to be described by the Sanlam Managing Director, F.J. du Plessis, as 'strategic investments'. The notion of 'strategic' followed from the agreement between the three principal shareholders not to allow control of the mining company slip from their hands. Thirdly, the frantic attempts by FVB to secure its business interests in Fedmyn, as well as to secure financial reward for its exposure to risk during the formative period of the mining initiatives (at a time when Afrikaner business actually did not contemplate involvement in mining), signified the emerging business domain contestation between Afrikaner businessmen. Thirty years later similar contestation was described in the English press as '*broedertwis*'.

[71] *SA Mining and Engineering Journal*, 4/9/1964.

[72] SA: Fedmyn Minutes of Board meetings, 3/8/1956; 16/6/1958.

[73] SA: FVB Minutes of Board meetings, 14/5/1959; 29/7/1959.

The company for the people and the people of the company

Dedication and competitive performance in the insurance industry characterized much of the work by the Sanlam team of managers, Head Office staff, and agents. The motivational thrust was to succeed in an industry dominated by non-Afrikaners and a society publicly skeptical of the ability of Afrikaners to succeed in business. Since 1918 the organization, management, and public image of Sanlam portrayed Afrikaner conservatism, patriarchal authority, and a proud sense of nationalism. The passing of the Sanlam Act in 1954 occurred at the critical organizational intersection in the history of the firm. Key capabilities had been built in the firm through learning from experienced staff who joined the company in 1918. Human capital accumulated in the firm permitted the building of economies of scale and scope. This expansion occurred under the next generation of leadership who succeeded the founding fathers by the late 1950s. Management remained centralized, rigid, and bureaucratic. The business strategy was to expand in insurance as well as functional diversification. To build the core capabilities in support of the strategy and structure of the growing firm, apart from establishing a hierarchy of practical organizational routines, Sanlam also constructed an organizational culture to support the structure. When the Sanlam Head Office moved to Bellville in 1953, the 'company village' phenomenon represented a strategic management tool towards achieving firm objectives.

Sanlam's management recognized that the confined office space in the Cape Town city centre was a serious constraint on operational expansion as far back as 1950. The idea of a company village was mooted at board meetings in 1943 and 1944. During 1950 Wassenaar visited insurance companies in the United State of America to observe the trends in the physical organization of those companies. Management displayed an enlightened sense of openness to international developments, and a willingness to move ahead with the leaders in the industry. Wassenaar reported that since 1925 American insurers had moved their head offices to extensive open land, away from shops in the business centre, perhaps in residential areas, but in close proximity to urban transport services. Sanlam was following an international trend in establishing Sanlamhof[74] in 1953. To the Afrikaans life office there were three golden rules: move to a location where a commercial centre would not be able to catch up with the company, remain within the reach of transport infrastructure, and buy enough land to secure the

[74] The new Sanlam Head Office was later known as Sanlamhof. The SA Mutual followed the international trend and moved out of Cape Town as well, but only in 1956, after Sanlam had relocated in 1953. P. Brooke Simonds: *Old Mutual*: 146–8.

company the ability to keep other businesses at bay.[75] The move out of Cape Town was mandated by the growth of the company, and management grabbed the opportunity to devise a functional location and physical structure to serve the needs of a growing enterprise.

The industrial paternalism sought to create a loyal and disciplined workforce able to sustain the growth of the company. Management created an environment in which the labour force was secure, submitted to the culture management instilled, and experienced satisfaction in work and personal development. The Sanlam management had been strongly paternalistic since 1918, as described in Chapter 2. A high degree of cultural homogeneity was considered vital to the success of a new entrant into a very competitive market. Management knew that a large body of its employees entered the urban environment for the first time. It was assumed that a home-like familiar socio-cultural environment would serve the firm's as well as family purposes. By the early 1950s, Sanlam was competing successfully in the industry, but the company was only at the beginning of its empowerment strategy. Wassenaar motivated the relocation to Bellville from a company perspective, but strategically the physical space afforded management the opportunity to organize accommodation, social interaction, sport, and other cultural activities in accordance with Afrikaner customs. Sanlamhof was the place where the Sanlam company culture and operational efficiency were envisaged to meet and serve business goals. Management was aware of some resistance to the move, but hoped to compensate by offering subsidized accommodation, food, and recreational facilities, similar to those of international company towns. Management's father-like conduct in providing for the staff was perceived to be justified in business. The staff periodical *Die Sanlam Fakkel* reported the paternalism in business as offering invaluable guidance to employees, opening avenues for progress and advancement of employees, encouraging studies in new industry developments, and displaying concern for the personal problems of workers.[76] The planning, organization, and execution of the new Head Office in Bellville at the same time as the life office came into its own as an independent mutual life company, underpinned the functional diversification envisaged.

The Sanlam administration and management moved into the new building in October 1953. The *Sanlam Fakkel* dedicated twelve pages to describe the layout of the premises on the 27.4 hectare Sanlam site.[77] The building was a modern version of international state-of-the-art insurance buildings: not too high—three storeys plus a basement—and open-plan group offices to facilitate communication and contact, meeting rooms and separate offices for only the most senior managers. The building, the adjacent staff accommodation, and the recreational facilities were presented to the readers as a

[75] WCA: CRL Collection: Wassenaar Memorandum to Board: Verskuiwing en beplanning van hoofkantoorgeboue: 12/1/1950.

[76] *Sanlam Fakkel*, November 1959: 14.

[77] *Sanlam Fakkel*, October 1953: 8–19.

dream come true for 'us all'. The new cafeteria provided meals, while breakfast and dinner were provided in the dining rooms in the staff accommodation. The three blocks of accommodation were named after founders of Sanlam: Carl Wilcocks, Fred Dormehl, and Willie Hofmeyr. The motive for the main building was to meet the expansion requirements of the company and assist staff to sustain and expand the delivery of high-quality services to the public. The modern technology of document transfers from one side of the building to the other to enhance record preservation, the state-of-the-art telephone system, the open communication facilities, and air conditioning on the top floor where the boardroom and executive offices were situated, all symbolized the progressive Afrikaner enterprise. The gardens were planned to enhance the appearance of the modern building. Sporting facilities (rugby field, cricket pitch, netball field, swimming pool, tennis courts, pool table, and table-tennis facilities) were all provided on the premises alongside the three blocks of flats and dormitory accommodation for staff. It was interesting that the former social club was replaced by the Sanlam sporting club, responsible for organizing all the different sports codes.

Industrial paternalism was visibly present in the structuring and organization of the new Head Office. Management wanted the staff to feel like one big happy family. However, not all staff members were always part of the happy family,[78] but the staff magazine generally portrayed a consensus that served the public image of a successful company. This lasted as long as Afrikaner nationalism displayed a high degree of unity and action, but began to decline towards the late 1970s. Since the occupation of the new Head Office it fulfilled a significant symbolic organizational role. A high degree of unity incentivised better performance, and during the late 1950s and 1960s Sanlam produced a number of industry-leading initiatives. One important development was in computer technology, which clearly benefited from the consolidation of human capital at the centre.

The Sanlam management kept a close eye on international industry developments. Managers were regular attendees at international industry conferences. Particular attention was given to up-to-date technology and in 1934 Sanlam introduced Powers-Samas forty-five-column punchcard equipment. Sanlam was the first insurance company in South Africa to introduce this technology. In 1948 the technology was upgraded to the reading of sixty-five columns. From the beginning meticulous attention was given to administrative efficiency and systematic record-keeping. The drive to succeed in the industry incentivized further innovation. Sanlam computer technicians assisted Powers-Samas in building a new five-line interpreter machine, introduced in 1955.

[78] W. Beukes (2017) *Van Afrikanerkultuur tot korporatief: die geskiedenis van Sanlam se Hoofkantoor-personeelkorps, 1918–2008*: 315, 321–2. Some staff members were not content with the dominant paternalism resulting in prescriptions on dress code, times of going out in the evening and returning back to the residence, permission to make personal decisions, such as getting married, or purchasing their own vehicle.

This technology enabled Sanlam to process more complex policyholder information about renewal dates, premium payments, monthly bank and employers' requests. These innovations enhanced the efficiency in communication with policyholders and saved time, which administrative clerks could allocate to other functions. Sanlam used the Powers-Samas technology for twenty-five years. In 1958/59 Sanlam switched to the IBM eighty-column cards before introducing IBM technology, which replaced the mechanical data input action of the Powers-Samas technology with IBM electro-mechanical technology.[79] As the modern technology of American computers entered the market, Sanlam was fully informed of the applicability thereof to the life industry through the publications of the American Life Office Administrators and membership of the Scottish Faculty of Actuaries, of which Sanlam actuaries had been members since 1955. Sanlam dispatched its chief actuary Dr G.H. Hansman and another actuary in the actuarial department, Pepler Scholtz, to investigate the possibilities and implications of Sanlam making the transition from mechanical high-speed calculators to electronic computers. By this time, the company had invested in growing industrial enterprises and the mining sector. Sanlam was also the first insurance company in South Africa to install a Burroughs Datatron computer in September 1958. This computer was supplemented by an IBM eighty-column punchcard reader and IBM printer. The equipment was 50 cubic metres in size and weighed 12 000 kilograms. Sanlam sent a group of seven Head Office employees from the different departments—actuarial, policy benefits, mortgages, planning, and accounts—to the USA for training prior to the installation. The company appointed its own engineers, Francois Botha and Nick van Zyl, to take care of maintenance. It was a committee consisting of Sanlam employees, led by David Malan, who investigated the possibilities of acquiring a computer for Sanlam's operation. They advised the board in great detail about the proposition and oversaw the installation and the introduction of the computer to the operations of the life office in November 1958 (this was the new computer, installed in September, that had come into full operation by November). Sanlam followed the advice of the American actuaries, namely that control of computer equipment should be in the hands of people who understand the life insurance business, 'men who know not only what we do but also why we do it'.[80] David Malan was in charge of the new computer, assisted by newly qualified actuary Uwe Voigt, who had just returned from studying in Scotland. With the first electronic computer utilizing magnetic tape in Africa, Sanlam improved operational efficiency exponentially.

Leadership in computer technology was not expected from the latecomer Afrikaans life office. This team, Malan and Voigt, addressed early implementation snags, such as longer-than-expected time to transfer data from the punchcards to the magnetic tapes,

[79] C. Smit (1993): *Sanlam in die Rekenaareeu, 1953–1993*: 6–9.

[80] Report by USA actuaries, 1952, quoted in C. Smit (1993): *Sanlam in die Rekenaareeu, 1953–1993*: 13.

because around only 106 out of 249 punchcards were reliable storage units. Malan acknowledged that transferring records from the punchcards to the computer's magnetic tapes took much longer, partly because the employees were not fully up to the task. A stronger reliance on the actuarial staff was proposed. The task remained an absolute priority and by late 1959 it was feared that the actuarial records might be too late for the release of the 1959 annual report. The 1959 annual valuation reports were subsequently only produced in October 1959. In the following year the annual valuation reports were only released in December 1960—two months later than the release date of the 1959 reports. By 1961, back-up procedures were adapted to suit the mass of Sanlam policyholder records, to the extent that when South Africa introduced decimalization in 1961,[81] the Sanlam computer was able to effect the migration to the decimal system. In 1962 the annual valuation programmes were run without punchcard data for the first time.

As with the entire Sanlam venture, the success of the ground-breaking transition to computer-based records and processing depended on human capital. Late in 1959, Carl Smit, Assistant Secretary (actuarial), was seconded to assist with the rounding-off of the 1959 valuation reports. Smit remained in the Sanlam computer department for thirty years, performing a key role in subsequent computer systems development in in the company. Management transferred more staff members from the actuarial department as well as the pensions division to the computer systems division in 1960. The complexities of decimalization, daily updates, cash renewals, and policy debt were finally resolved by September 1962. This was noteworthy, because Sanlam achieved the transition to the new computer by relying on its own staff, who adapted the systems to the needs of the company. Savings amounting to around £24 000 per annum as had been envisaged in 1957, were exceeded by 1962. All administrative functions were fully computerised by September 1962, enabling the daily performance of those functions electronically from then on.

But the 1960 world of computers was fast-moving. The company leased an IBM 1401 computer towards the end of 1962 as it needed more capacity. In 1964 the second-generation IBM 360 computer was purchased, followed by the third-generation upgrade, the IBM360/40, in October 1967. While waiting for the delivery of the 360/40 Sanlam systems engineers prepared an innovative integrated system to suit the Sanlam needs. The integrated system included a comprehensive membership data register, including address reconciliation, and a debit-order system, as well as an integrated policyholder system that included more than fifteen main and subsystems. The main policy system was supplemented by subsystems for new policies, area codes, renewal of policies, bonus

[81] Decimalization was introduced in South Africa in 1961. The South African currency was changed from the British Pound Sterling to the South African Rand, consisting of R1 = 100 cents, and £1 was exchanged for R2.00. All measurements were also changed from feet and inches to metric measures of millimetres, centimetres, etc., and liquids from gallons and pints to litres.

certificates, and internally linked policies. Additional systems were developed for commission payments, cash bonus payments, and Sanlam Trust-linked annuities. In February 1968 the first premiums were collected by debit order. Sanlam paved the way for the first 'electronic funds transfer' (EFT) transactions in South Africa and offered its guide to procedures for the implementation of a debit order system, since it was only a matter of time before the banks would have to follow suit. The security of the IBM computer did not fully comply with Sanlam's requirements. Once tasks on magnetic tapes were completed, the computer had to be stopped and restarted, causing the congestion of awaiting tasks. The Sanlam systems engineers then developed an innovation to secure automatic resumption of subsequent tasks. They introduced the so-called 'pumpkin card', an orange-coloured card placed at the end of each task. Once the computer recognized the pumpkin card it signalled the completion of one task, triggering the automatic commencement of the next. This innovation was called the Sanlam MONITOR system, which was later adapted to store different programmes utilized by the computer, a recognition system identifying the type of paper required for the printing of specified notices and documents. Further systems for delayed annuity payments, mortgages, rentals (of property), and the administration of shares were also developed and in operation by the end of the first decade of Sanlam's computerization.[82] In just ten years a firm foundation had been laid. The significance of this was that Sanlam was a leader in the assurance industry in South Africa.

As the leader in the computerization of the life insurance industry in South Africa, Sanlam had access to human capabilities from its own ranks. Johan de Wit took the managerial responsibility as General Manager of computer systems in 1962. He was assisted by systems project leaders Jan Pretorius and Dirk de Bruyn, and Wallace van Wyk, an administrative clerk in the actuarial department, who later took up the responsibility for technical assistance and staff training in the computer department. The systems development was completed by Dirk de Bruyn and Apie Meyer as systems analysts. Management was visionary in establishing a department of Automation and Mechanization (A&M). De Bruyn headed up A&M and investigated the computerization needs in different Head Office divisions, documenting and advising strategies to integrate those requirements into computer capacity. H.S. (Cassie) Carstens, the first Sanlam bursary holder, joined the computer systems team and was involved in the development of the three generations of computers at Sanlam. By 1965 he witnessed new applications, transactions, and enquiries processed during the course of a working day, being integrated with existing policy records immediately. Jan van Rooyen, Jurgens de Kock, Japie Cloete, and Theuns Pienaar all contributed to the foundation of the Sanlam computer establishment decade. Except for van Rooyen they were all experienced

[82] C. Smit (1993): *Sanlam in die rekenaareeu*: 38–9; 45.

employees from the valuations section of the actuarial department, who moved to Sanlam's systems and there contributed to the computer innovation of the company.

With the rapid expansion of computer capacity and of the Sanlam policyholder base, the company started to decentralize its computer system. A new IBM 370 computer enabled decentralized terminal networks using typing terminals, mini-computers, and personal computers operating on the central company network. New products, expanded product offerings, and the extended application of computerized routines in the daily operations at Sanlam Head Office paved the way for a permanent formal organization of the company's computer capacity. Two permanent structures were established. The first was a computer bureau, later called Multidata. This bureau was a subsidiary of Sanlam, established to sell its computer services outside the company. The other was the Electronic Data Processing Committee (EDP) in Sanlam. It consisted of H.A. Peters as chairman, J.H. de Wit, Managing Director of Multidata, J.H. Söhnge, H.T. Kriel and C.J. Smit. These men were part of the Sanlam management team. EDP and Multidata operated in tandem to ensure systematic progress in Sanlam of the computer systems planning and implementation, while Multidata delivered the same services to other companies within the Sanlam Group or associated companies, such as FVB, Bonuskor, and Sanmed.

By the mid-1980s the integrated systems solutions developed in Sanlam facilitated ongoing implementation of new systems to support product development and functional diversification. Systems management responded to the A&M proposals based on ongoing identification of company needs. The Sanlam systems department engaged in continuous research and development and kept a close eye on international developments. In 1972, Sanlam subjected its systems department to a voluntary international audit by the Diebold Organization, a USA-based computer consultancy and education organization. Sanlam's systems department was applauded for its innovative work and applications introduced to the local hardware, but these added nothing new to the knowledge of the Sanlam staff. The value was rather in the open communication between the specialists in computer systems and the users of the technology. Sanlam was subsequently invited to become a member of the Diebold Research Programme. This was in recognition of the expertise accumulated in Sanlam and afforded the company staff access to ongoing international contact, conferences, and research output, which enhanced the application and innovation in Sanlam.[83] These developments were incorporated directly into staff training. By the end of the 1970s a staff complement of seventy was engaged in the Sanlam systems division. The mid-1970s domestic unrest and subsequent state of emergency alerted the systems division to the potential security risks involved in its operations. Within three months a new secure underground location

[83] Ibid., 92–3.

was prepared to accommodate the Sanlam computer and related equipment. It was anticipated that South Africa might suffer international pressure capable of closing down access to new equipment. Additional security procedures were introduced to protect Sanlam's data.

Innovation in financial services

As computer technology completely overhauled Sanlam's administrative efficiencies, the door was opened to new products to support the growth vision of the company. Wassenaar placed strong emphasis on the opportunity of riding the wave of the stock market. Internationally the development of innovative life products was not typical of the industry. According to Clark, product innovation in the life industry was constrained due to the tense relationship between 'prudence and speculation'.[84] The most important innovation was structural—insurance companies increasingly became composite companies offering different classes of insurance. These companies expanded operations over such vast geographical areas that branches constituted the logical way of organizing extensive operations.[85] Life offices were more innovative in their investment policies.[86] Only in the late twentieth century did the life offices start to develop investment products, which responded to the demand for more sophisticated wealth products and subsequently undermined demand for ordinary life insurance.[87] The South African life industry was only partially similar to the international experience. The competitive market stimulated product innovation to secure market position and respond to client needs much earlier. In the robust South African competitive environment after 1945 and with the benefit of advanced systems developed in-house, Sanlam wanted to encourage investment in improved yield-bearing savings products. As interest rates dropped significantly after the 1969 stock market crash, yields in investments stagnated. The only type of product that offered protection against the decrease in inflation was 'with-profits' policies, but these were still subject to the statutory investment restrictions and policies of the life insurance company. A further limitation was that life companies did not value their assets at market value, thereby restricting their ability to pass on capital profits.[88] There were few

[84] G. Clark, *Betting on lives: The culture of life insurance in England, 1695–1775*. Manchester University Press, Manchester, 1999.

[85] D. Jenkins & T. Yoneyama (2000): *History of Insurance*, pp..33–6; T. Alborn & S. Murphy (2013): *Anglo-American Life Insurance*.

[86] R.E. Wright & G.D. Smith: *Mutually beneficial: The Guardian and life insurance in America*. New York: New York University Press, 2004, pp. 351–5.

[87] J.D. Cummins & B. Venard: *Handbook of International Insurance*. New York: Springer, 2007.

[88] K. Romain (1989): *Larger than Life: Donald Gordon and the Liberty Life story*. Johannesburg: Jonathan Ball: 129.

investment options available to consumers at the time, and life policies still dominated the market. The products with more investment features were endowment policies, which had an investment component. However, such policies were not yielding the inflation-beating returns needed and did not provide much liquidity. Investors were bound until maturity to realize the product.[89] In the early 1970s with the rising popularity of with-profits policies, and after the introduction of unit trusts, policies linked to performance of share portfolios started to take the lead in the market.[90]

If a life insurance company wanted to survive it had to adapt to the changing market needs by proving wealth products generating higher returns.[91] Sanlam was in great need of products that could make savings profitable again. By releasing itself from the regulatory burden imposed by the life insurance and pension fund legislation, this could be achieved. In 1969, referring to Sanlam, Wassenaar used the words 'Sanlam, group of financial services' for the first time.[92] He referred to 'adaption' in reference to the adaptation of products to suit the changing circumstances and the greater demand for growth.[93]

One strategy was to develop new group life insurance schemes for a variety of occupational entities, such as professions and companies. Sanlam had established a total of sixteen group life schemes[94] between 1954 and 1959.[95] Another strategy was to innovate in pension provision. In 1959 Sanlam introduced the first retirement annuity policy in South Africa.[96] After the promulgation of the Pension Funds Act No. 24 of 1956 there was a proliferation of pension funds. However, individual private participation towards retirement did not yet exist. Individuals either did not save at all (this meant there was a reliance on the state or family support), or engaged in personal savings and life insurance. The passing of the Income Tax Act No. 58 of 1960 subsequently allowed for the establishment of retirement annuity funds (commonly known as RAs) to enable private individuals to provide for their retirement with the help of a tax saving.

To protect the advantage it had secured in the retirement annuity market, Sanlam made a special arrangement with the Postmaster General to grant Sanlam a business reply service immediately after the Minister's tax rebate announcement. Sanlam prepared and

[89] Interview Ronnie Masson. [90] *Finance Week*, 14/3/1993: 18.

[91] SA: Sanlam Annual Report; Chairman's Address: 11. [92] Ibid., 6. [93] Ibid., 9.

[94] SA: 1/2/1/3/3/Vol. 30, *Group insurance: Rate Books*, 1954, 1967, 1974.

[95] Hospital Employees—1/10/58; Prison Services Employees—1/12/58; Municipal Employees—1/6/59; Teachers—1/5/54; Post Office Employees under trusteeship of the Afrikaans Language and Cultural Society (ATKV)—1/9/58; Salaried staff of the South African Railways & Harbours (SAR&H)—1/2/59; SAR&H Employees' Union—1/3/59; SAR Police Staff Association—1/11/58; SAR&H Running and Operational Staff Association—1/4/59; Public Servants' Association—1/7/58; Iron and Steel Corporation of South Africa (ISCOR)—1/7/59; Iron and Steel Allied Industries Union—1/9/59; South African Police—1/12/58; Professional Provident Society (PPS)—1/11/58; South African Army Scheme Fund (Scheme 1)—1/6/57; South African Air Force Fund—1/7/58; South African Navy Fund Scheme—1/5/58.

[96] Sanlam Product List, August 2013.

mailed letters to existing policyholders, informing them of the new tax rebate and inviting them to take up retirement annuities with the company. The leave of Head Office staff was cancelled for the period immediately following the Minister's announcement to secure a full complement able to capitalize on its existing advantage in the market.[97] Competitors followed Sanlam. The company soon added additional investment options to its retirement annuities, such as investments in unit trusts, the new investment vehicle of the mid-1960s.[98]

This development pointed to two important trends in society: higher levels of income and a growing investment orientation among policyholders, since retirement annuities were primarily investment products.[99] Sanlam identified an opportunity to take advantage of the strong growth in the economy (real national income rose by 8.7 per cent per annum between 1948 and 1961), the post-war demand for retirement provision, and the higher standard of living of the South African population, including Afrikaners. Sadie estimated that by the early 1960s Afrikaners' personal income as a ratio of that of English-speaking South Africans had increased from 47.6:100 in 1946 to 64.6:100 in 1960 and 69.9:100 in 1970.[100] When the Minister of Finance finally announced a tax concession in June 1960 (to a maximum of £300) to self-employed persons for contributions towards their own 'pension schemes', Sanlam established the Central Retirement Annuity Fund (CRAF), an open general retirement annuity fund. The CRAF was soon marketed to a much wider client base on the back of the new tax concession.[101] Sanlam used this product to target what it came to refer to as the 'senior market', that is the high-income market. This target market was professional people, self-employed people, and any investment-conscious person wanting to add enhanced retirement provision to existing pension provisions. It also included persons belonging to provident funds, to whom the tax concession was not extended.[102] As underwriter to the Professional Provident Society (PPS) retirement annuities for professional persons, Sanlam had them in mind.

The ordinary life, endowment, and annuity products remained operational in a very competitive life market. Sanlam had to innovate and think in a radically different way about product offerings. New products were developed by the actuarial department, where Sanlam employed many of the bright young minds the company had supported

[97] SA: 1/2/1/6, Letter J.A. Vorster–Field staff, 6/5/60.

[98] SA: 1/2/1/3/4, Special tariffs: Memorandum, 22/8/67.

[99] RAs contained two risks: firstly that of early death, when the full RA was payable to the policyholder, and secondly, longevity, where the policyholder's contribution extended beyond the period initially anticipated by the policyholder.

[100] J.L. Sadie, *The Fall and Rise of the Afrikaner in the South Africa Economy*. Stellenbosch Annals 2002/1, p. 56.

[101] SA: 1/2/1/3/4, Special Tariffs, 9/5/67.

[102] SA: 1/2/1/6, Senior Market Development, 12/6/1960.

with bursaries to study actuarial science and statistics.[103] Three disadvantages existed for life insurance policies by the late 1960s. The ordinary life insurance policies lacked the ability to beat inflation, participate in broader economic investment opportunities, or participate immediately in the growth of assets. Owing to the steady rise in inflation, life insurance was constrained by investment regulations and long-standing conservative internal investment policies, both limiting the returns that life funds could earn. Furthermore, Sanlam found that the market did not necessarily want to share in the past economic growth of South Africa, but rather wanted to invest in newly established companies. Lastly, traditionally, only participating policies would share in the profit of a life insurer as well as in the growth of the insurer's assets. The market felt that these forms of returns, which were mainly passed on to the policyholder by means of a bonus, were limited by the fact that the bonuses were only realized at maturity. When a bonus was declared it was added to the policy value attributable to the policyholder and would be paid out when the policy matured or at the death of the insured. Sanlam realized that the public wanted a means of immediate participation.

What was needed was more aggressive investing that could be liquid enough to adjust to the fast-changing investment environment. This could maximize opportunity wherever it arose, providing the policyholder with more active participation in the economic growth of South Africa. Such an investment policy should be capable of beating inflation. Sanlam responded to this with the introduction of the 100-Plus series of policies on 20 May 1969. These policies had the following characteristics: maximum exposure to growth-intensive assets by investing the net premium (net coverage after the cost of life cover and administration) in a fund that formed part of Sanlam's total assets, but was separately accounted for, so that each policyholder's share in its growth could be calculated. The fund would be limited in its investment scope only by the Insurance Act and thus would be able to make adjustments to its exposure to the best opportunities identified. Policyholders shared in the investment gains as they arose. This was achieved by the 'sophisticated' use of Sanlam's electronic computer. Sanlam could keep detailed records of each individual policyholder's contribution to the specific fund into which his or her premiums were channeled. A full range of policies was made available, including life insurance, endowment, retirement annuities, and child and savings policies. The asset bonus could not be negative. There was a guaranteed sum assured that would be paid, irrespective of what happened to the valuation of the assets in the stock market in which he or she was invested.[104]

[103] SA: B23: Memorandum to Sanlam Board, 25/10/1955: Bursaries to students in mathematics; Memorandum to Sanlam Board, 17/8/1962: Bursaries to matriculants. Mr M.H. Daling, later the CEO of Sanlam, was a recipient of a Sanlam bursary and qualified as an actuary at the University of Pretoria. So was Mr D.K. Smith, later CEO and Chairman of the board of Sanlam.

[104] SA: 1/2/1: Product development: Sanlam 100-Plus Policy document.

The 100-Plus policy range, introduced on 20 May 1969,[105] offered an investment opportunity in response to the changes in the market. A portion of the 100-Plus fund was invested in government securities, prescribed investments, and in cash deposits. The main reason for the 100-Plus policies, or internally linked policies instead of the unit trust-linked policies, was to allow for the changing prescribed asset requirements. With external linkage the proportion of prescribed assets could not be changed easily, whereas it was easy with an internal fund.[106] This combination changed as interest rate fluctuations determined the choice of alternative investment products. There were also three variations of the pension and provident fund offerings linked to the 100-Plus policies, namely the 100-Plus Guaranteed Portfolio, the 100-Plus Special Portfolio, and the 100-Plus Unique Portfolio. The difference in these portfolios depended on the degree to which the trustees would be involved. The 100-Plus Special Portfolio allowed the trustees to participate in the strategic decisions on the portfolio asset allocation such as moving the portfolio to a higher weighting in anticipation of an upcoming market movement. However, the 100-Plus Unique Portfolio offered the trustees full decision-making participation. Investments of R8 million were placed in the 100-Plus series within the first month on offer.[107] Within three and a half years of the introduction of the 100-Plus series, Sanlam raised the value of every R100 invested to R111.50 for the funds where no tax provision were required.[108] Longevity means success, and the 100-Plus policy series remained in force until the late 1990s.

At the *Pensioenmakelaars* (pension brokers) conference in 1977, Marinus Daling (an assistant manager, later to head up Sankorp as well as Sanlam) proposed that by investing the cash flows received by retirement funds (and probably provident funds too) into new assets rather than in the 'current portfolio', investors could increase the return yield on new cash flows by between 10.6 per cent and 12.25 per cent. Investing in existing portfolios resulted in all participants receiving similar yields, irrespective of the timing when the cash flows were invested. At that time (1977) the average return on the investment portfolios of the five largest life mutual companies in South Africa (within a particular class that was unspecified) was 10.6 per cent. Daling argued, 'we (Sanlam) think it's only fair that each participant should receive a return more or less matching the investment conditions that prevailed at the time that the investment was made.'[109]

[105] SA: 1/2/1: *Product Development A 101*, August 1970.

[106] Interview G. Rudman, 13/2/2010.

[107] SA: 1/2/1/2/1: Product Development: Notice, 17/11/70; *Cape Times*, 25/7/68.

[108] SA: 1/2/1/: Product Development Report, 11/2/1972.

[109] Sanlam Press release (1977): Sanlam has new investment plan for pension funds; Sanlam Annual Report, 1977: 2.

Subsequently, Sanlam developed investment products able to capture investment opportunities at the time of investment.

In 1977 Finplan was developed. It was a computer-assisted analysis service used by brokers and agents to calculate policyholders' current and future financial positions scientifically.[110] This analytical tool assisted agents in assessing the full financial profile of clients. In rolling out new investment products, Finplan proved a competitive advantage, especially as many new investment products were developed, which the agent could align with the client profile in an instant. As rapidly succeeding new investment products emerged, Finaplan proved to be successful and highly functional. In 1983 Sanlam again introduced three new investment-oriented products to offer policyholders such investment flexibility. Indexplan, launched in 1983, was a comprehensive insurance package designed to give the option to reinforce provisions for all eventualities (death, disability, or retirement and savings needs). It allowed for an automatic premium increase per annum to counter the effects of inflation. In June 1983 the Investment Series was launched to supplement the conventional series of policies. It included two options: one was the Sanlam Stable Investment Series, which fell in the category of conventional insurance with smoothed and largely vesting bonuses. The other was the Market Value Series, which was linked insurance that shared directly in the ups and downs of investment performance.[111] Seventy thousand units of the Investment Series were sold within the first year. Furthermore, building on the transparency offered by unit trusts, the Investment Series introduced the so-called 'transparent policies', which made clear disclosure of the separate elements of the policy—the life cover, rider benefits, and investment portion.

The next product offered was the 200-Plus Portfolio to address some of the limitations of the 100-Plus portfolios' investment scope. This was a unitized market value portfolio, with a scope of gilts, semi-gilts, equities, properties, and cash, where the unit price was declared monthly. The main difference between the two Plus portfolios was that the 100-Plus Portfolio had a moderate volatility profile, with a long-term focus, while the 200-Plus Portfolio was more volatile due to its pursuit of short-term investment opportunities. Because of this high risk/volatility profile of the 200-Plus Portfolio, Sanlam sold it as a complementary investment to the lower-risk pension and provident funds available. Unlike 100-Plus Portfolio, the 200-Plus portfolio was not constructed with a number of sub-portfolios.[112] The consistent innovation or adjustment to existing policies was indeed a contributing factor to the growth in Sanlam's premiums (see Table 3.1).

[110] SA: Sanlam 1/2/5: Product development: Finplan, 4/2/1977; Sanlam annual Report, 1977: 3; Sanlam (2010): *Sanlam: The IT journey from 1990 to 2014*: 12–14.

[111] Sanlam Annual Report, 1983: 6, 15.

[112] Sanlam Annual Report, 1990: 7.

Table 3.1. Sanlam performance, 1945–1985

Year	Premum Income £/R since 1961	% Growth	Assets £	Return on assets	Death and disability claims paid £ / R since 1961	Branches	Bonus rate	Admin cost £ / R since 1961
1945	1 888 766	29	9 394 751	3.35	215 186	9	2.0	209 961
1947	2 729 424	44	13 051 675	3.35	286 669	9	2.2.0	352 285
1949	3 451 377	26.4	17 784 699	3.6	428 412	9	2.2.0	411 551
1951	4 492 179	30.1	23 898 986	3.81	441 325	10	2.2.0	604 806
1953	6 053 322	34.7	32 901 535	3.94	633 021	11	2.4.0	887 095
1955	7 895 133	30.4	43 877 475	4.3	800 188	12	2.7.6	1 105 107
1957	10 156 622	28.6	57 698 736	4.65	1 239 960	15	2.7.6	1 482 765
1959	12 237 986	20.4	73 148 133	4.94	1 890 885	18	2.10.0	1 695 695
1961	29 206 757	19.52	179 684 662	4.97	4 766 000	21	2.5.0	4 420 596
1963	35 177 460	20.4	219 747 632	5.21	7 633 000	23	2.5	5 300 169
1965	43 644 000	24.1	270 572 449	5.38	10 404 293	26	2.65	9 576 885
1967	52 312 406	19.86	334 042 988	5.86	11 237 722	26	2.75	9 995 673
1969	64 896 980	24.2	421 403 355	6.2	14 853 433	30	27.5	11 981 779
1971	93 818 000	44.56	528 607 000	6.26	22 692 000	36	31.0	10 000 000
1973	143 925 000	53.4	701 867 000	6.25	26 909 000	38	31.0	14 000 000
1975	189 972 000	31.9	973 442 000	7.26	35 979 000	38	31.0	19 000 000
1977	259 940 000	36.8	1 349 981 000	7.95	49 800 000	43	33.0	22 000 000
1979	392 124 000	50.8	1 940 442 000	8.00	62 206 000	49	35.0	25 000 000
1981	644 744 000	64.4	3 072 848 000	9.54	96 318 000	52	37.5	43 000 000
1983	1 079 303 000	67.4	5 044 560 000	10.7	149 030 000	56	45.5	71 000000
1985	1 605 000 000	48.7	7 785 000 000	11.20	229 000 000	57	46.5	107 000 000

Source: Sanlam Annual Financial Statements, 1945–1985.

Health in Sanlam

A less successful initiative was health insurance. On 1 October 1939, Santam and Sanlam established the Santam/Sanlam Sick Fund, a closed medical scheme for employees, similar to what SA Mutual offered. When the Friendly Societies Act, No. 25 of 1956[113] came into effect, all medical schemes where members controlled the scheme, were required to register as mutual funds. Santam and Sanlam refused to register their fund, because they wanted direct control of the medical scheme. The Sanlam actuary, Hansman, approached the board in 1954 to consider a commercial approach to medical provision by means of medical insurance. Medical insurance policies would be issued by Sanlam, underwritten by the company, and thus controlled by the company. By June 1956 the National Medical Aid Society of South Africa (NMASA) was in trouble, having had only two solvent years since its establishment in 1949. The Sanlam board agreed to

[113] This act regulated the activities of all mutual aid societies, which included mutual societies formed to provide medical aid to members.

the concept of medical insurance and established a separate company, *Die Suid-Afrikaanse Nasionale Siekte- en Ongevalle Maatskappy* (SANSOM), on 29 March 1957. It was registered as an insurance company in April of the same year. The Board of Directors were all Sanlam managers, with Hansman as Managing Director. SANSOM then acquired the assets of NMASA even though Sanlam had not conducted a thorough due diligence of the latter. The scheme had around 20 000 members, thus it was a relatively large medical-aid society at the time, but the 'better risk' members did not move to the new SANSOM. Sanlam consequently acquired an unprofitable benefit structure, a very large variety of schemes, which the SA Medical Association (SAMA) refused to accredit, and exceptionally high administration costs.

As the Santam/Sanlam Sick Fund failed to get NMASA accreditation and preferential tariffs, it was not profitable. A request by AHT to join the Santam/Sanlam Sick Fund was turned down in 1945 and in 1960 Santam decided to establish a separate medical scheme for its own employees. This route to medical support placed Sanlam on a collision course with NMASA. The latter refused to grant the Sanlam in-house fund for employees, as well as SANSOM, access to preferential benefit tariffs because the schemes were not mutual funds managed by members. As long as medical insurance was managed as a commercial enterprise from which the owner of the policies could benefit, there would be no accreditation by NMASA. Sanlam paid itself dividends on the profits of the SANSOM business, which ensured that NMASA refused to include SANSOM members under preferential benefit tariffs. Members therefore did not have access to lower medical fees through a scheme accredited by NMASA. In 1968 the Sanlam in-house sick fund for employees finally closed its doors and employees were asked to join SANSOM.

Sanlam amended the SANSOM statutes to prohibit the payment of dividends to Sanlam. Subsequently, in March 1960, NMASA announced the accreditation of SANSOM for preferred benefit tariffs on condition that the number of schemes (options) available to members was reduced. Sanlam never succeeded in complying and NMASA accreditation was again withdrawn. Hansman, who had been appointed Managing Director of SANSOM, and Wassenaar failed to agree on a number of key elements of the medical business. SANSOM carried a heavy weight of the legacy of numerous options, ill-priced options, and a multitude of companies with in-house arrangements, which SANSOM accommodated without properly assessing the financial implications of the options available in each individual company (e.g. the SABC (South African Broadcasting Corporation) and the National Association of Local Governments had their own 'schemes' that were managed by SANSOM). The SANSOM offerings were simply never focused, correctly priced, or aligned with NMASA's preferred benefit tariffs. Members were always dissatisfied with being excluded from NMASA's preferred benefit tariffs. The Sanlam board twice categorically stated that SANSOM was subject to the authority and control of Sanlam, which indicated friction between the SANSOM management and

Sanlam. In August 1965 Hansman went on six months' leave and subsequently retired. In 1964 the SABC was the first of a number of members to announce the withdrawal of their employees from SANSOM. Sanlam actuaries consistently struggled to price the options of medical assistance in the SANSOM scheme correctly: tariffs were based on medical association preferred benefit tariffs, but premiums were too low. Failing to mend the one, Sanlam again established a new medical-aid vehicle in 1965: The South African Medical Fund Limited (Sanmed).

Sanmed was Sanlam's most successful medical insurance enterprise. From 1965 to 2000 membership grew to more than 140 000. Sanmed was a medical fund, but since it was denied registration as a mutual medical scheme, Sanlam again changed the statutes to prohibit the payment of dividends to the shareholder in an attempt to qualify for preferential benefit tariffs. Sanmed offered two schemes: Topmed, based on benefits equal to 100 per cent of NMASA benefit tariffs, and Helpmed, based on 80 per cent of NMASA benefit tariffs. Sanmed remained firmly under Sanlam control. Management improved the administration of the scheme to one of the best in the country, especially by linking it to the advanced Sanlam computer system. Administrative costs were reduced to less than 9 per cent of premiums and reserves in excess of 25 per cent were accumulated. The scheme was opened to black people in 1973, and in 1977 two separate schemes were established for Coloured people (Belmed) and black people (Bonmed). A new scheme was registered for Namibian members (Swamed) in 1980. Sanmed's management maintained good relations with the SA Association of Medical Aid Schemes (SAMAS). From 1968 Sanmed representatives served on SAMAS until the retirement of Sanmed's Managing Director, Nick du Preez in 1997. In 1979 Sanmed became a member of the International Federation of Voluntary Health Service Funds. Operational efficiency was underpinned by the computerized systems support of operations, which secured swift and efficient processing of claims. Despite Sanmed being a medical insurance product, benefits offered were based on SAMAS preferred benefit tariffs. The fine reputation of Sanmed as a voluntary medical insurance scheme ensured growing support. An increasing number of individual companies decided to close their in-house medical provision schemes in favour of Sanmed policies. Santam finally terminated its in-house scheme in 1980, resulting in more than 1 200 Santam employees joining Topmed. So did the employees of Nissan in 1985.

By 1985 Sanmed managed premium income of R95 million for 90 001 members. Benefits paid out in 1985 amounted to R91 million and reserves stood at R24 million. The value of the successful management of Sanmed was the growing public exposure to the broad Sanlam product offering. The trend in medical schemes was already moving closer to the professional administration of individual schemes, rather than the management of very large schemes. Medscheme had been in the management market since 1968, but Sanlam was not interested in medical scheme administration despite repeated advice to the board. Sanlam wanted control. Sanlam understood insurance policies and was comfortable with providing medical assistance to policyholders. However, the medical-aid landscape was changing and in the post-1985 period Sanlam's fortunes in this industry took a turn for the worse.

Growing Sanlam

New product offerings and employee benefits were the tools in the hands of the Sanlam agents to grow the market. The English press acknowledged the growth of the company towards the late 1950s and early 1960s. In 1959, Carel Birkby commented in the *Sunday Times* on the FVB £1 million rights issue as 'focusing attention on a healthy new development in the South African financial world—the rapid advance of Afrikaners into business. This expansion is warmly welcomed on all sides.'[114] In a supplement to *The Manufacturer* in 1961 specific mention was made of the sound investment returns earned by the Sanlam policyholders, but also that additional capital was made available to numerous and varied private and public enterprises.[115] While this recognition of the expanding Afrikaner business interests was welcomed, Sanlam's market penetration was coming under increasing pressure towards the late 1960s. At the beginning of the post-war period Sanlam's premium income was 16.28 per cent of total premiums of the domestic life industry. It increased to 17.7 per cent in 1950 and 28.04 per cent in 1961, but then contracted to 21.7 per cent in 1971. By 1972 the new life office in the market, Liberty Life, had achieved an overall third position. Management was concerned about agents' productivity and the high lapse rate. The very competitive market made for the development of additional distribution channels. Sanlam's competitor, SA Mutual, had contracted bank brokers since 1966 to attract business, but Sanlam's management was sceptical.

By the late 1960s Sanlam was convinced of the superiority of its agent training programmes, but agent retention remained problematic. Persistent problems with a high turnover of agents, ethical problems in agent conduct, and low productivity led to a conscious agent training strategy. The beloved and respected Jan Feenstra retired in December 1946. He was succeeded in 1948 by Bill Bezuidenhout as Manager: Agents under the new General Manager A.D. Wassenaar.[116] Wassenaar took a strategic view on distribution. He returned from a business trip to the USA in 1950 and immediately requested the board to send an official for a six-month training programme at *Mutual Life Insurance Company of New York*. Wassenaar was acutely aware of the fact that Sanlam was losing agents at an alarming rate. The Deputy Manager: Agent Affairs,

[114] *Sunday Times*: 18/10/1959: 'Afrikaner "Big Business" grows by £23m a year'.

[115] *The Manufacturer*, Supplement, July 1961: 5.

[116] *Die Fakkel*, October 1948: 3.

P.G. (Pally) du Plessis, was sent to the USA between April and October 1950. In 1955 Sanlam appointed as many agents in total as during 1949, but 50 per cent of the new appointees left the company within the first six months. In 1958 Bezuidenhout submitted a memorandum to the board concerning the recruitment of agents and the frequent resignations.[117] Wassenaar himself lamented in 1960 that Sanlam employed eight fewer agents that year than in 1959.[118] Comparing the Sanlam experience with the USA one brought some comfort, since the USA statistics showed that those companies retained only 57 per cent of their 'inexperienced finance agents' after the first six months of employment, while their 'first-year survival rate' was only 50 per cent.

Sanlam then restructured its agent training programme. Bill Bezuidenhout retired in 1959 and was succeeded by Pally du Plessis, then Assistant General Manager: Production. Following the advice of Dr Rains Wallace, research director at the Life Assurance Management Association, Sanlam introduced aptitude tests for new recruits. These were conducted in collaboration with the National Institute for Personnel Research from 1962, but by 1966 Du Plessis could not confirm that the aptitude tests had had any significant impact on agents' resignations. Sanlam subsequently introduced competitions and additional incentives to encourage improved production, but Du Plessis had to admit that the training of new recruits had not involved much more than the handing over of a tariff book and stationery while the inspector explained how to use the tables in the tariff book. The disturbing trend of agents' resignations by the late 1960s turned the focus of management back to six operational aspects of agent training. The company wanted a better co-ordinated training programme, more knowledge on estate planning and business insurance to be incorporated in agent training, more innovative products to compete in the market, and superior training to curb policy lapses by an enhanced selection process to match the right policy to the right person.[119] At Head Office a new department of Marketing Promotion was established in 1963. Mr Hennie Rossouw, Production Manager: Agent Affairs was given the task of compiling the most extensive training manual in Sanlam to date. It consisted of eight manuals—four to be completed through self-study, reporting the progress of the prospective agent to the area or regional manager. Once the candidate was familiar with the material, a written test was conducted, in which 95 per cent was a pass. Then followed a final training clinic and the induction to a branch or region. The new recruit was then handed manuals five to eight, which dealt in depth with financial institutions (commercial banks, other financial

[117] SA: Memorandum on Organization to Sanlam Board: B25: Bemarking—Algemeen en Bevorderings, 1944–1962.

[118] SA: Memorandum on Organization to Sanlam Board: B25: Bemarking—Algemeen en Bevorderings, 1944–1962.

[119] SA: Agents' Bulletin, 11/07/1969: 5.

institutions, the South African Reserve Bank) and finally extensive guidelines on the promotion of sales. The guiding motto of the manual was 'We at Sanlam do not sell products, we serve clients' needs.'[120]

The agent-guided training programme was an industry leader and led to sustained high-level training of agents in Sanlam. In the annual report on agency matters Mr A.J. (Jack) van Wyk,[121] Assistant Manager: Production, reported that in 1965, Sanlam had retained 57 per cent of the new appointees after twelve months, compared to the industry average of 32 per cent in South Africa. In 1969 this ratio had risen to 60 per cent for Sanlam and 37 per cent for the country, and by 1973 Sanlam secured a 63 per cent retention rate compared to 38 per cent in the entire industry.[122] Wassenaar insisted on measuring the Sanlam agents against the best internationally. In 1960 Sanlam entered the International Quality Award of the Life Insurance Agency Management Association. The aim of this award was to reward agents with the highest policy retention rate—90 per cent or above. In the first year of the award, based on production of 1958 and 1959, Sanlam had sixty-eight qualifying agents. The Life Insurance Agency Management Association Newsletter reported in 1961: 'Last year 221 qualifiers from outside the United States and Canada were awarded IQA certificates. These salesmen represented 16 companies and were located in 13 countries. Among the companies with high representation of qualifiers were the South African National Life Association in South Africa with 70 agents qualifying and Sumimoto Mutual Life in Osaka, Japan, which had 40 qualifiers.'[123] In 1967 Sanlam had 183 qualifiers in the International Quality Awards and fourteen agents had qualified every year since the inception of the award.[124] By 1985 the total number of Sanlam agents who had qualified for the award stood at 465.[125]

Improving the quality of agents through a more rigorous training programme began to bear fruit, but the company was still concerned about the high lapse rate. In 1962, 32 per cent of policies were allowed to lapse in the first year, and 9.1 per cent in the second year. The total lapse rate of policies during the first two years remained above 30 per cent up to 1964, then it dropped gradually and by 1974 had declined to 26 per cent.[126] Management put this performance down to inadequate motivation among agents and in 1971 called in personnel consultants to conduct courses in Achievement Orientation for its agents. The outcome was utterly disappointing: the best-performing agents' average gross commission earned for seven to twelve months after the course declined by 9.57 per cent and the poor-performing agents' average gross

[120] SA: 1/2/4/3: Sanlam Opleidingsgids vir Verteenwoordigers, 1970.
[121] Jack van Wyk succeeded Pally du Plessis as head of agents on 1 January 1968
[122] SA: Appendices to Sanlam Board Minutes, 17/2/1971; 18/3/1975.
[123] SA: *Die Fakkel*, July 1961: 11. [124] SA: *Die Fakkel*, 18/6/1965:1; 8/3/1967: 21.
[125] SA: 6/5/1: Chairman's Address to Annual General Meeting 19/03/1986: 13.
[126] SA: Minutes of Board Meeting, 8/5/1975: addendum on policy retention.

commission earned increased by only 9.09 per cent.[127] In a submission to the board on 15 May 1974, Jack van Wyk, who later became General Manager: Marketing, after Pally du Plessis retired in 1967, insisted on more dedicated training of agents through the appointment of full-time training staff.[128] The board agreed to an increased budget allocation for training and further restructuring of the extensive Sanlam training programme. This step was actually induced by the growing competition by brokers in the life market. Since 1966, other life companies had linked their sales strategies to brokers. Sanlam management was very careful not to allow inexperienced outsiders to market their products, but it was soon apparent that brokerage business had become an industry trend. Sanlam had to either get on board or fall behind.

By 1967 the market signals could no longer be ignored. Pally du Plessis and Wassenaar held long and penetrating discussions with Trust Bank's Managing Director and General Manager about the possibility of accrediting Trust Bank as brokers to Sanlam. Du Plessis convinced the Board of the wisdom of entering brokerage marketing, but it was realized that the agent network might not respond positively towards this move. The positive side of the decision was that Sanlam had maintained close relationships with Trust Bank and a further broker agreement would cement this relationship and perhaps secure Sanlam a steadier stream of business from the bank. It was finally a matter of growing market penetration and brokers had already made inroads in the distribution channel. Sanlam would simply be burying its head in the sand if this reality was overlooked. Jack van Wyk, the new Assistant General Manager: Production (from 1 January 1968), took a pragmatic business stance: he was not impressed by the 1968 brokers' production statistics, but when confronted by agents' displeasure about the direct competition by brokers, he stated that Sanlam was not an employment organization, but a life insurance company. If the interests of agents clashed with those of the company, the latter took precedence. Van Wyk therefore requested authorization for the appointment of broker consultants to canvas new business for Sanlam from brokers.[129] The decision by the board in December 1968 to appoint these consultants was a strategic shift in the traditional distribution channel. Broker consultants were located in branches and reported to agency management. The first two broker consultants appointed in November 1969 were Gerhard van Weesel in Durban and Piet van der Vliet in Cape Town. Annual reports to the board on the production by brokers showed a significant rise in the contribution by broker sales. In 1969 brokers contributed just under 6 per cent of total new sales in Sanlam. This ratio increased to 13 per cent in 1975.[130] Jack van Wyk had fully bought into the concept of broker sales. When he was

[127] SA: Report by D.C. van der Merwe: 'n Ondersoek na die invloed van 'n 'Prestasie-oriëntasiekursus' op die verteenwoordigers van 'n lewensversekeringsmaatskappy: 90.

[128] SA: Minutes of Board meeting, 15/5/1974. [129] SA: Minutes of Board Meeting, 17/4/1968.

[130] SA: Minutes of Board meetings, 18/3/1970; 18/2/1976.

threatened by leading Sanlam agents with resignation because they wanted to join the brokers, Van Wyk introduced volume-linked bonuses (*Kwantum Opslag bonusse*) for top-performing agents to keep them in the network. The loyal Sanlam agents remained a strong distribution network for the company. One agent, S.J. (Fanie) du Preez from Port Elizabeth, was Agent of the Year for thirteen years, starting in 1971. Between 1975 and 1984 he received the Gold Eagle award for agents exceeding a million units in policy sales, which gave him the highest cumulative earnings of all the agents. He achieved this performance within a period of six years, whereas no other agent had succeeded in achieving that exceptional goal in less than eleven years. Du Preez epitomized the Sanlam agent maintaining his direct relationship with the company in the wake of the sprawling broker business.[131] A new dynamic was occurring in the market and Sanlam was benefiting from both the broker initiative and ambitious agents competing to sustain their market position.

In April 1975 Sanlam appointed its head of product development, the actuary Desmond Smith, to head up sales development via brokers—only to be relieved of product development and assigned Manager: Broker Division later that year.[132] Smith had serious catching up to do, as SA Mutual had had a dedicated broker sales division in operation since 1967. Sanlam was the last life office to engage actively with the broker distribution channel. (In 1971 there were celebrations in Sanlam when the company's total premium income exceeded that of SA Mutual for the first time, but SA Mutual had turned the tables again by 1976.) Van Wyk was skeptical of the longevity of brokers in the market. He warned that regulatory intervention would cap commission to brokers and finally lead to their demise. In 1975 the Life Offices' Association (LOA) members discussed the 'Equivalence of Reward' principle, a maximum scale of commission payable to brokers. These negotiations failed to reach consensus and life offices continued to offer incentives such as bonuses on high sales volumes, which undermined the LOA attempts at reaching agreement on the matter.[133] The perpetual competition with SA Mutual and Sanlam's drive to grow market share simply meant that the latter had to address the new distribution channel strategically. Sanlam's late entry into the broker market mandated seeking measures to control the level of competition. Smith had an excellent feel for client demand, the requirements of product design, and market pressure. His standing in the industry was instrumental in directing the discussions in the LOA on the 'Equivalence of Reward' proposal. The life industry expected state intervention in the regulation of commission structures in the assurance market. The life offices had hoped that an agreement on the proposed Equivalence of Reward matter would secure industry control, but the non-adherence to the idea of prescribed commission was

[131] *Die Fakkel*, 24/9/1971; 21/11/1975; 8/01/1982; 18/01/1980; 6/1/1984.

[132] SA: *Fakkel*, 6/2/1976; 18/2/1976.

[133] SA: 7/5/1: LOA, Minutes of General Meeting, 6/12/1976.

bound to result in state action. In 1977 the Government Gazette No. 5426 of 1 March 1977, Regulation 28 par (3), stated explicitly that 'No registered insurer... shall pass or offer... to any independent intermediary... any consideration other than commission in monetary form.' Par (4) stated 'The value of such commission shall not exceed the values determined in accordance with the Schedule of this regulation.' This directive defined the formulae for commission payable to different categories of policies (retirement annuities, single-premium business, etc.). Desmond Smith was closely involved in the drafting of both the Equivalence of Reward draft proposal and Regulation 28. Of course, as the Registrar realized, in the end, compliance would depend on 'moral persuasion'.

In a market where competitors had early entrance advantage, it was important to Sanlam to secure some restraint to operational activity through agreements and institutional regulation. The playing field was more level, but the company gained confidence in moving forward on brokers following a survey on trends in client preference. In February 1978 Smith reported to the board that clients' preference for acquiring additional life insurance had changed significantly since 1975. The survey indicated that between 1974 and 1977 more than 10 per cent less persons had desired to purchase life cover, and Afrikaans males had displayed a 40 per cent smaller appetite for long-term life products. The encouraging result was that at 51 per cent Sanlam was still the preferred supplier of choice to higher-income Afrikaans males for future life products (ahead of SA Mutual at 37 per cent), although bank brokers had risen by 25 per cent in the popularity of intermediaries for the acquisition of long-term financial products.[134] This led the Sanlam management to authorize the immediate approval of computer-validated broker's commissions, which was a clear marketing advantage to brokers. Soon Sanlam increased senior management's focus on broker services. In 1978 the first Broker Services regional office was opened in Johannesburg and by 1982 more than 33 per cent of Sanlam's new sales arrived via the broker channel, but less than a quarter of all brokered sales came to Sanlam.[135] Despite a tendency of well-performing agents defecting to the brokers, Sanlam sustained a well-trained agency network alongside an expanding broker corps. By 1980 Sanlam's overall market share rose to 27 per cent. Broker personnel were included in the '*Komkamp*' national sales incentive for the first time in 1979. Brokers' average premium per policy exceeded that of agents and in 1982 five new Broker Services regional offices were opened—all staffed by Sanlam employees.[136] Hermie Laubscher, former Provincial Manager in the Cape, became Head of Broker Services in 1983 and invested heavily in USA best practice development training of brokers.[137] The strong

[134] SA: Minutes of board meeting, 15/2/1978.

[135] SA: Minutes of board meetings, 21/11/1979; 19/11/1980; 9/12/1981. *Die Fakkel*, 29/10/1982.

[136] SA: *Die Fakkel*, 6/11/1981.

[137] Laubscher introduced development training of brokers based on the Thomas Peters and Robert Waterman book *In Search of Excellence* (Peters & Waterman, 1982). The brokers received this training support from Sanlam, underlining the progressive approach to sales in Sanlam.

advance of brokers' sales of Sanlam products indicated growing broad confidence in the company. This unfortunately did not deliver a notable breakthrough for Sanlam into the English-speaking market. Its loyal agents, trained under rigid programmes aligned with international best practice, accepted the challenge of broker distribution. This development and Sanlam's response displayed confidence in its agent network. Sanlam entered a more strategic phase in its distribution history.

The company in the community

Growing Sanlam between 1945 and 1985 also entailed strengthening the social responsibility dimension of personal benefits on the macro level of society. Corporate social responsibility was one dimension of putting South Africa first. Sanlam set out to promote Afrikaner economic empowerment in the context of the wider South African society. While charity started 'at home' with personal loans to policyholders, interest-free loans for medical procedures, mortgages, and payment restructuring in case the policyholder was unable to contribute to regular premium payments, the company's employee benefit products were aimed at fostering self-help social security. To those in need, welfare contributions were forthcoming, but Sanlam's corporate social responsibility actions were first and foremost motivated by an empowerment drive, rather than welfare transmission. Assistance went first to Afrikaners, because their well-being was integral to that of the wider South African society. The company's focus started with its policyholder base, but as the profile of its policyholders changed, corporate social responsibility reflected that change.

The company did not have a distinct policy on corporate social responsibility in 1918. Donations were authorized from a personal budget allocated to the Chairman of the board. By the late 1960s the ad hoc donations approach made way for a more focused social empowerment policy. Applicants requiring assistance for their particular causes were expected to represent a nationwide constituency and not a limited sectional entity.[138] Sanlam responded to ad hoc applications, but the empowerment mission led to favouring education and the facilitation of learning. By the mid-1980s, three broad categories of social engagement emerged: education and training, cultural affairs, and welfare. In 1958 Wassenaar insisted that there had to be a direct financial interest for Sanlam, as well as the insurance industry, linked to the social responsibility engagements it supported.[139] Sanlam supported all South African universities as centres of education and empowerment. The closest institution to Sanlam was the alma mater

[138] SA: 5/3/2: Minutes of Board meeting, 23/1/1980.
[139] SA: 5/2/: D4: A.D. Wassenaar Memorandum, 1/12/1958.

of many Sanlam leaders and ordinary employees, the University of Stellenbosch. A steady stream of donations went to that University, especially to the Faculty of Commerce, the Bureau for Economic Research, the Faculty of Engineering, and towards the establishment of the medical school, but similar donations were made to the University of Pretoria for the establishment of its medical school. At the University of Cape Town, Sanlam supported cardiac and organ transplant research. As many Afrikaans-speaking students studied at English tuition universities, the company extended donations to all Afrikaans and English institutions in South Africa. Sanlam supported the dedicated university colleges for African peoples as well as the Coloured and Indian communities as a matter of principle.[140] The Universities of Pretoria and Stellenbosch received the highest allocation, and the rest of the institutions according to a formula based on student numbers. In 1968 this formula was replaced with support to universities linked to a 'strategic or psychological moment' at a particular institution for which funds were collected. Such an example was the construction of an auditorium at the Rand Afrikaans University, subsequently known as the Sanlam Auditorium, or specialist sporting facilities. Donations were made to the University of Fort Hare and the University of South Africa (UNISA) for the building of libraries.[141]

Apart from institutional funding Sanlam also extended support to students. These sponsorships were ultimately to serve the company's need for qualified staff, such as actuaries, accountants, managers, and computer experts, towards its empowerment strategy. Sanlam realized early in the 1950s that many capable and bright young minds on the *platteland* could not afford university studies. The company needed the human capital and subsequently developed a bursary scheme for top-performing scholars in mathematics. Sanlam sent officials to remote schools to identify such top performers. Three bursaries were offered annually for studies in Statistics, Actuarial Science, or Mathematics. Qualified graduates were then employed at Sanlam. Two well-known recipients of a Sanlam bursary were Desmond Smith and Marinus Daling. Smith hailed from the Transkei town Indwe, where his father was a bank manager. He was awarded a Sanlam bursary and enrolled at the University of Stellenbosch for a BSc degree in Mathematics and Applied Mathematics. At the end of his first year he was introduced to Actuarial Science. That became his passion and career at Sanlam where he progressed from the actuarial department, through various management positions to Managing Director between 1993 and 1998 and Chairman on the Board between 2010 and 2017.[142] Daling was from Nylstroom in the Northern Transvaal and matriculated in 1962. He completed his degree at the University of Pretoria and qualified as an actuary through

[140] SA: 5/2: D4A: Letter Wassenaar–Board, 20/2/1962.
[141] SA: 5/2/: D4B: Memorandum to Board, 17/7/1968.
[142] Sanlam Indaba: 1/9/1995: 8.

the Faculty of Actuaries.[143] Daling was the Chief Executive Officer of Sanlam between 1998 and 2001 and Chairman from 1993 until 2001. These bursaries were awarded to deserving bright scholars from both Afrikaans- and English-speaking backgrounds and were perhaps the most important empowerment tool towards addressing widespread poverty. It was largely the non-urban origins of many Sanlam employees that convinced management of the wisdom of a company village, Sanlamhof, as it was later known. This university bursary scheme was later extended to existing staff.

As Sanlam advanced with computerization, a growing appetite developed for people with advanced qualifications in quantitative disciplines. A stern memorandum to the Board in 1962 called for the appointment of fewer staff members assigned to routine administrative functions and more 'quality people capable of managerial decision making'.[144] Sanlam had developed a need for highly qualified human capital in a growing number of specialized departments of its operations. This offered a natural way of eradicating poverty among Afrikaners and gain from high-quality human capital. Apart from its own bursary schemes, Sanlam also contributed regularly to the *Helpmekaar Studiefonds* (a study fund established from the surplus funds after the *Helpmekaar* had paid rebel fines),[145] through general education and training.

From bursaries towards university study, Sanlam identified a need for financial support to poor children simply to complete school. The company established a bursary scheme for deserving scholars to write the Standard 8 examinations and the final matriculation examination in Standard 10. A survey by the *Afrikaanse Christen Vroue-vereniging* (ACVV) revealed the dire needs in the Cape Province. Similar needs were reported by the women's church societies in the other provinces and by school headmasters and the *Helpmekaar* organization. From 1959 Sanlam provided £2 000 per annum for school bursaries to deserving boys to complete either Standard 8 or matric. The school bursaries were later also offered to English-speaking scholars and to girls. By 1963 Sanlam had paid out 233 school bursaries—244 in 1964 and 285 in 1965—each for a duration of two years. Sanlam commented as follows on this enterprise: 'Through this bursary scheme we are delivering unique service to our people, by enabling wanting boys and girls to develop into valuable citizens of their country.'[146]

The next social need was the physical accommodation of scholars in school hostels, especially after the war of 1939/45. Many children from remote areas and farms needed to live in school hostels in the towns, but schools did not have sufficient funding to erect such hostels. Church congregations often had access to land, but not sufficient funding to

[143] SA: 5/2: B23: Bursaries: Memorandum to Board, 25/10/1955; B23: Bursaries: Memorandum to Board, 17/8/1962.

[144] SA: B23: Memorandum to Board, 17/8/1962.

[145] The HS is still an educational NGO operating in the field of study funding. SA: 5/2/D4B: Helpmekaar Studiefonds, 1963–1972.

[146] SA: B23: Memorandum to Board, 15/11/1965.

build such facilities. Sanlam then devised a scheme whereby the church, the Dutch Reformed Church (DRC), was granted loans for the construction of hostels, backed by endowment policies taken out by the DRC and guarantees for the capital by the Provincial Administration. The loans were in the form of debentures issued to the DRC at prevailing interest rates. The DRC paid the interest annually. By the late 1960s many DRC congregations were struggling to pay the interest on the debentures and more debentures were issued. These hostels were known as '*Goeie Hoop Koshuise*' (Good Hope Hostels: GHKs). Finally, the Provincial Administration redeemed the last loan guarantees by the end of 1975.[147] This enterprise initially accommodated a total of 2 270 school children in safe facilities for the duration of their school careers. Sanlam engaged in the business of lending at current interest rates, where the return on policyholders' funds was optimized. The GHKs were an example of how Sanlam conducted its life business through innovative strategies, which in the long run built its business and contributed to Afrikaner upliftment and empowerment through education.

As the Sanlam policyholder profile changed to include a growing English-speaking portion of the South African population, educational needs across language barriers were supported by Sanlam sponsorships. The South African Council for English Education (SACEE) was the recipient of a sustained Sanlam sponsorship for many years.[148] Funding went towards Coloured teachers wanting to improve their qualifications in mathematics, as well as to the University of the Western Cape where a mathematics laboratory was established to develop Coloured children's skills in mathematics.[149]

Sanlam was also involved in donations to an extended range of welfare initiatives, such as support for old-age homes, care societies for the aged, holiday camps for underprivileged children, and orphanages for children of all race groups in South Africa. Cultural activities, the preservation of historic monuments, locations and other heritage, Afrikaans language initiatives in compiling specialist dictionaries, prizes for national mathematics competitions, and Bible distribution all found a very sympathetic ear at the life office. Donations were getting out of hand and by the late 1970s Sanlam revised its stance on corporate social responsibility. For the first time management took a holistic view of expenditure on corporate social responsibility. Between 1965 and 1969 Sanlam contributed 0.16 per cent of annual premium income to donations, but this ratio declined to 0.05 per cent between 1973 and 1979. In the context of growing social turbulence and tension with the state regarding the role of big business, a formal policy position was necessary. Management introduced a fixed quantitative ratio between premium income and donations or sponsorships of between 0.05 per cent and 0.1 per cent of annual premium income for social responsibility expenditure. All payments exceeding R10 000

[147] SA: 3/1/3/2: Lenings aan Koshuise, A, B; 3/1/4/2: Letter Provincial.
[148] SA: 5/2/D4: Donasies SACEE, Letter SACEE–Sanlam 6/6/61: Letter Beak–Sanlam, 13/6/63.
[149] SA: S17: Donations, 1980–1989.

required board authorization. The policy framework for social responsibility expenditure was that projects had to comply with the following criteria: they had to be topical and afford Sanlam optimal media coverage, enhance the Sanlam public image, and have the consensus support of the governing body of the organization. Sanlam had to be able to identify with any project calling for its sponsorship and it had to contribute towards enabling Sanlam penetration into that market. Social responsibility projects had to assist the company to honour its responsibilities towards society.[150] This policy focus consolidated the plethora of engagements with numerous ad hoc applicants in a clearer social responsibility function.

Strategy and management: from a single centralized organization to the multidivisional form of organization

In the period under discussion, Sanlam slowly started to progress from a centralized unitary organizational structure (the so-called U form), as described by Alfred Chandler Jr, to a diversified organization displaying an M form of organization. This means that functional diversification led to the branching out of operations into decentralized business units. The development of the management style and strategic objective of the company testifies to this. Management was characterized by two elements between 1945 and 1985. The first was the direct, hands-on style grounded in centralized control. All financial, operational, and staff matters were discussed and final decisions taken by the Board of Directors. The management style remained rigid and bureaucratic. A multitude of processes, procedures, and rules relating to operational and staff matters were introduced. These were administered by the same generation of managers who had established Sanlam. Only in 1978 did a non-Sanlam rank-and-file person take up the position of Managing Director of the company, namely Dr F.J. du Plessis. When he became Chairman in 1982, he elevated the position to that of Executive Chairman, a role suited to Du Plessis' dominant personality. He perpetuated centralized personal control.

The second element of more human resources-based control emerged later on, as a clear adjustment in the style of management occurred in Sanlam. This did not change central control, just gave it a more human face. Centralized control, which characterized the U form of organization under G.F.S. de Villiers, A.D. Wassenaar and P.J.F. Scholtz, remained dominant. Even the chairmanship of the Board of Directors still displayed the control of the generation responsible for establishing the company. No real difference

[150] SA: 5/3/2: Minutes of Board Meeting, 23/1/1980.

followed Charlie Louw's succession of Hofmeyr in 1954. Although Louw had a different management style, the only real impact on the board was organizational. He introduced a more people-oriented approach to the management of the people who constituted Sanlam. Management improved benefits and working conditions for all employees. Modernization of the Head Office operations improved operational efficiency as well as the working environment. A Sanlam Cricket Club was established and the company even had its own choir. Board meetings were streamlined by organizing them into business and functional areas from 1955. When staff matters were discussed, the general manager responsible for staff matters attended the meeting, and when the investment portfolio was discussed the general manager responsible for investments was present. This signified recognition of delegated responsibilities and empowerment of people. In 1958, the minutes of the meetings were also streamlined by deciding only to minute decisions and not all discussions. In 1960 the approval and decline of mortgage loans (previously dealt with one by one) were consolidated and approved as a group.

Wassenaar did not introduce any new strategic directions for Sanlam when he succeeded Charlie Louw as Chairman. His concern was the stability of the company. His business skills and leadership were acknowledged by the Harvard Business School, which named him the 'South African Businessman of the Year' in 1968.[151] From 1955, a shift from generalists to specialists occurred in operations. Various specialists were appointed to develop specialist functions in the organization, such as a public relations officer (1955), an English language expert (1956), a technical consultant for the purchasing of electronic equipment (1958), a legal adviser (1978), and art advisers (1978). Delegation and the empowerment of a new layer of management signified a limited change in management control when Pepler Scholtz assumed office. The approach to staff also changed. A report on 'more effective utilization of human resources' was presented to the board in 1973. In 1980, decisions on salary increases to a certain predetermined level were gradually delegated to management on different levels of operation. In 1983, the decision-making powers for investment decisions were also changed, clearly pointing towards the delegation thereof to a differentiated level of management.

In 1979, discussions during the board meetings became much more strategic and factual. The detail was handled by the general managers within their areas of expertise. The strategic direction of Sanlam was gradually becoming more defined when Fred du Plessis took over as Executive Chairman. His vision for Sanlam was a prominent role in the South African economy as an Afrikaner business conglomerate. Management therefore took a distinct contextual view of its operations and sought to develop its human resources accordingly. In 1983 a Code of Conduct was introduced for Directors and the

[151] SA: *Die Fakkel*: 53 (49): 13/12/1985: 1.

following year the remuneration structure of Sanlam employees was benchmarked against the rest of the industry to secure appropriate industry positioning.

The most significant characteristic of the post-war period was the diversification of its investment base, which positioned Sanlam across all the sectors of the economy. The company did not engage directly in the management of the companies in which it invested, but the sheer size of its investments would become a cause for serious concern. The operational efficiency of many of the 'stakeholder' companies lagged the market towards the late 1970s, with shares trading at a notable discount. The Sanlam management took up directorships on the boards of the companies in which Sanlam held large shareholdings. This was one way of seeking closer access to operational control over the extended interests. The Sanlam management came to rely on the specialist services of experts, since insurance people were not industrialists, bankers, or mining experts. The board was acutely aware of the external environment and engaged more frequently in discussions on the state of the economy, the trends in political developments, and how those would impact on the company, as well as the government's growing anxiety about the role of 'big business groups' in the economy.

The organization had a very good understanding of client demand, as reflected in new product development and other services, such as medical insurance and employee benefits. The marketing of products and services extended more successfully into the market for other race groups. In 1954, an agent of colour was appointed in the Bloemfontein branch. In 1962 the English business market was identified as a specific target market. As the domestic environment was deeply affected by the 1976 Soweto riots, the company gradually moved to terminate the race loading of policies. Public relations were recognized as a strategic tool to enhance Sanlam's marketing strategy. In 1984 Du Plessis introduced nationwide 'roadshows' where policyholders were invited to cocktail functions hosted by the Executive Chairman. As an exercise in public relations Du Plessis wanted to establish a closer relationship between the life office and policyholders.

An important aspect of Sanlam's management since the beginning was its close alignment with international developments and personal contact with international leaders in the industry. Management attended international conference, sent staff members on study trips, and frequently conducted investigations into new international trends. Indicative of the international inclination was the visit in 1957 to the USA, which led to the introduction of new computer equipment. Sanlam actuaries also attended the international conference of actuaries in New York. In 1970, a commission was sent to England, USA, Canada, and Japan to investigate the global experiences of banks controlling insurance companies, or vice versa. This was a crucial issue in the South African market during the 1970s, when cross-shareholding between banks and insurers in South Africa was regulated by statute. Banks could not own more than 10 per cent in insurance companies, but as sanctions became more effective, the insurance companies in South Africa were the only institutions with sufficient capital to acquire the shares in local banks dumped by disinvesting foreign shareholders.[152] In 1975, Sanlam was the first South African life office and also the first outside Europe to become a member of Insurope, a European-based multinational association of life offices of group benefit insurers.[153] Insurope specialized in group and pension benefits to multinational firms' employers and their employees and it was this dimension Sanlam was beginning to explore as the domestic market came under increasing pressure. International expansion beyond the established offices in Southern Rhodesia (later Zimbabwe—these offices were closed in 1980) had already started in 1971, establishing life insurance branches in Lesotho, Botswana, and Swaziland.

In 1961 a tendency towards longer-term planning was beginning to manifest. Management accepted a plan for the long-term development of new branches. In 1970 a long-term planning session for the company was organized by facilitators from the Universities of Washington and Columbia. In 1983 the first five-year planning was considered by the Board. The Board gave attention to the restructuring of the branch offices, regions, and Head Office. Sanlam was contemplating the restructuring of the group by incorporating Santam into a single group. Organizational restructuring of the company followed the growing diversification of Sanlam's investment portfolio. The centralized management structure, where the board and the management functioned as one and the same authority, had to make way for more professional management. Amatori and Colli noted: 'Out of these changes (development of professional management) arose the modern multidivisional corporation.'[154] Diversification presented Sanlam with a twofold challenge. On the one hand, a population experiencing rising living standards began to demand more innovative investment products. This development mandated more innovative and differentiated products on offer. On the other hand, the expanding investment activities of Sanlam and its support for the Afrikaner economic empowerment initiatives, engaged the company increasingly in non-insurance business operations, which create a dilemma for Sanlam. Sanlam could not indefinitely manage this relationship with its so-called 'strategic investments', simply as 'investments'. It became important to exert influence on the level of operational efficiency of those investments. The company's organizational structure had to change. On 1 October 1978 the management committee was abolished as Du Plessis set out to build the Sanlam conglomerate. In 1984, the Board approved the formation of a Group Holding Company, acknowledging the functional diversification of operations and embarking on the M form of organization. The key management characteristics of Sanlam changed. The unitary form (U form) of the past, which was embedded in the

[152] SA: Nuusuitreiking 25/6/1979: Press release LOA on Cost structure of Life offices.

[153] SA: 7/5/2: LOA files: Insurope News, 17/1/1975.

[154] F. Amatori and A. Colli (2011). *Business History: Complexities and Comparisons*: 101.

scientific management theory and manifested through strong central managerial control in a centralized organization, developed strain. The classical management theory with its emphasis on authority and unity of command, direction, and the subordination of individual interest to that of the collective entity (in this case the managers), gradually changed. The emphasis on stability and tenure of staff and the promotion of a unity of interest between management and employees, could no longer be sustained in the more dynamic multidivisional enterprise. The rapidly growing economy after the war mandated change in organizational form and managerial practice. The bureaucratic and administrative management approaches made way for a more people-oriented approach. The human relations theory found growing application in the managerial style of the Sanlam management. By the 1980s the economic changes of South Africa impacted directly on the organizational and managerial structure of the company. The Peter Senge 'learning organization' soon manifested in the changes to the organizational structure as well as the nature of management in Sanlam. The multidivisional organization needed greater diffusion of decision-making powers. Top management developed a more strategic role as 'commanders-in-chief', and directed the next level of management, the divisional managers, who operated as the 'field generals'.[155] Du Plessis' autocratic management style between 1978 and 1989 temporarily placed a hold on the full manifestation of the M form.

Sanlam in the industry

The strong economic performance of the domestic economy after the war supported the expansion of Sanlam. While the company's total premium income had increased by 16.4 per cent annual compound growth between 1918 and 1945 (Table 2.1), compared to an increase of 6.45 per cent for the entire long-term insurance industry, its performance after the war made the company the second-largest domestic life office. Total premium income increased by 9.55 per cent annual compound growth between 1945 and 1985 (Table 3.1), compared to industry growth of 3.81 per cent. Sanlam's total premium income increased by a total of £170 000 000 during the forty years. This was the largest single increase in the premium income of any South African long-term assurer yet.[156] By 1965 Sanlam's annual premium growth had exceeded the growth of all other long-term insurance companies.[157] In 1945 Sanlam's premium income was 16 per cent per cent of the industry, but by 1985 the relative position of Sanlam's premium was 25 per cent of the industry.

[155] Ibid., 103.s. [156] SA: 6/5/1: Annual Report 1959: 1. [157] SA: Annual Report, 1965: 3.

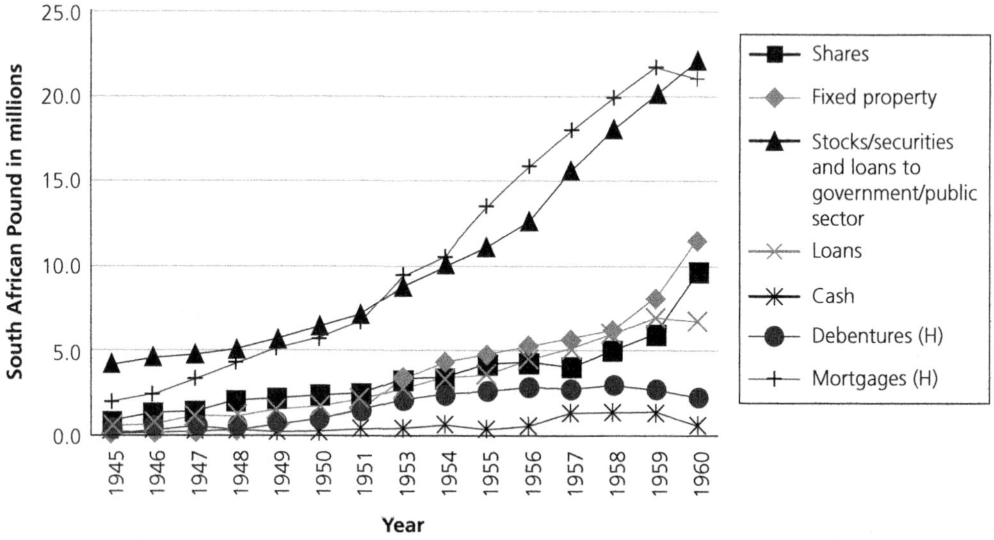

Figure 3.1. Sanlam asset profile, 1945–1960 (£)

Sanlam's total assets increased by 5.47 per cent between 1945 and 1985 (Figure 3.1), compared to industry asset growth of 3.35 per cent (Table 3.1). In 1945 Sanlam's assets made up 8.1 per cent of total industry assets, but by 1985 the company owned 18.2 per cent of total industry assets. Sanlam's assets were more diversified than in the preceding period between the wars. During the strong growth of the immediate post-war era, the largest portion of the assets was in mortgages and government paper as a result of the statutory requirements of the Insurance Act. During this period strong interest rate growth and well-performing listed entities gave rise to a stronger emphasis by management on investment in shares. This is reflected in the larger portion of assets in equities. Fixed property made up a smaller portion of assets but was still an anchor asset class. The company improved returns on assets from 3.35 per cent in 1945 to 11.2 per cent by 1985 (Figure 3.2). This performance was enhanced by improved investment income, which had increased on average by 35 per cent per annum since 1980. Operations were becoming more efficient, as administrative costs increased by only 3.7 per cent annual compound growth during the forty years (Table 3.1). During the time of socio-political instability between 1961 and 1976 (Figure 3.3, Figure 3.4), the profile of Sanlam's assets changed. The dominant asset class was government bonds, then shares (equity), and then real estate. The yield on these assets (Figure 3.6) beat inflation only up to the beginning of 1970, where after the downward trajectory of GDP growth and spiking inflation suppressed the yield on the long-term nature of the asset base. During the last decade of the period, 1976 to 1985 (Figure 3.5), high domestic volatility, high inflation, and a further contraction in economic growth resulted in investments in government bonds to exceed other asset classes by almost 50 per cent. Figure 3.6

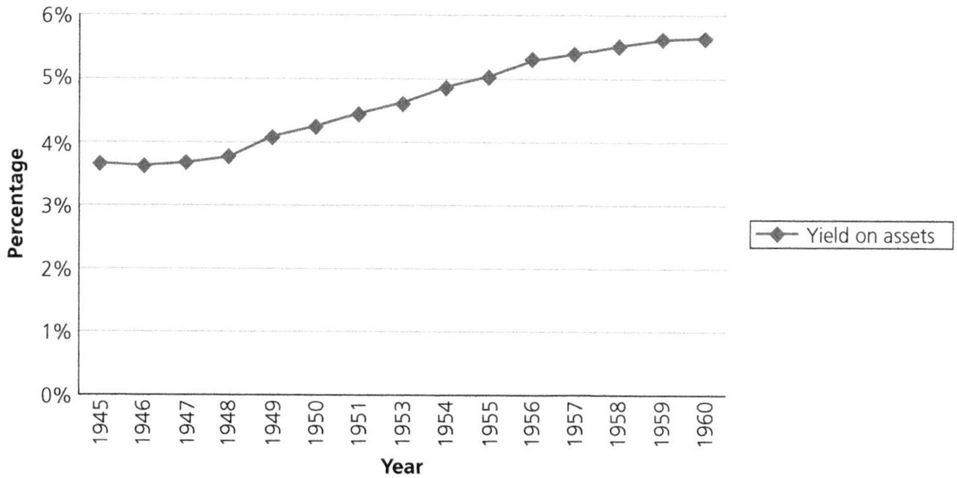

Figure 3.2. Sanlam yield on assets, 1945–1960

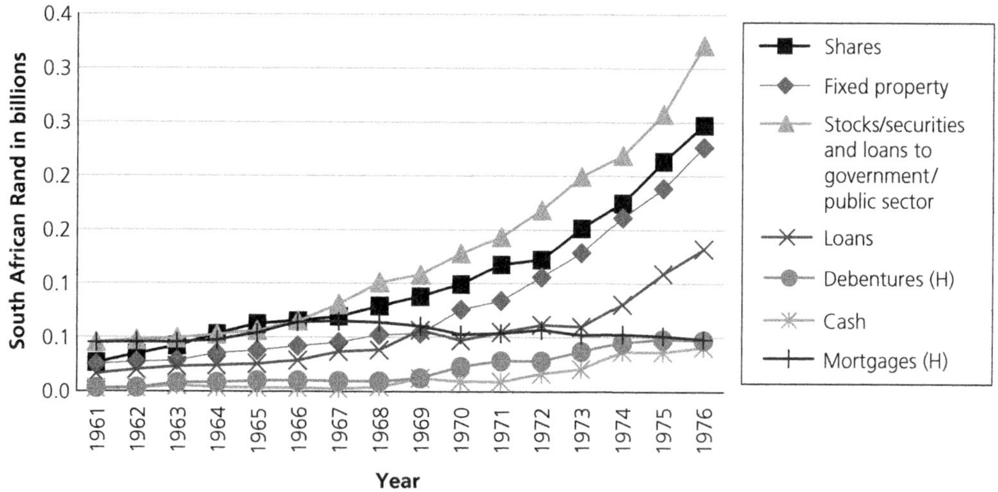

Figure 3.3. Sanlam asset profile, 1961–1976 (R)

shows the impact of these volatilities on the yield on Sanlam's assets. Yield remained below the Consumer Price Index excluding mortgages (CPIX), except for a brief period in 1984, but the yield on assets posted substantially stronger growth than domestic GDP growth. The insurance industry offered stable returns. Sanlam's large investment in so-called strategic investments (shares in industrial, financial, and mining conglomerates of variable performance) contributed to stable, but not exceptional returns. This allocation of capital resulted in investment inflexibility and illiquidity, and was bound soon to be the subject of strategic policy debate.

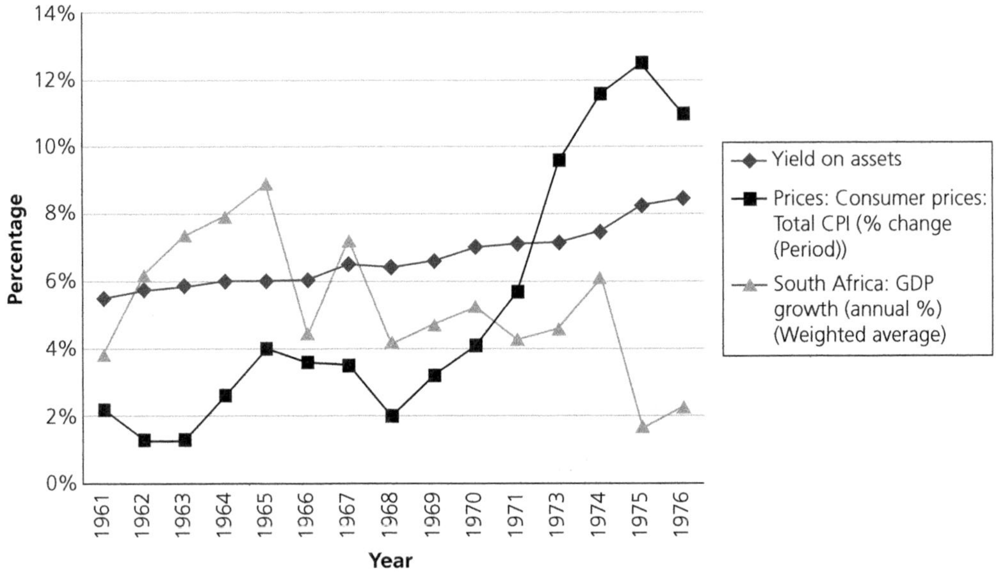

Figure 3.4. Sanlam yield on assets, 1961–1976

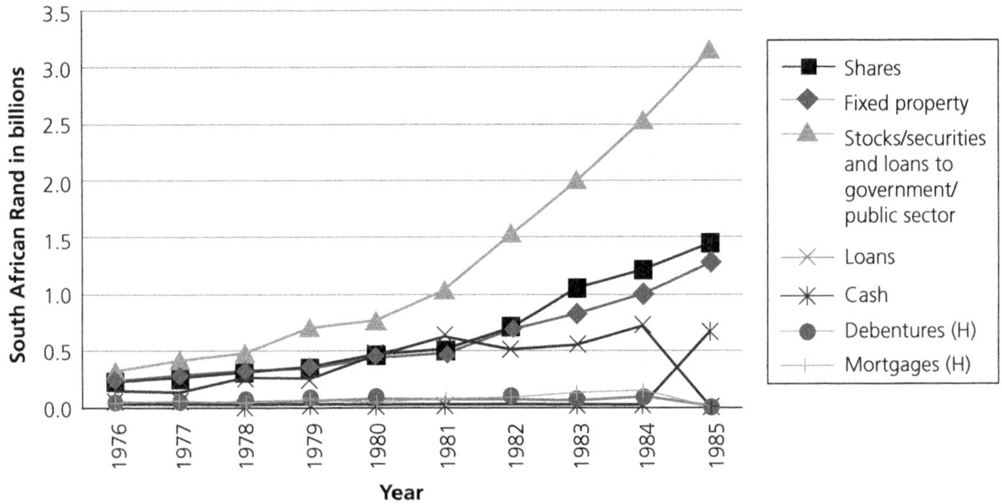

Figure 3.5. Sanlam asset profile, 1976–1985 (R)

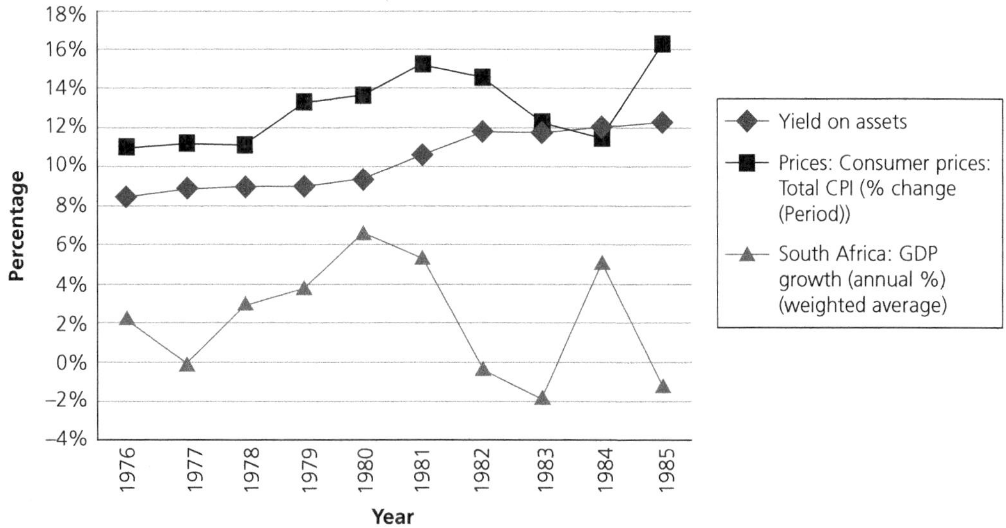

Figure 3.6. Sanlam yield on assets, 1976–1985

Sanlam was leading the industry on cost efficiency. During the 1970s, Sanlam's administration cost as a proportion of total income was 7.1 per cent, but by 1985 this ratio had dropped to 4.1 per cent, the lowest in the industry. The industry only matched Sanlam's cost efficiency of the 1970s in 1983.[158] The company's use of advanced computer technology and the intensive agent training programmes, coupled with the tightly controlled Head Office enabled this operational advantage in the market. This performance Sanlam portrayed as the growing confidence by the public in its business, especially a growing policyholder base among non-Afrikaners. The company maintained bonus declarations throughout, increasing the rate of bonuses incrementally but very conservatively. During the 1940s, bonus declarations hovered around 2 per cent, but after decimalization bonuses of 27 per cent per 1 000 were declared. By 1985 Sanlam paid bonuses of 46.5 per cent on policies qualifying for reversionary bonuses. The company introduced a variety of other bonuses, thereby enhancing the attractiveness of policies. When the government introduced income tax on insurance companies in 1959, the Chairman of Sanlam, A.D. Wassenaar, criticized the move as penalizing savers and discouraging saving in South Africa. He repeatedly expressed concern about the tax, stating that it was not in the interest of the country to tax savings, which constituted the source of capital for domestic capital investment.[159] In almost every annual Chairman's address the company expressed its opposition to and dismay at the penalization of savings through insurance. The tax liability affected the payment of bonuses.

[158] SA: 6/5/1: Sanlam Annual Report, 1985, Chairman's address: 15.
[159] SA: 6/5/1: Annual Report, 1959: 3; Annual Report, 1960: 4.

By 1985 the Sanlam policyholder base reflected the penetration into the broader South African population. Sanlam then had more than 1.6 million individual policyholders and an addition one million people belonging to group schemes. The English-speaking market was targeted more systematically from the 1960s. Where English-speaking policyholders made up only 10 per cent of the total number of Sanlam policyholders in 1960, this ratio rose to 20 per cent by the early 1980s and 40 per cent by 1990. Sanlam addressed access into the African market (this is black, Coloured, and Indian people) from 1958, when the board was advised that Sanlam had underwritten only 1 786 policies to a value of £597 833 for Africans by 30 September 1957. Sanlam acknowledged the potential of the African market, but had a stronger penetration in the Coloured market, since that population spoke predominantly Afrikaans, was concentrated in the Cape Peninsula and Eastern Cape, and many Coloured people were employed by AHT. Despite calls for a massive drive into the African market, total African business was equal to only 0.5 per cent of the total white business.[160] By 1968 this ratio had risen to only one sixtieth of Sanlam's policyholders [161] and by 1975 Sanlam had 5 390 African policyholders.[162] By the mid-1980s Sanlam's share in the total African insurance market had tripled from 5 per cent in 1975 to 14 per cent in 1985.[163] The entire life insurance industry started easing race loading of policies to African people in South Africa by the early 1950s. As the living standards of Indian and Coloured people was perceived to be closer to that of whites, insurance companies considered the risk similar to that of white policyholders. Sanlam started scrapping race loading on African lives from 1951, especially as the company obtained more reliable information about African mortality rates.[164] Sanlam followed broad industry trends in assessing applications from Africans. By 1957 only 28 per cent of policies issued to Africans had a race loading.[165] By the late 1970s, when African trade unions were authorised following the Riekert and Wiehan Reports, Sanlam had a strong presence in the employee benefits markets as well as group policies. The SA Mutual had moved faster than Sanlam on insuring African lives by offering more favourable rates than Sanlam. The latter was the cautious life office: African applicants were categorized based on education, income levels, and occupation. Individuals with a tertiary education, a stable and above-average income level, and occupied as a professional person, were exempt from any race loading. This demonstrated a business rather than a racial consideration for the implementation or removal of loadings. In 1976, for example,

160 SA: Memorandum to Sanlam Board, 25/8/1959.

161 SA: 6/5/1: Memorandum to Sanlam Board, 17/4/1968; Marketing Report 1967.

162 SA: 6/5/1: Memorandum to Sanlam Board, 18/3/1972; Memorandum to Sanlam Board, 17/10/1972; Conditions for non-white lives, 9/6/1977.

163 SA: 6/5/1: *FINWEEK*, 10–16 June 1993.

164 SA: Memorandum to Sanlam Board on the loading of Indian lives, 27/11/1951; 25/8/1959.

165 SA: 6/5/1: Memorandum to Sanlam Board, 17/6/1958.

Africans in 'Category A' who had an annual income of R4 000 or more, or teachers with an annual income of R2 400 or more, and university graduates or ministers from recognized church organizations were insured at the same rates as whites.[166] These requirements were later adjusted to an annual income of R5 000 or more per annum or teachers earning R3 000 or more per annum.[167] Sanlam emerged as a major player in the group and pension schemes market of trade unions in the late 1980s. The company's African policyholders increased to 13 per cent of its total policyholder base,[168] and this percentage was set to rise substantially during the following decades.

[166] SA: 6/5/1: Minutes of Sanlam Board, 15/6/1976; 21/6/1976; 15/6/1977.

[167] Ibid.

[168] S. Halleen: From Life Insurance to Financial Services: A Historical Analysis of Sanlam's Client Base, 1918–2004. PhD thesis, Stellenbosch, 2013: pp. 149.

4 Searching the soul

Wither Sanlam? Powerful conglomerate to 1997

Turbulence and strategy

The South Africa economy went into a downward spiral of stagnation and inflation from the early 1980s. GDP growth slumped to an average of 0.3 per cent per annum between 1981 and 1994. Real GDP growth had declined consistently since the 1960, but in the decade of the high oil and gold prices, real per capita GDP growth collapsed. Unemployment reached 12.7 per cent, moving into double-digit figures for the first time in South African history. International pressures on the policies of racial segregation mounted as foreign companies were asked to apply non-discriminatory codes of conduct in the workplace. The Sullivan Code was especially controversial, as African trade unions opposed the enforcement of the code, since they argued that it did not address the real hardship of black labour. In the domestic context socio-political discontent was mounting. The South African Council of Churches, the Urban Foundation (to which Sanlam contributed), and the United Democratic Front (UDF) established in 1983 mobilized local discontent. The international debate about sanctions against South Africa increased in intensity. President Ronald Reagan and British Prime Minister Margaret Thatcher led opposition to sanctions, arguing that the people who would suffer most were the black unemployed, but the USA congress passed the Comprehensive Anti-Apartheid Act in 1986. A total ban was thereby placed on all new investments in South Africa, loans to the government, export of computers and oil, import of non-strategic minerals and agricultural products, and an embargo on direct air travel between the USA and South Africa. The Commonwealth had a delayed response, but ultimately systematic sanctions followed from Commonwealth countries in 1989. Between 1986 and 1989 more than 520 companies sold their assets in South Africa to local businesses—at absolute bargain prices. Again, the outcome caused domestic corporations to revise their spending on community projects, a development that infuriated the trade unions. The sanctions and divestment exacerbated domestic dissatisfaction. The ANC Freedom Radio broadcasts announced its intention to make South African 'ungovernable' in the wake of persistent discriminatory state policies. In July 1985 a state of emergency was declared, followed by a second one the following year. The National Party leadership was confronted by growing domestic mass protest, extra-parliamentary talks between banned political organizations and influential community and business leaders, and growing intra-party pressure for reform. With the knowledge and silent acknowledgement of the state, business leaders under the leadership of Gavin Relly, Chairman of Anglo American Corporation, met with banned political leaders in Lusaka in September 1986, in Dakar in July 1987, in Munich in October 1988, and in Paris in June 1989. It was therefore not totally unexpected when on 2 February 1990 the South African State President, F.W. de Klerk, announced the unbanning of the ANC, Pan Africanist Congress, and all other banned political parties, the release of their leaders from prison, and the intention to commence negotiations on a peaceful transition to majority rule. The multiparty negotiations that took South Africa to the first national democratic election in April 1994 were equally turbulent and led the country through very unstable and uncertain times.

Throughout the pre-1990 unofficial talks about a resolution to the potentially explosive domestic political situation in South Africa, and the actual negotiations, business leaders took a proactive stance. The Sanlam leadership was directly involved in the talks with black leaders in exile. The Managing Director Fred du Plessis entered public debate on economic policy, but behind the scenes business leaders in South Africa engaged with the leadership of the ANC leadership to seek a peaceful solution to the political conundrum. Since the state of emergency in 1985 and 1986 business leadership in South Africa took it upon themselves to establish dialogue between the leadership in exile and the government. The first meeting was in Dakar, Senegal in 1987. It soon was apparent that the ANC leadership wanted to talk specifically to Afrikaner business leaders. Marinus Daling and Attie du Plessis were the two leaders from the Sanlam/ Sankorp stable who assisted in the talks to facilitate communication between the leaders inside and outside South Africa to bring the country to peaceful negotiations and a transition to democratic elections in 1994.[1] It was of particular significance that Thabo Mbeki, one of the prominent ANC leaders in exile, explicitly wanted to engage with Afrikaner business leaders, since he considered their political influence superior to the liberal English-speaking leadership.[2] Through various forums the second-largest life office engaged with the changing context. Strategic repositioning followed, but Sanlam was a big organization, deeply rooted in the history of racial segregation. Strategic repositioning mandated vision and leadership. In the period between 1985 and 1998 Sanlam could rely on able people, but unexpected events forced the company to delve deep into its human capital.

[1] S.G. Hoogenraad-Vermaak (2009)*'n Kritiese ondersoek na die bydrae van Afrikaner sakelui in die vestiging van 'n nuwe politieke bestel: 1985–1992*. Unpublished PhD Thesis. University of Johannesburg; W.P. Esterhuyse (2012) *Eidnstryd. Geheime gesprekke en die einde van apartheid*. Cape Town: Tafelberg; R. Hartman (2012) *Ali. The life of Ali Bacher*. London: Penguin.

[2] Esterhuyse (2012) *Eindstryd*: 345.

Sanlam leadership

The volatility in global financial markets was characterized by a growing deregulation of financial services. Sanlam's long-term strategies in these volatile times took shape in this context of deregulation. By 1988 these strategies were embedded in the path dependence of Sanlam's seventy years. In this part of its history Sanlam faced the consequences of its large non-insurance investments. This set the company apart from any other long-term insurance company in South Africa. How Sanlam unraveled this complex structure had a profound impact on subsequent strategies and the image of the company in the South African financial services landscape. It was not simply a matter of managing an investment portfolio. This part of Sanlam's history is the signature decade of the building down of its Afrikaner empowerment empire. Only after the restructuring exercise towards the mid-1990s could Sanlam start to focus on financial services as a core function. During this stormy period the relative stability of management and directors was a supportive factor. The Sanlam management displayed long-term stability in the succession of leaders who had made their way up the ranks in the company. Apart from Fred du Plessis, management consisted of the second and third generation of Sanlam managers. In 1985 Fred du Plessis was Chairman and Managing Director. The second rank of managers were Pierre Steyn George Rudman and Johan Söhnge as Senior General Managers. In April 1985 Pierre Steyn succeeded Du Plessis as Managing Director. The latter chaired the board, while A.D. Wassenaar was a member of the board until his retirement in February 1986. Wassenaar served Sanlam as Honorary President until his death in 1991. Du Plessis died in a motor-vehicle accident on 14 March 1989—a day before he would have delivered the chairman's address at the seventieth Sanlam annual general meeting. Between March and September 1989, Tjaart van der Walt was the Sanlam Chairman. In September 1989 Dr A.J. van den Berg was appointed Chairman of Sanlam. Management returned to the Sanlam faithful under Steyn (his career started in Sanlam in the early 1960s after he had completed a first degree as a recipient of a Sanlam bursary) and then in April 1993 Desmond Smith, Senior General Manager: Individual Insurance, assumed the position of Managing Director.

In 1993 Marinus Daling became Chairman of Sanlam, and subsequently Executive Chairman in November 1997. He headed up the investment division of Sanlam before the formation of Sankorp (the history of Sankorp will be discussed below). Daling's new executive team at Sanlam comprised Hendrik Bester, Managing Director: Asset Management; George Rudman, Senior General Manager: Finance; Johann Treurnicht, Senior General Manager: Marketing; and Leon Venter, Senior General Manager: Business Systems. They brought together vast experience as actuaries and managers in Sanlam, but the strategist was Daling, the relatively young fifty-two-year-old actuary who had managed the Sanlam investments in Sankorp since 1985. He was a close confidant of Fred du Plessis. When Daling succeeded Desmond Smith, the senior management team members, except for Rudman, were five years younger than him. The strategic repositioning of Sanlam was in the hands of a young Sanlam generation. The board provided backing to a group of people with deep and wide economic, strategic, and business experience—and the wisdom to guide transformation of the Sanlam business.

The corps of directors during the turbulent years of the political transition did not drive the change but offered stability at a time of Afrikaner division and the first-ever black government. Until 1996 the Board of Directors consisted of primarily Afrikaans men. They possessed an impressive body of intellectual capital, extensive experience in private business, state corporations, and the accounting profession. Former managers from Afrikaner companies, such as Dr William Coetzer from the mining company Federale Mynbou, served on the board until 1986. Several prominent Afrikaners in public service were board members. Dr A.J. van den Berg was appointed to the Sanlam board, having occupied leading positions in South Africa's industrial development. He was a chemist by profession and had worked with SATMAR (South African Torbanite Mining and Research)[3] since 1948, then joined the Industrial Development Corporation of South Africa (IDC) and since 1985 had provided experienced oversight to the Sankorp managerial team engaged in the restructuring of Sanlam's industrial assets. Dr P.J. Riekert, Chairman of the Prime Minister's Economic Advisory Council and Chairman of the commission that advised the government on the relaxation of legislation restricting black labour advancement, served on the board from the mid-1970s until 1989. Dr J.G. Loubser, former General Manager of Railways and Harbours, Dr P.E. Rousseau, former MD and Chairman of SASOL, and Dr C.H. J. van Aswegen, the long-standing Chairman of Santam, served on the board in 1985. Loubser was a mechanical engineer who introduced innovative productivity-enhancing mechanisms in the South African Railways, which earned him the Commonwealth William Alexander Agnew prize in 1976 and the Harvard Business Statesman of the Year award in 1981. As an alumnus of the University of the Witwatersrand, Loubser earned professional acknowledgement throughout the practising engineering profession, irrespective of language orientation. From the Potchefstroom University Prof T.J. (Tjaart) van der Walt, known for his liberal views, was brought in as director by Fred du Plessis. Pepler Scholtz and A.D. Wassenaar were the Sanlam old guard. Many of these individuals shared a close allegiance to Afrikaner political power, some were members of the secret organization, the *Afrikaner Broederbond*, and the group of three Afrikaans Reformed churches. Riekert was known for his strong views on improved skills development of black labour. In 1970 he had warned the

[3] SATMAR was the Anglovaal/USA joint venture for the exploration of torbanite/oil-shale and production of fuel from torbanite.

government that an average of 5.5 per cent targeted GDP growth per annum would be mandatory to secure improved employment. He advocated the scrapping of job reservation to ensure the training of more black people to meet the demand for skilled labour. Tjaart van der Walt was generally considered to be an 'enlightened' Afrikaner, a person seeking to open up society and move away from the policy of racial segregation. Rousseau, Van den Berg, and Loubser were experienced professionals with long and respected careers in the public service. Fred du Plessis was supported by Riekert, Wassenaar, and Van den Berg in his openly anti-state stance on interventionist economic policy. Two more 'enlightened' Afrikaners, Ton Vosloo, the Chairman of Nasionale Pers (NASPERS—the home of the Afrikaans Cape-based newspaper *Die Burger*, of which Willie Hofmeyr had been the first Chairman) and other media interests, and S.W. van der Merwe, a prominent Johannesburg lawyer, as well as the accountant and business executive D.L. Keys, Chairman and former CEO of Gencor and a member of the board of Billiton and reinsurance companies, were appointed to the board. In 1991 Keys was appointed Minister of Economic Co-ordination and of Trade and Industry, and in 1992 to the portfolio of Finance in the last Cabinet of F.W. de Klerk, but he resigned in 1994 and returned to the Sanlam board in September 1994. Keys had a successful business career and worked with the Sanlam management during the time he held his executive position at Gencor. Although he was an Englishman, he had close working relationships with Afrikaners throughout his professional career and spoke immaculate Afrikaans.

The first changes to the all-Afrikaner character of the Sanlam board occurred when the first woman, Professor Kate Jowell, a member of the University of Cape Town Graduate School of Business, was appointed in 1993. In 1994 Mr P.E.L. Schwartz, a prominent businessman in the Coloured community and Chairman of the Superama Group, joined the Sanlam board and in 1996 Professor A.C. Bawa, the Deputy Vice-chancellor of the University of Natal and Ms D.N.M. Mokhobo, chairperson of Fedics and of MBM Change Agents, were appointed to the board. The changes to the board introduced persons of colour and gender differentiation, but Afrikaner control remained firmly entrenched. The Afrikaners in management and on the board were known to be independent critical thinkers, supportive of political change in South Africa, but the extent of the consequences of majority black rule was unchartered territory. Sanlam's management navigated cautiously between business sustainability, fundamental changes in the long-term insurance market, and the political overhaul of South Africa. The board did not drive any path-breaking strategic or business changes in Sanlam. Management and policy direction were dominated by Fred du Plessis,[4] and after his death it was not the directors but management who operated as the agent of change management.

[4] Interview Walter Scheffler, 24/02/2009. He describes Fred du Plessis' appointment as a 'culture shock' to many in Sanlam, because he had a strong personality, strong views, and an academic demeanour, which often left the ordinary Sanlam employee grasping to understand the gist of what he said. He did not tolerate opposition.

Strategy, personality, and the Sanlam empire

The strategic direction of Sanlam from the mid-1980s epitomized the state of Afrikaner big business. By the mid-1980s Afrikaner business had become diversified, extending into all sectors of the economy, and no longer sold itself on the nationalist card. Afrikaners were as politically divided as ever before. In the business environment Afrikaner business interests entered strategic alliances with English capital in mining. An element of over-ambitious inexperience caught up with some of the earlier acquisitions and mandated careful rescue operations. To grasp the complexity of Afrikaner business exposure and the looming risk to both the macroeconomic stability and Afrikaner business in particular, it is necessary to take a step back in time to understand the person of Dr Frederick Johannes du Plessis. Fred du Plessis was born in the Western Transvaal, today known as North West Province, and matriculated at the local high school in Klerksdorp in 1949. He completed BCom, BCom Hons and MCom degrees *cum laude* at the Potchefstroom University for Christian Higher Education, which led him to a DEcon at the *Vrije Universiteit,* Amsterdam in 1958. He commenced a brilliant academic career at the University of Pretoria and later the University of Potchefstroom. A former student of his recalled that he was nicknamed 'Doep Diepte' (Deep Doep—referring to his serious nature) and that he was sensitive to being coherent in speech and articulation. He was the head of the South African Institute for Business Cycle Research, which positioned him squarely in the arena of macroeconomic policy. Du Plessis soon found the classroom restrictive and accepted directorships of Sanlam and Nedbank in 1971. In 1974 he was appointed Chairman of the board of Senbank, the Sanlam merchant bank subsidiary, and on 1 May 1978 Managing Director of Sanlam. Sanlam sought to consolidate its diverse banking interests and in 1974 requested Du Plessis to undertake the consolidation.

In 1968 Sanlam established Central Acceptances Ltd, with Senbank as a subsidiary. Soon Sanlam acquired the Bank of Johannesburg, a bank specializing in commercial and industrial finance. Sanlam also held shares in FVB's Federale Bank, in Mercabank (a merchant bank), Santam Bank (the general bank subsidiary of Santam), Sasbank, and Trust Bank, the general bank established within the FVB group by Jan S. Marais in 1955. These were small players in the banking sector and as regulatory intervention increased liquid asset requirements, many small banks experienced increasing operational pressure. Trust Bank was the largest in the group. This bank used its status as a non-commercial bank (which afforded the bank non-compliance with the strict liquid asset, capital, and reserve ratio requirements on commercial banks, as well as operations outside the Register of Co-operation between commercial banks—(ROCO[5]) to challenge

[5] G. Verhoef (2016): 'Strategies for market monopolization: the Register of Co-operation and the "imperial banks" in South Africa in the 1920s–1980s', in H. Bonin & N. Valerio (2016): *Colonial and Imperial Banking History*. Routledge: London: 85–103.

the market position of existing commercial banks. Marais spotted the gap in the market for personal and small- to medium-sized credit, which had taken off in the USA but did not yet sit comfortably with the commercial banking sector dominated by the imperial banks in the post-war period. Trust Bank entered the market for small- and medium-sized credit to business, industry, and individuals. By 1959 Trust Bank was the leading hire-purchase bank and by 1960 the fifth-largest registered banking institution in the country. The bank presented a non-conformist business strategy offering all banking functions under one roof, using miniskirt-clad glitzy female staff and modern banking halls to attract people not welcomed in the conservative upper-class commercial banks. In 1964 Trust Bank successfully listed on the JSE, to the public dismay of the financial press. The 'smile-and-thank-you' bank techniques of Trust Bank forced the conservative bankers in South Africa to admit that this unconventional approach had been endorsed by the Canadian Porter Commission and the Public Investment Bureau in Britain. Trust Bank was criticized for its policy of non-disclosure of internal reserves,[6] offering a kind of banking business resembling 'a new kind, a bazaar among banks, an everything-under-one-roof supermarket, in its own jargon "one-stop" banking'.[7] The main competitors were the commercial banks, registered as such under the Banks Act of 1942 and subject to more stringent capital and deposit requirements. Commercial banks' assets rose by 90 per cent between 1960 and 1967, but the assets of Trust Bank by 240 per cent.[8] Trust Bank diversified operations into property development, property participation ventures, the travel business, insurance through its own brokerage business, the acquisition of SA Metropolitan Life, its own acceptance bank, The Trust Accepting Bank, in 1968 (which became the third-largest merchant bank in South African within three years, with assets in excess of R11 million), and mutual growth funds through The Trust Bank Growth Fund Pty Ltd in March 1969. The innovation Trust Bank injected into the domestic banking environment was widely acknowledged, but held serious risks. Its flamboyant style, glossy rhetoric, and extensive exposure to property were more suited to the stable interest rate environment of the 1960s than the volatile spiking interest rates of the 1970s, complicated further by growing international isolation.[9]

Globally, liquidity contracted in the wake of the oil crisis of the 1970s and the subsequent world recession. This impacted directly on the open South African economy, which was dependent on oil imports. Du Plessis' knowledge of banking as former Professor in Money and Banking at the University of Potchefstroom afforded him credentials called upon by Minister of Finance O.P.F. Horwood in 1976 to act as curator of the collapsed Rand Bank. This bank had extended facilities to the value of R10m to

[6] *Financial Mail*, 27/5/196: 501; 6/6/1960: 734; 16/6/1960: 784.

[7] *Financial Mail*, 24/12/1964: 919; 8/5/1964: 58.

[8] *Financial Mail*, 27/10/1967: 296.

[9] G. Verhoef (1992): 'Afrikaner nationalism in South African banking; the cases of Volkskas and Trust Bank', in S. Jones: *Financial Enterprise in South Africa since 1950*. Macmillan: London: 115–53.

Glen Anil and when the property developer failed to repay the money Glen Anil collapsed, leaving Rand Bank unable to continue its operations. The bank was one of several casualties of increased regulatory intervention in the monetary sector during the mid-1970s, which led to ceilings on bank lending, the bank rate, and liquidity requirements. Du Plessis was tasked to wrap up Rand Bank. His professional conduct earned him the respect of the financial services industry.

It was not unexpected then, when Trust Bank failed to comply with new liquidity requirements of the Banks Act (as amended) 1972. By February 1977, Trust Bank's exposure to property stood at R171.8m.[10] Sanlam stepped in to rescue Trust Bank and Marais resigned as Managing Director in August 1977. Sanlam purchased 60 per cent of Trust Bank's ordinary shares to provide stability to the institution and protect Sanlam's interest in the bank. Trust Bank issued another 6 730 000 shares, sold its interest in Volkskas Bank so as not to have a commanding interest in rival banks, and commenced with a sobering merger strategy of its banking interests. A holding company in Sanlam, Bankorp Ltd, was used as consolidation vehicle. Merchant banking activities were merged in Senbank, acquiring Trust Accepting Bank. Bankorp acquired the 64 per cent Santam Bank shares in Mercabank in exchange for 3.4 million shares in Trust Bank. All the banking operations of Santam Bank, Bank of Johannesburg, and Credit Bank were merged into Santam Bank, which left Santam Bank a general bank offering hire-purchase financing and leasing.[11] The fundamental restructuring occurred under the control of Fred du Plessis, who was appointed Executive Chairman of Bankorp as Jan S. Marais stepped down. Du Plessis had just been appointed Sanlam's Managing Director in May 1978. The restructuring was used to reposition Trust Bank as a reclassified commercial bank (its cheque deposits had risen to R283m or 11 per cent of total liabilities by March 1982) in 1982. Trust Bank thus became the commercial bank in the Sanlam Group and Santam Bank the general bank in the group.[12] This development was the first strategic positioning of a life office in the banking sector, but it was a costly affair. Trust Bank made two more rights issues by 1981 to restore the bank's capital position, which had to be authorized by Sanlam as a mutual.

By the late 1970s the footprint of Afrikaner business was recognized, but Sanlam was criticized in the Afrikaans press for what was called its 'octopus-style' grab-and-control acquisition policy. Du Plessis himself was in frequent personal and written communication with P.W. Botha, President of South Africa, and the Minister of Finance, Barend du Plessis, about economic policy and the public criticism by government directed at so-called 'big business groups'. Botha accused Du Plessis of criticizing the government in

[10] Ibid.: 138.

[11] *Banks Quarterly Investment Research*: Martin & Company, February 1977: 4; April 1977: 9; June 1977: 10.

[12] G. Verhoef (1992): 'Afrikaner nationalism in South African banking; the cases of Volkskas and Trust Bank', in S. Jones: *Financial Enterprise in South Africa since 1950*. Macmillan: London: 141.

public and that 'he no longer wanted to be part of the team', but Du Plessis was unperturbed. He called for counter-cyclical lending policies, lower interest rates, and public recognition of the contribution made by Sanlam: 'In fact, South Africa ought to be thankful for an organization like Sanlam that mobilizes public savings and invest those towards the development of big capital-intensive local industries.'[13] This public confrontation displayed the rapidly crumbling Afrikaner political, economic, and social cohesion in the wake of a growing public awareness that government's hold had become seriously challenged and that fundamental change was imminent. Du Plessis emerged as an academic with a public profile prepared to take on Government to secure sound economic policies in the interest of the entire business community. He was proud of what Sanlam had achieved and the sustainability of the organization was his first priority. In the Sanlam strategy document of 11 November 1981 he wrote, 'it remains the aim to identify Sanlam as a conservative Afrikaner organization, since international tendencies were shifting more to the right than to the left.[14]

The negative publicity nevertheless upset Sanlam. The rescue operation at Trust Bank coincided with an offer by FVB to Sanlam in 1978 to acquire its shares in Fedmyn.[15] Sanlam acquired a controlling share in Fedmyn but faced a palace revolution. Rumours were going around that the Sanlam management was acting in too interventionist and authoritarian a manner at some of its related companies. (Sanlam referred to the non-insurance companies in which a controlling interest was held as 'related' [*verwante*] companies and not subsidiaries.) The intersection of management relations between Sanlam and related companies was troubling personal relations between Andreas Wassenaar and Wim de Villiers, Managing Director of Gencor. A small computer company delivering specialized computer services to the mining industry, Unicom, was owned by the Wassenaar Family Trust and a business partner, Alfred Street. Wassenaar's son Dirk was the manager. Unicom conducted some business with Gencor, but by the late 1970s was not in good shape. Wassenaar persuaded De Villiers of Gencor to take up a 20 per cent stake in Unicom to salvage the company. Unfortunately the company could not be turned around. Gencor finally acquired the Wassenaar Family Trust's share before liquidating the company, but not before Wassenaar accused Gencor of 'sabotaging' Unicom. De Villiers was brought to a decision on Unicom when in 1980 Gencor had

[13] SA: 6/1/6: Letter P.W. Botha–F.J. du Plessis, 2/5/1984; Letter F.J. du Plessis–P.W. Botha, 12/11/1984; Open letter F.J. du Plessis to 39 persons: Cabinet Ministers, Chairmen of Parliamentary Standing Committees and Chairmen of Public Bodies, 17/7/1985.

[14] SA: Minutes of Sanlam Board, 18/11/1981: F.J. du Plessis Sanlam Strategic Plan for 1981/82 to 1985/86. Du Plessis was referring to the rise of Margaret Thatcher in Britain and Ronald Reagan in the USA. He explicitly stated that he was not prepared to risk Sanlam by joining the bandwagon of new left politics in South Africa.

[15] SA: 6/5/2/: Minutes of Sanlam board, 15/11/1978. Federale Mynbou Beperk (Fedmyn) was the holding company of the mining interests.

to decide on a long-term relationship with Siemens on mainframe and other computer services Gencor would require in future for power-station equipment. Unicom presented a conflict of interest with Siemens and Gencor had to take a long-term business decision. It was apparent that Unicom did not fit the bill. In June 1981, at a board meeting of Fedmyn (the holding company of Gencor) De Villiers proposed that the shareholder loans to Unicom be written off and the relationship with Unicom be terminated in the interest of Gencor. He met with very strong opposition from Wassenaar, who was a Sanlam director on the Fedmyn board. Wassenaar subsequently posed a serious threat to the professional career of De Villiers. The latter withdrew from the winding-down negotiations of Unicom and allowed the Fedmyn Chairman, Dr W.B. Coetzer, to conclude the negotiations with Wassenaar. Wassenaar 'took over Gencor's interest for R1' as was reported to the Gencor board on 4 June 1981.[16] The personal relations between Wassenaar, then still Sanlam Chairman, and De Villiers were seriously compromised.[17] De Villiers was Deputy Chairman of the Sanlam board, but Wassenaar vowed later to have his say about De Villiers' future career. De Villiers decided to resign from the Sanlam board.[18] The row boiled over into a number of non-related issues, all of which contributed to very unpleasant personal clashes and a weakening of the relationship between Sanlam and other long-standing Afrikaner business interests in Gencor. This episode underlined the precarious nature of intra-Afrikaner relationships at the time of high volatility in South Africa. The storm in the teacup of the Unicom sideshow intersected with a much more strategic issue in the history of Sanlam.

In November 1978 the Sanlam board tabled the first document of a five-year strategic plan for Sanlam and its related companies. This was shortly after the Sanlam acquisition of the controlling interest in Fedmyn, the second-largest mining house in South Africa. The significance of this acquisition for Afrikaner business cannot be overstated. The epic nature of the rise of Afrikaners in the mining sector lay in General Mining (Genmin, controlled by Fedmyn) emerging as the second-largest gold-mining house in South Africa after a protracted acquisition battle for Union Corporation. This battle lasted from August 1974 to January 1975. At first Barlow Rand made an offer for Union Corporation in June 1974, followed by three offers by Gold Fields of South Africa (GFSA). Genmin also made an offer, which was rejected, leading to an acquisition strategy by Genmin by means of private purchases of Union Corporation shares in foreign markets until Genmin controlled 51 per cent of the issued Union Corporation shareholding. Genmin had arranged a foreign loan of US$85m with *Deutsche Länderbank*

[16] J.D.F. Jones (1995): *Through fortress and rock: The story of Gencor 1895–1995*. Johannesburg: Jonathan Ball: 168; SA: 6/1/6G: P.E. Rousseau Confidential Memorandum–Sanlam Board, 1/12/1981.

[17] SA: 6/1/2: Letter W.J. de Villiers–A.D. Wassenaar, 14/5/1981.

[18] SA: 6/1/6G: P.E. Rousseau Confidential Memorandum–Sanlam Board, 1/12/1981; 6/1/6G: Confidential Memorandum A.D. Wasseraar–Sanlam Directors, 5/1/1982.

to buy the Union Corporation shares, because foreign exchange regulations at the time did not permit the offshore transfer of South African currency to the magnitude required to raise its Union Corporation shareholding.[19] (Genmin was confident that it would be in a position to repay the loan in good time, since the gold price had risen well beyond the US$175 level of 1975 to more than US$600 by the end of 1980. Improved earnings from gold-mining would repay the loan.) GFSA thus failed to secure acceptance of its offer for Union Corporation and Genmin walked off with a formerly British-controlled mining house, which strengthened its gold-mining interests substantially. Genmin did it without the assistance of the Anglo American Corporation (AAC). The acquisition strategy first involved the support of AAC for the initial Genmin bid, but when that was rejected by the Union Corporation Panel in London, AAC offered its support to a new Genmin bid, but on condition that AAC received as compensation the platinum interests of Union Corporation and its shares in Sappi. Genmin's negotiators were not prepared to water down the potential Union Corporation asset and entered into agreements with 'friendly partners' to buy Union Corporation shares up to a point where Genmin's own shares and the 'mystery buyers' 10 per cent afforded Genmin a 51 per cent control, able to block the acceptance of the last GFSA offer.[20] This battle made for a conscious Sanlam policy to manage its 'strategic investments' close to its own boardroom.

The 1978 Sanlam strategy document introduced the first formal explanation of what the company considered to be its 'strategic' investments. Investments in related companies to the level where Sanlam had control, were considered its strategic investments and the company insisted on securing its full and undisputed control over those strategic interests at all times. The Sanlam role was that of an investment company and not a management company, seeking optimal returns on policyholder funds. Underperforming related companies therefore impacted directly on the ability of Sanlam to declare reversionary bonuses on its policies. It adopted the policy not to appoint the Managing Director of Sanlam to the boards of the related companies in order to maintain an arm's-length relationship. This issue of control in underlying companies where Sanlam owned a majority stake soon caused unprecedented bitterness in the relationship between Sanlam, Rembrandt, and Volkskas. The matter, which concerned control of Gencor—the merged mining house formed after Genmin had acquired Union Corporation in 1975—was driven to a public confrontation in 1981. As a result of the major upset caused to the English-controlled mining sector in South Africa, Wim de Villiers, Managing Director of Genmin and subsequently also of Gencor, wisely decided not to force an immediate integration between Genmin and Union Corporation. It was decided that Ted Pavitt, a bilingual South African and Managing Director of Union

[19] SA: 6/5/1: Minutes of Sanlam Board, 19/3/1980; SA: 6/1/2: Letter A.D. Wassenaar–D.W. Hertzog, 12/3/1985; SA: 7/1/3/1/1/: Genmin planning for Union Corporation acquisition.

[20] SA: G. Verhoef (1993)): *The History of Federale Mynbou Beperk*. Unpublished manuscript.

Corporation, would be requested to take up the position of Deputy Managing Director of Gencor, but that he would manage the former Union Corporation assets as a separate entity until such time as management decided it opportune to effect a full merger of operations. The Afrikaans management in Genmin realized that the merger of the two mining houses under the control of Afrikaner businessmen harboured potential sensitivities that would best be mitigated after enough time had elapsed and all parties concerned had developed a mutual relationship of trust in conducting the mining business they were there to do. By 1979 Wim de Villiers decided the time had come to commence the effective rationalization of the merged two mining houses.

Union Corporation had extensive gold-mining operations and as the rationalization commenced, Gencor realized a rights issue would be required to fund the development of the Beisa uranium mine and the adjacent Beatrix gold mine. The rights issue was conducted at Fedmyn, the controlling company of Gencor, following intense negotiations between Sanlam, Rembrandt, and Volkskas. Fedmyn raised the capital necessary to allow Gencor the expansions. The final distribution of shareholding in Gencor nevertheless raised Fred du Plessis' eyebrows. Fedmyn retained a direct stake of 44.67 per cent, but with the shareholding of other group companies, Sanlam and Gencor staff, 51.30 per cent was in the hands of Sanlam. '*Bona fide* outside shareholders controlled 48.7% of Gencor.'[21] For Sanlam this was too close for comfort. In a lengthy memorandum to the Sanlam board Du Plessis explained the bigger picture of Sanlam's investment policy. The company's priority was maximum return on policyholders' funds and it therefore had to prevent a real weakening in the market value of its assets to ensure competitive bonus rates on policies. It was therefore paramount that investment in shares had to be in related companies' equity. At the same time, the management of a successful related concern would require more operational independence and a balance of institutional equity partners to give it the desired independence. Du Plessis warned that minority shareholders could have different investment priorities from those of the majority shareholders, which could lead to disagreement on strategy and policy. Thus control for Sanlam had to be undisputed and absolute. The time to strengthen control was therefore under conditions of downward business cycle movements, provided, of course, that those investments rendered superior returns to other investment opportunities.[22] By February 1981 Sanlam was more than upbeat about Fedmyn's performance—it had outperformed the Industrial Index annually since 1978.[23] This was a strategic interest Fred du Plessis/Sanlam would protect at all costs.

[21] SA: 6/1/6G: Minutes of Sanlam board, 22/1/1980.

[22] SA: 6/5/1/: Minutes of Sanlam Board, 19/3/1980; Memorandum F.J. du Plessis, Financing Related Companies, 13/3/1980; Minutes of Sanlam Board, 18/6/1980.

[23] SA: Minutes of Sanlam Board, 18/2/1981.

In 1980 the following matters converged into a complex relationship: management control by Sanlam of its related companies as a vital strategic policy concern; the strained personal relationships between Wassenaar and De Villiers about Unicom came to a point; and product developments in the life insurance industry ruffled the feathers of Rembrandt. Completely coincidentally, the Life Offices Association (LOA) discussed international studies relating to the lower life expectancy of smokers. Reinsurance companies informed Sanlam that other life offices in South Africa were considering the introduction of discounts to non-smokers on new policies. Sanlam immediately investigated the matter, but first sought to discuss the matter with Dr Anton Rupert. The Rupert business empire included extensive cigarette interests. Failing to secure an appointment with Rupert, Du Plessis himself met with the Managing Director of Rembrandt to explain the developments. Between late March and the end of April 1980 there were heated written communication between Du Plessis and Rupert about the relationship between the companies, the decision to offer discounts to non-smokers, and several other matters that were clearly a thorn in Rembrandt's side. Rupert, a friend of Wassenaar's, interpreted the development as potentially detrimental to his business. This occurred at the same time as the Sanlam Growth Fund sold some of its shares in Rembrandt to comply with statutory investment regulations, but Rupert did not see it that way. Mutual dissatisfaction about the developments was expressed in polite written exchanges between Sanlam (signed by Fred du Plessis as Managing Director) and Rupert. Du Plessis informed Rembrandt that Sanlam had decided not to lead the market in introducing the non-smokers' discount and Rupert interpreted the sale of such policies as harmful to his business. He reminded Du Plessis that Dr M.S. Louw had been the first person to take up a cigarette from the production line of the Rembrandt cigarette factory and had reached a ripe old age.[24] Rupert wrote that 'you cannot be someone's partner, while using his company image for marketing purposes harms his business'.[25] Du Plessis called upon Rupert in the 'interest of the Afrikaner' irrespective of the personal relationship between Rupert and himself, not to allow a rift to develop between the two business entities for which they had taken responsibility'.[26] Sanlam then followed market leaders Shield Insurance and Colonial Mutual in issuing non-smokers' policies in August 1980.

This fragile relationship was put to the test when Sanlam proposed the enlargement of the Gencor board to allow for the inclusion of three Sanlam-appointed directors to the board in 1982. Sanlam reiterated its policy position of 1978. The company wanted

[24] SA: 6/1/2: Letter A.E. Rupert–F.J. du Plessis, 27/3/1980; SA: 6/1/2: A.D. Wassenaar–A.E. Rupert, 28/4/1980.

[25] SA: 6/1/6G: Letter du Plessis–Rupert, 31/3/1980; letter Rupert–du Plessis, 31/3/1980 (delivered by hand) [author translation].

[26] SA: 6/1/6G: Letter du Plessis–Rupert, 11/4/1980.

absolute control of its related companies. Rembrandt's 30 per cent direct shareholding in Gencor and Volkskas' 5 per cent left Sanlam without outright control. Fedmyn comprised 28 per cent of the total Sanlam investment portfolio. When Gencor requested its board to appoint seven executives of the company to the board, Sanlam opposed the request and announced its intention to change the statutes of Gencor to allow Sanlam to appoint a further three directors to the Gencor board. That would secure an undisputed majority for Sanlam on that board—a matter that raised red flags with Rembrandt and Volkskas and ushered in the famous '*Broedertwis*' between Sanlam, Rembrandt, and Volkskas. The last-mentioned two shareholders objected on the grounds of an alleged 'partnership relationship' between them and Sanlam, which they argued went back to the support they had rendered to Fedmyn during the Union Corporation battle. A formal agreement had been entered into between parties using the pseudonyms *Labrador, Giraffe, Camel, Lynx*, and *Aristotle* on 16 November 1975 in terms whereof Fedmyn issued shares to Rembrandt, Volkskas, and Sanlam to the effect that Rembrandt's equity stake in Fedmyn was increased to 25 per cent and Volkskas' to 10 per cent. That entitled Rembrandt to two directors on the Fedmyn board, with the support of Sanlam.[27] Rembrandt's payment was in Deutsche Mark into a Fedmyn account in Frankfurt, while the Volkskas and Sanlam payments were in South African currency into the Fedmyn account at Volkskas in Johannesburg. The agreement was authorized by the South African Reserve Bank. This was one way of securing sufficient funds outside South Africa to allow Fedmyn's private purchase of Union Corporation shares during the battle for control of the latter. Opposing the Sanlam move to enlarge the Gencor board, Rembrandt and Volkskas accused Sanlam of reneging on the 'partnership relationship' established by the confidential agreement in 1975. Afrikaner-controlled Rembrandt and Volkskas interpreted the Sanlam move as hijacking the Gencor board, undermining the independence of directors on the board and ruining a long relationship of trust. Sanlam denied the existence of any legally binding partnership between the parties. Du Plessis/Sanlam became suspicious of Rembrandt's intentions when the latter acquired 5 per cent of the Volkskas shares without informing Sanlam of the transaction.[28] The statutes of Gencor were amended at a Gencor board meeting on 1 April 1982. Sanlam sought legal advice about the validity of the changes to the statutes. Michael Katz confirmed the correctness of the decision. Rembrandt challenged the matter in the Supreme Court, but its application was dismissed with costs.[29]

[27] SA: 6/1/6: Confidential announcement. Labrador, Giraffe, Camel, Lynx, Aristotle, 16/11/1975.—Can an announcement be confidential?

[28] SA: 6/1/6G: Confidential Memorandum on Rembrandt by F.J. du Plessis, 27/9/1982.

[29] SA: Minutes of Sanlam Board, 17/3/1981; Minutes of Sanlam Board, 5/5/1982; *Financial Mail*, 14/5/1982: 283; *Cape Times*, 15/2/1982.

The facts of the matter were clouded in the personal intrigues between Wassenaar and De Villiers, who had been accused of siding with Rupert, a long-time confidant and close friend, as well as the personal clashes between Rupert and Du Plessis on matters of 'business philosophy', as Du Plessis described it.[30] The stress of the battle affected De Villiers' health and Wassenaar insisted on his resignation before 30 June 1982. De Villiers stood firm, supplying numerous reports by his personal physician attesting to his fitness to perform his duties. De Villiers' refusal to submit to Wassenaar's pressure resulted in an unsavoury relationship between him, Wassenaar, and W.B. Coetzer on the Gencor board. De Villiers then approached Du Plessis, as Sanlam's Managing Director, to request the resignation of Wassenaar and Coetzer from the Gencor board and undertook to resign in 1984 when he reached retirement age.[31] Du Plessis refused to consider the request, accusing De Villiers of not being neutral during the confrontation with Rembrandt and not submitting to the majority decisions of the Sanlam board. He stated that he could no longer defend De Villiers.[32] De Villiers called a press conference and announced his resignation at the end of November 1982. He was succeeded by Ted Pavitt as Managing Director of Gencor.

The media hailed De Villiers as the victim of Wassenaar's personal vendetta since Unicom. De Villiers was held in high esteem in the mining industry as a professional engineer and businessman. Sanlam was heavily invested in Fedmyn and more than satisfied with the returns on the investment. Du Plessis seemed genuinely convinced that Rembrandt was attempting to secure a foothold in Fedmyn,[33] which could undermine the Sanlam strategy of managing its strategic investments. By the mid-1980s Sanlam's concerns about the performance of its related companies was beginning to emerge as strategic to the future of the life office amid fundamental industry changes and turbulent domestic conditions. Despite a press statement to announce a truce between Sanlam and Rembrandt in June 1983, Du Plessis realized the harm done to the image of Sanlam among its policyholders. He subsequently embarked on an unprecedented outreach to policyholders. Meetings to which they were invited were organized across the country. These were the so-called Sanlam Managing Director Roadshows. The open meetings gave policyholders the opportunity to engage directly with Du Plessis, be entertained lavishly, and re-establish confidence in Sanlam.[34]

[30] *The Cape Argus*: Sanlam asserts its control of Fed Mynbou: 18/6/1982; *Sunday Times*: Sanlam spells out its policy on capital: 21/11/1982.

[31] SA: 6/1/6G: Confidential letter W.J. de Villiers–FJ du Plessis, 14/8/1982.

[32] SA 6/1/6G: letter F.J. du Plessis–W.J. de Villers, 16/8/1982.

[33] SA: 6/1/6; Letter F.J. du Plessis–W.H. de Villiers, 16/8/1982. In this letter Du Plessis wrote 'Sanlam is ernstig bekommerd oor pogings om beheer oor Gencor van ons te ontneem' [Sanlam is deeply concerned about attempts to take control of Gencor from Sanlam].

[34] SA: 6/1/6: Press release, 27/3/1983; *Sunday Times*, 28/3/1983.

'Take these disasters, son, and fix them': Sankorp

The public *Broedertwis* shook the confidence in Sanlam as a trustworthy life office, investment partner, and vanguard of Afrikaner economic achievement. The acquisition drive of the 1970s and 1980s by FVB and Fedmyn resulted in control by Sanlam of companies operating in diverse business and industrial sectors outside of the long-term insurance market. Sanlam did not have the expertise to intervene in operational management, but was aware of the sub-optimal performance of these non-core assets. The former Managing Director, Pepler Scholtz, a member of the Sanlam board in 1983, pointed out that more problems arose than were being solved when the company controlling a diverse number of operating concerns was also an operating company. Scholtz identified the conflicting dualism of the interests of the controlling company and those of related companies. Sanlam as a life office with the responsibility of guaranteed insurance cover and a safe savings opportunity, could not guarantee equal access to its investment funds by all its related companies and simultaneously look after policyholders' interests. Scholtz suggested the separation of responsibilities between management of a life office and management of non-core operating companies. The strategic importance of functional separation was inevitable. Fred du Plessis identified four areas of underperformance in the Sanlam Group: Sanlam passively observed the unsatisfactory performance of 'related' companies; there was a complete lack of co-ordinated group response to short-term business cycle estimates, and these impacted on the long-term perceptions of changes in technology, the political economy, social behaviour, and demographics; there was unco-ordinated recruitment and development of human resources in the Group; and finally, insufficient attention was afforded to the construction of a distinguishable group identity to separate Sanlam from other conglomerates in South Africa.[35]

The organizational concern was simultaneously a performance issue and a strategic interest not typically associated with a life office. Between 1970 and 1985 the Sanlam Group's structure became increasingly complex. Sanlam's asset base grew from R1 000m in 1975 to R6 000m in 1984. FVB and Fedmyn expanded into a wide range of industrial and mining interests, Bankorp's assets increased from R500m and 2 per cent market share, to R10 555m and 13 per cent market share by 1985. Sanlam acquired substantial stakes in the Malbak/Protea Group, Natie Kirsch's Tradegro group, and the Murray & Roberts construction group. Substantial losses were made in the chemical business Sentrachem, in Kirsch's Tradegro group, in Nissan, Gencor's industrial interests and in Sappi. The rumour in the financial press was that Sanlam had pumped more than R300m into these companies seeking to effect a turnaround.[36] The strategy was

[35] Sanlam Board Minutes, 15 August 1984.

[36] *Sunday Times*: 6 September 1987.

subsequently to overhaul one of its investment companies, URD Investments Pty Ltd (with only one asset—*Federale Mynbou Beleggings*, holding a 35 per cent stake in Fedmyn), into an investment company, *Sanlam Beleggingskorporasie Beperk* (Sankorp Ltd). Marinus Daling assumed the position of Managing Director and the board was the same as the Sanlam board.

The task was to secure operational efficiency at all of the underlying assets. The assets transferred from Sanlam to Sankorp were the so-called 'strategic investments' of Sanlam. The distribution of shareholding between Sanlam and Sankorp is illustrated in Table 4.1. Ultimately, the vision was to list Sankorp. The sheer size of these investments pointed to a conflict of focus at the life office. Fred du Plessis' *tour de force* to secure 'total control', left Sanlam in an effective controlling position of companies operating outside its core expertise and capabilities. Sustained underperformance and bad press left Sanlam no choice but to come up with a radical turnaround strategy.

Sankorp's first priority was extensive rationalization. Indiscriminate acquisitions left a diversity of sectoral interests scattered across all of the conglomerates under the Sankorp umbrella. Apart from Fedmyn's mining interests, there were also mining interests in Messina (Premier Metals). There were interests in electronics in Siemens (in which Sankorp and FVB both had interests), Plessey, Tedelex, TEK Electronics, TEK Logic, and TEK/Defy. Sandock Austral (in Gencor) and Magnis were both engaged in the

Table 4.1. Structure of Sanlam/Sankorp asset distribution, 1985

Sector	Selected companies	SANLAM total interest		SANKORP interest		Sankorp interest
		Rm	% issued share capital	Rm	% issued share capital	% of Sankorp's portfolio
MINING	*FederaleMynbou*	532	50	380	35	41
FINANCIAL	Bankorp	150	58	78	30	9
	Metropolitan Homes Trust	60	100	60	100	7
	Santam	16	40	16	40	2
TRANSPORT	Messina	30	50	30	50	3
	United Transport Holdings	49	30	49	30	5
ELECTRONICS	Plessey	73	25	73	25	8
ENGINEERING	Abercom	17	52	17	52	2
INDUSTRIAL	Malbak	75	50	60	40	7
HOLDINGS	FVB	60	54	44	40	5
	Anchusa	31	21	31	21	3
RETAIL	TEK/Defy	28	46	28	46	3
	Sanki	47	49	47	49	5
		R1 168		R913		100%

production, assembly, and import of rear axles, while Autocast (in Messina) and Ferroform (Murray & Roberts Engineering) manufactured engine blocks. There were pharmaceutical concerns in Malbak (Protea) and FVB (SA Druggists), retail furniture in FVB (Morkels), Sanki (Kirsh Trading–Russells) and Gencor (Ellerines), agricultural machinery in Malbak (Malcomess) and FVB (Fedmech), industrial concerns in Gencor, FVB, Malbak, and Murray & Roberts (Anchusa), and insurance in Metropolitan Homes Trust, Santam, and Bankorp. Immediate rationalization would take time because of vested business interests, the diversity of business cultures and management styles, and Sankorp's policy of non-interference in operational activities of underlying companies unless serious problems mandated.

The management philosophy driving the restructuring of Sanlam's strategic investments was what was known in management theory of the time, as strategic planning companies (SPC).[37] Sankorp functioned on a lean management structure, primarily participating in and influencing the development of business strategies in the related companies. Sankorp did not interfere with the management of underlying companies, but rather assisted with strategic planning.[38] It operated in two areas: establishing demanding planning processes and making substantial contributions to strategic thinking. It was not a question of taking control, but rather about strategic planning towards operational overhaul. The model of the SPC at the centre performing a vital role to develop business unit strategies, was expressed firmly and repeatedly. The SPC's role overall in the international business environment, was to 'centralize strategy and decentralize operations to a number of management companies based along market lines. The assumption is that operating managers look one or two years ahead. The centre must provide the longer-term perspective.'[39] A senior manager at a strategic planning company claimed: 'It's a charade to pretend in this era of corporate democracy to decentralize this right and responsibility. [i.e., to be involved in strategy decisions] widely into the organization. Down at the business level there are two or three decisions each decade that make or break business. Do you really want to leave the business manager alone to make these?'[40] Sankorp concentrated investment, human resources, and strategic planning expertise in its own structure in order to assist long-term planning from the centre, leaving short-term implementation decisions to operational management within underlying companies.

To map out the Sankorp strategy, the mission statement described Sankorp's business as a holding company of Sanlam's strategic investments, to ensure uninterrupted

[37] M. Goold and A. Campbell (1987) *Strategies and Styles: The role of the centre in managing diversified corporations*. Oxford: Basil Blackwell.

[38] Interview with Attie du Plessis, 27/7/2017: The teachings of Thomas Peterson in 'strategic planning' were adhered to.

[39] Goold and Campbell, 1987: 46.

[40] Goold and Campbell, 1987 47.

satisfactory profitability and balanced growth of the portfolio. Satisfactory profitability meant, firstly, profitability for sustainability, secondly, profitability to ensure the renewal and replacement of investments and, thirdly, comparable profit performance to market competitors. Sankorp assumed active participation in the boards of underlying companies, provided support where required, but also secured dismissal or succession in management to achieve target performance. Sanlam assumed control through Sankorp, but it was going to be a decade of rationalizing, rightsizing, and restructuring before the lopsided exposure of Sanlam to non-life-related sectors in the economy was rectified. The first priority was to restructure the conglomerates from within.[41]

This strategy was supported by in-depth economic analysis and forecasting, provided by P.D.F (Peet) Strydom, university professor, former economist at Senbank, and renowned for cutting-edge socio-economic scenario analyses. These analyses included industry norms to assess performance. The underlying principle Sankorp assumed in this strategy was that 'mutually understood and accepted' meant that both parties, Sankorp and the related conglomerate management, understood the Sankorp approach, bought into it, and mutually agreed to implementation. Sankorp's turnaround strategy would fail unless there was mutual buy-in from both the conglomerate management and the Sankorp leadership. In the world of powerful businessmen this was going to require fancy footwork. Media responses varied between highly critical and negative comments. *Finance Week* described the Sankorp portfolio as a basket of lemons,[42] while the *Sunday Times* interpreted the establishment of Sankorp as a defeat for Sanlam: 'As if Dr Fred du Plessis said to youthful investment chief, Daling: "Take all these disasters, son, and fix them".'[43] The so-called lame ducks, Nissan, Kirsh Trading Group (Checkers), Sentrachem, Sappi, and Kanhym, were addressed as part of a holistic conglomerate overhaul. The financial press did not necessarily like Fred du Plessis, but respected his intellect. He was seen as a 'dominant, ruthless, intolerant, irrationally brilliant... (man)... a man of overstated ambition',[44] but... he had his feet on the ground'[45] and was courageous enough to justify and implement his vision. Du Plessis maintained an active presence in the Sankorp planning process. He was known for his 'single-minded, purpose leadership and clear insight',[46] as well as 'clear economic vision, his expertise and his refusal to compromise his principles'.[47] When he died in 1989 the response was that, 'It says much for the management capability of the Sanlam Chairman, Fred du Plessis, who died in tragic circumstances last week, that his replacements in the group's top echelons were so self-evident.'[48] Du Plessis' thinking was that the SPC ultimately had to build

[41] Sankorp Mission Statement, 8/7/1985; Sankorp Minutes, 26/2/1986.
[42] *Finance Week*, 8–14 August 1991. [43] *Sunday Times, Business Times*, 5 March 1989.
[44] *Financial Mail*, 16 February 1989.
[45] *Cape Argus*, 15 March 1989. Statement by Jan van der Horst, Old Mutual.
[46] *The Star*, 23 February 1990. [47] *Pretoria News*, 16 March 1989.
[48] *Finance Week*, 29 March 1989.

the leadership throughout the group, which, it was believed, would ultimately deliver much-improved operational excellence.

Public opinion did not deter Du Plessis. He motivated the much-frowned-upon acquisition of Natie Kirsch's Tradegro group and Nissan as a strategy of investing in growth opportunities and the protection of jobs. Especially in the mid-1980s when foreign banks refused to roll over South African bank loans and foreign investment dried up, Du Plessis expressed his preference for investing in growth industries rather than 'play the stock market'.[49] To him investment in shares on the stock market would assist overseas investors who wanted to get their capital out of the country. Investment in growth industries would promote growth and employment creation, and investment in struggling industries would prevent retrenchment. Sankorp was extremely sensitive to the fact that the government blamed big groups or conglomerates for a contraction of job creation. When Sanlam acquired control of the Kirsh Group (KTC) in September 1985, Kirsh owed its creditors R500 million, placing the future of 31 000 employees in jeopardy. By 1987 a more appreciative press reported that big was not necessarily bad in South African business. 'By supporting ailing companies such as Tradegro, Nissan and Tedelex, we [Sanlam, according to Du Plessis] have saved 60 000 jobs. In addition, the number of people in our controlled companies has risen by 50 000 to more than 420 000—so thanks to Sanlam, there are 110 000 jobs more than there would have been.'[50]

The first three years of Sankorp was a period of consolidation. It was about appointing the right leadership for future restructuring. In July 1984 Dave Brink was appointed CEO of Murray & Roberts and in July 1986 Derek Keys was appointed Gencor CEO. Between 1985 and 1988 Sankorp arranged the relocation of almost all mining interests into Gencor, a high degree of concentration of financial and banking interests into Bankorp, and the industrial interests in FVB, Malhold, Malbak, Messina, Abercom, Sentrachem, GKN, Nissan, Plessey, TEK, Sandock-Austral, United Transport, Tradegro, Interhold, Kimet, and Sanki. These functional rationalizations did indeed contribute to improved performance on the JSE sectoral indices, but the Sankorp interests still underperformed the overall sectoral indices. Sanlam put its money where its mouth was. In September 1988 Sanlam announced a R2 billion capital injection for Sankorp to facilitate future restructuring and expanding enterprises needing capital.[51] The financial press responded favourably, describing the capital allocation as 'a substantial contribution to the development of South Africa' especially in a period when investments had become a cause for concern. Sanlam underlined the consistency of its policy: to create and expand new enterprises and not merely make safe investments in established undertakings.[52]

[49] *Business Day*, 28 October 1985. [50] *Sunday Times*, 6 September 1987.

[51] Sanlam Board minutes, 16/11/1988; Sankorp Minutes, 21/1/1989; *The Argus*, 16/2/1989: *The Star*, *Business Times*, 16/2/1989.

[52] *Business Day*, 16 February 1989.

Favourable comments from the *Sunday Times* (*Business Times*) were that 'Sanlam is continuing the operation bootstraps policies on which it was founded. As it did for a destitute Afrikaner community in the 1930's, after Sharpeville in 1961 and Soweto in 1976, Sanlam is again investing in the national interest.'[53]

The first restructuring exercise was at the Kirsh Group. Capital injection was needed, management had to be replaced, and unprofitable enterprises in the group had to be disposed of. When Sanlam investigated the KTC Group in 1984, the capital and operational risks were clear, but should the risks pay off, it could earn Sanlam handsome returns from the retail sector in the growing urbanizing communities. Daling was ambitious, writing that 'We must keep in mind that if we do not use this opportunity, we will probably never again have an opportunity to control a retail group in South Africa.'[54] In August 1985 the KTC Group did a R100 million rights issue, to which Sankorp subscribed and thereby acquired full control of the group. Daling moved in as Executive Chairman of the KTC Group and commenced a restructuring and selling-off exercise, disposing of supermarkets and furniture stores in 1987 and 1988. Pick'n Pay and newly emerging Spar and Shoprite stores still outperformed the KTC Checkers retail outlets, leading Martin & Company to note, 'Many of Checkers' store managers are considered inadequately qualified to run what are effectively small businesses'.[55] In 1990 Sankorp admitted defeat in turning Tradegro around. It was decided to unbundle the group. Despite Marinus Daling's ambition for Sanlam to control a retail group, he did not have the experience in retailing to succeed. Finally, Sankorp sold its controlling share in Tradegro to Christo Wiese's Pepkor Group in 1992. After the unbundling of Tradegro, Sankorp still held shares and debentures in Tradehold, which were sold to Pepkor. This closed off a chapter in Daling's retailing ambitions. The final unbundling realized R44 million for Sankorp and the remaining 31 million Tradehold shares still held by Sankorp were exchanged for Pepkor shares in 1992.[56]

The KTC exercise sounded a clear warning to Daling—the capabilities of an investment chief of a life office did not necessarily translate into successful operational management of a retail group. The performance enhancement of the conglomerates under its control was a direct function of specialist management in the dedicated sector. The investment function of a life office was diametrically opposed to the operational management of the construction industry, mining operations, or automobile manufacturing. Subsequent rationalization of the Sankorp assets depended on expert management in the dedicated operational sector. Tackling the underperforming FVB required a strategic decision about the Sankorp conglomerates. Industrial, mining, and service companies were scattered across FVB, Malbak, Murray & Roberts, and Gencor. Between

[53] *Sunday Times*, 5 March 1989. [54] Daling Memorandum to Sankorp Board, 21/8/1985.
[55] Martin & Company Analyst report, 1/1/1991.
[56] Sankorp Minutes, 27/11/1991; 14/10/1992.

1985 and 1988 Sankorp underwrote two R100m rights issues of FVB, but capital injection failed to resolve the fundamental problem of failing management. Foreign exchange losses of more than R80m were suffered in 1984. By November 1989 FVB's share price was 345 cents compared to the disclosed net asset value per FVB share of 650 cents, meaning FVB shares were trading at a discount of 47 per cent. FVB's share price dropped to a level of approximately 255 cents by 1989, which was lower than in 1968. The price-earnings ratio (PE) of FVB, when compared to other industrial holding companies at that time, was relatively weak. FVB's PE was 4.5 while Amic's was 7.5, C.G. Smith's 11.2, Malbak's 5.1, and Anglo Vaal Industries' 8.7.[57] Dr Kerneels Human, the FVB Chairman, passed away early in 1989 and Marinus Daling assumed the position, only to find that the ills of FVB were indeed in the quality of management.

Sankorp also needed to reconsider FVB as a 'strategic investment'. Fred du Plessis was no longer at Sanlam. The Sankorp strategic economic research and confidential investment report by Martin & Company advised Sankorp to move fast on creating dedicated and focused industrial conglomerates. A firm policy decision on industrial conglomerates in early 1991 confirmed the strategy forward: FVB was restructured as a services holding company and industrial assets were relocated into Malbak (industry), Murray & Roberts (construction and engineering), and Gencor (mining).[58] Sankorp took out FVB minorities, delisted the company and, as the sole owner of FVB, moved, sold, and restructured industrial, mining, and engineering companies in its other conglomerates. FVB sold its interests in Fedfood and SA Druggists to Malbak; Malbak sold its interests in Darling & Hodgson (of which Blue Circle comprised 42 per cent), as well as 50 per cent of its shareholding in Standard Engineering to Murray & Roberts; and Murray & Roberts purchased Firestone, Trichamp, and Gabriel from FVB. The name of FVB then changed to Fedservices in April 1992, the holding company of Servgro, the services conglomerate emerging from the industrial rationalization transactions of 1991. Servgro was a wholly-owned subsidiary of Sankorp with the following underlying subsidiaries: Avis, Fedics, Interleisure, Price Forbes, and Teljoy. Servgro listed on the Johannesburg Stock Exchange on 7 August 1992.[59] The final restructuring of FVB was indeed indicative of the change in business strategy in Sanlam. FVB was the vehicle of Afrikaner entry into industrial enterprise, established as the brainchild of M.S. Louw after the *Ekonomiese Volkskongres* of 1939. In 1992 Afrikaner businessmen were industrialists in their own right, managing industrial conglomerates far beyond FVB and no longer required FVB industrial finance to enter industrial enterprise. FVB was undoubtedly a powerful empowerment business that disseminated numerous training manuals for employees across the operational and management structures of new Afrikaans

[57] Sankorp Management, 28/11/1989; Sankorp Board, 20/6/1990; 12/9/1990.
[58] Sankorp Board, 14/11/1990. [59] Sankorp Board, 8/4/1992.

enterprises. In the end, FVB managed South African enterprises and made a notable contribution to industrial development and employment creation. Ultimately, under-performing FVB belonged to the history of Afrikaner empowerment.

The restructuring of the banking interests under Sankorp's control was a very different kettle of fish. In 1985 Sankorp and Sanlam together controlled 71.3 per cent of Bankorp. Trust Bank, the largest bank, was the general bank, with Mercabank, Santam Bank, Senbank and the International Bank of Johannesburg in diverse financial sectors. Du Plessis' style of management of Bankorp was described as if he managed the bank as his 'personal fiefdom'.[60] He engineered some functional rationalization by July 1985 when the corporate banking services of Santam Bank were incorporated in Trust Bank, the latter's consumer finance business was transferred to Santam Bank, and non-bank operations such as travel agencies, hotels, and industrial operations were sold.[61] Governance structures were weakened, as the board, audit committee, auditors, and Sankorp seemed to have performed a totally subordinate role to Du Plessis as Executive Chairman.[62] For all practical purposes those structures had no real influence over the direction the group was taking. A financial journalist commented later, 'A man of overstated ambition, Du Plessis was the Afrikaner champion and he wanted a conspicuously successful, big Afrikaner bank.'[63] In 1984 Bankorp acquired Mercabank, an institution with high exposure to property development. No sooner had the ink dried when in 1985 it transpired that Mercabank was heading for a R57m loss. Du Plessis was in a difficult position: he had crossed swords in public with the Governor of the South African Reserve Bank, Dr Gerhard de Kock, and openly attacked his monetary policies at *Afrikaanse Handelsinstituut* (AHI) congresses. Bankorp was in severe financial trouble and urgently needed bridging capital. Du Plessis approached the SARB (South African Reserve Bank) for a low-interest R300m loan, but De Kock agreed to only R200m. The repayment conditions were strict—full repayment by 1990. By April 1986 the SARB increased the facility to Bankorp to R300m at the latter's request. Du Plessis restructured the Bankorp Group, but had dismissed repeated warnings by Bankorp Management Services (Bankbes) of non-compliance with capital adequacy requirements, as an obsession *('beheptheid')* with rights issues.[64] Fred du Plessis consistently refused to do a rights issue.

Under Du Plessis, Bankorp pursued market share without concern for the quality of the acquisitions. The 1988 Bankorp annual report mentioned that 'the Bankorp group decided several years ago to increase its market share by means of organic growth', and then it was reported that total assets had increased to R6 358m at the end of 1988, representing a growth of 39.6 per cent for that year.[65] The 1989 Annual Report admitted

[60] Martin & Company Analyst report, 1/1/1991. [61] Sankorp Management, 4/11/1986.
[62] Sanlam Board, 2/12/1992. [63] *Financial Mail*, 16/2/1996.
[64] SA: 7/1/7: Sanlam Subsidiaries: Letter A.S. du Plessis–M.H. Daling, 30/1/1989.
[65] Bankorp Annual Report, 1988: 3.

that, 'earnings growth did not keep pace with asset growth' and after Du Plessis' death, news about the severity of the losses surfaced rapidly. By 1991 calculations of abnormal write-offs of R1930.5m could be accounted for.[66] Under Du Plessis, 'liberal accounting', 'aggressive tax planning', and a bad relationship with the SARB contributed to the dire straits in which the group was when he died in March 1989. He was succeeded by Tjaart van der Walt, a theologian, as Chairman of the Bankorp Group, with Dr Chris van Wyk as Managing Director. In August 1989 Dr C.L. (Chris) Stals succeeded Dr G.H. (Gerhard) de Kock as Governor of the SARB. Stals wrote to Van Wyk on 6 July 1989, conveying SARB's displeasure at Bankorp's excessive rate of increased credit extension. Stals noted that he had requested all five the major banking groups to exercise restraint in credit extension, with Bankorp being the only one not to comply with his request. The Sankorp executive management had to admit to the Sanlam board that they did not have nearly a full understanding of the extent of the problems in Bankorp. It was not Sankorp's responsibility, or intention, to manage Bankorp. Sankorp's assessment of the situation was that immediate management changes were advisable, limits to asset growth had to be fixed, the relationship with the SARB needed to be improved, and full disclosure had to be made of the extent of the problem areas in Bankorp. It was apparent that the Van der Walt/Van Wyk team did not have the capacity to fathom the full depth of the problem. In September 1989 Derek Keys took the reins as Chairman and with the insight of an ex-banker, immediately identified and addressed the problems. The SARB's repeated warnings in successive written communications with the newly appointed Executive Chairman of the Bankorp Group, voicing concerns about contraventions of the exchange control regulations, aggressive credit extension growth, the questionable quality of such credit, and persistent capital inadequacy, did not meet with immediate compliance. In June 1990 Bankorp appointed Mr P.L. Liebenberg as Executive Chairman of Bankorp. Keys only offered his assistance temporarily, since he deemed more permanent management necessary to steer Bankorp out of its difficulties. Liebenberg soon realized that the institution would not be in a position to adhere to the SARB loan repayment schedule. Bankorp could not repay the first instalment on the R300m loan by June 1990. Dr Stals immediately requested an investigation in collaboration with the external auditors of Bankorp, into its financial position. In a confidential submission to the Bankorp board in July 1990, Liebenberg had to admit that he had not, in his entire banking career, observed a bank as badly managed at executive level as Trust Bank during the immediately preceding years.[67]

The SARB investigation revealed the sheer mismanagement and almost irreparable state of the bank group. The group generated absolutely no profit during the 1989/1990 financial year. Only 52 per cent of its assets could potentially be turned around to deliver

[66] SA: 7/1/7: Sanlam submission to Heath Commission of Inquiry.
[67] SA: 7/1/7: Memorandum to Sanlam Board, 2/12/1992.

profitable returns. Bankorp was in no position to commence repayment of the loan facility as agreed. The SARB had only two options: close the institution or provide further assistance. The SARB agreed to act as 'lender of last resort' and extended the former loan to R1 000m, but insisted on a rights issue of R526m, underwritten by Sankorp that picked up 82 per cent of the issued shares. If only this had been the end of the unpleasant surprises. In June 1991 the external auditors informed Bankorp that a qualified audit would be issued, since the bank no longer complied with capital adequacy requirements and further bad debts had been revealed, rendering the SARB R1 000m facility inadequate. It was at this stage that the full extent of accumulated doubtful debts was revealed. The SARB once again increased its facility and the shareholders (Sankorp and Sanlam) had to provide another R800m towards the recapitalization of Bankorp. At this stage the SARB informed the Minister of Finance, Barend du Plessis, of the full extent of the Bankorp implosion. The SARB's rescheduling of the facility and repayment arrangements for Bankorp in 1991 was to give the bank more time to wind down its book of bad debts. Once Bankorp earned R1 125m or once capital and reserves of R3 000m were replenished, repayment would commence. This agreement was in force until 23 October 1995. The announcement in April 1992 that ABSA had acquired Bankorp, shifted the pendulum in the direction of an able financial institution.[68] Piet Badenhorst of ABSA approached Sanlam/Sankorp about the possible acquisition of Bankorp and further discussions followed with the Universa pyramid voting pool, which included the Rembrandt Group, the mine pension funds, and the Sage Group (Universa had a 30 per cent stake in ABSA, which was diluted to 24 per cent following the transaction with Bankorp). Permission for the transaction was acquired from the Minister of Finance, the Governor of the SARB, the Registrar of Deposit-taking Institutions, the Registrar of Insurance, the Competition Council, and the Securities Regulations Panel of the JSE.[69] The irony of this transaction lay in the communication between Wassenaar and Wim de Villiers in May 1980. Wassenaar expressed the view that future collaboration between Volkskas and Trust Bank was almost ruled out following the debacle about control of Gencor.[70] It turned out that Volkskas, then firmly in the ABSA stable, 'rescued' Trust Bank.

The ABSA acquisition did not change the agreement with the SARB, but some detailed conditions were amended in 1994 to provide for the fact that ABSA, and not Sankorp, was the new shareholder in Bankorp. Following the post-1991 agreement with the SARB the loan to Bankorp was fully collateralized by redepositing funds with the SARB or ceding government stock. On 23 October 1995 ABSA repaid the full R1 500m

[68] SA: Sankorp Board Minutes, 12/2/1992; Dr C. Stals Submission to Commission of Enquiry into the affairs of Tollgate Holdings Ltd, 26 February 1996; SA: 7/1/7: Sanlam submission to Davis Commission, 13/6/2001.

[69] SA: Sankorp Board Minutes, 12/2/1992.

[70] SA: 6/1/2: Letter A.D. Wassenaar–W.J. de Villiers, 26/5/1980.

SARB loan. ABSA was now the owner of Bankorp and set about its business integrating the financial services institutions of the Bankorp Group into the new ABSA group structure. The inheritance was not exceptionally beneficial—by March 1992, during the due diligence preceding the acquisition of Bankorp, it was revealed that its total bad debt book had risen to R5 400m[71]—well in excess of the SARB's 'lifeboat', as the loan facility became known in the press.

The so-called 'Bankorp Saga' delivered political capital to the new democratically elected government in 1994. The Minister of Finance, Trevor Manuel, repeatedly alleged misappropriation of 'taxpayers' money' in 'apartheid grand corruption', which had to be paid back. It was often claimed that the facility to Bankorp was a 'donation', but evidence of it being a low-interest loan was fully reported in the SARB minutes and financial reports. Several commissions of inquiry into corporate collapses between 1993 and 1996 kept throwing up Bankorp. This was not surprising given the nature of several of the abnormal write-offs disclosed to the SARB 1991 investigation. The single largest exposure was in excess of R75m to the Duros/Tollgate Group, which was the subject of investigation by the Hoberman Commission of Inquiry, later the Browde Commission. Since Tollgate was liquidated subsequent to the ABSA acquisition of Bankorp, the facility to Tollgate by Bankorp cropped up during the investigation into Tollgate. Stals delivered detailed evidence on the SARB assistance to Bankorp, but the Browde report explicitly stated that it had not investigated the SARB's role in extending a lifeboat to Bankorp. In 1999 Judge Willem Heath conducted an inquiry into the Bankorp 'lifeboat', concluding that it had been 'illegal' but that the interest benefits amounting to approximately R3 billion could not be recovered. This prompted the new Governor of the SARB, Tito Mboweni, to appoint Judge Dennis Davis to investigate the deal once again. The final report of February 2002 found the SARB conduct *ultra vires,* because all the agreements were not legally binding contracts. He ruled out recourse to 'unjustified enrichment' since ABSA paid the full facility back in 1995. Furthermore, the Sanlam policyholders who 'benefited' from a non-collapsing bank (in which Sanlam was the anchor shareholder), might no longer be policyholders by that time. Sanlam had demutualized in 1998 and was no longer a mutual long-term insurance company in 2002. So, to pin down who actually benefited and by how much, would be a costly moving target.[72] These findings failed to satisfy the conspiracy theorists, who saw the Bankorp lifeboat as a 'Broederbond' conspiracy. The fact that it was presented as 'an all-out Afrikaner affair' added to the political capital gains. Of course, respected English-speaking businessmen such as Lesley Boyd, Graham Boustred, David Brink, and Joe Pamensky also served on the board of ABSA. It was simply incorrect to refer to the final resolution to the Bankorp

[71] Ibid.

[72] *Business Day*, 27/2/2002; *The Star*, 27/2/2002; *Sake Burger*, 27/2/2002; A. Greenblo, 2017: 'Bankorp Lifeboat: Call back the past', *Today's Trustee*, March/May 2017: 50–4.

situation as an 'all-out Afrikaner affair'. Fred du Plessis was at loggerheads with the SARB and Government, and De Kock and Stals were incidentally Afrikaners, but respected central bankers as Governors of the SARB. Sanlam had the legacy of an Afrikaner life office, although dedicated strategies had been implemented since the mid-1980s to change that. Furthermore, the Gencor saga as described earlier, illustrated significant divisions between Afrikaner businessmen. The new ABSA was formed under the leadership of the former United Building Society chief, Piet Badenhorst, and the Trust Bank managers were all Afrikaners. Suspicion was cast on family relationships between leaders in the Afrikaner corporate world and Cabinet Ministers. The 'secrecy' of the rescue facility, which only became public in 1992 as ABSA acquired the ailing Bankorp, was oil on the fire of the anti-Afrikaner press and new ANC political masters. Stals' evidence regarding the stability of the South African financial system at a time of mounting international isolation, the debt standstill following PW Botha's Rubicon speech, and contracting access to credit, was not what the political protagonists wanted to hear. Throughout the saga Sanlam kept a low profile, seeking to extricate itself from the brinkmanship legacy of executive chairman Fred du Plessis. Sanlam's exposure to Bankorp was R906.8m,[73] hardly beneficial to policyholders' interests. The potential cost to policyholders would have been exponentially higher if the simpler option of allowing Bankorp to fail, had been chosen. Anton Rupert *ex post facto* commented that after Fred du Plessis, Sanlam did as much as it could to prevent major financial instability and economic uncertainty.[74]

Unbundling: deconcentration and business efficiency

The history of Sanlam in the mining sector was a legacy of Afrikaner ambition to conquer the commanding heights of the South African economy. It started with *Federale Mynbou*, acquiring General Mining and in 1975 Union Corporation, leading to the new mining conglomerate Gencor, in which *Federale Mynbou Beperk* (the holding company controlled by Sanlam) held a 53.7 per cent stake. The holding company's name changed to Gencor Holding Company in 1989.[75] Gencor suffered from the post-Wim de Villers management impasse when a five-man management committee managed Gencor. In May 1986 Derek Keys was appointed CEO and Ted Pavitt stepped down as Executive Chairman. Keys performed more functional rationalization of mining interests by consolidating mining interests in Gencor, industrial interests in Malbak, and paper in Sappi. Despite attributable earnings rising 201 per cent at the end of 1989, Gencor was

[73] SA: 7/1/7/: Sanlam submission to Davis Commission, 13/6/2001.
[74] Interview Anton Rupert by H. Giliomee: 3/5/1999, published in *Business Day,* 10/6/2014.
[75] SA: Sankorp Board Minutes, 12/07/1989.

still underperforming AAC.[76] An anticipated depressing economic climate during the early 1990s led Keys in September 1990 to raise the possibility of unbundling Gencor. The Gencor share price was trading at a discount to net asset value of 19 per cent in 1991 and was expected to drop further to 21 per cent in 1992. Keys' suggestion was met with lukewarm enthusiasm, but by 1992 Sankorp had calculated the effect of the discount on the market value of its investment in Gencor Holdings at R913 million. Unbundling made business sense. Keys was appointed Minister of Economic Co-ordination and of Trade and Industry at the end of 1991. His successor at Gencor, Brian Gilbertson, who strongly opposed unbundling, arguing that Gencor would lose its role as 'unique entrepreneurial machine', had the support of the Gencor executive team. Gencor's performance weakened, the share price dropped another 30 per cent and the ratio of Sankorp's earnings to the market value of its investment in Gencor dropped from 47 per cent to 21 per cent.[77] The business decision was a simple one: unbundle. Sankorp made the decision, negotiated with Rembrandt[78] and Genbel on voting pool agreements to protect their interests in an unbundled entity, and announced the unbundling of Gencor in February 1993, with implementation August 1993. The announcement was met with enthusiasm in the financial press. There was a perception that unbundling was motivated by political fears of nationalization[79] when the idea was first mentioned by Keys in 1991,[80] but later the economic argument took over. The expansion and performance of underlying companies during the previous two years required capital strengthening at most of those concerns. By early 1993 fund-raising activity had left the constituting companies in the Gencor stable soundly funded and as major autonomous investments in their own right. Examples included Sappi, which raised over R2 billion to purchase the German paper producer *Hannover Papier* and expanded production at its Saiccor plant from 1992. Samancor entered into a R3.5 billion joint venture with Anglo American's Highveld Steel and Vanadium to manufacture stainless steel at Columbus. That was financed at the Samancor level without recourse to Gencor. Alusaf (Aluminium smelter) expanded its operations through a R5 billion transaction in Richards Bay Minerals (RBM), with an expected rapid build-up of earnings from 1997. Genmin opened a new gold mine at Oryx. Gencor's unbundling was completed by 5 November 1993—the first major conglomerate unbundling in South Africa. Gencor remained a mining and minerals company with Genmin its core asset. Engen, Genbel, Malhold, and Sappi shares were distributed to Sanlam, Sankorp, Rembrandt, and Genbel. It was a worthwhile exercise—the cost to Gencor was R15m, but value in excess

[76] SA: Sankorp Board Minutes, 3/5/1989;10/5/1989.

[77] SA: Sankorp Board Minutes,14/10/1992.

[78] This happened under the Managing Director Desmond Smith who, together with Marinus Daling, conducted relations with Rembrandt going forward with great caution, hoping to restore the historical goodwill between the companies.

[79] *Financial Mail*, 20/11/1992: 'Picking up the gauntlet: Big business is not always bad business'.

[80] *Business Day*, 12/5/1993: 3.

of R2.5 billion was unlocked for Gencor and Gencor Holdings shareholders.[81] Sankorp's investment in Gencor dropped from 41 per cent of its portfolio, to 25 per cent, which was closer to the composition of a life office investment portfolio. In 1997 Gencor sold its non-precious metal assets to Billiton in a $1.2 billion transaction and received shares in Billiton in exchange. The transaction enhanced the focus of both groups and Billiton listed on the London Stock Exchange. Gencor subsequently emerged as a South African gold and platinum company, and offshore its non-precious metals interests were in Billiton, holding Samancor, Alusaf, Ingwe, and RBM. The unbundling exercise thus delivered a streamlined and focused Gencor. Sanlam's exposure to international mining interests via Billiton secured Sanlam policyholders professional management in international mining and Sanlam a portfolio investment (22.28 per cent in Gencor, and in the voting pool with the Rembrandt Group 33.41 per cent) with much-improved performance potential.[82]

Sankorp in society

As a strategic planning company Sankorp realized the crucial role of the environment in doing business. Volatile socio-political conditions have been shown throughout Africa to be highly detrimental to economic stability and growth. The South Africa of the mid-1980s dealt with adverse international pressures, declining foreign investment, and a growing impatient and discontent majority demanding political participation and improved standards of living. Sankorp studied the dynamics of South Africa's demography and the black market. The immediate crisis was the suboptimal use of human capital in the country, leaving a structural imbalance in the labour market. An insatiable demand for highly skilled labour and people in management loomed large. Too few black people were employed in semi-professional and professional occupations. Sankorp addressed those issues directly within the businesses under its sphere of influence. The Sankorp management could sense the changing mood in South Africa as the white population acknowledged the need for political change and acknowledged the justification for improved socio-economic conditions. The Sankorp strategy was firstly to establish contact with reputable black leaders, especially those in business and, secondly, to address working conditions and employment expectations of black people in its

[81] SA: Sankorp Board Minutes, 13/10/1993; Sankorp Management Minutes, 3/8/1994. Engen is the petroleum interests of Gencor consisting of Fedmyn's Trek Petroleum shares merged with Gencor's acquisition of Mobil (renamed Engen) after disinvestment in 1989. Malhold is the holding company of Malbak's industrial interests. Genbel is an investment company.

[82] SA: Minutes Sankorp Board, 21/08/1997.

underlying concerns.[83] The Sankorp management knew they could not affect the nature or timing of political change, but they were confident that a dedicated equal opportunity strategy (EO) was the responsibility of an SPC and that it could be implemented effectively.

Sankorp recognized that AAC and Barlows, the industrial group, were leading the market in implementing EO strategies in South Africa and excellent examples of such programmes could be seen at the technology group, IBM. Within the group of companies EO practices were defined as 'conscious, deliberate attempts by an employer to employ and develop members or grouping of people who have historically competed at a disadvantage in the labour market'. In practice the EO strategy served Sankorp's turnaround strategies in the underlying companies, but also contributed towards sustaining the free market, which was the long-term vision. This policy position was not called 'affirmative action', because of the perceived negative connotations to compulsion, legal prescription, and the potential of tokenism leading to a sense of inferiority, but rather a positive programme of empowerment that in the long run would put people in a position to exploit opportunities in the market. The alliance model was a more appropriate description of what Sankorp wanted to achieve with EO: It was performance driven and depended on the alliance between the organizations, which showed the willingness to adapt and accommodate the developed partner. The developed partner was required to also show a willingness to adapt to a change in the environment, thus building a two-way adaptive model to solve key human resource issues in the South African economy.[84] The innovations in Sankorp's EO alliance model were the concepts of mutuality and constructive negotiation. EO freed management up to do good business in the free enterprise environment; it addressed skills shortages by enabling employment practices and training of labour; it supported worker aspirations for equity, equality, and justice; and relied on a subsequent stable economic environment for growth and prosperity. The Sankorp EO strategy sought to improve the socio-economic environment in which it operated—indeed to protect its own interests, but also to contribute constructively to aspirations of the black majority for effective participation in the mainstream economy. Sankorp acknowledged this as an emotional area of black frustration, but Sankorp and Sanlam were in a unique position to address those aspirations. Sanlam had developed economically and socially marginalized Afrikaners from limited access to economic power to a position of ownership and control across all sectors of the economy. Self-empowerment taught the Afrikaner empathy with marginalization and the pivotal role of collective self-empowerment. The alliance model was the tool to arrive at black participation in the mainstream South African economy, while securing a

[83] SA: Sankorp Confidential memorandum: Aksieplan vir skakeling met swart leiers, 18/8/1986; Sankorp Memorandum: Blacks in the marketplace, 14/4/1987.

[84] SA: Minutes Sankorp Management, 5/5/1987; 18/1/1987.

market economy. Building the alliances started with assisting higher black expenditure (on food and clothing), followed by housing and transport. Implementing EO meant assisting in capacity building in the labour market and black entrepreneurs.

It was important to get the message across that Sankorp/Sanlam was not engaging in social responsibility programmes in South Africa for the first time. Extensive social involvement projects (*Korporatiewe Maatskaplike Betrokkenheid*—KMB) had been an integral part of the Sanlam business since the first decade of operations. In the last decade of the twentieth century Sankorp moved beyond the involvement in public programmes. Such programmes were the Human Performance System to improve human capital through training, the SA Housing Trust, seeking to provide housing, and the Skills Foundation, also involved in skills enhancement. The different companies in the group spent around R60 million during the 1988 financial year on such social involvement projects. The time arrived to take a more proactive role in conveying in practical terms what was done in the group on training, improved living and working conditions, business alliances, and economic empowerment projects for black people.[85] Long before a new black government took office, Sankorp gave practical effect to its alliance model of empowerment by facilitating the first black-owned insurance company in South Africa. There was a long journey of personal contact between members of the Sankorp management and black leaders from 1987. Meaningful empowerment to participate in the economy had to occur through a swift transaction using a successful company as vehicle. Sankorp decided to create a counterparty with whom to negotiate an empowerment transaction, because at the time few reputable black-owned companies were able to enter into such a transaction. Sankorp realized that it would have to be led by the black partners on how to implement the deal. There was also a need for a unique financing mechanism, since existing financing models did not take into consideration the unique context of the proposed transaction. The one non-negotiable aspect was that the transaction would be concluded on sound business principles.[86] The Sankorp choice for the empowerment vehicle was Metropolitan Life (Metpol), a blue-chip listed company in which Sankorp held an 81.1 per cent stake. Metpol was listed after Sankorp acquired control in 1985. Sanlam then merged AHT with Metpol, thereby consolidating insurance businesses operating in similar markets to create a stronger presence in that market. Metpol's business operated in the lower end of the market and 50 per cent of new business originated from black people, 30 per cent from the Coloured community, and only 20 per cent from whites. Metpol performed well with ROE at 15.1 per cent by 1987. In 1991 Sankorp made a rights issue for Metpol, whereby its shareholding was reduced to 50.0 per cent. This paved the way for the restructuring of Metpol's

[85] SA: Minutes Sankorp management, 14/3/1989.

[86] SA: Minutes Sankorp management, 10/4/1991; 3/7/991; Minutes Sankorp Board, 2/12/1992.

shareholder profile by involving foreign and local development capital. Sankorp wanted to sell 10 per cent of its shares in Metpol to an empowerment concern.[87]

As Sankorp prepared to do a Black Economic Empowerment (BEE) transaction around Metpol, the company was breaking new ground. There had never been such a transaction in South Africa. Sankorp negotiated the support of the Industrial Development Corporation (IDC) for the provision of bridging finance through a trust for black shareholders. The Black Advisory Panel consisting of black business leaders Drs Ntatho Motlana and Oscar Dlomo, Professor Mohale Mahanyele, and Messers Don Mkwanasi and Jabu Mabuza, was formed to negotiate the transaction. The first meeting between Sankorp and the advisory panel was in December 1992. Early in 1993 Jabu Mabuza was replaced by Dr Enos Mabuza, and Advocate Dikganag Moseneke and Mr Franklin Sonn joined the panel. Sankorp offered 10 per cent of its shares to the 'new company' or trust at R20.00 per share to a total value of R135 million, and the IDC provided the bridging finance. Sankorp provided R1.8 million towards the costs of marketing the share offer, but did not want any debt structure between itself and the purchasing entity, since that would refute empowerment. In March 1993 the first BEE transaction in South Africa was announced: Sankorp sold 10 per cent in Metlife to a new company Metlife Investment Holdings (Methold). Methold and Sankorp entered into a voting pool agreement (30 per cent Sankorp and Methold 10 per cent) to provide for transitional control over Methold during the establishment phase. This agreement provided for joint decision making on the appointment of the chief executive officer, the chairman of the board, the appointment of directors to the board, pre-emptive rights on the sale of shares in Metlife in favour of Methold and Sankorp, the issuing of new shares in Metlife, the buying and selling of assets, and the sale of shares in Metlife to competitors of Sanlam.[88] In May 1993 Methold was officially registered. The public marketing of shares commenced shortly thereafter and in July 1993 the prospectus was issued. The delay was the direct result of the turbulence caused in the country by the assassination of the leader of the Communist Party, Chris Hani. Sankorp allowed three years for the sale of the shares, after which, if the shares were not sold, Sankorp would buy them back. The successful completion of the public offer to black South Africans entitled Methold to a call option on a further 20 per cent of the shares in Metlife. A total of 141 million shares were offered to black South Africans, but by mid-December 1993 only 10 228 had been sold. Private placing sped up the process. A negligible number of the 600 000 Metlife policyholders responded to the share offer. By June 1994, 12.5 million shares were sold. The signature BEE transaction was at risk. It seemed unlikely that around 100 million shares would be sold before mid-1996, while other BEE transactions entered the public domain. Sankorp could lose the early-mover advantage.

[87] SA: Minutes Sankorp Board, 2/12/1992.

[88] SA: Minutes Sankorp Board, 11/2/1993; 14/4/1993.

Different explanations for the sluggish interest in the Methold shares were offered—black people were not well informed about shares as a store of value; few understood the concept of purchasing shares, and Methold shares were not listed while Metlife shares were; and insufficient financing mechanisms to the target market might have been a problem.[89] Attie du Plessis of Sankorp then proposed the escalation of the transaction to the next stage where Methold exercised the call option. The prospectus was withdrawn and the transaction restructured to allow Methold to exercise the call option for 20 per cent of Methold shares from Sankorp. The revised transaction also waived the condition that no single shareholder could hold more than 20 per cent of the shares, as well as that institutional investors could acquire shares in Methold. This waiver was explicitly to allow Corporate Africa to acquire a stake in Methold. The revised transaction included the immediate listing of Methold, and Sankorp's 20 per cent interest acquired by Methold was exchanged for Sanlam/Sankorp obtaining a 24 per cent stake (plus preference shares) in Methold. Listing opened the shares up to a much wider market, irrespective of race.

The slow progress with the Methold transaction was not because of a lack of capital in the black community, but because of the way the initial transaction was structured. Sankorp wished not to empower only a privileged few, but to extend the opportunity of acquiring equity to the largest possible cohort of black people. The reality was actually different. Eight of the nine Black business leaders Sankorp involved in the Metlife transaction had already acquired other business interests. A select number of the black elite had also already accumulated capital and placed it in Corporate Africa, established by Ntatho Motlana. N.H. Motlana and Sons (Pty) Ltd owned 55 per cent of Corporate Africa Holdings, while 38 per cent was owned by various trusts representing the interest of people like Sam Motsuenyane, Franklin Sonn, Enos Mabuza, Archie Nkonyeni, Paul Gama, Zwelake Sisulu, and Godfrey Pitje, and 7 per cent by other shareholders. Corporate Africa Holdings held 80 per cent of the shares in Corporate Africa Investments (CAI) and Standard Merchant Bank held the remaining 20 per cent. CAI was the sole owner of Corporate Africa, which held a significant stake in *The Sowetan* and in MTN (mobile telephones). These business connections developed into significant BEE vehicles. Allowing Corporate Africa entry into the Methold transaction was vital to conclude the deal.

The prospectus was withdrawn following the restructured transaction. Phase one of the Metlife transaction was concluded and the IDC loan repaid. A rights issue by Methold for shares in the 'new to be listed' Methold, the acquisition of corporate shares in *The Sowetan* and MTN in exchange for shares in Methold, and the call option secured Methold a direct 30 per cent stake in Metlife. This addressed the criticism in the market

[89] SA: Minutes Sankorp Board, 1/6/1994.

that Methold controlled Metlife with only a 10 per cent direct interest. In exchange for the 20 per cent Metlife shares Methold purchased from Sankorp, Sanlam/Sankorp received a 24.9 per cent direct stake in Methold. The rest of the purchase price for the 20 per cent in Metlife was paid for by the issue of 300 million preference shares of R1 each in Methold. The new transaction was announced in July 1994 and Methold listed in August 1994 as New African Investment Limited (NAIL). Shareholding in NAIL consisted of Corporate Africa (51 per cent); Original Black shareholders in Methold prior to the conclusion of the second transaction (26 per cent); Metlife staff (1 per cent); financial institutions (2 per cent); and Sanlam/Sankorp (20 per cent). The NAIL/Sankorp voting pool controlled 53 per cent of NAIL—30 per cent NAIL and 22 per cent Sankorp.

Sankorp always considered this a business transaction. Sankorp earned a neat R800 million as follows: R400 million for the 20 per cent shareholding in Metlife; R100 million through its acquired indirect interest in Metlife, *The Sowetan*, and MTN, and R300 million preference shares in Methold, backed by the Metlife share price. This transaction facilitated an exceptionally rapid empowerment of a number of black South Africans. The empowerment model differed fundamentally, as no State Owned Enterprise (SOE) provided finance to transact acquisition deals for the establishment of FVB, nor for the acquisition of AHT by Santam in 1918. Afrikaner empowerment was self-driven and incremental, funded by savings collected from Afrikaners countrywide. The NAIL transaction delivered a well-established listed entity to black ownership, with the added benefit of business support from Sankorp/Sanlam during the establishment phase. NAIL appointed Ntatho Motlana as Executive Chairman, with Dikgang Moseneke as his deputy. Jonty Sandler assumed the position of Managing Director. NAIL needed some time to reassure the market of its inherent capabilities. The NAIL share price rose by 65 per cent towards the end of 1995, despite trading at a 20 per cent discount to the value of underlying assets. Sankorp was confident that Metlife was a blue-chip company and managed the relationship with the transaction in a similar way as its strategic investments. Once the goal was achieved, in this case BEE, Sankorp had to decide whether NAIL was core to its total investment strategy. Early in 1995 Sankorp decided to redeem its preference shares in NAIL and retain only a portfolio investment. NAIL exercised its call option on 14 May 1996. The voting pool agreement between NAIL and Sankorp ended. The latter retained one board representative on the NAIL board and a portfolio investment, in line with its long-term strategic planning.[90]

It was BEE season in South Africa, but Sankorp stole the limelight as the first mover. NAIL entered the South African investment environment as an independent investment company, with assets in the financial sector, newspapers, and mobile technology. In May 1995 AAC announced the unbundling of Johannesburg Consolidated Investments (JCI).

[90] SA: Minutes Sankorp Board, 22/2/1996; 27/6/1996; Minutes Sankorp Management, 18/4/1996.

The outcome left Johnnic, an industrial investment company, and JCI Ltd, a mining finance house, in open invitation to BEE participation. NAIL subsequently played a central role in combining BEE interests in the National Empowerment Consortium (NEC) and acquired AAC's 41 per cent stake in Johnnic. Meflife funded three other BEE groups in the NEC to participate in the Johnnic deal. Cyril Ramaphosa left politics in 1996 to join NAIL as Deputy Chairman. He was also elected Chairman of the NEC executive committee and of Johnnic.[91] The Metlife empowerment transaction provided the means to benefit from the AAC unbundling exercise.

Sankorp's alliance model in BEE was extended to other emerging BEE consortia. In February 1994 Real Africa Holdings Ltd (REAL) was established as a consortium of black business men, trade unions, informal savings organizations, and church groups. In March 1995 REAL listed and Don Ncube, Chief Executive, approached Sankorp to take up 5 per cent of REAL's issued share capital. When Servgro listed in 1995, REAL approached Sankorp to acquire a stake in Servgro.[92] In 1995 Worldwide African Investment holdings (Worldwide), another BEE investment company, showed interest in taking up a stake in Plessey, an electronics concern in the Sankorp investment portfolio. Plessey expected a Telkom contract to install telephone lines, primarily in black areas, and wanted a BEE partner. Sankorp was engaged in rationalizing its investment portfolio and offered to sell 5 per cent of its shares in Plessey to Worldwide, subject to a put offer, which would enable Worldwide to sell the shares back to Sankorp within two years after the outcome of the Telkom tender. Yet another 4 per cent of Sankorp's shares in Plessey was sold to Worldwide (at ruling market prices) without the put option.[93] Sankorp achieved its own investment goals of streamlining its portfolio, but also facilitated the diversification of Worldwide's investment portfolio, while the Worldwide participation in the Plessey Telkom contract opened opportunities to black entrepreneurs and businesses. The synergy between the Sankorp views on empowerment and those of Worldwide provided a powerful motive for the transaction. Worldwide approached black economic 'enablement' as follows: 'The cardinal rule which should be a guiding principle in all BEE transactions should be one of adding value.... Unless we are convinced that we can add value by growing each company in which we would hold a stake, we would be reluctant to take any equity.... In adopting such a philosophy towards BEE, we believe that the concept can be implemented more successfully because the Black business community will find more willing joint venture partners in corporate South Africa. In turn, Corporate South Africa will have access to opportunities and returns which would have been unattainable, if it remained constituted as it is at present.'[94]

[91] *The Star* Business Report, 16/6/1996; 11/10/1996; 28/10/1996; 20/1/1997; *Financial Mail*, 20/3/1998.
[92] SA: Minutes Sankorp Board, 8/2/1995.
[93] SA: Minutes Sankorp Management, 29/11/95; Minutes Sankorp Board, 6/12/95.
[94] Worldwide African Investment Holdings (Pty) Ltd: Company Profile, 29/11/95.

As a public citizen Sankorp engaged in black empowerment initiatives to contribute to a responsible strategy for economic development. Making full use of the total human capital potential of the country made perfect business sense and had comprised a cornerstone of the business of Sankorp since 1985. The Metlife transaction was a high-profile deal because of the involvement of many prominent black leaders, but also because of the leadership of Afrikaner business. The arguments on employment creation, human capital development, and operational efficiency of underlying companies in the Sanlam Group, managed by Sankorp, were the justification for the strategy. At the same time Sanlam, through Sankorp, was aware of numerous sanction-busting strategies employed by several of its underlying companies. In Fedfood, Murray and Roberts, in some FVB subsidiaries, in several Malbak subsidiaries and in SA Druggists, TEK Electronics, and several underlying Gencor mining subsidiaries, different channels were pursued to export goods and to import vital inputs to sustain operations and grow the businesses.[95] This was business pragmatism justified by securing better-performing businesses.

Wrapping up Sankorp: investment rationalization at Sankorp

Sankorp was a strategic business vehicle for Sanlam. It unwound a massive empire of diverse business interests, which ultimately exposed the Achilles heel of the life office. 'Managing' such diverse but economically significant assets was outside the core competence of a life insurance company and Sanlam did not manage the interests well before Sankorp. Even then Sankorp did not 'manage' the underlying interests, but tried to influence the situation to attain improved strategy implementation. Suboptimal returns on those vast investments adversely affected returns on assets. In anticipation of fundamental socio-political realignment, optimal performance of Sanlam's underlying assets could no longer be sidelined. It became more important to address the socio-economic aspirations of the majority of those companies' workforce in terms of basic living standards, ambitions, professional aspirations, and the underlying critical factor of enhancing South Africa's human capital potential to its full capacity. These were broad socio-economic and political matters that stretched the insurance manager's capabilities. In Sankorp a core of strategic management experts addressed those concerns as part of a systematic performance overhaul of underlying concerns. What Sankorp achieved was to rationalize Sanlam's stake investments through disposals and investments, the unbundling of several conglomerate pyramids, the migration from absolute control to significant

[95] SA: Confidential Memorandum to Sankorp Board, 28/7/1986.

control of underlying companies, the delisting and listing of companies, and BEE. These actions added significant value, but also established core principles in management as a signature Sankorp legacy. These included management succession planning, equal opportunities, flexible work practice, directors' roles as active and engaged in the company, social involvement, managing the business environment in a situation of structural economic and political change, BEE, and corporate governance.[96] The most value-adding dimension of Sankorp's intervention was the close monitoring of the performance of the underlying companies and regular reporting to Sanlam in that respect. The Sankorp portfolio had a market value of R1 300 million in 1985, which by 1995 had risen to R21 779 million—36.77 per cent annual compound growth. In 1995 alone the value added to the Sankorp companies was R3 333 million, which represented an internal rate of return (IRR) of 19.7 per cent compared to the JSE Overall Index of 10.4 per cent. Sankorp's portfolio performed even better for the preceding three years, 1992–5, during which the value added was R13 331 million with an IRR of 46.5 per cent, while the JSE Overall Index was 27.2 per cent. Ultimately the combined stock exchange performance of Sankorp's portfolio between 1985 and 1995 exceeded the JSE's overall performance by 18 per cent.[97]

In 1995, after a decade of Sankorp intervention to secure Sanlam's improved investment flexibility, the decision was made to wind 'old Sankorp' down. The business context under the newly elected black government changed in 1994. The entire business sector realigned itself for a radically different environment. Sanlam expressed the vision of playing a more focused role in a wider field of financial services, with a more explicit focus on international markets. These ambitions initially revolved around Sanlam, ABSA, and Genbel, the investment vehicle that resulted from the Gencor unbundling exercise. The Sankorp executive management considered a new investment banking role for itself, perhaps leveraging off its BEE reputation to become a BEE investment partner of choice, but by mid-1997 those ideas waned. In January 1998 the remaining shares under Sankorp control were transferred to Sanlam as portfolio investments.[98] The company registration was changed to 'Sankorp Ou Sankorp', which remained as a dormant company in the Sanlam group of companies.

Survival in an unstable financial world

There was no better time to get Sanlam's strategic investments in good shape than the decade from 1985 to 1995. Political turbulence gained massive momentum, economic growth was sluggish and weakening, and the international financial services environment was changing fundamentally.

[96] SA: Minutes Sankorp Board, 22/2/1995.
[97] SA: Minutes Sankorp Board, 21/11/1996.
[98] SA: Minutes Sankorp Board, 25/2/1998.

Table 4.2. South Africa's GDP and CPI growth 1985–1998 (%)

Year	GDP growth	CPI
	%	%
1985	−1,2	16,3
1986	0,0	18,6
1987	2,1	16,1
1988	4,2	12,0
1989	2,4	14,7
1990	−0,3	14,4
1991	−0,1	15,3
1992	−2,1	13,9
1993	1,2	9,7
1994	3,2	9,0
1995	3,1	8,7
1996	4,2	7,4
1997	2,5	8,6
1998	0,7	6,9

Source: South African Reserve Bank, statistical data, 1985–1998.

GDP performance in real terms averaged 1.2 per cent per annum between 1985 and 1998. Fixed investment had declined annually since 1981 and the operating surplus of business, expressed as a percentage of GDP, had almost halved from twenty-eight in 1980 to fifteen in 1989. Both consumer prices as well as production prices increased in double digits from 1974 until 1993. CPI (inflation: Table 4.2) of 16.3 per cent in 1985 rose to 18.6 per cent in 1986 and then declined sluggishly towards the end of the 1990s, only to rise again to 13.9 per cent in 1992. The balance of payments was in negative territory as a result of weakened commodity prices. The gold price dropped from US$613 per fine ounce in 1980 to an average of US$317 in 1985, with a slight recovery to US$383 in 1990. Deflationary and strict monetary policies, coupled with international sanctions and debt repayments, reduced imports and foreign reserves. These factors put severe strain on the ability to stimulate the economy. Despite sluggish economic conditions, real wages of the black population rose to reduce the disparity between the different races' wages. The Gini coefficient was around 0.6 during the 1980s,[99] displaying a narrowing with other population groups but growing disparities within the black population group. This development presented opportunities for insurance companies. As the exchange rate weakened from 1985, South Africa became a capital exporter, diverting domestic output from domestic needs to external demands.[100]

[99] Mohr, 2010: An overview of the South African economy: 18.

[100] *Financial Mail*, 30/11/1990: 'Life Assurance Industry: A Survey': 5; Goedhuys, 1994: 146; Maasdorp, 2002: 17–18.

The deregulation of international financial markets led to liberal monetary policies. A combination of globalization of economies and their transition to market mechanisms reshaped the contours and mode of operation of financial systems.[101] South Africa followed the trend. The De Kock Commission advised the deregulation of financial markets. Full deregulation was not implemented, because the government was hesitant to scrap exchange control and open the market to foreign competition. The Financial Services Amendment Act, No. 106 of 1985, introduced internal financial market liberalization. Building societies suffered massive capital losses during the liquidity squeeze of the 1980s and by March 1982 the five largest building societies posted losses of almost R300 million. Regulatory constraints disappeared, functional convergence occurred, and banks entered the former building society domain of home mortgages. Banks bought ailing building societies and brought an end to the building societies' mutual character.[102]

The next step in financial market reconfiguration in South Africa was when foreign shareholders in Standard Bank and Barclays Bank withdrew from South Africa due to growing international pressure. This afforded the cash-rich insurance companies acquisition opportunities. The South African experience was the reverse of the Australian experience: deregulation reduced entry barriers and financial market segmentation contracted. In South Africa insurance companies emerged at the helm of the big banks. Five long-term insurance companies, SA Mutual, Sanlam, Momentum, Liberty, and Metropolitan, emerged as financial services giants. These companies controlled in excess of 90 per cent of the total assets in the industry.[103] The former big banking groups became the partners in new financial services conglomerates, with the long-term insurance companies the anchor shareholders. SA Mutual, the oldest surviving South African insurance company, controlled the Nedbank Group. The Standard Bank Investment Corporation (SBIC) emerged as the controlling shareholder of the Liberty Group. Sanlam's share in the ABSA Group afforded the company a strong position, and the Southern Life Assurance Company and Momentum Life Assurance Company were incorporated in the First Rand Group, which is the successor to First National Bank (formerly Barclays Bank) after the latter was acquired by Rand Merchant Bank.[104] The Southern Life Association, which was a mutual long-term insurance company, merged with Momentum Life, the insurance company in the First Rand Group. The Southern Life Association did not demutualize as a strategic business decision, but was demutualized in the takeover transaction. The two leading long-term insurance companies, SA Mutual and Sanlam, also controlled the two largest short-term insurance companies, i.e. Mutual and Federal and Santam, respectively. Sanlam did not control a bank, as SA

[101] Trinchet, 2003: 247. [102] Skinner & Osborn, 1992: 65.

[103] FSB, 2009; Ernest & Young, 2004; Von Wielligh, 2005.

[104] Verhoef, 2009; Verhoef, 2003; Benfield & Vivian, 2003; Vivian, 2007.

Mutual did. This was a source of serious contention in the future strategic positioning of Sanlam, as a strong relationship with a major bank had distinct distribution advantages.

The long-term insurance industry occupied an especially central role in domestic macroeconomic stability, which was the direct result of the international isolation of South Africa.[105] The long-term insurance industry's total assets as a proportion of GDP rose steadily from 22.9 per cent in 1980 to 76.9 per cent in 2000, growing faster per annum than GDP growth (at current prices). Net long-term premium income growth also consistently surpassed household savings growth (at current prices). By 1985 those premiums exceeded household savings (at current prices) by 43 per cent and by 1995 constituted 1005 per cent of household savings.[106] What was even more significant was that South Africa's long-term insurance premiums as a percentage of GDP had risen to the highest ratio in the world, namely 13.14 per cent in 1998.[107] The demand for traditional life insurance products of long-term insurance companies changed fundamentally in the turbulent times of the 1980s and 1990s. In this market the number of long-term insurance companies increased from fifty-seven in 1985 to seventy in 2000, but two companies, SA Mutual and Sanlam, controlled more than 80 per cent of the industry assets. A growing portion of the long-term income was invested in retirement products. The political economy of securing the domestic status quo, the inward-looking monetary policies, the legacy of protectionism and exchange controls since 1939, locked the bulk of South African savings within the country. A substantial part of those savings comprised retirement funds, and in the absence of a state social welfare system South African employers established occupational retirement plans, managed by separate bodies, fund managers, or insurance companies. Traditionally, long-term insurance companies managed the bulk of those retirement funds.[108] Changes in employment security therefore impacted directly on the funds under long-term insurance management.

Since the political volatility of the mid-1980s, structural changes occurred in the long-term insurance industry. A gradual shift out of life insurance into other wealth products occurred since the 1990s, while benefits paid also rose. This occurred as a portion of the existing cohort of policyholders switched from life policies to new wealth products, and simultaneously a new cohort of policyholders entered the market for life products. The latter were largely the new employees under the new democratically elected government. This market segment was relatively 'new' to the life market.

[105] G. Verhoef, 2010, 'Life offices to the rescue': 155–65.

[106] SARB Quarterly Statistical Bulletin, 1950–2001; South African Government: *Annual Report of the Registrar of Insurance Companies (1950–2001). Total long term net premium income includes total recurrent premiums and single premiums.* Also see J.W. Prinsloo (2000) 'The savings behaviour of the South African economy.' South African Reserve bank, Occasional paper 14: 3.

[107] G. Verhoef (2010) 'Life offices to the rescue': 156–7.

[108] R.W. Vivian (2007) 'South African insurance markets', in J.D. Cummins and B. Venard (eds) *Handbook of international Insurance.* New York: Springer: 697–9.

Table 4.3. Selected variables of the long-term insurance industry flow of funds, 1985–2000

	1985	1990	1995	2000
Income (R'bn)	7,09	40,14	86,97	190,94
Net premiums (R'bn)	4,15	21,18	61,77	144,47
Benefits paid (R'bn)	1,51	12,22	44,61	118,23
Ratio: Income-expenditure	2,8:1	2,41:1	1,62:1	1,36:1
Assets/Liabilities	1,78:1	1,35:1	1,27:1	1,41:1
Pension fund + Group life benefits: Premiums	1,87	7,72	20,98	66,92
% of total premiums	45,06	35,21	34,20	49,63
Retirement annuity business: Premiums	0,63	2,63	4,49	10,39
% of total premiums	15,16	12,01	7,32	7,70

Source: Registrar of Insurance, 1985–1997; Registrar of long-term Insurance, 1998–2000.

The net annual premium income of long-term insurance companies increased dramatically by 82.33 per cent between 1985 and 1990 (or at an average annual growth rate of 16.47 per cent), by 53.84 per cent between 1990 and 1995 (an annual average of 10.6 per cent), and by 94.56 per cent between 1995 and 2000 (an annual average of 18.9 per cent) (see Table 4.3) This premium growth was partly the result of the high inflationary environment, but after the 1990s that exceeded GDP and inflation growth. The strong premium growth was undermined by the simultaneous steady growth in benefits paid (which included terminations): between 1985 and 1990 benefits paid rose by 17.52 per cent per annum, which exceeded the inflation rate. Between 1990 and 1995 the annual growth in benefits paid increased by 14.5 per cent, and between 1995 and 2000 by 12.45 per cent per annum. Funds were flowing out of the industry more rapidly than they were coming in. The outflow of funds from the long-term insurance industry is also reflected in the declining ratio of income to expenditure. In the period between 1985 and 1990 the ratio of income to expenditure was 2,8 but then steadily declined to 1,36 by 2000. A similar trend manifested in the ratio of assets to liabilities. This ratio declined from 1,78 in 1985 to 1,27 in 1995 and then strengthened slightly to 1,41 by 2000. The outflow of funds from the long-term insurance industry and the weakening asset/liability ratio meant that surplus assets came under increasing pressure. This trend restricted the ability of insurance companies to strengthen solvency bases and limited any strategic change in business operations.

The long-term insurance industry showed a growing exposure to retirement funds, pension funds, and group life schemes. There was a growing appeal to the fund management function. The long-term insurance companies either managed pension funds (or employee benefit schemes) independently or on behalf of smaller employers. These funds increased from R1.87 billion in 1985 to R66.92 billion in 2000, or from 45.06 per cent of the business of the long-term insurance companies to 49.63 per cent in 2000 (see Table 4.3). This development is attributed to the large number of 'new' employees in

Table 4.4. Selected variables of Sanlam performance, 1985–1997

	1985	1990	1995*	1997*
Income (R'm)	2 477	10 418	43 848	35 285
Net premium income (R'm)	1 588	7 428	20 698	21 966
Benefits paid (R'm)	759	3 880	17 392	30 218
Expenditure (Rm)	1 049	4 892	3 460	3 442
Ratio: Income/expenditure	2:1	2:1	13:1	9:1
Assets/liabilities	7785m/ 201m**	27908m/ 654m**	124987m/ 117297m	139817m/ 129433m
–ratio	38.73:1	42.67:1	1.0:1	1.05:1
Pension fund + group life benefits/premiums	723 456/ 1 587 898	2 766 065/ 7 427 955	6 410m/20 698m	8 154m/21 966m
–% of total premiums	45.6	37.2	31.0	37.1

Note: *Financial year end changed to 31 December.
** No Shareholder funds.
Source: Sanlam annual financial statements, 1985–1998; Actuarial report to Sanlam Board, 1995–1998.

government service (the significant growth in the number of civil servants under the new government structures after 1994) and the rise of a new black middle class who entered permanent employment for the first time. In the absence of state social security, private pension funds as a mechanism of defined contribution savings options mushroomed. By 2000 the total assets of pension funds constituted 75.26 per cent of GDP.[109]

Sanlam sustained steady growth during these turbulent years by a 30 per cent annual compound growth in assets, 26.8 per cent annual compound growth in net income, and 26.9 per cent annual compound growth in premium income (see Table 4.4). Sanlam premium annual compound growth exceeded industry growth by almost 12 per cent between 1985 and 1997 (see Table 4.3). This performance occurred amid weak annual GDP growth, which only rose to 4 per cent in 1988 and 1996, but for the rest of the period moved well below 2 per cent or even into negative territory. Sanlam lost to the industry average as far as pension and group benefits were concerned. Pension and group benefits as a proportion of total premiums in the industry fluctuated between 45 per cent and 35 per cent between 1985 and 1998, while Sanlam's pension and group benefits as a proportion of premium income dropped from 45 per cent of total premiums in 1985 to 37 per cent in 1990, and 31 per cent in 1995, with some recovery to 37 per cent in 1997—still below the industry average (see Tables 4.3 and 4.4). Growth occurred not simply on the back of inflation, because growth performance consistently exceeded inflation, also when it dropped below double digits by the early 1990s. The steady rise in benefits paid followed the industry trend and brought forward the decision about the future of the life insurer as a mutual concern. While Sankorp realigned the strategic investment landscape of Sanlam's investments, the latter remained focused on growing premium income.

[109] Vivian, 2007.

To that purpose, Sanlam developed its computer capacity, the broker and agent corps,[110] and product innovation. After Fred du Plessis' death the company decided on a decentralization strategy. Pierre Steyn informed the board that PA Consultants had been appointed to advise Sanlam on an appropriate strategy for the future. This followed a management strategic planning session in May 1989, where this structural reorganization of Sanlam was decided. The company was reorganized into profit-oriented business units, reporting to senior general managers.[111] This put Walter Scheffler in the position of Senior General Manager (SGM): Group Benefits, Desmond Smith became SGM: Individual Insurance, and Ronnie Masson SGM: Investments. George Rudman took responsibility for Finance and Planning, and Johan Söhnge for IT and HR. Operations in the rest of the country were divided into regions, with Regional Head Offices (RHO)[112] opened in 1990 in Johannesburg (Southern Transvaal) and Durban (Natal). RHOs were only opened in 1992 in the Orange Free State, Western Cape, and Northern Transvaal. The RHOs indeed enhanced Sanlam's visibility. In Johannesburg the *Sanlam Sentrum* in Jeppe Street in the heart of the city caught the eye and was referred to as '*die Boere Carlton*'—the Boers' Carlton Centre, as opposed to the Carlton Centre, owned by English capital. Impressive visible properties put Sanlam in the public eye, but could not stem the reversing tide of consumer demand. Right from the start these RHOs were marketed as decentralized operations, to bring business closer to the client, speed up the processing of applications and claims, and improved service to intermediaries. In the short term processing speed was indeed improved, but costs kept rising (the issuing cost per policy rose by 130 per cent between 1992 and 1995, cost of maintaining a policy increased by 107 per cent and the cost of underwriting a policy rose by 227 per cent) and production slumped. Sanlam lost market share, ailing administration relating to technological support frustrated clients, and the rate of premium lapses rose by 31 per cent.[113] All this was not the result of RHOs, but the change in consumer demand under conditions of rising uncertainty. Sanlam's timing of the decentralization strategy was wrong. Walter Scheffler visited the USA early in 1994 and returned with another message: insurers were centralizing operations.[114] It took Sanlam another four years to follow the trend. This led to the introduction of the New Dawn strategy in 1998.[115]

[110] Venter. L (2016) *The history of Sanlam Broker Division*. Unpublished Sanlam internal research report.

[111] SA: Minutes of Sanlam board, 17/5/1989; Minutes of General Managers Meetings, 28/4/1989; 10/5/1989; 16/5/1989; *Die Fakkel*, 1/12/1898.

[112] Venter, L. (2016) *Historical overview of the Regional Head Office (RHO) structures within Sanlam (1990–1998)*. Unpublished Sanlam internal research report.

[113] SA: Minutes of General Managers meeting: 26/3/1996; 21/8/1996: Report by M. Saayman: Sanlam's comparative position, 1996.

[114] Interview Walter Scheffler, 24/2/2009; SA: Minutes of General Managers Meeting, 11/5/1994.

[115] The New Dawn strategy is discussed in Chapter 5.

Financial market deregulation opened opportunities to innovative financial entrepreneurs. Investment-linked products performed well—the 100-Plus and 200-Plus policy series, the Investment Series, and Indexplan—were all offered until the 1990s. Sanlam then revolutionized the life insurance market with an innovative product.[116] In August 1985 Sanlam introduced the 'One Policy'. This was a universal life policy, versatile and adaptable to the needs of the middle- and high-income markets. The company was the first South African life office to introduce policy flexibility, following on the success of a similar concept in the USA earlier in 1985. Sanlam responded to the upward mobility of its policyholder base. The time was right to offer investment products aimed at the growing middle- to high-income market segments, as domestic volatility strengthened the demand for flexibility in wealth provision and investments. The One Policy offered a policy structure responsive to a wide range of policyholder needs linked to life insurance. The life market followed quickly, accommodating a combination of a variable amount of life cover and investment possibilities. Sanlam added a unique element to its offer to its existing policyholders: they could convert from *any existing policy* to the One Policy. The combination of life cover and investment could be adjusted as often as the policyholder desired and no maturity date was mandatory upon signing the policy contract. Policyholders could also adjust life and disability cover at any time and for any term.[117] The One Policy was also referred to as the 'One Door Opener', because of the product flexibility and the multiple payment options allowed.[118] Sanlam opened the door to an optimal client needs' response and in 1986 already added an option for a planned short-term maturity term policy by introducing the 'Planned Premium Term' option to the One Policy.[119]

Sanlam took the life insurance market in South Africa by storm[120]—more than 2 000 One Policies were sold within two weeks and by the end of April 1987 a total of 184 000 One Policies were on the Sanlam books. In a socio-politically dynamic context responsiveness of business to market changes holds the key to sustained industry leadership. The other life offices were swift to respond to the challenge. Sanlam's market advantage was practically eroded by 1987,[121] as competing life offices offered superior trauma and contingency cover in their policies competing with the One Policy. SA Mutual undercut Sanlam in terms of minimum entry premiums, maximum cover, and better cash

[116] SA: Product List, August 2013.

[117] SA: 1/2/1, Product Development: One Policy, 30/9/84.

[118] SA: F22/11/85, *Sanlammer*, 53(46): 1.

[119] SA: 1/2/11/2, *News Flash, Marketing Actuary*, 20/3/86. This allowed the policyholder an endowment option for a fixed term, minimum ten years, maximum the shorter of thirty years and the termination of the policy before the age of seventy-five.

[120] *Cape Times*, 5/9/1985: 'Sanlam's One Policy is a sure winner'; *Natal Mercury*, 14/8/1985: 'Flexibility is the keynote of Sanlam insurance policy'; *The Citizen*, 14/8/1985: 'Sanlam's One Policy'; *Die Burger*, 14/8/1985: 'Sanlam bemark unieke polis'.

[121] SA: 1/2/1, Product Development CJvR Memorandum, 12/6/87.

values in its competing product 'Flexi Life'.[122] The One Policy brought an outright tariff war. As with previous market-leading innovation, Sanlam's premium income rose strongly after the introduction of industry revolutionizing products. The company's premium income increased from R32 million in 1962 to R255 million after the introduction of the 100-Plus policies. The One Policy catapulted Sanlam's premium income from R2 087 million in 1986 to R3 527 million by 1987 and R12 966 million just before demutualization in 1998.[123]

By increasingly linking life policies to investment products, Sanlam strengthened its investment income in the long run and delivered on the vision of building Afrikaner ownership in the mainstream economy.[124] That was a conscious strategy to grow its market share from its mutual life insurance base. Where fixed property comprised 14 percent of the Sanlam asset base in 1960, it declined to 9 percent in 1990. Equity made up 22 percent of the Sanlam assets in 1960, but in 1990 it was 54 percent. The company's policyholder profile also changed from predominantly Afrikaans-speaking persons to more than 40 percent English-speaking South Africans, and one third of the total policyholders were African or black South Africans.[125] The success of the One Policy and sustained higher premium growth compared to SA Mutual between 1986 and 1990, account for these demographic changes as Sanlam made inroads into the traditional market of other life offices.[126]

It was significant that at the end of 1984 Sanlam's premium income exceeded that of its old rival, SA Mutual. This achievement was reason for a special Sanlam management sense of victory—albeit short-lived. The One Policy was indeed a contributory factor. Another was the very successful television marketing campaign with the human face of babies. Sanlam regularly commissioned a market survey on its public image. The research found Sanlam to be a too cold, too formal, too business-like company, with little empathy. Du Plessis wanted Sanlam to have a more 'human' face. A marketing campaign using babies was launched. Diaper-clad babies, dressed up as, for example, gypsies and executives, discussed how they could secure their future. The executive said he did not want 'guesswork', to which the gypsy woman then responded by saying Sanlam offered security backed by sound research. The slogan was 'Assuring your tomorrow. For sure!' The babies played with blue clay while discussing their future—signifying the flexibility of the One Policy. This 'baby' campaign paid off handsomely. It was well received and Du Plessis got very positive feedback on his roadshows.[127]

Sanlam introduced no major product innovation during the early 1990s. Additional benefits on existing policy offerings added nuanced responses to risk. Sanlam managed

[122] SA: 1/2/1, Product Development CJvR Memorandum, 12/6/87: Appendix 6.

[123] Sanlam Annual Reports, 1962–1998; Rudman Memorandum to Sanlam Board, 19/9/1990.

[124] Interview David Hickey, 13/5/2013.

[125] S. Halleen: From life insurance to financial services: A historical analysis of Sanlam's client base, 1918–2004. PhD thesis, Stellenbosch, 2013, pp. 113, 149.

[126] SA: Rudman Memorandum to Sanlam Board, 19/9/1990.

[127] SA: 1/2/1/1: Marketing campaign, 6/2/1984.

the Central Retirement Annuity Fund (CRAF) and was the underwriter of the Professional Provident Society (PPS), which were retirement annuities available to all people, irrespective of race.[128] In the retirement annuity market Sanlam RAs outperformed those of competitors. When the company offered RAs with up to R100 000 life cover without medical examination, the market jumped at the offer.[129] Later on Sanlam regretted not adding a condition of gainful employment to this offer, since it attracted more substandard claims than anticipated.[130] Sanlam's leading position was acknowledged in the annuity market.[131] In November 1986 J.P. Pretorius, the Sanlam Chief Actuary, also requested less stringent underwriting for deferred compensation policies and return of premium guarantees should a client leave the services of the company owning the policy. This concession was available only to selected marketers, who agreed to a commission clawback when premiums were returned. These concessions proved a sound marketing strategy, since in 1986 annuity sales rose by 26 per cent.[132] Without detracting from the focus on the senior market (high-income market), a definite shift to the junior market (lower socio-economic strata) occurred during the late 1980s.[133] This was not new territory to Sanlam, since most of the new policyholders after the company commenced business in 1918 came from the lower end of the market and were people with a limited understanding of life insurance. Re-entering the entry-level market during the 1980s constituted a different demography.

The volatility in the South African political economy during the 1990s created a demand for risk diversification, especially distributing risk outside the country. By 1995 the value of reversionary bonus policies had deteriorated, since demand declined. For almost ten years very little new business was conducted in that market. The demand swung to products linked to the market performance.[134] In 1995 Sanlam was the first South African life insurance company to offer local residents global investment opportunities through the Sanlam Personal Finance life product range. Policyholders were offered offshore investments through asset swap arrangements, using the Sanlam Foreign Fund and purchasing single-premium endowment policies. The first offer was made in December 1995 and popular demand mandated a second offer in March 1996. These asset swaps were a market-leading innovation that gave Sanlam an added opportunity to establish alliances with foreign asset managers. From August 1995 Sanlam negotiated asset swap transactions with Mercury Asset Managers and State Street in the UK to an

[128] SA: 1/2/1/6: Senior Market development: Letter CRAF–W.J. Bezuidenhoudt, 12/6/1967.

[129] SA: 1/2/1/1/2: Memorandum to Sanlam Board, 16/3/1986: J.P. Pretorius (Actuary).

[130] Interview D. Hickey, 9/6/2014.

[131] *Cape Times*, Your Money: 5/2/1987: 'Sanlam comes out leader in survey of RA performances'; SA: 1/2/1/1/2: Memorandum to Representatives, 8/5/1987.

[132] SA: 1/2/1/1/2: Memorandum Pretorius–Sanlam Board, 19/11/1986; Memorandum to Sanlam Board: Marketing, 12/2/1987.

[133] SA: 1/2/1/1/1: Memorandum to provincial, regional and new business managers, 27/5/1988.

[134] SA: 5/4/2: Minutes of Sanlam Board, 13/12/1995.

amount of R835 million. Assets (gold and other equities in exchange for cash) were soon channelled through Alliance Capital and Standard Life UK asset managers as portfolio managers for Sanlam in the UK.[135] Similar asset swaps were transacted with the *Bayerische Vereinsbank AG* in 1999[136] and by April 1997 Sanlam had accumulated assets to the value of R2.9 billion through such transactions.[137] The demand for non-insurance-linked products, such as unit trusts, rose rapidly. Sanlam lagged behind other life offices in offering Sanlam Personal Portfolio-linked unit trust products from April 1997. The One Policy was amended in June 1996 by offering the 'One Policy for Two'. This policy extended the policy benefits of the One Policy on an equal basis for women, targeting professional working women.[138]

While restructuring the Sanlam strategic investments, Sankorp carefully researched the changing socio-economic conditions in South Africa and advised Sanlam on ways to address such changes.[139] A rising black middle class and people in the junior market had to be educated about life insurance. In that market the prevalence of persons living with HIV/Aids mandated a product development response. Sanlam engaged through its social responsibility initiatives to address the needs of those suffering from it.[140] In 1988 Sanlam announced policies for persons living with HIV/Aids. All new life policies included an Aids exclusion clause. Screening procedures were introduced on all policy applications to identify the HIV/Aids status of the applicant. The One Policy was only affected when life cover was required, which was then adjusted for the illness as a medical condition. For policies without life cover, or life policies with cover less than or equal to the minimum cover, for investment policies or children's policies or policies that form parted of an investment plan, no HIV/Aids disclosures were required.[141] HIV/Aids cover was calculated on age and blood count levels.[142] Sanlam's approach was that identification of the presence of HIV/Aids within two years of the inception of a life policy would result in the termination of the life cover. If HIV/Aids infection was diagnosed more than two years after the inception of a policy, benefits were paid for a limited period.[143] Sanlam was an active participant in the Life Offices Association's HIV/Aids standing committee, which engaged in education programmes and collaborated with the Actuarial Society's Aids Committee on technical information such as genetic and HIV testing.[144]

Two important factors supported premium growth: technology and distribution. In the life industry speed of processing communication between client and company is vital.

135 Sanlam Life Board, 16/08/95; Sanlam Board, 19/01/96; Sanlam Exco, 27/05/97.
136 Sanlam Board, 3/12/97; 1/12/99. 137 Sanlam Board, 30/4/97.
138 SA: Confidential Memorandum Sanlam Board, 26/2/1997.
139 SA: Sankorp, Confidential memoranda, 13/6/86; 14/7/87.
140 SA: Sanlam Life Board Minutes, 10/1/89.
141 SA: 1/2/1/1/2, Marketing memorandum 90 MCT/cb: 29/3/89.
142 SA: 1/2/1, Product development memorandum, 20/10/94.
143 SA: 1/2/1, Product list, 20/1/97. 144 SA: 7/5/1, LOA Minutes, 10/2/95.

Sanlam led the industry in computer technology for life business. It was strange that IT only received its own management structure in 1991. The Human Resources and Information Technology departments reported to a senior general manager, but in 1991 the first General Manager: Information Systems, Japie Cloete, was appointed. This signified the elevated role IT played. In 1997 Marinus Daling restructured operations into autonomous business units. IT was placed in Business Systems (BS) under General Manager Leon Venter.

By the late 1980s Sanlam had installed a full computer network with remote terminals in regional offices in the Western Cape and the Witwatersrand. Visual Display Units (VDUs) to replace typed output with high speed onscreen display were introduced in the mid-1970s. This technology delivered impressive productivity gains in the SANMED claims department. BS developed the IT systems for Sanlam Personal Finance (SPF), the life unit. By the 1980s new sales and membership data was captured electronically. BS provided support for the strong 1990s growth in the life market, developing the Finpro financial analysis program to provide more flexibility, enhanced productivity, and the implementation of linked products to replace the outdated systems of the past. By the mid-1990s the existing computer system was unable to respond swiftly and efficiently to demands for innovation. Service delivery on existing policies began to undermine productivity. From 1995 Finpro was developed to address operational efficiency. Finpro operated off a new platform, Seer HPS, which enabled a swifter introduction of new policies to the market within a day, but by 1999 Finpro was outdated and replaced by Lamda3, a product purchased abroad.[145]

IT supported distribution and enabled sales. The Megkwot quoting system developed in the late 1970s, combining three elements: LID (Client) transaction, which captured the personal information of the applicant; a New Business (NUB) transaction, which captured policy details (life cover, premium for quotation), and Tariff (TAR) transaction, which collated the information and provided the quote. This system was loaded on the personal computers, which agents and brokers had acquired since 1983. In 1983 Sanlam introduced WANG personal stand-alone computers (PCs) to replace the typewriter terminals. Sanlam captured this technological advantage in the distribution network by allowing agents and brokers to purchase personal computers, first the WANG and later updated models, equipped with the same software used at Head Office. The PCs were linked via dial-up connections to the mainframe at Head Office. Finpro, Megkwot, and ISABEL, the client management system, enhanced productivity through the direct dial-up connections. In 1994 ISABEL was replaced by a Windows-friendly SanAdmin version. Both these systems were replaced in 1998 by SanQuote, Sanlam's new electronic quotation program. From August 1986 agents' and brokers' personal computers were linked directly to the Sanlam mainframe. The WANG 'coded transactions' were

[145] Sanlam (2014): *Sanlam: The IT journey from 1990 to 2014:* 3–16; SA: Confidential Memorandum to Board, 26/2/1997.

subsequently replaced by the superior user-friendly full-screen online transactions.[146] These IT systems enhanced the processing of data through electronic image processing, which became an ongoing 'Business Process Re-engineering' program in Sanlam IT. It made a substantial contribution to the fast circulation of policies, improved quality of new policy issues, and reduced the cost of new policy issuing. The BS was a major enabling function in Sanlam. The pressing conditions in South Africa during the late 1980s and early 1990s made technological efficiency vital to a life office. Sanlam's BS struggled to keep up with the demands of the following decade's market competition.

The relative position of Sanlam in the rapidly changing financial services market gradually manifested. As indicated in Table 4.4, long-term fund inflows showed a declining trend.

Despite assets growing at a 30 per cent annual compound rate between 1985 and 1997, and premium income by 24.8 per cent, the yield on assets displayed the warning signs. Yields declined from over 11 per cent in the mid-1980s to below 6 per cent in 1994 and then recovered to just over 8 per cent by 1997. This was consistently well below the inflation rate (see Table 4.5 and Figure 4.1). Only in 1997 did the RoA (Return on Assets) of Sanlam equal inflation. Beating GDP growth was not placing Sanlam in a leading position in the market. As indicated in Table 4.5, Sanlam's premium income as a proportion of the long-term insurance industry rose from just over 27 per cent in 1985 to 34 per cent in 1994, but then dropped to 25 per cent in 1996 and recovered to 31 per cent in 1997. With declining returns on assets, Sanlam needed to make fundamental changes to its business model.

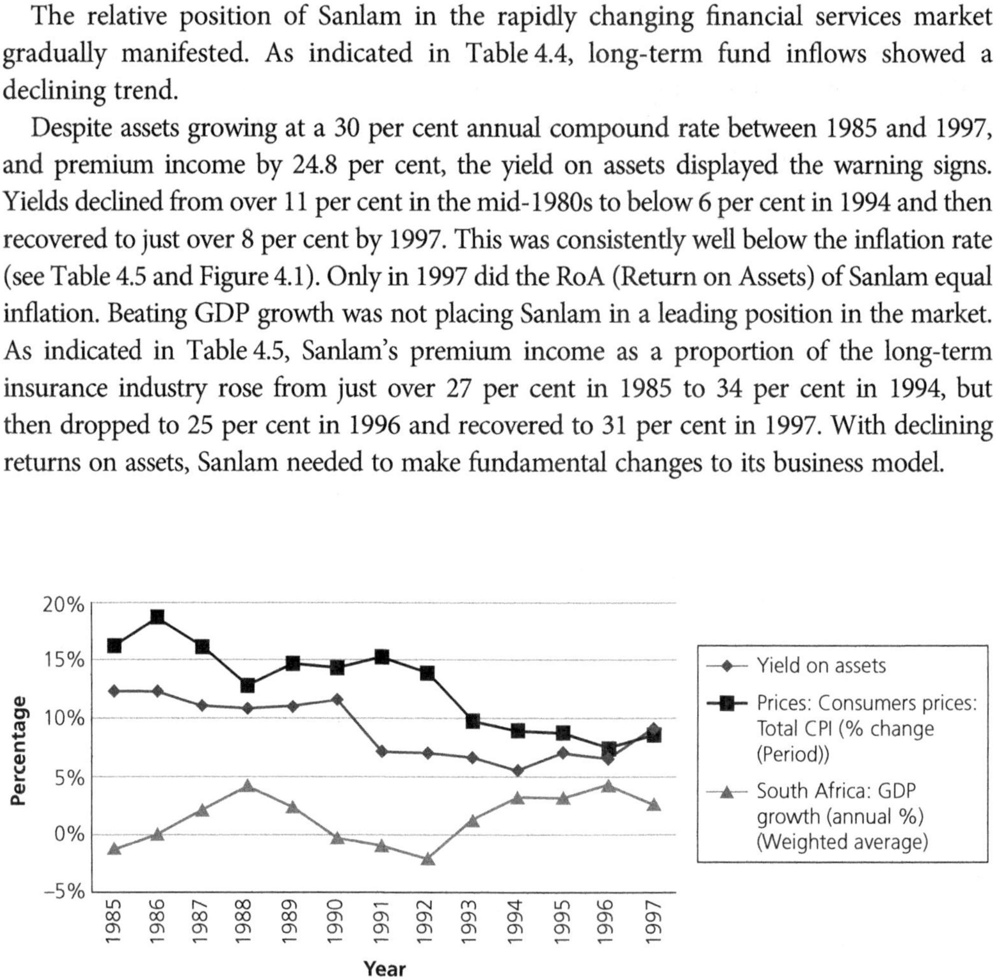

Figure 4.1. Yield on Sanlam assets, 1985–1997

146 Sanlam (2014): The IT journey: 22–30.

Table 4.5. Sanlam selected performance indicators, 1985–1997

	Premium income Rm	% growth	Premium as % industry	Life assurance fund Rm	Total assets Rm	Asset % industry assets	RoA %
1985	1 605		27.07	7 524	7 785	18.2	11.2
1986	2 087	23		9 316	9 611	19.6	11.19
1987	3 527	40.8		12 269	12 845	21.2	10.28
1988	5 174	31.8	34.04	16 537	17 213	23.3	10.10
1989	6 036	14.2	35.13	21 735	22 796	18.7	10.23
1990	7 428	18.7	34.33	27 254	27 908	19.56	10.71
1991	8 178	9.17	33.34	50 012	50 786	29.4	6.76
1992	10 400	21.3	33.3	59 125	60 070	29.3	6.68
1993	12 798	18.6	33.23	70 568	71 846	29.5	6.29
1994	13 626	6.14	29.5	99 163	101 380	31.9	5.22
1995	16 654	18.1	26.9	122 260	124 987	33.8	6.70
1996	18 618	10.54	25.06	130 400	132 877	29.04	6.22
1997	21 966	15.2	31.02	136 244	139 817	28.5	8.57
Annual compound growth '85–'97	26.84			30.11	30.02		

Source: Sanlam annual financial statements, 1985–1997; Financial services board annual reports, 1985–1997.

Adapting to the new South Africa

Business in South Africa devised an accommodating business strategy long before 1990. In Sanlam, strategic environmental repositioning occurred regularly from the mid-1980s. The Head Office epitomized Afrikaner business ambitions. A patriarchal management culture made for a disciplined workforce, respect for senior management, and a high degree of alignment with Afrikaner culture, religion, and language. This all changed as a younger-generation Afrikaner succeeded the old guard. As brokers entered the distribution channel during the late 1970s, more non-Afrikaans speakers worked with Sanlam. The corps of English-speaking staff at Head Office increased gradually. Staff gradually also displayed political affiliations other than support for the National Party, and Wassenaar and Fred du Plessis often engaged in public criticism of the ruling party. A dwindling cultural cohesion replaced the high nationalism of the 1930s and in the early 1980s Afrikaner division was accentuated with the establishment of the Conservative Party in 1982, as the conservative split posed political opposition to the National Party. In 1988 the 150th commemoration of the Great Trek was mentioned only by a single photograph in *Die Fakkel*,[147] while the 1938 centenary celebrations dominated

[147] SA: *Die Fakkel*, 21/10/1988: 3.

news in *Die Sanlam Fakkel* and staff were encouraged to participate in the celebrations. The assumed 'Afrikaner unity' had lost its central core and the disintegration of what was left thereof was cemented in the deep political divisions around the 1992 referendum in favour of political reform.[148] The Dutch Reformed Church denounced racial segregation in 1986 and opened its doors to all South Africans irrespective of race, and the black opposition in exile signaled crumbling solidarity and a willingness to talk about a peaceful political transition to a unitary democracy. In Sanlam two incidents in 1993 pointed to the end of the era of Afrikaner domination. The first was a report in the staff magazine *Sanlammer* of 22 January 1993 explicitly mentioning the language orientation of new appointments at Head Office: seventy-three Afrikaans and fifteen English new recruits. This was the first time the in-house magazine explicitly mentioned the growing English-speaking staff complement. The significance emerged from the fact that by the early 1990s almost half of the Sanlam policyholder profile was English speaking.[149] The second incident was the report announcing a basic language course in *isiXhosa* for staff. *isiXhosa* was the native language of the majority of African people in the Eastern Cape, of which a large number had relocated to the Western Cape, or Cape Peninsula. This development indicated the openness towards the wider socio-economic context of the company's operation.[150] In 1996 a staff magazine, then called *Bloudruk*, was published in March in English as *Blueprint*, carrying the caption '*A new face in Sanlam. Fair deal for all.*' A smiling black face covered the front page.[151] Management stated that Sanlam wished to conduct its business in South Africa as a true national institution.[152] In the *Sanlammer* of 12 July 1992 an article by Prof Willie Esterhuyse (a well-known protagonist of political reform and Professor in Philosophy at the University of Stellenbosch) claimed that Sanlam could never be the same in the new dispensation, because the '*volk*' of 1918 no longer existed. While the slogan 'born from the people to serve the people' [*uit die volk gebore om die volk te dien*] suited the ambitions of Afrikaners seeking economic empowerment, the last decade of the twentieth century required self-assessment and an explicit decision to adapt to the new circumstances.[153] Esterhuyse was a useful agent of change to deliver this message, but in the Chairman's report at the end of 1991 Dr A.J. van den Berg also

[148] H. Giliomee (2003): *The Afrikaners, Biography of a People*: 626–8; H.J. Vermeulen (1997): 'The subtext of Pieter Fourie's *Donderdag se mense* and the demise of Afrikaner nationalism', *Journal of Literary Studies*, 13(3–4).

[149] SA: *Sanlammer*, 22/1/1993: 2; W. Beukes (2017) *Van Afrikanerkultuur tot korporatief: die geskiedenis van Sanlam se organisasiekultuur met spesifieke verwysing na sy personeel in Hoofkantoor,1918–2014*. Unpublished PhD Thesis, University of Stellenbosch: 90–4; Halleen, op. cit: 109.

[150] SA: *Die Sanlammer*, 23/7/1993: 2. [151] SA: *Blueprint*, 3/1996.

[152] Halleen, op. cit: 111. [153] SA: *Sanlammer*, 12/7/1992: 1.

acknowledged the legacy of Sanlam growing from humble traditional Afrikaner roots, but stated that the company nevertheless always sought to serve the interests of all South Africans.[154] The reality of demographic changes resulted in the closing of the DRC congregation frequented by many Sanlam staff living in the accommodation adjacent to the head office building and other Sanlammers living in the vicinity. The congregation was founded in October 1966, but was later demolished to provide for the construction of a shopping centre.

Sanlam did not lead the market in social transformation of the life offices, but followed closely. Management managed change. People of colour always comprised part of the Sanlam staff, but after the 1990s the numbers rose steadily. By 1991 the staff magazine noted that 693 African people worked in Head Office, compared to eighty in 1954.[155] A much larger contingent of Coloured people had always worked in Sanlam since 1918, but as apartheid legislation enforced segregation more systematically during the 1950s, the board put pressure on Wassenaar and the executive management to replace certain black or Coloured messengers and security staff with white employees. Wassenaar motivated the retention of the existing staff on the grounds of their being first-class people, while the white people available for those jobs failed to rise to the same standards.[156] Remuneration differentiation between whites and Coloured people was only officially terminated in 1975. More fully qualified and highly skilled Coloured people entered employment at Sanlam, especially in the information technology division Multi Data. Management then announced equal pay for equal work by equally qualified staff.[157] Racial segregation at Head Office was a stark reality until the late 1980s when separate facilities gradually made way for common rooms and single sports representation of Sanlam by all employees. Social integration in the workplace emerged gradually during the late 1970s. In 1977 the first photograph of white and Coloured staff members attending training was published in the staff magazine.[158] Following the Wiehan Report of 1979 in which the recognition of black trade unions and a termination of separate facilities in the workplace for different races were accepted by the state, Sanlam also scrapped separate eating facilities at Head Office.[159] In 1982 Clara Snyders, a Coloured woman, joined the Sanlam 25 Club for staff with twenty-five years' service to the company in the catering division,[160] and in January 1983 Chris Adonis, a Coloured

[154] SA: 5/5/2: Chairman's address, 19/2/1992: 6.

[155] SA: 4/10: Staff Administration, K5, Memorandum to Sanlam Board.

[156] SA: Minutes of Sanlam Board, 17/11/1954.

[157] SA: Sanlam News release, 20/5/1975: Sanlam Information technology; *Die Fakkel*, 23/5/1975: 1.

[158] SA: *Die Fakkel*, 22/7/1977; 6/4/1979

[159] SA: 5/3/15/3: Training of Black and Coloured people in Sanlam 'Non-white staff', 12/11/1980; 'Non-white staff eating facilities', 9/6/1981.

[160] SA: *Die Fakkel*, 5/11/1982.

man holding a Sanlam bursary, was appointed in the internal audit department after completing a BCom degree plus further postgraduate qualifications.[161]

The period of transition from a racially divided society to an open society under majority rule overlapped with a growing global emphasis on corporate accountability and a greater social purpose of the corporation. As neoclassical economic policies gained popularity during the 1980s, and companies were called upon to reduce corporate social responsibility (CSR), business worldwide rather redefined CSR. The attention shifted to social matters that, once addressed successfully, in the long run would be mutually beneficial.[162] Towards the end of the twentieth century the public social responsibility reputation of a company became a matter of strategic importance. In South Africa the legacy of racial segregation added a statutory dimension to corporate social investment. Sanlam's CSR (*Korporatiewe Maatskaplike Betrokkenheid*) focus did not change in principle after 1985. The primary focus remained education and training. Sanlam, unlike many other organizations in South Africa, chose to regularly provide funds to those population groups marginalized under racial segregation. Examples include various contributions made to the Bantu Sport and Recreation Fund, as well as annual donations provided to universities for black, Indian, and Coloured students.[163] In 1980 a new formula for CSR expenditure and assessment was adopted. Sanlam agreed to allocate between 0.5 per cent and 1 per cent of the previous year's premium income to CSR.[164] With the growth in premium income Sanlam's CSR expenditure between 1980 and 1994 rose by 1205 per cent, peaking at R4.2 million in 1994. By 1989 the bulk of Sanlam's CSR went to education (31 per cent), 19 per cent to sport, 11 per cent to health and welfare initiatives, and 28 per cent to 'other' causes. In the 1990s the company's CSR shifted to 20 per cent for education, 20 per cent for sport, 16 per cent for welfare and health, and 7 per cent for entrepreneurship. The reasoning behind this shift was that sport was a powerful tool towards social transformation. Sanlam sponsored only 'clean' sport, that was non-contact sport and sport codes with which the company was comfortable to be associated with, especially athletics and football. Being involved in these sporting codes gave Sanlam exposure with top performers—a perception the company wished to establish, namely that merit and achievement are rewarded, irrespective of race.[165]

[161] SA; *Die Fakkel*, 19/3/1982.

[162] D. Windsor (2001): 'The Future of Corporate Social Performance'. *The International Journal of Organisational Analysis*. 9(3): 225–56.

[163] G. Verhoef (2016): Die onderneming en die gemeenskap: Korporatiewe maatskaplike betrokkenheid deur Sanlam, 1918–1980 *Tydskrif vir Geesteswetenskappe*, 54(4): 1–22; V. Laburn (2011): The economics of Corporate Social Investment: Sanlam and Corporate Social Responsibility expenditure, 1970 to 2008. Unpublished MA mini-dissertation, University of Stellenbosch, 2010.

[164] SA: 5/3/2: Minutes of Board, 23/1/1980.

[165] SA: S.19: Memorandum on Sport Sponsorships, Sanlam Board, 18/7/1984; Sanlam Board, 17/8/1988.

By 1995 Sanlam realigned its CSR policy with the new government's Reconstruction and Development Programme (RDP).[166] This decision followed a countrywide CSR poll, endorsed by Sanlam, to identify the 'Most Caring Company'. White respondents perceived Sanlam as a highly 'caring' organization, the black respondents placed Sanlam in thirteenth position. The 1995 repositioning of Sanlam's CSR was not a fundamental shift for the company. It perceived its CSR as a medium of communicating to society its involvement in building security for its policyholders.[167] Sanlam lived its civil citizenship through community engagement, because that was how it interpreted its responsibility towards the country. The RDP-induced shift was actually not a fundamental shift. In complying with RDP priorities, Sanlam's CSR was aimed at repositioning the organization in the new South Africa by engaging in human capital investments to ultimately build its client base and thereby educate people outside the life insurance net, about ways to construct their own social security. The focus remained education and training, also through engagement in welfare and health and in sport. Since the Sanlam policyholder profile had changed substantially after the 1960s, 40 per cent of policyholders were English-speaking by the mid-1990s, and around 30 per cent were black people, the company clearly had to target the black youth market to secure a foot in the door of future business. Sanlam's CSR was not purely philanthropic, but an alignment of its business goals with those of the future generation.[168]

By the late 1990s Sanlam's CSR on education had risen to 36 per cent of CSR expenditure, 26 per cent went to welfare and health, 10 per cent to sport, and 9 per cent to entrepreneurship. The football sponsorship of the Santos Football Club gave the company a presence in the community where it desperately needed a repositioning. This was an 'emerging' market Sanlam sought to develop. The Sanlam staff engaged directly with the organization, training, and support of the players and supporters. This sponsorship followed on the Sanlam football sponsorship since the early 1970s and the official sponsorship to the national junior football team since 1994. This involvement with football was perceived as an engagement with social upliftment and personal education similar to the work undertaken with marginalized poor Afrikaners during the 1920s and 1930s.[169] By 1997 Sanlam's total policyholder composition reflected a 6 per cent increase in black policyholders to 22 per cent, whereas the proportion of Indian and Coloured policyholders remained stable. Sanlam anticipated the increasing penetration into the black market. By 1997 black clients stood at 37.8 per cent of new recurring policies and 26.2 per cent of single-premium policies.[170]

[166] SA: S.17: Sanlam Board Minutes, 18/10/1995: Confidential Memorandum P. Smit–Sanlam Board, 15/8/1995.

[167] SA: Minutes Sanlam Board, 18/3/1992; SA Report to Sanlam Board, 11/12/1996.

[168] SA: Memorandum to Sanlam Board: KMB, 21/6/1995.

[169] SA: S.19: Confidential Memorandum to Sanlam Board, 27/8/1997.

[170] SA: Confidential memorandum to Sanlam Board, 26/2/1997.

The environmental changes in the sphere of Sanlam's operations and the company's own response to that changing environment was articulated in its submission to the Truth and Reconciliation Commission (TRC). In 1995 the Act on the Promotion of National Unity and Reconciliation, No. 34 of 1995, was passed. It opened the series of hearings by the TRC with the aim of providing 'as complete a picture as possible' of the 'nature, causes and extent of gross violations of human rights'. The Sanlam board initially decided not to make a submission to the TRC,[171] but it became clear that many corporates from the business community prepared submissions to contextualize their operations. Sanlam's absence would not serve the interests of the company, at that time preparing for possible demutualization as well as addressing its penetration into the broader South African society. Desmond Smith as Managing Director did the submission on behalf of Sanlam on 13 November 1997. As a point of departure the Sanlam submission denied any involvement in so-called 'gross violations of human rights', but acknowledged that the policy of separate development 'seen as the best guarantee for overall justice and peace in the country','turned out to be totally wrong'.[172] Smith explained the historical roots of Sanlam as an empowerment enterprise to address post-South African War Afrikaner impoverishment, being the market in which the company competed according to its strength (par 5–6). Sanlam acknowledged that property belonging to the company had been the location in which former political prisoners were held and tortured, but denied any prior knowledge of such conduct. As lessor, Sanlam distanced itself from the actions of the lessee, nevertheless expressing deep regret and sorrow. The unfolding of racial segregation was a colonial legacy, which constituted the institutional violation of human rights of suffrage, freedom of movement, and residence. Sanlam noted the development of the institutional arrangements of racial segregation as impracticable and immoral (par 7–8), but that business as an organization dealt with the dual and powerful nature of government. Government had the political power, but also conducted business with the corporations. The enterprise had to operate in the best interests of all its stakeholders—in the case of Sanlam, its policyholders. The latter soon became representative of the broad spectrum of South African society and were no longer only poor Afrikaners. Therefore Sanlam and all other businesses in South Africa criticized Government, confronted the state, and opposed government actions in many respects, but could not be expected to be the 'watchdog of the government as far as human rights violations are concerned'. Sanlam and many other insurers conducted business with the government, providing services such as pension funds, group life schemes, and investments, which served the interests of people from different strata, communities, and professions in the country (par 9–13). Sanlam rejected the notion that

[171] SA: Minutes of Sanlam Board, 13/5/1997.

[172] SA; Oral introduction on 13 November 1997 by Mr D.K. Smith, Managing Director: Third Draft, 10/11/1997.

business benefited from the policy of racial segregation, since the real costs of the policy were not taken into consideration. Furthermore Sanlam and other financial services companies were denied the opportunities of lucrative international operations and investments (par 9). Sanlam quoted its management, from M.S Louw to A. D. Wassenaar and F.J. du Plessis, as critics of the state, calling for 'the final demise of apartheid . . . and in its place must come a just society with equal opportunity for all' (par 17–18). The submission quoted the English-language Sunday newspaper the *Sunday Express* and the *Cape Times*, reporting on Sanlam scrapping petty apartheid (par 29). The company distanced itself from the violence of the struggle, but called for a commitment by the new government to 'checks and balances for the protection of human rights' (par 226–7). The submission provided detailed testimony of how Sanlam had engaged, of its own accord, to address imbalances of the past: in employment equity, the pioneering empowerment transaction with Metlife, other tertiary training and education opportunities, the Development Fund exceeding R750 million for development investment, and the broad range of corporate social investment initiatives (par 22–6).[173] This testimony before the TRC was an open and honest submission on how Sanlam had entered the market and changed with its stakeholder base. Smith admitted that the past could not be changed, but presented Sanlam's submission as an explanation of the course of development of the company, not as a justification. Sanlam the legal entity had no independent emotions, but the individuals on the different levels of management had travelled the journey of transformation simply because the underlying values of Sanlam of 1918 were the same values guiding the company at the end of the twentieth century.[174] Testifying showed good faith, but Sanlam had already made substantial progress in repositioning itself as the company adding value to all its stakeholders. This was apparent in the policyholder profile, the employment composition at Sanlamhof, and sustained social engagement.

The transformation in Sanlam—in the public positioning of the company, in Head Office organization and staff complement, and in market focus—occurred as a response to exogenous environmental changes. Sanlam pioneered the first BEE transaction at a time when corporate South African business sought to establish relationships with the leadership of black-owned business, who were anticipated to emerge as closely aligned to the new political dispensation expected soon to dawn upon South Africa. This transaction did not initiate a systematic and comprehensive internal company transformation process. As the newly elected state after 1994 introduced statutory sanctioned transformation, Sanlam followed as a 'transformation-taker', not an initiator. Explicit compliance with state segregation policies in the physical separation at the workplace, leisure

[173] SA: Letter P.E. Linde–F. Randera, 13/10/1997: Submission by Sanlam to the Truth and Reconciliation Commission, 13/10/1997; Minutes of Sanlam Board, 29/10/1997.

[174] SA: Oral testimony by D.K. Smith in response to a question by TRC Commissioner, 13/11/1997.

activities, and employment conditions only changed in response to external socio-economic transformation. Management seemed to have a wait-and-see attitude. The proactive market-leading initiative of the BEE transaction was unmatched in the changing context of the early 1990s. In 1995, after the transfer of power to the newly democratically elected government, the Managing Director admitted to the board that Sanlam had not yet identified the key role players with whom the company should network for future positioning of its business. Smith anticipated a change of 'culture' or 'the way of doing things in Sanlam' to follow from an investigation into improved efficiency and a new culture in Sanlam. Serious challenges were identified in the bureaucracy in the company and in a lack of a clearer business focus.[175] It became increasingly clear that Sanlam had begun its soul searching, as the control obsession of the era under Fred du Plessis disappeared from the strategic vision. The transition into the new business and socio-economic environment was challenging. The good relationship between Marinus Daling and Thabo Mbeki since their engagement outside South Africa in 1987, was testimony to the deep-seated shared South Africanism that would bridge the trying times ahead. Market conditions were adverse. Visionary leadership was needed to lead Sanlam out of a period of disappointing, weak performance.

[175] SA: D.K. Smith memorandum to Sanlam Board, 6/3/1995.

5 Managing change: diversification and transformation, 1993–2003

Two strong trends converged—individual freedom and deregulation. Global financial deregulation transformed the world of finance. Clients' money rendered mobility and choice. The collapse of the Soviet Union and the fall of the Berlin Wall brought liberal market freedom closer to societies. Individual freedom of choice, expression, and affiliation shaped confident citizens seizing the opportunities. South Africa experienced its own radical transition from white minority rule to majority government in 1994. The face of the country changed, and financial institutions followed global trends. Globally financial deregulation invited market contestation, which led to mutual organizations developing an appetite for extended operations outside the limited confines of the mutual organization. In the traditional life market, insurers experienced functional competition as deposit-taking institutions and new asset managers offered investment options to pension funds and life and/or short-term insurance products through brokers. The most unique distinguishing characteristic of the life industry was the long-term nature of its guarantees, but the industry abandoned those gradually. The investment public displayed a contracting demand for risk products and a growing demand for investment products. Distribution channels became highly contested, with brokers and agents enjoying the attention of suppliers, rather than the client. These developments inevitably led to wider regulatory intervention by states worldwide and also in South Africa. In the volatile local market of declining interest rates and policy uncertainty, the long-term insurance industry faced strategic choices, which were fundamental to the stability of the South African economy because of the size of the industry.

The long-term insurance industry occupied a critical role in the South African economy, especially since the domestication of the industry during the late 1970s and the international isolation reaching a peak during the 1980s. By 1990 three companies, SA Mutual, Sanlam, and Liberty Life, dominated the industry. Together the value of their market capitalization was equal to 23 per cent of the total capitalization of the JSE, although only Liberty was listed on the JSE. The premium income of the life offices was equivalent to roughly 30 per cent of gross domestic fixed investment (GDFI) in any year, or rose from 3.7 per cent of GDP in 1979 to 8 per cent in 1990.[1] The confidence of the nation in the industry was evident in the exceptionally high expenditure by South Africans on life insurance compared to expenditure by other nations in the world. In 1990 the total long-term premiums in South Africa comprised 7.47 per cent of GDP—lagging only Japan and South Korea. By 1994 that figure had risen to 9.42 per cent—the highest in the world. In 1998 South Africans spent 13.14 per cent of GDP on life insurance and by 2004 this ratio rose to 14.86 per cent. South Africa was still the world leader.[2] As the bulk of the long-term premiums was not invested in risk products, but in savings for retirement, stability in this market was therefore essential. The centrality of the industry can also be described by the relative growth in GDP and savings. Between 1990 and 2000 real GDP rose by 2.6 percent p.a., household savings by 8.1 percent p.a. and the CPIX by 9.8 per cent p.a., but long-term insurance premiums by 19.3 percent p.a.[3] After 1994 the long-term insurance market was expected to grow significantly, as a growing portion of the South African population entered the market. In a similar way as a large portion of the Afrikaner people had been outside the long-term insurance market before 1918, a large portion of the South African society was outside that market before the democratic elections of 1994. Towards the end of the twentieth century long-term insurance companies competed with other financial services providers for this new market. The structure of that demand changed from long-term stable returns to higher-risk wealth products.

Financial market deregulation impacted directly on the long-term insurance industry. The Insurance Act, No. 27 of 1943, was amended in 1998. Two separate statutes replaced this Act—one for short-term insurance and one for long-term insurance. In 1999 the Long-Term Insurance Act, No. 52 of 1998, came into force. The Act prohibited the registration of composite primary insurance companies. Insurance companies could no longer undertake both long- and short-term insurance business, but both could be conducted under a single holding company. The collapse of the AA Mutual insurance company in 1986 resulted in the appointment of the Melamet Commission of Inquiry into regulation and oversight in the financial services sector. In response to the commission's proposals on improved sector control, the Financial Services Board Act, No. 97 of 1990, was passed, leading to the formation of the Financial Services Board (FSB) in 1992. The Registrar of Insurance moved under the broad umbrella of the FSB. The FSB became the recipient of regular industry submissions. The FSB issued further regulatory requirements to the industry and took on an overarching oversight role following the publication of the King Report on Corporate Governance (King I) in 1994 and King II

[1] *Financial Mail*: 'Life Assurance Industry. Supporting the economy?' Survey, 30/11/1990: 5. (Why not use stats of the LOA?)

[2] G. Verhoef (2010): Life offices to the rescue: 156; U. Birkman and C. Codoni (2004), World Insurance in 2003: Insurance industry on the road to recovery; *Sigma*, 3, Zurich: SwissRe.

[3] Verhoef, ibid.: 157–63; R. Vivian (2007): 'The South Africa insurance markets', in J.D. Cummins and B. Venard (2007): *Handbook of international Insurance*, Springer: 677.

in 2002. A tight web of industry regulation developed as protection of the public interest found reflection in the 2001 Financial Intelligence Centre Act, No. 38 of 2001, and the Financial Advisory and Intermediary Services Act, No. 37 of 2002. The regulatory environment put increasing cost pressures on the industry, which escalated in the second half of the 2000s.

The structure of long-term insurance funds changed in the context of changing investor preferences mandated by political uncertainty and subsequent state policies. The net annual premium income of long-term insurance companies fluctuated heavily (see Table 4.3). The growth in premium income during the latter half of the 1980s was assisted by high inflation, which had been well in excess of GDP growth since the 1990s. The strong premium growth was undermined by the steady growth in benefits paid (benefits paid included payments in case of maturity of policies and terminations), a function of the flow of funds out of the industry more rapidly than the inflow. Higher outflows resulted in the declining ratio of income to expenditure. In the period between 1985 and 1990 industry income to expenditure ratio was 2.8, but then steadily declined to 1.36 by 2000. The ratio of assets to liabilities of the long-term companies deteriorated from 1.78 in 1985 to 1.41 in 2000.

In Table 5.1 the change in liabilities of the long-term insurance industry is illustrated. There was a substantial exposure to pension funds and group life schemes (or employee benefit schemes). This is a function performed by the industry on behalf of smaller

Table 5.1. Product segmentation in the long-term insurance market, 1985–2000 (R'bn)

	1985	1990	1995	2000
Pension fund + group life benefits				
–Premiums	1.87	7.72	20.98	66.92
–%	45.06	35.21	34.20	49.63
Retirement annuity fund business				
–Premiums	0.63	2.63	4.49	10.39
–%	15.16	12.01	7.32	7.70
Immediate annuity business				
–Premiums	0.21	3.83	10.04	12.01
–%	5.13	17.49	16.37	8.90
Disability and health insurance				
–Premiums	0.02	0.19	1.4	2.79
–%	0.54	0.85	2.30	2.07
Single premiums				
–Premiums	0.07	0.27	5.42	17.85
–%	1.75	1.24	8.84	13.24
Periodic premiums				
–Premiums	1.34	7.28	18.99	24.90
–%	32.31	33.21	30.96	18.46
Total				
–Premiums	4,15	21,92	61,32	134,84
–%	100	100	100	100

Source: Registrar of Insurance, 1985–1997; Registrar of long-term insurance, 1998–2000.

employers. These funds rose from R1.87 billion in 1985 to R66.92 billion in 2000, or from 45.06 per cent of the business of the long-term insurance companies to 49.63 per cent in 2000. The rapid expansion of 'new' employees in public and private employment (the massive explosion of civil servants on all three levels of civil government after 1994) and the rise of a new black middle class entering permanent employment, and soon the impact of BEE policies, contributed to a large degree to this growth. In the absence of state social security, private pension funds as a mechanism of defined-contribution savings options, mushroomed. By 2000 total assets of pension funds constituted 75.26 per cent of GDP. The relative decline in retirement annuity business from 15.16 per cent in 1985 to 7.70 per cent in 2000 indicated that investors moved increasingly to alternative investment instruments to provide for future needs. This trend was underlined by the similar trend displayed in periodic premium policies, which declined from 32.31 per cent of long-term insurance business to 18.46 per cent in 2000. The trend was similar for immediate annuity investments. This was a shift in the allocation of investor funds within the pie. The trend in immediate annuities, first a high increase and then a reduction in relative size, was a result of industry product innovation. The long-term insurers introduced the single-premium 'investment' product. Liabilities of single-premium products were just about equal to the assets held. This increase in single premiums written by the life insurers caused tension in the deposit-taking industry. The latter attacked the tax base of life insurers. During the 1980s the long-term insurance industry still fell under the earlier tax dispensation, where a higher portion of non-taxable liabilities (like pension fund and immediate annuities business) had the effect of reducing the tax rate on free reserves. The mutual companies had fewer problems with inflating their non-taxable actuarial liabilities to benefit from the lower tax rate. This was one consideration to sustain the mutual form of organization. When the Minister of Finance started to talk about a reconsideration of the tax base of the long-term insurance industry towards the mid-1980s, the industry moved fast to offer immediate annuities as part of the new product combinations. In practice this was similar to the increase in single premiums by circumventing the new tax regulations. This strategy assisted the long-term industry to attract funds in competition with other deposit-taking institutions. As this landscape changed, so did the business strategy of the long-term industry, especially the mutual companies. This chapter explains Sanlam's response to the changed financial services environment by reflecting on the beginning of the discourse on changing the form of organization.

Sanlam in a changing industry

An industry overhaul necessitated strategic thinking and change management. Management had to come to grips with the contracting demand for long-term insurance products, understand the new demand for wealth products, and carve out a new role in the dynamically changing financial services industry. It was soon apparent that Sanlam emerged as a 'learning organization'[4] where leaders perceived themselves as part of the evolution of the nature of work and organizations. The ability to apply the five disciplines of the learning organization held the key to Sanlam's industry repositioning. The death of Fred du Plessis and the management repositioning under Pierre Steyn set in motion a direction that was not at that time envisioned to be the beginning of the demutualization of Sanlam. Steyn inherited Sanlam with a yield on assets of just over 10 per cent, while inflation ranged between 14 per cent and 15 per cent. He called on George Rudman, who was then Senior General Manager: Finance and Planning, to find 'a profit base' (*winsgrondslag*) for Sanlam. The telling question was: what is profit in a mutual insurer? Rudman consulted with British and American life offices overseas on how to manage the 'estate'[5] (the capital—this was the term used in a mutual company for the excess of assets over actuarial liabilities) of a mutual insurer. He returned to the country convinced that Sanlam, the mutual, had to be managed with a clear view to generate profit as the security to the company in times of market downturn and extreme volatility. Rudman took a visionary position when in January 1990 he appealed for a 'new' approach to the management of policyholder funds. He called for a dedicated strategy to seek optimal profits on investment, low costs, and an equitable distribution of risk. He told management that the mutual company should no longer be managed as a mutual. Its 'capital' should be considered as an 'estate', which constitutes the capital to be invested to optimize returns to profit-sharing policyholders.[6] Rudman understood the need for a radical change in the culture of doing life business. It was vital to develop a business approach to life business when markets and client demand were changing and political volatility increased instability. Bringing about such a complete mental shift called for patient convincing. Rudman spent almost four years propagating the reorganization of the mutual's business into profit-driven operations in separate 'business' units in the company from where profits would flow to the 'estate', which was what the capital of the company was called. The concept of self-sustaining business units contributing to own cost centres was new to the life business. Rudman's line of thought introduced thinking on a new strategy for Sanlam: a financial services company utilizing its acquired investment expertise to develop new financial products to grow profits in competitive global financial markets, benefiting policyholders. Subsequently a profit-oriented management strategy was implemented in 1990/91. (Reference was made to this policy

[4] P.M. Senge (1990): *The fifth discipline: the art and practice of the learning organization*. New York: Doubleday. The five disciplines Senge identifies are systems thinking, personal mastery, mental models, building of a shared vision, and team learning.

[5] The 'estate' as defined by Rudman at that time was the difference between assets and policyholder liabilities, that is, the free assets of the company.

[6] SA: 5/2/1: Confidential memorandum G. Rudman–P. Steyn, 16/1/1990.

change in Chapter 4 regarding the introduction of RHOs.) Operations were divided into profit centres, e.g. individual insurance, group benefits, investments, services, and the 'estate'. The profits from each unit went to the capital/estate of Sanlam, which then provided investment capital for innovative investment opportunities opening up in the deregulated international financial sector.[7]

Change did not come immediately, because Sanlam was the typical mutual. Earlier, Hansman noted that mutuals were less effective in reducing costs, since profit accumulated from policyholders' premiums constituted the only source of capital available to the mutuals, which constrained their ability to expand their services in response to growing demand. Mutuals were also handicapped in their ability to diversify by state regulation that limits insurance companies' freedom to engage in other business. The introduction of the new profit centres did not immediately deliver the expected results—unit costs escalated, policy lapses rose, cost charges to policy bases were too low, tax benefits were eroded, and policy sales declined. Sanlam's operational choices were increasingly restricted by insufficient responses to environmental changes.[8]

In the immediate period after the 1994 election, management deliberated about the company's future strategic direction. Since 1990 George Rudman had kept a close eye on the international industry landscape with a view to Sanlam's strategic repositioning. Two dimensions of Sanlam's market position were at stake. On the one hand there was industry change and on the other socio-political contextual change. At the beginning of the 1990s the dominant organizational form of life offices globally was still mutual. This was especially the case in the United States, Japan, Australia, and Canada. Some Canadian life offices changed their corporate form of organization during the 1980s from joint stock to mutual to protect themselves from American life office takeovers. The leading Australian mutual was the Australian Mutual Provident Society (AMP). Joint stock companies dominated the British life market, but thirty of the world's fifty largest life office were mutual.[9] Transition to public liability companies occurred usually because of agency problems, where the execution of managerial discretion resulted in operational inefficiency or differences of strategic direction with clients. Other concerns about operational cost also influenced the choice of organizational form.[10] The choice between the mutual form and a joint stock company revolved around issues of efficiency, performance, and the ability of the organization to resolve problems between owners,

[7] SA: 5/2/1: Confidential Memoranda, Sanlam Board, 20/06/90; 15/05/91.

[8] H. Hansman (1985): 'The organization of insurance companies: Mutual versus stock', *Journal of Law, Economics and Organization*, 1(2): 134; Interview Ronnie Masson, 18/03/2009.

[9] SA: Confidential Memorandum G. Rudman–Sanlam Board, 19/4/1995; R. Pearson and T. Yoneyama (2015): *Corporate forms of organizational choice in international insurance*, Oxford: Oxford University Press: 7–15.

[10] H. Hansman (1996): *The Ownership of Enterprise*. Cambridge, MA: Belknap Press of Harvard University Press: 287–97.

managers, and customers.[11] By the mid-1990s the 80 per cent market control of the fifty largest life offices in the world contracted to 76 per cent. This contraction was ascribed to the demutualization of the USA long-term insurer Equitable Life in 1992, and serious difficulties experienced by the National Mutual Life Company in Australia.[12] In South Africa the first demutualization of a long-term insurer was in 1984 when Southern Life, a mutual life office, merged with Anglo American Life. Rudman pointed out that financial difficulties, especially insufficient capital to bridge a period of unsatisfactory return on assets to sustain bonus rates on existing policies, generally tipped the scale in favour of demutualization. In 1993 Pierre Steyn requested Rudman to focus on developments in the Australian financial services market. Rudman's regular visits to Australia during the early 1990s influenced his thinking on demutualization and his choice of consultants when it was finally decided to demutualize Sanlam. Similarities in the Australian and South African markets made the choice of the Australian model a sound one, especially because the AMP had made substantial progress with preparation for demutualization when Sanlam started the debate.[13]

The Sanlam dilemma: legacy or leader?

The transformation in the life insurance industry and the radically different operational context of the late twentieth century occurred in tandem with an increasing disintegration of the Afrikaner nationalistic edifice. Mutuality and the empowerment motive comprised the foundation of Sanlam's rise. Since the first Chairman's address W.A. Hofmeyr had underlined the centrality of mutuality in Sanlam's operations on behalf of policyholders. This was a powerful legacy and almost inconceivable that it could ever change. From the beginning Sanlam was driven by policyholder interests and premium income. In 1953, when the Sanlam Private Act established Sanlam as a separate mutual company without shareholder capital, the mutual nature of the organization and its operations caused public opposition from competitors. SA Mutual's Chairman objected in public to the announcement by Sanlam that the company's name would change from Sanlam (Ltd) to Sanlam (Mutual). The 'Old man from Pinelands', as some people in Sanlam referred to SA Mutual, feared public confusion, but Hofmeyr claimed Sanlam had always been a mutual life office and would remain mutual. Both the Australian mutual life offices operating in South Africa, Colonial Mutual and the National Mutual

[11] Pearson and Yoneyama, op. cit.: 16–17.

[12] SA: Confidential memorandum G. Rudman, 19/4/1995.

[13] G. Verhoef and M. Keneley (2011): 'Pressures for change in the Australian and South African insurance markets: a comparison of two companies.' *Competition and Change, 15(2): 136–54.*

Life Association, used 'mutual' in their official names and Sanlam therefore insisted on indicating its mutuality officially in its name. Mutuality was part of the Sanlam legacy but by the 1990s was no longer the crucial motivational mass mobilizer of the beginning of the century. Industry changes mandated functional adaptation, but management had to prepare policyholders for a change.

Management was also not easily convinced about changing its mutuality. Desmond Smith considered Pierre Steyn a devout 'mutualist'. At the time of his passing away in December 1993 Smith claimed that management was already fairly swayed towards the wisdom of demutualization. It was simply a matter of striking the right time, both in terms of the readiness of Sanlam as well as the market.[14] Rudman made submissions to the Sanlam board twice, arguing the benefits of demutualization given contextual complexities and operational underperformance. He insisted that any decision to change the mutual form of the organization had to be in the interest of policyholders. In both instances he failed to convince the board, who represented policyholders' interests, which were that policyholders' interests would not be served at that stage by changing the mutual character of the company.[15] It was never clear whether Pierre Steyn was personally in favour of demutualization,[16] but when Marinus Daling succeeded Steyn as Sanlam Chairman after Steyn's death in December 1993, it was known to senior management that one of the priorities on Daling's to-do list was to demutualize Sanlam. The Sanlam institution was not going to change easily. Rudman recalled the management summit session ('*bosberaad*') in April 1994 where discussions on mutuality loosely surfaced and Marinus Daling sounded Rudman out about the desirable route for Sanlam. Rudman remarked that there were no sacred cows as far as mutuality was concerned. If it was decided on sound business principles that Sanlam should demutualize, then 'we decide it and do it'.[17] However, many more mutuality stalwarts needed convincing.

While functional restructuring was imminent, the socio-political transformation was equally vital. These two distinct processes ran concurrently. Change in leadership was needed, but that assumed clarity about the new direction in which the organization was moving. Sanlam was still perceived to be the vanguard of Afrikaner business, although that was not substantiated by the policyholder profile. In 1966 only 65.8 per cent of Sanlam's policyholders were white, 22.1 per cent was black, 8.4 per cent Coloured, and 3.7 per cent Indians. The strongest growth was in the black client base (32 per cent growth between 1994 and 1996 alone). By 1996 the majority of recurring-premium policies issued by Sanlam were in English and the gender composition also changed to include more than 34 per cent women.[18] Sanlam preferred to interpret these

[14] Interview D.K.S. Smith: 5 October 2017.
[15] SA: Minutes of Sanlam Board, 19/4/1995; 21/9/1994.
[16] Interview G. Rudman, 14/11/2007. [17] Interview G. Rudman, 14/11/2007.
[18] SA: Minutes Sanlam Board, 26/2/1997.

Table 5.2. Sanlam accumulated surplus and policy liabilities, 1986–1994

	Accumulated surplus (1) R'm	Total policy liabilities (2) R'm	Policy liabilities (market related/linked policies excluded) R'm	1÷2%	1÷3%
30/09/86	1 402	10 942	4 078	1.8	34.4
30/09/87	1 455	17 046	6 044	8.5	24.1
30/09/88	1 493	19 231	8 007	7.8	18.6
30/09/89	1 686	29 950	12 097	5.6	13.9
30/09/90	1 697	34 449	15 117	4.9	11.2
30/09/91	1 745	47 279	20 961	3.7	8.3
30/09/92	1 805	56 455	25 881	3.2	7.0
30/09/92	2 100	67 669	32 076	3.1	6.5
30/09/94	3 200	86 463	41 531	3.7	7.7

Source: Sanlam archives: Sanlam minutes of board meeting, 19/04/95.

trends as an expression of public trust, which constituted a reason to protect its mutual character. It was from the operational side that pressure was mounting to reconsider the organizational form. That meant Parliamentary sanctioning. It was underperformance in an environment anticipated to be hostile to big business that ultimately swung the argument against mutuality.

Industry contraction was a fact. Sanlam experienced an alarming collapse in its accumulated surplus. Table 5.2 shows Sanlam's accumulated surplus as a proportion of total liabilities declining from 12.8 per cent in 1986 to 3.7 per cent in 1994. The decline was even greater from 34.4 per cent to 7.7 per cent when excluding market-related or linked liabilities.

Sanlam was lagging the market in the ratio of total accumulated surplus to policy liabilities at 3.7 per cent, since SA Mutual maintained a ratio of 19.5 per cent, Liberty 30.9 per cent, and Momentum 11 per cent. Sanlam explained this unflattering market position by the strong growth in policyholder liabilities of around 29.5 per cent per annum between 1986 and 1994. This expansion actually highlighted its serious capital deficit. Growth in the market value of total Sanlam assets was 20 per cent between 1987 and 1994, but only 9 per cent in the market value of Sanlam's capital portfolio, while inflation averaged 13.1 per cent over the period. Sanlam was paying dearly for its aggressive drive to grow market share during the 1980s. In 1994 Sanlam had a 30.2 per cent market share, shy of SA Mutual's 31.8 per cent. Before the 1980s Sanlam was moderately conservative in allocating bonuses to reversionary bonus policies. The full bonus earned on policies was not allocated to policyholders. Market competition and 'fairness' considerations later resulted in Sanlam paying the full bonus earned. Smaller 'surpluses' were added to the Sanlam 'capital'. On all other policies full returns earned were paid, thus contributing to a gradual weakening in Sanlam's capital position.

By 1994 the composition of Sanlam's business had changed in tandem with the industry. Market-related or linked policies comprised 63 per cent of the portfolio in 1986, but by 1994 had dropped to 52 per cent. Annuity business rose from 6 per cent to 12 per cent of the portfolio, reversionary bonus policies declined from 24 per cent to 8 per cent, and other business increased from 7 per cent to 28 per cent in 1994.[19] Rising policy lapses (27 per cent between 1995 and 1996) and other withdrawals (rising by 25 per cent between 1995 and 1996) exacerbated these pressures.[20] This put severe strain on Sanlam's already weak capital base. Rudman called for a dedicated capital growth strategy.

A persistent struggle to succeed in healthcare services added to disappointing performance and remained a drain on both revenue and public trust. Insisting on controlling health service provision meant that Sanmed operated its health insurance outside the realm of the Office of the Registrar of medical schemes. The membership of the different schemes offered by Sanmed, namely Helpmed and Topmed, grew steadily and exceeded 96 000 by the year of its coming of age in November 1986. Two factors inhibited growth at Sanmed. The first was the lack of ability and experience to take on the administration of medical schemes. Medical scheme administration had emerged as a lucrative industry, but Sanmed was unprepared for it. The second factor was its increasingly underperforming computer system. Sanmed had to deal with the growing discontent of members. The Rembrandt Group and the SABC withdrew from Sanmed and formed independent medical schemes for their employees. Sanmed lost the business because it was not geared for medical scheme administration, because Sanlam was not interested in the administration of medical schemes, but rather in selling medical insurance policies. In 1986 Dalsig Investments Ltd, a Sanlam subsidiary, was restructured to enter the administration of medical schemes, but Dalsig posted losses until 1991. Gencor terminated its agreement with Dalsig for the administration of its medical scheme. As separate medical schemes of subsidiaries such as Santam and Nissan closed down, those members joined one of the Sanmed schemes. The challenge was not to lure new members into the schemes, but to deliver good service. New products, such as the One Medical Policy, only provided a short-term advantage in offering flexibility in options for medical cover, because the amended Medical Schemes Act of 1994 allowed the same flexibility to the industry. In 1991 Sanlam acquired a share in the Sunninghill Medical Institute, but corruption and maladministration in 1993 led to its liquidation. This exacerbated the Sanmed ills. The 1991 decision to develop a computer system independently from Sanlam had not materialized by 1993. Membership of Sanmed started waning. Dalsig lost schemes under administration as the new political powers withdrew municipal and provincial medical schemes such as Commed in North West Province from the Sanlam-linked Dalsig administration.

[19] SA: Confidential memorandum G. Rudman–Sanlam Board, 19/4/1995.

[20] SA: Confidential report on changes in the individual insurance sector–Sanlam Board, 26/2/1997.

Sanmed's medical schemes only qualified for preferential medical scheme tariffs on condition that the schemes' free reserves were not paid out as dividends to the owner and only shareholder, Sanlam. These reserves were kept as reserves in the schemes, but in 1995 Sanlam decided to transform Sanmed into a source of income for the company. This was in the context of Sanlam desperately seeking 'profit' to build its 'estate'. The Sanmed statutes were consequently amended to allow Sanlam to receive dividends. The Registrar of Medical Schemes' exemption was withdrawn. Sanmed management then asked Sanlam to pay a lump sum as 'reserves' to the different schemes, but the latter refused. This refusal led to repeated court action seven years later, which Sanlam lost. The more serious problem was the failing computer system. Delivery on membership cards, processing of claims, and electronic data imaging increasingly fell short of expectations. To complicate matters further, in 1995 Sanmed introduced USA-style managed healthcare. At high cost the Capp Care system, running on the HSD Diamond system, used in California to conduct pre-screening of members of the new managed healthcare system, was acquired. It soon proved unable to synchronize with the existing Sanmed IT systems. The anticipated savings through managed healthcare failed to materialize for Sanmed.[21] By 1997 and 1998 Sanmed delivered losses to Sanlam and therefore paid no dividends. Massive systems failure caused backlogs of more than 300 000 claims. Sanlam then restructured Sanlam Health, its subsidiary. Sanmed changed to Sanlam Health Risk Management (SHRM), Dalsig to Sanlam Health Administration Management (SHAM) and the managed healthcare to Sanlam Health Quality Management (SHQM)—with effect from 1 January 1998. The legacy of Sanmed to a subsequently newly demutualized Sanlam was persistent loss-making performance and a growing public discontent, linked directly to Sanlam. This drain on Sanlam's profitability lurked in the background of organizational restructuring deliberations.

Building 'capital'

A mutual life office does not have 'capital'. The excess of assets over liabilities is considered its 'capital'. Sanlam maintained a capital adequacy ratio of between 2 per cent and 3.5 per cent between 1986 and 1994. Sanlam invested this 'capital' in a separate capital portfolio, valued at actuarial calculations, which was usually lower than market value and therefore less volatile. Policyholder liabilities were invested in the policyholder fund to minimize risks of policyholder liabilities. In an environment of low interest rates and high inflation since the mid-1980s, Sanlam thus suffered a declining return on assets

[21] SA: Minutes of Sanlam Board, 16/8/1995; 13/12/1995.

and weakened its capital position. From 1970 the company's yield on assets remained below inflation and only turned slightly positive by 1997. The most depressing asset performance was from the strategic legacy investments, such as the investment of around R204 million first in Bankorp and subsequently in ABSA, which delivering an average of 12.2 per cent p.a. return between 1979 and 1994, compared unfavourably to an expected 21.5 per cent return on an investment in the banking sector. Automakers (the holding company of Nissan motors in South Africa) was one such underperforming investment. Automakers was transferred to the without-profit portfolio in 1993, subsequently reflecting less adversely on Sanlam's investment earnings. The investment of R75 million in Condura (TEK Corporation), which delivered negative returns throughout the period between 1985 and 1994, fell in the same category. The same applied to the undeveloped property and poor-performing real estate of around R400 million, also a legacy of the Fred du Plessis era. Finally, by the end of 1994, non-performing assets in the capital portfolio were restructured to leave the portfolio with only negotiable investment assets, which had a potential for much-improved returns.[22]

Sanlam was caught up between fast-growing policy liabilities, underperforming assets, business restructuring, and longer-term liabilities becoming shorter-term liabilities. Capital adequacy pressures exacerbated the contextual uncertainties. Uncertainty about the intentions of the new government was alleviated somewhat by a sense of comfort in Sanlam that the existing regulatory framework had been the instrument of control of both mutual and public liability companies, and that the Registrar of Insurance had executed such regulation in the past. It was clear that a culture of conservatism in Sanlam was still seeking assurance in past institutions for its future, but that the game changer was the reality of investor demand in a fundamentally different financial market. Socio-political uncertainties indeed affected these client decisions, but the global financial market deregulation spilled over into the sophisticated South African financial system, mandating adjustments on two fronts: global markets as well as domestic political overhaul. For most of 1995 to 1997 the strategic transformation discussions in Sanlam revolved around the transformation of Sanlam from a big bureaucratic long-term insurance company to a financial services group consisting of business divisions trading in services and contracting. This involved changing the face of Sanlam's employees to reflect the demography of its policyholder base, to strengthen its 'capital' base through a new profit-oriented business philosophy, the adaptation of marketing strategies to target the uninsured market, to modernize its use of technology, and to involve staff as stakeholders in developing a managerial culture from below.[23]

The implementation of Rudman's profit-oriented business operations also entailed significant changes to the management of Sanlam's assets. Shortly before Fred du Plessis'

[22] SA: Confidential Memorandum G. Rudman–Sanlam Board, 19/4/1995.

[23] SA: Minutes of Sanlam Board, 21/6/1995; 16/8/1995; 31/1/1996; 28/8/1996; 27/2/1997.

death, Hendrik Bester succeeded in convincing him that the successful management of Sanlam's properties was seriously hampered by the Sanlam management style, i.e. submissions to the board before key decisions on investment in/divestment from properties could be made. Property management, Bester had experienced, called for much swifter action. Du Plessis authorized the establishment of Sanlam Properties as a separate operating business the day before he died. Bester had to go through the same convincing with Pierre Steyn, and finally in October 1989 Sanlam Properties entered a phase of relative autonomy. This enabled improved performance on the property management side, which harmonized with the decentralization strategy management decided upon at the first '*bosberaad*' after Du Plessis' death. A similar approach was taken by Ronnie Masson heading up investments.

The winding down of Sankorp by 1997 was a critical factor in stabilizing the Sanlam 'estate'. New life policy products were primarily rolled out after demutualization, such as the Stratus investment-linked products. During the capital-building period under Smith as Managing Director and Ronnie Masson as Head of Investments, a substantial contribution to the strengthening of the capital occurred through the persistent good performance of the 200-Plus series of investment policies. The 200-Plus series yielded more than 27 per cent per annum during the seven-year period up to 1991, and the 100-Plus series more than 29 per cent for the same period. The inflation-beating performance of the 200-Plus series continued up to 1997. By 1994 those investment trusts that accommodated a vast proportion of pension funds and retirement annuity funds, posted a sustained 26.8 per cent return for the preceding ten years. The First Bowring & Associates survey of investment portfolios for pension and provident funds reported that the 200-Plus portfolio produced the highest return for the ten years ended 30 June 1994, outperforming the industry.[24] The 200-Plus investment series sustained above-industry performance throughout the 1990s until the Asian financial crisis in 1997 caused share prices to decline sharply. In 1996 the 500-Plus series was launched, which offered returns of 26 per cent on the investment of untaxed individual policies.[25] The high levels of volatility in the financial markets towards the end on 1997 resulted in consumers moving towards more stable and established financial institutions. The Sanlam fund managers subsequently focused more on guaranteed products such as the Rolling Guaranteed Equity Fund and Guaranteed Plan.[26] At a time when the long-term insurance industry experienced a move out of traditional life products, Sanlam concentrated on securing high yields on the funds under its management. Sanlam managed a suite of fifteen unit trusts by late 1997. The total 'off-balance-sheet' funds managed by Sanlam investment managers rose from R8 549 million in 1994 to R26 661 million in 1998. These unit trusts provided for different levels of risk and, through the OptiRand

[24] SA: Sanlam Annual Report, 1995: 1.

[25] Sanlam Annual Report, 1996: 3.

[26] Sanlam Annual Report, 1997: 14.

vehicle introduced in 1995, also offered rand-hedging characteristics. The OptiRand fund invested in both import and export companies, thereby giving investors the benefit to hedge exchange rate fluctuations. In 1996 the Guarantee24 facility offered investors upon death, a payment at the highest level of their investments during the twenty-four months before death. After the Asian financial crisis the Sanlam Money Market Trust offered a haven for funds waiting to see the outcome of volatility. Sanlam also engaged in setting up the Empowerment Equity Fund in collaboration with REAL Africa Asset Management in 1998.[27] The asset swap facilities (see Chapter 4) also served to offer international investment options to investors and thereby grow Sanlam's 'estate'.

Together with significant improvement in the ratio of income to expenditure between 1990 and 1997 (from 2.1 in 1990, to 9.1 in 1997—see Table 5.3), Sanlam succeeded, according to Rudman, by 1997 to have improved the capital position of Sanlam adequately to pursue demutualization.[28] Critical risks identified in 1996 were topped by underperforming investment yields, but by 1997 this matter had improved. The most critical risk was social and political adversity towards the company.[29]

Operating in such an environment undermined all the financial and market penetration targets set in the strategy to arrive at a point where demutualization could occur. Sanlam disappointed on all fronts—in performance, and in addressing internal organizational challenges. According to Tillinghast-Towers Perrin (TTP), a consulting company advising Sanlam on the road to demutualization, Sanlam was losing key staff to competitors, computer information was unreliable and slow, Sanlam lagged the market in delivering new products, its products failed to deliver value for money,[30] its capital adequacy was slipping, and its technology infrastructure proved insufficient and inefficient. The global trend to demutualize, especially the demutualization of the Australian AMP in 1997, and the policy uncertainty in South Africa, brought the final decision to demutualize forward. In no official document was it stated that Sanlam anticipated possible nationalization under the new government, but the risk loomed large. The absence of shareholders, who might have acted as deterrent against outright nationalization or asset grab, was cause for concern. A mutual company was an easy target, especially if it was capital rich (which Sanlam was not) and belonged to a substantial number of Afrikaner policyholders, who had a legacy of support for the National Party government's racial policies. The possibility of the nationalization of the long-term mutual insurers was contemplated in the Life Offices Association (LOA) as a distinct possibility. Long before his death in 1993, Pierre Steyn also had been concerned about the relative

[27] Sanlam Annual Reports, 1993–1998.

[28] Interview G. Rudman 12/2/2009: Email communication G. Rudman–G. Verhoef, 22/4/2010.

[29] SA: Minutes of Sanlam Board, 27/2/1997.

[30] SA: Minutes of Sanlam Board, 29/1/1998: Independent brokers informed Sanlam management that the Sanlam products failed to deliver value for money and were unimaginative.

ease with which Parliament could change the private acts governing the two leading mutual life offices in South Africa. That posed a definite risk to Sanlam and SA Mutual.[31] Demutualization offered a strategy to limit this risk.

There was a gentleman's agreement of reciprocal notification between Sanlam and SA Mutual if and when demutualization was decided upon. It seemed almost a done deal when Rudman submitted a comprehensive memorandum on a revised corporate structure for Sanlam in May 1997.[32] The final decision to demutualize was taken as part of an overall strategy to migrate Sanlam from a life office to a financial institution, from a local South African company to an international company, and from an under-capitalized company to a well-capitalized company. These discussions were highly confidential, resulting in the minutes distributed not as 'minutes' but as an 'aide memoire'.[33] It must be kept in mind that the decision to demutualize was actually taken during the first half of the 1990s, but the capital constraints held the conservative Sanlam management back since 1993, because the company wanted first to strengthen its capital base. At the first '*bosberaad*' under Smith as CEO, he set five-year targets to achieve, inter alia, a stronger capital position. In his cautious Sanlam actuary mind he did not envisage demutualization before 1999.

After the May 1997 meeting Daling was asked to inform Mike Levett of SA Mutual that Sanlam was contemplating demutualization. When SA Mutual finally made a public announcement in July 1997 on the company's intention to demutualize, Sanlam's planning had already made some progress. Management did not wish to create public anxiety or confusion and therefore described the discussions on the possible demutualization of Sanlam as 'part of a process'.[34] Rudman was of the opinion that Daling was more interested in listing Sanlam than in demutualization. The difference between the two points of departure Rudman explained as emerging from personal conversations between him and Daling.[35] When contemplating demutualization, Daling asked Rudman how he would prioritize a plan of action—appoint the consulting actuaries first, or the consulting investment bankers first? Rudman was clear: first the actuaries, because they had to advise the mutual on how it would change the ownership structure, then provide the arguments why such change was advantageous to policyholders, and then how to compensate policyholders so as to get their support. Independent actuarial evaluation would deliver independent financial statements, which would be a prerequisite for listing. Daling followed Rudman's advice—TTP was appointed. The second occasion was while

[31] Interview G. Rudman, 24/2/2010. Long before 1997 it was apparent that a black majority government would take power. This was a distinct change in the market of life offices in South Africa that had to be contemplated by management of all local mutual insurance companies.

[32] SA: Minutes Sanlam Board, 28 May 1997: Confidential memorandum G.E. Rudman: A revised corporate structure for Sanlam.

[33] SA: Minutes Sanlam Board, 25/6/1997. [34] SA: Minutes of Sanlam Board, 27/8/1997.

[35] Interview G. Rudman, 24/2/2010; Email communication G. Rudman–Sanlam Corporate Office, 31/8/2017.

the demutualization preparations were in full swing. TTP asked permission to advise SA Mutual on its demutualization, since TTP had been approached by SA Mutual to do so. Daling was adamant that Rudman should refuse. Rudman was confident: Sanlam was proven right by commissioning TTP. Rudman had his first choice 'hand-picked' team from TTP, who had advised the Norwich demutualization in the UK, as well as the top strategist advising AMP in Australia, on his Sanlam team. Furthermore, TTP gave guarantees to erect a Chinese wall between Sanlam and SA Mutual and Sanlam would have TTP's best technical support. Daling again agreed. Finally, Daling opted for the investment banker Robert Flemming & Co. Sanlam's internal team objected to the British wanting to teach them British tax law, while they had to get a job done in a tight time frame. In the end, Rudman again got his choice of investment bankers in the form of Dresdner Kleinwort Benson. It was clear that the actuary understood his trade as it had developed in a mutual office and had solicited the best in the market to advise on demutualization first, and then listing. Daling finally accepted Rudman's proposal.

While there were doubts about the capital readiness of Sanlam for demutualization, Rudman was of the firm conviction that the company had adequate capital to demutualize successfully. He argued that published statutory mandated information about the company did not convey the full message about Sanlam's capital position. He argued that Sanlam conducted solid mutual business, without playing for public appreciation for good-looking numbers. Then Sanlam differed from other long-term offices. Sanlam held the extensive 'strategic' investments (discussed at length in Chapter 4) and reflected them at low asset values in the published statements. These assets could be considered 'hidden assets', which, once released, added to the capital adequacy of the company. Other assets were 'invisible' assets, the tax advantage Sanlam utilized under the new long-term insurance act of 1990. A new tax dispensation for the long-term industry was announced and a three year phasing-in period allowed. Sanlam made full use of maximum tax payments at concession rates, whereby Sanlam made significant tax 'savings'.[36] These were factors contributing to the confidence to move forward with demutualization in 1997.

Sanlam was a big ship that would not turn quickly. In May a Strategic Review Committee of the board consisting of Daling, Desmond Smith (Managing Director since 1993), Derek Keys, and Ton Vosloo as non-executive board members, and George Rudman from senior management, was formed. In that committee it was made apparent that Daling was driven by an ambition to be first in the market to demutualize. At the August board meeting he called for greater urgency on the matter and in October 1997 a comprehensive advisory report on the preferred organizational structure of Sanlam was commissioned and delivered in January 1998.

[36] Confidential communication G. Rudman, 30 September 2017.

The final decision on when to demutualize had not yet been taken, but was imminent. Daling then moved behind the scenes to ensure he would be the captain of the Sanlam ship. On 14 November 1997, the day after Smith had testified before the TRC on behalf of Sanlam, Daling informed him that the Human Resources Committee of the board had decided that he be relieved of his duties as Managing Director. Daling consulted with all but three members of the board telephonically to establish consensus. Various aspects of the weaker performance of Sanlam, including the declining CAR (Capital Adequacy Ratio) during 1997, inefficiency in claim processing and the subsequent massive backlog at Sanmed, and unflattering Sanlam operating profit and marketing results in 1997 were placed at Smith's door. The fact that Sanlam's operating profit had increased consistently since Smith's appointment as Managing Director in 1993 was not considered, nor were the fundamental transformation programmes, organizational reforms, and introduction of profit centres in Sanlam acknowledged. In granting a performance bonus to Smith at the end of 1996, Daling indicated that he expected Smith to emerge as a stronger leader of the team to map out a holistic vision of the direction in which Sanlam was moving, and solicit improved performance of all members in the management team. This was the only hint that Daling considered Smith not to be the dynamic leader to steer Sanlam through demutualization. The actuarial report for 1997 showed that operating profit was up, but was only 86 per cent of budget. On the back of that information Daling apparently claimed, 'I told you so.'[37] Ultimately, Daling's personal ambition to push demutualization through despite Smith's cautioning that Sanlam was still in a capital-building phase, explains his action. There was no dissatisfaction among board members, but Daling ousted Smith to have demutualization as he desired it. The board ratification of Smith's 'retirement' was simply a rubber stamp. Smith left immediately and Daling succeeded him as Executive Chairman.[38] The focus was fully on driving demutualization. Smith did not suit the Daling re-engineering plan. Timing was of the essence. Daling moved away from a past positioning strategy and embraced the business process redesign approach to strategy as he took agency of the developments in Sanlam. It was hinted that slow change management might have explained why management was not ready to drive the demutualization process when Daling thought the time was ripe,[39] but there were other reasons why he decided to act swiftly. To Daling and Rudman's

[37] SA: Minutes of Sanlam Board, 24 and 25/2/1998. Actuarial Report for the twelve months ended 31 December 1997. Desmond Smith claimed that Daling effected a number of 'write-offs' which impacted significantly on operating profit for the year.

[38] SA: Minutes of Sanlam Board, 3/12/1997; Confidential Memorandum D.K. Smith. It was general knowledge among the management team that Smith was convinced of the sound decision to demutualize, but that he did not think Sanlam was ready to take the step. He was convinced that Sanlam's capital position needed to be on a sound footing as a matter of priority. Sanlam, according to Smith, could not afford to demutualize yet. Daling's ambition did not leave room for that. Interview Desmond Smith, 14/6/2017; 10/8/2017.

[39] Confidential communication G. Rudman, 30 September 2017.

satisfaction, sufficient capital had been accumulated to do the transaction. This included the Gensec transaction, about which difference of opinion remains. A project of the significance and magnitude of the Sanlam demutualization, required dedicated and focussed management, and therefore had to be concluded swiftly. To achieve this, Daling separated operations between business as usual, and demutualization. On the latter project. George Rudman was the undisputed anchor. Furthermore, year 2000 was coming soon and that required special attention. Demutualization needed to be out of the way well in advance. A real risk with demutualization, was the leak of shares through sales by new shareholders. This mandated the shortest possible time lapse between the announcement to demutualize and the closing period under which new policies could qualify for eligibility to shares during listing. The shorter the time between announcement and actual listing, the more remote the risk of information leakage on the scheme—which could lead to further complications. Daling and his team had to, and did, move swiftly and efficiently. The report by TTP of London on 'Project Sunrise', the pseudonym for demutualization, presented to the board in January 1998, was conclusive—demutualize Sanlam.

Daling immediately set out to construct a well-oiled machine to ensure efficient delivery of Project Sunrise. This became an operational priority against time. The re-engineering process commenced with a revised organizational structure at management level to support a stronger business case for demutualization. From a highly centralized organizational structure during the 1980s where management presided over marketing (distribution), administration, investments, and Head Office functions such as finance, administration, and actuarial services, a definite functional focus was required. The structure Daling inherited was still tiered without transferring business responsibility solely to the functional entities. He cleaned it up by creating six different Sanlam businesses: Sanlam Personal Finance, where all products and services to individuals was housed; Sanlam Employee Benefits, which dealt with all the functions pertaining to employee benefits—sales, marketing, group benefits, data, consultancy and Sanlam Health sales; Sanlam Asset Management, which was the dedicated investment function in conjunction with Gensec Asset Management; Sanlam Development, which dealt with the development of bank functions, international expansion, and new ventures; Sanlam Health, which focused on healthcare services and products; and lastly, Sanlam Facilities, which was responsible for buildings, the mainframe, and network functions. The new separate business units of Sanlam Financial Service Group were autonomous and took accountability and responsibility for their own bottom line. This positioned them to drive performance in the build-up to a call on the market. Daling had a well-planned strategy. The TTP proposals for an alternative corporate structure for Sanlam were with Daling on 22 January 1998. By the time he requested board approval for the restructuring, he had already discussed the plans with the international consultants advising Sanlam on demutualization. This was the prelude to the big restructuring—demutualization.

The TTP recommendations came as no surprise to the Sanlam management. The trends in the domestic financial services market mirrored international developments and Sanlam knew it comprised competition, internationalization, and 'conglomeration'. The scenario analysis Rudman had put forward in the early 1990s was on target and under Desmond Smith Sanlam started addressing the capital issues. TTP underlined the limitations on Sanlam's investment freedom as a result of its 'strategic investments'. The operational freedom to respond to the dynamic opportunities of the market depended on the corporate form of organization. Sanlam could remain mutual, if that was so crucial to the company, but that would entail a narrow focus on life insurance and seeking steady growth. Sustained mutuality was bound to lead to declining and poorer benefits to policyholders. The stronger position of life insurers in the retail market compared to the wholesale market, pointed to the potential for growth in the off-balance sheet component of the long-term business. Sanlam had traditionally built its business in the less sophisticated segment of the market. This market position was cemented by Sanlam's strong reliance on its own agents as the primary distribution network. In the off-balance sheet growth segment of the market, both retail and wholesale, Sanlam was lagging the industry. While consumerism was less prevalent in the South African market (probably as a result of the isolation and subsequent concentration in the financial services markets), Sanlam's regular premium savings products were not price sensitive. This made Sanlam more reliant on its agents for distribution. The financial press noted a decline in earnings from 59 cents per share (based on the accounting recalculation for listing purposes in 1998) to 17.9 cents per share, and losses at Sanlam Health increasing from R96 million in 1992 to R242 million in 1998.[40] Radical re-engineering to regain a competitive market position required the company to reflect on aspects of its historical legacies—empowerment of its own people, loyalty to the company through agents, and a shared collectivism through mutuality. Demutualization was going to address more than a business model for Sanlam. It was the closure of a chapter grounded in South Africa and the entrance into the global world of finance.

Between January 1998 and October 1998 Daling controlled the unfolding of the demutualization plan, which Rudman overheard him expressing as his personal ambition soon after moving into the chair of the board.[41] This was the culmination of a brilliant career at Sanlam, from the office of the actuary, to investment chief, to Managing Director of Sankorp, and finally back to Head Office to become the leader Fred du Plessis had groomed him to be. It was time to adapt the cautious organizational-learning strategy to the new post-1990 socio-political environment. Henry Mintzberg,

[40] G. Hirshon: 'The big clean-up has started', *Financial Mail*, January 1998.

[41] Interview G. Rudman 14/11/2007.

the Canadian management scholar, wrote in his book *The Structure of Organizations*[42] that 'culture is the soul of the organization—the beliefs and values, and how they are manifested', and therefore no organization had a blank slate. No existing company can choose its strategy as if it is a new start-up. Existing companies' strategy will always manifest in the legacy of its past and the outcome will be conditioned by that legacy. In Sanlam, Daling consciously negotiated around the mutual legacy to steer the company towards a new position in the market. Sanlam could not ignore its mutual heritage, but the re-engineering of Sanlam mandated strategic positioning in the changed environment. Demutualization was a catalyst in the process of transformation from a strategy based on asset ownership and market share, to one of dynamic competitiveness and profit. The board agreed to this repositioning. There was no time to waste. The demutualization process had to progress like clockwork. Derek Keys told George Rudman, who was steering the board strategic committee, to secure the following: Firstly, keep the process simple; secondly, keep the board out of court; and thirdly, do it all before the end of 1998.[43] TTP advised Sanlam that there would be commercial value in beating SA Mutual to demutualization, therefore the business plan was temporarily set aside to implement demutualization before the end of 1998. The public announcement that Sanlam intended to demutualize and seek policyholder approval, was made on 29 January 1998. Approval would lead to listing on the Johannesburg Stock Exchange as well as the Namibian Stock Exchange. This came seventy-nine years after the life office started its business on a mutual basis.

Working towards regulatory compliance was extensive but key to raising market confidence. First the structure of the Sanlam Group of companies was changed. One of the JSE listing requirements was that Sanlam had to have a level of capital not linked to policyholder liabilities, or maintain capital adequacy. This has been Rudman's concern since the mid-1990s and Daling conveyed the precarious position of Sanlam's reserves when he disclosed that the company had around R12 billion reserves at the end of 1997, compared to SA Mutual's R31 billion.[44] The solution was Gensec. Both Daling and Ronnie Masson, General Manager: Investments at Sanlam, served on the board of Gensec. They knew Gensec shares were overpriced in the market, which offered an opportunity to Sanlam. Although Daling had been unsuccessful in attracting Anton Botha, CEO of Gensec, to head up Sanlam Asset Management (SAM) earlier in 1997, the demutualization decision mandated swift rectification of the Sanlam capital position. Daling and Masson decided to sell SAM to Gensec. The dual advantage was the accounting gain and the capital strengthening to Sanlam. As subsidiaries were accounted

[42] H. Mintzberg (1979) *The Structure of Organizations: A synthesis of the Research.* Prentice Hall: 15. 20–5.

[43] Interview George Rudman, 14/11/2007.

[44] S. Lunsche 'Sankorp treasures give Sanlam a step up', *Sunday Times,* 31/8/1997.

for at book value (in accordance with accounting principles), Sanlam would be permitted to account for the SAM sale and the corresponding equity value at market value. Gensec was contemplating branching out into asset management and Sanlam needed capital. With undue haste the due diligence of SAM was concluded and the transaction clinched within three weeks. When Anton Botha consulted with Professor Michael C. Jensen of Harvard Business School, USA, on the transaction, Jensen advised against it, saying Gensec operated on state-of-the-art risk management systems, while Sanlam as a typical life office 'was hundred years behind you'. Jensen warned against the irreconcilable cultures of risk management and long-term insurance directed by actuarial and distribution systems. In June 1998 Sanlam sold SAM to Gensec for 100 million Gensec shares priced at R70 per share. This transaction netted R7 billion for Sanlam, which increased its 43.4 per cent interest in Gensec to 66.3 per cent, making Gensec a full subsidiary of Sanlam.[45] The hasty acquisition of Gensec was purely to place Gensec's equity on Sanlam's books and thereby artificially boost the intrinsic value of Sanlam prior to demutualization. Gensec subsequently managed Sanlam's life insurance asset portfolio, unit trusts, properties, and third-party assets. It gained access to the UK through Sanlam's London-based operations. This transaction was a lifesaver as far as Sanlam's capital position was concerned, but very soon became an albatross.

To present the Sanlam offer to the public, comprehensive accounting recalculations were required. The historical values of assets and liabilities of the entire group were recalculated to allow a benchmark of comparison to potential investors of the performance record of Sanlam (the life business) and the Sanlam Group. Maximum disclosure was important for potential investor confidence, locally and internationally. The accounting implications for Sanlam were far-reaching. Long-term insurers such as Sanlam had to comply with fifteen statutes, of which the Insurance Act, as amended in 1998 by the Long-Term Insurance Act, No. 52 of 1998, and the Insurance Second Amendment Act, No. 51 of 1998, were the most important. These statutes determined the registration, conduct of insurance business in the public interest, compiling of valuations and financial statements, and the holding of adequate assets in South Africa. This legislation dealt with the investment of policyholders' funds and limited commission payable to the intermediaries.[46] Furthermore, compliance was required with the Professional Guidance Note 104 (PGN104 of 1998) issued by the Actuarial Society of

45 SA: Minutes Sanlam Board, 9/6/1998.

46 The complex nature of the Sanlam business subjected aspects of its operations to the Pension Funds Act, No. 24 of 1956, the Companies Act, No. of 1973, the Income Tax Act, No. 68 of 1962, the Unit Trust Control Act, No. 54 of 1981, the Stock Exchange Control Act, No. 1 of 1985, the Financial Markets Control Act, No. 55 of 1989, the Safe Deposit of Securities Act, No. 85 of 1992, the Inspection of Financial Institutions Act, No. 68 of 1984, the Financial Institutions Act, No. 39 of 1984, and finally the Financial Services Board Act, No. 97 of 1990. Banks were regulated under the Banks Act, No. 94 of 1990. The spread of Sanlam's financial services activities made compliance with the entire spread of statutes compulsory.

South Africa, as well as accounting standards issued by the South African Institute of Chartered Accountants (AC121).

Compliance with the Johannesburg Stock Exchange listing requirements had explicit accounting implications for Sanlam: five years' consolidated financial statements of the entity requesting listing, distinguishing between policyholders' entitlements and shareholders' entitlements within Sanlam Life. The basis of restatement was 31 December 1997. The alignment of Sanlam's consolidated financial statements was complex because of differences in accounting standards. No international accounting standard existed for the financial reporting of long-term insurance companies. Sanlam's group operating profits were calculated on the basis of financial soundness valuation (FSV), while in the UK the basis of modified statutory valuation (MSV) was used, and in the USA the statement of financial accounting standards (SFAS). There was also a difference in the calculation of long-term insurers' premiums and claims, liabilities, new business costs, and the reporting on unrealized gains and losses.[47] SA General Accepted Accounting Practice (GAAP) did not require consolidated financial statements of associated companies. To comply with the listing requirements of the JSE, a full set of reconstructed pro forma financial statements for the five years prior to listing was required. These statements for listing, prepared by Flemings Inc. and Dresdner Kleinwort Benson, are given in Table 5.3.

Table 5.3. Comparative financial information, Sanlam Group: prospectus 1998 and annual reports, 1995–1997 (R'm)

	1995*	1996	1997	30 June 1998
Premium income prospectus	19 028	21 545	25 273	11 256
Premium income annual reports	16 654	18 618	21 966	
Investment return prospectus	1 130	1 286	849	1 738
Investment return annual reports	17 145	12 304	11 980	
Expenditure prospectus	18 726	25 354	31 374	14 399
Expenditure annual reports	3 347	3 100	3 442	
Operating profit prospectus	1 058	1 044	963	914
Operating profit annual reports	1 144	921	1 007	
Investment return prospectus	16 877	12 530	12 056	14 321
Investment return annual reports	17 145	12 304	11 980	
Earnings before taxation prospectus	2 037	2 007	1 305	2 167
Earnings before tax annual reports	1 144	1 054	759	
Headline earnings prospectus	1 322	1 3101	1 147	737
Headline earnings annual reports	2 689	1 707	1 178	

Note: *Fifteen month period.

Source: Sanlam annual reports, 1995, 1996, 1997; Sanlam prospectus, 1998.

[47] SA: 5/3/12/6/8: W. Harris–Memorandum, 7/1/1998; 10/6/1998; SA 5/3/12/6/8: TTP Memorandum. Financial reporting in South Africa and the UK, 19/2/1998.

The reconstructed financial statements enhanced the projection of the Sanlam Group's performance, because in terms of GAAP group statements had to present consolidated figures. Premium income was higher than in the official Sanlam pre-demutualization annual reports, because Santam's premiums were consolidated in the recalculated statements. In 1995 Sanlam published premium income of R16.6 million, but the recalculated figures were R19 million; in 1996 the difference was between R18.6 million and R21.5 million; and for 1997 between R21.9 million and R25.2 million. The difference between the pre- and post-figures was between 12.4 per cent and 13.5 per cent, which made a significant impact on investors' assessment of the attractiveness of the company. The weaker investment returns were the result of the consolidation of ABSA into the Sanlam Group accounts, since ABSA had underperformed consistently since the early 1990s. Sanlam's investment in ABSA of R2.6 billion represented a 23 per cent stake in the bank. The volatility in investment market conditions affected Gensec and ABSA adversely, and subsequently adversely impacted on Sanlam—as prospective investors were warned in the prospectus. Expenditure was significantly higher in the consolidated statements, primarily because of the consolidation of the Santam and ABSA accounts. Operating profits and investment returns remained relatively flat, but earnings before taxation were significantly better after consolidation. Headline earnings were weaker in 1995 and 1996 after consolidation, but improved in 1997 and the half-year figures for 1998 promised further improvement.

The consolidated reconstructed statements supported the Sanlam vision of 'establish [ing] itself as a broad-based financial services group able to provide clients with a comprehensive range of financial products'.[48] The consolidated statements also disclosed potential risks in both domestic and international markets, especially changes in investment market conditions. In June 1997, as an exceptional step, Sanlam reinsured with SwissRe Life & Health SA R1 billion of its stable bonus portfolio to protect its capital position. This move secured Sanlam a capital portfolio partner and added security to its capital adequacy, while non-market-related liabilities were exchanged for market-related liabilities.[49] Markets were sceptical and cautious about the prospective demutualization of Sanlam. Prior to listing, the *Financial Mail* wrote, 'The more the FM tries to understand the life business, the more we find ourselves contemplating deep but merely theoretical pleasures of what a simpler disclosure by a life insurers would be like.'[50] Understanding life insurance companies' financial statements was vital to secure investor interest upon listing. Sanlam had to address this skepticism on two fronts: shake up performance, and communicate in a transparent fashion to build investor confidence.

[48] SA: Sanlam Share Offer Prospectus: 25; Sanlam Demutualization Prospectus: Information Memorandum: 4.

[49] SA: Minutes of Sanlam Board, 25/6/1997; 9/12/1998.

[50] D. Basson and S. Feely: 'It's just money for jam', *Financial Mail*, 29/08/97.

The *Financial Mail* was blunt about Sanlam's predicament: Sanlam had lost heavily on its strategic investments (Bankorp, FVB, Sentrachem) and therefore had about one third of SA Mutual's reserves. So, while no official announcement on demutualization was made by Sanlam (before the end of January 1998), the market expected it, and also that 'Sanlam may even pip Old Mutual to the post as it has already done much preparatory work.... Though management is adamant that a capital shortage is no major issue, the belief in the market is that Sanlam will have to use listing to bolster its reserves.'[51] As SA Mutual announced its intention to seek listing before the end of 1998, Sanlam worked out a tight schedule towards actual listing.

A rocky legal route lay ahead towards demutualization. The market was keenly anticipating a cash injection of around R8 billion. The Sanlam Private Act of 1954 did not provide for demutualization. To secure such authorization, Sanlam had to engage with the Minister of Finance and the Treasury. Amendments to the Long-Term Insurance Act provided for a policyholder fund to hold shares in the holding company of the life office (in this case it would be permission for Sanlam Life to hold shares in Sanlam Limited, the holding company to be established). The risks were very clear to Sanlam. The volatility of the transition in management and organization during demutualization created opportunities for predators to engineer takeovers. Sanlam knew about international precedents, and considered the newly appointed government's Black Economic Empowerment policies a potential game changer. The international protection precedent implemented by British building societies, the Colonial Mutual and AMP in Australia, and the Canadian life offices, was to set a limit in the articles of association to the percentage of shares a single owner may hold in the new listed entity. Opportunistic dealmakers attempted to do an empowerment transaction with Sanlam during the demutualization process. Daling was adamant that demutualization was to be 'clean'—only demutualization—and afterwards a BEE deal could be considered. A combination of the two could make the demutualization process controversial.[52]

The most crucial aspect of the preparation for demutualization was the financial soundness reports and due diligence report for the JSE, whereby market confidence could be enhanced. With prolonged underperformance and market skepticism, these aspects were fundamental to successful demutualization. TTP delivered a sound due diligence report in September 1998 and PricewaterhouseCoopers and Ernst & Young delivered a financial due diligence report, which was considered by Sanlam. They could not 'ask for more comfort'.[53] When the Cape Division of the High Court finally delivered

[51] Ibid.

[52] SA: Minutes of Sanlam Board, 11/12/1998. With the reference to a 'clean' transaction, Daling meant that he preferred demutualization to be the only focus of the transaction and not to include other concerns, such as empowerment transactions on the side.

[53] SA: Minutes of Sanlam Board, 11/12/1998.

an order confirming the Scheme in Case 13592/98 (Sanlam's application for permission to demutualize and change the Sanlam Private Act of 1954), on 22 October 1998, the share offer documents were dispatched to policyholders, employees, and other prospective investors. The High Court permitted the demutualization of Sanlam and the simultaneous adoption of the Memorandum of Association and Articles of Association of Sanlam Ltd. Sanlam Ltd was registered as a public company. It issued shares to eligible policyholders and the public and established the Sanlam Demutualization Trust to hold the shares for members without confirmed addresses.

The scheme sanctioned by the High Court Order was the following: Simultaneous with the preparation for demutualization, Sanlam was converted into a separate company with share capital, to be named Sanlam Life Insurance Limited ('Sanlam Life'). A company shell in the Sanlam stable, Sankern (Pty) Ltd, a subsidiary of Sanlam, was renamed Sanlam Limited and became the holding company for the Sanlam Group. Sanlam Ltd owned the entire shareholding in Sanlam Life. Upon listing, shares allocated to eligible shareholders of Sanlam were shares in Sanlam Ltd. Institutions and other members of the public who acquired shares in the initial public offering of Sanlam Ltd, also held shares in that company. Immediately after the High Court order, Sanlam sent out the share offer to eligible policyholders and published the prospectus of Sanlam Ltd. To change the Articles of Association of Sanlam, a special general meeting of policyholders was called for 15 October 1998. Daling delivered an emotional address in which he thanked 'Our Creator' for the courage and vision of the leaders of Sanlam who steered the company through bad and good times to become the 'respected trademark in South African life assurance'. There was no legal requirement that members had to approve of demutualization, but the Sanlam management agreed that if a 75 per cent approval from the 1.8 million eligible policyholders[54] was not achieved, management would not proceed. Circulars were sent to policyholders in September 1998 to explain the process and inform them of the general meeting. A total of 100 members in person and 1 002 276 by proxy voted unanimously in favour of demutualization.

Sanlam engaged in a well-planned and well-executed communication programme to inform its policyholders. Sanlam mailed the *Demutualization Proposal Information Memorandum* to policyholders in September 1998. This document explained the proposal to demutualize, the implications, and the offer to policyholders to participate in the intended public listing of Sanlam Ltd. This document explained the comprehensive impact demutualization would have on members and the South African economy and society. The outline of the risk factors in both the industry and the socio-political factors relating to South Africa was compelling. The prospectus argued that changes in the domestic insurance industry, as primary provider of savings and investment products,

[54] Sanlam had 2.2 million policyholders, but only 1.8 million were eligible to vote, since the rest were members of retirement funds.

had changed fundamentally. Strong competition by other financial services providers necessitated a strategic rethinking. Furthermore, regulatory changes pertaining to taxation, the structure and control of the financial services sector, increased disclosure requirements, government prescriptive policies on the provision of healthcare, and general changes in the investment environment, all changed the context in which Sanlam operated. The last-mentioned was the crux of the matter: Sanlam's investments on behalf of its Shareholders' Fund in entities such as Gensec, ABSA, and Santam suffered in the weakening stock markets, especially since the Asian financial crisis in August 1997.

Underlying the market dilemma, was the different expectations of policyholders. Some sought stability of bonus returns on policies, while others strove for optimal returns on investment. In explaining that Sanlam encountered capital adequacy risks embedded in weak investment returns, which led to management action to sustain bonus rates and reserves, the argument in favour of investment flexibility became clearer. Market volatility was negative for Gensec. It was bad for returns on derivatives (on which Sanlam relied increasingly) and bad for dividend payments on Sanlam's equity investments and subsidiaries. Domestic risks such as growing policy surrenders and high disability benefits following high retrenchments in the context of the new socio-political conditions in South Africa, were compounded by rising HIV/Aids risks. Finally, it was impossible to predict how many free shares (shares allocated to eligible policyholders) would be sold immediately after listing and how the share price would respond after the initial public offering. Certain domestic conditions exacerbated uncertainty for Sanlam. The first was persistent exchange control measures, which, despite moderate relaxation in 1997 and 1998, constrained capital raising outside South Africa and created uncertainty of approval in case of international investments. Uncertainty with regard to accounting and comparative disclosure standards applicable to South Africa compared to the United Kingdom and the USA on the issuers of securities and their reporting standards, could impact on the value of the company and therefore potential shareholders had to be alerted to this risk.[55]

Financial journalists had warned Sanlam about the impact of risks inherent in the difference in accounting standards and policies in the different markets of operation[56] on the public's assessment of the value of the company. Sanlam disclosed the accounting and disclosure risks to prospective shareholders because the company would compete with Liberty Life, a major competitor in the life and diversified financial services market, in future. This was going to be the new competitive environment for Sanlam. Finally, the government had already indicated that it would tax the windfall 'profit' of mutual life offices at demutualization. The Demutualization Levy Act, No. 50 of 1998, levied 2.5 per cent of the value of the portion of free shares allocated to eligible policyholders and

55 Sanlam Share Offers. Prospectus, 28/10/1998: 16–20.

56 SA: 5/3/12/6/8: Letter Deon Basson–Sanlam (G. Rudman).

employees. This statute established the so-called Umsubomvu Fund, justified as a fund to alleviate the plight of the disadvantaged. Sanlam publicly supported the demutualization levy by declaring it the responsibility of all South Africans to contribute to political and economic integration of society.[57] Prospective shareholders' decisions were thus complicated. Knowing that SA Mutual was also planning for demutualization, Sanlam covered all potential risks that could impact on investor sentiment.

A public debate erupted as various interested parties speculated about the social and economic impact of demutualization. In the financial press the demutualization of the two life office giants, SA Mutual and Sanlam, was described as delivering an injection of around R80 billion to the South African economy. Off course, there was the risk of volatility in consumer spending if people might decide to sell the shares they acquired as a result of their status as eligible policyholders upon demutualization. It was also possible that a class of sophisticated shareholders could emerge from persons who own shares for the first time. The Congress of South African Trade Unions (COSATU) had called for the demutualization of mutual companies to ensure the more effective use of their resources for economic development. By August 1998 COSATU turned around and opposed demutualization on the grounds that policyholders would allegedly be stripped of their rights 'to collectively control these institutions and to shift control of major assets to international investors'.[58] The agenda of labour was driven by a frustration of being excluded from managerial decisions. Labour did not dispute the right of policyholders in the mutual to decide on the management of the company, but they claimed managerial authoritarianism and insisted on a direct say as members of pension funds administered by Sanlam. While Daling consulted with COSATU directly and hoped for an agreement, public collective action followed but failed to derail demutualization. Sanlam embarked on extensive roadshows locally and internationally between early November 1998 and the date of listing, 30 November 1998. Eligible policyholders received a minimum of 300 free shares (which rose to a maximum of 800 for certain policyholders) in Sanlam Ltd, as well as an offer to purchase further shares at a discount of 10 per cent. Sanlam shares listed at 600 cents per share on listing day. Eligible policyholders were persons who owned valid policies with Sanlam before 31 March 1998, as verified and confirmed. Individuals owning policies that lapsed or were surrendered before 15 October 1998 did not qualify for shares. These policyholders received a share statement on their share allocation and an offer to purchase more shares on 30 November 1998. Under the demutualization proposal the Capital Fund of Sanlam (mutual) became the Shareholders' Fund of Sanlam Life.

[57] Sanlam Share Offers Prospectus, 1998: i; Sanlam Annual Report, 1998: 9.

[58] SA: 5/3/12: Letter COSATU–M.H. Daling, 4/4/198; COSATU Submission to Portfolio Committee on Finance, 18/8/1998.

Prior to listing, Sanlam's strategic assets were restructured as per the scheme sanctioned by the High Court. First the shareholding in the strategic assets were distributed. On 30 June 1998, in preparation of the demutualization conversion, 10 per cent of the share capital of ABSA and 25 per cent of the share capital of Santam were transferred from the Sanlam Policyholders' Fund to the Capital Fund. In return, a portfolio of shares and cash equal to the market value of the share transfer went to the Policyholders' Fund. Once the conversion scheme was authorized by the Cape High Court, certain assets were transferred to Sanlam Ltd. Twenty per cent of the share capital of Gensec and 20 per cent of the share capital of Santam were transferred from the Capital Fund to Sanlam Ltd. The full shareholding of Sanlam Health and Sanlam Unit Trusts, and a number of smaller wholly-owned subsidiaries held at the time of listing in the Capital Fund, were held in Sanlam Ltd. These transfers were funded by the capital raised by the listing of Sanlam Ltd. The new structure of ownership in Sanlam Ltd and Sanlam Life after demutualization and listing at the end of November 1998 is shown in Figure 5.1. An important consideration for the distribution of shareholding in the group was South African GAAP, which permitted the valuation of share ownership under 50 per cent of equity at market value, and at net asset value if more than 50 per cent was owned.

The offer to acquire shares in Sanlam Ltd opened on 28 October 1997 and closed on 30 November 1997 followed by the listing on the JSE, which was the largest single listing in the history of the local bourse. Sanlam Ltd also listed on the Namibian Stock Exchange on 30 November 1998. A total of 2 654.6 million shares were issued—1 977.5 million

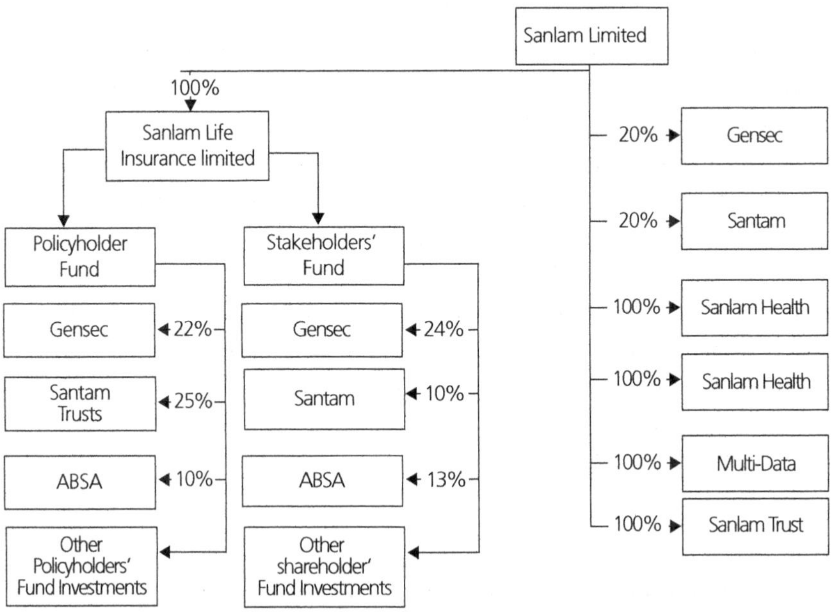

Figure 5.1. Structure of Sanlam Ltd and Sanlam Life Ltd shareholding at demutualization, 1998

were to policyholders as free shares and additional shares acquired in terms of the offer to purchase shares. Shares purchased in terms of the offer amounted to 633 million. In a price stabilization effort, Gensec undertook to subscribe for 150 million shares at the public offer price of 600 cents per share. It bought a further 17.3 million shares on the market, thus acquiring 132.7 million Sanlam shares by the end of December 1998. In a similar stabilization scheme, the Global Co-ordinators (international brokers) were granted an option for thirty days after listing, to subscribe and procure subscribers for 103.4 million shares. This was the so-called 'Greenshoe' offer. The 'Greenshoe' bought a further 26.26 million shares in the market upon listing, netting Sanlam an additional R144.7 million in capital. These options stabilized policyholder flowbacks and increased the capital raised to R4 billion, minus costs. Sanlam was left with R3.9 billion additional capital. The Demutualization Levy amounted to R271 million.[59]

Sanlam management was satisfied with the outcome of the listing on the JSE and Namibian Stock Exchange, but market analysts did not share the optimism. The Sanlam share opened at 599 cents on 30 November 1998, but never approached that level until early in March 1999, when the pressure eased following the announcement of better-than-expected financial results for 1998. A record 62 million shares were sold on the first trading day and around 200 million during the first ten days of listing, ascribed to free shares flowing back into the market, pushing the share price down to the late 580s per share. Heavy policyholder flowback occurred in January 1999 as 16 per cent of free shares went back onto the market. Insured retirement funds also reduced their exposure to Sanlam during the early listing period. By the end of May 1999 individuals held around 43 per cent of the Sanlam shares, retirement funds 13 per cent, and nominees (institutions) around 43 per cent.[60] By the first quarter of 1999 the Sanlam share still traded at a discount of more than 30 per cent to embedded value.[61] Analysts did not expect a change in market perceptions soon.

Sanlam nevertheless had to act in support of its own equity. Setting up the Demutualization Trust (DT) to administer the share portfolio of untraced persons, locating and validating them and allocating their free shares, the company acted in good faith. The DT commenced business on the date of the High Court order sanctioning the demutualization scheme of Sanlam, 22 October 1998. For a period of ten years, lapsing at 24:00 on 22 October 2008, eligible shareholders could validate their eligibility and claim their shares. Sanlam selected people of high public standing to assume the DT operation. The Trustees were Meschack Canca, a practicing attorney of Cape Town; Johan Bester, a chartered accountant and Company Secretary of Sanlam; Willem Esterhuyse, Professor

[59] SA: Minutes of Sanlam Board, 3 February 1999; ING Barings South African research: Sanlam listing update, No 2: 12/1/1999; G. Paterson: Warburg Dillon Reid: Life Assurance. Sanlam (Reuters RIC), 24/4/2010.

[60] G. Peterson: Warburg Dillon Reid: Life insurance: Sanlam, 24/8/2010.

[61] Flemming Martin Research South Africa, 26/7/1999; ING Barings South African research, 12/1/1999.

in Business Ethics at the University of Stellenbosch Graduate School of Business; Abram Nkabinde, a retired Vice-Chancellor of the University of Zululand; and Leonora van den Heever, a retired judge, as chairperson. The DT had thirty-nine meetings devising strategies to locate eligible policyholders who had not yet taken ownership of the free shares allocated to them. These strategies included extensive mail projects (locating 46 607 shareholders), telephonic searches (locating 87 177 shareholders), identification searches in collaboration with the Department of Home Affairs (identifying 50 913 persons, 9 905 of whom were deceased, but 4 671 executors could be located to arrange for the receipt of the free shares), and a specific strategy to identify thirty-three individuals to whom large numbers of shares had been allocated. These thirty-three persons were eligible to receive 810 210 shares. The DT located twenty-three of them and allocated 653 638 shares to them. It also validated claims to allocated shares, corrected the allocation of shares, and corrected ownership, as brokers and loan sharks attempted fraudulent claims. By 22 October 2008 only 1.01 per cent of the shares allocated to the DT for validation and distribution (29 463 947 shares) could not be allocated to eligible persons. The DT also paid out cash to eligible shareholders who were resident outside South Africa and unable to cash cheques. The DT received dividends on shares held in trust, but chose not to keep the dividends but to purchase Sanlam Ltd shares. A total amount of R258 339 174 was received in dividends, R96 096 278 of which was spent on DT administration (average cost per validation amounted to R212.18) and search and trace projects. On 22 October 2008, 58 893 010 shares purchased with dividend receipts remained in the DT and were subsequently transferred to Sanlam Ltd.[62]

The significance of the DT's activities was the display of deep and broad penetration of Sanlam policies into the South African society. When the DT assumed its duty, more than 50 000 beneficiaries were in KwaZulu-Natal, the coastal province with a predominantly Zulu and Indian population. Eligible beneficiaries such as L.N. Ndimande, K.K. Dikhaar, M.M. Tolom, V. Hemraj, I. Essop, F. Moosa, K.V. Tshinavhe, M.J. Moseki, Phumla N. Nyoka, N. Siyolo, P.P. Nyoka, Mzikayise J. Macingwane, and Kefiloe S. Macingwane substantiated the Sanlam claim to the penetration outside the traditional white community.[63] As the DT wrapped up its business by the end of October 2008, Sanlam set up an additional committee to consider borderline claims 'with merit'. This committee awarded *ex gratia* payments to the value of R552 190.50 to forty-eight claimants. The DT actions ensured 97.7 per cent success in placing eligible Sanlam policyholders in possession of their allocated shares. SA Mutual closed its demutualization agency at the end of August 2006, an event Sanlam used to underline its public commitment to build its shareholder base. The DT went to great lengths and cost to

[62] SA 5/3/12/13/1 (2): Sanlam Demutualization Trust, 1998–2008 Chairman's report, 3/6/2009.

[63] SA 5/3/12/13/1 (1) Minutes of Demutualization Trust, 15/8/2002; 5/12/2003; 8/5/2003.

locate eligible shareholders. The message of locating and serving its diverse shareholder base fed into Sanlam's new strategy to position itself as a diversified financial services company with deep roots in South Africa.

Building the new Sanlam

The face of Sanlam Ltd was Marinus Daling. At the age of fifty-four, with thirty-three years' service in Sanlam, working his way up from a *platteland* Nylstroom boy of the Northern Transvaal on a Sanlam bursary at the University of Pretoria, his ambition was Sanlam beyond the mutual. The confluence of context and business salvage convinced Daling at the end of 1997 that he had to act decisively. After stepping into the role of Executive Chair on 30 November 1998 Daling orchestrated Sanlam's rescue strategy. The leadership structure of Sanlam Ltd was a hand-picked team. Attie du Plessis, who was pulled into the demutualization team, served on the executive committee with George Rudman; Flip Rademeyer, Financial Director; Hendrik Bester, Head of Personal Finance; Nic Christodoulou, Head of Employee Benefits; Charl le Roux, Head of Sanlam Health; Anton Botha, Head of Gensec; Chris Swanepoel, Chief Actuary; and Johan Bester, Sanlam Secretary. The Sanlam Ltd board was identical to the board of Sanlam Life. The members migrated from the Sanlam pre-demutualization board to the post-demutualization boards. The members were: Mr J.P.L. Alberts a chartered accountant and businessman; Dr D.C. Brink, mining engineer and Executive Chairman of Murray and Roberts, the construction conglomerate; Prof K. Jowell, professor and dean of the University of Cape Town Graduate School of Business; Prof A.C. Bawa, the Deputy Vice-chancellor of the University of Natal; Mr W.M. Grindrod, Chairman of the Grindrod Unicorn Group; Mr D.L. Keys, a chartered accountant and former CEO of Gencor; Ms N.M. Mokhobo, a social worker and manager of a change management consultancy; Mr T. Vosloo, Chairman of Naspers; Mr P.E.I. Schwartz, an educator and Chancellor of the Cape Technikon; Mr J.J.M. van Zyl, a practising engineer, and Professor P. Smit, a demographer and former vice-chancellor of the University of Pretoria. Daling had continuity on the boards and trusted colleagues in the Executive Committee (Exco). Members of the Exco served on various boards in the Group, thus distributing existing executive management of Sanlam throughout the Group operations. The Sanlam 'trusted' or former directors were entrusted with the new Sanlam. Daling had to hold the reins at the centre, since demutualization had changed the organizational form but not the inefficiencies or market skepticism.

In 1999 separate business units comprised Sanlam Personal Finance, Sanlam Employee Benefits, Sanlam Health, and Gensec, as well as a new wholly-owned subsidiary, New Business Development. Sanlam controlled 56.9 per cent of Santam and

23.7 per cent of ABSA. Structurally, the new Sanlam did not differ much from the old. That was the challenge of change management in a society that bore very little resemblance to the one in which Sanlam achieved strong growth during the 1960s and 1970s.

The market signaled caution to the poor-performing share price. With a restructured stakeholder profile—Sanlam Ltd now had shareholders—individual shareholders constituted less than half of the shareholder profile. The retirement funds and nominees (institutions) made up around 56 per cent of the shareholders. The 1998 financial results were described by one analyst as 'Sanlam . . . running hard to stand still' as Sanlam lost market share, delivered a weaker operating surplus, posted a decline of 21 per cent in new business, and a 43 per cent fall in individual life single premiums.[64] The light in this dark tunnel of a depressed operating environment was substantially improved performance by the underperforming unit trusts, especially the new Sanlam Select Trust, which topped the performance of all the unit trusts in that category. Non-life retail investments in unit trusts and the SP^2 (an investment product) contributed 49.8 per cent to new investment flows.[65]

The strategic direction Daling engineered for the new Sanlam was intended to be both stabilizing and enterprising. His strategy was holistic, revolving around a multidimensional approach. He described demutualization as the 'most important event of the year [1998]', but emphasized that Sanlam was moving to become a 'world-class financial services group', with customers perceiving the evolution of Sanlam as steady, organized, and confident. The confidence Daling referred to was not in walking away from the Sanlam legacy, but building on the strong reputation, which was more important than innovative products.[66] Fundamental to this reputation was the company brand of empowerment and delivery on undertakings. Daling's vision was for Sanlam to 'become the leading financial services group in the developing world by providing superior advice, products and services which continually would exceed the needs and aspirations of our customers and shareholders'.[67] Daling as the captain of the massive Sanlam ship managed change by attempting to act on all fronts.

The first focus was on building investor confidence. This depended on substantially improved financial disclosure. Technical accounting policies had to be used to change market perceptions about the abilities and strengths of Sanlam. In 1998, during the heat

[64] T. Gamedze: 'Sanlam. Running hard to stand still', HSBC Simpson McKie. Life assurance South Africa: 3/5/1999.'

[65] SA: Minutes of Sanlam Board, 10/3/1999; 6/5/1999: Gamedze, op..cit.

[66] It is interesting to note that the minutes of the Sanlam Board meetings were kept in Afrikaans, but once the demutualization negotiations involved growing numbers of international advisers and consultants, minutes were kept in English from the first meeting in 1998. In January 1999 the language of reporting switched back to Afrikaans. Finally in 2000 after Vermaak took office, the minutes were again compiled in English and have remained such up to the present.

[67] SA: Minutes of Sanlam Ltd Board 'Beraad', 9/1/1999.

Table 5.4. Headline earnings, 1998, 1999 before and after LTRR

	1999	1998	Difference %
Current headline earnings—R'm	1 955	1 186	65
–cents per share	73,4	58,4	26
Headline earnings based on LTRR	2 618	1 507	74
–cents per share	98,3	74,2	32

Source: Sanlam annual report, 1999: 19.

of demutualization deliberations, a new financial director, Flip Rademeyer, joined the executive management of Sanlam. He aligned financial reporting post-demutualization with investor analysts' demands for more transparent financial information. The first step was the introduction of the Long-Term Rate of Return (LTRR) on investments. The Code of Corporate Practice in the United Kingdom had sanctioned reporting in terms of the LTRR as the preferred method of reporting on investment returns. The LTRR added the long-term return on investments of shareholders' funds to headline earnings, and eased out short-term fluctuations on earnings in equity markets. The impact of this accounting adjustment was the following (see Table 5.4): headline earnings in 1998 were reported as R1 186 million, and in 1999 as R1 955 million. Once recalculated in terms of the LTRR, headline earnings in 1998 were R1 507 million and R2 618 million in 1999. The difference between 1998 and 1999 was 65 per cent in the old accounting terms, but 74 per cent under LTRR.

The responsiveness to a definite investor-preferred reporting disclosure contributed to improved investor confidence. The alignment with the UK Code of Corporate Practice also served to improve Sanlam's international communication with investors. As illustrated in Table 5.4 Sanlam's headline earnings calculated according to the LTRR showed a marked improvement on the non-LTRR figures for 1998 and 1999. Irrespective of how headline earnings were calculated, the improved Sanlam headline earnings between 1998 and 1999[68] exceeded industry performance and pointed to significantly improved post-demutualization performance. This positive reflection was vital to stabilize the high levels of volatility in the share price. Policyholders' flowback (sale of newly acquired shares) during the first few months of listing reached a high of 28 per cent of free shares issued, which was within the band of international practice of between 20 per cent and 40 per cent of free shares issued at demutualization. By March 2000, Rademeyer reported that flowbacks had come down to 0.6 million shares per day. The share price had risen well beyond 995 cents per share by the end of 1999. Improved headline earnings through LTRR had a positive effect on investor confidence in Sanlam. Individual shareholders owned around 40 per cent of the Sanlam shares by the end of 1999, and nominee

[68] SA: Minutes of Board Meeting, 9/3/1999: Sanlam Annual Report, 1999: 19.

companies around 46 per cent. The notable achievement was that offshore ownership increased to 14 per cent by 2000. Nine per cent of the Sanlam shares were held by USA companies and 4.8 per cent by UK investors.[69] The second accounting adjustment that enhanced investment analysts' confidence was the publication of a consolidated shareholders' cash flow for the first time in 2000. The drive to improve disclosure started in 1999. In the ninety-seven-page 1999 annual report Sanlam published the contribution by all divisions to the operating profit of Sanlam Ltd. This was the first consolidated Group financial results since listing, justified in the annual report as 'part of Sanlam's ongoing attempt to release useful and relevant information'.[70] The 1999 financial statements were also the first to disclose Sanlam Ltd's embedded value—information applauded by analysts (see Table 5.6.) The contribution by each of the business units in Sanlam to headline earnings was down in relative terms. SPF (Sanlam Personal Finance) contributed 61 per cent in 1998, but 50 per cent in 1999; SEB (Employee Benefits) contributed 24 per cent in 1998, but 20 per cent in 1999; Gensec's contribution was down from 25 per cent to 19 per cent in 1999; Santam's dropped from 6 per cent in 1998 to 3 per cent in 1999; Corporative (a new business unit established by Daling) rose from 2 per cent in 1998 to 6 per cent in 1999. The operating margins at SPF, SEB, and Santam improved, but not at Gensec. The overall operating margin improved from 13 per cent in 1998 to 18 per cent in 1999 (see Table 5.5).

This information disclosed the performance variation between operating entities, the high administrative costs and operating margins, which positioned the Group in the industry. Sanlam was lagging SA Mutual in Capital Adequacy Requirements (CAR), but as the latter prepared for demutualization in 1999, accounting reporting requirements for listing on the JSE allowed for better comparison. Productivity had to improve company-wide. Compliance with market demand for fuller disclosure was also a response to the International Accounting Standards Board's call for enhanced earnings disclosure by the long-term insurance industry. Productivity as an overall strategic focus impacted directly on the decision to address a number of loose business ends in Sanlam Ltd. These loose business ends will be explained below. In each case, Sanlam sought to sustain high productivity through the restructuring of operations.

The first productivity issue was within the Sanlam Personal Finance business. With declining demand for traditional life products, SPF developed new single-premium products offering investment flexibility, reduced tax and commission charges, and dramatically improved simplicity in the structure of the product. Investors in the new single-premium investment policy could choose from four investment funds, one of which was an offshore fund. In following SA Mutual, an added offer of a 0 per cent loan

[69] SA: Minutes of Sanlam Ltd Board Meeting, 1/9/1999: Memorandum P. de V. Rademeyer: Share price and share statistics; Memorandum P. de V. Rademeyer: Share price and share statistics, 8/3/2000.

[70] Sanlam Annual Report, 1999: 18.

Table 5.5. Contribution to earnings, Sanlam Group, 1998–1999 (R'm)

	SPF		SEB		Gensec		Healthcare		Santam		Corporative		Total	
Year	1999	1998	1999	1998	1999	1998	1999	1998	1999	1998	1999	1998	1999	1998
1	4 619	4 279	1 426	1 262	1 247	1 029	854	970	2 603	3 261	239	215	10 988	11016
2	783	608	168	115	747	710	11	(220)	59	20	(946)	4	1 722	1 237
3	974	722	399	288	788	648	34	(209)	214	236	113	18	2 522	1 703
4	1 301	1 237	850	803	48	(118)	112	(44)	98	(145)	(927)	(2555)	1482	(822)
5	50	61	20	24	19	25	2	−18	3	6	6	2	100	100
6	37	39	19	21	40	31	19	27	15	13			30	28
7	21	18	12	10	60	69	1	−23	3	1			18	13

Source: Sanlam annual report 1999: 18.

Note: 1 = Income from financial services
2 = Operating profit after exceptional items
3 = Headline earnings after tax
4 = Headline earnings—investment surplus
5 = Attributable profit
5 = % contribution to headline earnings
6 = Administrative costs as % of income
7 = Operating margin %

facility was built into the policy, allowing investors access to their money interest free. SA Mutual had introduced single-premium investment policies with the loan offer in October 1998 (while Sanlam was pursuing demutualization) and Sanlam suffered a reversal of fortune. Its single-premium business declined from a R1 billion policy stream to R380 million during 1998. The precondition to improve this was better technology support. From 1995 Sanlam's IT development people worked on a new SPF support programme to assist with the implementation of linked products, to replace outdated Sanlam systems, and to improve flexibility and time to market for new products. As 'Finpro' encountered repeated delays and suboptimal functioning, SPF decided to migrate out of Finpro—an exercise which cost Sanlam R550 million. These 'school fees' assisted the 1998 strategic decision to terminate new IT program development in Sanlam and purchase well-established software packages and customize them in Sanlam.[71] This decision followed the group-wide policy position that *systems* [were] *in support of new* products. The new policy was that the development and maintenance of technology had to serve the business interests. This could best be done by decentralizing the choice and development of technology to fit in with the needs of the different business applications. A multidivisional business organization had evolved over many years, while technology supply remained centralized. The time had come to optimize technology support through dedicated systems supply and application to the tailored needs of SEB, SPF, and Sanlam Trust. When SPF installed the Auto New Business capability in 1999, it enhanced SPF's capacity to upload policy applications seamlessly and SPF signed forms for the new business processes via email. This deviation from the legacy position of internal technology development was productivity enhancing. It was also a courageous decision since many Sanlam employees were put out of work. In 2000 Sanlam introduced the S.Net suite of applications. This was an advanced Client Relationship Management (CRM) system expediting applications, processing, and business completion.[72] This systems innovation laid the groundwork for future fast systems innovation to support product and service development in the diversified financial services group. These new systems supported the introduction of new products, which SPF planned for the new millennium.

By 2001 net outflow of funds from SPF was turned around and the intrinsic value of new business had almost doubled since 1999. In 2000 SPF restored an operating profit of 34 per cent on the performance of 1999. SEB also posted an operating profit of 20 per cent in 2000 on the performance of 1999. The improvement in new SPF business was primarily ascribed to the launch of the new Stratus investment policies, for local as well as international markets. In SPF, Sanlam Life, Sanlam Unit Trusts, Sanlam Personal Portfolio, and Sanlam Trust (a trust entity organized around the acquisition of Boland

[71] SA: Sanlam: The IT Journey, 2014: 23–4.

[72] Ibid., 23; SA: Minutes of Sanlam Ltd Board, memorandum K. Venter: Migration of the Finpro program, 3/2/1999; Memorandum C.G. Swanepoel: Individual Insurance: New single-premium project.

Bank's trust business in 1996) jointly delivered improved results. The most significant trend at SEB was the stemming of the massive outflow of funds, as pension funds had switched from Sanlam to competitors since 1990. By the end of 2000, SEB narrowed the outflow to 50 per cent of the trend of the previous five years. This outcome followed the much improved performance of the asset management operations in Sanlam Unit Trusts since 1995.[73] Supported by new products, more efficient IT support assisted in the turnaround at SPF and SEB. Gensec failed to show the same turnaround: It lost market share and profits were down 9 per cent. Investment management and investment performance remained a drag on the turnaround strategy.

To address investment inflows, renewed emphasis on internationalization led to alliances with foreign partners. The asset swap transactions since 1995 had been no real internationalization strategy. By 2000, asset swaps constituted 30 per cent of Sanlam's new recurring-premium business. When the first five-year endowment policies reached maturity in 2000 and had to be paid out in South Africa in ZAR, an investment opportunity arose for Sanlam. The company applied for a life insurance licence in the Channel Island of Jersey because of the favourable regulatory environment. South African long-term insurance companies were prohibited by the Exchange Control Regulation from issuing long-term insurance policies in any currency but ZAR. A branch of Sanlam in Jersey could issue such policies in foreign currency. Through a Jersey-licensed branch Sanlam issued foreign currency endowment policies to South African clients.[74]

In 1999 Gensec entered into a joint venture with Macquarie Bank of Australia to acquire the knowhow to manage cash management trusts (CMTs). Macquarie Bank was a leader in CMTs and wrap accounts, whereby independent financial advisers managed investors' funds more efficiently. This joint venture did not expand Sanlam's operations overseas, but the company did acquire specialist knowledge to strengthen its investment management capability. The joint venture was accommodated in the Sanlam subsidiary, Innofin, but after four years (2003) Sanlam bought out the Macquarie stake and transformed the investment product into a personal finance product. Sanlam was leveraging off knowledge of the Australian market to address unsatisfactory investment performance of wealth products for the top end of the market.[75]

All the international activities occurred in an uncoordinated manner. It was only later in August 2000 that Sanlam announced its first official internationalization strategy. This strategy announced the intention of Sanlam to implement a regional expansion model. The weakness of this approach was not the regional direction. It was acknowledged that a firm's investments follow patterns exhibiting regional aggregation and arbitrage logic

[73] SA: Minutes of Sanlam Board, 13/09/2000. [74] SA: Minutes of Sanlam Board, 13/09/2000.

[75] SA: Minutes of Sanlam Board, 13/09/2000; Sanlam Board, 28/10/03; Sanlam Annual Report, 2005: 109–11.

to cope with the opposing pressures of globalization (i.e. integration) and local markets (i.e. localization).[76] Semi-globalization also acknowledged partial cross-border integration whereby barriers to market integration were high but not inhibitive,[77] and the Uppsala model explaining internationalization commencing with expansion into neighbouring regions first.[78] The problem with the Sanlam strategy was that it did not comprise an integral part of the Sanlam overhaul strategy and was the exact opposite of where Sanlam had focused its international actions since 1995. Sanlam moved into the UK market and not into regional markets on its borders. By 2001 internationalization was primarily about meeting Sanlam's domestic growth targets. Real growth of around 10 per cent was possible only for some businesses in the Sanlam Group, while earnings above 20 per cent were achieved in overseas markets. The second driver of internationalization was earnings diversification: to follow existing Sanlam clients, to acquire international client bases, and to maintain the competitive product offerings of the company, while offering talented individuals international mobility within the Group and simultaneously buying intellectual capital.[79]

The official internationalization strategy showed the lack of clear direction. This strategy admitted that Sanlam was wrong to conceptualize operational expansion into 'regional' markets as a first step towards internationalization. Sanlam had limited knowledge of developing markets and could not compete with First World companies already established in those markets—as admitted by Exco: 'Sanlam has not really demonstrated that it can work in a Third World environment; with South Africa's infrastructure and regulatory environment being developed to a First World level as it is.... Sanlam doesn't really have experience with the lower end of the market... It is thus proposed that the geographical focus be changed to one based on a hub in the developed world.' The target market was first the English-speaking ones, then India/Malaysia or markets where the wealthy leadership echelon is business-English literate. So Sanlam went abroad on the Gensec track. Gensec Bank was the vehicle to conduct Sanlam's business using a Dutch subsidiary, Sanlam Netherlands BV (SNH), for the hub into the UK and Western Europe. There was also no group-wide co-ordination of international operations, as underlying businesses often explored international opportunities in an uncoordinated fashion. Management sensed this lack of direction and parameters for screening internationalization targets.[80] Daling's statement in his 1999 Chairman's

[76] J.L. Arregle, P.W. Beamish, and L. Hébert (2009): 'The regional dimension of MNE's foreign subsidiary localization', *Journal of International Business Studies* 40(1): 86–107.

[77] P. Ghemawat (2003): 'Semi-globalization and international business strategy', *Journal of International Business Studies* 34(2): 138–52.

[78] J. Johanson and J. E. Vahlne (1977: 'The internationalization process of the firm: A model of knowledge development and increasing foreign market commitments', *Journal of International Business Studies*, 8(10): 23–32.

[79] SA: Minutes of Sanlam Exco, 4/6/2001.

[80] SA: Minutes of Sanlam Exco, 7/5/2001.

address, 'As far as internationalization is concerned, Gensec is already expanding its offshore activities',[81] epitomizes the marginal position of the internationalization policies in the bigger scheme of operational turnaround to Sanlam. This lacklustre dedication to internationalization seemed ingrained in the strategy, since in 2000 the Sanlam Group Strategy still claimed that internationalization was 'done through Gensec. Other businesses will follow later.'[82] Offshore action seemed uncoordinated. Gensec opened offices in Dublin and London and introduced the Dublin Fund for offshore investments. When the opportunity came to acquire the UK actuarial firm Punter Southall & Co. in May 2001, the deal was struck. Justified as a means to serve Sanlam clients' offshore investment demands, Sanlam entered into an alliance with P-Solve and Hitchens Investment Management.[83] Local financial analysts expressed question marks about these transactions, because the benefit to Sanlam seemed vague.

The performance of Gensec had been a bone of contention since acquisition. The flat performance in 1999 diluted the Sanlam headline earnings by 2.4 cents per share. This trend continued in 2000, diluting Sanlam's earnings per share by 3 cents per share. Then fifteen asset managers, previous employees from SAM (Sanlam Asset management), resigned from Gensec. This was a serious loss, since one of them, Schalk de Vos, was the driver of the successful Sanlam Select, Prime Growth, and Provider unit trusts, as well as the 500-Plus individual portfolios. Gensec private equity also lost Leonard Fine and Sam O'Leary,[84] thus displaying merger inefficiencies bound to impact on overall performance later. Furthermore, Gensec suffered a loss of about R18 million in 1999 following a rights-issue underwriting with Stanbic, of Macmed, which ultimately collapsed. Gensec had deposits with Fidelity Bank, and a stake in The Business Bank, both institutions which suffered losses due to the Macmed collapse. These developments mandated a profit warning by Gensec on 22 October 1999. When the Sanlam board was advised that the relationship between Gensec and Sanlam needed revision, Gensec argued limited strategic and operational freedom to conduct its business. On the other hand, Sanlam considered asset management its core function, thus justifying strategic oversight. SAM's unit trusts had a fine track record in the industry, but were in jeopardy as a result of the dysfunctional merger with Gensec. It was clear that Sanlam would forfeit valuable investment bank expertise in disposing of Gensec, but independent analysts confirmed in a presentation to the Sanlam board that management at Gensec was dysfunctional and staff morale at an all-time low. The strategic decision to take out the Gensec minorities (25 per cent of the shares were held outside Sanlam) in December 2000 came as no surprise. Despite both entities operating in financial services, they operated in fundamentally different business cultures: insurance managers were driven by volumes and

[81] SA: Minutes of Sanlam Board, 10/3/1999. [82] SA: Minutes of Sanlam Ltd Board, 9/2/2000.
[83] SA; Minutes of Sanlam Board, 7/3/2001; 4/6/2001; 18/6/2001.
[84] S. Cranston: 'Mergers work best on paper', *Financial Mail*, 15/4/1998: 8.

systems, while asset management was primarily performance and capabilities driven.[85] The central role of Gensec in the Sanlam performance is illustrated in Table 5.5. Sanlam could not just walk away from this asset, but the feeling that the capabilities of the Gensec people were inadequate for the Sanlam asset management function was mounting. Sanlam finally took out the minorities in Gensec on 31 December 2000, a transaction that was far too expensive for Sanlam but one which Daling wanted to conclude at all costs. He had to admit to the error of judgement in hastily concluding the acquisition of Gensec prior to demutualization and was adamant that Sanlam and Gensec's ways had parted.[86] Gensec Asset Management was rebranded Sanlam Investment Management (SIM) from 2 April 2001. This transaction did not cure the investment return ills of Sanlam, but afforded the company the opportunity to regain control over the function. It was the price ultimately paid for acquiring Gensec prior to demutualization, just to be able to say that there was an asset management company in the Group. Gensec Bank remained an investment bank within the Sanlam Group.

A more pressing matter was the relationship with ABSA. Sanlam had already admitted in 1995 that it did not have the resources to conduct a full acquisition transaction with ABSA, resembling the FNB/Momentum or Standard Bank/Liberty transactions.[87] At that time, ABSA was the only banking group in South Africa without a business relationship with a long-term insurer, since ABSA had developed its own insurance business. On the other hand Sanlam desired a more substantial return on its 23 per cent stake in ABSA. Under the project name 'Apollo' confidential discussions were held between Sanlam (Flip Rademeyer and George Rudman) and ABSA (Danie Cronjé) about the possible merger of the two entities. Sanlam was eager to secure improved access through the ABSA network for bancassurance, but ABSA had established its own insurance division. The negotiations were 'sensitive' and conducted in the utmost confidentiality, because of the potentially disruptive impact on financial markets in the event of a restructuring of operations. The timing was further compromised, because the Governor of the SARB, Tito Mboweni, had just appointed Judge Dennis Davis to reopen an investigation into the Bankorp lifeboat, following a report by Judge Willem Heath. Daling wanted a conclusive outcome to these discussions by 2000. Discussions eventually steered in the direction of a merger, but on 8 March 2000 the two parties announced in a press release that a merger was no longer considered, but that Sanlam would retain its 23 per cent stake in ABSA. The principle of arm's-length collaboration was firmly established. Cooperation occurred on individual business levels. Sanlam was particularly pleased that the two insurance companies in the ABSA Group acknowledged the

[85] V. Pienaar: 'Survey: etirement fund manager mergers rife: but are they the answer?' *Business Day*, 23/6/1998.

[86] Interview: P. de V. Rademeyer, 11/11/2012.

[87] SA: Minutes Sanlam Board, 7/3/1998.

specialized nature of the investment skills in Gensec and had transferred assets to the value of R2 billion to Gensec.[88]

It was very important for Sanlam to expand its distribution channels to improve investment inflows. Sanlam resumed its investigation into possible co-operation with other institutions. The company commissioned McKinsey to advise on a future strategy. The McKinsey memorandum 'Implementing a Customer-Centric Wealth Creation Strategy' proposed a merger strategy between Sanlam and ABSA—Project Alexis. The idea was that Sanlam should become a broad financial services offering through primary transaction relationships with middle- and high-income clients, as opposed to a 'bricks and clicks' client base. This would imply the establishment of an extensive network, including branches. This strategy would bring Sanlam immediately into direct access of ABSA's extensive branch network. This idea depended heavily on acceptable pricing for such a merger, political and regulatory implications, the market response to a resurfacing of the lifeboat saga, and the possible impact of the FSB's requirements of annual actuarial valuations of the long-term insurers.[89] The Sanlam board supported a merger with ABSA in principle, but by the end of 2001 decided to make contingency plans in the event of the ABSA board declining merger proposals. In September 2001 the ABSA board rejected the business case put forward as 'Project Alexis'.

Sanlam, as controlling partner in the voting pool agreement with Universa,[90] consulted with its partners in the voting pool to reduce the number of shares in ABSA in respect of which the voting pool would act collectively, from 48 per cent of the issued shares in ABSA to 37 per cent.[91] This gave Sanlam greater freedom of movement with respect to ABSA. The agreement also resulted in the unbundling of shares held by Universa in ABSA. Sticky negotiations continued, but by early 2003 no agreement was in sight. Major differences existed between the parties on the principle of calculation of value (fair value or market value) and in February 2003 the Sanlam board was advised that ABSA had expressed an interest in a merger at existing exchange rates. The idea of a possible hostile takeover surfaced. The ABSA offer failed to convey real value to Sanlam and the old Daling view remained valid: the size of the investment in ABSA mandated superior returns for Sanlam. Unless ABSA delivered better returns, a merger would

[88] SA: Press Release, 8/3/2000: Sanlam retains its shareholding in ABSA; Minutes of Sanlam Ltd Board, 8/3/2000.

[89] SA: Minutes of Sanlam Ltd Board, 9/2/2000.

[90] Universa entered into a voting pool agreement in January 1992 with Sankorp (later replaced by Sanlam after the winding up of Sankorp) with regard to key policy matters in ABSA. Universa consisted of Rembrandt (39%), Mine Pension Fund (39%), the Sage Group (22%). This voting pool agreement mandated unanimity between Sanlam and Universa on changes to ABSA's future business, appointment of the chief executive, mergers and acquisitions, material capital expenditure, and some further matters pertaining to dividend policy and issuing of shares.

[91] SA: Minutes of Sanlam Ltd Board, 5/12/2001.

destroy value. The board dispatched a letter to the board of ABSA expressing the Sanlam rejection of ABSA's merger proposals.[92]

The negative trend in inflows into investments and new policies since the mid-1990s was at the root of the endeavours to find workable synergies with ABSA. Sanlam expanded its own agent base by appointing more Coloured, female, and English-speaking agents. On the initiative of Mr Harry Brewer of SA Mutual, the Institute of Life and Pension Advisers (ILPA) was formed in 1995 to oversee knowledge and professional standards of insurance advisers. ILPA's name changed to the Financial Planning Institute (FPI) in 2000. From 2009 it was commissioned by the FSB to conduct regulatory assessments of advisers in the field. Throughout the long history of Sanlam the company has been admired for the depth of the training of its agents. As a member of the LOA, Sanlam worked closely with other members in the industry to formalize training and professional standards. The company opened training centres across the country to extend training to people operating in the Xhosa-speaking population, apart from the training in Afrikaans and English. By 1995, 23.8 per cent of the Sanlam advisers were black and 6.7 per cent of the branch managers were black. This did not arrest the declining trend in new business.

By 1997 the number of Sanlam advisers had also declined significantly, which had a direct impact on new business volumes. This development convinced Sanlam that a new approach to distribution was called for. An international financial services consulting group, TBOi NMG Africa, was appointed to revitalize the existing distribution paradigm. In response to the fundamentally different context of operations, Johan Treurnicht, General Manager: Marketing, found the existing Sanlam pool of advisers ill-equipped in the new deregulated financial services environment. In spite of industry-regulated training standards and the high level of expertise and professionalism of the Sanlam adviser and broker networks, high industry costs and structural inefficiencies called for a radical repositioning of distribution. While the ABSA discussions dragged on without clear direction, the consultants offered the New Dawn plan for distribution revitalization in 1997. The New Dawn strategy captured the spirit of Rudman's by then well-known call for a profit orientation and business approach in Sanlam. New Dawn based a turnaround distribution strategy on a move away from volumes towards a business orientation embedded in 'best practice'. New Dawn proposed distribution driven by client-centricity ('client is king'), characterized by a relationship with 'Sanlam' and not the adviser, and remuneration only on condition of active engagement in the action of selling. The New Dawn proposals suggested a clear identification of different distribution channels, each targeting a dedicated market segment. It was important to agree on a policy of identifying markets and devising prospecting strategies, but the so-called 'cold

[92] SA: Minutes of Sanlam board, 5/3/2003.

canvassing' had to be replaced by a much more orderly managed system of identification and action on new business leads. Three distribution channels were identified: brokers, in-house advisers, and a new 'independent' company, owned by Sanlam and other shareholders, comprising high-flyer advisers and brokers, delivering a dedicated personal service of excellence—the so-called Phoenix companies.[93]

New Dawn addressed key transformational drivers in Sanlam. These drivers could not easily rise above the Sanlam 'straightjacket' of bureaucracy, loyal marketing by the loyal Sanlam agents, branding, and the rapidly transformed South African society. The competitive environment posed both an opportunity and a threat. A distinct business orientation would change the volume driver to a performance driver. Improved performance driven by profit—that was the core of post-demutualization Sanlam. New Dawn hit the ground running early in 1998 and SPF very soon noticed a spark of revival in new business volumes. The business orientation of both brokers and Sanlam advisers indeed also contributed to the new information technology policy to purchase the most up-to-date computer software, such as the Lamda policy administration platform, to support the new marketing paradigm. The LOA had recently sanctioned the general access (GA) concept. This concept allowed advisers and brokers to market products of their 'own' and other industry players. This meant that a very successful Sanlam adviser would be allowed to sell a brilliant product put on the market by a competitor, such as Liberty or SA Mutual. This development strengthened the Phoenix distribution channel, as independent financial advisers could build a portfolio for clients including the best from different industry players. Client-centricity, business orientation, and value-added financial advice made up the new distribution chain, introduced by New Dawn. By 2000 Sanlam had more than 200 Independent Financial Advisers in the market, allowed to sell accredited Discovery, Liberty, and Fedlife products. The business-oriented overhaul was completed when Sanlam announced that its advisers would no longer receive subsidies, bonuses, allowances, or employer contributions in future, but commission, the same as brokers.[94] The success of the New Dawn plan lay in changing the business performance orientation of the Sanlam advisers, but it did not stop the decline in Sanlam's market share. SPF had experienced improved production since 1999, but had by no means regained lost market share.

New Dawn did not meet management's expectations. Marinus Daling abruptly fired Johan Treurnicht soon after the implementation of New Dawn, disrupting a strong team in distribution. This dismissal was unexpected, since Treurnicht had a long career in broker distribution and general product distribution in Sanlam. No official explanation for Treurnicht's dismissal was published, but Daling's conduct resembled his decision in

[93] SA: 1/2/23/5: Sanlam: New Dawn, Organizational Design Distribution Sales Organization; Also see Venter (2016) *The History of Sanlam Broker Division*: 57–61.

[94] *Sandaba*, February 2000: 11; April 2000: 3–5.

1997 to fire Desmond Smith as Managing Director in the heat of the preparation towards demutualization. Daling did not appoint an executive manager for marketing in his new executive committee in 1998. SPF under Hendrik Bester was assigned the marketing function within the business unit. The context for change, both as an organization and in operations, had not yet been addressed. Very incomplete organizational transformation had manifested in Sanlam Head Office and regional structures by 1997. Management failed to take into account an important organizational matter, namely the culture of the people working in the organization. By 1997/1998 just under 70 per cent of the Sanlam advisers were Afrikaans speakers and 88 per cent of them were white. They spoke Afrikaans and their thought and behavioural processes were South African, whereas the TBOi NMG consultants were very British, distant from the market they sought to advise on enhanced operational performance. Advisers involved in the training environment in New Dawn recalled the sense of distance, being lost and abandoned during encounters with the consultants, who knew no Afrikaans nor understood the South African society. Communication between the consultants and Sanlam advisers was unsuccessful and many a training session ended in walkouts and advisers regrouping among themselves to translate the information into their world.[95] Ironically, the New Dawn thinking later led to a successful marketing model that evolved from within the Sanlam advisers' structure.

Early in 2000 the advisers accepted the concept of business development managers (*Besigheidsontwikkelingsbestuurders*)—BDMs). These BDMs assumed a business development role between branch and regional managers. They managed an income stream within a business unit, a concept aligned with the New Dawn Phoenix company concept.[96] They operated fairly independently and successfully developed business entities *à la Phoenix*. When the Sanlam advisers, organized in the Sanlam Advisers Forum since 1992 (SAF), claimed a stake, either monetary or in terms of equity, in the business units they managed, the former bureaucratic centralizing Sanlam management trait manifested again. The BDMs insisted on their independence and right to dispose of their business units should they so wish, but Sanlam executive management refused. Only in March 2004 a long drawn-out dispute between SAF and management ended in legal counsel advising that the BDMs were employees of Sanlam. This curtailed the independent business drive of advisers, but would later re-emerge as the so-called Blue Star Business concept. This dispute highlighted the Sanlam management's desire for control, as had been vividly displayed with Sanlam Health. It took another four years before the concept of independent businesses in the distribution channel as a culmination of successful broker and adviser performance, was accepted.

[95] Interview with Sanlam advisers involved in ND, 15/6/2016.

[96] SA: *Sandaba*, October 2000: 1.

Market analysts remained unconvinced about Sanlam's direction. Addressing financial analysts in 2000, Sanlam identified its target market as households earning R4 000 per month, but a year later shifted the target to households earning R2 000 per month. Repeated references by management to narrow the gap between the Sanlam share price and the disclosed Embedded Value (EV), did not satisfy the market—the analysts looked for 'strategic objectives relating to operational issues'[97]—they wanted to know companies' strategic objectives with respect to the operational priorities of the companies. The engagement with the market perception of Sanlam at a time when SA Mutual was demutualizing and listing (September 1999) seemed to occupy management. Sanlam even considered seeking a credit rating from Standard & Poor's. Although Sanlam was not a borrower, management thought a credit rating would put the company in the public eye, especially among overseas investors. The process of securing such a rating would also assist the internal 'getting the house in order'.[98] Much publicity was given to the fact that Sanlam was the first South African company to announce interim results live on satellite television.[99]

Cautiously changing culture: transformation

The public image of Sanlam not only suffered as a result of disappointing performance, but also as a result of the different constituencies affected by the need to transform Sanlam into a leading financial services company in and of South Africa. A relatively marginal matter was cost-saving outsourcing activities, which were performed in the course of 1998/1999. Corporate facilities and infrastructure services of Sanlam were outsourced to independent business partners on condition of concluding mutually beneficial contractual agreements that would protect Sanlam's interests. Drake and Scull (SA) took up the contract as chief supplier of most of the services comprising corporate services (stationery, equipment, signs, etc.). Infrastructure services were put out on tender to companies such as Debis/Spicer, DiData, and PQ Africa. Sanlam assisted the Coloured chauffeurs in Sanlam's service to establish their own transport company, On Time Chauffeur Services, with which Sanlam contracted to perform the transport services that were formerly part of Sanlam Head Office functions. Printing functions were outsourced to Koerikai, a local small printing enterprise. Graphic design was outsourced to Out of the Blue Creative Communications, whereby Sanlam shed

[97] Investec Securities: F10: 23/2/2001: 'Life assurance in the context of contractual savings institutions': 45.

[98] SA: Minutes of Sanlam Board, 4/8/1999. The credit rating was never conducted, but the discussions on the matter were indicative of Sanlam seeking wider international market approval.

[99] Sanlam Annual Report, 1999: 7.

costs and empowered small businessmen.[100] These outsourcing exercises afforded Sanlam an opportunity to assist some of its loyal workforce in entering the market for small businesses and were indicative of the goodwill between Sanlam and its employees. Although marginal to the bigger Sanlam transformation, these outsourcing exercises eased in opportunities for Sanlam to address black economic empowerment (BEE) concerns.

Black economic empowerment was not a matter of minor significance. The policy framework was slow in developing a clear strategy. A sense of indecision reigned when an executive noted during the outsourcing exercise that 'we know black economic empowerment is going to cost us money'. By the time Sanlam turned eighty in 1998, organizational transformation was cosmetic and the energy was all directed at demutualizing successfully.

The broad ideological context of the new government after 1994 resulted in statutory requirements necessitating a comprehensive transformation strategy. During the last years of the 1990s Sanlam dealt with the broad transformation environment basically on two fronts. The first was compliance with the Employment Equity Act, No. 55 of 1998. Sanlam considered employment equity a business imperative and dedicated a specific focus for it in the Human Resources function.[101] Policies to give effect to broad transformation were approached holistically—they were formulated at the centre, but implementation was decentralized into the different business units. Many hours went into the deliberations on the Sanlam Vision, and these fed into official Sanlam policy documents on employment equity, Code of Management Practices, guidelines for people with disabilities, and a Code of Practice to end racial harassment and unfair discrimination. Diversity management was aligned with business strategy, since compliance was considered a business imperative. After the appointment of Peter Schwartz to the Sanlam board in 1994, followed in 1999 by Dawn Mokhobo as the first African woman, John Moalusi was the first African person appointed to the executive team in Distribution. By late 1999 Sanlam confidently claimed to have all the 'building blocks' in order to implement employment equity—but by the end of the century implementation was scattered.[102] Sanlam had always employed people of colour, but from the mid-1980s the staff complement of black and Coloured people increased. This was both a diversity and a training matter. Alarm bells started ringing during the first quarter of 1995, when it was revealed that 23 per cent of new black employees had resigned, primarily citing difficulty with Afrikaans as the language of the workplace. Since Sanlam had started its business in 1918 with a strong emphasis on education as the only tool of empowerment, management in 1994 embraced yet another education opportunity. Desmond Smith,

[100] SA: Minutes of Sanlam Ltd Board, 19/8/1999.

[101] Venter (2016 *Development of Human Resources 1994–2015 with Sanlam.* Unpublished Sanlam internal research report.

[102] SA: Minutes of Sanlam Board, 3/2/2000.

then CEO, claimed that one of the factors that could make South Africa 'a front runner, is the development, education and training of the individual'.[103] The link between employment equity and ensuring that Sanlam remained successful in the changing environment of the 1990s, was education and training of its employees. Sanlam immediately brushed up the financial support programme to assist employees in furthering their studies. In August 1997, before the promulgation of the Employment Equity (EE) Act in 1998, Sanlam released its employment equity policy. Because of the language constraint, other avenues of training needed to be developed. At first management explained the meaning and operation of the EE legislation and then the targets for compliance. Extensive communication with employees informed them of the categories of designated persons to benefit, namely blacks, women, and people with disabilities, provided they were suitably qualified. The unfolding of employment equity was underpinned by internal Sanlam training and capacity building, most of which occurred from 2002.

The gradual implementation of employment equity was also partly the result of the sensitivity around the transformation of Head Office. Sanlamhof was a truly Afrikaner institution, functioning as a close-knit 'patriarchal family', but as the changes occurred gradually in the wider South African society, it had to reflect in Head Office as well. The demographic restructuring had a profound impact on the 'Sanlamhof family'. In one anonymous letter to the staff magazine, *Bloudruk*, in April 1994 one employee advised disgruntled fellow employees, that if they were looking for loyalty, 'kry vir julle 'n hond' [get yourselves a dog].[104] Social restructuring took time. From 1918, management had stimulated a workforce spirit of '*Sanlammer wees*' [to be a person of Sanlam] and a '*Sanlamgees*' [the spirit of Sanlam] to enhance organizational efficiency, but this had to be undone in a very short time span. When the IT infrastructure unit was outsourced, it left 230 employees without jobs in Sanlam in January 2001. The core IT team moved to another IT company, Debis, contracted to perform IT services for Sanlam. This restructuring assisted Sanlam in streamlining its organizational structure with greater focus on its core business, but did not sit well with staff at Head Office.[105] Sustained poor performance during 2001 and 2002 and the subsequent decision to sell Sanlam Health to Medscheme in 2001 exacerbated the negativity among Head Office staff.[106] The leadership transition at the end of 2002 coincided with stern and outspoken criticism in the staff magazine against management, showing the delicate nature of the mood at Sanlamhof. For many years since the employment of non-Afrikaans-speaking persons, dissatisfaction about the use of Afrikaans as official language at Head Office and in general internal communication, simmered beneath the surface. Finally, in 2002 'practical' considerations forced Afrikaans out of the meeting rooms and off the agendas and minutes. It could simply no

[103] *Sanlammer*, 3/5/1994: 1. [104] *Bloudruk*, 1/4/1994: 19.
[105] SA: News Release: 'Sanlam kontrakteer IT infrastruktuur uit', 25/1/2001.
[106] SA: News Release: 'Sanlam verkoop sy gesondheidsorgbesigheid aan Medscheme', 1/10/2001.

longer be assumed that everybody was proficient in Afrikans, since the new cohort of directors, managers, and employees mirrored the new South African demographic diversity. English became the language of official communication. Many employees were still Afrikaans speakers and conducted general conversations in Afrikaans, but officially English replaced Afrikaans as the language of communication in Sanlam. The 'cultural' change created a context where the implementation of employment equity and black economic empowerment initiatives called for great skill and leadership.

The second front of transformation in Sanlam was gaining the confidence of the black market. Having successfully completed the first Black Economic Empowerment transaction with NAIL in 1993, Daling wanted to sustain the momentum. In discussions with leading business people heading up new black-owned corporations, investment companies, and trusts, Sanlam tested the waters. The former business partners, NAIL, Metropolitan Life, and Sanlam, explored a possible merger of the three entities. The aim was to create a new financial services group 'reflecting the spirit of the new South Africa, with strong empowerment characteristics'. The catalyst to the negotiations was the desire to accelerate the pace of transformation in the interests of South Africans. For Sanlam the merger would secure lost market share, and financial and strategic benefits in all of the Sanlam's chosen markets. Planning had progressed to the stage where cautionary statements were published in June, July, and August 2000, advising the public about the intended merger. The transaction came to a halt. On the exact date the final principles of the transaction were to be sealed, Sanlam reversed its position. The deal depended on ratification by all three companies' board of directors. Advocate Moseneke, Chairman of the Metlife Board, conveyed Metlife's support and enthusiasm for the deal. The Sanlam board had second thoughts. Independent market research indicated that the Sanlam brand enjoyed a stronger South African image among both white and black respondents; Sanlam had a much stronger image as an empowerment concern than Metlife; Sanlam performed better on employee benefits, on business decisions, and overall brand acknowledgement. Overall the market research indicated that the public placed greater value on 'hard' items, than 'soft' items. This meant that Sanlam's actual delivery found stronger appeal than image and perceptions. Sanlam expected synergies of around R2–R3 billion, but realized that some government salary contracts (PERSAL—the staff salary system) might be at risk following such a merger. However, this was the least of Sanlam's concerns. During merger talks the Metlife management wanted binding merger principles, whereas Sanlam wanted open and non-binding principles during the merger process to allow for decision making by the incoming new company board. The Sanlam position was simple: no deal unless supported by both boards. Sanlam executive committee no longer supported the proposed transaction. Overall, the Sanlam management was skeptical and called the talks off. In the joint cautionary the parties told the public that agreement had been reached 'that the commercial benefits of the merger would not be as significant as were initially expected'. The expected benefits of long-term growth in shareholder value and the formation of a strong platform for sustainable competitive advantage were probably not going to materialize.[107]

Once the mood had changed on the transaction, the reservations voiced by different members of the Sanlam board underlined salient concerns. On the one hand one director was excited about the wonderful learning curve experienced by the actuaries, accountants, and advisers on constructing a potential massive merger transaction, but the straw that broke the camel's back was management. There were serious reservations about the quality of management in the merger partner, on exactly how the new entity would be managed, and who would be the management team. As it appeared from the 2000 interim results, the board was satisfied that financial performance showed significant improvement. A game changer was the position of the leading role players, Marinus Daling and Dikgang Moseneke. It was admitted that the fact that the initiative had started with discussions between Sanlam and NAIL, and Metlife had joined later, might not have been the right strategy. Moseneke and Daling were the keystones to the deal, but rumours went around that Moseneke was tipped for Chief Justice of South Africa, which would take him out of the picture. Then in August 2000 the news broke that Daling had cancer. He did not attend the final board meeting on 'Project Moon', but Rudman, who was acting as CEO, had discussed the matter with him in advance. To him the business case was weak and he doubted the potential value Sanlam would derive from the transaction. Too many aspects of the proposed transaction created unease at Sanlam and finally the executive management team was not prepared to enter without Daling and possibly also Moseneke. These were the strong leaders they would trust to take on the merger, but without them the board would not go ahead with the venture.[108]

The political environment under a new government seeking to transfer ownership of business and economic activity to the majority put pressure on business to do BEE transactions. Business bought into the concept of compliance with those policies as 'a business imperative'. Sanlam received numerous opportunistic proposals to enter into BEE transactions and walked away from most. The NAIL/Metlife opportunity might have secured Sanlam a greater share of the market typically served by the NAIL/Metlife business operations. The Metlife of 2000 was no longer the company Sanlam had sold to NAIL in 1993. The business case in 2000 needed to address value to Sanlam, as was the case with the talks with ABSA. Sanlam suffered from negative inflows and suboptimal returns on investments. The ABSA and Metlife talks hinged on value added to Sanlam. When it became known that Daling was terminally ill, the executive team was unwilling to venture into a potentially complicated transaction, a transaction that would most probably also be too expensive (as was the transaction to take out the Gensec minorities) and could not deliver on the performance criteria of adding substantive value to Sanlam.

[107] SA: Minutes of Sanlam Ltd board, 13/9/2000; Withdrawal of Joint Cautionary Announcement, 18/9/2000.

[108] SA: Minutes of special meeting of the Sanlam Ltd Board, 28/8/2000.

Sanlam committed itself to BEE, but the one big transaction remained a delusion. The company had an established corporate social responsibility record. From that basis further community engagement was rolled out. Sanlam enjoyed sufficient industry recognition in 1995 for the government's Public Investment Commission (PIC) to appoint Sanlam as external portfolio manager of the PIC equity portfolio on 22 November 1995. The PIC handed Sanlam a mandate outlining the minimum requirements for the management of the portfolio. The mandate also required Sanlam to develop plans of action to include individual commitment to the Reconstruction and Development Programme (RDP), affirmative action, upliftment of the historically disadvantaged people, and programmes to train people of colour in investment management. As asset management in Sanlam travelled through SAM, Gensec, and finally back to SIM, it was in SIM that the Development Fund sat. In 1996 Sanlam established its own Sanlam Development Fund, managed by SAM. Sanlam did not wish to place funding in projects with a weak economic reconstruction impact. Since 1996 the Sanlam Development Fund had dedicated more than R2.2 billion towards the development of small business entrepreneurs (through Cash Bank, the National Housing Finance Corporation, and New Farmers); funding for historically disadvantaged persons to acquire shares in BEE transactions (such as the National Empowerment Corporation, Johnnic, Sancino/NuClicks, and Nitac/PQ Africa); direct investment in BEE companies (such as Kunene Finance, Nozala, Worldwide Investment, Sancino, and Thebe Investments); and made investments in infrastructure development in neglected locations, such as the Witbank/Maputo road construction and the Beit Bridge/Bulawayo railway line. Sanlam also established the Community Building Fund. This R500 million fund allocated sponsorship to actual building projects improving community infrastructure, service delivery, and the creation of employment opportunities, such as the Lesotho Highlands Water Project, the Rand Water Board, and the Umgeni Water Board. The R279 million contribution to the demutualization Umsobomvu Fund served the same purpose.[109] By 2002 more than R2.2 billion had accumulated in this fund.[110] On 17 April 2001, SIM established a new Sanlam Development Fund of Funds, with more resources, to contribute to the development of local business in South Africa. This was a joint venture with SIM and Cape Partners.

Community social investment was not new to Sanlam, but in the post-1994 era contributions were aligned with the government's economic reconstruction priorities, while at the same time underpinned by a dedicated strategy to build the Sanlam brand. The company employed a more professional strategy to strengthen its branding and the

[109] SA: SIM Report to the Public Investment Commissioners on the Action Plans i.t.o. section H.2 of the mandate, July 2001; SA: Minutes of Sanlam Board, 5/6/1996; 8/6/2001; Sanlam Annual Report 2001: 12; Sanlam Annual Report 2002: 18.

[110] SA: Minutes of Sanlam Board, 25/3/2003: Investment report SIM.

use of the well-known Sanlam logo. A new emphasis on building the brand emerged around the early 1990s, when the use of a variety of logos by Sanlam group companies caused a stir. During the 1970s the blue 'S' in the Sanlam logo was replaced by the white hands embracing a blue ball, symbolizing protection, caring, safety, and trust. This 'hands' logo was firmly entrenched by the early 1990s. Desmond Smith was emphatic about the business value of the Sanlam corporate identity. He called for a consistent adherence to the single, but clear and well-known logo.[111] In 1996 the company slogan was changed from 'Where your future counts', to 'Your future in good hands', to convey the client-centricity in Sanlam [See Appendix 1]. The simple well-known single blue and white Sanlam hands-logo was placed in jeopardy in June 2000, when the board accepted a decision to implement a multibrand strategy for the Sanlam Group. This decision led Daling to commission a new name for the holding company. The proposal was FINSECO—acronym for financial services company. However, the new name was not taken to the board as Daling decided not to fiddle with the brand name of repute.[112]

Market research in 1997 and 2000 indicated the strong positive reputation of Sanlam in the public mind, but showed that its image was weaker than that of SA Mutual and that brand awareness of Sanlam trailed SA Mutual and most of the leading banks. A disturbing observation was that Sanlam's extensive corporate social investment did not hit the public target as well as it should. The advice to Sanlam was to build the positive achievements of the company internally and externally.[113] At Head Office the name of the internal staff magazine was changed. *Die Fakkel* first appeared in 1932. The name *Fakkel* was retained until it was changed to *Sanlammer* in August 1991, but this name changed to *Bloudruk/Blueprint* in February 1995 as a monthly publication. *Sanlammer* called up too-vivid images of the patriarchal Head Office culture. There was a need for a more neutral company name. The *Sanlammer* was terminated at the end of 2000, which left twenty months of no internal staff magazine. The publication for Sanlam advisers, *Sandaba*, was established in 1998 and in September 2002 assumed the role of an in-house staff magazine again. It conveyed much of the complex transformation process at Head Office, but also the search for inclusivity around the corporate image of a dynamically changing financial services company.

Daling's vision for Sanlam Ltd was to be the leading South African financial services group, the benchmark of excellence, a company perpetuating its legacy as a company of empowerment. Sanlam implemented black economic empowerment and employment

[111] SA: 5/3/4: March 1990: Desmond Smith statement on Sanlam Corporate Identity.

[112] SA: Minutes of Sanlam Board, 6/12/2000. This memorandum 'Progress report on the multi-brand strategy for the Group' was discussed by the board, but not ratified. It was minuted that Daling had withdrawn the proposal to change the name of Sanlam Ltd.

[113] SA: Minutes of Sanlam Board, 29/10/1997: Memorandum: J.H. Brown: Verslag van korporatiewe beeld.

equity as a simple strategy—doing what we do best and have done since 1918. In the roll-out of corporate social involvement the focus was on education, training, entrepreneurship, and personal development, especially through sport. The signature corporate social engagement of Sanlam was its sponsorship of the *Takalani Sesame* educational series for school readiness development in South Africa. Sanlam acquired the USA *Sesame Street* licence and adapted the programme for South African requirements. *Takalani Sesame* was a radio and television programme to reach children across the wide and stretched out South African landscape. The series commenced in 2000 and is still running. From 1995 the Sanlam corporate social investment programme covered sponsorships to educational institutions (universities, colleges, and schools), cultural activities, entrepreneurship and employment creation, health and welfare projects, and service to communities through the construction of buildings and complexes for public use.[114] At 1 per cent of operating profit, Sanlam's corporate social investment was not completely philanthropic, but aimed at a target market aligned with the changing profile of its policyholders. A notable shift was the increased focus on the youth in black, Coloured, and Indian communities, especially with respect to health and sports activities. The triangular relationship between branding and the preservation and strengthening of the corporate identity, enhancing the public image of the company through corporate communication management, and corporate social investment, was a complex and delicate matter. These functions were not logically coordinated, since different business units in Sanlam seemed to administer their own corporate social investment programmes. Consolidation seemed imminent, but Daling had not addressed it by 2000.

Sudden change in the game

Marinus Daling was a brilliant actuary and business strategist. He wanted demutualization and he drove it through in record time. By August 2000 he had lots of unfinished business: Santam had emerged as the leading short-term insurer in South Africa, but was still recovering from the substantial underwriting losses suffered in late 1990. After the acquisition in 2000 of the full share capital of Guardian National Insurance (GNI) (with approval from the Competition Commission) for R1.57 billion, and the appointment of Johan van Zyl as CEO on 1 August 2001, it was hoped that Sanlam's 55 per cent stake in Santam would start delivering positive results. Santam made a rights issue to fund the GNI acquisition. Sanlam followed its rights to a cost of R316 million to the shareholders' fund and R684 million to the policyholders' fund (of the latter, R618 million was placed with

[114] SA: 5/2: Memorandum: Sanlam Korporatiewe Maatskaplike Betrokkenheidsprogram, 7/10/1995; 5/2: Memorandum: Sanlam's contribution to the Reconstruction and Development of South Africa, 16/4/1998.

institutional investors, leaving the policyholders' fund an exposure of only R66m).[115] Santam moved to a 17 per cent market share, which secured the former Afrikaans company the leading short-term position. Unfortunately, undisclosed irregularities in GNI could not be recovered by May 2001. An internal audit committee noted the 'unacceptable state of the finance control environment and accounting records of GNI prior to the merger'. Total write-offs amounted to R30 987 819. This amount related to the pre-merger period and was not disclosed to Santam. Another problem that surfaced after the merger was that GNI had failed to recover long-outstanding balances, and that some reinsurers' accounts had not been rendered for two years. This merger was the most important development in Santam's strategy to grow its market share, but came at an initial cost. In a statement to the JSE, Santam declared that 'the merger of the two companies would create the leading short-term insurer in South Africa with a well-balanced business profile and the ability to deliver world-class standards of customer service, productivity levels and shareholder value creation'.[116] The positive spin-offs included improved underwriting expertise and growth opportunities in the commercial sector and electronic commerce. Johan van Zyl, who joined the Sanlam board in August 2001 as Chief Executive Officer of Santam, managed these turbulent post-merger times in Santam. The Santam acquisition of GNI also ushered in the transformation of the still predominantly Afrikaans insurer to a national South African icon.

Other ills remained for Daling in Sanlam. There was the ailing Sanlam Health with perpetual shrinking membership. A difficult two years between 1999 and 2001 of searching for a buyer for Sanlam Health finally came to a close in 2001 when the Sanlam board agreed to an exit strategy from this business, and Medscheme bought SHQM and SHAM. The struggling asset management operations and consistently underperforming Gensec was finally integrated in the Sanlam Group, but at a price too high for Daling's peace of mind. The ABSA talks were not making noticeable progress. In Namibia, Sanlam Namibia, which was dually listed on the Namibian Stock Exchange at the time of Sanlam's listing on the JSE, developed stable and extensive business in the country. Sanlam Namibia as a legal entity was never listed separately in the NSX. Sanlam Namibia immediately after listing issued policies in terms of the Namibian insurance legislation. Sanlam Namibia operates under the Sanlam brand name, although in various legal entities across a number of business units, including insurance and investment products. Internationalization was still not part of an integrated strategy. While Daling bravely soldiered on at Sanlam and all the subcommittees and subsidiary boards, the writing was on the wall. In January 2001 the search was on for his successor. From June 2001, Daling resigned from the multitude of subcommittees in Sanlam and was unable to attend the December 2001 board meeting. He passed away on 1 February 2002.

[115] SA: Minutes of Sanlam Board, 9/2/2000.

[116] SA: Minutes of Santam Board, 10/11/2002.

Early in 2001 Daling indicated that he would step down as Sanlam CEO, but remain in his capacity as Chairman. The board made it clear that his successor had to be a leader and strategist who could take Sanlam to the new dimension the company strove for: 'to be recognized by our stakeholders and our international partners as the benchmark of excellence for financial services where we operate'.[117] The decision to appoint Dr Leon Vermaak, Managing Director of Santam, as the CEO of Sanlam Ltd came as a surprise. The reason for the surprise was that Vermaak had not worked in long-term insurance before, he was a marketing expert, but Daling favoured him. Vermaak had served Santam as Assistant General Manager: Marketing since May 1995, but moved into the position of Managing Director from 1 July 1999. He was the person called upon to succeed Daling from 1 May 2001. Johan van Zyl succeeded Vermaak as CEO of Santam and from 1 August 2001 he joined the Sanlam executive committee as Santam's CEO. As Vice-Chancellor of the University of Pretoria, Van Zyl had been a non-executive independent director of Sanlam since 2000. Vermaak entered a Sanlam of extensive unfinished business.

At the first board meeting he attended in June 2001, new members were welcomed to the board. As Kate Jowell, Murray Grindrod, and Flip Smith had resigned as directors, Vermaak used the opportunity to add more black directors to the board. The new directors were Prof. André Perold of the University of Stellenbosch Business School, Messrs Thulani Gcabashe and Peter Vundla (both prominent black businessmen), as well as Johan van Zyl. A new company secretary, Xoliswa Motswai, was also appointed.[118] Vermaak immediately made changes to the executive structures in Sanlam. He merged the SPF and SEB business units to become Sanlam Life under Executive Manager Hendrik Bester. Vermaak argued that the trend had become individual choice. That meant the same or similar solutions to all clients, be that on individual or group levels. Nick Christodoulou was appointed Executive Manager: New Business Development, primarily to exploit synergies between or across existing business divisions in the Group. Vic van Vuuren in Human Resources was appointed Executive Manager: Human Resources, while Johan van Zyl assumed an executive position as a result of his position at Santam. Mr Bohang Mohale joined the executive team as Head: Corporate Marketing. John Moalusi former Deputy Executive Head of SEB, was relieved of his executive functions to allow him to focus on sales. These changes ruffled feathers. Hendrik Bester resigned at the end of 2001 and Xoliswa Motswai left in August 2002. The first woman member of the executive team, Lizé Lambrechts, succeeded Hendrik Bester at the helm of SPF.

At a time when markets were recovering from the effects of the 1998 East Asian crisis, Sanlam kept limping. The operational results failed to excite analysts. As shown in

[117] SA: Minutes of Sanlam Board, 7/2/2001: Sanlam Vision/Group strategy.

[118] Motswai was a corporate lawyer, but in 2002 stepped down 'for medical reasons' and was succeeded by Mr J.P. Bester as Sanlam Company Secretary.

Table 5.6. Sanlam performance 1998–2002

	1998	2000	2002
Total group equity (Rm)	21 952	27 238	27 087
Total assets (Rm)	17588	178065	18357
Headline earnings (Rm)	1 186	2 406	2 127
Embedded value (EV) per share (cps)	827	1035	1032
Return on EV %	−0%	5.1%	−9.2%
Total issued shares (m)	2 654.5	2 654.5	2 654.5
Earnings per share (cps)	58.4	90.6	80.8
Share price (cents)	585	956	760
Dividend per share	–	30	37
Capital Adequacy Ratio (CAR)	1.7	2.4	1.7

Source: Sanlam annual financial statements, 1998–2002.

Table 5.6, headline earnings declined by 12 per cent between 2000 and 2002. The EV per share followed the same trend as return on EV declined by 9.2 per cent between 2000 and 2002. Sanlam's CAR improved from 1.7 in 1998, to 2.4 in 2000, but then weakened to 1.7 again in 2002.

A sense of discontent could be read between the lines in the board proceedings. Sharp criticism was voiced against the destruction of value that had occurred in Sanlam, witnessed in declining headline earnings and weaker return on EV. When Vermaak referred to ABSA and Gensec as legacies of the past, one director bluntly remarked that had Sanlam only sustained the performance record of ABSA over the recent period, Sanlam would have been bigger than SA Mutual. The executive team and members of the board had become disillusioned with the leadership of Vermaak. He fell short of the expectations to deliver on strategic management to a diversified financial services company. Market perceptions were negative. During the ongoing merger discussions with ABSA, it became apparent that he had harboured ambitions to lead the massive new financial services entity once the merger had been completed. Stalwarts in Sanlam were skeptical about the ability of such a merger to add real value to Sanlam. While it made sense to walk away from a merger with ABSA, Vermaak had other ideas and ambitions. Vermaak insisted on pursuing the ABSA deal, while the rest of the board and executive team did not want to do so. It came down to either Vermaak and ABSA, or no Vermaak, and adherence to the Daling position on ABSA. This difference of opinion illustrated the strategic disconnect between Vermaak and the rest of the executive management team and directors on several matters, by then clearly illustrated by the drawn-out merger discussions with ABSA. It was finally Rademeyer's hunch that a possible hostile takeover might be lurking, that cooled merger talks off.

There was no longer time for Sanlam to sail aimlessly on the ocean of the South African financial services industry. Analysts were earnestly looking for signs of strategic direction at Sanlam. The company organized a two-day presentation for financial analysts in January 2001, an event that afforded Sanlam the opportunity to explain the depth of the business. This was well received, but could not forestall the growing uncertainty about leadership. A recurring theme was the persistent outflows from Sanlam life business and contracting market share. The Sanlam market share dropped from 26.97 per cent in 1997 to 12.09 per cent in 2003. Although this was an industry-wide experience (except for Momentum and Investec growing market share marginally), Sanlam lost proportionally more than the other market players. In response to the 2000 financial results, Deutsche Securities referred to the 'massive uncertainty surrounding the CEO', exacerbated by the highest outflows in the industry. Sanlam lost R5 billion in 2002 (3.8 per cent of the life fund), which was an improvement on the R6 billion in 2001, but the outflow from SA Mutual was only 2 per cent. Liberty gained a 6 per cent increase in fund inflows and Momentum 2 per cent. Sanlam had lost the confidence of investors and ordinary people. At the same time the return on embedded value of 12.7 per cent at Sanlam in 2002 was below industry performance. Liberty posted a 29 per cent return on its embedded value, SA Mutual 24 per cent, and momentum 18 per cent. The weakness in Sanlam's performance remained the same as in previous years: SIM underperformed, Gensec Bank 'had another poor result' with its international business profits after tax, declining by 26 per cent. Assets under management declined, while Sanlam built infrastructure, doubling expenses, in its international operations amid severe pressure on revenues from asset management and the IFA business. The message was unequivocal: Gensec does not fit in with the Sanlam business and should be disposed of. The international business needed fundamental reconceptualization.[119]

When Sanlam announced decreased bonuses on life policies in 2002, negative bonus stabilization reserves of 10 per cent meant at least a three-year delay in restoring bonus growth. The overall looming negative sentiment was all about management. Sustained and market-leading underperformance in growing its share of new business, continued record outflows, and sustained poor investment results threatened to erode the benefits of demutualization. Daling was a strong leader, but not Vermaak. Daling was instrumental in the appointment of Leon Vermaak as his successor. The last board meeting he attended was in September 2001. It took twenty months for the executive management team (excluding Vermaak) and the board to realize that the new CEO did not have the capacity to manage a diversified financial services group, especially not a recently demutualized group grappling with the hasty and fundamental change in organizational form and operations. The decision to ask Vermaak to step down was taken by members of the board and some executives. The board minutes never reported on the decision. There was also no mention of the departure of Vermaak in the official annual report of

[119] D. Shochot: Deutsche Securities: Sanlam Ltd: 7/3/2003; H. Uys: Cazenove: Sanlam Company update, 5/9/2001; H. Uys: Cazenove: Sanlam Company update, 6/3/2003; M. Brown: CLSA: Emerging markets: SA companies update, 29/1/2001.

2002. The board confirmed the decision in December 2002 and started the search for a person who could 'fix the return on Sanlam's capital and long-term transformation' of the company. Flip Rademeyer acted as CEO since December 2002, but on 25 March 2003 the board announced the appointment of Dr Johan van Zyl, CEO of Santam, to assume the position of CEO of Sanlam from 31 March 2003. He was hailed for his leadership and transformation capabilities displayed as Vice-Chancellor at the Afrikaans and conservative University of Pretoria, and moreover, his good relationship with the government and ruling party.[120] The significance of such interpersonal relationships resonated well in Sanlam, since Marinus Daling's relationship with Thabo Mbeki since the late 1980s afforded Sanlam access to social capital that was much needed in times of tough business conditions.

Van Zyl had a clear understanding of the dilemma facing Sanlam. He understood that the industry was under siege, but also identified fundamental shortcomings at Sanlam. The uncertainty surrounding the departure of Vermaak resulted from visionary and leadership shortcomings and were exacerbated by unrealistic stakeholder expectations. The old ways of doing business in Sanlam were not changed after demutualization, but the market of operations did change fundamentally. The business structure was cumbersome and executive leadership functioning suboptimal. Having worked with Sanlam since he joined the board, and as executive director following his appointment as CEO of Santam, afforded Van Zyl a holistic assessment of operations. He saw radical changes as the only viable strategy. The lacklustre commitment and delivery needed a clear strategy, allowing the company choices and from that a clear direction. Hard business decisions needed to be taken as part of a simple clear business model, aiming at a 10 per cent real return on capital. That was not negotiable. Soft issues such as client-centricity, BEE, and employment equity were sure contributors to the sustainability of a growth trajectory. Van Zyl was clear in his mind about the restructuring of management and operations across the entire group.[121] His clarity of analysis and vision on the solution made him the obvious choice. He was part of Sanlam, but not from within, and understood strategy as a tool towards turning an organization around.

Demutualization was implemented with urgency and speed. What a diversified financial service group would be as distinct from a life office, had not been thought through sufficiently to establish a new business model after listing. The acquisition of Gensec turned out not to be the right choice for Sanlam. The death of Daling left Sanlam exposed to extensive unfinished adjustments. Vermaak was not ready to bring about the strategic redirection Sanlam needed. Leon Vermaak stood outside the financial service business and never grasped the complexity of the fundamental reconstruction required to consolidate operations around a core of financial services. Perhaps Daling, as a Sanlam

[120] SA: Minutes of Sanlam Ltd Board, 25/3/2003.

[121] SA: J. v Zyl: Presentation to Sanlam Human Resources Committee, 26/1/2003.

actuary his entire professional life, had detailed knowledge about operations, but failed to institute a consolidation and efficiency enhancing plan while in office. He was a 'Mintzberg manager'—a person who was part of the deeply ingrained culture of the organization, in this case the former mutual, Sanlam. To transform that organizational culture required distance. The successful overhaul of a conservative life office to become a diversified financial services company required radically innovative macrostrategic thinking. His engagement with Sanlam through many phases of its development, his apprenticeship under Fred du Plessis, the Sankorp restructuring exercise, and his brilliant ability to spot the traps facing Sanlam, did not yet deliver the successful business model required at the time of his death. A new holistic business model was wanting. Sanlam was suffering from the acquisition drive legacies of the 1980s and owned underperforming assets. By the end of 2002 the company was at a crossroads: either it had to think in a radically different way about its direction, or face humiliating sustained loss of its industry position.

6 Affirming the roots

Sanlam from South Africa for South Africa and beyond, 2003–2013

The new millennium dawned upon a Sanlam braving stormy seas. Investors and policyholders increasingly moved away from traditional long-term life assurance products, seeking new wealth products. South Africa was entering the first decade of its new democratic political order, but the business environment in emerging markets weakened. The impact of the global financial crisis (GFC), which hit the developed world in 2007/08, affected emerging markets soon thereafter. Real GDP growth in South Africa was down to −1.5 per cent in 2009, but recovered to 3 per cent in 2010 and 2011. Soon afterwards the domestic economy entered a consistent downward spiral of slow growth, low productivity, and socio-political uncertainty. In the global economy GDP growth in advanced economies also slumped since 2004 and moved into negative territory from 2010, leaving emerging markets to follow the trend. The slow recovery in developed countries effectively pulled developing markets into slow growth. The South African situation was exacerbated by domestic political volatility caused by the political tension in the ruling ANC party. President Thabo Mbeki dismissed his deputy Jacob Zuma in 2004. Tables were turned when Zuma was elected ANC President in 2009. The South African economy also went into recession for the first time in seventeen years. Real GDP per capita growth declined consistently from 1.8 per cent in 2008 to 0.6 per cent in 2013. Inward foreign direct investment as a proportion of GDP slumped from 3.44 per cent in 2008 to 2.24 per cent in 2013, and gross government debt rose from 27.2 per cent in 2008 to 44 per cent in 2013. Not even hosting the Soccer World Cup tournament in 2010 could provide a large enough financial injection for a sustained economic recovery in South Africa. Business witnessed growing regulatory intervention, both locally and internationally. Government regulatory intervention in South Africa affected the insurance industry. State regulation of pension and retirement funds administration was introduced. The state also intervened in the market for financial services by publishing policy statements on the introduction of a state-administered health system and comprehensive state social security provision. A climate of policy uncertainty emerged. When former President Nelson Mandela passed away in 2013, the socio-political landscape in South Africa entered a new period of volatility. The financial services sector was left to manage both policy uncertainty and weakened economic conditions. Sanlam entered this challenging decade under new leadership.

Restoring value

Winning the demutualization race left the protagonists with a company not fully prepared for the new financial services market into which it had turned. The new Sanlam did not escape from the legacies of its past. Sanlam's relationship to ABSA remained unresolved to Sanlam's satisfaction. Santam performed sluggishly and delivered unexpected 'surprises' inherited from the acquisition of GNI. Gensec still suffered from a clash of cultures and personalities. The long-term insurance market suffered from a contracting public appetite for the traditional life policy. The brilliance and market-respected personality of Marinus Daling obscured the operational constraints emerging from the failure to effect a fundamental company repositioning in the new financial services context of a listed entity. Managing the legacies was not what the new Sanlam needed, but a reconceptualization of the world of a diversified financial services company in the competitive environment created by global deregulation. The business needed redressing. A serious disfavour Daling unintentionally did to Sanlam was to land the struggling company with an inexperienced successor. However, unnoticed, another more able successor was being groomed to stage the recovery plan. This was a Fiedler contingency model leader, a person combining insight into the context of the business and a personal task-oriented leadership style suited to inspire subordinates to perform at a high level and focus on task accomplishment. He personified the traits of the leadership model—intelligence, knowledge, and expertise, dominance, self-confidence, high energy, tolerance for stress, integrity, honesty, and maturity—and put them to use as a transformational manager.[1] At the ABSA retail board and as Santam CEO, Johan van Zyl had gained a broad insight into industry developments. As an agricultural economist, considering the macro perspective came naturally. As the contingency model suggests, Van Zyl assumed the executive position at Sanlam at a time when the demutualization gains proved insufficient. In Sanlam Life alone, capital to the value of between R14 and R15 billion was estimated to be necessary for long-term sustainability of the life business.[2] The stalemate at Sanlam was that there was no clarity of vision or agreed business model to steer the company through the rough seas and help it come into its own, capable of outperforming the rest. In identifying the critical issues faced by a stagnating Sanlam,

[1] G.R. Jones and .JM. George (2009): *Contemporary Management*, 6th edition, McGraw-Hill: 504–8; 513–14.

[2] SA: Minutes of Sanlam Ltd Board, 3/12/2003: Confidential memorandum: capital management Framework, JPM/2003/11/26.

Van Zyl articulated the negative market sentiment. Weak customer relationships undermined the delivery of value specific services to each business unit. The business model of a diversified financial services conglomerate had to function from a single group vision, managed from the centre and implemented in the different business units.[3]

In May 2003, immediately after his appointment, Van Zyl explained that the business model he would implement consisted of a complexity of business clusters, but with critical governance and co-ordination from the centre, which was at Group level. Head Office had to be a simple lean structure managing the Group on a principle of tight/loose control. As a financial services company, the focus was on the client, therefore the simple guiding operational principle was 'client-centric wealth creation'. In order to achieve that, the company had to go back to basics. The focus was on delivery, to all stakeholders—add value to shareholders and policyholders and all other clients through a client-centred approach. Van Zyl grounded the transformation strategy in existing expertise—the individual/retail market, as well as the corporate market. The business was about wealth creation and protection within financial services, and in all the different segments of the value chain—product development, packaging, and distribution. Sanlam was strong in the middle market, but its presence in the high-net-worth individual markets required focused tightening and development. Entering the mass market was contingent on the ability to create wealth and protect it. In the corporate market, retirement funds and employee benefits had to regain priority. The merchant banking operations were not Sanlam's core business and therefore Gensec had to be relocated. The old way of conducting business was no longer adequate, income diversification was needed, and the crippling dependence on traditional channels had to become more flexible distribution channels at lower associated costs. The business model operated from a centre with autonomous underlying businesses managed at arm's length. The Group would manage the individual business units on a portfolio basis, but encouraged innovation and maximum choice, seeking maximum 'share of the wallet' on a strong brand. The successful implementation of the strategy depended on a collective effort of the team of business leaders responsible for the operating businesses, aligned to corporate head office strategy. Sanlam needed to cut costs and Van Zyl undertook to effect a R250m cost reduction per annum in Sanlam Life. Sanlam then introduced a portfolio management system, with clear goals and targets for individual businesses, priorities, and incentives. What had to go, needed to go as soon as possible.[4]

The revised business structure of the Sanlam Group took shape before the end of that year. Restructuring commenced with the reintroduction of an Executive Committee consisting of the executives of the business units and group management. This was the forum where Van Zyl brought a leadership team into the realm of the new business

[3] SA: J. van Zyl presentation to Sanlam HR Committee, 30/1/2003.

[4] Ibid.: Minutes of Board, 12/5/2003; 4/6/2003.

Table 6.1. Contribution to Sanlam financial performance, 2003

2003	Sanlam Life	SIM	Santam	Banking	Sanlam independent financial services
Contribution to group profit before tax–%	60	12	31	–	–
Contribution to new business inflows–%	23	55	17	–	–

Source: Sanlam annual report, 2003.

philosophy and disseminated the strategic vision of group performance built on autonomy on underlying levels. The restructured business units were: Sanlam Life, with Lizé Lambrechts as Chief Executive; short-term insurance in Santam with Steffen Gilbert as Chief Executive; Sanlam Investment Management (SIM) under Johan van der Merwe as CEO; the banking unit comprising Gensec under Anton Botha as Chief Executive; and Sanlam Independent Financial Services with Nic Christodoulou as Chief Executive. The contribution of each business unit to Sanlam Group's profit before tax and new business inflows at the end of 2003 was as shown in Table 6.1. The life business contributed 60 per cent to group profits before tax, but only 23 per cent to new business inflows, SIM contributed 12 per cent to profits and 55 per cent to new business inflows, and Santam contributed 31 per cent to profits but 17 per cent to new business inflows.

The unbalanced distribution between the contribution to profit and new business inflows called for rectification. The life unit conducted individual life and group life insurance, estate and trust management in Sanlam Trust, money management and payment systems through Multi Data. Life insurance in the UK was conducted through Merchant Investors Assurance, and mobile phone insurance through Sanlam Customized Insurance. The life business in Namibia was conducted through Sanlam Namibia, and group retirement administration through Total Care Strategy in which Sanlam held a 60 per cent share. Sanlam Life offered personal loans through Direct Axis, in which Sanlam had a 70 per cent share. Santam conducted the full range of short-term insurance. SIM housed a variety of investment functions—investment management; Octane Management (an alternative investment platform in SIM); Innofin, the investment channel to the high-net-worth market; Sanlam Collective Investments (managing Sanlam's unit trusts); Sanlam Multi Managers International; Sanlam Property Management; Sanlam Private Equity, and Tasc, an independent UK administrator of third-party funds. These entities were the preliminary structures of the functional restructuring Van Zyl wanted, but were bound to adapt to the unfolding of the strategic rebuilding of the core financial services business. Dynamic changes occurred as the strategy materialized.

Management took a holistic macro view of the extensive scale of internal business repositioning needed. Between 2003 and 2006 some initiatives had to be concluded, others terminated, and substantial efficiency enhancement and cost-saving exercises executed with clinical precision. The crucial strategic entity was the Group Executive

Committee. This was a deviation from the management styles of both Daling and Vermaak. This Group Executive Committee gave practical effect to Van Zyl's management style of strategic leadership rolled out on the strength of the team of expert business leaders heading up the operational units. The committee comprised of Van Zyl as Group CEO, Nick Christodoulou (IFS), Steffen Gilbert (Santam), Lizé Lambrechts (Sanlam Life), Kobus Möller (Finance), Temba Mvusi (Group Corporate Services), Flip Rademeyer (Financial Director), Chris Swanepoel (Actuary), and Johan van der Merwe (SIM). The areas of priority were the consolidation in the life business, streamlining SIM, and the relationship with Gensec, addressing internationalization and consolidating the image of Sanlam as a South African citizen.

Central to improved operational efficiency and profitability, as well as allocating resources towards the business units targeted in the turnaround strategy, was the management of capital. Financial analysts were somewhat disturbed by Sanlam's preoccupation with embedded value (EV) after demutualization. While fundamental strategic direction seemed absent and performance weak and declining, the crucial business imperative was return on embedded value. In essence the turnaround strategy lay in optimal return on capital, EV, and this position was endorsed by the board in May 2003. Sanlam embarked on a systematic capital management strategy. The responsibility to conceptualize and map out the strategy fell to Flip Rademeyer and Kobus Möller. This core matter in the future strategic positioning of Sanlam functioned like the brain in relation to the body: return on capital targets came from the centre and implemented in the decentralized business units to allow for business-specific decentralized decision making. The parameters of return on capital management were to earn between 3 per cent and 4 per cent above the ten-year bond yield. In 2003 this meant Sanlam targeted a 13 per cent to 14 per cent return on its capital. The company was again embarking on a process of building capital, just as had been the case before demutualization. 'Sanlam Corporate' (Group management at Head Office) called on the highest level of co-operation of all role players (business unit managers and their respective management teams) to render commitment. It took responsibility for the composition of the Group's asset base, investment risk profile, and overall return earned on capital. Raising capital, governing strategic investment decisions, and allocating appropriate capital to the different business units were central corporate responsibilities. Similar responsibilities were placed at the business units dealing with the capital allocated to them. In the case of Sanlam Life, 40 per cent of Sanlam Ltd's strategic investments (in ABSA, Santam, and SIM) was held by Sanlam Life and thus restricted the flexibility of operation of the business unit. Until this impairment could be addressed, Life would have to work with Group Corporate on capital management.[5]

[5] SA: Minutes of Sanlam Board: Memorandum J.P. Möller: Capital Management (Part 2): 12/5/2003.

Capital management was the beginning of taking control of Sanlam back to the centre. In typical contingency model leadership behaviour, the new CEO used the path-goal strategy[6] to bring the management of business units into the overall strategy to restore growth to Sanlam. The capital management function calculated the market value (fair value) of the strategic subsidiaries (Santam, Gensec Bank, SIM, SI, and Gensec Properties) at R5 497 million in August 2003, and set a target of a 14 per cent return. The total group capital at the end of 2003 was R2.7 billion, with a total EV of R26.84 billion. The constraint on capital was the very high exposure of 40 per cent of Sanlam Life's capital to its strategic investments. Those investments were non-discretionary, which prevented Sanlam Life from complying with new FSB capital adequacy requirements. The Sanlam Life capital shortfall could be addressed by reducing the exposure to ABSA. The reduction of Sanlam's stake in ABSA to below 20 per cent was negotiated in an agreement with ABSA management and Rembrandt. A second possibility to secure capital for application in the Group, specifically Sanlam Life, was a BEE transaction.[7]

Addressing the relationship with ABSA moved to centre stage. The return on the investment in ABSA continued to concern management. During August 2003 a Memorandum of Understanding was finally signed, providing for a distribution agreement on a dedicated service channel for ABSA brokers, assistance with data brokers and Sanlam reinsurance for ABSA life products. Sanlam decided to launch home loans as a product in the life business, hoping to attract new business into the life business unit. This was offered as a joint venture with ABSA, but was not a bancassurance agreement, which was what had been a long-standing proposition discussed in Sanlam since the mid-1990s. In August 2004 Sanlam put a bancassurance proposal to ABSA. There was reserved optimism about the proposal. On the one hand Sanlam was averse to the risks in the mass market, which was a market segment in which ABSA had considerable exposure. Sanlam could benefit from access to the massive ABSA client base, but Van Zyl was on record as cautioning against targeting the mass lower end of the market. The possibility of underperforming policies, similar to the early experience in the industrial insurance market, were contemplated. He reiterated this view during a subsequent management '*bosberaad*'. Sanlam Life's recovery strategy was also not prioritizing the mass market. During discussions on bancassurance it became clear that the terms of possible collaboration were tailored to favour ABSA and not to deliver optimal value to Sanlam. A degree of collaboration resulted from initiatives to sell Sanlam products through ABSA brokers, and on small businesses such as business bank brokers and financial services. Competition on investments resulted in some tension, because Sanlam insisted

[6] A path-goal management strategy refers to a clear goal-oriented strategy formulated by management, into which other managers are systematically introduced and integrated.

[7] SA: Minutes of Sanlam Ltd Board, 3/12/2003: Memorandum J.P. Möller: Capital Management Framework.

that investments were its turf. Developing a sound understanding of the framework of collaboration inevitably brought turf contestation. Sanlam delayed the launch of new life products jointly with ABSA early in 2004.[8] The negotiations on bancassurance became increasingly intertwined with the talks about the disposal of Sanlam's shareholding in ABSA.

During February 2004 when Van Zyl and Rademeyer were in London on a roadshow communicating the Sanlam 2003 annual results, an analyst tipped them off that Barclays was seeking an avenue back into South Africa. Since Sanlam wanted to reduce its shareholding in ABSA but recognized the potential consequences of the termination of this very long-standing relationship, or even just reducing that stake substantially, as well as the impact any reconfiguration of shareholding may have on Rembrandt, Sanlam tested the waters on a potential buyer of its entire shareholding. The talks with HSBC and Citi Bank of New York failed to deliver substantive results, but Standard Charter was interested. The lead to Barclays finally opened a door to a solution to a long-standing concern for Sanlam. When it transpired that a deal might be in the making, Van Zyl appointed Deutsche Bank to advise Sanlam. A working committee of the Sanlam Board consisting of the new Chairman Roy Andersen, Carmen Maynard, Patrice Motsepe and Eugene van As (the Sanlam board members in Johannesburg), Johan van Zyl, Jeanne Masson, Kobus Möller and Johan Bester from the executive management in Sanlam, and four representatives of Deutsche Bank in London, Johannesburg and Cape Town, was formed to conduct the negotiations on the possible transaction. During 2004 and 2005 the possible deal with Barclays had a profound impact on the future of Sanlam.

When the term of certain directors lapsed, new directors were appointed. Van Zyl followed an explicit strategy to bring in leadership and managerial strengths from diverse backgrounds to infuse innovative thinking in Sanlam. These people served Sanlam exceptionally well during the strategically sensitive negotiations with Barclays. In April 2004, Patrice Motsepe, Rejoice Simelane, and Bernard Swanepoel were appointed non-executive directors of Sanlam as part of a BEE transaction whereby Sanlam acquired a BEE shareholder. Patrice Motsepe, a prominent black professional (lawyer) and businessman, was pivotal to this first post-1994 Sanlam BEE transaction. Dr Rejoice Simelane held a PhD in Economics and served as economic adviser to the Premier of Mpumalanga Province. She assumed the CEO position of the BEE investment company established by Sanlam in 2004 (discussion follows). Bernard Swanepoel was an experienced mining engineer and an entrepreneur and had been CEO of Harmony Gold Mining for twelve years. He had a wealth of experience in the mining industry. A distinguished academic and later politician, Prof. Wilmot James of the Human Sciences Research Council was also invited onto the board of Sanlam in 2004. In June 2004 Maria Ramos, Valli Moosa, and Roy Andersen were also appointed non-executive

[8] SA: Minutes of Sanlam Ltd Board, 2 and 3/03/2004.

directors of Sanlam. Valli Moosa was a member of the ruling African National Congress, former Minister in the Cabinet of Nelson Mandela, and had just stepped down as Minister of Environmental Affairs under President Thabo Mbeki. Maria Ramos was also a leading ANC member and Director General of Treasury and the Department of Finance under the ANC government, before assuming the directorship at Sanlam. Ton Vosloo resigned his position as Chairman at the end of May 2004, affording the company the opportunity to appoint a new chairman during volatile economic conditions and difficult times for the industry. Roy Andersen was elected Chairman of the Sanlam Board in June 2004. He was held in high esteem in the financial services industry, since as a chartered accountant he was President of the JSE, CEO of Liberty Life, and later Chairman of Murray & Roberts. The depth of his experience in the corporate world was vital to Sanlam as the transaction with Barclays unfolded. From 3 June 2004 Roy Andersen was the new Sanlam Chairman, the first non-Afrikaans chairman.[9] He headed a much-transformed Sanlam board, with persons from outside the traditional Afrikaans business environment and in some cases from political convictions challenging the legacy Sanlam image. Van Zyl was instrumental in diversifying the profile of the directors as he re-engineered the business strategy of Sanlam.

The roll-out of the Van Zyl 2003 Sanlam strategy to create shareholder value, grow the business, and lift capital efficiency, began delivering positive results towards the end of 2004. Operating profit rose by 40 per cent and improved new business volumes contributed to a more encouraging net fund inflow position. The stabilization programmes intended to bring calm and confidence back to the organization and stage a turnaround strategy with a high success potential, seemed imminent. A stronger market performance gave further impetus to the talks with Barclays about acquiring Sanlam's stake in ABSA. If Sanlam could succeed in freeing up the capital invested in ABSA, it would bring the enhanced capital efficiency goal much closer. The decision involved a substantial section of the South African corporate landscape. The Sanlam decision to sell to Barclays involved consultation with, and preferably consensus with ABSA's BEE partners, the banking group's executive management, the regulators at the FSB and the SARB, and Remgro. Sanlam and Remgro had a pre-emptive rights agreement on each other's ABSA shares. Remgro was willing to waive the agreement in case of a sale of its stake to Barclays. The bancassurance negotiations with ABSA made unsatisfactory progress. In the discussions ABSA rather sought to display independence from its major shareholders than move towards a mutually beneficial agreement with Sanlam. To the latter the distribution potential of a firm bancassurance agreement was imperative to secure the new business inflows needed, especially in the life business. Sanlam wanted a firm legal agreement on bancassurance from ABSA prior to the conclusion of the

[9] SA: Minutes of Sanlam Board, 10/4/2004; 24/5/2004; 2/6/2004. Roy Andersen is fully bilingual and speaks an immaculate Afrikaans.

transaction with Barclays, but ABSA was willing only to issue letters of intent. That was too uncertain for Sanlam, but ABSA was advised that a legal agreement posed an unacceptable risk to the transaction with Barclays. Finally, a firm legal agreement seemed difficult to enforce. ABSA later delivered written confirmation of willingness, intent, and commitment by both parties (ABSA and Sanlam) to implement the existing agreement on collaboration, and a commitment to provide Sanlam with a 30 per cent market share of its distribution by 31 December 2005. Barclays recognized this agreement in writing and undertook to support the arrangement in its final offer to Sanlam. Sanlam accepted the letter as confirmation that the bancassurance agreement the parties had concluded would deliver economic benefits in business flow reciprocity and sustain the relationship.[10]

The sale of Sanlam's ABSA shares was of dual significance: the release of tied-up capital, which was the crucial aspect on which a successful turnaround strategy at Sanlam depended, and significantly improved operational flexibility with less capital tied up in a single investment that failed to perform according to the investor's expectations. By September 2004 the conditions of a proposed transaction were on the table. Barclays targeted a 60 per cent stake in ABSA's issued share capital. It wanted irrevocable commitments from existing shareholders in ABSA to the effect of at least 40 per cent of the issued ABSA shares. Sanlam was prepared to commit its 19 per cent stake, there was a possibility that the policyholder fund would commit its 2 per cent as well, and Remgro was willing to commit its shares. Direct communication between Andersen and Motsepe for the ad hoc committee, and Barrett, Barclays Chairman, and David Roberts, Barclays' representative on the transaction, finally put to rest the hope for a legally enforceable agreement with ABSA on bancassurance. Sanlam simply had to rely on the letters of confirmation exchanged between ABSA and Sanlam on co-operation in terms of the MOU (Memorandum of Understanding) of 2003.[11]

It soon became apparent that significant progress on that matter was a pipedream. The more important matter was price. Talks started around R68 per share, which was a premium of 42 per cent on the ABSA share price of R48 at the time (September 2004). Remgro wanted R70, but Sanlam agreed to R68, as did ABSA. In November 2004 the Sanlam board ratified Sanlam's irrevocable offer to Barclays of the Sanlam and Sanlam policyholder fund's shares in ABSA. The Sanlam offer was valid to 31 March 2005 subject to shareholder approval. Although not a requirement, the board made the final offer subject to shareholder approval. The board of ABSA approved the terms of the proposed transaction on 19 November and on 22 November an official press statement confirmed the offer, the responses by shareholders in ABSA, and that regulatory

[10] SA: Minutes of the ad hoc subcommittee of the board regarding project X, 13/9/2004; 8/10/2004; 14/10/2004; 15/10/2004; 29/10/2004; SA: Confidential memorandum: Sale of investment in Absa, 12/11/2004.

[11] SA: Letter Steve Booysen (ABSA CEO) and Danie Cronjé (Chairman ABSA Board)—Johan van Zyl (Sanlam CEO), 5/11/2004.

approval was awaited. Negotiations were fragile by December 2004, since four parties had indicated an interest in transacting with Barclays, but exchange rate volatility could affect the price. Sanlam's Andersen was adamant: Sanlam's Plan B was to make Plan A work. When shareholder approval was given in January 2005, the transaction was only contingent on regulatory approval. Sanlam's offer was open until 31 March 2005, but regulatory approval in April 2005 finally secured the transaction.

Barclays was subjected to eight months of tortuous negotiations, resulting in an offer of R82.50 per ABSA share. Barclays failed to secure the 60 per cent stake in ABSA it desired, since certain institutional investors in South Africa refused to dispose of their shares. The transaction of R23.9 billion landed Barclays 53.96 per cent of the issued ABSA equity, giving the British bank full control of the largest retail bank in South Africa. To Barclays the transaction brought the bank that had entered the South African banking industry in 1926, but disinvested in 1986 following statutory requirements of domestic control of local banks, back into South Africa and thereby opened opportunities into the rapidly growing mass market in South Africa and the rest of Africa. It was also of historical significance: Barclays was the imperial bank that had acquired the ailing National Bank of the former Zuid-Afrikaansche Republiek (Transvaal Boer Republic) in 1926 and, through the acquisition of control of ASBA in 2005, also the last remaining former Afrikaner control of banks in South Africa. ABSA had absorbed into its conglomerate, numerous small banks, as were both Volkskas and Trust Bank—the two Afrikaner-controlled big commercial banks in South Africa—in 1992. To Sanlam the sale of its entire shareholding of 124.3 million ABSA shares, or its 21.3 per cent stake in ABSA, gave new life to the capital efficiency programme. With the R10.3 billion cash instead of the ABSA shares which were recognized in the Sanlam financial statements at market value, Sanlam immediately wiped out its capital shortfall. The ABSA transaction brought no capital 'inflow'. The value of ABSA in the Sanlam books at a value much lower than market value, changed with the transaction to an exceptionally high value. This accounting 'adjustment' managed to change Sanlam from a capital-hungry company to a capital-rich one. With the added cash the company could now portray its true capital-rich situation and buy back shares to reduce the excess capital. It was now in a position to acquire businesses able to grow its life business and buy back its own shares to the value of R4 billion.[12] The company strategy was now planned around alternative deployment opportunities for its surplus capital.

The significance of this transaction to Sanlam was both strategic and financial. The cash available changed the business landscape of Van Zyl's turnaround strategy. This put

[12] https://mg.co.za/article/2005-07-26-sanlam-finalise-sale-of-absa-stake-to-barclays; *Financial Times*, 9/5/2005: 'UK bank takes step back in time with S. African buy': p. 29; *Business Day*, 11/4/2005: 'Barclays set to buy major stake in Absa': http://www.economist.com/node/3915787: 'Absa's allure: Barclays finally lays out its bid': 28/4/2005; *Daily Telegraph*, 26/7/2005: 'Barclays takes S. African stake'.

Sanlam in a position to decide on the application of 'surplus' capital in business ventures offering good returns and eased the tense relationship with an underperforming strategic asset. The legacy of 'strategic' investments from the Fred du Plessis era was finally concluded. For the first time since 1973 when Sanlam acquired FVB's stake in Trust Bank, it no longer had a substantial stake (through the voting pool) in a South African bank. Management of the structural change in the Group suddenly became much easier. The conclusion of other strategic initiatives on the restructuring of Gensec Bank, and the conclusion of a major BEE transaction, were key components in the 'Delivery 2004' plan.

The Gensec saga was finally wound up as part of the strategic decision to drive capital management. Negotiations with ABSA to buy Gensec failed to deliver the desired outcome. The restructuring of Gensec commenced with the replacement of the CEO with immediate effect in August 2003. Anton Botha temporarily took over the position. A Gensec Bank Restructuring Committee was formed, reporting to the board on the progress with business overhaul and corporate governance. Sanlam Capital Markets (SCM) took control of Gensec Bank's former capital market operations. The restructuring was an integral part of group-wide capital management and the strategy to seek significant improvement in investment returns. In December 2003 SCM's fixed cost base was more than half less than that of Gensec Bank, while equity capital employed in Gensec amounted to R1.6 billion, compared to R400 million in SCM. The Gensec ROE (without write-downs, provisions, and restructuring costs) was 7.7 per cent, while SCM's was 21 per cent. Write-downs and provisions in Gensec amounted to in excess of R465 million. Gensec underperformed the investment bank index by more than 4 per cent per annum, which translated into a destruction of value to shareholders of approximately 12 per cent since the hasty acquisition of Gensec. There was no argument about the rationale for the intended restructuring. If the Gensec Bank aspirations of becoming a fully-fledged investment bank were realized, that would demand a further capital injection, which could not be justified in the greater scheme of capital management. SCM engaged in stock broking, capital market transactions, structured debt finance, and structured products. SCM disposed of a number of unprofitable operations and discontinued activities such as equity underwriting, corporate finance, project and structured finance, foreign exchange transactions, private equity, the operations in Ireland, deposit taking, and short-term corporate advances. SCM successfully moved into the capital market. In June 2004 the bank licence of Gensec was returned to the Registrar of Banks. All former Gensec business was integrated in the SCM operations. This action freed up further capital, available for better employment in the Group's capital management programme.[13] The Gensec episode concluded a clouded period of destruction of value at a time when Sanlam needed to grow its capital.

[13] SA: Minutes of Sanlam Ltd Board, 3/12/2003; 19/4/2004; 2/6/2004.

Truly South African

Part of the overall turnaround strategy was not only improved capital and operational efficiency, but also positioning Sanlam in the new transformed South Africa. In 2004 the Sanlam board received a 'transformation report' for the first time. To Van Zyl the success of business restructuring was market buy-in. Business success was premised on full compliance with transformation targets—in employment equity on all levels of the business, also management and oversight (the board), and BEE transactions to secure strong and reliable black partners for Sanlam in its quest to be the leading South African financial services group. Van Zyl was of the opinion that a strong BEE transaction would contribute to much-improved performance on other levels of the business, such as new business flows, investments, and the overall social disposition towards the company. Prior to his appointment as CEO in May 2003, the executive team commenced discussions on finding a major BEE partner for Sanlam. By October 2003 an MOU was signed between the empowerment group leader, Patrice Motsepe, who was advised by Bowman Gilfillan and J.P. Morgan, and Sanlam, supported by Jowell Glyn Marais as legal advisers, and to a limited degree also Deutsche Bank. Concluding a BEE transaction was not simply a matter of complying with political imperatives, but as Van Zyl articulated it, 'a pre-requisite to continue to do business in certain key markets'. There was no longer a shy away from the mass market, but a strategic drive to enter all segments of the black market, and to compete successfully with the other companies to acquire clients from competitors. The business considerations in the South African context related directly to the relationship between state and business. The ruling party's programme of statutorily enforced transfer of ownership and control of the domestic economy to those identified as the entitled majority, was intended to grow the economy inclusively, allowing the benefit of growth to reach the entire population. This policy resulted in the formulation of sector charters setting out the targets of effecting the charter goals of ownership and control. Sanlam was directly involved in the negotiations leading up to the signing of the Financial Sector Charter (FSC) in 2003. The charter formulated a scorecard for targets on direct ownership, employment equity procurement, and corporate social investment. The FSC took more than three years to arrive at a consensus position, including eleven industry players, such as the Black Business Council, the LOA, the Banking Council of South Africa, SAICA, the Association of Black Securities and Investment Professionals (Absip), the Department of Trade and Industry (DTI), the Treasury, and others. The FSC negotiated matters pertaining to management, control, employment equity, the appointment of black women in management, access to financial services by low-income earners, skills training, and empowerment funding. Compliance with the FSC is reflected in the B-BBEE score of Sanlam explained in Tables 6.4 and 7.1. Sanlam's Chief Executive: Employee Benefits, Themba Gamedze, expressed Sanlam's support for the charter, as 'it was the outcome of the first constructive engagement between black and white professionals and business'.[14]

Concluding a transaction to establish an empowerment partner for Sanlam comprised a central part of Van Zyl's business strategy to build the diversity profile of Sanlam. The FSC targeted black ownership of 10 per cent of financial institutions. In 2003 the Sanlam share price rose steadily, and a key consideration in the structuring of an empowerment transaction was that the sale of up to 10 per cent of its equity at any material market value discount that could potentially destabilize the upward trend, should be avoided.

The Ubuntu–Botho[15] transaction was signed in April 2004. This was a signature BEE transaction in South Africa and established a successful partnership between Sanlam and black business and communities. Two principles underscored the transaction. The deal had to result in a meaningful holding by the empowerment partner and the benefits had to be broad based. This meant the transaction had to provide for a definite mechanism for the benefits of the deal to flow through to 'black people'.[16] The transaction had to sustain black control and bring Sanlam an active business partner. The company had no interest in a high-profile transaction that would result in the disposal of the acquired shareholding as soon as possible. The new empowerment partners were expected to promote Sanlam and contribute to its growth. The transaction therefore formed an integral part of the Sanlam growth strategy.

Kobus Möller, the Group Executive: Finance, led the team thrashing out the composition and details of the technical structure of the funding of the transaction. A firm condition was that interested parties had to bring some of their own funding and that the transaction had to be concluded on fair value, therefore on strict business principles. To establish ownership of the transaction the parties agreed on a structure consisting of four components: the contribution of own capital, acquisition of finance on arm's-length terms, an active grant (free shares) as a wealth transfer component, and the potential to increase the holding through an 'earn in' mechanism. The 'earn in' principle was

[14] SA: Minutes of Sanlam Ltd Board, 2/6/2003; 6/8/2003; 28/10/2003; *Financial Mail*, 24/10/2003: 'Putting polish to the charter': 14; 'All cried out': 22–4.

[15] Ubuntu is an African cultural belief that calls on individuals to come together, to be communal in their outlook, or to look out for each other.

[16] See Broad-Based Black Economic Empowerment, Act 53 of 2003; Definitions: 'black people' is a generic term which means Africans, Coloureds, and Indians—

(a) who are citizens of the Republic of South Africa by birth or descent; or

(b) who became citizens of the Republic of South Africa by naturalization—

(i) before 27 April 1994; or

(ii) on or after 27 April 1994 and who would have been entitled to acquire citizenship by naturalization prior to that date;

[Definition amended by section 1(b) of Act No. 46 of 2013].

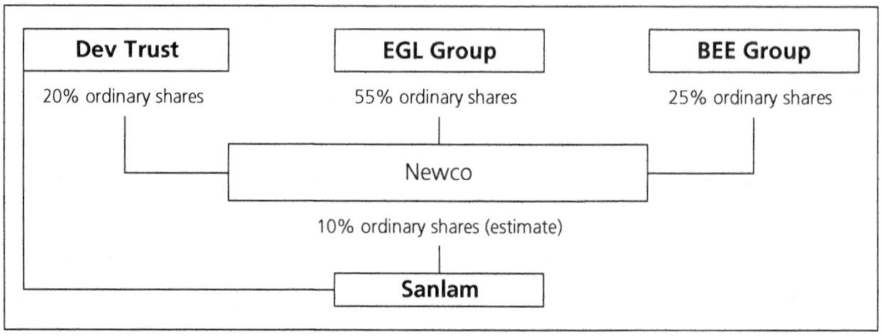

Figure 6.1. Provisional B-BBEE deal structure

based on the assumption that the new empowerment partner would bring new business and access to new markets to which Sanlam would not have had access without the intermediation of the new partner. Therefore a formula was agreed in terms of which value added by new business flows in specific Sanlam businesses would allow the new empowerment partner to 'earn' an additional 2 per cent stake in Sanlam through the conversion of deferred Sanlam shares issued to the empowerment partner. The condition was clear: work together to bring growth and the benefit would accrue to the new partner. This agreement had to remain in place for a minimum of ten years. While preference debt was in place, all dividend income would be used to repay debt. At the outset the transaction rested on patience, but the Sanlam executive was excited about the 'meeting of minds' on the rationale for and operation of the transaction between Sanlam and the new empowerment partners. New shareholders had to wait on and contribute to growth and performance of Sanlam to repay debt and earn dividend income directly. The structure of the deal is reflected in Figure 6.1.

The agreement in April 2004 established Ubuntu–Botho Investments (Pty) Ltd (UB). This was the 'newco'. The Empowerment Group Leader (EGL) group was the billionaire Patrice Motsepe's Sizanani-Thusanang-Helpmekaar Investments (a company owned by Motsepe and his family). The BEE group consisted of a spread of stakeholders, such as trade unions (which included SADTU and Nehawu), women and youth groups, religious and community organizations, as well as nine provincial companies from all the provinces in South Africa. This BEE group represented approximately 700 shareholders and acquired a 25 per cent in UB. This was what Sanlam meant by broad-based empowerment. As a key differentiating feature of the transaction, the EGL and BEE groups invested a total of R200 million of their own funds to acquire their respective 55 per cent and 25 per cent interests in UB. In a separate arrangement between the parties, the EGL group provided the funding for the BEE group's capital contribution. In addition, UB issued 'B' preference shares (approximately R750 million) to institutions, which would be redeemable in ten years, to raise the balance of the funds required to acquire just more than 4 per cent of Sanlam at the weighted average market value of 765 cents per share.[17]

The Demutualization Trust (DT) at the time held a balance of around 2 per cent (57 million shares) due to eligible Sanlam policyholders that could not be traced since demutualization. In terms of the demutualization rules, unallocated shares would revert to Sanlam in 2008, ten years after demutualization. Given the considerable effort to date by the DT to find the eligible policyholders, it appeared likely that the bulk of these shares would eventually revert to Sanlam. Management thus considered it appropriate to incorporate a component in the empowerment transaction structure that would effectively transfer the benefit of the value of the unclaimed shares to the broader community. Therefore, once the negotiations had reached a high degree of finality, Sanlam requested the DT to sell 52 million of its shares in Sanlam to UB. In return the DT would receive 52 million 'A' preference shares to the value of R389 million in UB. As security against any possible subsequent claims by eligible policyholders, the dividends paid by the UB preference shares would be 1.15 times that which it would have received on the Sanlam shares, while Sanlam would issue convertible shares to the DT that would be convertible into Sanlam ordinary shares as and when the DT received a claim to deliver Sanlam shares. On dissolution of the DT in 2008, ownership of the UB preference shares would be transferred to Sanlam and the Sanlam convertible shares cancelled. The trustees of the DT accepted the proposal after due consideration, including obtaining independent legal advice. The deal assisted the DT in raising an additional dividend income without risk,[18] while for Sanlam it was a neat way of utilizing the excess shares in the DT and assisting the company in structuring the BEE transaction. In a related leg of the transaction Sanlam issued a further 2 per cent new Sanlam shares to UB, in return for which Sanlam received a 20 per cent stake in UB. Sanlam donated this shareholding in UB to the UB-Sanlam Community Development Trust (UB Trust), which as a result became a 20 per cent shareholder in UB. The beneficiaries of the UB Trust would be the poor and disadvantaged communities in South Africa. While this would initially be a donation by Sanlam, it was essentially the transfer of the value that would eventually accrue to Sanlam on the dissolution of the DT in 2008.

In aggregate, in terms of the above UB acquired 8 per cent of Sanlam, which was funded by means of a R200m own capital contribution, redeemable preference shares for R1.15 billion, and the issue of a 20 per cent UB holding to the UB Trust.

UB further subscribed for 56.5 million Sanlam deferred shares at 1 cent per share. The deferred shares (with full voting power) would be fully convertible into a 2 per cent

[17] SA: Minutes of Sanlam Board, 28/10/2003: 3/12/2003; 3/2/2004; P. Ndzamela (2016): 'Ubuntu-Botho pays R830m dividend', https://www.businesslive.co.za/bd/companies/financial-services/2016-03-29-ubuntu-botho-pays-r830m-dividend/ (accessed 14/4/2016); www.bloomberg.com/markets.

[18] Sanlam Annual Report, 2004: 112–13.

holding in Sanlam ordinary shares based on achieving an appropriate level of value added in terms of an 'earn-in' formula. Should these deferred shares be fully converted prior to the expiry of the ten-year term of the transaction, UB would be entitled to subscribe for another 2 per cent of Sanlam deferred shares on similar terms. The transaction thus offered incentives to UB to become an active business partner of Sanlam and earn a growing stake in the company. The transaction also incentivized Sanlam to deliver growth and profits that would enable UB to repay debt and start reaping the benefits of its shareholding. Van Zyl travelled to all nine provinces with Motsepe to explain the transaction and encourage widespread buy-in. The 'earn-in' component of the transaction had a ten-year term and it was anticipated that all the transaction debt would be repaid within the ten years. After the conclusion of the transaction, Motsepe, Simelane, and Swanepoel were appointed directors on the Sanlam board. Motsepe was elected Deputy Chairman. The empowerment transactions resembled the early Sanlam empowerment of fellow-Afrikaners, now only a black empowerment entity targeting black communities. The vital difference is that Sanlam had no big sponsoring corporate backing a fast-track investment transaction delivering empowerment and wealth in the scope of less than a decade.

Sanlam acted strategically in concluding the UB transaction. Broad-based BEE was imperative for business in South Africa, but the business of empowerment was given substance with the UB model. At the same time, Sanlam experienced growing disengagement from its traditional support base, namely the Afrikaans client base following restructuring and implementation of EE policies. In the context of seeking to turn the outflow of business around, Sanlam did not take favourably to negative messages in the market, in this case from traditional Afrikaans clients. Although it was not a deliberate policy to defy Afrikaans and the traditionally Afrikaans client base, the implementation of transformation policies prescribed by statutes did affect part of Sanlam's market. Van Zyl received representatives of Solidarity, the powerful largely white Afrikaans trade union organization, and the Afrikanerbond (successor to the Afrikaner Broederbond), expressing concern over the impact of Sanlam's restructuring on its members. He lent a sympathetic ear, explaining that Sanlam did not wish to discriminate against any segment in society, but that the company was committed to transformation. This just emphasized the critical importance of communication with policyholders and shareholders during the repositioning of Sanlam. The company wanted to be a truly South African organization, calling on the loyalty of a diverse population and client base. While Sanlam undertook to consider the re-employment of people put out of work as a result of the implementation of transformation policies, the logic of its growth strategy mandated commitment to systematic penetration into the market outside its traditional and existing client base. The UB transaction aligned the Sanlam growth strategy with a dedicated entry-level market growth strategy. Growth in that market was also fundamental to the success of UB. As a signatory to the FSC, Sanlam was bound to the achievement of targets on EE, procurement, access to financial services, CSI, and BEE.

The momentum of 'back to basics' and the strategy of 'getting what we have to work efficiently' to create wealth began to bear fruit. The life business under the strategic management of Lambrechts began to show net positive new business inflows, but Van Zyl wanted greater client-centricity and coordination of operations. He restructured the life business into Personal Finance, under Lizé Lambrechts, and Employee Benefits under Themba Gamedze, whom he elevated to an executive position, as well as alternate director. (This was a return to separate business units as had been operational before Vermaak consolidated them in 2002.) The Sanlam Life Board remained a single entity, but from 2004 had two CEO positions—one for the life business and one for emerging markets. It is in this leadership roles where Lizé Lambrechts on the life business side, and Heinie Werth, on the emerging market side, emerged as strong drivers of the 'back-to-basics' strategy—and to measurable success for the company.

Since business restructuring in 2003 raised the need to reassess the economic benefit of joint venture operations, the joint venture with Macquarie Bank in Innofin came under the spotlight. In October 2003 Macquarie was taken out as a minority shareholder. Innofin competed directly with the life business for funds from retail investors and sourced most of its funds from Sanlam Life's SP^2 broker and adviser network. To cut costs and co-ordinate the competition for funds in Sanlam Life, Innofin and SP^2 distribution were moved to the life business. The successful restructuring of the life cluster depended on much-strengthened distribution and product development, for which the recruiting of key individuals or teams was authorized. In every category of individual life products (recurring premiums, retirement annuities, single premiums) Sanlam's market share decreased between 2002 and 2003.[19] Much was expected from the UB business partners in terms of rendering capacity in distribution and product development into hitherto untapped markets.

With the UB partner the focus on the life business took on a definite strategic direction to acquire a significant number of black clients, especially in the entry-level market. In the life business two considerations determined Sanlam's strategy: regain lost market share and cut costs. To regain market share the aim was to grow more aggressively in the Gauteng (formerly part of the Transvaal province before 1994) and English-speaking market. One strategy was to acquire life offices with a footprint in the target market. Serious consideration was given to acquiring Sage Life, but this did not materialize. In December 2004 Sanlam Life bought a 55 per cent stake in Thebe Investment Corporation's (TIC) life company, Safrican. As TIC sought to expand its financial services business, Sanlam considered a joint venture with TIC as an opportunity to develop synergies and expand its penetration into the entry-level market. Safrican's distribution went through Thebe Community Financial Services (TCFS), a company operating in

[19] SA: Minutes of Sanlam Ltd Board, 'Buy out of Innofin minorities', 23/10/2003; 'Sanlam Group strategy and business structure', 22/4/2004.

that market. Sanlam bought a 30 per cent stake in TCFS and supported its management in an empowerment offer to acquire 20 per cent in TCFS. TCFS provided distribution opportunities to other financial services of Sanlam distributed through Sanlam IFS. Further synergies in TCFS included debt collection, employee benefits, and a money-moving business similar to Sanlam's Multi Data. Safrican had an annual turnover of R240 million and 1.8 million members insured, but apart from life insurance, the products included funeral cover and savings policies for low- and middle-income individuals and families.[20] While the negotiations with ABSA remained sticky and delivery slow, the TIC transaction brought Sanlam closer to the empowerment environment and presented distribution opportunities in a market segment unexplored by Sanlam.

In 2004 Momentum Life indicated a willingness to dispose of its 33 per cent stake in African Life (Aflife). This was a moment of great significance in the history of Sanlam. African Life was a major competitor of Santam during the establishment years and threatened the penetration of Santam/Sanlam into the Free State *platteland* (see Chapter 2). In 2004 Sanlam indicated a keen interest in acquiring the full share capital of Aflife. During the last quarter of 2005 Sanlam acquired African Life, with approval of the Competition Commission. Momentum bought the health cover and administration business of Aflife. Sanlam was particularly impressed with the geographical distribution into African countries, as Aflife had a footprint in Botswana, Kenya, Ghana, Zambia, Tanzania, Namibia, and Lesotho. This was a strategically significant asset, since Sanlam had no experience in African markets, except in Namibia.[21] By the end of 2004 Sanlam announced progress in the life business to the value of R26 billion in new business and R2.4 billion net inflow of funds.[22]

Venturing outside South Africa

The international business of Sanlam impacted across the Group, but did not contribute significantly to the growth strategy of the Group. In the life market Merchant Investors Assurance (MIA) UK provided a distribution channel to Sanlam's products, but performance hardly justified the cost. Van Zyl repeatedly called for a clarification of Sanlam's international business model. This came to fruition as the focus on the basic business principles of harnessing the unique diversity of a truly South African company,

[20] SA: Minutes of Sanlam Board, 26/8/2004; 1/12/2004; 1 & 2/3/2005.

[21] SA: Minutes of Sanlam Board, 26/8/2004; 1 & 2/3/2005; Sanlam Life Board, 27/5/2004; Sanlam Life Board, 6/5/2005; J. van Zyl (Sanlam CEO) and J. Rowse (Aflife CEO) presentation to Sanlam Life Board, 24/2/2005.

[22] Sanlam Annual Report, 2004: 112–13.

manifested increasingly in the business of penetrating formerly unexplored markets. Being a legacy empowerment company of a marginalized segment in the market (this was the poor and economically marginalized Afrikaners in 1918), Van Zyl capitalized on that acquired capability in Sanlam in mining opportunities in the domestic and neighbouring markets, resembling its original legacy market. For the international business this strategy meant that Sanlam would engage in foreign markets where it had a competitive advantage. In the life market, growth opportunities emerged in the entry-level market and in financial services it was across all market segments. Since the first twelve to eighteen months of Van Zyl's stewardship delivered noticeable results in all clusters of the Group's business, restructuring Sanlam International was inevitable. After the business unit restructuring exercise of 2003, there was no place for Sanlam International as a separate business unit. International operations comprised an integral part of focused business operations in different markets, namely life, investments, capital markets, and financial services, either in the domestic or foreign markets. Confidence in the managerial capabilities of Sanlam's management ruled out the past alliances and joint ventures, which resulted in foreign businesses managing South African capital on behalf of Sanlam. Control returned to Sanlam. International operations of Sanlam were expected to develop as a secondary outcome of restored competitive advantage within each cluster. These operations became part of a home-base consolidation strategy ('protecting the farm') to reverse poor performance and restore value to policyholders and shareholders. Sanlam International closed down. Investment operations were consolidated in SIM. Sanlam terminated the alliance with Punter Southall by purchasing the remaining 80 per cent UK interest. Sanlam's own investment managers managed the entire UK portfolio in Punter Southall. Sanlam also established Sanlam Multi Manager International (SMMI), a subsidiary in Dublin from where Sanlam investment managers managed Sanlam products to South African clients. SMMI gradually instilled confidence in the UK market and slowly established a UK client base. By the end of 2003 Sanlam experienced a net funds outflow of R55 million from its international business, but this was expected and actually welcomed.[23] This development enabled a managed withdrawal from those businesses and opened the opportunity to tailor Sanlam's international operations to its overall growth strategy. The net outflow of funds reversed once SIM restored profitability towards the end of 2004, leading investors to place more funds with SIM. Growing the life business was a priority. Sanlam therefore acquired the UK closed-book life insurance portfolio from Capital Alliance UK in Merchant Investors Assurance (MIA) for £40 million on 1 January 2004. Capital Alliance wanted to refocus on its core business, while MIA offered Sanlam a foot in the life insurance door in the UK. Sanlam placed its own management team in the UK to effect a turnaround in the

[23] Sanlam Annual Report, 2003: 93.

existing life portfolio in MIA. The synergies with the UK market were real, but represented alignment with only a small part of the total diversified financial services products Sanlam had on offer.

Targeting the entry-level market, Aflife, Channel Life, and Shriram (discussion on Channel Life and Shriram to follow) became growth vehicles for the life business, and at the same time exported Sanlam products to global markets. During 2004 Sanlam restructured its involvement in Namibia by facilitating the establishment of a Namibian holding company that acquired most of the Sanlam business in Namibia. Sanlam retained a majority stake in the new holding company, and Sanlam agents and independent brokers were allowed to market Sanlam and Innofin products. The Sanlam systems were still utilized during the bridging period. Sanlam thus subsequently reduced its presence in Namibia to that of an investor into a foreign life office and investment management company.[24] To grow the entry-level market segment in 2005, Heinie Werth was the conceptualizing manager behind the strategy and steered the implementation of that vision. Sanlam identified Channel Life, a life insurance company in the PSG Group, as a potential synergy to its overall growth strategy. Channel set itself to contribute to the 'Africanization of traditional assurance in South Africa'. Through direct marketing (not agents or brokers, as Aflife or Sanlam had used) Channel had the potential to reach into markets Sanlam had not entered. By 2005 Channel had raised premiums in excess of R1 billion and had R2 billion assets under management. Sanlam acquired a 50 plus one share in Channel in 2006 and was satisfied with the sound management, governance, and IT systems in Channel. It reversed its 55 per cent interest in Safrican into Channel and put all its own credit life business through Channel for at least two years, using the Channel brand. Channel products were also sold through the Sanlam distribution channels, thereby giving direct effect to the Van Zyl strategy to develop partnerships in promoting value creation and growth for Sanlam.[25] The acquisition of Safrican in 2005 was the first step in Sanlam's systematic employment of a growth strategy in the entry-level market (ELM). Channel was the second such acquisition and gave effect to the recognition of the boom in the retail market being driven by ELM growth. The only growth in the insurance industry during the first decade of the twenty-first century was in the ELM market, primarily through recurring-premium products, and Sanlam selected well-performing players in that market to effect a strategic entry into that market.

The next step was entry into a much larger mass ELM market. Confirming the Sanlam vision of being a leading provider of financial products and services aimed at wealth creation and wealth protection, it was necessary to access all relevant markets. The key question was whether the company should pursue structural growth opportunities in a potentially mature industry, or in a relatively saturated market. The domestic market

[24] SA: Minutes Sanlam Board, 3/12/2003.

[25] SA: Minutes of Sanlam Ltd Board, 5/8/2005.

displayed most of these characteristics and rang true for Sanlam Life particularly. It made good sense to investigate the strengthening of new or underdeveloped distribution channels (bancassurance, group schemes), or further consolidation in the market. Sanlam Life investigated opportunities in the Indian market. India was one of the fastest-growing economies and had a relatively stable political system, but the population was underinsured, which presented Sanlam with an attractive opportunity. Insurance penetration as a measure of GDP was very low at 2.3 per cent of the insurable population. The Indian middle class consisted of around 300 million people and earned an income similar to the generic ELM profile of Sanlam policyholders. Sanlam decided to enter that market with an Indian partner, the Shriram Group. This group was a second-league group in India with a focus on South India. It offered short-term finance to informal savings groups and had an employee base of 11 000, more than 80 000 agents and 43 million clients. The funds under management amounted to US$1.5 billion. Shriram considered entering insurance, but was looking for a partner with experience, products, and distribution knowledge. An investment of US$30 million in the Shriram insurance joint venture would give Sanlam Life 1.1 per cent ROC in year one, but by year five it was expected to rise to 12.1 per cent and 47.3 per cent in year ten. This opportunity allowed Sanlam access to a massive market and the partnership of an experienced Indian financial services entity, but also a partner dependent on Sanlam's expertise in ELM insurance products and markets. A perfect synergy emerged. Sanlam invested US$30 million (R242.2 million) in Shriram for a 26 per cent stake in the group, with a potential to raise that by 6 per cent, regulatory approval permitting.[26] Shriram Life Insurance was subsequently established in 2006. This strategic acquisition placed the life business on a much-needed profit trajectory, facilitated by, amongst others, freed capital from the ABSA share sale, and a Sanlam Life cost reduction to the value of R270 million in 2004.

The 'back-to-basics' strategy indeed succeeded in turning Sanlam's performance towards positive territory. It occurred on the back of much-improved general economic conditions in South Africa and globally. Both 2004 and 2005 delivered strong growth in the JSE All Share Index. Interest rates started a downward trend and international investors adjusted their risk premiums on emerging markets downwards. Foreign acquisition of South African equities rose to record levels by the fourth quarter of 2004. The Barclays acquisition of a controlling stake in ABSA illustrated the trend. In 2005 state finances benefited from the buoyancy in local and international markets, when government debt dropped to its lowest level since 1981. Real economic growth in South Africa was 5 per cent for the first time in twenty years. At the end of 2004 Sanlam even contemplated issuing a trading statement, because operating results were expected to be up between 25 per cent and 35 per cent on those of 2003 by October already.

[26] SA: Minutes of Sanlam Ltd Board, 5/3/2005; Sanlam Annual Report, 2005: 108–9.

Strong growth in equity markets supported this growth, driven by rising international commodity prices. Global market volatility set in during 2006, and in 2007 the subprime crisis halted the euphoria of the first half of the 2000s. By then Sanlam had reaped the benefits of holistic restructuring and transformation. Van Zyl managed change with a forward-looking perspective. All the elements of group performance were aligned with the turnaround strategy he introduced in 2003.

In the relatively positive economic climate since 2003 the restructured Sanlam businesses reached a fair degree of stability by 2006 in four business clusters. Van Zyl as Group CEO was the captain of the big ship turning around slowly. The business clusters were: Group Office as a management cluster, Group Finance, Group Human Resources, Group Marketing and Communications, and Group Services conducted the services impacting group-wide. It was in this cluster that Van Zyl drove the transformation of the company and addressed the brand image of Sanlam. Group Finance performed the management and reporting responsibilities, which had developed major intricacies as accounting standards changed and the international financial reporting standards (IFRS) were introduced in 2005. These impacted directly and fundamentally on the nature of financial reporting by insurance companies, and subsequently affected the published valuations of Sanlam's embedded value. As the spate of negative publicity against the insurance industry of late 2004/early 2005 abounded, the change in accounting policies contributed to further uncertainty. Addressing these uncertainties was necessary to restore the negative image of Sanlam in the domestic market. It was both accounting communication as well as broad social communication on who and what Sanlam was, that demanded attention from management. The repositioning of the business depended as much on improved operating performance and efficiency as on brand efficiency, market respect and confidence. Compliance with transformation imperatives was a business decision. The UB transaction did not automatically translate into a warm embrace of Sanlam in the black market. Afrikaner nationalism mobilized broad support for Sanlam during the establishment years. After the 1990s broad-based support had to be earned by attracting those outside the traditional Sanlam sphere of influence by means of client-centricity and a commitment to South Africa as a nation. Sanlam had to emerge as the champion of South Africa, as it had at the beginning of the century. The transformation of Sanlam in its entire business context was equally important to strengthen investment returns and new business flows.

The four business clusters into which the business of Sanlam evolved by 2005 were Life Insurance, Short-term Insurance, Investment Management, and Independent Financial Services. In pure Alfred Chandler theory, the growth strategy to maximize returns on EV on a sustainable basis determined the functionally determined cluster strategy.[27] The configuration of the business entities in each cluster changed as the

[27] A.D. Chandler Jr (199) *Strategy and Structure Chapters in the History of the Industrial Enterprise*. Cambridge, MA: MIT Press.

business focus sharpened. In Sanlam Life there were Sanlam Personal Finance, Sanlam Employee Benefits, Innofin, Merchant Investors Assurance (UK), Sanlam Namibia, Sanlam Trust, Sanlam Customised Insurance, Sanlam Home Loans (with ABSA), and Sanlam Personal Loans. Multi Data was a separate legal entity in Sanlam Life, performing money transfers and tax directive business for Sanlam Life. In 2005 the separate legal entity was of no use and the payment division of Multi Data was sold to BDB (a joint venture of Nedcor and ABSA). On 1 January 2005 Multi Data was reincorporated into the life cluster.[28] Santam and Westminster Motor Insurance Association were the short-term businesses in that cluster.

Sanlam Investment Management comprised all the investment functions: SIM, Sanlam Capital, Sanlam Private Investments (SPI), Sanlam Properties, Sanlam Collective Investments (SCI), Sanlam Multi-Manager International, Octane Management Ltd, SIM Namibia, and Sanlam Management Ireland. The Sanlam Independent Financial Services cluster housed Sanlam Financial Services (UK), Simeka Consultants and Actuaries (SCA), Bull and Bear Financial Services, Gensec Properties, Break-Thru Financial Services, and Thebe Community Financial Services (TCFS).[29] Other business activities were small and operated outside the clusters. Fundamo (Pty) Ltd, a company performing mobile payments, was not a full subsidiary, but a company in which Sanlam held a 37 per cent stake with empowerment partners. Encoresa was a 50 per cent Sanlam-controlled company, providing management solutions to insurance brokers and advisers. Full consolidation of focused operations was not yet complete, as many international activities were in the process of being wound up or repositioned in the Group. These actions were explained as the 'refining' of Sanlam's internationalization strategy, a 'simplification of operations' through decentralization which left each business unit with the responsibility to develop appropriate international business lines. Sanlam Netherlands Holding BV remained an offshore holding company, because the Dutch subsidiary functioned as a vehicle through which proceeds of business in the UK and Western Europe could be diverted. This Dutch subsidiary operated in a favourable tax environment and served as a vehicle for the accumulation of foreign capital.[30] In 2004 Sanlam sold Tasc Administration (Dublin) and in 2005 reduced its stake in Sanlam Financial Services UK to a minority 25 per cent holding. Sanlam Financial Services (SFS) UK was a distribution entity, but no significant business was flowing to the Sanlam product providers in the UK or South Africa, and therefore did not contribute to the business model. The strategy

[28] Sanlam: The IT journey: 53.

[29] SA: Minutes of Sanlam Ltd Board, 7/9/2005: The Sanlam Group of Companies; Minutes of Sanlam Ltd Board, 23/11/2005: Presentation J. van Zyl: Strategy and structure; Minutes of Sanlam Ltd Board, 7/12/2005.

[30] These considerations motivated the establishment of the Dutch subsidiary in 2001. Minutes of Sanlam Exco 7/5/2001. In 2003 the strategic position of Sanlam Netherlands Holding BV was justified on the same considerations.

with SFS matured as SFS developed into a position of a self-sustaining entity servicing predominantly the UK institutional market. There was limited cross-selling of Sanlam products. This position justified the ordered exit. In future distribution would be built through IFS to the high-wealth niche markets in the UK, while the clusters in South Africa were the product factories.[31]

Affirming the roots in a complex context

Sanlam used market segmentation to implement its growth and improved efficiency strategy. Sanlam built its business through a stronger focus on client-centricity, brand awareness, empowerment, and moulding the culture of Sanlam with that of the new South Africa. There was no turning back from this strategy, but by 2006 the realization of goals or targets did not always materialize as planned. Disappointment with returns on investment and growth in individual life business were a drag on the growth strategy. The bancassurance agreement with ABSA did not deliver the expected results, but the sale of ABSA shares released capital unproductively employed. A serious drain on a constructive forward-moving strategy came from the overburdening regulatory context. This coincided with litigation on past policies by the Pension Fund Administrator (PFA).[32] SA Mutual, Liberty, and Sanlam were taken to court by the PFA in 2005 on costs and benefits accruing to policyholders in terms of illustrated values upon contracting retirement annuities.[33]

The matter of early termination costs caused serious brand damage to Sanlam, but was indeed an industry dilemma, reflecting negatively on the cost structure of the life insurance industry. Criticism against the cost structure of the life industry was voiced in various forums, especially at actuarial society congresses and eventually in the Parliament Portfolio Committee on Finance. The matter turned out to be a serious reputation risk to the industry. Sanlam as the manager of the Central Retirement

[31] SA: Minutes of Sanlam Ltd Board, 2/6/2004; 4/8/2004; 1/12/2004; 3/8/2005; 7/12/2005.

[32] A highly publicized case of a Sanlam holder of a retirement annuity went to the Pension Fund Administrator. Mr de Beer claimed that Sanlam had charged excessive costs and failed to pay out what was promised in the policy document. Judge Denis Davis ruled against Sanlam. The case earned Sanlam very negative publicity, despite the case being representative of policies across the long-term insurance industry. The Life Offices Association (LOA) joined in the dispute, but a resolution of the dispute required generic adjustment. Sanlam was particularly upset about being made the example of a practice widely applied in the industry. SA: Minutes of Sanlam Ltd Board, 7/12/2005; D. Basson: 'Lessons of the Sanlam decision', *Finance Week*, 30/3/2005: 13–14.

[33] *Personal Finance*, 27/8/2005; *Personal Finance*, 23/10/2005. The court ruled against the insurance companies disputing the authority of the PFA to address complaints by policyholders on matters pertaining to the terms and conditions of the policy.

Annuity Fund considered the matter in a serious light, especially since the company had just embarked on a turnaround strategy and a campaign to restore brand loyalty. The pending court decision on the De Beer case left Sanlam no choice but to seek to negotiate a principled decision on the calculation of early termination values. These deliberations involved the Minister of Finance and the Treasury. In Sanlam a special board committee consisting of Roy Andersen, Chairman; Johan van Zyl, CEO; George Rudman, Chris Swanepoel, and Flip Rademeyer prepared the Sanlam policy on the matter. While the outcome of the court decision was awaited, the Sanlam board agreed on a package position for Sanlam. The company wanted to retain the moral high ground and therefore agreed to a maximum percentage reduction in fund values to be paid on early termination on policies in force for between one and two years. This percentage diminished with longer in-force terms. The new Stratus investment products released by Sanlam Life in August 2003 provided for much-increased early termination values, but a proactive strategy on existing policies was needed. In close collaboration with Liberty Life, Sanlam proposed a 25 per cent maximum cost recovery on policies in force for between one and two years, and scaled the cost recovery down gradually. Sanlam provided for a maximum penalty cost recovery of 25 per cent going back for a three-year period as a worst-case scenario. Provision for R600 million impacted at least R0.20 per the value of Sanlam shares.[34] The R600 million reduction in the embedded value of Sanlam Life as a consequence was put forward as the price of certainty. Once an industry-wide decision emerged, Sanlam applauded the certainty with respect to future policies. There was no doubt the company wished the LOA had taken a tougher stance on the matter, but the political context, and the vitality of Ministerial and Parliamentary approval of a consensus decision, necessitated agreement on this one-off cost to Sanlam. The company had to move on more critical strategic matters.

One such a critical matter was CSI. The 2003 strategy of rebuilding Sanlam's market share was indeed a strategy to affirm its roots, or revisit those roots. In Pettigrew's explanation of organizational change, he describes an organization as a living entity with a past, a history, and a future.[35] To ensure the sustainability of Sanlam, the firm foundation in its past made up the roots it could use as tools in the new emerging CSI context. As Sanlam entered its ninetieth year in 2008, the corporate citizenship report formed part of the official annual report. The CSI strategy endorsed by the board adopted the principle of CSI as support for the business and corporate citizenship agenda, based on the philosophy of enlightened self-interest. CSI was good for business and for the broad society. The CSI agenda dovetailed with the brand strategy to position

[34] SA: Minutes of Sanlam Ltd Board, 23/11/2005; 7/12/2005: L. Lambrechts JRF/jv: Memorandum: Improved early termination values for existing policies, 24/11/2005.

[35] A.M. Pettigrew (1987): 'Context and action in the transformation of firms', *Journal of Management Studies*, 24 (6).

Sanlam as a socially responsible and relevant enterprise on each of the levels of operation—local, regional, and national. The brand strategy of 'thinking ahead' was used to position the company as a long-term value investor in nation building and the development of a thriving economy. The link between CSI and the brand strategy wanted to elicit not only an intellectual response to Sanlam, but an emotional, spontaneous outburst of positive alignment. The CSI strategy was to develop markets by building capacity through forward-looking educational, entrepreneurial, employment creation, health, environmental, and social programmes. It was again all about Sanlam as a truly South African company investing in products and services to create value for all stakeholders. CSI is directed at building the capacity of civil society, to implement social development projects to sustain society in the long run. The Bottom of the Pyramid (BoP) strategy of C.K. Prahalad provided the rationale for Sanlam's use of CSI to build future markets.[36] This BoP strategy advised greater focus on the entry-level market. Sanlam was more established in high-net-worth and middle-income client markets, but could build the business in the new South African context by adjusting towards the mass bottom end of the market.[37] CSI became more strategic and centrally integrated into the back-to-basics business plan.

On two fronts developments supported the vision of realizing growth goals by 2010. The first was the development in the ELM and the second was capital management. The strategic acquisition of access to the ELM through Aflife, Channel Life, Safrican, and Shriram allowed the development of an integrated vision, objectives, and strategy for all Sanlam's entities operating in that market segment. The ongoing frustration with constructive materialization of the bancassurance agreement with ABSA led to the exploration of possible collaboration with Capitec Bank, a retail bank operating in the lower end of the market. Despite excellent management and IT systems, Capitec as a bank did not develop insurance capabilities. Capitec indicated an interest to enter the insurance market. It made sense to Sanlam to consolidate its existing initiatives in the ELM market. This was done by restructuring Sanlam Life's ELM operations under a new entity, Sanlam Developing Markets (SDM), from late 2005. This brought an integrated management structure to the different operating entities (building blocks, as termed by Ian Kirk and Johan van Zyl) in the ELM market segment. SDM made substantive progress in regaining market share, attracting new business and repositioning the brand in the ELM. The 2005 budget displayed the enthusiasm on this market segment: a loss of R34 million in 2005 was expected to deliver a R392 million profit in 2006.[38]

[36] C.K. Prahalad (2004): *Fortune at the bottom of the pyramid.*

[37] F. Louw (2005): 'Thinking Ahead'. Sanlam's approach to corporate social investment, February 2005.

[38] SA: Minutes of Sanlam Ltd Board, 7/12/2006; Memorandum HW/bg: Entry-level market (ELM) integration initiative, 30/11/2006.

Sanlam's insurance client base was not yet aligned with the profile of the industry. Black insurance clients as a proportion of South African insurance clients rose from 33 per cent in 1998 to 47 per cent in 2006, with the strongest growth between 2004 and 2006. Similar to that of Liberty Life, Sanlam's client profile remained predominantly white, albeit Afrikaans-speaking males, rather than black, but the client base of SA Mutual, Metropolitan, and African Life was predominantly black males. Metropolitan Life and African Life client profiles displayed a strong exposure to the ELM, which supported the Sanlam decision to acquire African Life. Sanlam's client profile was also skewed towards older clients (45 per cent between the ages of thirty-five and forty-nine years and 22 per cent between the ages of fifty and sixty-four years). In each age category Sanlam exceeded the industry target market. Two-thirds of Sanlam's clients fell within the LSM 8 and LSM 10 categories (LSM 8 earns R17 900 average household income per month and LSM 10 earns R26 600 average household income per month).[39] The profile of the Sanlam insurance client base clearly justified the stronger emphasis on transformation via the ELM markets.

The second initiative was capital management. One aspect of capital management was share buy-back operations. With the proceeds of the ABSA share sale in hand, investment opportunities delivering attractive returns were scarce and the board decided to invest in itself. Despite the share price moving around R11.65 cents per share, which was only a 3 per cent discount to EV, systematic share buy-back transactions followed. The decision to buy back Sanlam shares was explained at the Annual General Meeting of shareholders on 21 September 2005. Van Zyl explained that Sanlam did not simply wish to replace the capital released through the ABSA transaction by another single investment. Part of the capital was used to conclude the Aflife and Channel transactions, but returning the capital to shareholders was one option. Sanlam could declare a special dividend, which would incur a 12.5 per cent tax to shareholders. Buying back its own shares in a compulsory buy-back scheme was the viable option to invest in the confidence of the company. A robust discussion on the matter followed, with some shareholders expressing their feeling of being pressurized to sell their shares to the Sanlam offer because it was a compulsory buy-back scheme. To conclude the share buy-back transaction, Sanlam had to have at least 75 per cent support at the AGM. The final voting gave management 82 per cent support in favour of the share buy-back initiative.[40] In May 2005 Sanlam bought back 4.2 million of its shares for R49 million—at a price of R11.65 per share. In October 2005 a similar buy-back removed 278 million Sanlam shares from the market. Shares were acquired from shareholders holding 300 or fewer Sanlam shares. Sanlam applied to the JSE for permission to buy back another 80 million

[39] SA: 4/24: Marketing Research: J. Dommisse (2006): *Profile and penetration of insurance companies.* SAARP AAMPS Survey 2006.

[40] SA: Minutes of Annual General Meeting of Sanlam shareholders, 21/09/2005.

Table 6.2. Net flow of funds, 2002–2006 (Rm)

	Net total funds (Rm)	Net life business (Rm)	Net international life (Rm)	Net SIM (Rm)	Net SIM (international (Rm)
2002	(3924)	(2404)		(3661)	1571
2004	16 591	2959	1078		711
2006	(7451)	3678	1261	(11 154)	6722

Source: Sanlam annual reports, 2002–2006.

of its shares, 10 million of which were held in a share incentive scheme. This was not a compulsory buy-back scheme, since Sanlam bought its own shares as an ordinary purchaser on the JSE. The shares bought were delisted and cancelled, except those held in the share incentive scheme.[41] The share buy-back exercise removed 588.78 million Sanlam shares from the market, thereby reducing the company's issued share capital by 21.3 per cent. Since share buy-backs commenced in 2005 Sanlam injected R8.996 billion into the market by 2007.

This exercise was value enhancing. In hindsight it made it clear that Sanlam was actually very solvent at demutualization. The problem was that new regulations did not allow all the assets held as qualifying capital. The share price rose from around R12.40 in 2005 to well above R23.00 in 2007. The narrowing of the long-standing discount of the Sanlam share price to EV was not only the result of the share buy-backs, but also improved operating performance. Improved market confidence was strengthened by the diversification of the business and improved net flow of funds. The contribution of the life cluster to Group operating profit declined from around 63 per cent in 2002 to 56 per cent in 2003, but the life cluster turned net outflows around to net inflows from 2004. International confidence was important for the growth strategy of Sanlam, given the overcrowding of the domestic insurance market. By 2006, 25 per cent of the Sanlam equity was held offshore. The net flow of funds into the life and investment business from international sources substantiated the trend[42] (see Table 6.2, which shows the growth in the net inflow of funds into the business units of Sanlam). Between 2002 and 2006 the net inflow was negative, primarily because of net negative inflow of –R11 154 million into SIM. The life business posted net inflow of R3 678 million, but could not offset the underperforming SIM operations.

In 2008 Sanlam celebrated ninety years in the industry. In the ninetieth year the Sanlam Group's total long-term insurance business stood at R18.6 billion and other business at R83.3 billion, a 39 per cent increase on R62.2 billion in 2004.[43] This

[41] SA: Minutes of Sanlam Ltd Board, 24/11/2004; 1 & 2/3/2005; 1/6/2005; 7/12/2005.

[42] J. Lambridis (2007): 'Sanlam Limited (SLM). FY06 results.' Citigroup, 13/3/2007.

[43] Due to the introduction of IFRS in 2005, financial reporting was restated in terms of IFRS requirements only from 2004. The published figures for earlier than 2004 are not IFRS restated.

performance must be assessed not only against the background of favourable market conditions, relatively high interest rates, and buoyant equity trading, but also in the context of mounting regulatory intervention. How this was managed, impacted directly on the performance of a financial services company.

Regulatory impact: a business imperative

Two contextual processes absorbed enormous capacity from all companies in the financial services industry: regulation and empowerment. The financial services sector became very specific targets of empowerment policies. At the same time the world was shaken at the foundation of trust and confidence by successive accounting scandals. The first was the Waste management scandal of 1998, then the Enron audit scandal of October 2001, followed by the successive scandals of Worldcom, Parmalat, and Tyco in 2002. In 1994 retired Supreme Court Judge Mervyn E. King delivered the first King Report on Corporate Governance (King I). King interpreted his task as an opportunity to educate the South African public on the functioning of a free economy. The King I report of 1994 made recommendations on the composition of a board of directors, the responsibilities of non-executive directors and governance principles regarding remuneration, balanced reporting, effective auditing, affirmative action programmes, and the code of ethics of the company. The King I code of corporate governance had no legal backing, but was indirectly enforced by conditions in other statutes, such as the Companies Act, or the JSE Exchange Listing Requirements. The King II report on corporate governance in 2002 elaborated on corporate governance, requiring informed oversight roles from non-executive directors. This code required a corporate code of conduct for a board, outlining the way to deal with conflicts of interest, independence, and a board charter setting out its responsibilities. Firm proposals addressed the qualifications and responsibilities of directors, the relationship between the chairman and the CEO of the company, remuneration, and more importantly, the role of directors on board committees. Sanlam has had such a Code of Conduct since the mid-1990s. An evaluation of board performance was required and the company secretary was assigned the task of implementing the corporate governance functions, especially in guiding new inexperienced directors. The report underlined the risk management responsibility of the board, which also extended to assessing the audit function in the company, financial reporting, sustainability reporting, relations with shareholders, and organizational integrity and ethics. These recommendations were made mandatory for JSE-listed companies. Sanlam subsequently devoted much time to prepare enhanced governance structures and procedures. A Charter and Code of Ethics for the Board of Directors complying with the

South African Code of Corporate Practices and Conduct, recommended in King II, were drafted. These governance requirements introduced formal training requirements for new directors, annual submissions to confirm performance assessment and compliance to the JSE, and reports on board performance (number of meetings, number of meetings attended by each director, remuneration, responsibilities, etc.). Board committees facilitated further integration of the directors into the business conducted in the company. In March 2003 the board reconstituted its committees into the following: audit and risk, human resources, nominations, BEE, independent directors, and safety, health, and environmental committees. A board summit in August 2004 addressed many of the corporate governance issues raised in King II. Many of the new generation directors were very unfamiliar with the history and development of the company when entering the corporate board context.[44] To comply with their duties in terms of King II, companies were required to facilitate mentoring and introduction into the corporate board environment. A growing burden of document production and regulatory compliance increased the workload of the office of the secretary, but contributed to the integration of persons traditionally distant from Sanlam into an organization of which they became stakeholders.

Considering the transformation and empowerment dimensions of the FSC, the significance of sound governance lay more in building a stronger business, and broad trust and association with Sanlam as an organization in the business of creating wealth for all, in South Africa, than only managing risk. King II required explicit disclosures in the annual report on risk management.[45] The board had a direct responsibility for risk management and internal control processes and systems. Risk management became a standard item on the audit committee agenda and business units established documented business continuity plans. These processes were integrated with the development of directors. The FSC is a BEE document and set targets for the appointment of gender and demographic diversity to both management and the board. These targets dovetailed with broad transformation targets of EE. Complying with King II linked compliance with the FSC and EE to the explicit capabilities of directors. Building a stronger Sanlam in South Africa necessitated full compliance with these environmental documents. Sanlam identified leading individuals outside the traditional Sanlam sphere of influence to serve on its board. These persons were professionals and respected in their own right in various environments, but did not necessarily have experience of corporate directors' responsibilities. Due to other valuable traits, such as community leadership, or experience in different business environments, their contributions to the Sanlam board were part of a process of building the new Sanlam. It was incumbent on Sanlam to effect the coherent roll-out of King II and the FSC parameters. Up to 1992 Sanlam had an

[44] SA: Sanlam Ltd Board Summit, Erinvale, Somerset West, 3 & 4/8/2004.

[45] SA: Minutes of Sanlam Ltd Board, 4/3/2003: Memorandum J. de Kock: Group Risk Management, 22/11/2002.

all-white male board of fourteen directors. In 1993 Kate Jowell was the first woman appointed as director. In 1994 Mr Peter Schwartz was the first person of colour appointed to the Sanlam board. By 2007 eight out of eighteen directors were people of colour, and five of the board members were women. Changing the face of Sanlam on board level did not translate into wider social support. To achieve that, as a business imperative, required a closer look at the brand and CSI.

One of the vital marketing mechanisms of any corporate is its brand. Meaningful repositioning of Sanlam in the new regulatory context and democratically transformed country gave rise to the idea to revisit the Sanlam brand and its logo. Van Zyl commissioned an in-depth investigation into the trademark (logo) and domain name shortly after assuming the position as CEO in 2003. The survey confirmed strong awareness of the existing Sanlam brand logo (the blue hands around a ball, supported by the company name 'Sanlam' to the right thereof). A brand as a collection of perceptions in the mind of the consumer is subject to changes in the consumer market. The Sanlam brand suffered in the minds of investors as a result of underperformance since the early 1990s, but also in the minds of the broad society as it was associated with one segment of society for a very long time (although not fully justified, as the changing policyholder profile had indicated by the mid-1980s). Van Zyl therefore created a central function on group level to manage the brand and market the business of Sanlam centrally.[46] This was fundamental to the roll-out of transformation and CSI programmes and building group-wide loyalty. The investigation into the status of the Sanlam brand indicated broad awareness and recognition, but least so in the newly emerging black market. An integrated strategy followed to promote the single centrally managed brand to symbolize transformation in Sanlam, from regulatory compliance to organizational repositioning. Van Zyl as change manager, was aware of the importance of brand recognition and therefore drove transformation and loyalty to the successful South African icon, Sanlam, as a business imperative.

Organizational sustainability depends on the ability to adapt to change. In 2003 Sanlam published its first Transformation Report. Temba Mvusi, Chief Executive: Group Services, explained the report as encapsulating 'the historical context of Sanlam's transformation programme and activities, and to lay a framework for sustainability reporting in the future'.[47] Transformation was directly linked to a dialogue with Sanlam's stakeholders, that is policyholders, shareholders, and the society in which the company conducts its business. The transformation process did not constitute a break with the past, but a perpetuation of how Sanlam had engaged with its stakeholders since its establishment. *Korporatiewe Maatskaplike Betrokkenheid* in the twenty-first century translated into corporate social investment (CSI), which became a keystone of sustainability. Acknowledging the regulatory framework and transformed CSI, Sanlam

[46] SA: Minutes of Sanlam Ltd Board, 3/3/2004; 22/4/2004; 1/6/2004.

[47] SA: 3/5/5: KMB/CSI: 'Thinking ahead, staying relevant'. Transformation Report, 2003: 1.

displayed the ability to adapt to change. The 2003 transformation report addressed Sanlam's social investment in areas affecting its stakeholders. By 2003 the policyholder profile showed 50 per cent Afrikaans and 50 per cent English policyholders. The composition of the board was also evenly split between Afrikaans- and English-speaking directors. When in 1993 the 'Marketing Sanlam' survey showed that 72 per cent of the South African population was black but that only 20 per cent of Sanlam's policyholders were black, it was decided to focus more explicitly on the black market.[48] The African client base in group benefits and pensions funds rose significantly from the mid-1990s as Sanlam attracted public sector employee benefit business. Sanlam's own Walter Scheffler, Senior General Manager: Group Benefits, made the presentation to the ANC to market Sanlam's pension fund capabilities. Sanlam was subsequently awarded the administration of this pension fund.[49] By the early 2000s Sanlam managed a substantial number of employee benefit schemes for black employees in different sectors of the economy. The shareholder profile showed almost 20 per cent foreign shareholders, 58 per cent South African, 77 per cent institutional shareholders, and 20 per cent individual shareholders. Based on an analysis of policyholder documents, Sanlam made a rough estimate of the racial distinction of its shareholders in 2003. It was estimated that of the individual shareholders 3.2 per cent were black and of the institutional shareholders 16.8 per cent were black. With another 0.04 per cent black shareholders in the Sanlam share incentive scheme, black shareholders made up roughly 20.3 per cent of Sanlam's shareholders at the end of December 2003.[50] The predominantly South African stakeholder profile made focused attention to the burning issues in the domestic society imperative. Van Zyl wrapped the transformation strategy around success and sustainability. He stated that the transformation challenge was an opportunity to build a successful and sustainable company 'based on inclusivity and diversity.... For Sanlam transformation represents a major business opportunity. It presents the chance to grow our business from broader and stronger foundations, the opportunity to serve new markets and harness the full economic power of our amazing diverse society.'[51] The company wanted equitable economic growth as the driver of social progress. Acknowledging inequalities of the past and committing resources to redress them occurred simultaneously with sustained commitment to the company's traditional support base. The roll-out of CSI programmes displayed a definite transformation dimension and stood in the context of the socially responsible corporate citizen where social involvement

[48] SA: Sanlam Advertising and marketing survey, March–April 1993.

[49] Interview Walter Scheffler, 24/2/2009.

[50] Ibid.: 32. This calculation was made for the purposes of the transformation report, and has not been repeated since. Sanlam does not maintain demographic information on shareholders.

[51] Ibid.: 7, 6.

outweighed financial costs. It was no longer a question of whether firms should engage in socially responsible projects, but where and how that engagement was conducted.[52]

Social development manifested in different projects. Sanlam participated in the Disabled Children's Action Group (DICAG) and built the Happy Home for Disabled Children in Umtata, opened by Nelson Mandela in October 2000. The commitment to education continued in the *Takalani Sesame* television series to develop literacy and numeracy skills. Several radio programmes in four languages supported the series, which in 2003 received the Grand Jury Award for children's programmes. To enhance entrepreneurship the award-winning Sanlam Money Game, following on from entrepreneurship workshops offered by Sanlam's Nexus Financial Services, gave local entrepreneurs an opportunity to risk their hand at small business development. These initiatives did not deviate from the underlying principles of Sanlam's pre-1990 CSI, namely the development of human capital through educational programmes, skills development, and health promotion. The UB transaction figured large in the transformation report, since that was one transaction to build business capacity and promote social development through the UBCDT. The entrepreneurship development programmes also fell within the ambit of BEE. Sanlam was involved in the dissemination of health-related information through publications, workshops, and sponsorships. The company also supports cancer and HIV/Aids research and awareness programmes.

Against the background of changing socio-economic conditions, Sanlam conducted extensive research into the HIV/Aids pandemic's impact on South Africa.[53] This was a vitally important area of corporate citizenship that impacted directly on the insurance industry. The rise of a black middle class and the importance of educating that market about life insurance, just as Sanlam had done with Afrikaners in the 1920s, meant that the matter of persons living with HIV/Aids became central to access into that market. Sanlam was engaged through its social responsibility initiatives with organizations involved in HIV/Aids prevention programmes and care projects.[54] Since the late 1980s Sanlam led the industry in providing for people living with HIV/Aids.

An important aspect of transformation was implementing EE throughout the company. To make EE an integral part of the growth strategy, Sanlam considered it to be human capital transformation. In complying with the FSC targets of EE, the business community had to engage in extensive training and education programmes to facilitate the employment of capable employees on all levels of operation. For Sanlam to create wealth, the company had to be sustainable and that assumed employing capable employees. Driving the transformation of its staff, EE, and empowerment, the company

[52] J. Kerr (2008): 'The creative capitalism spectrum: Evaluating corporate social responsibility through a legal lens', *Temple Law Review*, 81: 831–70.

[53] SA: Sankorp, Confidential memoranda, 13/6/86; 14/7/87.

[54] SA; Sanlam Life Board Minutes, 10/1/89.

offered a four-month R4 million business awareness programme at Head Office in 1994. A similar programme was run in collaboration with Sanlam business partners in Pretoria for youths in the northern provinces.[55] These programmes introduced young people to the business of an insurance company and were aimed at facilitating employment in the entry-level ranks of the company. The family-like social context of Head Office staff since the formative years of Sanlam changed with the arrival of the first trade unions at Head Office in 1994. This adjustment was inevitable, since the composition of the employee profile adjusted to the new society, which displayed a growing diversity. A scorecard on EE was introduced in compliance with the Employment Equity Act, No. 55 of 1998. Across the corporate sector compliance was dependent on training and education programmes. Not only support for further studies, but also training in the business and administration of Sanlam became an important mechanism to secure access to persons outside the traditional white society. Management communicated the impact of the EE Act and progress with compliance through the staff magazine. By 2003 staff transformation at Head Office had achieved almost 80 per cent of the target based on statutorily prescribed demographic proportions. The white permanent employee complement of 3 244 was just 131 short of the target of 3 375 employees across all administrative grades. The 1 283 permanent black employees were only 180 short of the target of 1 463. A similar ratio was achieved with temporary employees. Sanlam Life was included in the Black Managers Forum organizational stream, which exposed the life business to a wider network of black managers. The pool of appropriately experienced managers was limited. Sanlam had trained black managers on different levels of the business, but to sustain the supply, internal training was vital. The company established an internal training function at Head Office and was registered with the South African Qualifications Authority as a Provider of Learning. The internal employee training programmes improved retention and enhanced skills levels of Sanlam's employees.

As a signatory of the FSC, Sanlam awarded learnerships to unemployed matriculants. In 2004, fifty black matriculants started their career in the insurance industry with Sanlam.[56] The in-house staff magazine reported with great acclaim on the successes of new employees in training. In 2004, 2006, 2009, and 2012 the international Investor in People Award, conferred by the Department of Labour, recognized the quality of training provided by Sanlam.[57] The Insurance Sector Education and Training Authority acknowledged the quality of the Sanlam training programmes in 2006 by placing a pool of black trainee managers in the Sanlam training programmes. When Sanlam was awarded an 'A' rating by the Department of Labour in June 2007 for its B-BBEE compliance, it came as no surprise, since the transformation agenda was driven hard. Performance bonuses of managers on different levels of authority were calculated on compliance with EE targets. Furthermore, Sanlam did not wish to have a repeat of an

[55] *Sanlammer*, 5/8/1994; 16/9/1994. [56] *Sandaba*, October 2004: 6.

[57] *Sandaba*, February 2004: 15; Sanlam Personal Finance, July 2013: 29.

investigation by the Department of Labour in 2003, when some regional Sanlam offices had failed to comply with EE targets. This did not fit well with the brand revitalization drive and BEE initiatives. The commitment to EE was given another boost when Sanlam introduced SAP software technology in December 2005 to roll out online training. Trainees accessed electronic training at Sanlam Head Office. This use of technology improved consistency in training and contained the cost of trainers having to repeat training and travel large distances to decentralized training centres. By late 2008 an entire four-phase training cycle framework was offered online anywhere in the country.[58] The online training suite was the centrepiece of motivating employees towards human capital advancement. By 2009 Sanlam had fallen short of EE targets. Finding sufficient human capital capacity to comply with statutory employment targets remained under pressure until critical momentum was achieved with the internal training programmes. The SAP online computer training platform enabled access to training opportunities in all divisions of employment in Sanlam. The system allowed for the recognition of employees' skills levels and suggested further training, the outcome of which was automatically conveyed to the employees' supervisors. Employees could also request access to further training. This automated system made a significant contribution to skills development and by 2009, the widening of the ratio between white and black employees. The difficulty in turning the trend emerged from an internal assessment of the progress with human capital transformation in 2009. Employees in Sanlam Life and in Sky Solutions were quite positive about the implementation of EE, but not those in SEM, SIM, and ITSS. Only 60 per cent of employees understood the importance of the implementation of EE policies. A fair degree of suspicion still existed regarding transparency, fairness, integrity, and respect among employees.[59] The fact that the outcome of the survey, which Van Zyl communicated to the employees early in 2009, was published in its entirety, was part of the strategy to massage employees' opinions into support. Sanlam would not compromise on EE, since leaving its human capital behind would defeat the objective of transformation. The answer to this dilemma was sustained training, and recruitment supported by training. Transformation could not progress faster than the supply of capable staff. The supply of professionally educated individuals went according to plan, because they were trained at universities and/or had Sanlam bursaries. It was in the sphere of company-based skills that Sanlam was successful. Just like the high esteem in which Sanlam agents were held in the past as a result of the professional training they received in Sanlam, the company adapted its training of excellence programmes to the community of new employees. In January 2012 Sanlam was awarded official status as a Further Education and Training (FET) College in the insurance industry.[60] The FET status added to the status of the company's training programmes. It also enhanced achievements in other areas of employment equity,

[58] *Sandaba*, December 2008: 17; also see Venter (2016) *Development of Human Resources 1994–2015 with Sanlam*.

[59] *Sandaba*, July 2009: 1.

[60] Official email communication: F.A. Stroebel, 30/3/2016.

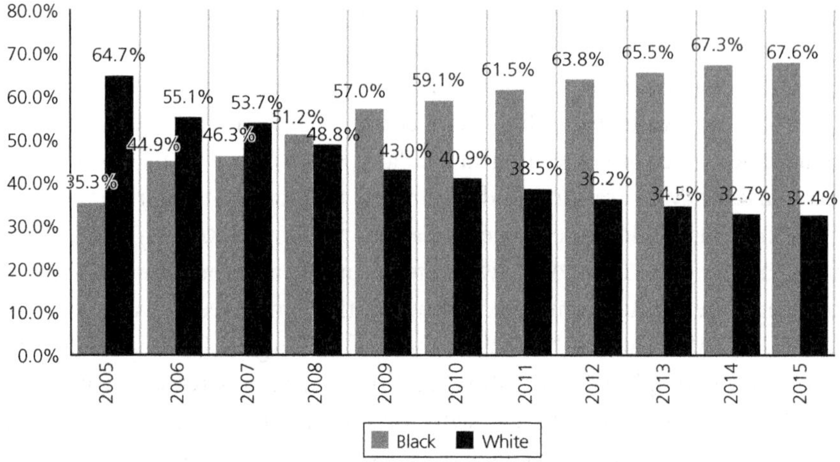

Figure 6.2. Employment structure, 2005–2015

namely the employment of people living with disabilities. In 2011 Sanlam received the National Disability Company Award, with specific acknowledgement to individual Sanlam employees who had made workplace changes to that effect.[61] Additional support material in the form of hard-copy catalogues on the suite of training opportunities through the Sanlam online portal, such as the SPF HR Learning and Development Prospectus, strengthened the learning culture among employees. The combined effect of sustained high-level easy-access training programmes and a commitment to human capital transformation finally gave Sanlam a 65.5 per cent black employee component in 2013. The graphic representation in Figure 6.2 shows the take-off in reversing the trend and growing the black employee component in Sanlam since 2009. The adjusted human capital structure dovetailed with the UB BEE transaction and the restructuring of Sanlam Emerging Markets SEM) into Sanlam Developing Markets as a separate business cluster from 2005.

During the consolidation after 2003, a multifaceted focus on client-centricity drove incremental success. Sanlam Life innovated products and services within the life cluster. These included the new more flexible Topaz and Cobalt insurance products for the middle market. It also included the Glacier structured investment platform offering to the high-income market. The new-image Innofin embarked on a massive marketing drive in Gauteng province, the traditional home market to Liberty Life. Sanlam Life also diversified its business into services such as home loans and personal loans (Direct Axis), and a loyalty programme called Reality. New business volumes and net inflow of funds to Sanlam Life in 2006 signaled the ability to reverse the adverse movements in the life business since the 1990s. The Client Contact Centre, which had been operational since 7 December 1998, was given better client-facing capabilities through the introduction of

[61] *Sandaba*, February 2012: 11.

the Siebel interface program that integrated all the other source programs applicable to client services. Sanlam had traditionally had a leading position in IT in the insurance industry since the early 1960s, but lost that advantage after Y2K, because of the rapid developments in the technology industry. Massive pressure was put on technology innovation to effect client-centricity. By the mid-2000s IT innovation delivered improved support. Massive IT upgrades at the Client Call Centre led to the replacement of Siebel with the Sentrix IT solution in 2008. In conjunction with TCS in India, the SPF IT department developed this system specifically for Sanlam Life as the first service-oriented architecture (SOA). The sophisticated IT system allowed automatic information upgrades, which served to improve integration with other business clusters in Sanlam. Extensive IT software upgrades supported distribution since 2006. This upgrade project, Project Saturn, supported agents and brokers in the roll-out of new products and services developed to turn the life business around.[62]

One area where all the other leading life offices had established a presence was healthcare. Sanlam failed in several attempts to operate successfully in that market. After selling the administration of its medical schemes to Medscheme, Sanlam was locked in a legal battle with Topmed and Selfmed, its former schemes, in the latter's claim for the reserves of Sanmed. Sanmed preceded Topmed and Selfmed. These two schemes claimed ownership of the reserves of Sanmed from 1997, but Sanlam fought a legal battle between 2002 and 2011. Sanlam lost each appeal case and was finally subjected to arbitration. The arbiter ordered Sanlam to pay Topmed R458 million and Selfmed R130 million, which was just over 41 per cent of the original claim of R1 420 million. While this dispute raged on in the courts, the restraint of trade entered into by Sanlam with the Medscheme transaction lapsed in October 2004. Initial negotiations with Medscheme to acquire a stake in the medical scheme administration business failed because the two parties could not agree on price. Then Sanlam looked into acquiring a stake in Resolution Health, but the Registrar of Medical Schemes refused to approve of the transaction. Resolution Health had two negative salient features. The first was that almost 65 per cent of its members were civil servants, who were soon compelled by the state to join the Government Employees Medical Scheme (GEMS). Furthermore, Resolution was under investigation for mismanagement, which resulted in the refusal to accredit the transaction with Sanlam. Finally, in January 2008, Sanlam acquired a stake in the administration of Bestmed, thus returning Sanlam to medical scheme administration, or health management. The company also bought a stake in the medical scheme brokering firm Optivest. Sanlam Health grew its administration through mergers of medical schemes under its administration. In 2009 Bestmed merged with Telemed, which gave Sanlam Health Management another 65 000 members. Through an attempt to acquire Eternity Private Health Administrators, Sanlam Health also brought CAMAF

[62] Sanlam: The IT journey, 1990–2014: 23–5; 31–2.

(Chartered Accountants Medical Aid Fund) in under its administration. The application of the i-Med IT platform for this medical scheme administration, which Sanlam Health acquired during the Eternity negotiations, was only suitable for the administration of in-house schemes and therefore failed to deliver optimal results in the general administration functions. Only CAMAF operated well on i-Med. The relationship between Sanlam and Bestmed also broke down in 2011 and left Sanlam Health Distribution Management in negative territory once again. Sanlam seemed incapable of succeeding in the healthcare sector. In 2011 Ahmed Banderker was appointed to salvage Sanlam Health. By 2012 Sanlam courted Topmed again. They signed an agreement whereby Topmed became Sanlam's medical scheme of choice for its staff. In 2014 Sanlam acquired a stake in Medscheme's holding company AfroCentric Health. The tale of Sanlam and healthcare therefore concluded with Sanlam in medical scheme administration at arm's length.[63] Sanlam's experience with healthcare was disappointing and added to the difficulty in Sanlam Life to restore positive new business inflows.

Strategic intent: growth and wealth creation

After the conclusion of the ABSA transaction and the cash-rich Sanlam's decision to buy back its shares, a notable improvement in market confidence developed. The share price rose to well above R12.00 by the end of 2005 and the discount to EV dropped below 10 per cent. The financial analysts were upbeat about the anticipated upward trend in the Sanlam share price. That rise reflected in the growing proportion of institutional shareholders to 60 per cent of Sanlam's shareholders in 2006. Offshore shareholders made up 24 per cent of Sanlam's shareholders. Individual shareholders' stake in the company diminished from 47 per cent shortly after demutualization to 17 per cent in 2006. Expectations materialized, since in 2007 the share price rose to around R22.75 and traded at only a 3 per cent discount to EV. Overall performance of the Group in 2006 pointed to the growth strategy gaining sustainable momentum. New business volumes exceeded R100 billion, and core earnings R4 billion for the first time.[64] The performance reflected a group reaping the benefits of a focused business strategy implemented since 2003, but the significant development was the change in the structure of the business. During 2002 more than 75 per cent of all new business inflows was generated through the life insurance business. In 2007 new business from the traditional life market declined to around 20 per cent, while the performance of innovative private investment products moved into fast-growing territory. By 2007 Sanlam had built the largest private

[63] SA: Minutes of Sanlam Ltd Board, 2002–2014; Sanlam Life Board Minutes 2002–2014.
[64] Sanlam Annual Report, 2007: 119.

client business in South African in Sanlam Private Investments. SPI held assets under management of more than R50 billion in 2007, reversing a loss-making operation of 2002 to deliver R80 million pre-tax profit in 2007. Financial services' net contribution to group results rose by 20 per cent, core earnings per share rose by 27 per cent, new business volumes rose by 26 per cent, the value of new life business rose by 31 per cent, and return of Group Equity Value per share rose to 18.8 per cent. Van Zyl described 2007 as the first year in which Sanlam had achieved real growth since the early 2000s. He considered the establishment years of his back-to-basics strategy as years of 'fixing the business and developing a wide base'. The foundations of the turnaround strategy were improved capital efficiency and diversification.

At this point in the strategic redirection of Sanlam, Ian Kirk was appointed Chief Executive: Capital, Strategy and Special Projects. Kirk was the deputy CEO of Liberty, and had experience in the insurance industry that complemented the existing strategic overhaul conceptualized and implemented by the entire executive team. The ability to effect strategic turnaround so soon after Van Zyl's appointment as CEO underlines the buy-in and contribution by each individual member of the executive team. When the synergy between Kirk's insurance career and the direction Sanlam was beginning to move towards became apparent to Van Zyl, he invited Kirk to join the Sanlam executive. There were clear synergies between the back-to-basics strategy and Kirk's strategic insurance industry capabilities. In May 2006 Ian Kirk joined Sanlam with the explicit task to apply his expertise to collate the strategic review of the Group. The Sanlam strategic 'back-to-basics' vision had already gained momentum. Kirk joined forces with the executive team to move key aspects of the strategy forward in areas where his expertise complemented the existing executive expertise. The Group strategy based on five pillars, which constituted the basis of Sanlam's subsequent business cluster direction, was the outcome of this collaborative effort. In the context of the emerging Group strategy, Kirk was responsible to launch Project Helix (the establishment of MiWay, direct insurance sold out of Sanlam's call centre technology base), the extension of the existing partnership with the Indian Shriram Group, and the direct marketing strategy to expand distribution channels in the modern era of digital technology. Kirk also ran a cost project between Sanlam and Santam to enhance Group efficiency. (The roll-out of these initiatives will be discussed later in this chapter.) In June 2007 Kirk was appointed CEO of Santam, where he continued efficiency enhancing operations effecting stronger alignment between Santam and the other business units in the Sanlam Group. This development was in itself part of the group 'back-to-basics' strategy.

The performance of Sanlam in 2007 confirmed delivery on the Group's comprehensive growth strategy. Sanlam 'Thinking Ahead' posted a 16 per cent rise in net earnings from financial services, a 23 per cent rise in core earnings, but a 29 per cent decline in headline earnings. New business volumes were up by 26 per cent, but more importantly, net inflow of funds was reversed from a net outflow in 2006 to a R11 billion inflow in

2007. These results indicated that the Group strategy was beginning to deliver the desired outcome. The vision of becoming the world-class financial services provider was approaching realization. This was now the time to re-engineer the strategy to achieve new targets; since sustained success depended on a dynamic strategy, capable of constant adaptability and innovation, Sanlam was sitting on excess capital without a clear vision of where to invest it. Furthermore, the Group showed strong growth since 2006, which indicated the importance of refining 'strategic intent'. In 1989 C.K. Prahalad and Gary Hamel wrote in their Harvard Business Review article 'Strategic intent', that such intent meant something like establishing global leadership in a particular market or industry. Just seeking to increase shareholder wealth was not going to get the troops excited. The Group's 'strategic intent' to 'grow the platform' towards being the leader in wealth creation and a world-class, truly South African diversified financial services group, came from the new 2006 Kirk-formulated strategy. Van Zyl and Kirk were fully *ad idem* about this strategy.

The foundation of 'strategic intent' as it came to be expressed in the 2006 Sanlam strategy, comprised five building blocks. Underlying this strategy was building block one, namely increased diversity and improved efficiency. This translated into releasing capital from the life business and growing its scale of play in administration, and improved distribution in order to increase the client and asset base. Building block two focused on diversification of financial services by selectively growing credit capabilities. Building block three again emphasized the strengthening of bancassurance in support of the diversification of financial services offerings. Building block four was sustained transformation of the Group to display the demographics of South Africa and address the needs of the full spectrum of society. Building block five was to reprioritize internationalization. In the forthcoming years Sanlam would stabilize its expansion into the ELM, but pursue a differentiated strategy in the UK and other developed markets.[65] The implementation of these strategic goals translated into the revised cluster structure. Cluster one was retail services, which included SPF, SDM, and Sanlam UK. In 2008, Sanlam's operations in the UK were consolidated in a separate company, Sanlam UK, managed by a Sanlam Executive Officer, Lukas van der Walt. Sanlam UK operated separately and independently from SPF. Cluster two was the institutional cluster, housing Sanlam Investments (formerly SIM), Sanlam Employee Benefits (SEB), and Sanlam Capital Markets (SCM). Cluster three was the short-term insurance cluster, where all the short-term insurance business was consolidated, including that of Santam, the largest short-term insurance company in South Africa. The new cluster was cluster four, the corporate cluster (corporate Head Office), responsible for the Group's centralized functions. These included finance and risk management, marketing and communications,

[65] SA: Minutes of Sanlam Ltd Board, 3/3/2008: Sanlam Board Summit, 1/8/2007.

human resources, information technology, and CSI. Sanlam Independent Financial Services invested in independent customer-facing entities and intermediary financial services.

The operating cluster structure was reconfigured again in 2011. The business of Sanlam was subsequently conducted through the following clusters: SPF, responsible for the retail business; SEM, driving Sanlam's financial services in emerging markets; SI, providing investment solutions to individual and institutional clients; and Santam in the short-term insurance cluster. The reconfiguring showed that the diversification strategy succeeded in creating a diversified financial services company. The out-engineering of the corporate cluster during the 2011 reconfiguration showed that the existing clusters were successful in delivery on focused business targets under dedicated and capable management. This performance meant that the overarching role of the corporate cluster could be reduced or 'out-engineered'. The publication of the King III report in 2009 called for a more profound emphasis on communicating overall performance of corporates to the broader society. The public had to be informed about the sustainability of the enterprise in all aspects of operation. The 'Triple bottom line' requirement mandated information not only about financial performance, but also social and environmental performance. In the Sanlam clusters diversified business operations delivered on all three dimensions of business sustainability. This was supported by sustained transformation. Transformation promised sustainability. The business environment was severely constrained by the effects of the GFC since 2007, but within five years of formulating the 'growing the platform' strategy, the Group was in a sound competitive position domestically—and growing globally.

The sources of business development in the clusters were synergies in the Group, new acquisitions, and expansions. The overall performance of Sanlam between 2002 and 2013 is reflected in Table 6.3. Headline earnings improved from R2 127 million to R8 062 million. The embedded value per share rose from 1 032 cents per share to 4 121 cents per

Table 6.3. Sanlam performance, 2002–2013

	2002	2004	2006	2008	2010	2012	2013
Total group equity value (Rm)	27 087	36 682	46 811	45 238	57 361	75 352	84 409
Total assets (Rm)	18 357	228 024	335 482	31 708	361 191	490 953	561 304
Headline earnings (Rm)*	2127	3185	6838	2702	5122	5763	8062
Embedded value (EV) per share (cps)	1032	1344	2047	2213	2818	3707	4 121
Return on EV per share %	−9.2%	27.7%	31%	−1.7%	18.2%	22%	17%
Total issued shares (m)	2 654.5	2 767.5	2 303.6	2 190.1	2 100	2 100	2 100
Headline earnings per share (cps)*	80.8	116.6	304.9	132.2	252.4	292.1	395
Share price (cents)	760	1300	1830	1700	2792	4477	5324
Dividend per share	37	50	77	98	115	215	200
Sanlam life capital adequacy Ratio (CAR)	1.7	3.7	4.4	2.7	3.4	4.3	4.5

Note: * Introduction of IFRS in 2006 changed accounting policy. Figures not fully comparable to period before 2006.
Source: Sanlam annual financial statements, 1998–2016.

share. The return on EV per share rose from -9.2 per cent in 2002 to 17 per cent in 2013. As the CAR improved from 3.7 in 2002 to 4.3 in 2013, Sanlam was displaying its capital stability as well as access to sufficient cash to perform transactions to grow the business. The discussion below on the development in the different business clusters during the decade of Johan van Zyl's turnaround strategy illustrates this performance vividly. The successful implementation of the turnaround strategy rested on the joint vision and dedication of the experienced management team on business unit level, implementing the shared vision.

In the personal finance cluster, the life business was the core of SPFs business. The sustained growth in the nominal value of the life business led to the consistent rise in SPFs contribution to Group financial services earnings between 2007 (46 per cent) and 2013 (52 per cent). By 2013 the life insurance component operated through flexible personal finance solutions to different segments of the market. The Sanlam Sky Solutions (SSS) were the risk products offered to the entry-level market. Sanlam Individual Life focused on delivery to the middle, professional, and small- and medium-sized enterprise markets. The Glacier investment platform provided investment solutions to the high end of the market. Distribution was also segmented. The SSS operations were strengthened by the acquisition of African Life Assurance (South Africa) in 2005. This niche insurance company operated in the entry-level market, thus aligning with SSS. SDM had already acquired African Life Assurance operations in other parts of Africa, making the South African acquisition a logical extension of the strategy to deliver financial services more inclusively in South Africa. Channel Life and African Life were integrated into SSS. A dedicated broker division for SSS was established under the management of Ronald Samuels, with regional managers Ian Trollip in the Eastern Cape and Basil Naidoo in KZN. The Sanlam Affiliated Intermediary Service, an affiliated service providing compliance, training, and administrative support to brokers, supported the growth of SSS in this market segment. The number of SSS brokers rose to 215 by 2014 and contributed 12 per cent of SSS broker revenues.[66]

Sanlam consistently sought new distribution channels. Broker services were a growing strength in the distribution channel. In 2010 Sanlam acquired SEESA Financial Planners. This was a network of thirty brokers, who retained their independence, but Sanlam offered them compliance, and practice management support from a Sanlam subsidiary Succession Financial Planners (SFP) This distribution network grew to 120 brokers by 2014, supported by regional managers in Pretoria, Cape Town, Johannesburg, and Durban.[67] The impact of the Conflict of Interest regulations flowing from the FAIS Act, No. 37 of 2002, gazetted in Government Gazette No. 33133 of 19 April 2010, restricted practices whereby service providers (such as Sanlam) could incentivize brokers

[66] *Sandaba*, July 2014: 3; Sanlam Personal Finance, September 2014: 16–17.
[67] Interview with Heinrich Punt, 9/10/2014.

in distributing its products. Sanlam's strategy was to provide support using independent support businesses.

Sanlam Life IT developed another innovative distribution model in 2005. SanlamConnect was an automated advice for specific products. At a Sanlam kiosk in shopping centres in large metropolitan areas, clients could access advice by themselves. Clients could get automated advice based on their risk profile for certain basic products for retirement and savings via the internet. SanlamConnect assumed a level of financial literacy and client sophistication, which proved to be overstated. In 2012 the model was aborted and the IT application decommissioned. A more successful IT application was Sanlam Direct, launched in 1999. This operated through a basic call centre. A client identification system supported the direct marketing model, which assisted Sanlam Direct with selection refining. By 2005 this distribution channel boosted sales in the life business and was IT supported by repeated updates. It was this capability that Ian Kirk spotted as an opportunity to expand distribution. He conceptualized MiWay, a telephonic direct marketing channel for SPF's products. Having observed his young son's adverse reaction to having to work through intermediaries, while electronic technology facilitated online and direct managing of one's affairs, including short-term insurance, Kirk pioneered MiWay. The channel was finally launched in 2008, but not after long and strenuous negotiations with the broker community to ensure they would not boycott Sanlam going forward. Brokers were vehemently opposed to the direct marketing channel, but after consultation with brokers, Kirk agreed that MiWay would operate under a separate licence (not Sanlam), separate infrastructure and separate brand, and that there would be no sharing of data. To ensure success, Kirk got the head of Broker Services, Edward Gibbons, to manage the introduction of MiWay into the market. This distribution channel opened direct access to clients, especially young people, to a wide range of Sanlam insurance, credit and savings products, as well as short-term insurance. Sanlam was not leading the market in this strategy, but doing damage control, as the direct market had been harvested with good results by competitors. MiWay gave Sanlam a new distribution channel, but in 2010 Sanlam sold it to Santam. That put all the short-term business of Sanlam in one vehicle, but reserved exclusive access to MiWay to Sanlam for the distribution of other financial services.[68] By 2014 more than 130 telemarketing agents were using Sanlam Direct and contributed to approximately 10 per cent of Sanlam Life's business.[69]

The SPF focus on the entry-level life market, competed with the SDM market. SDM was therefore moved out of SPF in 2010 and renamed Sanlam Emerging Markets (SEM) as a separate cluster. Heinie Werth managed SEM as part of the overall 'back-to-basics'

[68] SA: Minutes of Sanlam Ltd Board, 2/12/2009; 8/12/2010: Memorandum JPM: Sale of MiWay, 30/11/2010; Interview Ian Kirk, 10/8/2017.

[69] SA: Minutes of Sanlam Ltd, 7/12/2007; Sanlam IT: 27–8.

strategy. SEB was also moved from SPF in 2007 into the institutional cluster, where performance improved by 2008. SPF operated in the South African market and diversified into a number of revenue streams apart from life business—trust business, healthcare management, personal loans, the loyalty programme Reality, and trade and bridging finance through Anglo African Finance (in which SPF had a 65 per cent interest). As a strategic direction to ensure ongoing progress in creating shareholder value, management considered three options at the board summit in August 2007. The first was simply to go about the Group's business as usual—go it alone. The second option was collaboration with strategic partners in a relatively permanent joint venture agreement. The third option was a full sale or merger. The first and last options were not considered, but the second was selected as the one to develop. This brought Sanlam back to the strategy of growth through a bancassurance agreement. It led the company to investigate Project Gliese—negotiations between Sanlam and the First Rand Group on a potential bancassurance deal—in 2007 and 2008. Differences in operational culture between Sanlam and Momentum, the insurance entity in First Rand, the issue of control and sanctioning by the competition authorities, eventually resulted in the termination of this attempt.[70] Sanlam was always out shopping for enhanced distribution vehicles.

The operations of Sanlam UK were integrated into the different clusters when Sanlam UK ceased to operate independently. MIA operated as the life vehicle of Sanlam Life in the UK. Other investment business in the UK formed part of the institutional cluster operations. SPF suffered from contracting demand following the global financial crisis in 2007/2008, but by 2013 SPF recovered market share to contributed 42 per cent to Group Embedded Value (GEV). The life business made up 93 per cent of the SPF EV. Growing the SPF business meant a massive effort in the uninsured market. This afforded Sanlam an opportunity to establish partnerships with empowerment enterprises, train brokers and agents on the Sanlam products, and simultaneously develop the credit business, also through small empowerment initiatives. This was where the original life business of 2003 was at in 2013.

The institutional cluster of 2007, renamed the investment cluster in 2011, had a long and complicated path towards strategic redirection and success. The legacy position from which SIM developed was that of an investment division of a long-term insurer. The culture of securing stable investment returns for policyholder bonuses did not serve a diversified financial services company seeking to attract investments on the basis of delivering the best return in the market. To deliver on the high expectation of investment returns, Hendrik Bester (former General Manager: Investments) insisted on Sanlam Investments being granted independence to perform an investment function determined by optimal return and not conservative stable bonuses. Bester did the same when he

[70] SA: Minutes of Sanlam Ltd Board, 8/2/2008.

insisted on permission to take Sanlam Properties out of the long-term insurance business environment in 1989. The fact that clients had moved out of long-term insurance products since the 1990s, and moved towards structured high-return investment wealth products, left Sanlam at risk. Underperforming investment returns on policyholder funds also jeopardized the ability of the life business to attract new business. The Gensec acquisition and subsequent disappointing performance led to the restructuring thereof and gradual building of an independent investment function in SIM. It was only with the appointment of Johan van der Merwe as CEO of SIM in mid-2002, that a slow, but focused process of building an investment house emerged. Van der Merwe was an investment manager at Genbel at the time of the 1993 unbundling of the Gencor conglomerate. Then he was involved in the Gencor acquisition of Billiton and subsequently joined Investec Asset Management. Sanlam Unit Trusts (SUT—later renamed Sanlam Collective Investments) operated in Sanlam Life. Only in 2003 was SUT moved to SIM, albeit still a subsidiary of Sanlam Life. Sanlam's unit trusts had a very good track record, as described in the previous chapter. Investment management just became more sophisticated after 2000. The culture of risk appetite and high returns characterizing asset managers in the investment banking and asset management industry was far removed from Sanlam's asset managers. In SIM this cultural transformation developed slowly, because first the business had to attract talent, pay sufficiently well to keep them at SIM, or lose them to the highly competitive industry players. This occurred with Omri Thomas' resignation as SIM Chief Investment Officer after only one year in the position, following an attractive offer from a competitor. Superior investment returns held SIM back, exacerbated by the effects of the GFC market volatility and high fixed costs. Underperformance also undermined SIM's ability to attract retail funds. An overhaul of the SIM business model in 2005 placed the cluster on the road to improved performance and industry competitiveness. SIM's business was restructured into 'boutiques' of investment operations. These were focused investment functions headed up by specialists in the different 'boutiques'. The different functional units were active quants, small caps, core and unconstrained equities, alternative investments, fixed-interest investments, and liberty-driven solutions. Individual results in each unit had to match overall 'boutique' objectives.[71]

The GFC adverse market volatility contributed, inter alia, to the underperformance of SIM. SIM experienced a net outflow of funds in 2007. In 2007, SIM contributed 30.24 per cent to the net result from financial services in the Sanlam Group. Very chequered results had flowed from early overambitious business initiatives in the UK since the early 1990s. During Van Zyl's back-to-basics strategy, the investment business was consolidated, and focused and capable investment specialists were attracted. The

[71] SA: Minutes of SIM Board, 3/4/2006.

challenge lay in developing a high-return investment culture, but that required an appropriate appetite for risk and specialists with an industry track record. The business in the institutional cluster included SIM as the second-largest investment manager in South Africa by 2007, collective investments, asset management, employee benefits, private investments, private equity, strategic property services, and structured investment solutions. SIM also expanded into emerging markets and the UK. SIM established its specialist capabilities by 2013. The growth figures underline the success: operating profit growth exceeded more than 50 per cent for three consecutive years since 2004. This profit growth was reduced to 19 per cent in 2007 and 1 per cent in 2009, but solid investment performance was soon restored.

Sanlam's strategy to expand operations into markets outside South Africa always included operations in the niche investment market in the UK as a developed market for Sanlam's high-end-of-the-market wealth products. The revised strategy in the UK since the mid-1990s acquisition drive had been to create the relationships, build trust, product propositions, and structures for group linkages to develop. From 2009 Sanlam UK operated as a strategic management company, despite the shares in MIA, Principal, Buckles, Nucleus, Intrinsic, and the Punter Southall Group still being held by Sanlam Netherlands Holdings BV. Management still considered the linkages in 2010 to be 'sub-scale'. As part of the overall Sanlam strategy post-2006 to enhance return on capital, the relationships were harvested, using Sanlam Fund Solutions (SFS) to attract investment funds via the different linked independent financial advisers. Lukas van der Walt, CEO of Sanlam UK, managed the positioning of Sanlam UK as a wealth management business in retail financial services, providing life and pension product and wrap administration services. Despite massive volatility in 2010 following the Japanese earthquake, the tsunami in South East Asia, and the Arab Spring, the UK business nevertheless attracted 43 per cent more funds in 2011—at £266 million it was significantly lower than the £622 million budget. In January 2011, Sanlam UK added Border Asset Management to its wealth management businesses. The SPF Glacier investment platform proved a popular investment vehicle into foreign markets, also the UK. By 2012 Glacier was the biggest LISP[72] in South Africa and Glacier International attracted R824 million in investments. Sanlam UK turned disappointing performance of the Sanlam UK investments under its management in 2008 around. By 2013 this had become a major driver of new business flows into the investment cluster.

Strategic diversification through the investment cluster delivered a highly diversified suite of investment services integrated by the leadership of Johan van der Merwe as cluster CEO. This cluster offered asset management, wealth management, international investments, and international services, either from Sanlam businesses or in partnerships

[72] Linked Investment Service Provider.

with specialist services providers across the globe. SIM and Sanlam Structured Solutions performed the asset management function in South Africa. The investment cluster rolled wealth management products out with partners in Australia, Switzerland, and the UK. The SEB, SCM, and Retirement Fund Administrators (RFA) collaborated through joint ventures with smaller players and empowerment entities in the market. In the international investment function, Sanlam collated all the partnerships in international investments into Sanlam International Investment Partners (SIIP) in 2013. These international partners were Four Capital, a London-based European and global equity manager in which Sanlam held a 54 per cent stake; Eight Investment Partners, an Asia-Pacific asset manager, based in Sydney and Hong Kong, in which Sanlam held a 62.5 per cent stake; Centre Asset Managers, an American and global asset manager based on Wall Street, with Sanlam owning 63.5 per cent of its equity; and Artisan, a European property management company on the Isle of Man. Sanlam owned 33.3 per cent of its equity. Sanlam International Mutual Fund Administrator, Sanlam Asset Management Ireland, Sanlam UK, and P^2 also comprised part of the cluster.

The integration of SEB into the cluster was strategically managed to arrive at two goals. The first was to create a dynamic, motivated team in SEB, and the second was to enhance the investment performance of SEB. Management noted that the SEB team suffered from a lack of vision and drive to improve performance. The Exco and Johan van der Merwe then initiated an Active Learning Programme called 'Stretch'. This exercise required SEB employees to come up with a model to grow the business, based on innovative business opportunities. Three teams worked to deliver proposals, which resulted in a restructuring and rationalization of functionality of SEB's operations. The Retirement Fund Administration was merged with Coris Capital before, and subsequent to the migration into the institutional cluster, became part of the wider retirement annuity administration platform of Coris Capital. The result was almost immediate. In 2008 SEB profits rose by 63 per cent. Synergies with new products developed by Sanlam Structured Solutions, a business within the cluster, contributing to the new life in SEB and enhancing the cluster performance. In 2013, SEB's remarkable turnaround delivered operating profit before tax and minorities of R1500 million and the value of new business exceeded R300 million, compared to R855 million profits and R266 million new business in 2012. By 2013 the institutional cluster had grown its contribution to Group financial services to 24 per cent. This performance was a significant improvement from the 11.2 per cent contribution in 2002 and 13.4 per cent contribution in 2003. SEB was one of the divisions in the cluster that gained most from the stronger investment climate in the cluster.[73] The success was built on Sanlam's own investment management

[73] SA: Minutes of Sanlam Ltd Board, 6/6/20007; 23/11/2007; 3/12/2008; Sanlam Integrated Report, 2011: 13; Sanlam Integrated Report 2013.

capabilities, supported by its products and partnerships aligning with the Sanlam investment philosophy and internationalization drive.

The transformation of Sanlam into 'the leader in wealth creation and protection in South Africa, leading that process in emerging markets and playing a niche role in the developed markets',[74] had clear strategic business implications. The unfolding of expansion through SEM was the most significant development in the Group in terms of the articulated vision. In 2007, SDM had been part of SPF, but then assumed an independent cluster position from 2008. The reluctance during the early 1990s to expand into developing markets was reversed once Sanlam changed its business model during the turnaround strategy. Sanlam linked its aspirations with regard to the ELM market through African Life, Channel, and Shriram, where it leveraged knowledge off that market segment through Sanlam products. Sanlam developed competitive products for the ELM in South Africa, other African markets, and India. SDM contributed 7 per cent to net results from financial services in 2007 and increased this contribution to 18 per cent by 2013. Non-South African new business flows in SDM increased from 23.4 per cent in 2007 to 54.8 per cent in 2010 and non-South African net flows of funds in SDM stood at 63.7 per cent of net flows in 2010. The strategic redirection of Sanlam to the ELM was the correct strategy for future growth in new business flows. At the end of 2013 operational profits before tax and minorities, had doubled from R850 million in 2012 to R1.736 billion. That was 21 per cent organic growth complemented by further investment in Shriram, India. Operating profit after tax and minorities exceeded R1 billion for the first time.[75] The growth in demand by the middle class in African and Asian markets was an unprecedented business opportunity to Sanlam.

The expansion by SDM into the ELM was a manifestation of the Dunning'*OLI* model that explained internationalization on the grounds of ownership (*O*), location (*L*) and internalization *(I)*.[76] Sanlam had developed insurance products for the entry-level market since its inception and had extensive experience in tailoring products to the needs of first-time clients to the industry. The company also had the location advantage through its embeddedness in a sophisticated financial system able to support life insurance with linked financial services. Another important geographical advantage of Sanlam was its location in Africa, and in the South African market, a diversely segmented market, including an entry-level segment, for which Sanlam had developed appropriate products throughout its history. These conditions provided the company with country-specific advantages (CSAs) such as product knowledge, experienced staff, and distribution channels adaptable to similar markets in foreign locations. As Sanlam acquired strong operational capacity in African ELMs, the roll-out of home-grown products into those markets occurred rapidly.

[74] Sanlam Integrated Report, 2013. [75] SA: Minutes of Sanlam Ltd Board, 5/3/2013.

[76] J.H. Dunning (1993) *The Globalization of Business*. London: Routledge.

SDM's operations in the ELM were not smooth. By 2007/2008 first-year lapses in Aflife and Channel were higher than expected. The loss-making Channel outbound call centre was closed in 2008. This pointed to compromised sales quality and imperfect selection, which also resulted in client complaints to the Ombudsman. During 2008 Aflife was reorganized and rebranded as Sanlam Sky Solutions. This rebranding caused confusion among clients and resulted in complaints to the Ombudsman about the quality of service. In 2009, SEM acquired PSGs 34.6 per cent stake in Channel Life, which gave SEM a 63 per cent stake in Channel Life. This acquisition broadened SEM's Sky Solutions (Aflife South Africa) penetration in South Africa and retained the distribution relationship with the fast-growing Capitec Bank. Channel's premium growth rose from R200 million in 2006 to R280 million in 2008, which justified the SEM acquisition. Other innovative mechanisms to grow the Sanlam distribution channel included establishing insurance companies as joint ventures with church organizations. An example is the Kganya Insurance Company established with the Zion Christian Church organization in 2011.[77]

Experience of insurance varied in the different African markets. In Botswana (through its joint venture with Botswana Life) and Tanzania (through Aflife) there was excellent group business and bancassurance, but less individual business. In Kenya (through Pan African Life) political volatility led to slower growth, but in Ghana (through ELAC) and Zambia (through Aflife) the reverse manifested. Long-term investments in the cluster included a recapitalization of Channel Life and a gradual integration of Santam's short-term products into the Sky Solutions offerings. Africa's economies had shown impressive growth since the first half of the 2000s. It made business sense to explore entry into Nigeria as well, but although it was one of the largest African economies (the SEAN economies—South Africa, Egypt, Algeria and Nigeria) it did not yet form part of Sanlam's focus. The precarious nature of Nigerian governance required Sanlam to diligently investigate the potential market for a partner into the Nigerian market. From 2008 Sanlam engaged with various financial sector entities in Nigeria. In 2010 the final decision was made to partner with First Bank in Nigeria. SEM entered the large Nigerian market, but its life market was small and underdeveloped. A licence to conduct life business in Nigeria was issued in February 2010 to First Bank and that opened the door to commence SEM's business. SEM signed an agreement with First Bank for the distribution of Sanlam ELM products in Nigeria. In 2010 operations expanded into Malawi via NICO Malawi and during the second half of 2010 Sanlam Life Insurance Uganda entered the Ugandan market. In these markets Sanlam also entered the health management business in 2010.[78] The growth in the ELM markets exceeded expectations. By 2010 SDM contributed 8.6 per cent of Group financial services income and by 2013

[77] This church organization was established in 1924 and has a following well in excess of 5 million.

[78] SA: Minutes of Sanlam Ltd Board, 3/12/2008; 3/12/2009; 8/12/2010; Sanlam Limited: CEO Report.

this had risen to 18 per cent. Operations included retail and group life insurance and related business, credit and banking financial services, investment management, and general insurance. These operations included the business in Namibia and India.

The first success with Shriram Life in India offered opportunities for further expansion during 2008. In May 2008 Shriram established Shriram General Insurance (SGI). Santam managed that business on behalf of Sanlam. Changes in the Indian regulatory context complicated Sanlam's intention of growing its stake in Shriram. Regulation in India prohibited a promoter of an insurance company from owning more than 26 per cent of the equity. Owners in possession of more than 26 per cent had to divest over a period of ten years. Foreign owners were exempted from this, but if Sanlam could find a bank replacement equity partner and link its business to a bancassurance model, the company could achieve the higher growth rates it was after. In 2009 Sanlam established a new dedicated distribution channel, New Channel, in India. When Sanlam entered India, it had to pay a 357 per cent premium on the share capital as a prerequisite for entry—a practice Sanlam regarded as 'common practice to gain entry to the Indian market'. By 2010 the cumulative annualized return on the R242.2 million investment in Shriram was still negative.[79] It was therefore important to grow the business. Sanlam was positive on the growth potential of the Indian economy and therefore sought avenues to increase its footprint. The global financial crisis adversely affected potential insurance markets in Africa and India—SEM experienced a slowdown in growth during the last half of 2009 and in 2010. Sanlam waited for regulatory amendments in India, which were finally granted by the Cabinet in 2012, permitting FDI into local insurance companies from 26 per cent to 49 per cent. This opened the door to one of the largest financial services transactions in India in 2012. Sanlam acquired a stake in Shriram Capital India (SCI) for R1.920 billion. Sanlam's direct interest in Shriram Life Insurance, its stake in SCI, as well as its stake in Shriram Management Share Trust, were placed in a holding company. The holding company held Shriram's 85 per cent and Sanlam's 29.2 per cent stake in SCL. Sanlam also bought a 4.97 per cent stake in Shriram Transport Finance Company (STFC).[80] This was a market poised for growth.

From India the Sanlam strategy to access South East Asia went to a strategic acquisition in Malaysia. In 2012 Sanlam acquired a 49 per cent stake in Pacific and Orient Malaysia for R817 million. SEM Mauritius (Pty) Ltd, a wholly-owned subsidiary of SEM, bought a further 26 per cent in STFC, bringing SEM's direct interest to 6.67 per cent. SEM also increased its stakes in CIH (Namibia), the NICO Group operating in Malawi, Uganda, and Tanzania (49 per cent) and concluded a stronger agreement with Santam, whereby Santam acquired an economic interest in Sanlam's general insurance assets to a value of R181 million. In 2013 it was agreed with Santam that SEM and Santam would be

[79] SA: Minutes of Sanlam Ltd Board, 10/3/2010: Memorandum JvZ/af: Future strategy in India, 4/3/2010.
[80] SA: Minutes of Sanlam Ltd Board, 9/3/2011; 22/8/2011; 5/12/2012.

the only Group vehicles for investment in emerging-market short-term insurance ventures. Sanlam's SEM managed the investments and Santam performed the role of technical adviser and reinsurance partner. In return, Santam retained a 33 per cent economic interest in general insurance investments and other individual businesses.[81] In all SEM operations Sanlam secured firm control of the decentralized operations through the local boards, where Sanlam's CEO and CFO represented Sanlam.

Delivering on commitment

A decade after assuming the leadership of Sanlam Ltd, Johan van Zyl was in a position to confirm to shareholders that Sanlam had delivered on its commitment made in 2003. That commitment was to deliver growth, operational and cost efficiencies, diversification, capital efficiency, and transformation. The Sanlam Group delivered 12.03 per cent annual compound growth on Group Equity Value between 2002 and 2013 (the first decade of Johan van Zyl's management). Asset growth of 40.77 per cent was reported. Headline earnings per share rose by 17.31 per cent and embedded value per share by 14.85 per cent (all annual compound growth between 2002 and 2013). This achievement occurred in highly volatile economic conditions, exacerbated by the GFC. In South Africa GDP growth was sluggish, inflation was an average of 5.26 per cent, personal disposable income increased by 11.4 per cent annual compound growth and household savings declined from R3.1 billion in 2002 to negative saving of –R632 million in 2013.[82] This was the result of weak economic growth. As the Group strategy was based on optimal growth on Group Equity Value (RoGEV—Return on Group Equity Value), the benchmark was to outperform the Group's cost of capital by at least 100 basis points. The cost of capital was calculated at the risk-free nine-year bond rate (RFR—Risk Free Return) plus 300 basis points. The compounded RoGEV of the Group since Sanlam demutualized and listed in 1998 outperformed that target comprehensively by 2013. The target was exceeded by more than 170 basis points and the actual RFR by around 200 basis points in 2013.[83]

Sustained quantitative delivery on growth in the South African financial services sector had to contend with the increasingly demanding and complex regulatory environment. Statutory regulation of the financial services industry gradually began to followed global trends in implementing the so-called Twin Peaks regulatory dispensation, where prudential regulation is separated from market conduct regulation. In South

[81] SA: Minutes of Sanlam Ltd Board, 5/12/2012; 13/3/2012; 5/6/2013; 12/2/2014;

[82] South African Reserve Bank, Quarterly Bulletin of Statistics, 2002–2014.

[83] Sanlam Integrated Report, 2013: 121.

Africa the SARB performs prudential regulation and leaves market conduct regulation in the financial services industry to the FSB. Furthermore, the political agenda of the state, desiring regulation through industry charters of ownership, control and management of enterprises in different sectors of the economy, and especially over the direction and nature of delivery of financial services to the people, added to the regulatory overload. Market conduct by financial services intermediaries came under a growing body of regulations in terms of the Treat Customer Fairly (TCF) framework. This led to the promulgation of the National Credit Act, and amendments to the FAIS (Financial and Advisory Intermediary Services) legislation on matters concerning the protection of customers' private information, intermediary commission structures, rebates of asset managers, regulation of 'appropriate' remuneration for certain products, and state intervention in the regulation of the retirement industry, social security, and medical schemes. The Sanlam Group operated in each of these areas of expanding regulation. Apart from the uncertainty of operation caused by the drawn-out discussion papers and interventions, it implied unfair competition in a market where Sanlam had successfully established itself as a South African corporate citizen.

Sanlam responded positively and proactively to the BEE and transformation aspects of the growing regulatory overload. In these instances it was considered a business imperative. Sanlam built on its empowerment history by repeatedly presenting its transformation credentials as simply doing what the company had done since 1918. The statutorily sanctioned B-BBEE industry charters and DTI scorecards impacted on Sanlam's choice of business partners. The innovative and broad interpretation of the transformation agenda delivered exceptionally favourable results to the company during the Van Zyl opening decade. The UB transaction was the signature transaction, but was supplemented by numerous other partnerships with small and medium-sized enterprises with an empowerment component. By 2013 close to 30 per cent of Sanlam's shareholders were blacks—including the PIC (Public Investment Commissioner) and small black entities. The sound business principles underlying the UB transaction reached maturity in 2013. In 2006, the favourable financial position of UB's book led Sanlam to offer UB an early payment of dividends on the Sanlam shares in the latter's portfolio. The providers of funding to UB argued that, despite the strict prohibitive conditions on the sale of Sanlam shares and dividend payments until debt is paid, the strong performance of the shares and the subsequent high dividend earned by UB on its Sanlam shares justified an early payment. Sanlam therefore paid a dividend of R50 million to UB with the explicit instruction that it had to be made accessible to the beneficiaries of the Sanlam–UBCDT.[84]

[84] SA: Minutes of Sanlam Ltd Board, 7/12/2005.

The UB business relationship delivered on expectations. By the maturity date at the end of 2013, the 56.5 million 'A' deferred Sanlam shares would vest if UB had delivered on the conditions of the transaction, and to the extent that an assumed value of 765 cents per deferred share had been accumulated. The value of the accumulation was calculated based on a formula linked to the quantum and profitability of South African-sourced new business volume growth in Sanlam. This growth was calculated to be R57.1 million by the end of 2012. The bulk of the new business came in the growth of Sanlam Sky. The withdrawal by the PIC of a substantial portion of its mandate to SIM in 2006 undermined the performance of UB in the investment cluster. The counter performance by Sanlam helped to reduce the negative impact of the PICs decision. Sanlam's share buy-back schemes gave the share price much-needed support. In effect, this management action increased UB's shareholding from 8 per cent to 11.4 per cent at the end of December 2012. The sixfold increase in the Sanlam share price therefore assisted UB by 2013 to accumulate substantial value to redeem all debt and vest the 'A' deferred shares. By 31 December 2013 UB owned a 14 per cent stake (292.5 million shares) in Sanlam, all debt redeemed. This maturity outcome was assisted by the rise in Sanlam's share price from 765 cents to more than 8000 cents in 2013, as well as the reduced number of shares in the market. Van Zyl and Motsepe commented on the mutually beneficial nature of the business relationship. The business partners were so content with their relationship that they entered into a joint venture, the UB Phase 2. Sanlam undertook to assist UB in becoming the leading black-controlled financial services business in South Africa.[85]

Developing the Sanlam business translated into delivering on commitments. The UB Phase 2 transaction took Sanlam's empowerment legacy into the realm of functional transformation of the Group as truly South African. For a decade under Van Zyl Sanlam sold its customers a promise. That promise was to meet obligations to clients. To achieve that the company needed people, values, and a brand. Sanlam implemented corporate governance structures right from the board to lower levels of management. The board was the highest body overseeing corporate governance and ethical practice and compliance. In the first South African Business Ethics Survey (SABES) in which Sanlam participated in 2013, the company outperformed the other financial services companies surveyed. The outcome showed that respondents were aware of the Sanlam Code of Ethics, knew where to obtain advice on ethical matters, and how to report unethical conduct. The most important achievement was the transformation of the Sanlam people's profile. In its employment profile the ratio of black to white employees changed from 30.3:69.7 in 2004 to 65.4:34.6 in 2013. This reflected the policy to ensure diversity, but to avoid exclusion, to reflect the demographic profile of the country. The Sanlam

[85] SA; Minutes of Sanlam Ltd Board, 2/3/2012; 5/12/2012; 4/12/2013; 5/3/2014; *Financial Mail*, 26/3/2014: 'Motsepe's new ambition. Forget mining, financial services is his next big play': 20–4.

Table 6.4. Sanlam Group B-BBEE scorecard, 2008–2012 (verified June 2013)

	% weighting	2012 Total score	2011 Total score	2010 Total score	2009 Total score	2008 Total score
Ownership	20	20.49	19.34	17.33	18.2	16.65
Management control	10	8.61	8.96	8.16	7.54	7.74
EE	15	4.52	7.04	6.71	4.04	3.83
Skills development	15	12.23	9.91	9.49	9.46	1.36
Preferential procurement	20	16.59	17.02	17.16	15.46	17.56
Enterprise development	15	15	15	15	15	15
Socio-economic development	5	3.48	3.81	2.36	2.84	3.04
Total score	100	80.92	81.08	76.21	72.54	65.18
B-BBEE procurement Recognition level		110%	110%	100%	100%	100%
B-BBEE status level contributor		3	3	3	4	4
Black ownership		30.5%	29.92%	28.09%	25.45%	23.59%
Black female ownership		7.28%	7.34%	1.67%	2.75%	1.66%

Source: Sanlam transformation report, 2013: 84.

Group Employment Equity Forum operated as a consultative forum to improve EE implementation and communication. To identify high-potential and specialized black employees for management level, was a challenge, given the growth and delivery promise Van Zyl so openly communicated as his commitment to the Sanlam stakeholders. The Group engaged in several graduate programmes to support education and training of people for employment in the company. The SanlamUp Graduate Development Programme, the Actuarial Graduate Programme, the Open Your World 2013 Vacation Development Programme, and the Sanlam CA Training Programme are dedicated programmes to give the best talent access to careers in Sanlam. While seeking to deliver on the promise to comply with the B-BBEE scorecard of the DTI, as well as the transformation targets of the FSC, the determining variable for Sanlam was delivering growth and thus value to its stakeholders. These empowerment criteria operated across a wide range of activities, adding up to a B-BBEE level contributor to black economic empowerment. In Table 6.4 the progress on the official scorecard is reflected.

Sanlam improved its score on black ownership and black management control marginally, but performed almost on full target with respect to skills development, preferred procurement, and entrepreneurship development of black people. The transformation record depended largely on the perception of South African society of the Sanlam Group. Performing outside strictly insurance and financial services was not new to Sanlam. Empowerment had been its history. Desmond Smith, the Sanlam Ltd Chairman, commented: ‘Values are universal: they transcend political, religious and cultural barriers. We believe that our values which have formed the bedrock of our company since it was established some 95 years ago are fundamental to what we now call sustainable business.'[86]

The transformation compliance challenge operated in conjunction with CSI as an outward community engagement commitment, but also had to translate into an in-house changed content and committed workforce. The *Sanlam Blueprint for Success* was an initiative to build the organizational culture of Sanlam. During Sanlam's first half-century, a family-like organizational culture characterized the Sanlam workforce. The people called themselves *Sanlammers*. In the truly South African era of the second decade of the twenty-first century management wanted to revitalize the spirit of Sanlam around the values of the new era. Management launched the *Blueprint for Success* initiative to increase engagement levels of employees of '*our*' organization. The initiative presented the culture of Sanlam as characterized by humility, tradition, and success. The *Blueprint for Success* wanted to retain what already existed in Sanlam, but also to build it to a higher level of performance. The initiative drove this organizational culture by defining and measuring the achievement thereof. The assessment of workforce engagement showed a relative sense of organizational coherence, but underlined the need for sustained communication to succeed.[87]

Reporting on the sustainability of organizations required an engagement with the organization-in-society actions. Corporate social investment comprised an integral part of the transformation process, but also developed naturally from existing social engagements. Sanlam CSI directed efforts to grow the Sanlam business, but also to transform South African society. Social investment was principle-based. That meant the CSI activities were directly linked to Sanlam's core businesses, whereby the Group's business would be sustained. Five principles constitute the basis of CSI operations. The first is that CSI is conducted through partnerships and collaboration with NPOs (Non-Profit Organizations), while Sanlam employees are encouraged to join in the activities. The second principle is that CSI must be aligned with Sanlam's core business focus. Therefore Sanlam engaged in six financial literacy programmes targeting young and adult persons. The third underlying principle is that CSI programmes must fit Sanlam's values and brand and contribute to its corporate identity. The fourth principle is that all the CSI initiatives must converge in a holistic approach to social transformation. The fifth underlying principle is that these initiatives must have a long-term dimension. Sanlam was in the CSI environment for the long run to demonstrate the Group's commitment to its stakeholders and society. Between 2009 and 2013 Sanlam's expenditure on CSI rose from R19.3 million to R64 million, or around 1 per cent of net profit after tax. By 2013 Sanlam's CSI operated on two levels. The first was the establishment of the Sanlam Foundation (SF) in 2011 to spearhead the CSI activities. The SF perpetuated the strong

[86] Sanlam Group Sustainability Report, 2013: 7.
[87] SA: Minutes of Sanlam Ltd Board, 5/6/2011; 3/12/2012; Sanlam Sustainability Report, 2013: 40.

education focus of Sanlam's CSI of the past. The SF focus areas were programmes in financial literacy, the strengthening of mathematics, science, and English capabilities, HIV/Aids awareness programmes, environmental awareness programmes, enterprise development, consumer education, and the *Executive Back-to-School* projects. The other dimension of CSI was sponsorships. The determining principle for sponsorships was to support the passion of the people Sanlam serviced. These broad sponsorship categories followed on the sponsorship engagement throughout Sanlam's history. In 2013 Sanlam sponsored nine national projects. The first was the Sanlam Kay Motsepe Schools Cup—a national schools' soccer tournament. In collaboration with the Cancer Association of South Africa (CANSA) Sanlam sponsored the annual golf championship, the Sanlam Cancer Challenge. The *Takalani Sesame* TV and radio broadcasts are directed at school readiness and early literacy development. Another programme is the *Takalani Club*. This initiative operates at selected schools where children are exposed to high-level interactive education programmes (100 schools and around 8 691 children are involved). The *Sing'it Lyrics Competition* is an online lyric writing competition to develop local song-writing capabilities. The best songs are broadcast on *Music TV*. For the 'good life' Sanlam sponsors the Sanlam Investments Food and Wine Design Fair, which is held at Hyde Park in Johannesburg. The showcase of local artisanal content increases business turnover for exhibitors and markets the Sanlam brand. A signature event is the *Woordfees* (Festival of Words), a national cultural festival promoting the Afrikaans language through different literary and musical genres. Sanlam also has a long association with the promotion of financial journalism and sponsors the annual Financial Journalism Awards, which promote critical and cutting-edge financial journalism. The last sponsorship category is the Entrepreneur of the Year Award. This award has become a passport to success for entrepreneurs by affording them exposure to the value of R6.4 million.[88]

The Sanlam CSI is no different from that of other corporates in South Africa. The distinguishing element of the post-2008 B-BBEE CSI statute for business in South Africa was the quantification of impact. Performance in terms of the statute is scored in numbers on a scorecard, adding up to totals, which represented different categories of compliance. Generally, it is argued that it is difficult to determine accurately the impact of CSI on both the organization and its indirect beneficiaries. The scope of inputs and outputs and internal processes in CSI makes it a multidimensional concept that differs between industries and companies, each difficult to measure.[89] In South Africa the FSC and DTI B-BBEE compliance mandates have compelled corporates to submit

[88] Sanlam Sustainability Report, 2012; 2013.

[89] S.A. Waddock and S.B. Grave (1997): 'The Corporate Social Performance–Financial Performance Link.' *Strategic Management Journal*, 18 (4): 303–19; K. Udayasankar (2008): 'Corporate Social Responsibility and Firm Size', *Journal of Business Ethics* 83: 167–75.

information on expenditure, the number of beneficiaries, the impact on society, and contribution to social development. The sustainability report seeks to quantify CSI and contributes to the public perception of corporate citizenship. Sanlam manages its CSI as an extension of its business. Since 2013 the communication thereof in the Sustainability Report has become as important as the financial performance.

Conclusion

At the end of a decade of redirecting Sanlam from constrained operations facing adverse market conditions, capital impairment, and uncertain strategic direction, the Group emerged in an undisputed growth trajectory at the end of 2013. The company celebrated ninety years in the South African financial services landscape in 2008. That year was at the foothills of a successful turnaround trajectory. The Group had the benefit of a team of strategic thinkers at the helm. Johan van Zyl successfully integrated the managerial and intellectual capabilities of his executive team into a consensus corporate strategy of aiming for the globe from the firm foundations of local roots. Strategically the Sanlam Group was held together by a shared business philosophy that creates a 'One Firm' firm. This philosophy had its roots in an entrepreneurial culture with its essence captured in traditional values (such as honesty, hard work, and ethical behaviour), innovation, stakeholder value, and strong ties with business partners.[90] The Group made significant progress towards becoming the leader in client-centric wealth creation, management, and protection in South Africa, and in emerging as a leading player in financial services in selected emerging markets of Africa and Asia, and specific developed markets. The functional structuring of the business of the Sanlam Group into autonomous clusters enabled the human capital capabilities in the Group to operate within a framework of 'tight and loose' parameters. The decade between 2003 and 2013 revisited the roots of Sanlam and confirmed those roots in negotiating the future of the Group. This was confirmed by Van Zyl: 'Sanlam's history has been a key driver of empowerment, economic advancement, wealth creation and protection. This is a legacy and a responsibility that we take very seriously.'[91]

[90] SA: Minutes of Sanlam Ltd Board, 3/12/2012: Sanlam Business Philosophy: November 2012.

[91] *Sanlam. Riding the wave. Sanlam's socio-economic impact in South Africa and beyond.* Sanlam, 2013.

7 Wealthsmiths™: a century later

Emerging-market growth has outperformed developed markets since the gradual global recovery from the global financial crisis. These high-growth markets present significant opportunities to insurance companies. These opportunities have resulted from the convergence of a growing middle class, billions of prospective new customers, maturing regulatory regimes, and increasing financial literacy. Sustainable revenue growth for the insurance industry depended on innovation in market-aligned product offerings and well-managed, good governance implementation. The sluggish recovery of the global economy after 2008, the banking crisis in Cyprus, and the credit crisis in Greece and other Southern European countries soon put a dampener on the African growth record of the post-market liberalization reforms during the first decade of the twenty-first century. Africa was still highly dependent on resources. As world resource prices slumped and Chinese demand contracted from 2014, the downward trend in the business cycle dashed the high expectations of sustained growth. As developing economies remained under pressure after 2013 due to lower commodity prices, weakening productivity, and geopolitical stresses across emerging markets, corporate profits contracted. Monetary policy positions diverged in the two regions of African economic engagement. The terms of trade weakened consistently for Africa. In Europe the European Central Bank raised interest rates in fear of deflation and economic stagnation. The USA Federal Reserve Board embarked on the opposite policy direction by concluding its asset acquisition in the American market and keeping interest rates low. This monetary policy supported a strong US dollar. As inflationary pressures started to mount in Europe towards the end of 2016, higher oil prices gradually caused inflation to rise around the globe.

Africa and some markets in South Asia recovered steadily after 2013. In Africa, growth was at 5.2 per cent for 2014, 3.4 per cent in 2015, and 4.3 per cent in 2016. The Nigerian economy grew by 6.3 per cent in 2014, but then weakened to negative growth in 2016. Kenya recorded 6.4 per cent growth in 2014, 5.7 per cent in 2015, and 5.8 per cent in 2016. India sustained growth of more than 7 per cent between 2014 and 2016, Malaysia between 4.2 per cent in 2014 and 6 per cent in 2016, and Indonesia 5 per cent in 2014, 4.9 per cent in 2015, and 5 per cent again in 2016. Emerging-market resilience coupled with relatively low insurance penetration in those markets constituted a market opportunity for a multinational insurance company.

South Africa's sustained political uncertainty and no clear macro-economic policy direction posed a threat to business opportunity and stability. Supply-side shocks, such as rising electricity prices and inconsistent supply, together with the high cost of servicing debt, a rising tax burden on a contracting taxpayer base, and persistent high unemployment, undermined any growth forecast. Corruption and nepotism in the ruling party were endemic in the entire economy. While Nigeria and Kenya emerged as high-growth economies in Africa, the South African economy stagnated at a time when it should have been taking advantage of being the star among emerging markets.[1] International confidence in the strongest economy in Africa suffered another shock when the Minister of Finance, Mr Nhlanhla Nene, was abruptly replaced in December 2015. As a result of unprecedented business leader intervention the President was persuaded to bring Mr Pravin Gordhan back as Minister of Finance three days after the Nene debacle. The international ratings agency Fitch adjusted South Africa's local foreign currency debt downward in December 2015. Most ratings agencies maintained a negative outlook on South Africa's sovereign debt, warning of a further downgrade if the policy environment did not stabilize and investor confidence did not receive fundamental support. South Africa's sovereign debt was finally downgraded to junk status following a midnight cabinet reshuffle in March 2017. The source of stability in the South African economy, the Minister of Finance, Pravin Gordhan, and his deputy, Mcebisi Jonas, were abruptly dismissed. These developments occurred amid growing allegations and alleged exposures of state capture by individuals closely associated with the President. These events occurred during weak economic growth of less than 2 per cent in 2014, 1.3 per cent in 2015, and 0.3 per cent in 2016. By mid-2017 the South African economy was in recession. As bond yields rose under conditions of market uncertainty, Government debt stood at 52 per cent of GDP, inflation rose, and consumer spending came under severe pressure. While emerging markets have experienced a gradual recovery since the last quarter of 2014, South Africa could not share the positive outlook. In December 2017 the ruling ANC elected a new leader Cyril Ramaphosa. In February 2018 he assumed the position of President of South Africa. A sense of optimism returned to the markets as Ramaphosa promised a 'new deal' of good government and a business-friendly economic policy. Growth forecasts turned positive again, but South Africa and the world are caught in the populist–rationalist dichotomy, which poses a challenge to sustainable economic growth. Generally growth opportunities are mainly outside South Africa.

These developments served to underline the strategic importance of Sanlam's growth and diversification strategy. The strengths of the South African financial services environment are the sophisticated regulatory framework and the financial soundness of its insurance companies. Sanlam developed sufficient *OLI*[2] advantages by the second decade of the twenty-first century to extend its business into markets outside the

[1] PwC: *Africa insurance trends*, October 2014: 4.

[2] OLI: ownership, location, and internalization. Sanlam owned the intellectual capital of its products, had the advantage of its physical location as and near to emerging markets, and had internalized innovation of its intellectual property of its investment and financial services products.

home market. The rebuilding strategy since 2003 has created competitive advantages in structure and products, in management capabilities and financial soundness, to position the Sanlam Group as an African emerging-market financial services corporate. This section offers a condensed overview of the development path of a small insurance company from elementary beginnings to a diversified financial services group succeeding in sustaining growth. Davids noted 'retention is the new growth', thereby underlining the significance of Sanlam's performance since 2013.[3] During the last five years before commemorating its centenary in 2018, Sanlam confirmed its presence in selected global markets grounded in firm empowerment roots in Africa.

People and strategy

It is significant that Desmond Smith, the Chairman of the board of Sanlam[4] at the start of the last five years before the Sanlam century, was the first Managing Director to formulate the vision to transform Sanlam to become *''n wêreldklas finansiële instelling'* [world-class financial institution].[5] As the member of the Sanlam Board with the longest service in the company, Smith epitomized the dynamic adaptive capacity of Sanlam to align operations with the needs of its changing client base. In 2014 the board of Sanlam comprised people with a long relationship with the company, both in an executive capacity and as independent and experienced business people and professionals. The Chairman was Desmond Smith, former Managing Director and actuary of Sanlam, and Patrice Motsepe was Deputy Chairman. Motsepe was a lawyer and mining entrepreneur, the owner and founder of African Rainbow Minerals, and the lead partner of Sanlam in establishing Ubuntu Botho Investments (UB). Rejoice Simelane and Bernard Swanepoel joined the board in 2004 as part of the UB transaction. By 2014 they had been involved as non-executive Sanlam directors for a decade. Rejoice Simelane is the CEO of UB and Bernard Swanepoel an experience mining executive. Manana Bakane-Tuoane and Valli Moosa were also appointed in 2004, with Moosa performing a strategic role as chairman of the Social, Ethics, and Sustainability board subcommittee. Moosa was a former Minister of Environmental Affairs in the cabinet of President Mandela, bringing to Sanlam a close relationship with the ruling party. Bakane-Tuoane is also an economist, who served as the Director General in the office of the Premier of the Northwest

[3] G. Davids (2016): 'Life Assurance Sector Report: Retention is the new growth.' Nedbank CIB, 6/6/2016.

[4] Desmond Smith was elected Chairman of the Sanlam Ltd board in June 2010 and retired at the end of June 2017.

[5] SA: 6/5/1: Minutes of Sanlam Board, 15/3/1995; Sanlam Annual Report, 1995: *Besturende Direkteur se Oorsig*: 3; Minutes of Sanlam Board, 31/1/1996: Memorandum DKS/af 'Maatskappybeplanning: 1996': 2.

Province. Her network connections and specialist knowledge of economic matters positioned her ideally as an independent director of Sanlam. In 2006, Sipho Nkosi, Lazarus Zim, and Anton Botha were appointed to the board as members with specific business expertise. In January 2018 Zim retired from the board. Anton Botha came to the Sanlam business through the acquisition of Gensec in 1998 and was instrumental in restructuring the Gensec operations into the new SIM institutional and later investments cluster. Apart from Smith, Flip Rademeyer, former Financial Director of Sanlam, and Chris Swanepoel, former Chief Actuary of Sanlam, joined the board in 2011. In 2013 Arun Duggal, a mechanical engineer from India, was appointed to the board to acknowledge the partnership entered into between Sanlam and Shriram. Sanlam also appointed Paul Bradshaw, an actuary from the UK, to the board. Bradshaw's appointment signified the strategic relationship that had developed through Sanlam UK in the UK financial services market. In 2011 Philiswe Buthelezi, a corporate finance MBA graduate, was appointed to the board, but she resigned in January 2015. The directors provided Sanlam with an oversight grounded in both long experience in Sanlam prior to demutualization, and business in general. The executive directors had long careers in Sanlam, adding the institutional knowledge for sustainability. Johan van Zyl served on the Sanlam board from 2000, and Kobus Möller and Ian Kirk from 2007, with Temba Mvusi as Chief Executive: Group Services from 2009, and Yegs Ramiah as Chief Executive: Brand from 2012. Ramiah also resigned from the board in January 2018. In non-racial South Africa the composition of the board was duly recorded as comprising eight white men, five black men, three black women, and one white woman, plus two non-South African citizens. The Financial Services Charter, within the B-BBEE policy paradigm, mandated the specific demographic composition. Compliance was a business decision but for Sanlam it was an opportunity to display the rich diversity of the South African society at work to develop partnerships to position the Group as a truly South African global player in its quest to add value.

As Sanlam entered its centenary year, the composition of the board comprised the same human capital capabilities on which the Group has depended to manage risks and ensure sustainability since 2003. Depth of experience and business partnerships combined to deliver relationships established on board level. Sanlam retained the strong organizational loyalty by appointing former executives to its board. Desmond Smith retired as Chairman of the board of Sanlam Ltd at the end of June 2017, and was succeeded by Johan van Zyl as new Chairman of the board in June 2017. Van Zyl was appointed as director to the board of Sanlam after retiring as CEO at the end of 2015. In terms of the strategic agreement between Sanlam and UB in 2014, UB is entitled to appoint three members to the Sanlam board. Van Zyl assumed one of those directorships with effect from January 2016. Kobus Möller retired at the end of September 2016. His successor as Financial Director was Heinie Werth, who had been Chief Executive of SEM since 2008. New appointments to the board as non-executive directors in 2015 were

Karabo Nondumo and Clem Booth. Booth, an international insurance specialist from the UK, gained experience from working for Munich Re and Allianz. In April 2018 Mathukana Mokoka, a chartered accountant and non-executive director of companies was appointed to the Sanlam Ltd board. The demographic composition subsequently consisted of eight white men, four black men, three black women and one white woman. Two non-South African directors served on the board. The board performed the official King III prescribed governance function, but was an organizational instrument to support the repositioning of Sanlam. Johan van Zyl managed the relationship with the board as an instrument of regulatory compliance, but more so, strategically, as an instrument of business transformation. The business strategy since 2003 has been diversification, creating and protecting value, and transforming for sustainability. The UB transaction was strategy in action. It presented Sanlam with the mechanism of integrating business development, transformation, and sustainability with value creation. From the time he assumed office as CEO in 2003, Van Zyl consistently reported on compliance with statutory regulated empowerment criteria. He explained the imperative as 'We view the continued transformation of our organization's culture and diversity as key in terms of our competitiveness and long-term sustainability',[6] and 'Transformation is one of the pillars of our business strategy.'[7] From 2012 the embeddedness of Sanlam in the history of empowerment of a marginalized segment of society rang out as a transformation directive. In 2012 the CEO declared, 'For almost 95 years Sanlam has been setting standards of excellence in its operations, first as a local insurance company and more recently as an international financial services group . . . Sanlam's long history of empowerment, economic advancement, wealth creation and protection motivates us. This is a legacy and a responsibility that we take very seriously.'[8] These sentiments were reiterated by the Chairman in 2013, when he said 'We believe that our values, which have formed the bedrock of our company since it was established 95 years ago, are fundamental to what we now call sustainable business.'[9] In 2014 the Sanlam integrated report claims 'We're in the business of building legacies. For over 96 years we've been committed to our trade of helping people make the most of their money with a roll-up-your-sleeves readiness and resolve.'[10] Smith returned to the history of Sanlam in 2015, stating that 'over the decades the Group has reinvented itself: the Cape-based life insurance company that was founded in 1918 is now an international financial services group with a presence in more than 30 countries'.[11] The Chairman again claimed longevity of a value system when he stated 'Sanlam's resilience in uncertain times is testimony to a value system and

[6] Sanlam Annual Report, 2007: Report of the Chief Executive: 29.
[7] Sanlam Integrated Annual Report 2011: Management Review by Group Chief Executive: 43.
[8] Sanlam Sustainability Report, 2012: Message from the Group Chief Executive: 6.
[9] Sanlam Sustainability Report, 2014: Future: Chairman of the Board: 6.
[10] Sanlam Integrated Report, 2014: 7.
[11] Sanlam Integrated Report, 2015: Chairman's Letter of introduction: 16.

work ethic that have stood the test of time for almost 100 years.'[12] As strategic management rhetoric, Sanlam's history and the transformation imperative are presented as a management continuity.

A key determinant in the successful delivery of financial services is stability, which builds trust in the organization. Building trust in the organization depended on consistency and predictability of operations. This was how Van Zyl motivated the appointment of Ian Kirk as the new Sanlam CEO in 2015: 'Consistency and predictability are two of the Group's main characteristics. In keeping with these character traits, which have served the Group well over 96 years, the Sanlam leadership succession planning was announced well in advance.'[13] The Sanlam Ltd board displayed stability and so did executive management. Ian Kirk joined the Sanlam executive in 2006 and moved to Santam in 2007. In 2015 Johan van Zyl announced his retirement at the end of 30 June 2015. Ian Kirk succeeded him as CEO from 1 July 2015.

Ian Maxwell Kirk, an Irish citizen who studied at Trinity College in Dublin and subsequently qualified as a chartered accountant of the Institute of Chartered Accountants of Ireland, came to the Johannesburg office of the international audit firm, PriceWaterhouse, on international service as an assistant manager. He qualified as a CA (SA) in 1984 and, as he was engaged in computer auditing, he completed a Higher Diploma in Business Data Processing at the University of the Witwatersrand and the Certified Information System Audit qualification in 1985. In 1986 he became a partner at PriceWaterhouse and was appointed to establish the insurance industry practice in that firm in 1989, based on his responsibility for audit methodology and research. In 1994 he took up the position as head of Audit and Banking Advisory in the firm, PriceWaterhouse being second in South Africa in respect of insurance clients. This specialist professional position groomed him at the exact point where Investec Bank sought a leader for a small listed insurance company, AGA Holdings, in which it held a significant stake. In 1996 AGA was restructured as Capital Alliance Holdings Ltd, one of the first broad-based black empowerment financial services companies in South Africa. Ian Kirk managed an impressive acquisition drive at Capital Alliance between 1996 and 2004 in which small life offices and the life books of insurance companies in South Africa and Australia were acquired and merged with that of Capital Alliance. When a reinsurance transaction was concluded with Investec in July 2001, Capital Alliance took over the individual life policy books of Fedsure and Norwich Life. Capital Alliance subsequently managed over 1 million individual life contracts and 700 000 group schemes. The Liberty Group bought Capital Alliance Holdings in December 2004 in a R3.3 billion transaction. Kirk became the deputy CEO of the Liberty Group in March 2005. This broad industry experience aligned seamlessly with the emerging strategic repositioning developed in

[12] Sanlam Integrated Report, 2016: 92. [13] Sanlam Annual Report, 2014: 69.

Sanlam by Van Zyl and his executive management team when Kirk joined Sanlam in 2006. Ten years later Kirk received the confidence of Sanlam to lead the management team of the Group from its first century of business into the new century of growth.

The strategic business acumen of Van Zyl and Kirk, infused by the long-standing experience of members in the executive management team in Sanlam, proved able to grow market confidence in Sanlam. The convergence of Kirk's experience in insurance, structuring empowerment transactions, and Van Zyl's broad group restructuring strategy worked well to effect the turnaround at Santam under Kirk since 2007. Santam performed an increasing supportive role in the unfolding of the SEM penetration into Africa, India, and Malaysia. Santam invested in large, long-term projects whereby the company provided data capabilities and agility for future business contexts. Management synergies in the Group nurtured intra-group synergies as part of the *Sanlam for Sanlam* Group strategy. Kirk therefore maintained executive stability by retaining the cluster configuration of operations from 2011.

Sanlam was known through the years for the quality people within its stable. The strong loyalty to the company, also due to historical reasons, and rigorous succession planning, ensured management stability. When Kirk assumed the position of Sanlam Group CEO, the reality was that a number of other executives had already indicated a desire to change focus in their lives. A seamless transition into the Kirk era could have been at risk. In 2014 the Executive Committee consisted of Johan van Zyl, CEO; Ian Kirk, CEO of Santam; Themba Gamedze,[14] Chief Executive: Strategic Projects; Lizé Lambrechts, Chief Executive: SPF; Kobus Möller, Financial Director; Themba Mvusi, Chief Executive: Group Market Development; Yegs Ramiah, Chief Executive: Brand; Johan van der Merwe, Chief Executive: Sanlam Investments; Heinie Werth, Chief Executive: SEM; and André Zeeman, Group Actuary. In 2013 Sana-Ullah Bray, former secretary of Santam, was appointed Group Secretary of Sanlam. When Kirk moved back to Sanlam, Lizé Lambrechts moved to Santam as CEO from January 2015 and Kirk acted as Chief Executive of SPF until he assumed office in July 2015 as Sanlam CEO. Themba Gamedze retired at the end of 2015. Hubert Brody assumed the position of Chief Executive: Strategic Projects. When Kobus Möller retired at the end of September 2016, Heinie Werth succeeded him as Chief Executive: Group Finance. Junior John Ngulube, former CEO of MunichRe Africa, was appointed to the position of Chief Executive: Sanlam Corporate, in February 2016. He left Sanlam Corporate in April after having taken care of two portfolios. Brody moved to SPF with the intent of future

[14] Themba Gamedze, an actuary, was appointed Chief Executive of SEB in 2003, then in 2007 he assumed responsibility for Sanlam Independent Financial Services and in 2008 Group Marketing and Communication. At the end of 2008 he retired, but was recalled in 2013 as Chief Executivce: Strategic Projects. *Sandaba*, November 2003: 11; February 2006: 12; October 2007: 19; November 2008: 2; *Inside Sanlam*, March 2013: 3; December 2013: 14–15.

career changes. His role in SPF allowed due course of Sanlam's succession planning. Jurie Strydom was appointed Chief Executive at SPF in 2017 when Brody retired from the position. Anton Gildenhuys succeeded André Zeeman as Group Actuary and Chief Executive: Risk and Compliance. At the end of November 2015 Johan van der Merwe, Johan van Zyl, and Machiel Reyneke accepted positions at African Rainbow Capital. Reyneke was formerly the Chief Financial Officer of Santam under Ian Kirk. Robert Roux assumed the position of CEO of SIM, having been Van der Merwe's Chief Operating Officer for a few years. Temba Mvusi was due to retire, but he agreed to assume the executive responsibility for Sanlam Corporate in April 2017. Sufficient depth of managerial capabilities, and mutual alignment with business philosophy and strategy, prepared through forward-looking succession planning, facilitated a seamless transition from the Van Zyl executive team to the next one, allowing for career changes, succession, and continuity.

The stability in the executive management structure had been a product of the inclusive management style of Van Zyl since assuming office. He allowed maximum decentralized decision making and executive operations at cluster level within the management paradigm of 'tight and loose' management autonomy. There was no doubt about Group strategic direction from the CEO. A strong management team evolved though the devolution of authority into the clusters, allowing 'owner-manager' management styles to develop. Van Zyl kept the strategy tight at Group Corporate level, but encouraged decision making at the level where the relationship resulted in the deal. Since 2003 an efficient executive team spirit or camaraderie has evolved, despite rigorous debate. This was not always the case in Sanlam, but was fostered as it became obvious that no turnaround could happen unless a team pulled the cart. The executive committee comprised a team of individualists, professionals, strategists, and intellectuals with a single goal. A sense of purpose was visible in the meetings of the executive committee. The Van Zyl 2014 executive team was a blend of pre-demutualization *Sanlammers* (Lambrechts, Möller, Werth, and Zeeman) and new experts from outside Sanlam (Kirk, Gamedze, Mvusi, Van der Merwe, Ramiah, and Van Zyl himself). They had all attended advanced executive management or leadership programmes abroad. This introduced a susceptibility to innovative strategic thinking and a wider focus on the global world of business. This team was not connected to the legacy of the former Afrikaner-controlled state or strong nationalist sentiments. To the contrary, either a-political sentiments or sympathy towards the new political dispensation was known to be the case. The business focus of turning Sanlam around overshadowed any ideological considerations. The entrepreneurial mindset of a relatively young 2014 executive team (all in their fifties, and two in their forties) blended well with the strategic repositioning of the Group. Throughout the decade of Van Zyl's refocusing of Sanlam he maintained a high degree of management stability. That was the gift to Kirk, himself a player in that stable team. Few management changes occurred as the strategy unfolded. By 2015 Sanlam had sufficient capacity to take the Group forward without disruptive executive changes after the departure of Van

Zyl. The only persistent challenge was to procure suitable talent among dedicated empowerment categories. This was not only a concern for Sanlam, but an industry-wide phenomenon.[15] As Sanlam enters its second century, executive and board stability characterizes leadership and governance.

Underpinning Group synergies and growth performance was another dimension of stability: Group business philosophy and strategy. The stated business philosophy and Sanlam Group strategy have become a living set of working documents. Clarity on the business philosophy since 2003 has solidified strategy. Stability with regard to strategy confirmed operational focus, and consistent implementation of strategy delivered the strategic outcome formulated as overarching goal, namely earnings growth or RoGEV (Return on Group Equity Value). The clarity and stability in respect of business philosophy is an asset on which the Group will capitalize in future, since they encapsulate the building blocks of operation. For a big business group or conglomerate challenged by complex contextual dynamics, both in the domestic market as well as in global markets, certainty of business philosophy is vital. Having to turn an eighty-five-year-old company (Sanlam was eighty-five years old in 2003) around without destroying its foundation, but rather utilizing the foundation as a source of vision for the future, depended on a business philosophy with which all stakeholders could identify. The business philosophy of Sanlam has been and for the foreseeable future will be 'to be the leader in client-centric wealth creation, management and protection in South Africa; to be a leading Pan-African financial services player with a significant focus on India and Malaysia; to play a niche role in aspects of asset and wealth management in specific developed markets.'[16] This philosophy infused Group-wide business operations around the principle of Sanlam being a 'one-firm firm'. In each of the clusters business was conducted in accordance with firm principles, namely that business had to optimize value for shareholders, measured by return on group equity value (RoGEV) and return on capital employed (RoCE), and that was to be the outcome of capital efficiency. The Group strove for operational excellence, client-centricity, and the delivery of the right solutions to meet client needs. These goals were implemented through the establishment of business partnerships and strategic alliances to create growth opportunities, but limit the risk of acquiring new clients and allocating capital. The business philosophy was not to chase market share at all costs, but to deliver sustainable profits measured by RoGEV. It was all about cost-effective revenue, rather than size. The broad framework of this philosophy relied on people, technology, governance, values, and the code of conduct. The 'tight' aspect of the business philosophy was that the board set overall

[15] PwC: *Africa insurance trends*, October 2014: 7; SA: Minutes of Sanlam Exco, 15/2/2016.

[16] Sanlam Business Philosophy: Minutes of Sanlam Ltd Board, 7/2/2007; Minutes of Sanlam Ltd Board, 4/3/2014.

business definition and strategy, and the Group CEO defined that at cluster level. Implementation is by the clusters.[17]

The business philosophy translated into strategy. Strategy in 2017 was fundamentally the same as the strategy in 2007. Sustainable value creation for shareholders rested on five pillars: earnings growth, operational and cost efficiencies, optimal capital utilization, diversification, and transformation. The strategic enablers were sound governance, people development, responsible products and services, a prosperous society, and a responsible environmental footprint. The strategy confirms the *Sanlam for Sanlam* focus to secure operational efficiency of the whole, rather than only that of the constituting units. Group Office provided strategic and operational support to the business clusters as the 'glue' holding the Group together. This alignment of purpose between people and organizational culture across the Group emerged as a strong strategic intent. The power of Sanlam's strategy in 2018 is the consistency of intent and purpose over the previous decade and a half. The strategy is firstly to grow and add value in the South African market, and secondly to do the same internationally.[18] The underlying building blocks of that strategy in South Africa are the following: improve efficiency and performance; define and build Sanlam's client-centric and client-experience roadmap; increase diversification; and transformation. Internationally the building blocks are to deliver the vision in emerging markets, especially to be the leader in Pan-African financial services, and in niche-developed markets.[19] This strategy does not deviate fundamentally from that of similar financial services corporates in South Africa, but where Sanlam leads the industry is in implementation. Kirk insists that Sanlam's human capital, the people, aligned over an extended period of time with the long-standing overall business philosophy and strategy, have delivered superior results in implementing vision and strategy.[20]

Underpinning strategy roll-out was society—this means that strategy could only be implemented successfully with the alignment to society, with the buy-in of society. Sanlam was again, as in the formative years, embedding itself firmly in the society it sought to serve. Since 2003 the Sanlam brand has grown in stature as a company delivering on its promises. In the world of globalization brand loyalty secures brand success. Building the truly South African company, Sanlam relied heavily on trust in the brand, in the message of stability transmitted by the almost century-old South African insurance company. It took Sanlam almost ten years to establish its brand outside South Africa, but Group Executive Yegs Ramiah still considered the Sanlam brand 'the best-kept secret'.[21] In 2013 Sanlam decided to embark on a comprehensive brand promotion strategy to supplement the *Sanlam for Sanlam* Group focus. Market research indicated

[17] Sanlam Business Philosophy: Minutes of Sanlam Ltd Board, 4/3/2014.
[18] SA: Minutes of Sanlam Exco, 15/2/2016.
[19] SA: Sanlam Group Strategy: Minutes of Exco meeting, 17/2/2017.
[20] Interview: Ian Kirk, Johannesburg, 16/08/2017. [21] SA: Minutes of Sanlam Exco, 24/11/2014.

the strength of the iconic Sanlam blue hands brand, but visibility and easy recognition in the fast-moving global expansion strategy justified formalization and redefinition. In 2014 a monolithic architecture for the rebranding of the Sanlam brand was commissioned. The delivery confirmed the well-known Sanlam blue hands around a single ball, signifying security, trust, confidence, and peace of mind. To enhance the brand image, a single brand was registered as an official trademark, comprising of four elements. The first was the blue hands encircling a single ball, but this time a second element was added. This was the positioning of the trusted hands in a circle. It symbolized the perfect closure of the trust and confidence. The third element was the standardization of the colour blue used in the trademark [See Appendix 1]. Finally the trademark pay-off line 'Wealthsmiths™' symbolized the essence of the business of Sanlam—creating wealth from whatever means a person has—limited or large. The new trademark did not deviate from the trusted iconic blue hands, but found official grounding in a registered trademark, which was launched on 19 August 2014. The rebranding occurred at a time when Sanlam had expanded its footprint to more than fifteen countries.[22] As a strategic marketing tool the rebranding was followed by a series of television advertisements depicting the simple wealth-creation activities of ordinary people. The natural instinct of making the most of what one has, was linked to the story of Sanlam. The punchline was the simple human truth that people have been doing small things to improve their lives and daily circumstances. That was the story of Sanlam, as explained by Johan van Zyl: 'The time has come for us to tell our story with conviction and pride, and about how we are ensuring the sustainability of this business into the future.'[23] As the adverse economic and industrial conditions in South Africa unfolded, the company underlined its identity by pointing to the fact that its business operations showed how the Group did business: 'It made the most out of our clients' money in a straightforward, honest and hardworking way—being Wealthsmiths™'.'[24] The triangulation of strategy, people, and brand was a powerful asset as Sanlam moved towards its first centenary.

Playing in all markets

Sanlam delivered diversified financial services—insurance, financial planning, investment management, wealth management, and retirement—in each of the five clusters, operating through different strategic business units. To lead in client-centric wealth creation, management, and protection, Sanlam developed specialist differentiation in product offerings for different markets. As the strategic direction of Sanlam's business

[22] Sanlam Annual Report, 2014: 17. [23] Sanlam Press Release: 23/6 2014.
[24] SA: Minutes of Sanlam Ltd Exco, 9/2/2014.

moved into almost automatic momentum (the strategic direction had become so fully ingrained, that implementation occurred almost 'automatically'), competition in the financial services sector intensified and the regulatory environment became more demanding. Such contexts often give rise to internationalization strategies and Sanlam was no exception. Selling intangible products, dependent on trust and confidence, Sanlam was in a favourable position by 2014 to capitalize on its three-pronged legacy—people, strategy and brand—in taking the Group from one century into the next.

The real risk of digital disruption, big data, and business intelligence moved to centre stage as the impact of the Fourth Industrial Revolution on business operations was the reality of the time. The fact that in some IT spaces technology was becoming old and less agile, and the complexity of data dependence in the new business landscape, made the digital disruption risk extremely real. This risk was also intensified by the vast geographical distribution of Sanlam's activities; digital delivery was cost efficient, but also contained the high risk of digital disruption. The shift to direct marketing occurred long ago and was embedded in delivery across all clusters. Sanlam introduced new IT technology and a comprehensive cloud computing policy to drive cost efficiency and limit digital disruption. The implementation of a cloud-compatible security architecture commenced in 2014. The global threat of digital disruption was made very clear at the World Economic Forum deliberations in 2015. Sanlam commenced with a full Group digital securing overhaul in collaboration with a leading international audit firm, to secure its big data. The Business Intelligence renewal discovery (Big Data) project started in 2015 and will run well into 2020. This is a five-year exercise. The global demographic changes resulting from urbanization (also highly prevalent in South Africa), technological change, ageing and massively increased global connections, made the consideration of this risk imperative to secure and protect market share and clients.[25] The risk of digital disruption and cyber security compounded substantial cost quantification to the entire financial services industry.

SPF: creating value at home

The year 2014 presented the insurance industry with an exceptionally challenging operating environment. Extended industrial action (a four-month strike in the platinum mining sector), put downward pressure on new business. In the retail market, the Sky Solutions business was highly exposed to the communities affected by the platinum strike. Sanlam was primarily exposed to this market through the Sanlam Sky policy suite.

[25] SA: Minutes of Sanlam Ltd Exco, 24/11/2014: Memorandum: Group Cloud/Technology outsourcing policy; SA: Minutes of Sanlam Ltd Exco, 15/2/2016.

Sky adhered to the 'Treat customers fairly' (TCF) framework by keeping policies active by assisting policyholders in resuming regular premium payments after disruptions. After the strike in the platinum mining sector towards the third quarter of 2014 many policyholders resumed premium payments. At the high end of the market an innovative Investment-linked Lifetime Income Plan was launched through the Glacier investment platform. This resulted in an increase of net inflows onto the Glacier platform of 31 per cent and accumulated funds of R156.9 billion at the end of 2014. Glacier also attracted 27 per cent higher net inflows in new life policies, as a market appetite for risk products illustrated consumer uncertainty. SPF made the most of the trying times, when it acquired part of the assets of Afrocentric Healthcare in 2014 to increase the effective SPF stake in Medscheme to 28.7 per cent. Medscheme was the third-largest health risk management services provider, and also the third-largest medical scheme administrator. Sanlam capitalized on this acquisition by offering Sanlam Gap Cover to supplement medical expenses. This was a slow re-entry into health insurance.[26]

In 2017 Sanlam concluded an acquisition transaction for a 53 per cent stake in BrightRock, a life insurer established in 2012, for R707 million. BrightRock had accumulated R148 billion in life cover in only five years of operation. The transaction addressed the SPF hurdle of building market penetration in an already structured local market, as well as confirming Sanlam's commitment to invest in South Africa.[27] An important dimension of this acquisition was the nature of the BrightRock life products. These are individualized, needs-matched life insurance cover, built around a client's needs, designed to change as those needs change, and are distributed through an intermediated individual risk market. This product resembles the Sanlam pioneering 'One Policy' of 1985 as the One Policy was a similar single needs-based policy designed to change as needs change. SPF effected a perfect match. Maintaining the Brightrock brand illustrated the Sanlam growth strategy through partnership.

In 2015 a cluster-wide Project Re-Imagine conducted a thorough review of pricing, delivery, agility between products, and client-centric services to address the challenging depressed market environment in South Africa. From the Retail Distribution Review (RDR), ease of delivery, response to client needs, and pricing at the appropriate level of product delivery emerged as potential constraints in the life market. Project Re-Imagine led SPF to conduct extensive research into how the product–client relationship could be improved. The research showed that SPF could benefit from the total reorganization of its product suite into focused businesses. The new business structure came into operation in August 2016. Sanlam Individual Life then operated in functionally focused businesses. Sanlam Sky offered funeral cover; the Risk business dealt with income

[26] SA: Minutes of Sanlam Ltd Exco, 9/2/2015.

[27] Sanlam Press Release, 25/1/2017; M. Maake: 'Sanlam in control of BrightRock', *Business Day*, 26/1/2017; Minutes of Sanlam Ltd Board, 8/3/2017.

protection and risk in case of disability or death; Glacier focused on investment growth and retirement provision; the Savings business provided savings for a variety of needs, including retirement; the Closed Book business took care of the older-generation products; and Shared Services provided economies of scale and integrated client services. The completion of this restructuring effectively limited internal competition and brought similar businesses together. The business was simply more agile and therefore better organized to enhance its competitive positioning.[28] The completion of Project Re-Imagine, which also included life products in Santam (MiWay Life) delivered significant cost savings to SPF, but more importantly, better service delivery to clients. A significant part of the local market risk is the regulatory environment. The final implementation of the FSB's RDR, which only occurred late in 2018, is part of the regulatory landscape impacting on the financial services industry. It adds yet more new compliance measures on distribution channels and intermediary remuneration. These have direct cost implications for the Group. Regulatory risks motivated by socio-political pressures for structural changes to the financial services industry, impact changes to product offerings and services. The potential competition from Government through compulsory national savings schemes, a national social security dispensation, and a national health system all contributed to market competition, which motivated SPFs sustained drive for cost-efficiency. SPF enhanced distribution channel diversification by launching 'Sanlam.com' in 2014 as the online purchase platform. Access to a client's full portfolio became a reality when the Client Portal opened in December 2014. Santam launched MiWay Life in 2015, which added to the life insurance business of the Group, but also underlined the power of direct online delivery. As part of the strategy to increase intra-group synergies, the omni-channel distribution system was introduced to grow digital access to a wide variety of products in SPF and other Group clusters. This technological facilitation of synergies operated Group-wide, but was especially relevant in supplementing the reorganization in SPF. Sanlam Sky was most adversely affected by the downturn in the economy, but good service delivery sustained this client base. By 2014, African Life, the vehicle through which the delivery took place, had 3 100 tied agents, eighty-five client service centres and 1.3 million in-force policies. One aspect of the success was that 96 per cent of claims were paid out within four hours.[29] Sanlam Sky launched the Sanlam Sky MyChoice funeral policy in 2014, which accounted for more than 80 per cent of new business sales in this market.[30]

The SPF business has emerged as a diversified personal finance, retail enterprise. From savings products, individual life, wealth management through the Glacier platform, and business development, the core life entity has been transformed to align with the strategy

[28] Sanlam Sustainability Report: Responsible Products and Services content: 12.

[29] SA: Minutes of Sanlam Ltd Board, 8/3/2017.

[30] SA: Minutes of Sanlam Ltd Board, 4/6/2014.

of diversification. The story of SPF during the last five years before the centenary of Sanlam is innovation and diversification. Despite almost no growth in the South African economy, SPF delivered 17.6 per cent RoGEV in 2014 (down from 20.6 per cent in 2013), but slumped to 12.1 per cent in 2015 and then recovered to 22.7 per cent again in 2016. This is an important achievement, since SPF significantly outperformed the Group RoGEV per share of 11.8 per cent in 2016. The impact of the underperforming local economy and political uncertainty contributed to SPF recording only 1 per cent growth in new business volumes in 2016, but the net value of new business was up 22 per cent in 2016 thanks to a move to higher-margin products. Net fund flows rose by 26 per cent in 2016, which was only marginally down from a net fund flow of 31 per cent in 2015. Sanlam demonstrated the ability to mobilize confidence in the depressed market. SPF's business is focused entirely on the South African market. This cluster is set to benefit from sustained initiatives by the Group to explore further growth opportunities in the domestic market. Sanlam has not neglected the South African market on the back of the strong performance of SEM. A consistent search is under way to explore synergies and growth opportunities in all geographical locations, also South Africa. The highly competitive nature of the domestic market, the strict competition laws and regulatory environment, and the adverse opportunity environment for young talent from certain demographic segments, which leads to a consistent talent drain, do not disincentivize Sanlam to invest its capital in South Africa. Negotiations are under way to explore further domestic growth opportunities, because Sanlam remains committed to South Africa.

Diversifying in selected international markets: SEM

The most dramatic delivery on the Sanlam diversification strategy happened in 2015. Sanlam Emerging Markets (SEM), under the leadership of Heinie Werth and Robert Domisse, is the cluster with the most diversified business operations and is the primary driver of Sanlam's internationalization strategy. The dilemma Sanlam faced was that growth opportunities in a mature and concentrated traditional insurance market (South Africa) were limited. The advantage that Sanlam had was its cross-selling abilities within the Group, and the geographic footprint. Furthermore, international financial services corporates were also interested in entering emerging markets, but they were exposed to a greater market risk because of their unfamiliarity with emerging markets. Sanlam was in a doubly advantageous position: it understood emerging markets and had established valuable partnerships in those markets, especially in India, the rest of Africa, and Malaysia. These business partnerships constitute the channel for Sanlam to expand its own operations and partner with other interested financial services businesses to bring expertise to the emerging markets and develop the scarce skills in those markets.

An outward-looking growth strategy has already gained considerable momentum in India, Malaysia, and Africa. Werth and Domisse consistently looked to establish new partnerships with local financial services entities that share the Sanlam values and business vision. Sanlam undertakes extensive capability and talent mapping in markets into which it intends extending its business. Sanlam then compiles a 'human capital map' of the potential new market. This human capital map enables Sanlam to explore the human capital landscape, identify the most suitable partners and people for its business, and finally enter into relationships for mutually beneficial business in those new markets. Strict compliance with the Sanlam-communicated compliance framework underpins the business operations. SEM partnership entities comply with governance rules on financial reporting, risk management and risk escalation, ethics, internal audit, capital allocation, and dividend policies. This is how Sanlam invests in new growth opportunities to secure a return on its discretionary capital. The precondition for success is the quality of the partnership with the local market player. SEM works through local boards. Local expertise is leveraged to work with management, while Sanlam is the technical partner through SEM. The responsibility for governance lies with the local board, while risk management resides at SEM cluster level. This partnership model sets Sanlam's expansion into emerging markets apart from its competitors in South Africa. In 2016 SEM provided financial services in Malaysia and eleven countries in Africa. Today, Sanlam is the largest and most diversified Pan-African financial services company.

Sanlam's strategy was to extend operations into the Anglophone African axis, because of the market risk of operation under language barriers, that is, conducting business in countries where the lingua franca is exclusively a language in which the Sanlam staff would not be proficient. This would be the case in Francophone African countries. Entering a language compromised business environment could be mitigated through a strong partner proficient in the other language. Project Nile (SAHAM[31]) was bound to change this dispensation. Negotiations started in 2014 with the SAHAM Group, established by Moulay Hafid Elalamy in Morocco in 1995. He is an entrepreneur in Morocco and was appointed by the King of Morocco as Minister of Industry, Trade, and New Technologies. The SAHAM Group operates in three branches of financial services. SAHAM Finances offers insurance and financial assistance business, SAHAM Offshoring outsources call centres, and SAHAM Healthcare Services operates in the health sector. The SAHAM Group has ties with reputable international financial services organizations, which includes the International Finance Corporation (IFC), Abraaj Capital, Wendell, Bertelsmann, and ASISA. SEM explored the possible association with SAHAM on the basis of acquiring a minority stake of 20–25 per cent. Sanlam immediately established that the SAHAM Group had a strong operational management

[31] SAHAM is a Moroccan company name, compiled from the initials of family members of Mr Hafid Elalamy.

team. Heinie Werth was convinced that SEM could enter the Francophone axis in Africa through this partner—a strategic development—since Sanlam would not succeed in doing that through its existing channels in Africa. SAHAM did business in nineteen African countries. These are primarily North African countries, from where 52 per cent of the revenue is derived, West African countries, which contribute 16 per cent of revenue, and Central African countries, contributing 25 per cent of revenue. Operations in the Middle East (Lebanon) contributed 6 per cent of revenue. SAHAM earned 81 per cent of income from general insurance products, 15 per cent from life business, and 4 per cent from financial assistance. The size of the transaction was also cause for caution: it could be a US$1.1 billion plus transaction for 100 per cent ownership. Several directors advised a transaction at minority level, retaining the IFC as an anchor partner. Concerns were also raised about the potential dilutive effect such a massive transaction could have on Sanlam's dividend flow.[32] These considerations pointed to the sensitivity to over-extension of resources, despite the ambition to grow and diversify risk. The opportunity to create a substantially larger African presence remained very attractive. The experience with former 'strategic' investments that led to prolonged illiquidity remained in the institutional memory.

Sanlam's initial offer for 20 per cent of SAHAM was declined, but in an unexpected turnaround the majority shareholder, who was also the chairman of the SAHAM Group, offered to sell Sanlam a majority stake in the business. Lengthy negotiations and due diligence investigations with the assistance of Ernst &Young finally led to a transaction in February 2016 (SAHAM l).[33] The conclusion of this transaction was described as SAHAM I, or the first tranche of the transaction between SAHAM and Sanlam. In March 2016, SEM acquired 30 per cent in SAHAM Finances for US$390 million. This was SAHAM II, or the second leg of the transaction. The initial transaction established a presence for SEM not matched by any other African financial services group. The importance of the acquisition was that SAHAM was a financial services company with a US$1.04 billion premium income in 2015. Its specialized field of business is general and medical insurance, with limited life insurance interests. This was the opportunity Heinie Werth identified and utilized. SAHAM is the leading motor insurer in Côte d'Ivoire and Morocco. In May 2017 SEM acquired another 16.6 per cent interest in SAHAM Finances, securing SEM a 46.6 per cent stake. The second transaction in May 2017 did not yet settle the question of outright control. In 2017 Sanlam entered into negotiations for the acquisition of the remaining shareholding in SAHAM from the founder. This transaction, SAHAM III, or the third leg of the transaction, was finally concluded on 8 March 2018. This transaction was concluded through SEM Ireland, Limited (SEMIL). To fund the transaction, Sanlam Limited did a pre-emptive cash placing of 65 517 241 ordinary shares. The private

32 SA: Minutes of Sanlam Ltd Exco, 27/1/2015.

33 SA: Minutes of Sanlam Ltd Board, 5/8/2014; 3/12/2014; 4/3/2015; Minutes Sanlam Ltd Exco, 27/1/2015.

placing of the shares were co-ordinated by J.P. Morgan and Deutsche Bank, at a 5 per cent discount to the market price. SEM successfully raised R5.7 billion. On the day the success of the private placing was announced, Sanlam's share price dropped by 88.78 cent to 8357 cents (share price dropped 6.94 per cent on the day of the announcement). The share price had reached almost 9000 cents by early April 2018, but the lower price was still higher than the average Sanlam share price during 2017. Sanlam motivated the share issue by stating that the Solvency Assessment and Management (SAM) regulatory regime, that came into effect on 1 July 2018, mandated a strengthening of the Sanlam Limited capital for purposes of CAR.[34] This was the first time Sanlam approached the market since listing. The more than 65.5 million new shares are bound to impact on dividend payments.

The SAHAM transaction is forward-looking and will facilitate the full exploitation of synergies with other financial services businesses in the SAHAM Group and expand SEM's presence to countries in Africa previously inaccessible. Developing synergies is what SEM wants to achieve—to develop omni-channel capabilities to facilitate multiple touch points across channels with all business entities. Opportunities exist in reinsurance, health management, financial assistance, specialist business and relationship business (brokers, banks, multinational solutions), individual life (a market underdeveloped in Africa), IT, systems and tax efficiencies. The SAHAM transactions delivered on the Sanlam regional/ international diversification strategy as no other transaction has done. They have also expanded the Sanlam geographical footprint to establish SEM as the undisputed leader in financial services in Africa. This enables Sanlam to offer the route into Africa for a multiple of global businesses interested in mining the potential of the African continent.

Heinie Werth was the driving force at the time to position the SEM business as the flagship of Sanlam's globalization. The Namibian business continued to grow off the legacy base of the link with South Africa prior to independence in the early 1990s. The Botswana market was Sanlam's largest African market outside South Africa before operations expanded into East Africa. Recently, operations in Namibia expanded into acquisitions in Zimbabwe, and further acquisitions in Uganda (Masawara PLC and Pinebridge East Africa) extended SEMs penetration. In Ghana, The Enterprise Group decided to link up with another US-based insurer as principal partner in its life business. SEM had no desire to divest, but the Enterprise Group had taken a final decision. The developments in Ghana underlined the volatility in the emerging markets. This was the first experience of its kind for SEM, but the company negotiated the right of immediate re-entry into the Ghanaian market. In addition, SEM obtained a premium price for exiting its assets. SEM made an important breakthrough when it entered neighbouring Mozambique. In April 2015. SEM

[34] SA: Minutes of Sanlam Ltd Exco: Press Release 27 March 2018; S Njobeni 'Sanlam pays dearly for share placement', https://iol.co.za/business-report/companies/Sanlam-pays-dearly-for-share-placement-14147165 (accessed 30/3/2018); A. Jeftha (2018) 'Sanlam stock drops on news of R5.6 bn new share issue', https://www.fin24.com/Companies/Financial-Services/sanlam-stock-drops-on-news-of-r57bn-new-share-issue-20180328; http://www.sharenet.co.za/v3/sens_display.php?tdate=20180327170500&seq=63&print=1.

bought a 51.1 per cent stake in Mozambican insurer NICO Vida, and later that year this business was rebranded as Sanlam Mozambique Vida. In 2016, SEM gradually phased in the rebranding of its operations in markets outside South Africa. The first was in its largest market in Africa, Kenya. The holding company in Kenya, Pan Africa Insurance Holdings, subsequently became Sanlam Kenya PLC. The expansion of business ensured growth in a flat market, but offered Sanlam economies of scale by replicating experience and expertise in underinsured markets.

In Malaysia, SEM acquired 51.1 per cent of Koperasi MCIS Zurich Insurance Berhad in April 2014. This R1.25 billion transaction gave SEM a share in Malaysia's insurance sector. Similar to developments in South Africa, regulatory tightening occurred in all of the emerging markets. The protection of the Sanlam brand, being the Group's most valuable intangible asset, was aligned with the Group's insistence on governance compliance across the Group. Regulatory changes posed an operational risk to SEM, but compliance with risk-based solvency regulations, stronger financial crime prevention measures, and European conduct risk principles were fully in line with Sanlam's business philosophy of 'good corporate governance' and 'prudent and transparent reporting'.[35]

The most challenging aspect of SEM's business is the huge variation in country-specific volatilities. Sanlam mitigates these risks by extensive market research prior to entry, supplemented by a thorough enterprise due diligence, and the compilation of an in-depth 'talent map'. Group risk analysis in all categories of risk and pertaining to all segments of business operations, is comprehensive. Risk reports to the Sanlam Ltd board generally comprise in excess of 200 pages. Strict compliance with risk policies and the quality of the people in partnership have secured the successful internationalization through SEM. SEM posted 28 per cent growth in RoGEV in 2014, 29.9 per cent in 2015, but negative growth in 2016, largely because of market volatility and ZA Rand strengthening. The potential to grow the Sanlam Group business remains an important driver of SEM's expansion, especially into markets with a low financial services penetration and a paucity of technical skills. Vast potential exists for SEM to effect the 'one-firm firm' principle in the different geographical locations across Africa, but this is part of the long-term future strategy. Santam purchased a 35 per cent stake in SEM's general insurance operations in Africa to ensure future alignment between Sanlam and Santam. This gave substance to intra-group synergies, but was only the first step in that direction. SEM has a number of bancassurance arrangements in different countries in Africa. The acquisition of SAHAM is pivotal to this end. The SAHAM presence has opened the potential of developing numerous synergies between existing businesses, as well as attracting multinational businesses, such as brokerages, into Africa. As the driver of Sanlam's globalization, SEM's contribution to Group net results from financial services in 2016 was 20 per cent—4 per cent up from 2015. There are embedded risks in the SEM strategy, but the SEM development is the segment of the Sanlam Group performance to follow.

[35] Sanlam Business Philosophy.

Investing in wealth: Sanlam Investments (SI)

The investments cluster competed with a highly successful asset management and investment banking industry in South Africa. Performance came under severe market risk as a result of exchange rate volatility, weak equity markets, lower performance fees, and weak performance in the UK in 2016 following the Brexit developments. In 2014 the African Bank in South Africa was placed under administration, contributing to uncertainties about the sustainability of unsecured lending. This had an adverse impact on credit markets in South Africa. The persistent changes in the regulatory environment in South Africa and the Sanlam business philosophy to deliver client-centric services while complying with the Treating Customers Fairly (TCF) framework, brought the SI management to a comprehensive operational restructuring exercise. This commenced in 2013, and bore fruit as early as 2014. The essence of the restructuring was to establish two distribution businesses, namely Retail and Institutional. All the South African investment business went into a single Investment Core. SI's other operations remained organized in wealth management, asset management, capital management, SEB, and international investments. These changes delivered a more holistic and sophisticated approach to client needs, and reduced costs by lowering client turnover because of reduced acquisition costs. SI placed its clients first and sought to deliver optimal investment returns. The entity suffered from slow delivery on BEE targets, because there were simply too few black professional investment managers in the market. To address the empowerment limitation, SI opened a training institute for black investment managers, Alternative Investment Academy (AIA), in the Investment Core in 2014. Delivery on the demand for black investment professionals could not be instantaneous. SI could not influence the state institutions' views on compliance. SI was therefore adversely affected by the PIC's withdrawal of around R10 billion and the Metal Industries Benefit Fund's withdrawal of R2 billion investment funds from SI.[36] Where SI could act proactively was in anticipating the regulatory changes to retirement funds. In 2014, SI established Graviton Retirement Planning Services as a proactive initiative to assist salaried employees with low-cost and annuity solutions—clear client-centred service development. Market-facing operations were noticed. In 2014 Sanlam Private Wealth, a division of SI, was named the Top South African Wealth Manager in the *Business Day Investors Monthly* Top Private Banks and Wealth Managers survey, and took second position in the category Best Stockbroker. Sanlam Private Wealth (SPW) also won the accolade for best broker for lump sum investor for the fifth time at the *Investors Monthly* Top Stockbrokers awards. Industry recognition supported the favourable outcome of the restructuring processes.

[36] SA; Minutes of Sanlam Ltd Board, 4/3/2015.

SI entered 2014 with a strong net inflow of funds (189 per cent higher than 2013) and a 20 per cent rise in new business. This was mainly as a result of the acquisition of the employee benefit annuity business of the explosives and chemical conglomerate AECI. This was a significant transaction, because of the historical legacy of AECI operating in the business environment of AAC and the SA Mutual. SI developed an annuity policy guaranteeing the pensions of 3 650 AECI pensioners for life, linked to annual inflation adjustments. That policy managed R8.3 billion in assets, which makes it one of the largest life insurance policies ever written in South Africa. SI expanded in the UK market by acquiring 89.7 per cent of FOUR Capital in the UK, and 20 per cent in Cameron Hume, a UK-based specialist investment management company in the fixed-income investment business. SI also acquired 69.9 per cent in Centre, an American and global asset manager based on Wall Street. By acquiring a 33.3 per cent stake in Artisan, a European property management company on the Isle of Man, SI built up the property management business. Sanlam Netherlands BV merged with the UK business in 2015, since the critical mass in the UK business supported the decision to conduct business through that entity. SI expanded into India through the acquisition of the full equity of SEA, a Bangalore-based equity research hub. Growth in the South African market was strengthened by the acquisition of the property management agreement of Vukile Properties.[37]

Challenging market conditions, investment rating downgrades, and almost zero domestic economic growth made for an investment environment where only perseverance would be rewarded. SIM and SCM, both divisions of SI, collaborated in 2016 to win a credit mandate to the value of R2.4 billion. Satrix, the online investment platform into local and global asset classes, attracted the Attorneys Fidelity Fund to the value of R1.2 billion, and the Absolute Return team won a mandate for R2.4 billion from Investment Solutions. The ability to attract substantial investment mandates testifies to the change in investment culture and sustained performance. Recognition of SI's ability to deliver exceptional investment returns came from Allan Gray, the largest growing investment platform in South Africa. In 2016 Alan Gray included the SIM Inflation Plus Fund to its fund list. This added a large pool of investors to this fund in the SI Core Fund pool. The Wealth cluster in SI became the best-performing business in SI over a ten-year period, with US$600 million in assets under management. Compared to industry benchmarks in 2016, the SI performance showed a weighted average of 71.3 per cent of funds outperforming. SPW separately outperformed the industry benchmark by a weighted average of 103 per cent over a three-year period up to 2016.[38] This performance constitutes a fundamentally different scenario from 2004 when Chris Swanepoel, the Group Actuary, stated that, 'If the Board argues that SIM is not a satisfactory choice for the policyholder assets, it should rather take the necessary steps to improve SIM or

[37] SA: Minutes of Sanlam Ltd Exco, 24/11/2014.

[38] SA: Minutes of Sanlam Ltd Board, 8/3/2017.

else in the final instance to close it down, than to redirect investments away from it.' SIM's relative performance measured against the Alexander Forbes Large Manager Watch (LMW) was seventh out of eleven funds in the domestic market, and eighth out of a total of twenty-eight different-sized funds. Swanepoel said, 'It is important to note that SIM is still in the fix mode.'[39] SI has matured from the fixing period through functional and geographical diversification.

In 2015 and 2016 the dismally performing South African economy took its toll on SI business. Robert Roux assumed the position of Chief Executive of the cluster. The restructured SI delivered stronger RoGEV of 20.4 per cent higher in 2014 than in 2013, and 21.3 per cent in 2015, but recorded negative growth for the 2016 financial year owing to weak equity markets. Despite the return-on-equity deficit, SI had 273 per cent growth in net fund inflows. SI's contribution to Group financial services contracted from 21 per cent in 2014 to 19 per cent in 2015 and 14 per cent in 2016. The future of SI lies in outperforming the strong South African asset management industry. A legacy of managing the life insurance funds of Sanlam has been transformed. Sustained industry outperformance depends on the people, their skills and hard work.

Yellow umbrella cover: Santam

The short-term insurance business in Santam has converged into enhanced synergies with the other financial services operations of the Sanlam Group. In 2014 the listed Santam was a general insurer with a market share of 22 per cent. The company contributed 12 per cent of the Sanlam Group's net income from financial services in 2014 and in 2015 this contribution was 13 per cent, but dropped to 10 per cent in 2016. The contraction in relative contribution follows the expansion of SEM's operations and a 6 per cent contribution by Sanlam Corporate. Santam closed its underperforming Santam Europe in 2008 and then expanded into Africa, following the SEM footprint. Santam remains an important channel for the distribution of other products in the Group, such as SPF's personal finance. The synergies between SPF and Santam have developed in a focused business strategy since the acquisition of Guardian National in 2002. The Santam business is primarily in commercial and personal general insurance, with specialist business classes, but also reinsurance in emerging markets through SantamRe. SantamRe added to the diversification in Group operations by new reinsurance business in group and non-group international business. MiWay, started in 2009, is the general and life insurance products distribution platform via direct marketing channels. Sanlam

[39] SA: Minutes of Sanlam Ltd Board, 1/12/2004: Memorandum CGS/fga: 'Investment strategy and the role of SIM'.

underwrites the MiWay life business. As the *Sanlam for Sanlam* concept developed the principle of 'one-firm firm', the delivery of life products through the MiWay Santam platform constituted *one-firm firm* in action. Santam used its direct marketing distribution channel to deliver life products developed in SPF. Innovative new products were developed, such as MiFitLife, which is life cover for athletes, designed by #ForAthletesByAthletes. The platform also marketed MiLittleLife maternity and child cover. These are appealing new products available via direct marketing, speaking directly to the modern generation Y market.[40]

The short-term general insurance industry in South Africa is extremely competitive. The market context is highly volatile, with social and political unrest, inefficiencies in local administration impacting on infrastructure deficiencies, and climatic catastrophies. Santam's RoGEV performance in the Group has been volatile as it reflects the market performance of the Santam shares. Santam's RoGEV was 1.5 per cent in 2013, 19.1 per cent in 2014, and then -8.4 per cent in 2015, but recovered to 32.1 per cent in 2016. Santam's contribution to net Group financial services was 12 per cent in 2014, 13 per cent in 2015, and 10 per cent in 2016. Sanlam holds a 62 per cent stake in Santam. The Santam net contribution from financial services in the Group was R814 million in 2016, the lowest in the Group, except for the newly created Sanlam Corporate cluster, which delivered R510 million to Group financial services in 2016. After SPF with 6 515 employees, Santam was the largest employer in the Group with 5 749 employees. For the first time in its history, Santam paid a special dividend in 2016 to optimize its capital position. The company entered into an agreement with MunichRe of Africa for some of the Santam businesses to use its international AA–S&P credit rating from January 2017, as Santam moves to increase the diversification of its business. The value of Santam to the Group is primarily in its footprint and distribution channel, and of course, the historic relationship since 1918. Santam initiated a cross-group Insurance 2025 scenario in 2016. This initiative began a strategy to see how world developments in insurance will affect the business of the Group. This strategy intends to take a long-term perspective on a systemic, business portfolio-based take on resource allocation. It forms part of Santam's Vision 2020 for the strategic positioning of the cluster in the Group.

Santam is managed as part of the Sanlam Group of companies and from 2003 Johan van Zyl, who was appointed Managing Director of Santam in August 2001, became part of the Sanlam Ltd executive committee. Since 2003 almost all the CEOs of Santam have moved to and from Sanlam, seeking to strengthen synergies between the two companies. The legacy of Santam initially being the only shareholder in Sanlam and thus being its parent company, was reversed when Sanlam became a separate mutual entity in 1954. Sanlam sought to acquire the entire share capital of Santam in the early 2000s, but the high share price persuaded Sanlam not to pursue the deal. Institutional investors actively

[40] Sanlam Integrated Report, 2016: 121.

ran up the share price, making buying out of the minorities an unattractive proposition. Santam is the undisputed market leader in short-term insurance in South Africa, acknowledged by PwC in 2007 as the best short-term insurer in motor and property insurance.[41] In 2009 a Markinor Top Brand survey and the Financial Intermediaries Association of Southern Africa identified Santam as the number one short-term insurer in South Africa for commercial and corporate insurance in 2010 and 2011.[42] In 2011, Santam was even described as the best financial services business in South Africa.[43] Santam confirmed its corporate citizenship responsibility by developing a programme to assist dysfunctional municipalities to lower their insurance risks proactively. The Partnership for Risk and Resilience (P4RR) is linked to the Business Adopt-a-Municipality (BAAM) programme, which identifies vulnerable municipalities and provides support in addressing disaster management more effectively. BAAM is a strategic partnership between Santam, the Department of Co-operative Government (DCoG), the South African Local Government Association (SALGA), and the private sector to assist municipalities to improve sustainability and service delivery in respect of fire-fighting, flood, and storm-water management. P4RR has provided risk management assistance to fifty-three municipalities in South Africa and includes its B-BBEE trust *Emthunzini Community Trust* as Santam's stakeholder in the implementation of this programme. Similar stakeholder engagement occurs in Africa where Santam works with infrastructure developers to develop infrastructure on the continent.[44] From 2015 Lizé Lambrechts took over as CEO of Santam, succeeding Ian Kirk. Her distinguished twelve-year career in Sanlam, and during the last decade as executive manager of SPF, earned her the confidence of the investor community, policyholders, and the Sanlam Group. Her appointment was widely publicized, since she was the first woman to lead a short-term insurer, but moreover, because of her track record in steering SPF through challenging market conditions and regulatory changes. As South Africa's largest short-term insurer, the 'Yellow Umbrella' has become a household brand in South Africa, and gradually also elsewhere on the continent. In the Sanlam Group it is a vital business unit in the quest to deliver comprehensive and diversified financial services to the South African and global markets.

Going corporate

Sanlam Corporate (SC) was the new cluster dedicated to delivery to the corporate sector. A restructuring of business units in the Sanlam Group resulted. SEB, Sanlam's investments

41 SA: Minutes of Santam Board, 26/2/2007. 42 FSB Bulletin, Second Quarter, 2011. I.

43 *Financial Mail:* S. Cranston: 'Santam. Margins just get wider.' 4/3/2011.

44 www.santam.co.za

in Afrocentric and Sanlam Healthcare moved to SC to form the core of its business. SC embodied the 'One Sanlam' experience to selected corporate clients. The 'one-firm firm' principle applied to the delivery of a variety of services to clients in the corporate sector by a single Sanlam entity. The client-centric approach was not new, but in the competitive financial services markets superior service delivery is what secures business. SC wants to be the 'partner of choice' to targeted corporate clients and the single entry point for the corporate to business with any of the Sanlam Group clusters, intermediaries, and labour unions.[45]

All financial services businesses face the market risk of a narrow focus on products, market segment, or delivery channel. Sanlam experienced such risks several times during its long history. At first the primary, but never exclusive focus on the Afrikaans-speaking people in South Africa served to establish Santam and Sanlam in the insurance industry dominated by foreign players. Once matured in that market, the focus shifted to the broader domestic market and this has been a continuous strategic realignment. Since the late 1940s the narrow focus on life insurance has made way for investments in the equity market, followed by investment products such as unit trusts, and an extensive broadening of product offerings into wealth instruments once the life market lost its appeal. The beginning of diversified financial services companies post-deregulation in the financial services environment internationally, swept Sanlam and all other players in that market along. The delivery through a single tied-agent channel soon made way for brokers and subsequently for direct digital distribution. As strategies followed contextual changes, so did enterprise structure. With tight central strategic direction, divisional structures (clusters) exercised optimal decentralized executive authority to deliver on diversity. The Sanlam experience was no different from that of life offices in other parts of the world and in the years leading up to its centenary, the strategy was to refine, excel, and take delivery to the next level of adding value to all stakeholders. The success factor in future is how well the clusters can deliver on integrated best-in-the-industry services. The scope for innovation is constrained, but quality of delivery depends on the human capital.

The context of value: transformation

Transformation of business is a matter of sustaining the business as a going concern. The Sanlam Group's future is grounded in the Wealthsmiths™ culture of 'sincerity, respect, and consideration for one another'.[46] Sustainability is presented as succeeding in adding value by doing ethical business. Value creation has taken on a much larger life than only

[45] Sanlam Integrated Report, 2016: 123.

[46] Sanlam Sustainability Report, 2016: 7.

financial performance. Building Sanlam has become building South Africa and all other stakeholders wherever they are in the emerging markets and in niche locations. On the back of the brand Wealthsmiths™ Sanlam's financial performance is the vehicle to add value. From R232 million net new business value in 2003, the net new business value rose to R1.592 million in 2013. This growth was enabled through the strategic management of the resources of the company to understand and reflect the various markets in which it operated. A better understanding of the massively expanded markets of operation ensured the delivery of relevant services, made the business grow, and completed the circle of value creation—the added value that went back to the stakeholders. Transformation has two elements. The first is changing the face of the people in Sanlam and those with whom Sanlam does business. The second is changing the lives of society, of the entire scope of stakeholders of the Group. Transformation is one of the building blocks of the Sanlam strategy. According to the strategy document, the sustainability of Sanlam depended on 'if it becomes a mirror of all the people of South Africa'. It is no longer the company reporting on its CSR expenditure, but on its embeddedness in society and in the environment. The strategy is now performance in the six capitals context. The capitals are financial capital, human capital, intellectual capital, social and relationship capital, manufactured capital (physical equipment), and natural capital (the environment). The vehicles of delivery are similar to those in the past, but the target market is radically different. People development constituted the actions or programmes directed at enhancing human and intellectual capital in the company. This is where Sanlam reported on the change in corporate culture, its EE policies, empowerment practices, recruitment, training, and employee profile: a total of 12 900 employees, 73 per cent black, 27 per cent white, 38 per cent male, 62 per cent female, and 41 per cent black persons in the middle and senior management positions.[47]

During 2014 the FSC increased empowerment targets significantly. While Sanlam subscribed fully to the empowerment mandate, the reality of a skills deficit presented a real risk to the performance of business. Employment equity constituted a centrepiece of the Sanlam strategy, but implementation posed a risk. In February 2016 Exco agreed to the implementation of the 80/20 ratio for the Sanlam Group. This meant that 80 per cent of new appointments would be from the African people and 20 per cent from the white cohort.[48] Kirk wanted full buy-in from the executive on this intensified employment transformation. Despite reservations about being able to meet the targets, the executive supported the principle. The risk to balance was performance with compliance. Key performance indicators of executives are linked to meeting the new targets.

The Sanlam Group has already achieved a Level 2 B-BBEE compliance, but the implementation of the new FSC targets held a real risk with regard to sustaining

47 Sanlam Supplementary Sustainability reports: 2016: People Development: 1–22.

48 SA: Minutes of Sanlam Exco, 22/4/2016.

that level. Using a SAP computer-based training portal to facilitate employee training, Sanlam sustained a consistent increase in employees from B-BBEE-designated categories. In 2017 the SAP People Management platform was replaced by SAP Cloud Solutions to support enhanced training, employee engagement, retention, and collaboration across the Group. Between 2006 and 2016 the profile of senior and middle management changed from 81.1 per cent white, 18.2 per cent black, and 5.3 per cent African, to 59.5 per cent white, 40.5 per cent African, and 13.9 per cent black in 2016. The changed management profile resulted from a recruitment drive that targeted the designated groups. In 2012, 55 per cent of recruitment still occurred among white people, 45 per cent among Africans and 13 per cent among black people. By 2016 only 25 per cent of the recruitment target market constituted white candidates, 75 per cent Africans and 41 per cent blacks.[49] Restructuring in SPF opened opportunities for black staff, but the escalation into senior management positions has been the result of Project Sapphire. This project was aimed exclusively at building the middle management capabilities, especially of black persons, to move into senior roles within two years. Project Sapphire included the leadership programme at the Gordon Institute of Business Science (Gibs) and mentoring support. These employment practices formed part of a systematic strategy to comply with FSC's EE targets, but specifically to ensure sustained delivery by the Group on its promises to all its stakeholders. It was not simply a matter of complying with demographic targets, but to sustain performance. The quality of employee training and development received industry accolades. In 2016 the Top Employers Institute awarded Sanlam the Top Employers South Africa award. This award measured Sanlam's performance against the Group's talent strategy, workforce planning, *OnBoarding* training platform, learning development in the Group, performance management, leadership development, career and succession planning, compensation and benefits, and finally, the employment culture. The skills development programmes of the previous decade were still effective vehicles to grow the talent Sanlam needed. These include the Sanlam Graduate Programme, the Sanlam CA Training Programme, the Graduate Internship Programmes and the SPF Financial Planning Academy. The Academy is accredited by the Insurance Sector Training Authority (INSETA) and is the avenue to agents qualifying as Certified Financial Planners. Industry recognition was aligned with international standards in employment empowerment standards, as well as with the South African Qualifications Authority (SAQA), which put the achievement of Sanlam on par with that of an accredited tertiary education institution.[50]

[49] SA: Minutes of Sanlam Ltd Board, 8/3/2017. It needs to be kept in mind that 'Africans' refers to people of indigenous African origin. While 'blacks' refers to people of colour (non-white people), namely Coloured people, Indian people, and African people. The recruitment policy of Sanlam is therefore to direct 75% of recruitment initiatives, at the African target market, and 41% of the recruitment initiatives at the black target market.

[50] Interview Frederick Stroebel, 13/12/2015; *Inside Sanlam*, October 2016: 8.

Mirroring the South African society in the Sanlam Group was a business decision, as was the decision to seek an empowerment partner. The UB transaction of 2004 matured in 2013 and a vested shareholding in Sanlam Ltd gave UB a 14.5 per cent direct stake in the Group. The relationship with UB depended on whether real value was flowing from it for Sanlam. This was undisputed and therefore made good sense to build the business partnership to the next level of mutual interest. Sanlam developed the partnership with UB as a preferential empowerment partnership and did so on the basis of mutual business support. In 2014 a Memorandum of Understanding (MOU) was signed between Sanlam Ltd and UB on the structure of the future business partnership. This MOU provided for the development of the new investment vehicle of UB, namely African Rainbow Capital (ARC). ARC benefits from former Sanlam expertise in that retired Sanlam managers have taken executive positions on the ARC board and are managing the ARC investments to deliver value to its shareholders that will ultimately benefit African communities. ARC's board consists of Patrice Motsepe as chairman, Johan van Zyl (former Sanlam CEO and current Chairman of the Sanlam Ltd board), Johan van der Merwe (former CEO of Sanlam Investments), Machiel Reynecke (former CFO of Santam), and Rejoice Simelane, Andrew Mathube, and Tom Boardman (former CEO of Nedbank) as non-executive directors.[51] ARC is now the strategic empowerment partner of Sanlam Ltd and the vehicle to deliver benefits, together with Sanlam, to the UB Community Development Trust. ARC is an investment company engaged in a full range of financial services, such as life insurance, healthcare, asset management, general financial services, short-term insurance, property services, and banking. These are all the services offered by the Sanlam Group, which flow to UB shareholders via ARC. ARC serves as a vehicle to direct investments to Sanlam Ltd to extend the mutually beneficial business relationship that started with UB in 2004. ARC is the wholly-owned subsidiary of UB Investments Ltd.[52] The empowerment credentials of Sanlam are primarily vested in its relationship with UB and ARC.

In the human capital, social and relationship capital contexts, Sanlam performed its CSI activities. This is its investment in a prosperous society and has been part of the long history of Sanlam. In 2011 the Sanlam Foundation (SF) was established to roll out programmes to support communities, business development (entrepreneurship), and consumer financial education. The three categories of intervention are consumer financial education, socio-economic development, and enterprise and supplier development. The SF perpetuates the Sanlam legacy of concentrating on education as the most important

[51] Johan van Zyl, Johan van der Merwe, and Tom Boardman also serve on the Board of Directors of Ubuntu-Botho Investments (Pty) Ltd. It is in UB Investments that the UBCDT and the broad-based black empowerment entities hold direct shares. The benefits generated through UB Investments flow as dividends to the empowerment entities.

[52] www.africanrainbowcapital.co.za/about-us; Sanlam Minutes of Board, 5/3/2014.

empowerment strategy. Financial education is delivered through programmes to teach people about saving, such as '*Money fo Sho!*' (teaching communities skills and knowledge to make better financial decisions); SEB Trustee training (training on retirement decisions); Project Qaphela (a financial literacy programme targeting the National Union of Mineworkers); Sanlam for Professionals and Graduates (training new graduates on financial decisions to be taken in early employment); WITS Radio Academy's *Business Buzz* (a weekly show on the complexities of business and finance for students); and Saver Waya-Waya, a financial literacy programme at technical and vocational colleges. Bursaries for students are distributed through the Thuthuka Bursary Fund (a fund for black trainee accountants), Sanlam Learner Brilliance Project, COSATU HIV/Aids education programme, the Nelson Mandela University Trust Financial Planning Bursaries, and the Worlds Open Worlds (WOW) initiative. Enterprise and support development is delivered through ASISA (Association for Savings and Investment South Africa) the Tertiary School in Business Administration (TSIBA—a private not-for-profit business school) and Shanduka Black Umbrellas, a non-profit organization assisting black entrepreneurs. These educational and entrepreneurial development initiatives also include the Sanlam Art Collection. In 1965, Sanlam started the collection of South African art and continues to support local talent through the acquisition of their art and displaying the collections to the public.[53] All of these activities comprise the Sanlam strategy to add value to all its stakeholders. To quantify how Sanlam grew the 'prosperous society', CSI expenditure was presented as a key performance indicator. CSI as a proportion of net profit after tax was 1.18 per cent (R64 million) in 2013 and 0.88 per cent (R68 million) in 2016. The application of those funds is reflected in the improvement in Sanlam's B-BBEE contribution score (see Table 7.1).

Table 7.1 shows that Sanlam improved its total B-BBEE score from 89.14 in 2014 to 91.49 in 2016. This occurred primarily on the back of sustained investment in EE, skills development, investment in financial literacy programmes, empowerment financing through partnerships with a variety of empowerment enterprises, and improving people's access to finance through credit extension linked to the entry-level product range. The lower score on EE and management control is a function of the availability of human capital, but the engagement with advanced management training contains the potential to deliver on this requirement.

As a corporate citizen the Sanlam Group has moved close to full compliance with the FSC benchmarks in most of the empowerment categories. Management implemented total business process re-engineering to manage the fundamental change in the environment of its operations. These environmental changes were most pronounced in South Africa after the early 1990s, but also reflected the integration of South Africa in the global

[53] Sanlam Sustainability Report: Prosperous Society Contents: 1–22.

Table 7.1. Sanlam verified FSC scorecard, 2016

	% weighting 2012	2012 Total score	% weighting 2016	2014	2015	2016
Ownership	20	20.49	14+3	15.97	15.75	15.66
Management control	10	8.61	8+1	7.07	7.10	7.41
EE	15	4.52	15+5	7.71	8.15	8.83
Skills development	15	12.23	10	9.16	9.21	9.35
Preferential procurement	20	16.59	16	14.6	15.06	16.00
Enterprise development	15	15	5	5.00	4.27	3.71
Supplier development (new 2014)	n/a	n/a	n/a	n.a	n/a	n/a
Socio-economic development	5	3.48	3	3.00	3.00	3.00
Empowerment financing (new 2014)			15	15.00	15.00	15.00
Access to financial services (new 2014)			12	12.05	12.14	11.00
Consumer education (new 2014)						1.53
Total score	100	80.92	100	89.14	89.69	91.49
B-BBEE procurement recognition level		110%				
B-BBEE status level contributor		3		2	2	2
Black ownership		30.5%				
Black female ownership		7.28%				

Source: Sanlam sustainability report: prosperous society contents: 21.

context. Worldwide client-centricity, sustainability of the business organization and the society in which it conducts its business, and regulatory interventions to improve governance entered the world of business. In South Africa the statutory enforcement of BEE added an important dimension to those trends. Regulatory and empowerment compliance added a distinct cost to business, but in accepting that as part of business process re-engineering, which depended on successful change management, project management, management support and technological competence,[54] Sanlam turned from a local player to an emerging market conglomerate. The principles of the Global Reporting Initiative (GRI), which were implemented from 2011, displayed successful change management.

Following global trends, good governance formed the bedrock of sustainability. The King IV report, released in 2016, underlined the integrated nature of business's value creation process. All the elements of value creation are equally important and inseparable. Governance in the organization serves to enhance the core purpose of the business, its risks, opportunities, strategy, business model, performance, and sustainable development. The Sanlam Group reconfirmed its commitment to an integrated approach to governance. Risk management operated through an extensive framework of dedicated committees from board level down to operational level in each cluster. Governance

[54] V. Grover, S.R. Jeong, W.J. Kettinger, and J.T.C. Teng (1995): 'The implementation of business process re-enginering.' *Journal of Management Information Systems*. Special Edition: Towards a theory of business process change management: 12(1).

compliance fed directly into integrity of the brand Wealthsmiths™.[55] Sanlam's treatment of the King IV requirements on good governance was no different from industry norms. The King Reports on Corporate Governance since 1994 have found their way into business practice with a high degree of compliance in South Africa. This was the case because of the sanctioning by the Institute of Directors, the inclusion in the new Companies Act of 2008 and the GRI on integrated reporting. Sanlam capitalized on this trend by aligning its brand with sustained delivery and the long history of delivery in South Africa. Reputational risk was positioned as equally important to all the other elements of risk. As a result of the increasing globalization of Sanlam, the brand came to carry the company across the globe. An innovative brand and marketing strategy in 2016 set Sanlam apart from the industry. The brand office adopted the concept of a virtual marketing team. Sanlam was the first corporate in South Africa to introduce a globally recognized marketing management system. This made Sanlam the leader in social and content marketing software. 'The system creates a governance structure for all brand-related activities and material.'[56] The alignment of the consistent appropriation of the brand supports the business strategy in all aspects of the delivery thereof. As Sanlam mirrored South African society, so the brand mirrored the value added by the Group across geographies.

Business transformation for the next century

The internationalization of insurance started towards the end of the eighteenth century. This reflected the growing willingness to take on risk. The second wave of insurance globalization followed from the 1970s as the economic, political, and cultural structure of the world began to change. The growth of business conglomerates, financial sector deregulation, and the magnitude and frequency of risk assisted the growth of large insurance companies and their ability to manage risk.[57] Sanlam developed in this global risk environment into a player from an emerging market increasingly taking on risk in other emerging markets. Sanlam was in a very competitive market, not only in South Africa, but also in the emerging markets into which it expanded. Borscheid and Haueter refer to this competition as 'inordinate growth of insurance groups operating on an international scale'.[58] As South Africa was invited back into the global world, South

[55] Sanlam Sustainability Report, 2016: Sound Governance contents.

[56] Sanlam Sustainability Report, 2016: 77.

[57] P. Borscheid and N.V. Haueter (eds)(2012): *World Insurance. The evolution of a global risk network.* Oxford: Oxford University Press: 11–26.

[58] Ibid.: 29.

Table 7.2. Distribution of Sanlam Group net results from financial services, 2017 (%)

	South Africa	Rest of Africa	India	Malaysia	Other international
2016	76.8	12.4	6.7	0.7	3.1
2015	77.8	11.8	4.46	0.3	5.4
2014	74.2	11.22	6.62	0.8	7.0
2013	74	13	6.7	0.3	6
2012	80.5	11.3	4.2		4
2011	86	11			3
2010	89.3	8.6			1.9
2009	91	7.3			1.5
2008	91.4	6.7			1.8
2007	92	5.9			1.9

Source: Sanlam annual reports, integrated reports, 2007–2016

African companies explored globalization of operations. Sanlam ventured into international markets from the mid-1990s, but the structured and successful global penetration occurred from 2008.

The restructuring of the Sanlam business model gave rise to stronger performance in the operating clusters and this performance drove the expansion into markets outside South Africa. In Table 7.2 the expansion is reflected. By 2016, South African business contracted to a relative contribution of just more than three quarters of total Group business. The strongest growth is in the African markets, where the full potential of the SAHAM partnership awaits full unlocking. While potential new synergies and acquisitions in the domestic market still make up a core focus of Sanlam's business, diversification into emerging markets illustrates the risk appetite of the Group in those markets. Sanlam makes the most of its country-specific and firm-specific advantages of familiarity with emerging entry-level markets in Africa to forge partnerships on the rest of the continent. Sanlam has by far the largest rest-of-Africa business, writing more than three times the volumes than its nearest competitor. The success in Africa is a key dimension of the sustained internationalization of Sanlam and a policy to establish partnerships to direct further penetration.

After 2003, Sanlam did not seek market share in South Africa as a primary goal, but RoGEV, that is adding higher value to shareholders and therefore to all stakeholders who benefit from the growing engagement with the total environment in which the Group operated. Stronger business volumes and quality of the business led to 13.6 per cent annual compound growth in total equity value between 2012 and 2016, which was 1 per cent higher than the growth performance between 2002 and 2013 (see Table 6.3). The growth was significant taking into account adverse market conditions with an average of 5.7 per cent inflation between 2012 and 2016, a weakening exchange rate and GDP growth consistently below 2 per cent. The slowdown in growth during 2016 is

Table 7.3. Sanlam Group performance, 2012–2016

	2012	2014	2016
Total goup equity value (Rm)	75 352	95 936	110 717
Total assets (Rm)	490 953	611 253	672 559
Headline earnings (Rm)*	5 763	8325	9860
Embedded value (EV) per share (cps)	3 707	4 684	5 407
Return on EV per share %	22%	18.5%	11.8%
Total issued shares (m)	2 100	2166.5	2166.5
Normalized headline earnings per share (cps)*	292.1	407.6	408.5
Share price (cents)	4477	7000	6290
Dividend per share	215	225	268
Sanlam Life Insurance Capital Adequacy Ratio (CAR)	4.3	4.5	5.8

Note: *Introduction of IFRS in 2006 changed accounting policy. Figures not fully comparable to period before 2006.

Source: Sanlam annual financial statements, 2012–2016.

linked directly to the slump in the life insurance market. Sanlam had already developed diversification as the distinct strategy of the company, supplemented by the exploration of opportunities in emerging markets. In all the markets in which SEM operates, insurance penetration as a percentage of GDP is below the world average of 3.8 per cent (with the exception of South Africa at 12 per cent and Namibia at 5.7 per cent).[59] In the competitive insurance industry, Sanlam has achieved its goal of growing return on equity, as shown in the data on the comparable position of Sanlam in the domestic long-term industry. In 2013, 2014, and 2015 the industry return on equity was 20 per cent, 20.8 per cent, and 21.1 per cent respectively. Sanlam posted a return of equity for those years of 23.3 per cent, 21.6 per cent, and 25.8 per cent. The SA Mutual remained well below the Sanlam performance with 18.8 per cent, 22.2 per cent, and 18.6 per cent.[60] For as long as Sanlam has been in the insurance business in South Africa, it has compared itself with the established long-term company, SA Mutual. The Sanlam attention to operational efficiency led to Sanlam Life RoEV exceeding that of SA Mutual by 6 per cent since 2011.[61] On RoGEV, Sanlam also outperformed the industry consistently between 2013 and 2015, while the most important competitive position of Sanlam in the industry is illustrated by the successful reduction in costs and its strong capital position. Also with respect to general marketing and administrative costs, Sanlam outperformed all other long-term insurance companies in South Africa. The strength in Sanlam's CAR with respect to covered business rose from 4.5 in 2013 to 5.8 in 2015—the highest in the industry. Its arch-rival, SA Mutual, experienced a declining CAR–3.3 in 2013 to 3.1 in 2015.[62]

[59] KPMG (2015): The South African insurance industry, August 2015: 48.

[60] PwC: Insurance through challenging times. Insurance industry analysis, 2016: 42.

[61] F. du Toit: 'Sanlam vs Old Mutual EM life. Past and future RoEV supports SLM', Renaissance Capital, 20/2/2017.

[62] Ibid.: 43.

The decision to do a private placing of 65.5 million shares to fund the SAHAM III transaction in order to secure SAM compliance, illustrates the conservative capital adequacy policy pursued in Sanlam. The diversified nature of Sanlam's business requires comparison with different categories of financial services entities—a complex comparison. In the general insurance market Santam is by far the leading South African company, but in the long-term life market SA Mutual still has the largest market share. When considering the SEM penetration into Africa, Sanlam has a commanding lead in the long-term industry in Africa. The declining trend in return on Sanlam EV per share since 2012 is the result of weakening market conditions. (Table 7.3) The upside is that growth opportunities in Africa via the SAHAM footprint and in the Malaysian and Indian markets in South and South-East Asia are only in the establishment phase. The positive assessment by financial analysts of the future of the Sanlam Group is in the distinct capacity shown to extend business operations beyond the traditional core of business and into markets with growth potential outside the domestic market.[63] As the global asset management industry is in transition as a result of demographic restructuring, market volatility, and regulatory changes, the vertically integrated businesses, with active operations in all segments of the market, are best positioned to mobilize savings along the entire savings chain to bring returns to their clients. The Sanlam Group has built its strategy towards diversification since 2003 and has taken a strategic position since demutualization to mobilize savings and investments across an extended geographical footprint. The diversification of its business remains the business focus in the competitive markets of the twenty-first century.

Ultimately, the market perception of Sanlam is reflected in the performance of its share price. The performance of the Sanlam share price since demutualization, when compared to the SA Mutual share price performance since demutualization, displays sustained stability and sustained strengthening. This perception of stability earned the company valuable loyalty prior to demutualization, and also after demutualization. The new shareholder constituency presented the added expectation of strong growth and high return on investment. The Sanlam share price struggled to move significantly beyond the listing price until late in 2004. Once the turnaround strategy took shape in 2004 and Sanlam commenced with share buy-back transactions in 2005, confidence rose. The real take-off occurred towards late 2012, when Sanlam delivered solid results. In the five years since 2013 growing market confidence in Sanlam supported a strong upward movement in the share price. Sanlam maintained its primary listing on the Johannesburg Securities Exchange, while SA Mutual moved its primary listing to London shortly after demutualization. The graph trajectory of the SA Mutual share price since demutualization, is seen in Figure 7.1. The SA Mutual price opened substantially higher than the

[63] M. Salmon: 'Life Insurance': Investec sector review, 12/4/2016; F. du Toit: 'Sanlam operational update. Strong business gets stronger in tough times', Renaissance Capital, 8/12/2016.

Figure 7.1. Sanlam and SA Mutual share price performance, demutualization to November 2017
Source: Thompsons Reuters Corporation, 2018.

Sanlam listing price, but was consistently more volatile. This follows the SA Mutual exposure to international market developments, especially during the GFC, when the SA Mutual share price plummeted. Sanlam's share price dropped marginally during the GFC crisis, but recovered with the same stability as had been characteristic of the share since 1998.

A regression analysis of the monthly Sanlam share price fluctuations explains the trajectory of the Sanlam share price between 1998 and 2018. A dummy regression analysis was estimated based on the ordinary least squares method (OLS) in order to determine the effect various events had on the share price of Sanlam. The following regression model, estimated in this study as specified by Brooks (2013), was used:[64]

$$Sanlam_t = \alpha + \beta_1 Sell\_ABSA_t + \beta_2 Prime\ rate_t + \beta_3 GBPZAR_t + \beta_4 JvZ(CEO)_t \\ + \beta_5 India_t + \beta_6 Morocco_t + \beta_7 BEE_t + \epsilon_t$$

[64] Where:
$Sanlam_t$ = the monthly closing chare price for Sanlam
$Sell\_ABSA_t$= dummy variable representing the period where Sanlam sold its shares in ABSA
$Prime\ rate_t$ = the monthly closing prime rate prevailing in South Africa
$GBPZAR_t$ = the monthly closing Great British Pound/South African Rand exchange rate
$JvZ(CEO)_t$= dummy variable representing the period where Sanlam employed Johan as their new CEO
$India_t$ = dummy variable representing the period where Sanlam expanded business into India
$Morocco_t$ = dummy variable representing the period where Sanlam expanded business into Morocco
BEE_t = dummy variable representing the period when Sanlam initiated the BEE transaction
In accordance with Brooks (2013), the beta coefficient of each explanatory variable will be used to determine the magnitude of the effect the relating variable had on the Sanlam share price, and the p-value will be used to determine the significance of the relating explanatory variable.

Table 7.4. Regression outputs: Analysis of Sanlam share price movement, 1998–2018

Variable	β	p-value
SELL_ABSA	−5.80909	0.06190*
PRIME_RATE	−3.11445	0.00000***
GBPZAR	5.070638	0.00000***
JvZ(CEO)	−2.35219	0.45080
EXPAND_TO_INDIA	−2.04952	0.61310
EXPAND_TO_MOROCCO	11.78571	0.00020***
BEE_TRANSITION	−8.80562	0.00490***
C	21.54279	0.00000***
Adjusted R-squared	0.803158	
Prob(F-statistic)	0.000000	

The regression analysis output is reflected in Table 7.4.

The stability in the share price trajectory is substantiated by the outcome of the regression.[65]

The take-over as CEO by Johan van Zyl and the expansion to India did not have a statistical significant initial impact on the Sanlam share price based on its p-value being larger than 0.1. On the other hand, the business expansion to Morocco did have a positive statistical significant impact on the Sanlam share price at a 99 per cent confidence interval. During the expansion to Morocco, the Sanlam share price increased by 11.786 units (*ceteris paribus*). The selling of Sanlam's stake in ABSA and the BEE transaction both had a significantly negative impact on the Sanlam share price. The selling of the ABSA stake and the BEE transition caused the Sanlam share price to decline by 5.809 and 8.806 units respectively (*ceteris paribus*).

These results underline underlying stability in the development of Sanlam as a diversified financial services Group since demutualization. The basic stability and sustained gradual upward trajectory indicates the fundamental role of the basic insurance and financial services business to the Group. The Sanlam management was satisfied with the demutualization transaction, but the market remained relatively skeptical until management communicated and implemented a clear and basic growth strategy grounded in the core business of the group. The appointment of Van Zyl did not

[65] With respect to the overall model, the adjusted R-squared of 0.803158 indicates that 80.316% of a change in the share price of Sanlam can be explained by the explanatory variables included in the model. According to Gujarati and Porter (2009), an adjusted R-squared above 0.75 indicates that the model is a reasonably well fitted model. Furthermore, the p-value of the f-statistic is 0.000 indicating that the total model is significant at a 99% confidence level. Both these statistical measures therefore indicates that the model is sound and does not suffer from omitted variable bias.

make the rainbow, neither did the expansion into India—the persistent implementation of the basic growth strategy did. Sustained delivery on the communicated Group strategy, as often underlined by Van Zyl, shaped growing market confidence. Entering into a substantial BEE transaction, the UB transaction, also did not render sudden results. The patient hard work to ensure delivery on the expectation indeed by 2016 did strengthen market confidence, and coupled with strong overall Group performance, eventually contributed to the strong performance of the Sanlam share price. By 2013 and 2014 the business model earned the confidence of the market and further expansion into West Africa in collaboration with SAHAM, gave a significant hike to investor confidence and pushed the share price upwards. Adverse global economic conditions and domestic political volatility contributed to the decline in the share price between 2015 and 2016, but this was not Sanlam specific. The entire South African economy was under pressure. Persistent performance of the Group in its core business supported the recovery of the share price to its highest levels ever. The history of Sanlam in South Africa is one of stability and loyalty to South Africa. These traits remained persistent throughout the Sanlam century. Sanlam was a South African company, grounded in patriotism and the typical '*settlergeist*' insisting on independence from the colonial power. Sanlam did indeed become what Daling referred to at the general meeting of policyholders before demutualization, namely a 'respected trademark' of South African life insurance. Since demutualization the market acknowledged the relative stability of the fundamental soundness of the Group's business and by 2014/2015 that confidence excelled, narrowing the gap between the SA Mutual share price and the Sanlam share price.

Epilogue

The South African insurance industry has been a significant role player in the financial services sector of South Africa throughout the history of the country. It performed a stabilizing role during the years of international isolation by mobilizing savings more comprehensively than any other saving channel in the country. The central role of the insurance industry in South Africa, compared to perhaps the largest insurance industry in the world, is illustrated in Table 7.5, which depicts insurance density and insurance penetration between South Africa and the USA between 1960 and 2014.

The insurance density of the South African market rose from 10.3 per cent of the USA market in 1960 to 23 per cent of the USA market in 2014. In 2015 this density declined marginally to 20.5, primarily as a result of the high population growth in South Africa. More South Africans, relative to the size of the local population, are invested in the insurance industry compared to the American population. Insurance penetration was 4.8 per cent in 1960 compared to 7.6 per cent for the USA, but by 1991 South African insurance penetration surpassed the American penetration and by 2015 was 14.7 per cent

Table 7.5. Comparative insurance density and penetration, South Africa and the USA, 1960–2014

	Insurance density* US$		SA density as % of USA	Insurance penetration** US$ %	
	SA	USA		SA	USA
1960	18	175	10.3	4.8	7.6
1970	42	331	12.7	5.9	8.5
1991	338	1927	17.5	11.3	8.6
2014	925	4017	23.0	14.0	7.3
2015	843	4095	20.5	14.7	7.3

Notes: *Insurance density = US$ (life and non-life) premiums per capita.
**Insurance penetration = US$ (life and non-life) premiums as % of nat income/GDP.
Sources: *Sigma*, no. 3, 2016; *Sigma* no. 4 (2015), no. 4 (1993), no. 4 (1972).

compared to 7.3 per cent in the USA. When considering the long-term industry only, South Africa has been the country among emerging markets with the highest insurance penetration since the early 1990s.[66] The relatively high penetration and increasing density can be ascribed to two main factors. The first was the absence of any form of universal state social security programme. Providing for social financial security was a private matter. The second factor was the dominance of the South African life offices in the local financial services sector, being able to offer relatively high and stable returns on policyholder funds, the ability to instill confidence in the local industry as agents of the confidence of the people. As the demand for ordinary life insurance contracted, the industry developed innovative new products that offered a comparatively high return. Under international sanctions and a restrictive exchange rate system, South Africans had limited investment opportunities. The long-term insurance industry took advantage of this situation to attract funds and offer flexibility in returns. Ordinary life policies were supplemented by linked insurance products, a variety of investment products, as well as equity-based investment opportunities. Long-term insurance companies are not known for product innovation, but the case was different in South Africa and Australia. Furthermore, the diversification strategies during the period of isolation offered a hedge option to ordinary people. Diversification into a variety of financial services coupled with product innovation offered the public both relative sound returns and security. When the life offices acquired control over the banking groups during the mid-1980s, the industry solidified its position by utilizing the banking distribution channel to strengthen its penetration. Sanlam was a prominent innovator in the market. Entering the industry very late, and having to compete with established companies such as SA Mutual, as well as overseas companies from the leading British market, innovation and efficiency were the keys to establishing the company and growing market share.

[66] G. Verhoef (2010): 'Life offices to the rescue!': 151.

It is not organizations that change society, but human agency. People devise tools to achieve social, economic, and political goals. The recurring theme throughout the history of Sanlam is that the company has been an agent of social transformation. Afrikaner nationalist leaders, respected as educated and professional people involved in the discourse on equal language rights and people worthy of a share in the mainstream of the economy, considered the insurance sector a useful tool towards empowerment. Long-term insurance companies generally position themselves in society to offer policyholders security against risk. Sanlam entered the market with an added mission, namely the socio-economic upliftment and economic empowerment of 'Afrikaners'. This category of people was defined during the early years of the century as those who placed South Africa first, those who were loyal to South Africa. The bulk of that constituency was Afrikaners, both very poor and wealthy, respected members of society. The social engagement of this long-term insurance company deviated from the ordinary business operations of long-term insurers. Sanlam was closely associated with Afrikaner nationalist idealism and political ambitions, but always marketed its services to all seeking the benefit of its products and services. Right from the start English-speaking and Afrikaans-speaking South Africans, white and Coloured people, worked alongside each other in Sanlam. After the surge in Afrikaner nationalism during the 1938 *Groot Trek* centenary celebrations, and then the mobilization of dedicated economic empowerment strategies at the *Volkskongres* in 1939, Sanlam unmistakably positioned itself at the centre of Afrikaner empowerment.

The nationalist connection indeed served a twofold purpose. On the one hand it gave the company a significant advantage in the Afrikaans-speaking market, but not all Afrikaners automatically chose the Sanlam policy offering. SA Mutual has always had a strong policy-holder base among Afrikaans-speaking people. On the other hand Afrikaner empowerment was taken to the effective level where abject Afrikaner poverty was eradicated by the early 1960s and effective Afrikaner penetration into industry, mining and the financial sector secured.

Bringing the history of Sanlam to the brink of one hundred years, the subsidiary Santam developed a strategy to grow in the South African market by an empowerment strategy. Marginalized Afrikaans-speaking people moved to a central position in the economy. Insurance companies do not traditionally take on a role as socio-economic empowerment agent of a particular segment of society. The extensive exposure to non-insurance core investments acquired as part of this empowerment strategy contributed to almost three decades of underperformance, a loss of focus on the core business of a long-term insurance company, and unsavoury public intra-Afrikaner disagreement. With Afrikaners no longer poor and marginalized, the binding power of nationalism disintegrated. Hard business decisions were needed, but the 'strategic investments' empire had to be wound up to release capital for the business Sanlam was in the market to do—long-term insurance and financial services. Policyholders' interests were at stake while Sanlam was involved in a protracted exit strategy. At a crucial intersection in the history of South Africa during the mid-1980s when international pressure mounted and domestic opposition forced the government's hand, Sanlam was slow in changing its business model. Highly critical of the Government of the day, Sanlam leaders entered the public and secret discourse on unsustainable policies, macro-economic policy and basic social equity. Strategic direction and change management in Sanlam steered the company from the mutual form of organization into a listed entity. This development followed international trends in financial services, but this development coincided with radical socio-political transformation in South Africa.

The company entered a new business environment upon demutualization. Despite more than five years of internal discussions on demutualization and the release of capital tied up in underperforming assets, demutualization was finally engineered with tight time management and speed. The ambitious Marinus Daling could not complete what he intended to achieve with demutualization. One 'vastly experienced' financial analyst, David Shapiro, noted, 'It's extraordinary isn't it, that you had the "big 3" in the past, Sanlam, Old Mutual and Liberty... Old Mutual is imploding, they made all these acquisitions. Now they're hiving them off, unbundling them. And Sanlam has just steadily kept to its course. Changed direction here and there, and just got stronger... and you've got to give it to management for doing that. They were never infatuated to go and do big deals offshore or run away and do things like that. Their ambitions were kept under control and it's now paying off.'[67] It was finally the change in leadership and leadership style, that steered the organization into the functional overhaul that was required to sustain the core business and develop a strategy for sustainability.

From 2003, the organizational change that was meant to emerge from demutualization was engineered by strategic leadership that embarked on systematic change management. As the inside-Sanlam-generation management was replaced by outside strategic leadership, Sanlam entered the trajectory towards transformation for growth and sustainability. The last legacy hurdle towards realizing the transformation was unlocking the value in ABSA. The careful delivery on promises, adding value, and its growth strategy since 2003 brought Sanlam to a commanding position as diversified financial services group in South Africa. This business transformation came about in a short time—approximately eighteen years, between 2000 and 2018. Those eighteen years between 2000 and 2018 were the foundation years of the new-century Sanlam.

The first century of the history of Sanlam concludes with an empowerment achievement of a different nature. Value-adding business, diversification of risk and revenue stream, conservative management, and an embeddedness in the soil of establishment and operation, secured the emergence of a diversified financial services group in a global

[67] www.biznews.com/hogg-interviews - shapiro/2017/09/11.

context a century later. A new-generation management translated the needs of the new context after 1994 into wealth creation and preservation activities for that new world. Impoverished Afrikaners were now replaced by a new generation outside the insurance industry. Following the empowerment model that guided the wealthy Afrikaners of the Cape in promoting financial and economic inclusion, broad-based South African empowerment became a business imperative. It was only when the business strategy to return business to the fundamental basic elements of delivery on insurance promises came into effect, that the recovery of Sanlam could begin.

The back-to-basics strategy removed any distraction from operational efficiency, growth, wealth creation and preservation, and sustainability in the core financial services focus of the company. As a fundamental precondition, human capital building, which had been a legacy throughout the history of Sanlam, received priority. Transformation was a business imperative, just as it was the empowerment imperative in the 1930s to facilitate Afrikaner entry into the core heights of the domestic economy. Building capacity was part of empowerment. With the strengthening of core financial performance once management could take strategic decisions backed by access to sufficient capital, Sanlam rolled its empowerment strategy out into new emerging markets outside South Africa, as well as supported entrepreneurship and small business development through partnerships in a wide range of financial services. The business developed synergies in and between clusters and companies in the Group around the concept of a 'one-firm firm'. This strategy delivered positive results for overall financial performance. The confidence of Sanlam in its business strategy was illustrated by the R14.2 billion placed back into the market through successive share buy-back schemes since 2005 and the first-ever interim special dividend paid in 2014. Once financial performance had been restored to sustained growth after 2008, Sanlam embarked on systematic internationalization. The critical success factors in putting Sanlam on a post-centenary trajectory are competencies in management, specialist product development, service delivery, and social connection through its empowerment brand with the broader South African society. Afrikaner nationalism as a mobilizing force has been replaced by a South African inclusivity. The last two decades of Sanlam's century of development blend with the history of South Africa, in a similar way as it had represented the fabric of South Africa during the first decades of its operation.

The ability of Sanlam to sustain a localized small insurance company in the face of international competition by big foreign insurers can be ascribed to two key factors. The first was the resilience to change the business model as often as required to stay abreast of the developments in the industry. The second was to transform itself to reflect the dynamic changes in the market in which it operated. The people of Sanlam are the face and the driver of this transition. Afrikaans-speaking managers had been at the helm of Sanlam since its establishment in 1918. As society and South Africa changed, Afrikaners in Sanlam were slow to relinquish power. The transformation of control, management, and client profile coincided with global and domestic demographic changes. The new post-2003 leadership team understood that a company belonged to its stakeholders and therefore had to reflect that. The business decision of transformation fed into the transformation of strategy, structure, and people. In 2018 Sanlam is an emerging-market multinational enterprise. Offshore institutional shareholders comprise 38.14 per cent of Sanlam Ltd shareholders. Individuals make up 12.59 per cent of the shareholder base. The history embedded in the Afrikaner empowerment legacy nevertheless held potentially negative implications for Sanlam. The company was closely associated with the ruling National Party for a long time. Sanlam's past could have made the company unresponsive, or unable to adapt to the new context of South Africa and of the globalized world. In Sanlam's testimony before the TRC the inclination to do business in a given environment was clearly articulated. The leadership came from a distinct cultural background, but accepted adapting to changing circumstances as a business imperative. When the context of Afrikaner impoverishment and marginalization presented a business opportunity, the intersection was utilized skilfully. As Afrikaner business impacted significantly on the mainstream of the South African economy, Sanlam performed a vital re-engineering role through Sankorp. The very deep penetration of Sanlam through its shareholding in extensive so-called strategic investments, not simply as a portfolio investor, but as an engaged stakeholder, distinguished Sanlam from all other long-term assurers in almost the entire global insurance landscape. No other life office in South Africa had such a profound impact across the entire cope of the economy. This involvement delivered serious risks, because actuaries and insurance managers are not mining engineers, industrialists, bankers, or retail managers.

Afrikaner presence through the conglomerates controlled by Sanlam represented a goal well achieved. It was imperative for its own business progress. Building down this business empire was a daunting task, but also a business imperative. The capital tied up in those investments undermined Sanlam's ability to take advantage of changing global market trends. Worldwide conglomerates unbundled to unlock value to underlying shareholders. Sanlam had to do that to its investments managed by Sankorp as a first step to financial freedom to deliver optimal benefit to its policyholders. As globalization and market liberalization changed the world, so did the Sanlam leadership align themselves to take advantage of its embedded knowledge and experience to take the company to the next level of international business. The strategic leadership actually understood the value of the company's history as a resource for innovation, transformation, and ultimately sustainability. History as a unique resource, rare, and impossible to duplicate,[68] was duly acknowledged by the management in the course of devising the repositioning and the turnaround strategy at Sanlam. When the Carnegie Commission

[68] R. Suddaby, W.M. Foster, and C.Q. Trank (2010): 'Rhetorical history as a source of competitive advantage', *Advances in Strategic Management*, 27: 147–73.

on poverty in South Africa claimed in 1932 that Afrikaners were poor because they failed to adapt to the modern economic environment, Afrikaner leaders took a leaf from that book, not to be repeated in future. Since Sanlam was rooted in South African soil, business sustainability was dependent on the ability to adapt to the changing socio-economic context. Sanlam heeded that call through its own history. As the operational turnaround succeeded and Sanlam moved into global emerging markets, the empowerment history was appropriated as a unique resource of competitive advantage. Sanlam also used its legacy brand to build firm competitiveness, both in the domestic as well as in international markets. The potentially negative association with Afrikaner political power during the time of Afrikaner empowerment came to be appreciated as a powerful competitive advantage. Sanlam built a sound insurance enterprise able to become a global visionary Wealthsmith™.

APPENDIX 1 THE DEVELOPMENT OF THE SANLAM LOGO, 1918–1991

Sanlam Logo 1918

Sanlam Logo 1929

Sanlam Logo 1932

Sanlam Logo 1940

Sanlam Logo 1953

Sanlam Logo 1968

Sanlam Logo 1973

Sanlam Logo 1986

Sanlam Logo 1991

Sanlam logo 2014

BIBLIOGRAPHY

1. Sanlam Archive

A. PAPERS AND NOTICES

Articles of Association, 1918.
SA RN 3/6/2: Selected advertisements, 1918–1945.
SA Policy Registers, 1918–2010.
SA 1/2/1/1/2 Stone & Cox Life Insurance Tables, 1920, 1927.
SA 5/2/4/2 C: Application J. Bezuidenhout, 15/3/1920.
SA 6/5/1: Letter of application Fanie Cloete, 6/11/1920.
SA Sanlam Chairman's Report, 1920–1953.
SA 5/2/2: Geboue, 1-20:1919–1938.
SA 1/2/1/3 Rate Book, 1922, 1929, 1931–1936.
SA 5/2/6: Annual Agent statements, 1929.
SA B 1/2 1/2/13/2, Selected brochures, 1935–1938.
SA 5/3/1: Monthly Report 1930–1935: Memorandum Feenstra on Orange Free State.
SA 6/1/7: Sanlam notice to policy holders, March 1946.
SA 5/2: B23: Bursaries: Memorandum to Board, 25/10/1955.
SA 5/2/: D4: A.D. Wassenaar Memorandum, 1/12/1958.
SA 1/2/1/3/3/Vol. 30, *Group insurance; Rate Books*, 1954, 1967, 1974.
SA 3/1/2: Beleggingsnavorsing: Memoranda insake beleggings, 18/8/1954; 20/10/1954; 14/4/1959.
SA 3/1/2: Sanlam Beleggingsnavorsing: Memorandum insake beleggings in gewone aandele, 9/2/1951: 1–5.
SA 3/1/2: Beleggingsnavorsing: Hoofbestuurder: Memorandum i.s. SANLAM/Bonuskor verhouding, 5/02/1960.
SA 1/2/1/6, Senior Market development, 12/6/1960.
SA 5/2/D4: Donasies SACEE, Letter SACEE.
SA 6/6/1961 Letter Beak-Sanlam, 13/6/63.
SA 5/2: B23: Bursaries: Memorandum to Board, 17/8/1962.
SA 5/2/D4B: Helpmekaar Studiefonds, 1963–1972.
SA Mining and Engineering Journal, 4/9/1964.
SA 1/2/1/3/4, *Special tariffs: Memorandum*, 22/8/1967.
SA 1/2/1/3/4, *Special Tariffs*, 9/5/1967.
SA 6/5/1: Memorandum to Sanlam Board, 17/4/1968; Marketing Report 1967.
SA 1/2/1/6: Senior Market development: Letter CRAUF–W.J. Bezuidenhoudt, 12/6/1967.
SA 5/2/: D4B: Memorandum to Board, 17/7/1968.
SA Agents' Bulletin, 11/07/1969.
SA 1/2/4/3: Sanlam Opleidingsgids vir Verteenwoordigers, 1970.
SA, 1/2/1/2/1, Product Development: Notice, 17/11/1970.
SA 1/2/1/ *Product Development A 101*, August 1970.

SA 1/2/1/: Product Development Report, 11/2/1972.
SA 7/5/2: LOA files: Insurope News, 17/1/1975.
SA Sanlam News release, 20/5/1975.
SA 6/1/6: Confidential announcement. Labrador, Giraffe, Camel, Lynx, Aristotelus, 16/11/1975.
SA Nuusuitreiking 25/6/1979: Press release LOA on Cost structure of Life offices.
SA S 17: Donations, 1980–1989.
SA 5/3/15/3: Training of Black and Coloured people in Sanlam 'Non-white staff', 12/11/1980.
SA 5/3/15/1: Non-white staff eating facilities, 9/6/1981.
SA 6/1/6G: Confidential Memorandum on Rembrandt by F.J. du Plessis, 27/9/1982.
SA 6/1/6: Press release, 27/3/1983.
SA 1/2/1/1: Marketing campaign, 6/2/1984.
SA 6/5/1: Chairman's Address to Annual General Meeting, 19/03/1986.
SA 5/3/4: March 1990: Desmond Smith statement on Sanlam Corporate Identity.
SA 5/5/2: Chairman's address, 19/2/1992.
SA Sanlam Advertising and marketing survey, March–April 1993.
SA 6/5/1: FINWEEK, 10–16 June 1993.
SA G Verhoef (1993) *The History of Federale Mynbou Beperk*. Unpublished manuscript.
SA Bloudruk, 1/4/1994: 19.
SA 7/5/1, *LOA Minutes*, 10/2/1995.
SA *Blue Print*, 3/1996.
SA 7/1/7: Dr C. Stals Submission to Commission of Enquiry into the affairs of Tollgate Holdings Ltd, 26 February 1996.
SA 1/2/1, *Product list*, 20/1/1997.
SA Sanlam Exco, 27/05/1997.
SA 5/2/1: Confidential report on changes in the individual insurance sector—Sanlam Board, 26/2/1997.
SA Sanlam Share Offers. Prospectus, 28/10/1998.
SA Press Release, 8/3/2000: Sanlam retains its shareholding in ABSA.
SA 1/2/1: Product development: Sanlam 100-Plus Policy document.
SA 3/1/3/2: Lenings aan Koshuise, A, B; 3/1/4/2: Letter Provincial.
SA Sanlam: Policy register, 1.
SA SIM Report to the Public Investment Commissioners on the Action Plans i.t.o. section H.2 of the mandate, July 2001.
SA 7/1/7: Sanlam submission to Davis Commission, 13/6/2001.
SA News Release: 'Sanlam verkoop sy gesondheidsorgbesidheid aan Medscheme', 1/10/2001.
SA 7/1/3/1/1/: Genmin planning for Union Corporation acquisition.
SA 3/5/5: KMB/CSI: 'Thinking ahead, staying relevant'. Transformation Report, 2003: 1.
SA News Release: 'Sanlam kontrakteer IT infrastruktuur uit', 25/1/2001.
SA J. v Zyl: Presentation to Sanlam Human Resources Committee, 26/1/2003.
SA Sanlam Ltd Board Summit, Erinvale, Somerset West, 3+4/8/2004.
SA Sanlam Group strategy and business structure, 22/4/2004.
SA 5/3/12/13/1 (2): Sanlam Demutualization Trust, 1998–2008 Chairman's Report, 3/6/2009.
SA 3/5: Sanlam: New Dawn, Organizational Design Distribution Sales Organization.
SA F. Louw. 2005. Thinking Ahead: Sanlam's approach to corporate social investment. February 2005.
SA J. van Zyl (Sanlam CEO) and J. Rowe (Aflife CEO) presentation to Sanlam Life Board, 24/2/2005.
SA 4/24: Marketing Research: J. Dommisse (2006) *Profile and penetration of insurance companies. SAARP AAMPS Survey 2006.*

SA Report by D.C. van der Merwe: ŉ Ondersoek na die invloed van ŉ 'Prestasie-oriëntasiekursus' op die verteenwoordigers van ŉ lewensversekeringsmaatskappy.
SA *Sanlam. Riding the wave: Sanlam's socio-economic impact in South Africa and beyond.* Sanlam, 2013.
SA *Sanlam: The IT journey from 1990 to 2014.*
SA 7/1/7: Sanlam submission to Heath Commission of Inquiry.
SA Sanlam Business Philosophy, November 2012.
SA Sanlam Personal Finance, July 2013.
SA Sanlam Product List, August 2013.
SA Sanlam Personal Finance, September 2014.
SA Sanlam Executive Committee documents: Fifth Floor, Sanlam Head Office: Truth and Reconciliation Commission Submission documents, 1997.

B. LETTERS AND PERSONAL DOCUMENTS

SA Letter Fichardt–Santam Provisional Board, 12 April 1918.
SA 6/5/1 Letter C.R. Louw–W.A. Hofmeyr, 3/10/1918.
SA 6/5/1: Letter MacDowall–De Klerk, 23/10/1919.
SA 6/5/1: Feenstra correspondence, 9 June 1920.
SA 6/5: Feenstra biographical papers: Letter Feenstra–Macdowall, 9/6/1920.
SA 6/5/1: MacDowall to Chairman, Santam dated 25/05/1920.
SA 5/2/4/2: Geskiedkundige Memos en Briewe: 'D.P. de Klerk: Eerste Trustbestuurder van Sanlam.'
SA 6/1/1/5: W.J. Bezuidenhout Biographical documents: Minutes of Special AGM 1 May 1923.
SA 6/1/1/5; W.J. Bezuidenhout Biographical documents: Minutes of Extraordinary Special Annual General Meeting of shareholders, 1 May 1923; *Africa Insurance Record*, July 1924: 36.
SA 5/2/4/2/1: Letter Secretary–General Manager, 30/11/1925.
SA 5/4/2/1/2 Correspondence Johannesburg Branch manager–Secretary, 11/7/27.
SA 4/10: Letter J.C.W. Louw–M.S. Louw, 2/01/1934.
SA 6/1/19: P.A. Malan biographical papers: Letter E. Louw–P.A. Malan, 9/9/1939.
SA: 6/1/19: P.A. Malan biographical papers.
SA 6/1/7/; M.S. Louw papers: Memorandum aan die Raad insake finansieringsmaatskappy, 20/10/1938. SA 6/1/7: Personal documents M.S. Louw: FVB Statutes and Articles of Association, 27/11/1940.
SA 6/1/7: M.S. Louw address, 12/09/1945, Stellenbosch: Association for Economy and Trade.
SA 6/1/7: M.S. Louw Documents; Vertroulike Memorandum insake die voorgestelde stigting van 'n beleggingskorporasie die kapitaal waarvan voorsien word deur kontant-bonusse op Sanlam-polisse, 26/02/1945: SA: 6/1/7: M.S. Louw Memorandum, 20/5/1945.
SA 6/1/4: H.S. Marais: Sanlam Gedenkboek, July 1946.
SA 6/5/1/8: C.H. Brink papers: Cape Argus, 15/8/1946.
SA 6/7/1: M.S. Louw documents: M.S. Louw address to FAK: 'Opkoms van die Afrikaner op ekonomiese gebied', 14/3/1950.
SA 6/1/7: M.S. Louw biographical papers: Memorandum G.D. Wilson: AHT, 8/2/56.
SA 5/2/4/2: Death letter de Villiers, 19/11/1957.
SA 6/1/7: M.S. Louw personal documents: Saambou. The aim and purpose of Saambou, address delivered to Sanlam managers' conference, October 1957: 304.
SA 6/7/1: M.S. Louw documents: Address at Sanlam Managers Conference, October 1957.

SA 6/1/7: M.S. Louw biographical papers, Memorandum, 13/4/59.
SA 6/1/7: M.S. Louw Personal Document File: Memorandum of African Homes Trust, 13/04/1959.
SA 1/2/1/6, Letter J.A. Vorster–Field staff, 6/5/1960.
SA 5/2/D4A: Letter Wassenaar–Board, 20/2/1962.
SA 6/6/1/5: Interview with P.A. Malan, March 1965.
SA 1/2/5: Sanlam Product development: Finplan 4/2/1977.
SA 6/1/2: Letter A.D. Wassenaar–W.J. de Villiers, 26/5/1980.
SA 6/5 6/5/1, Biographical notes on Servaas Daniel de Wet.
SA 6/6/1: Biography A. MacDowall.
SA 5/3/12/6/8: Letter Deon Basson–Sanlam (G. Rudman).
SA 6/1/6G: Letter du Plessis–A.E. Rupert, 11/4/1980.
SA 6/1/6G: Letter du Plessis–A.E. Rupert, 31/3/1980; letter A.E. Rupert du Plessis, 31/3/1980 (delivered by hand).
SA 6/1/2 A.D. Wassenaar–A.E. Rupert, 28/4/1980.
SA 6/1/2: Letter A.E. Rupert–F,J, du Plessis, 27/3/1980.
SA 6/1/2: Letter W.H. de Villiers–A.D. Wassenaar, 14/5/1981.
SA 6/1/6G: P.E. Rousseau Confidential Memorandum–Sanlam Board, 1/12/1981.
SA 6/1/6G: P. .E Rousseau Confidential memorandum–Sanlam Board, 1/12/1981.
SA 6/1/6G: letter F.J. du Plessis–W.J. de Villers, 16/8/1982.
SA 6/1/6; Letter F.J. du Plessis–W.H. de Villiers, 16/8/1982.
SA 6/1/6G: Confidential Memorandum A.D. Wasseraar–Sanlam Directors, 5/1/1982.
SA 6/1/6G: Confidential letter W.J. de Villiers–F.J. du Plessis, 14/8/1982.
SA 6/1/6: Letter F.J. du Plessis–P.W. Botha, 12/11/1984.
SA 6/1/6: Letter P.W. Botha–F.J. du Plessis, 2/5/1984.
SA 6/1/6: Open letter F.J. du Plessis to 39 persons: Cabinet Ministers, Chairmen of Parliamentary Standing Committees and Chairmen of Public Bodies, 17/7/1985.
SA 6/1/2: Letter A.D. Wassenaar–D.W. Hertzog, 12/3/1985.
SA 7/1/7: Sanlam Subsidiaries: Letter A.S. du Plessis–M.H. Daling, 30/1/1989.
SA 5/3/12: Letter Cosatu–M.H. Daling, 4/4/1998; Cosatu Submission to Portfolio Committe on Finance, 18/8/1998.
SA 6/1/7: M.S. Louw biographical documents; Speeches.
SA 6/2/1 Biographical files P.D. Rousseau.
SA Letter Steve Booysen (ABSA CEO) and Danie Cronjé (Chairman ABSA Board)–Johan van Zyl (Sanlam CEO), 5/11/2004.
SA Sanlam Press release: 25/1/2017.
SA Minutes of Sanlam Ltd Exco: Press Release 27/3/2018.

C. MINUTES, MEMORANDA, AND REPORTS

Minutes of Dagelijks Bestuur: 20/6/1919–30/8/1950.
Minutes of General Meetings: 09/12/1976.
Minutes of Sanlam Ltd Board: 09/01/1999–12/02/2017.
Minutes of Sanlam Life Board: 3/12/1998–27/05/2004.
Minutes of Sanlam Board: 27/09/1918–09/03/1999.
Minutes of Sankorp: 04/11/1986–08/04/1992.
Minutes of FVB: 27/11/1940–1970.
Minutes of Sanlam Ltd Executive Committee (Exco), 2010–2017.

Sanlam Annual Reports: 1919–2010.
Sanlam Integrated Reports: 2011–2016.
Sanlam Sustainability Reports: 2012–2016.

D. SANLAM PERIODICAL PUBLICATIONS

Die Sanlam *Fakkel*, 5/11/1928–1/12/1998.
Inside Sanlam: 10/2016.
Sandaba: 02/2000–12/2013.
Sanlammer, 12/7/1992–16/9/2000.

E. *SANTAM*

Santam Board Minutes, 4/04/1918.
Santam Board Minutes, 29/07/1918.
Santam Board Minutes, 30/09/1918.
Santam Board Minutes, 24/01/1919.
Santam Board Minutes, 26/2/2007.
Santam Report to Board of Directors, 28/09/1919.
Santam Bank. *50th Annual Report* 1967.
SA Santam AGM, 1953.
SA Santampos Maart 1959: 6.

2. Books

Alborn, T. and Murphy, S.A. 2013. *Anglo-American Life Insurance 1800–1914*. London: Pickering & Chatto.
Amatori, F. and Colli, A. 2011. *Business History: Complexities and Comparisons*. New York: Routledge.
Arndt, E.H.D. 1928. *Banking and Currency Development, 1652–1927*. Cape Town: Juta.
Arndt, E.H.D. 1938. *An analysis of the investment policies of life insurance companies in the Union of South Africa: The need for more Constructive Legislature*. Pretoria: University of Pretoria Press.
Barras, R. 1986. Towards a theory of innovation in services. *Research Policy*, 15(4).
Beinart, W. 2001. *Twentieth Century South Africa*. Oxford: Oxford University Press.
Birkman, U. and Codoni, C. 2004. World Insurance in 2003: Insurance industry on the road to recovery. *Sigma*, 3, Zurich: SwissRe.
Borscheid, P. 2012. *World Insurance*. Oxford: Oxford University Press.
Borscheid, P. and Haueter, N.V. 2012. *World Insurance: The Evolution of a Global Risk Network*. Oxford: Oxford University Press.
Brooks, C. 2013. *Introductory Econometrics for Finance*, 3rd edn. Cambridge: Cambridge University Press.
Chandler, A.D. Jr 1969. *Strategy and Structure: Chapters in the history of the American enterprise*. Cambridge, MA: MIT Press.
Clark, G. 1999. *Betting on lives: The culture of life insurance in England, 1695–1775*. Manchester: Manchester University Press.
Cummins, J.D. and Venard, B. 2007. *Handbook of International Insurance*. New York: Springer.
De Kiewiet, C.W. 1942. *A history of South Africa: Social and Economic*. Oxford: Clarendon Press.
De Kock, M.H. 1924. *Selected Subjects in the Economic History of South Africa*. Cape Town: Juta.

Dennett, L. 1998. *A Sense of Security: 150 Years of Prudential.* Cambridge: Granta Edn.s.

Dickson, P.G.M. 1961. *The Sun Insurance Office 1710–1960.* London: Oxford University Press.

Dunning, J.H. 1993. *Globalisation of Business.* London: Routledge.

Du Toit, P. 1939. Van die breë beleid van die Volkskongres (1934) tot die ekonomiese selfstandigmaking as kernvraagstuk. (Address delivered at the EVK, Bloemfontein.) In *Referate, Besluite en Presensielys van die Ekonomiese Volkskongres.* 3, 4, and 5 October 1939. Bloemfontein: FAK.

Esterhuyse,W. 2012. *Eindstryd. Geheime gesprekke en di einde van apartheid.* Cape Town: Tafelberg.

Feinstein, C. 2005. *An Economic History of South Africa.* Cambridge: Cambridge University Press.

Giliomee, H. 2003. *The Afrikaners: Biography of a People.* Cape Town: Tafelberg.

Giliomee, H. 2013. *Die laaste Afrikanerleiers. 'n Opperste toets van mag.* Cape Town: Tafelberg.

Giliomee, H. 2014. Afrikaner nationalism 1875–1899. In *A History of South Africa: From distant past to the present day*, ed. F. Pretorius. Pretoria: Protea Book House.

Goold, M. and Campbell, A. 1987. *Strategies and Styles: The role of the centre in managing diversified corporations.* Oxford: Basil Blackwell.

Grobler, J. 2014. Black political awakening, 1875–1949. In *History of South Africa: From distant past to the present day,* ed. F. Pretorius. Pretoria: Protea Book House.

Grosskopf, J.F.W. 1932. *Report on the Poor White Problem in South Africa.* Stellenbosch: Pro Eclessia Drukkery.

Gujarati, D.N. and Porter, D.C. (2009). *Basic Econometrics*, 5th edn. New York: McGraw-Hill.

Hansman, H. 1996. *The Ownership of Enterprise.* Cambridge, MA: Belknap Press of Harvard University Press.

Hartman, R. 2012. *Ali: The life of Ali Bacher.* London: Penguin.

Hofmeyr, J.H. 1913. *Het leven van Jan Hendrik Hofmeyr (Onze Jan).* Cape Town: Van de Sandt Villiers.

Jenkins, D. and Yoneyama, T. 2000. *History of Insurance.* London: Pickering & Chatto.

Jones, F.S. 1992. Introduction: The growth of the financial sector, 1950–1988. In *Financial Enterprise in South Africa since 1950*, ed. F.S. Jones. London: Macmillan.

Jones, G.R. and George, J.M. 2009. *Contemporary Management*, 6th edn. Boston: McGraw-Hill.

Jones, G.R. and George, J.M. 2011. *Essentials of contemporary management.* 4th edn. New York: McGraw-Hill Irwin.

Jones, F.S. and Müller, A.L. 1992. *The South African economy, 1910–1990.* Basingstoke: Macmillan.

Jones, J.D.F. 1995. *Through fortress and rock: The story of Gencor 1895–1995.* Johannesburg: Jonathan Ball.

Keller, M. 1963. *The Life Insurance Enterprise, 1885–1910: A Study in the Limits of Corporate Power.* Cambridge: The Belknap Press of Harvard University Press.

Kemp, J.C.G. 1942. *Die pad van die veroweraar.* Pretoria: Nasionale Pers.

Le Roux, N.J. 1953. *W.A. Hofmeyr: Sy werk en waarde.* Cape Town: Nasionale Boekhandel.

Leach, G. 1989. *The Afrikaners: Their last Great Trek.* London: Macmillan.

Little, M.D., Cooper, Richard N., Corden, W. Max, and Rajapatirana, S. 1993. *Boom, Crisis and Adjustment: The macro-economic experience of developing countries,* New York: Oxford University Press.

Maasdorp, G. 2002. Economic Survey, 1970–2000. In *The Decline of the South African Economy*, ed. F. S. Jones. Cheltenham: Edward Elgar.

MacDonald, J.R. 1903. *What I Saw In South Africa. September & October 1902.* London.

Macintyre, A.C. 1898. *South African Red Book: a Record of Insurance, Banking and Commercial Affairs.* Cape Town: T. Maskew Miller.

Malan, H.R. 1977. William Angus Hofmeyr, in *South African Biographical Dictionary.* Pretoria: Tafelberg.

Miller, R.J. 1968. *Life Assurance in South Africa.* Johannesburg: Blue Crane Books.

Mintzberg, H. 1979. *The Structure of Organizations: A synthesis of the Research.* Prentice Hall.

Müller, C.F.J. (ed.) 1987. *Vyfhonderd Jaar Suid-Afrikaanse Geskiedenis.* 4th edn. Pretoria: Academica.

Müller, C.F.J. 1990. *Sonop in die Suide. Geboorte en groei van die Nasionale Pers, 1915–1948.* Cape Town: Nasionale Boekhandel.

Pearson, R. and Yoneyama, T. 2015. *Corporate forms of organizational choice in international insurance,* Oxford: Oxford University Press.

Peters, T. and Waterman, R. 1982. *In Search of Excellence.* New York: Harper & Row.

Philllips, H. 1990.*'Black October': The impact of the Spanish influenza Epidemic of 1918 on South Africa.* Government Printer: Pretoria.

Prahalad, C.K. 2004. *Fortune at the bottom of the pyramid: Eradicating poverty through profits.* New Jersey: Wharton School Publishers.

Romain, K. 1989. *Larger than Life: Donald Gordon and the Liberty Life story.* Johannesburg: Jonathan Ball.

Sadie, J.L. 2002. The Fall and Rise of the Afrikaner in the South African economy. *University of Stellenbosch Annals,* 2001/2002.

Scannell, J.P. 1968. *Uit die volk gebore: Sanlam se eerste vyftig jaar.* Cape Town: Nasionale Boekhandel.

Schumann, C.G.W. 1939. 'Die huidige posisie van die Afrikaner op ekonomiese gebied'. Address delivered at the EVK, Bloemfontein, in *Referate, Besluite en Presensielys van die Ekonomiese Volkskongres.* 3, 4, and 5 October 1939. Bloemfontein: FAK.

Senge, P.M. 1990. *The fifth discipline: the art and practice of the learning organisation.* New York: Doubleday.

Simons, P.B. 1995. *Old Mutual 1845–1945.* Cape Town: Human & Rousseau.

Skidelsky, R. 1998. The growth of a world economy. In *The Oxford history of the Twentieth Century,* eds M. Howard and W.M. Louis. Oxford: Oxford University Press.

Skinner, I. And Osborne, E. 1992. Changes in Banking in South Africa in the 1980s. In *Financial Enterprise in South Africa since 1950,* ed. F.S. Jones. London: Macmillan.

Smit, C. 1993. *Sanlam in die Rekenaareeu, 1953–1993.* Cape Town: Sanlam.

Trebilcock, C. 1985. *Phoenix Assurance and the Development of British Insurance: Vol 1, 1782–1870.* Cambridge: Cambridge University Press.

Trinchet, J. 2003. The Evolution of the Financial System and the Efficiency of Intermediaries and markets. In *International Banking and Financial Systems,* ed. L. de Rosa. Farnham: Ashgate.

Venter, J. 1987. *Charles Robert Louw.* In *South African Biographical Dictionary.* Pretoria: Tafelberg.

Verhoef, G. 1987. *Die Geskiedenis van Nedbank, 1945–1973.* Unpublished DLitt and Phil thesis, Rand Afrikaans University.

Verhoef, G. 1992. Afrikaner nationalism in South African banking; the cases of Volkskas and Trust Bank. In *Financial Enterprise in South Africa since 1950,* ed. F. Jones. London: Macmillan.

Verhoef, G. 2010.The chemical industry. *South African economy and policy, 1990–2000,* eds S. Jones and R. Vivian. Manchester: Manchester University Press.

Verhoef, G. 2010. Life Offices to the Rescue! A History of the Role of Life Insurance in the South African Economy during the Twentieth Century. In *The Development of International Insurance,* eds R. Pearson and R.W. Wright. London: Pickering & Chatto.

Verhoef, G. 2015. The world insures South Africa: Early insurance activities of Insurance companies in South Africa, 1820–1910. In *Corporate Forms and organizational choice in international insurance,* eds R. Pearson and T. Yoneyama. Oxford: Oxford University Press, p. 164.

Verhoef, G. 2016. Strategies for market monopolization: the Register of Co-operation and the imperial banks in South Africa in the 1920s–1980s. In *Colonial and Imperial Banking History,* eds H. Bonin and N. Valerio. London: Routledge.

Vivian, R. 1995. *The story of Mutual & Federal: 1831–1995.* Johannesburg: Mutual and Federal.

Vivian, R.W. 2007. South African Insurance Markets. In *Handbook of International Insurance,* eds J.D. Cummins and B. Venard. New York: Springer.

Weare, W.B. 1993. *Black business in the New South: A social history of the North Carolina Mutual Life Insurance Company*. Durham: Duke University Press.

Weideman, N.C. 1955. *Politieke naweë van die Anglo-Boereoorlog 1899–1902*. Unpublished DPhil Thesis, University of Pretoria.

Westall, O.M. 1992. *The Provincial Insurance Company 1903–1938: Family, Markets, and Competitive Growth*. Manchester: Manchester University Press.

Wright, R.E. and Smith, G.D. 2004. *Mutually beneficial: The Guardian and life insurance in America*. New York: New York University Press.

3. Academic Journals

Arregle, J.L., Beamish, P.W., and Hebert, L. 2009. The regional dimension of MNE's foreign subsidiary localization. *Journal of International Business Studies*, 40(1).

Benfield, B.C. and Vivian, R.W. 2003. Insurance in the 1990s. *South African Journal of Economic History*, 18.

Du Toit, F. 2016. Sanlam operational update: Strong business get stronger in tough times. *Renaissance Capital*, 8/12/2016.

Du Toit, F. 2017. Sanlam vs Old Mutual EM life: Past and future RoEV supports SLM. *Renaissance Capital*, 20/2/2017.

Flemming Martin Research South Africa, 26/7/1999.

Freschi, F. 2010. The business of belonging: Volkskapitalisme, modernity and the imaginary of national belonging in the decorative programme of selected commercial buildings in Cape Town, South Africa. *South African Historical Journal*, 61(3).

Gamedze, T. Sanlam: Running hard to stand still. HSBC Simpson McKie.

Ghemawat, P. 2003. Semi-globalization and international business strategy. *Journal of International Business Studies* 34(2).

Goedhuys, D. 1994. Monetary policy in the 1980s years of reform and foreign financial aggression. *South African Journal of Economic History*, 9(2).

Groverm, V., Jeong, S.R., Kettinger, W.J., and Teng, T.C. 1995. The implementation of business process re-enginering. *Journal of Management Information Systems*. 12(1).

Hansman, H. 1985. The organisation of insurance companies: Mutual versus stock. *Journal of Law, Economics and Organisation*, 1(2).

ING Barings South African Research, 12/1/1999.

Investec Securities: F10: 23/2/2001: Life assurance in the context of contractual savings institutions: 45.

Johanson, J. and Vahlne, J.E. 1977. The internationalization process of the firm: A model of knowledge development and increasing foreign market commitments, *Journal of International Business Studies*, 8(10).

Kerr, J. 2008. The creative capitalism spectrum: Evaluating corporate social responsibility through a legal lens. *Temple Law Review*, 81.

KPMG 2015. The South African insurance industry, August 2015: 48.

Mohr, P. 2003. An overview of the South African economy in the 1990's. *South African Journal of Economic History*, 18(1–2).

Nash, A. 1997. Wine-farmers, heresy trials and the 'whole personality': The Emergence of the Stellenbosch philosophical tradition, 1916–1940. *South African Journal of Philosophy*, 16(2).

Paterson, G. 2010. Warburg Dillon Reid: Life Assurance. Sanlam. Reuters RIC, 24/4/2010.

Paterson, G. 2010. Warburg Dillon Reid: Life Assurance. Sanlam. Reuters RIC, 24/8/2010.

Pelser, A.N. 1941. Die Arm-blanke in die Suid-Afrikanse Republiek tussen die jare 1852–1899. *Historiese Studies*, 2(4).

Pettigrew, A.M. 1987. Context and action in the transformation of firms. *Journal of Management Studies*, 24(6).

PWC: *Africa insurance trends*, October 2014: 7.

PWC: Insurance through challenging times: Insurance industry analysis, 2016: 42.

Salmon, M. 2016. Life Insurance: Investec sector review, 12/4/2016.

Simkins, C. 1999. The political economy of South Africa in the 1970s. *South African Journal of Economic History*, 14(13).

Singleton, J. and Verhoef, G. 2010. Regulation, deregulation and internationalization in South African and New Zealand banking. *Business History*, 52(4).

Smit, B.W. and Mocke, B.A. 1991. Capital flight from South Africa: magnitude and causes. *South African Journal of Economics*, 59(2).

Suddaby, R., Foster, W.M., and Trank, C.Q. 2010. Rhetorical history as a source of competitive advantage. *Advances in Strategic Management*, 27.

Udayasankar, K. 2008. Corporate Social Responsibility and Firm Size. *Journal of Business Ethics*. 83(2008).

Verhoef, G. 1995. 'Nationalism and Free Enterprise in Mining: The Case of Federale Mynbou, 1952–1965', *The South African Journal of Economic History*, 10(1): 89–107.

Verhoef, G. 2003. The invisible hand: the roots of black economic empowerment, Sankorp and societal change in South Africa, 1985–2000'. *Journal for Contemporary History*, 28(1).

Verhoef, G. 2005. Afrikanernasionalisme in die besigheidswêreld. 'n Verenigde front? *Joernaal vir Eietydse Geskiedenis*, 30(1).

Verhoef, G. 2006. Die stigting van instellings as werktuie in die ekonomiese opbouproses van die Afrikaner sedert die Anglo-Boereoorlog. *Tydskrif vir Geesteswetenskappe*, 46(2).

Verhoef, G. 2006. The History of Medical Aid provision in South Africa's public sector. *Social Science History*, 30(4).

Verhoef, G. 2008. 'Nationalism, social capital and economic empowerment: SANLAM and the economic upliftment of the Afrikaner people, 1918–1960', *Business History*, Special Issue: Putting Social Capital to Work. 50(6): 694–713.

Verhoef, G. 2009. Concentration and competition: The changing landscape of the banking sector in South Africa 1970–2007. *South African Journal of Economic History*, 24(2).

Verhoef, G. 2009. The development of diversified conglomerates: the case of Federale Volksbeleggings—a case study. *Joernaal vir Eietydse Geskiedenis*, 24(2).

Verhoef, G. 2016. Die onderneming en die gemeenskap: Korporatiewe maatskaplike betrokkenheid deur Sanlam, 1918–1980. *Tydskrif vir Geesteswetenskappe*, 54(4).

Verhoef, G. and Keneley, M. 2011. Pressures for change in the Australian and South African insurance markets: a comparison of two companies. *Competition and Change*, 15(2).

Vermeulen, H.J. 1997. The subtext of Pieter Fourie's *'Donderdag se mense'* and the demise of Afrikaner nationalism. *Journal of Literary Studies*, 13(3–4).

Von Wielligh, S.P. 2005. Financial reporting by South African long term insurers: A comparative study. *Meditari Accountancy Research*, 1(1).

Waddock, S.A. and Grave, S.B. 1997. The Corporate Social Performance–Financial Performance Link. *Strategic Management Journal*, 18(4).

Westall, O.M. 2003. The history of insurance. In *Business History*, 44(1).

Windsor, D. 2001. The Future of Corporate Social Performance. *The International Journal of Organisational Analysis*, 9(3).

4. Periodicals and Newspapers

Bolyn, L. 2005. Sanlam finalises sale of Absa stake to Barclays. https://mg.co.za/article/2005-07-26-sanlam-finalise-sale-of-absa-stake-to-barclays (Accessed 10 August 2017.)

Brown, W. *CLSA*: Emerging markets: SA companies update, 29/1/2001.

Business Day, 10/6/2014.

Business Day, 12/5/1993.

Business Day, 16/02/1989.

Business Day, 23/6/1998.

Business Day, 27/2/2002.

Business Day, 28/10/1985.

Cape Argus, 15/03/1989.

Cape Times, 04/05/1901.

Cape Times, 15/2/1982.

Cape Times, 5/2/1987.

Cape Times, 5/9/1985.

Croft, J. et al. 2005. UK bank takes a step back in time with S Africa buy. http://www.ft.com/cms/s/0/fd54265c-c026-11d9-b376-0000e2511c8.html?ft_site=falcon&desktop=true#axzz4s4uZh94j (Accessed 10 August 2017.)

Davids, G. 2016. Life Insurance Sector Report: Retention in the new growth. *Nedbank CIB*, 9/6/2016. www.nedbankcapitalresearch.co.za

Die Burger, 14/8/1985.

Die Burger, 28/04/1997.

Die Transvaler, Supplement, 08/06/1968.

Finance Week, 29/03/1989.

Finance Week, 30/3/2005.

Finance Week, 8–14/08/1991.

Financial Mail, 16/2/1996

Financial Mail, 14/5/1982.

Financial Mail, 16/02/1989.

Financial Mail, 16/6/1960.

Financial Mail, 20/11/1992.

Financial Mail, 20/3/1998.

Financial Mail, 24/10/2003.

Financial Mail, 24/12/1964.

Financial Mail, 26/3/2014.

Financial Mail, 27/10/1967.

Financial Mail, 27/5/1960.

Financial Mail, 29/08/97.

Financial Mail, 30/11/1990.

Financial Mail, 30/11/1990.

Financial Mail, 6/6/1960.

Financial Mail, 8/5/1964.

Financial Mail, January 1998.

Financial Mail, 15/4/1998.

Financial Mail, 4/3/2011.

Jeftha, A. 2018. 'Sanlam stock drops on news of R5.7 bn new share issue', https://www.fin24.com/Companies/Financial-Services/sanlam-stock-drops-on-news-of-r57bn-new-share-issue-20180328 (accessed 30/3/201).

Lambridis, C. 2007. 'Sanlam Limited (SLM). FY06 results.' Citigroup, 13/3/2007.

Maake, M. 2017. Sanlam in control of BrightRock. https://www.businesslive.co.za/bd/companies/financial-services/2017-01-26-sanlam-in-control-of-brightrock/(Accessed 08/2017.)

Natal Mercury, 14/8/1985.

Ndzamela, P. 2016. Ubuntu Botho pays R830 m dividend. https://www.businessalive.co.za/bd/companies/financial-services/2016-03-29-ubuntu-botho-pays-r830m-dividend/(Accessed 14/4/2016.)

Njobeni, S. 2018. 'Sanlam pays dearly for share placement', https://iol.co.za/business-report/companies/Sanlam-pays-dearly-for-share-placement-14147165 (accessed 30/3/2018).

Personal Finance, 23/10/2005.

Personal Finance, 27/8/2005.

Pretoria News, 16/03/1989.

Sake Burger, 27/2/2002.

Shochot, D. *Deutsche Securities*: Sanlam Ltd: 7/3/2003.

Staff Reporter. 2005. Barclays now holds 56% of Absa. https://mg.co.za/article/2005-12-22-barclays-now-holds-56-of-absa (Accessed 08/09/2017.)

Sunday Times, 21/11/1982.

Sunday Times, 28/3/1983.

Sunday Times, 31/8/1997.

Sunday Times, 5/03/1989.

Sunday Times, 6/09/1987.

Sunday Times, Business Times, 05/03/1989.

Sunday Times, 06/09/1987.

The Argus, 16/2/1989.

The Cape Argus, 18/6/1982.

The Cape Times, 01/08/1882.

The Cape, 04/01/1918.

The Citizen, 14/8/1985.

The Economist, 2005. Absa's allure. http://www.economist.com/node/3915787 (Accessed 10/08/2017.)

The Star Business Report, 11/10/1996.

The Star Business Report, 16/6/1996.

The Star Business Report, 20/1/1997.

The Star Business Report, 28/10/1996.

The Star, 11/05/1960.

The Star, 23/02/1990.

The Star, 27/2/2002.

The Star, Business Times, 16/2/1989.

Today's Trustee, March/May 2017.

Uys, H. *Cazenove:* Sanlam. Company update, 5/9/2001.

Uys, H. *Cazenove*: Sanlam Company update, 6/3/2003.

www.africanrainbowcapital.co.za/about-us

www.santam.co.za

http://www.sharenet.co.za/v3/sens_display.php?tdate=20180327170500&seq=63&print=1

5. Western Cape Archives

WCA: A2213: Private Collection C.R. Louw, Band 3: File Santam 1918, 1919.

WCA: A2213: Correspondence between C.R. Louw and A.E. Rupert, 20/6/61; 7/7/61; 27/7/61.

WCA: A2213: C.R. Louw Collection: Memorandum on Rembrandt, 19/9/1950.

WCA: C.R. Louw Collection: Feenstra–Louw, 1/7/1937.

WCA: CRL Collection: Wassenaar Memorandum to Board: Verskuiwing en beplanning van hoofkantoorgeboue: 12/1/1950.

WCA-A2213: Agreement Santam/Sanlam, 19/6/1945.

WCA-A2213: Memorandum to Sanlam Board, 18/8/1958.

WCA-A2213: Memorandum to Sanlam Board, 29/10/1952.

WCA-A2213: SANLAM minutes of Board meeting, 28/1/1953.

WCA-A2213: Union of South Africa, Private Act, No. 3 of 1954.

6. Other Archives

Banks Quarterly Investment Research: Martin & Company, April 1977: 9.

Banks Quarterly Investment Research: Martin & Company, February 1977: 4.

Banks Quarterly Investment Research: Martin & Company, June 1977: 10.

Martin & Company, Broker Analyst, 1/1/1991.

Standard Bank Archives (SBA): GMO 3/1/62: Report to Standard Bank of South Africa, Ltd London: 13/12/18: 802.

7. Government Publications

Official Year Book of South Africa, 1925, p. 841.

Official Year Book of the Union of South Africa, 1910–1924: various tables consolidated.

Private Act, No. 3 of 1954: Section 5.

RP 87/1972: Report of the Commission of Inquiry into Monetary Policy in the Republic of South Africa.

Registrar of Insurance, Annual Report, 1945, 1948.

Report of the Registrar of Insurance Companies, 1950: 40; Report 1954: 34.

South African Reserve Bank, Quarterly Bulletin of Statistics, 2002–2014.

The Banks Act No. 94 of 1990.

The Companies Act, No. 26 of 1973.

The Financial Institutions Act, No. 39 of 1984.

The Financial Markets Control Act, No. 55 of 1989.

The Financial Services Board Act, No. 97 of 1990.

The Income Tax Act, No. 68 of 1962.

The Inspection of Financial Institutions Act, No. 68 of 1984.

The Pension Fund Act, No. 24 of 1956.

The Safe Deposit of Securities Act, No. 85 of 1992.

The Stock Exchange Control Act, No. 1 of 1985.

The Unit Trust Control Act, No. 54 of 1981.

Transvaal Chamber of Mines, 61th Annual Report, 1950: 60.

Union of South Africa: Summaries of Returns deposited with the Treasury by Insurance Companies, 1948.
Union Statistics for Fifty Years (1961): A3–A5; A10; A18; A22.

8. Theses and Research Reports

Adams, R. (2010) *Die Ver-Suid-Afrikanisering cvan die Suid-Afrikaanse ekonomie.'n Studie van Sanlam, 1918–1980.* Unpublished MA Dissertation, University of Stellenbosch.

Beukes, W.J. (2017) *Van Afrikanerkultuur tot korporatief: die geskiedenis van Sanlam se organisasiekultuur met spesifieke verwysing na sy personeel in Hoofkantoor,1918–2014.* Unpublished PhD Thesis, University of Stellenbosch.

De Wet S.R. (2018) *The Role of Asset Management in the Transformation of a Life Insurance Company to a Financial Services Group: the Case of Sanlam.* Unpublished PhD Thesis, University of Johannesburg.

Drostie, A. and Verhoef, G. (2015) *Management and sustainability: The development of Management in Sanlam, 1918–2015.* Unpublished Sanlam internal research report.

Du Plessis, A. (2015) *Die Sanlam Veldpersoneel, 1918–2013.*Unpublished Sanlam internal research report.

Du Preez, N. (2016) *Sanlam en Gesondheidsorg.* Unpublished Sanlam internal research report.

Hagedorn-Hansen, Y. (2017) *The Transformation of the South African short term insurance industry as represented by the development of SANTAM, 1918–2012.* Unpublished PhD Thesis, University of Johannesburg.

Halleen, S. (2013) *From life insurance to financial services: A Historical Analysis of Sanlam's client base, 1919–2008.* Unpublished PhD Thesis. University of Stellenbosch.

Hoogenraad-Vermaak, S.G. (2009) *'n Kritiese ondersoek na die bydrae van Afrikaner sakelui in die vestiging van 'n nuwe politieke bestel: 1985–1992.* Unpublished PhD Thesis. University of Johannesburg.

Koen, W.P.G. (1986) Sanlam tussen Twee Wêreldoorloë. Unpublished Ph.D. University of South Africa.

Laburn, V. (2011) *The economics of Corporate Social Investment: Sanlam and Corporate Social Responsibility expenditure, 1970 to 2008.* Unpublished MCom Minor dissertation. University of Stellenbosch.

Sanlam Computer Research Group (2014) *Sanlam: The IT journey from 1990 to 2014:* Unpublished Sanlam internal research report.

Venter. L (2016) *The history of Sanlam Broker Division.* Unpublished Sanlam internal research report.

Venter, L. (2016) *Historical overview of the Regional Head Office (RHO) structures within Sanlam (1990–1998)* Unpublished Sanlam internal research report.

Venter, L. (2016) *Development of Human Resources 1994–2015 with Sanlam.* Unpublished Sanlam internal research report.

9. Interviews

Email communication G. Rudman–G. Verhoef, 22/4/2010.
Email communication G. Rudman–Sanlam Corporate Office, 31/8/2017; 30/9/2017.
Interview D. Hickey, 9/6/2014.
Interview David Hickey, 13/5/2013.
Interview Desmond Smith, 14/6/2017; 10/8/2017.
Interview Frederick Stroebel, 13/12/2015.

Interview G. Rudman, 14/11/2007; 12/2/2009; 24/2/2010.
Interview Ian Kirk, 10/8/2017; 16/08/2017.
Interview Ronnie Mason, 18/03/2009.
Interview Walter Scheffler, 24/2/2009.
Interview J. van Zyl, 12/5/2013.
Interview Heinrich Punt, 9/10/2014.
Interview: P. de V. Rademeyer, 11/11/2012; 16/08/2016.
Official email communication: F.A. Stroebel, 30/3/2016.
Interview A.S. du Plessis, 29/9/2016; 18/08/2017.

INDEX OF NAMES

INDEX

f refers to figures; *t* refers to tables